MW00795202

THE FLETCHER JONES FOUNDATION
HUMANITIES IMPRINT

The Fletcher Jones Foundation has endowed this imprint to foster innovative and enduring scholarship in the humanities.

The publisher gratefully acknowledges the generous support of the Fletcher Jones Foundation Humanities Endowment Fund of the University of California Press Foundation.

Rationalizing Korea

Rationalizing Korea

THE RISE OF THE MODERN STATE, 1894–1945

Kyung Moon Hwang

UNIVERSITY OF CALIFORNIA PRESS

University of California Press, one of the most distinguished university presses in the United States, enriches lives around the world by advancing scholarship in the humanities, social sciences, and natural sciences. Its activities are supported by the UC Press Foundation and by philanthropic contributions from individuals and institutions. For more information, visit www.ucpress.edu.

University of California Press
Oakland, California

Library of Congress Cataloging-in-Publication Data

Hwang, Kyung Moon.
    Rationalizing Korea : the rise of the modern state, 1894–1945 / Kyung Moon Hwang.
        p.   cm.
    Includes bibliographical references and index.
    ISBN 978-0-520-28831-7 (cloth : alk. paper)
    ISBN 978-0-520-28832-4 (pbk. : alk. paper)
    ISBN 978-0-520-96327-6 (ebook)
        1. Korea—Politics and government—1864–1910.   2. Korea—Politics and government—1910–1945.   3. Korea—Social policy—19th century. 4. Korea—Social policy—20th century.   5. Public administration— Korea.   I. Title.
    DS915.35.H84   2016
    951.9 03—dc23   2015021601

Manufactured in the United States of America

25   24   23   22   21   20   19   18   17   16
10   9   8   7   6   5   4   3   2   1

CONTENTS

ILLUSTRATIONS

MAP

FIGURES

TABLES

PREFACE

This work represents an organic companion to my first book, *Beyond Birth*, which examines the transformation of social structure from the late Joseon era to the 1930s, with a focus on certain status groups whose members and descendants experienced a remarkable ascent to the newly emergent elite of modern society. Foremost among the vehicles for this mobility was the state bureaucracy, which had served also as the institutional site of these groups' socio-political subordination in the Joseon. *Beyond Birth*, then, naturally led to the current project of analyzing the development of the state in order to better comprehend the underlying structures of Korea's modern transition.

While few people familiar with Korea would dispute the notion that the state played an outsized role in its modern history, there has been surprisingly little scholarly attention dedicated to this subject, particularly for the earlier part of the modern era. This book seeks to fill this gap while considering how the rise of the modern state in Korea sheds light on major themes that extended beyond the peninsula as well. Among them is the notion of increasing rationalization as the hallmark of modern governance. Rationalization had also marked the statecraft of the preceding Joseon dynasty, however, and in the early modern era it was manifested in multiple forms, including the ways by which the state legitimated its authority. In fact the source of such legitimacy was often located in the performance of state administration itself, a self-referential and modern response to an age-old challenge. Indeed, for the modern state, rationalization was in general an ongoing attempt at reflexivity: The state tried to induce a self-disciplining of compliance among the people while constantly adjusting to responses to its own practices.

The fluidity of this concept of rationalization, in turn, acts as a stand-in for the complexity of Korea's modern history. Over the past two decades or so it has become commonplace, at least outside of the peninsula, to associate Korean modernity mostly with Japanese colonial rule (1910–1945), but this book demonstrates that, as seen in the history of the state, the processes of modern change preceded and transcended the colonial period. Taken together, the multiplicity and diversity of Korea's modern transformation merged into a vast historical experience that cut across the temporal and national boundaries of political control. In playing a central role in this process, the rise of the modern state provides answers to some of the grander questions of modern Korean history: To what extent did Korea adapt to the externally induced pressures for fundamental change at the turn of the 20th century? How did the Japanese takeover occur, and how did colonialism develop thereafter? How did Koreans, with their assorted backgrounds and interests, respond to and in turn shape the nature of foreign rule? And how did Confucianism, the dominant social ethic and ideology of the Joseon era, affect this process? As this book shows, different social spheres, such as the economy, religion, and education, achieved their familiar modern forms through the rationalities of an increasingly assertive yet tempered regulatory state, and these relationships likewise reflected the overlapping, transnational, and composite character of Korean modernity.

Such findings, then, show the state as one of the indispensable, and perhaps the most instrumental component (in multiple ways) of Korea's modern transition. Whether under the direction of Korean monarchists and reformers, Japanese military commanders and bureaucrats, or the countless lower-level officials of both ethnicities, from the late 19th to the mid-20th century, the state took the leading role in forging momentous change. It constructed the structures of public schooling and public health, devised and implemented a systematic path of economic growth, and ordered the people, their religions, their families, even their names. The state was, in short, a comprehensive agent for mobilization—for taxation and appropriation, to be sure, but for broader and deeper transformations as well. Still, it was also very much shaped by the greater developments in society, economy, and culture, and even the colonial state was not as formidable or uniform a social force as is commonly perceived. Such intricacies render the state in early modern Korea intriguingly hard to grasp, but it is hoped that this book meets this challenge and thereby reveals connections to more recent and contemporary Korea, as well as to larger patterns of Korean history as a whole.

A product of nearly two decades of gestation and production, this book owes a lot to a lot of people. I want to begin with appreciation for those closest to me. My wife Helen and our son Sejin have been constant sources of love, support, and happiness over the long journey that we and this book have taken. My mother and sister, my brother and his family, my cousins and in-laws, as well as other relatives both in the US and in South Korea, have all been unstinting sources of comfort and joy. I cannot thank them enough for endowing what I do with extra meaning.

Outside my family, I wish to start by thanking Yi Hun-sang of Donga University in Busan, who has served as my teacher, friend, and upstanding academic example for over twenty years. I have benefited enormously from our long conversations and collaboration efforts, from conferences to field trips. I want also to express deep appreciation for my erstwhile advisor and lifelong friend and mentor, Carter Eckert, a steady source of wisdom and a model for scholarship and scholarly integrity. In Los Angeles, John Duncan has been a most valuable colleague who has enriched my life here in more ways than one. At USC, I have benefited immeasurably from the presence of Sunyoung Park, my admirable and very impressive "fellow traveler" in Korean studies.

There are countless people to thank at the USC departments of History and EALC, including Elinor Accampo, Lois Banner, David Bialock, Youngmin Choe, Bill Deverell, Charlotte Furth, Jason Glenn, Josh Goldstein, Sarah Gualtieri, Lon Kurashige, Paul Lerner, Philippa Levine, Akira Lippit, Peter Mancall, Lori Rogers, Ayse Rorlich, Ramzi Rouighi, Carole Shammas, Brett Sheehan, Diana Williams, and Jack Wills, for helping me with my work intellectually, institutionally, or otherwise. A very special appreciation in this regard is reserved for my inspirational friend and tennis partner Maria Elena Martinez. Members of the Parkside community also remain close to my heart, particularly Priya Jaikumar, Oliver Mayer, Matthew Nelson, Ricardo Ramirez, Michael Waterman, and their families. Others at USC I wish to acknowledge include Clayton Dube, David Kang, Elaine Kim, Linda Kim, Ken Klein, Lynette Merriman, Beth Meyerowitz, Sarah Pratt, Stan Rosen, Grace Ryu, and Denzil Suite. And I could not have pursued my work without the dedication and assistance of Joy Kim and Sun-Yoon Lee of the USC Korean Heritage Library.

Beyond my home institution a most valuable group of scholars has helped nurture this project over the years in some form of another. In North America and Europe, they include Donald Baker, Kyeong-Hee Choi, Donald Clark, Alain Delissen, Martina Deuchler, Takashi Fujitani, Valerie Gelezeau, the late Jahyun Kim Haboush, Gail Hershatter, Su-Bok Jeong, Christine Kim, Daeyeol Kim, Jennifer Jung-Kim, Sean Kim, Sonja Kim, Sun Joo Kim, Namhee Lee, You Jae Lee, James Lewis, Sungyun Lim, Yumi Moon, Chan E. Park, Eugene Y. Park, Jin-Kyung Park, Mark Peterson, Christopher Reed, Michael Robinson, Holly Stephens, David Straub, Soyoung Suh, John Treat, Jun Uchida, Boudewijn Walraven, Kenneth Wells, and Mimi Yiengpruksawan. In Korea I have incurred a great debt to scholars who have offered their time, friendship, scholarship, and other forms of assistance: Bak Chan-seung, Bak Tae-gyun, Choe Hui-jeong, Choe Won-gyu, Jai-Keun Choi, Gim Do-hyeong, Gim Dong-no, Gim Yang-su, Im Ji-hyeon, Michael Kim, Seo Yeong-hui, Son Suk-gyeong, and Yun Hae-dong. I wish to thank also the members of the Naksungdae Economic Research Institute, including Bak Hui-jin, Bak Hwan-mu, Gim Nang-nyeon, and especially Yi Yeong-hun for generously allowing me to participate in their projects and, even in disagreement, for offering helpful feedback, encouragement, and access to their intellectual labors, which have proven most valuable for this book.

Other institutions that have offered me a forum in which to present this book's findings and ideas at various stages are the Association for Asian Studies (AAS), POSCO International Symposium on Korean Studies, the Korea Institute at Harvard University, Korean Studies Colloquium of the University of British Columbia, Institute of Korean Studies of Yonsei University, Center for Korean Studies at UCLA, the Association for Korean Studies in Europe (AKSE), the Korean Studies Lecture Series at the University of Oxford, the USC-Huntington Early Modern Studies Institute, the École des Hautes Études en Sciences Sociales (EHESS), Institut National des Langues et Civilisations Orientales (INALCO), Korean Studies Institute of USC, Asia-Pacific Research Center at Stanford University, Center for Korean Studies at UC-Berkeley, Institute for Korean Studies of The Ohio State University, Department of Economics at Seoul National University, Seoktang Research Center at Donga University, Research Institute for Comparative History at Hanyang University, the Academy of East Asian Studies at Sungkyunkwan University, and the USC Department of History. I greatly appreciated the opportunities, responses, and collegiality provided by these occasions.

I also depended on the generosity of the following funding sources: The USC Center for Religion and Civic Culture, The Senior Research Fellowship from the Korea Foundation, the Special Visiting Scholar residency at the École des Hautes Études en Sciences Sociales, the Sejong Society and USC Korean Studies Institute, USC Dornsife Faculty Development Award, the Advancing Scholarship in the Humanities and Social Sciences grant at USC, and the USC Dornsife Dean's Office. My sincere gratitude goes out to these agencies for facilitating the research that went into this book.

And last but not least, my sincere thanks go to John Duncan, Kirk Larsen, and readers in the multiple stages of review at the University of California Press for supplying constructive comments and criticisms on the entire manuscript. Others who took the time to provide enlightening feedback include George Kallender, Hwasook Nam, Sunyoung Park, and Franklin Rausch, and my heartfelt appreciation goes out to them. A special shout out goes to my student assistants for this project over the years: Pleres Choi, Philip Gant, Jonathan Hong, Jonghyun Paek, Young Sun Park, and Yu Tokunaga. I thank also Bart Wright and Dan Vaughan for their graphics work, and Susan Storch for the index. And of course the team at the University of California Press was integral: Stacy Eisenstark, Jessica Moll, Paul Tyler, and especially Reed Malcolm for his steady professionalism. I am forever grateful.

NOTE ON ROMANIZATION AND TRANSLATIONS

This book employs the Revised Romanization System of Korean. The more conventional spelling of "Pyongyang" will be used, as will the name of "Seoul" in reference to Korea's capital city unless otherwise noted. For clarity, Korean given names of historical figures are unhyphenated, while those of contemporary figures, mostly authors, are hyphenated. Japanese words and names are rendered in the Hepburn system, and Chinese in Pinyin. English translations of the titles of cited works are provided in the bibliography. Unless otherwise noted, all translations in the book are by the author.

JEOLLA — Provinces
Gangwha — Cities, Towns or County Seats
‑‑‑‑‑‑ — Provincial Boundaries
‑‑‑‑‑ — North/South Provincial Boundaries
—— — Major Rivers

RUSSIA

Gyeongheung

Baekdu Mountain

Duman (Tumen) River

N. HAMGYEONG

Cheongjin

MANCHURIA

Amnok (Yalu) River

Gapsan

S. HAMGYEONG

N. PYEONGAN

Cheongcheon River

Uiju
Sinuiju

Jeongju

Hamheung

S. PYEONGAN

Daedong R.

Pyongyang

Wonsan

Jinnampo

Imjin River

Geumgang Mountain

HWANGHAE
Haeju

GANGWON

Gaeseong

TAEBAEK MOUNTAINS

Ganghwa

Tongjin

Seoul

Gangneung

Incheon

Siheung

Wonju

East Sea

GYEONGGI

S.
CHUNGCHEONG

N.
CHUNGCHEONG
Cheongju

Andong

Pyeonghae

CHUNGCHEONG

Gongju

Cheongyang

Daejeon

N. GYEONGSANG

Buyeo

Han R.

Gunsan

Yellow Sea

Geum R.

Daegu

Gyeongju

Jeonju

Nakdong R.

N. JEOLLA

Eonyang

Namwon

Jiri Mountain

Ulsan

Gwangju

S. GYEONGSANG

Dongnae

Naju

Jinju

Masan

Busan

Mokpo

S. JEOLLA

Sacheon

Haenam

Korea Strait

Tsushima

JAPAN

South Sea

Kitakyushu

JEJU
ISLAND

Fukuoka

0   50   100 kilometers
0   50   100 miles

Korea ca. 1909.

Introduction

IT IS WELL ACCEPTED THAT modern society began to appear in Korea from the end of the nineteenth century to the end of Japanese colonial rule in 1945. Through an examination of the economy, religion, education, population, and public health, this study aims to show how the state contributed to and reflected this process, as well as how the modern state arose from the premodern foundation of the Joseon dynasty. The findings of this book call for an expansive reconsideration of state making's historical significance in this era and of widely accepted representations of Korean modernity.

The most familiar such representations are normally located in the two postliberation entities of North and South Korea (1948–present), particularly in the undeniably pronounced role played by interventionist, paternalistic, domineering states in shaping these two countries. Their historical connections to the colonial state (1910–45), particularly its latter form, have been carefully considered in the historiography,[1] but a systematic examination of the state's development over the early twentieth century is missing. In fact, very few studies track a major topic, and none as critical as the state, over the entire span of Korea's early modern era, including across the threshold of 1910, the year of the Japanese annexation of Korea. And much of the scholarship, particularly in English, takes for granted that modern Korea began with Japanese colonization. Connections over the 1945 threshold, when colonial rule ended, are often acknowledged, but in dealing with 1910, the divide is taken as an almost impermeable wall, with what happened before that year becoming too readily ignored.

A major rupture certainly occurred with the onset of colonialism, but much of the heavy attention paid to this shift is premised on the belief that formal change in political rule or sovereignty expresses itself immediately and comprehensively. If we step back a bit from this moment, however, to broaden our field of vision and simultaneously sharpen our gaze, we find that, in the development of the state in the early modern era,[2] there were many turning points just as significant—for example the 1894–95 Gabo Reforms, or the period of "Cultural Rule" following the 1919 March First independence uprisings. And when fused into an expansive process of change, these shifts comprise a story of the modern state's emergence that appears more gradual than sudden, as modified as new. The Korean experience of modern change was in many ways similar to that of other societies jarred or eventually consumed by imperialism, but unlike most others, Korea had long been ruled by a unified, sophisticated state. Indeed, there were many "modern" features of the Joseon dynastic state (1392–1894), particularly its systematic, ideologically grounded, and textually based bureaucratization and the intangible yet perhaps more durable customs and mentalities regarding state authority. These patterns, reinforced over centuries, would prove difficult to undo, despite the efforts of Korean reformers at the turn of the twentieth century and colonial officials over thirty-five years of rule, even as they both recognized the utility of this tradition as well. In fact, the similarities between the precolonial and colonial states were just as striking as the novelties introduced by Japanese colonialism.

This book seeks to demonstrate, then, the necessity and value of examining state development over an extended period. It finds that, as a process, early modern state making in Korea was:

1. *imperializing,* as the context of imperialism served as the undercurrent of major transitions throughout this era, and military imperatives occasioned the most fundamental transformations in the form and function of the state. Whether in inducing a dramatic expansion of extractive and mobilizational capacities at the end of the nineteenth century, or in actualizing foreign conquest in the protectorate period of 1905–10, or in the turn to wartime mobilization in the 1930s, imperialism and war consistently drove the state's development;

2. *civilizing and colonizing,* as both pursuits were primary extensions of modern state making, and vice versa. While the construction of a modernizing administrative order rationalized foreign rule, the civilizing drives of colonization spurred this process since before the annexation, reflecting the distance between the holders of sovereignty

and political power, on the one hand, and the people whom they ruled, on the other;

3. *reifying*, since the state, through its regulatory objectification of discrete social sectors, played an indispensable role in determining their modern forms. Through its command over knowledge and the accompanying administrative specialization, the state helped shape these distinctive domains in the process of wielding its authority over them;

4. *embedded*, for while state power was exercised through command and coercion, just as critical was the state's social immanence. Social penetration, in short, required integration and the creation of social space through cooperation, co-optation, and responsiveness to resistance. This also made paramount the orientations and group identities of state officials when gauging the state's distance from—or proximity to—society. State authority often emerged from the inside-out, or, in the case of policing and local government, from the bottom up;

5. *fragmented*, for the early modern state was less than the sum of its parts. Differentiation began with the state's structural and operational bifurcation and extended to the legitimacy gap of colonial rule, and finally to its human actors: state officials as well as public figures, interest groups, and other individuals external to the state whose influence, including in opposition, was often pronounced.

These themes, particularly the latter two, converge into this book's primary argument: The modern state emerged in Korea through processes of rationalization that were fluid and often absorbed extralegal, informal, "traditional," and indeed seemingly irrational impulses. Further contributing to this dynamic was a related sense of rationalization—that of justification, or legitimation—which, informed by a broader concern over state efficacy, did not always align with the pursuit of administrative efficiency. And as with the mostly overlapping concept of "rationality," "rationalization" itself was applicable mostly in the plural form, as there was rarely a uniform or unidirectional process of rationalization, but rather multiple rationalizations (or rationalities) in line with evolving, competing, and at times opposing goals and imperatives. The compounding, often constraining impact of these rationalities in turn compels a reconsideration of the notion of state rationalization, if not of the state itself.

What, then, was the state? In conceiving of the state, one can draw upon a wide range of perspectives, from the political representation of a people to the absolutist expression of monarchical sovereignty (*L'etat, c'est moi*). While this study makes no attempt at an essentialized notion of the state, it is premised on a recognition of three primary manifestations: first, the state as a thing, a collection of tangible realities—buildings, lands, roads and bridges, funds, weapons, officials, etc.—that materially constitute the governing institutions within a defined territory; second, the state as a practice, or actions by both state officials and the people that standardize and reinforce its authority; and finally, the state as an idea, a set of rules, often in the form of laws, dictating what social behaviors are permissible, how collective resources are appropriated and allocated, and who holds decision-making and coercive power over others.

It is perhaps this enforcement quality that appears most definitive to common perceptions and hence has made it acceptable, as a shorthand, to follow Max Weber's well-known reduction of the state to its monopolization of legitimate violence.[3] Such a conceptualization also reflects a strong orientation toward a modern state, for premodern states appear not to have exclusively controlled the use of force as much as to co-opt and deflect disparate sources of coercion. Indeed it appears that much of what we imagine when thinking of a state is really a modern one, and an acknowledgment of this reality, while not justifying the conflation of the modern form with the state itself, leads us to reiterate that, around the world, state making was often fundamental to modernity, and vice versa.

Of course Weber went far beyond this blunt formulation and still stands as a major authority for comprehending state making as a core feature of modern times. Particularly durable has been his emphasis on instrumental rationalization[4]—objectification, differentiation, and specialization—as the goal-driven principle behind not only the state, as realized primarily through bureaucratization, but modern society as a whole.[5] The compelling ramifications of Weberian rationalization in modern state making—the overtaking of traditional by legal authority, the overlaps between state development and capitalism, and the shaping of social categories through the state's relationship to them—will inform this book's inquiry as well. Weber's strong suggestion that bureaucratic rationalization begat social autonomy for the state, however, can also hinder the comprehension of historical particularities, and hence it also reminds us of the geographical specificity of his vision. This demands caution when applying it to a historical context, like Korea, that escaped Weber's attention, notwithstanding his writings on premodern China. As with the Chinese dynasties, Joseon was a Confucian state that met the Weberian criteria for "a great modern state" to a surprising degree. The Joseon state was, for example, "absolutely dependent upon a bureaucratic basis" for maintaining its authority, and officials, who enjoyed universal recognition for their skills and public duties, were systematically educated, recruited, and trained. And despite the weakness of a commercial economy as the foundation of a stable taxation system, regular officials (except the hereditary clerks) received either monetary or in-kind compensation.[6] This is not to claim that the Joseon state was modern, even in the Weberian sense, but it does suggest that the organizational sophistication of premodern Korean statecraft denies a ready rendering of it as despotic or even patrimonial.

Such heady labels, in fact, reflect historical thinking that branched into multiple directions of twentieth-century thought, including colonialist, imperialist ideologies and their offspring, the various guises of modernization theory that came to dominate Western (and Eastern) perceptions of global history and society in the post–World War II era.[7] But these associations should not lead us to throw out the Weberian baby with the bathwater, for the notion of rationalization as the hallmark of state growth in the modern world appears soundly grounded, if we acknowledge the cumulative impact of the tempered, modulated, and even contradictory application of multiple rationalizations in the process. What helps, then, is a delineation of the rationalities that emerged out of particular historical contexts, and an explication of how they related to each other and to elements beyond the grasp of administrative systematization. Here Michel Foucault's response to Weberian rationalization, namely *governmentality*, is particularly illuminating.

It is telling that both Weber and Foucault used the state as the central, climactic example of their respective explanations for the dynamics of modern rationality, including its debilitations and disenchantments. Foucault, whose overarching interest in exposing the often hidden structures and behaviors of social power led him eventually to theorize the emergence of the modern European state, demonstrated how the exercise of territoriality in an age of intensifying interstate rivalry came to depend on a range of administrative approaches that he called governmentality. At its core governmentality describes the engendering of reflexivity in the state as well as in the people. The governmentalization of the state entailed adaptable and responsive techniques of surveillance, analysis, and management that in turn effected an internalization of the state's authority in which people came reflexively to govern themselves. Such a "conduct of conduct" operated at the macro level through the state's systematic oversight and scrutiny of the masses under its jurisdiction, who became objectified as an organic "population." The targeting of this population for bureaucratic outcomes regarding the people's lives, deaths, and welfare constituted what Foucault identified as the state's practice of *biopower*, while for regulating individual behavior, the state exercised the micro-authority of *disciplinary power*. The latter was expressed by a variety of institutions, such as prisons and hospitals, and encapsulated in the modern state's comprehensive establishment of the spaces, bounds, and guidelines of acceptable action. Biopower and disciplinary power, then, constituted core rationalities of the governmentalized state not only as an institution, but as a "reflected practice" of constant negotiation and adjustment to inputs, facilitated by advances in the technologies of surveillance and communication at the turn of the nineteenth century in Northern and Western Europe.[8]

As with Weber, such historical specificity in Foucault's observations leads one to question the broader applicability of this concept, but remarkably, Foucaultian analysis holds cogent explanatory potential for analyzing modern state making in Korea. The concepts of governmentality, biopower, and disciplinary power, for example, illuminate the dynamics behind the state's endeavors in social categorization and public health, and more generally they reflect the modern state's efforts in enlightening, civilizing, and modernizing society. To be sure, the Joseon Confucian state—as did premodern states elsewhere—presumed social edification as central to its larger goal of maintaining order and stability. But beginning in the late nineteenth century, for the first time in Korea, high civilization became located beyond the country's own traditions and, importantly, beyond China. Imperialism and interstate competition, along with the attendant forces of militarization and commercialization, forced a response to external pressures. But internal demands to generate transformative change through the state were just as pronounced, often rendered into institutional reforms that increased the state's powers of categorization, standardization, and surveillance. Hence scholars like Bernard Cohn, who in echoing Foucault finds such processes "designed to keep objects and persons in 'their place'" inherent to modern society as a whole, consider the civilizing and colonizing thrusts of modern ruling orders as dual expressions of the same phenomenon.[9] Likewise, major state endeavors in Korea, starting in the precolonial period and carrying forth into colonial rule, were articulated as civilizing, "rational" necessities: leveling the ascriptive social hierarchy, overcoming superstition, enhancing access to education, promoting public health and personal hygiene, and encouraging industry (and industriousness), among other pursuits.

Such efforts to reinforce the state's standing as the steward of advanced civilization, however, also encountered the complications, limitations, and resistance that reflected the Foucaultian delineation of modernist ordering as constructs of social relations. As Colin Koopman has thoughtfully argued, Foucault's great insight into modernity was not that it inserted a domineering partition between reason and passion, but that modernity always contained both rationalizing and opposing impulses, or "experimental transgressions," across this ostensibly fixed divide.[10] Rather than taking the growth of the modern state as the unfolding of rationality itself, we can view it as a process in which the modern state formed in the interstices between instrumental rationality and its counterparts, whether expressed as tradition, customs, or even superstition.

This heterogeneous and cluttered quality of modern state making, which aspired to dismantle and reorder but also to absorb the dichotomies of old and new, domination and defiance, public and private, and metropolitan and colonial, has gained considerable clarification through the work of historian Yun Hae-dong. Through his research into, among other topics, the colonial state in Korea, Yun has developed the notion of a "colonial gray zone" (*singminji ui hoesaek jidae*), an emergent, politicized public space that contained and mediated the expanding social interventions of the colonial state, on the one hand, with the wide-ranging, often resistant responses of a reconstituting public sector, on the other.[11] The concept of a colonial gray zone transcends divisions of social interaction according to ethnicity, nationality, region, or class, just as it escapes the ready categorization of state actions—or the responses thereto—as either modern or traditional, dominating or accommodating, foreign or native, or even public or private. As Yun has shown, the implications of this insight extend to a host of broader questions about Korea's modern history; for state making in this era, the colonial gray zone accentuates particularly the social impact of bureaucratic growth, as well as of both the ambitions and limitations of the expanding state.

How, then, did the modern state, including that of Korea, get people to do things? Beyond (the threat of) punitive sanctions, such as incarceration or other means of coercion, the churning of the state through the population's routines of social interaction also reinforced this authority: going to the post office or local civil affairs bureau; registering a birth, marriage, or death; paying taxes; and generally dealing with public officials, whether policemen on the street or clerks at the local government office. Timothy Mitchell has called these exchanges a manifestation of the modern state less as a tangible reality and more as an abstract "effect" induced within the populace, which works through a constant redefinition and expansion of the state's boundary with its objectified society.[12] In this way the "state effect" echoes Foucault's notion of the governmentalized state, which deploys the disciplinary power of state institutions, such as the army, police, schools, hospitals, and other service agencies, in order to shape subjectivities into an awareness of their subservience. Governmentalizing practices and their practitioners hence endowed the early modern state in Korea with unprecedented ambition and *presence*, notwithstanding the highly systematic statecraft of the preceding Joseon dynasty. Whether for intrusions for hygiene checks, verification of household registration information, meting out summary punishment, collecting taxes, or engaging in a host of other actions, state officials, particularly the police, became persistently present, if not quite omnipresent, and the resulting patterns of social interaction and tension had a profound impact on institutionalizing and legitimizing state authority.

State power, however, also depended considerably upon efforts, by both state officials and extra-state actors, to conceive and express the state's authority as the accepted order—to rationalize state power, in other words, symbolically and discursively. This ideological authority of the state implanted—through the state's concentration of symbolic capital, in Pierre Bourdieu's terms—a comprehensive, epistemological hegemony over "normative regularities."[13] This book will devote considerable coverage, as well as a dedicated chapter (chapter 3), to exploring the multiple means by which such semiotic and discursive practices helped to construct state authority in early modern Korea. In so doing, this study will examine the state as an ideological expression of political authority, but also state authority as wielded ideologically: the modern state's symbolic instrumentality, as well as its use of certain discursive and ideological engineering practices—e.g., propaganda and public campaigns—to affect popular perception and social behavior.

The goal of this enterprise, surely, was to get people in Korea to do certain things, but owing to the major transfers in not only political power but sovereignty itself, this effort also constituted state rationalization as a process of establishing or strengthening legitimacy—the legitimacy of state authority as well as of a particular state. What took place, in the formulation of Christopher Pierson, reflected a hallmark of the modern state in general: regardless of formal sovereignty, the state's authority rested on a legal basis, and hence it expressed, somehow, popular consent (or "managed consent").[14] Granted, the state in Korea was never the product of an electoral democracy in this period,[15] and sovereignty remained vested in the monarchy, whether Korean or Japanese. And of course neither the precolonial nor colonial regime suggested that its legitimacy was ever at stake. But everything short of this revealed a consciousness of validation, a recognition of the need to mollify, deflect, or absorb potential resistance.

This constituted an awareness of the connection between legitimacy and performance, or at least of the recurrent need to justify not only the *fait accompli* of the state's existence but also its continuing authority—a *raison d'etat* that, as Foucault put it, amounted to, "because there is a state and so that there is a state."[16] Such an approach began with the Gabo Reforms of 1894–95 and explains the subsequent rhetorical efforts by the Japanese rulers to authenticate the protectorate in 1905 and eventually the annexation in 1910. The colonial regime, for its part, made explicit this strategic tautology of legitimation: Only the colonial state could implement the necessary changes, and its pursuit of these changes in turn validated its dominion. This study will refer to such an administrative, self-referential process as *managerial legitimacy*—or to be more precise, managerial *legitimation*—which sounds (and might as well have been) Weberian but falls someplace between legal and traditional legitimacy.

Indeed the colonial state's development could be traced substantially through its evolving efforts to manage, then eventually overwhelm, the legitimacy gap of foreign rule through managerial legitimation. Both internal and public documents, such as propaganda works and interventions in the mass media, reveal that colonial officials acknowledged the following reality: They could not rely upon brute force, or even the threat thereof, to maintain their authority, although everyone recognized this as the ultimate basis of colonial rule. Following the harsh government response to the March First independence uprisings of 1919, this awareness of the precariousness of colonial power grew more acute. The ensuing major shift in the Government-General's operating approach, touted as "Cultural Rule" (or "Cultural Politics," *bunka seiji*), demonstrated a heightened sensitivity to popular response and featured the institutional dispersal of power to the provinces and localities. This held true until the demands of war mobilization beginning in the mid- to late 1930s led the colonial state to discard this delicate balancing act and turn toward, of all things, a bluntly nationalist legitimation: its primary role, as an expression and instrument of the imperial cause, to induce a totalizing embrace of Japanese national identity.

That nationalism served as a legitimating tool for state authority represented nothing new, of course, and indeed this had stood as the predominant ideological recourse for sustaining the monarchical state of the Daehan Jeguk (1897–1910), or Great Korean Empire, which preceded and eventually was overcome by the Japanese takeover. In contrast to many other colonial settings, in which nationalism appears to have developed out of the oppositional interaction with colonial knowledge structures, in Korea the modern construction of national identity reached an early peak before colonization. Furthermore, due to the country's Confucian statecraft tradition, from the very beginning of internal reform efforts in the late nineteenth century, it was the state that became the target of competing nationalist visions. The interplay with nationalism, in other words, became ingrained early in the process of modern state making, and indeed the Crown's embrace of this mantle represented an example of Benedict Anderson's model of an "official nationalism."[17] As this book will demonstrate, the colonialist version of this dynamic, while attempting to shift the object of loyalty from the colony to the metropole, nevertheless displayed striking similarities to earlier, precolonial practices.

HISTORICAL AND HISTORIOGRAPHICAL OVERVIEW

Some of the recurrence of precolonial patterns and practices stems from the fact that the Japanese protectorate, instituted in the wake of Japan's victory in the Russo-Japanese War of 1904–5, had taken hold of most higher-level functions in the Korean government by 1907. But many of the major measures that are now commonly recognized as core projects of the colonial state—household registration reform, land reform, infrastructural projects, disease control measures, etc.—had forerunners in the precolonial and pre-protectorate period, and in fact state makers throughout this era drew largely from the same models of modern statecraft circulating around the globe.

Indeed, had there been no colonial takeover, no one would dispute the inclusion of these pre-1910 and pre-1905 endeavors as integral to the longer arc of state development in early modern Korea. But the historiography of this era, particularly outside the peninsula, often treats changes before the Japanese takeover as either inadequate or even retrogressive, and hence pre-dictably overwhelmed by the rampaging rationality, efficiency, and coerciveness of Japanese rule. That historians of modern Japan, many of whom rely only upon Japanese-language sources, tend to harbor a perspective that replicates that of the official colonial sources is somewhat understandable, however regrettable.[18] For historians of Korea, though, to make the same assumption in order to accentuate the coloniality of the colonial period is no more helpful than the nationalist insistence that 1910 halted the autonomous Korean path toward modernity.[19] If nationalist historiography is prone to treating the onset of colonial rule as a Manichean wall of sovereignty while overlooking the agency of Koreans after (and even before) annexation, then scholarship that takes for granted an enormous rupture in 1910, including in relation to the state, risks playing an absolutist game of declaring major changes as either "modern" (or "rational") or not, with little room for considering extended transitions.

Interestingly, within Korean academia, such adherence to a definitive "colonial modernity," which began to gain currency in the 1990s, has characterized a small group of mostly economic historians who profess to let the numbers speak for themselves and hence find the precolonial period mired in backwardness and inefficiency. Their distaste for nationalist orthodoxies and their outsider status in mainstream Korean historical circles have understandably gone hand in hand, yet despite an interest shown by many of these scholars in exploring long-term patterns from the late Joseon era onward,[20] their affinity for quantifiable benchmarks has also tended to exaggerate the gap between the two sides of 1910 through an overreliance on published colonialist accounts and statistics. Many noneconomic Korean historians, on the other hand, who tend to reject outright any association of colonial rule to modern (and hence favorable) change, have nonetheless provided a valuable service through their strenuous efforts to demonstrate the forwardness of earlier developments. In short, they have highlighted the continuities, perhaps unwittingly, from the late nineteenth century to the colonial period. Likewise, the present study favors connecting major shifts into an overarching story of state development in the early modern era, including the ties to the Joseon dynastic state.

Late Joseon Era to the Protectorate Period, 1800s–1910

As noted above, unlike many other preindustrial societies, Korea had been ruled by a centralized systematic state. Perhaps most influential in bestowing a modern legacy were the social prestige and economic privileges given to state officials, products of a Confucian ethos that channeled the most talented (and socially eligible) men into the state bureaucracy. Even the training, certification, and social standing of specialist occupations, such as those in the applied sciences, medicine, and law, were all integrated into the wide-ranging ambitions of the state. But *ambition* here is key, for the realization of these ideals was limited by the preindustrial means of transportation and communication, which in turn strengthened the relative hand of a widespread aristocracy. Even as an instrument officially of the monarchy, the late Joseon state's autonomy and therefore its capacity—so critical to assessing its "power"[21]—were severely curtailed by extra-state resources and traditions from deep in Korean history that upheld the nobility's social supremacy in much of the country. This domination extended to the state as well, as the aristocracy staffed the highest posts and determined the conditions for bureaucratic access, which in turn helped to maintain its privileged social standing.[22] For all its systematic complexity, in other words, the Joseon state ultimately reflected the dominant social group's interests, and to a degree that Marx would have found familiar, except that the Korean aristocracy's supremacy was based on something far more extensive than material resources.

From a modernist perspective, these were among the decisive weaknesses of the Joseon state that became conspicuous when, in response to crises in the second half of the nineteenth century, it tried to mobilize resources in the face of aristocratic opposition.[23] These efforts culminated in the Gabo Reforms of 1894–95, which—while under the protection of Japanese troops who had entered the country to prosecute their war against China—abolished the Confucian civil service examination in conjunction with the pursuit of a wide-ranging, fundamental restructuring of Korean state and society. Although the Gabo government collapsed in early 1896, its basic ideals, approach, and organization would survive in modified form for another half century as the blueprint for state administration.

Even the immediately ensuing state of the Great Korean Empire, which ceremoniously harked back to the Joseon dynasty as its basis for governance, maintained and strengthened most of the Gabo Reform measures. Following relegation to the background during the Gabo Reforms and the utter humiliation of his flight to the Russian Legation in early 1896, King Gojong and his handlers, after more than a year in internal exile, emerged in 1897 to proclaim the monarch an emperor and his realm an empire. The urgent diplomatic needs were clear: to escape imperialist predations by declaring Korea's independence from China and by elevating Korea to a standing equal to that of its powerful neighbors. For these and other advances, the Great Korean Empire, long derided for its failures, has received a surge of scholarly reconsideration over the past two decades. While generating fruitful debate about whether it was, in fact, the harbinger of an autonomous path toward modernity, most of this scholarship has viewed the empire as a noble failure that succumbed to the inexorable forces of imperialism.[24] Clearly, as an effort to fortify the state sufficiently to withstand the geopolitical tides, the Korean Empire fell short, but it should not be dismissed as a quirky final gasp; the strengthening of the monarchical state, which progressed through institutional and fiscal changes as well, included a complementary symbolic push of legitimation that would set an example for subsequent state development, as shown in chapter 3. And as chapter 4 demonstrates, the infrastructural, industrial projects directed by the Crown also endowed the monarchical state with an aura of advancement and established a connection between state legitimacy and economic development that would reappear during the colonial period.

Indeed, these were recurrent patterns not only on the Korean peninsula but around the modern world, a reminder that the national autonomy of these precolonial reforms, not to say the difficulty of measuring such autonomy, mattered little more than the larger regional and global context of state making out of which they arose. It is critical, then, to move beyond examining the precolonial Korean state as an effort, in the exclusive service of Korean autonomy, that fell short of standards established later by a foreign conquest regime. Such lessons are underscored by the historiography of the Japanese takeover, which has focused recently on the protectorate regime of 1905–10 and the increasingly subordinated Korean state that coexisted with it. The picture that has emerged is one of an irregular and somewhat defensive process of incremental Japanese conquest, buttressed by the influx of Japanese soldiers and settlers that added the substance behind the military, bureaucratic, and legal measures.[25]

Japan's reascendance in Korean political affairs, which accompanied its war with Russia in 1904 and 1905, formally began with the signing of an agreement, under Japanese pressure, in February 1904 that allowed Japanese troops to be stationed on Korean soil.[26] Half a year later, the Korean government agreed to a treaty that consented to hiring outside advisors for foreign relations and finance matters.[27] On the heels of Japan's victory in the war the next year came the notorious "Eulsa joyak" treaty of late October 1905 that transferred the Korean state's diplomatic and financial management to the Japanese and led to the establishment, early in the following year, of the Japanese protectorate organ, or Residency-General (Tōkanfu),[28] which exercised sovereign control over the Japanese residents in the major urban areas of the peninsula. The final treaty before annexation, in July of 1907, accompanied the forced abdication of the recalcitrant Korean monarch, Gojong, in favor of his more agreeable son. In requiring the Resident-General's approval for any significant government measure, including in personnel matters, this treaty nailed shut the coffin of Korean autonomy and had a greater impact than the 1905 protectorate treaty or, arguably, even the 1910 annexation treaty.[29] Although it remains underexplored in the historiography, the incorporation of, and dependence on, multitudes of Korean personnel throughout this era constituted a signal feature of the new state order implemented by the Japanese, as chapter 2 details.

Colonial Period, 1910–1945

More so than the military, then, it was the state that served as the instrument of foreign conquest and foreign rule. As suggested above, however, far more than just Japanese soldiers and officials came to Korea; as Jun Uchida has shown, the tens, soon hundreds, of thousands of Japanese residents external to the state played an indispensable, if not always cooperative or willful, role in mediating the colonization process in some form or another. Uchida's study, though, also leaves room to question or even deny, as some historians do, the validity of speaking of a colonial state, for a focus on Japanese residents, most of whom lived in the dozen or so major urban areas and almost all of whom engaged in nonagricultural work, appears to take for granted that the "dispersal of power" through the intervention of settler interests was replicated throughout the colony.[30] The often severe discrepancies in the Government-General's treatment of the two ethnic populations, in other words, leads one to wonder to what extent the native population could have been the object of colonial rule. There is much to be said, then, for the notion that the Japanese colonized not the Korean people as much as the Korean state—using, in effect, a system of proxy rule dependent upon the stout maintenance and exploitation of the ethnic divide. This is a profoundly tempering critique, forwarded by esteemed historians such as Bak Chan-seung,[31] that demands a demonstrable reckoning of this segregation in any attempt to forward an overarching analysis of the colonial state.

While mindful of such colonial binaries, this book takes up the challenge in several ways. First, this study will show, as Uchida also reiterates,[32] that even as ethnic biases, including authorized discrimination, persisted, with some exceptions colonial policies, structures, and methods of rule from the beginning assumed a governed unity consisting preponderantly of Koreans, the overwhelming majority of the peninsula's population. More tellingly, the colonial state depended on a systematic integration—or infiltration—of Korean society in exercising its authority, which grew in line with its structural growth. The colonial state underwent, by every measure, an enormous expansion. The regime, the absolute expenditures for which increased over thirtyfold between 1911 and 1943,[33] created dozens of new agencies, hundreds of new spheres of jurisdiction, and, just as importantly, thousands of new bureaucratic posts. Among the many major state initiatives and projects illustrating this expansion, perhaps the most critical was the first one: the comprehensive land survey from 1910–18, which sought to catalogue all the real estate holdings in Korea. As detailed in chapter 1, an enormous bureaucracy, the Provisional Land Survey Bureau, formed to administer this daunting project and served as the entrance point into the colonial ruling order for thousands of Koreans. The early colonial state also expanded its enforcement apparatus, particularly the civilian and military police, the excessive practices of whom—while reflecting the primacy of pacification and the derisive label of "military rule" originally forwarded by contemporary critics—also contributed to the growing tension with the populace at large. For even such a stark show of force could not prevent the explosion in civil unrest that characterized the March First independence demonstrations of 1919, the bloodily botched suppression of which killed or maimed thousands.

March First heightened the sense that liberation from foreign rule could be openly demanded if not necessarily achieved, galvanized the loose strands of the budding Korean independence movement abroad, and stunned the Japanese rulers into a pronounced and prompt reorientation of their approach to governing. The ensuing period of "Cultural Rule," heralded by the appointment of a new Governor-General, Saitō Makoto, in the fall of 1919, reflected a major liberalization of politics in the metropole that extended across the Japanese empire.[34] The moniker of Cultural Rule is commonly attached also to the general social milieu of the 1920s and 1930s that witnessed a veritable explosion in associational and publication activity—indeed, a *cultural* flourishing on the part of the colonized. In fact, much of the historiography on colonial Korea, particularly in English, has understandably gravitated toward this middle period of almost two decades, when colonial polity and society reached a stability under which the contours of an unmistakably *modern Korean* mode of life emerged, particularly in the urban areas.[35]

In administrative practice, the colonial state under Cultural Rule—while premised on strengthening, not diminishing, Japanese dominion—nevertheless instituted conspicuous managerial reforms: openness over repression, persuasion over coercion, co-optation over domination in handling resistance, and the balancing of ambitions for administrative efficiency with concerns for state efficacy, or legitimacy. One could argue, in fact, that these wide-ranging modifications to colonial rule through greater social integration showed *governmentality at work*, as the Government-General and its Affiliated Agencies undertook a studied, measured series of adjustments through bureaucratic and social management aimed at inducing, rather than coercing, the internalization of colonial authority. And given the subsequent wartime regime, the Cultural Rule state might have represented the peak of governmentality in colonial Korea.

As is well known, the Japanese empire's turn toward a wartime footing, starting with the staged Manchurian Incident of 1931, triggered major changes in the empire's largest colony, Korea, beginning in the mid- to late 1930s. What is highlighted in both the popular and scholarly perceptions of the wartime mobilization period—the final, inglorious phase of foreign rule marked by the extreme exercise of state power—tends to overwhelm considerations of the entire colonial experience, as the regime implanted a litany of regimentations that compounded the deprivations of the period. And as part of the comprehensive, severe extraction of personal, material, and spiritual sacrifices from the colonized populace for Japan's "holy war," the colonial state systematically coerced Koreans into an embrace of Japanese identity itself.

The reach of wartime mobilization became so extensive that, as this book will detail, hardly any realm involving the state escaped its unrelenting push. In public health and disease control (chapter 8), for example, the colonial regime's measures to boost human resources for the battle fronts intensified its long-standing efforts to manage prostitution and control infectious disease. These concerns in turn relied upon fundamental changes to the administrative instruments of social delineation, categorization, and surveillance (chapter 7), which included the notorious policy of coercing the registration of Japanese names upon the colonized population in 1940. In the spheres of religion and education (chapters 5 and 6), the state attempted to produce loyal "imperial subjects" (*kōmin*) of the Japanese monarch, a process expressed institutionally in a variety of ways, from altering the school curriculum to saturating the public sphere with Shinto symbolism, expelling foreign missionaries, and intimidating Christian resisters. All of these steps, in turn, supplemented the colonial state's core drive of wartime mobilization—namely, the rapid industrialization of the colony into a material base for the Japanese military (chapter 4)—and exerted a deep, lasting impact on Korean society as well as on the memory of the entire colonial era.

Such wide-ranging implications, including those for the colonial state, of Korea's wartime experience has prompted recently a stimulating study by Takashi Fujitani on the uncanny parallels between Japanese mobilization of Koreans for the war and American mobilization of Japanese-Americans. In an extensive exploration of the two empires' responses to the need for manpower, Fujitani persuasively shows—by demonstrating the comprehensive efforts militarily, bureaucratically, ideologically, and otherwise to alter the degree and character of ethnic discrimination—that the similarities of the two empires were as striking as the glaring differences. In his consideration of how this process involved the colonial state in Korea, the author accentuates the stringent efforts to instill an extraordinary about-face in state policy toward complete integration of the native populace through the formal elimination of segregation and discrimination. This reorientation resulted in reforms in population surveillance methods—most prominently, the household registration system—in order to implant a voluntary, then a mandatory conscription targeting the Korean population. In short, all of these efforts amounted to the first actualization of a governmentalized state in Korea, or what Fujitani deems the "completion of governmentality,"[36] through the exigencies of total war.

As this book will demonstrate, wartime imperatives did indeed play a seminal role in the formation of the modern state in Korea, as it did elsewhere as well,[37] but this connection began long before the outbreak of the Second Sino-Japanese War in 1937, and in fact manifested itself initially in the First Sino-Japanese War of 1894—the geopolitical circumstances that made the Gabo Reforms possible—and then in the Russo-Japanese War of 1904–5, the catalyst for the Japanese takeover. More importantly, these and other events exerted a cumulative impact on the incremental, measured, and often contested and oppositional development of statecraft rationalities that began to governmentalize state administration well before the wartime mobilization of the 1930s. As Todd Henry has shown, the sites and practices of inducing the reflexivity of colonial subjecthood, from palace exhibitions to hygiene campaigns, were extensive and penetrative from the beginning of colonial rule.[38] Indeed, if one takes the definition of a governmentalized state as one that, according to Fujitani, "operated not by physical and brutal force alone, but also through an explosion of bureaucrats, statistics, background checks, and technologies that sought to constitute individuals into self-reflexive subjects who would ideally regulate themselves and make normative choices,"[39] then it is likely that the state in Korea entered this trajectory even before the Japanese takeover.

ROAD MAP

Broad explorations of the state's institutional, symbolic, and conceptual development in early modern Korea will occupy Part I of this book, "The Structures of State Rationalization." Chapter 1 concentrates on the progress and impact of differing rationalizations in the central state, using two case studies: the land surveys of the precolonial and early colonial periods, and the wartime mobilization measures beginning in the 1930s. As with chapter 1, the expansion of both financial and bureaucratic resources is a key theme in analyzing the provincial and local governing system in chapter 2, which argues for the centrality of the periphery in this era's state development, particularly by focusing on policing and local autonomy, the chapter's two case studies. These first two chapters provide the necessary context to examine in chapter 3 the state's symbolic presence—as a rationalization of state authority to be recognized, internalized, and hence legitimated, and as a facilitator for what can be deemed "ideological engineering," whether in the form of ordinary propaganda or, as seen in the chapter's case studies of official campaigns and spectacles, of more lavish discursive appropriations and interventions.

These considerations of legitimacy and symbolic authority will also permeate the chapters that comprise Part II, "Rationalizing Society," which will consider five social sectors through which the modern state came to be conceived and realized: economy, religion, education, population (or social structure), and public health.[40] As these chapters suggest, each sphere could arguably be taken as the defining feature of the modern state. Just as importantly, in their familiar manifestations these areas also came largely to be demarcated—indeed, constructed—by their reconstituted and increasingly subservient relationships to the state. Since fully accounting for each of these five relationships requires nothing less than five separate monographs, the present study focuses on a particular state rationalization in each chapter to discern the particularities of state making in early modern Korea. Regarding the state's management of the macroeconomy, for example, chapter 4 queries to what extent a developmental state appeared at this time, while for religion, chapter 5 considers secularization as an administrative rationalization that appropriated much of the authority and symbolic standing of religions, which themselves came largely into their modern forms through the state. For education—which, like religion, represented a site of ideological and symbolic contestation—chapter 6 investigates how public schooling, and particularly citizenship education, sought to instill a normative connection between the state and the people. Finally, chapters 7 and 8, which examine the administration of population tracking and public health, respectively, through the rationalizations of registration and disease control, apply the Foucaultian concepts of biopower and disciplinary power in examining the emergent regime of governmentalized biopolitics. Each chapter, then, also pursues a set of secondary rationalities as interpretive tools for each social sector (table 1).

Taken together, these five realms demonstrate core features of the modern state's formation in Korea and forward the arguments of this book. Still, it may strike the reader that several themes are conspicuously underexamined in this study, and hence an explanation is in order. First, mostly left undiscussed will be "politics," in reference to the people and processes, including contestations, behind policy formation and administration. Given the plentiful scholarship that illuminates the ins and outs of political and bureaucratic decision-making and interest-balancing,[41] the present study, while mindful of such dynamics, focuses more on politics in the broadest sense—the impact

TABLE I Social Sectors and State Rationalizations

Social Sector	Rationalization	Secondary Rationalities
Economy	Developmentalism	Legitimacy cultivation; infrastructure investment.
Religion	Secularization	De-Confucianization; pluralism as a regulatory tool.
Education	Public Schooling	Citizenship education; "self-cultivation" in the Ethics curriculum.
Population	Registration and Classification	Governmentalized biopower; social leveling through surnames and occupations.
Public Health	Disease Control	Biopolitics of disciplinary power; discursive construction of state authority.

of state policies and practices, and responses thereto, on considerations of political legitimacy. The same could be said for the military, both as a structural component of the state and as a theme, through militarization, for the state's form and function. The latter is crucial, given especially that military concerns, and of course violence, helped to initiate and continued to infuse the character of colonial rule in Korea (the Governor-General was always a military, and usually army, commander); but the militarized features of the state, which to Foucault were indispensable sources of the disciplining pursuits of modern governmentality,[42] are largely covered by this study's emphasis on policing and on the pronounced impact of the state's militarization for wartime mobilization.[43] Following the elimination of the military police units after 1919, the military's institutional presence itself was confined mostly to the contingent of Japanese soldiers stationed in Korea (Chōsengun). This also inhibits a meaningful study of the theme of territoriality and border control, or of foreign relations in general. While it is true that external relations as a contextual factor—the existence of modern (nation-)states in a competitive international arena—determines considerably a state's character,[44] the colonial state in Korea mostly did not engage in foreign policy. That this reality leads one to question the extent to which the Government-General was even a valid state presents a fruitful tension in this book, particularly when considering the delicate balance between autonomy and dependence in relation to the metropole. Finally, perhaps the most glaring feature of the modern state that eludes dedicated treatment in this study is the penal, legal, and juridical system, or broadly the sphere of the law, which has received recently an injection of engaging analysis from Marie S. Kim.[45]

To be sure, the dissemination and authority of laws and regulations constituted the state's symbolic and discursive infrastructure, and the courts, while operating as state extensions—especially in their role as a source of the civilizing mission—also stood as semi-autonomous voices that checked state ambitions. Such a disaggregated character of the state, one of this book's main findings, will be demonstrated through various other means, as will the centrality of legal measures in the form of ordinances and orders that penetrated every sphere of the bureaucracy.

This brings us, in closing, to the issue of sources. The documents that chronicled and implemented state activities, as well as its rules, regulations, and laws, will constitute a significant portion of the primary sources used in this book. At one level, this is unavoidable, as a study of the state, while maintaining the analyst's filter, must rely substantially on state documents. Indeed a great challenge in reading official sources is to resist a cynicism that endows the entire state archive with a dedicated consciousness. (Far from purposeful, state documents are mostly repetitive, routine, mundane records, and scouring them reaches a level of tediousness that likely went into drafting them in the first place.) Of course, one must turn, as this study does, also to extra-state sources such as newspapers and magazines, as well as memoirs, diaries, and other personal accounts; even literary works can serve to supplement, reframe, and overcome the positivism and biases of state accounts. At another level, the scholar benefits from an awareness of state record-keeping practices themselves as rationalizations,[46] as shown in this study's consideration of household registration methods (chapter 7) and of the proliferation of reports and other forms of knowledge produced by the bureaucracy, including the police. This book takes state documents, then, as both an articulation *and* a tool of the state's comprehension: narratives, ordinances, maps, charts, images, statistics, and other official expressions demonstrate the way state officials saw things as well as the way they wanted to see things. Indeed, these records reinforce the significance of the state as an ideological construct as much as an institutional or social one.

PART ONE

The Structures of State Rationalization

ONE

State Making under Imperialism

FRAGMENTATION AND CONSOLIDATION IN THE CENTRAL STATE

THE STATE IN KOREA UNDERWENT more major changes at the turn of the twentieth century than it had the previous three centuries. Following the devastating Hideyoshi invasions of the 1590s and the Manchu conquests a few decades later, the late Joseon state had settled into a stable form by the latter seventeenth century. For two hundred years thereafter, there were no major revisions in the governing form, which reflected the general stability of the internal order and the protracted peace in East Asia. This relative calm was shattered by domestic uprisings and the pressures from abroad in the second half of the nineteenth century, and in less than a decade following the Korean court's capitulation to Japanese demands for trade and diplomatic intercourse in 1876, the central administration substantially expanded to meet the functional needs of the new era. Another decade later, in the mid-1890s, a sweeping set of reforms altered forever the basic organization of the Korean state. Thereafter, a series of political dislocations hit the peninsula, resulting in the further dissolution of Korea's long-standing governing order through the force of Japanese imperialism. By the 1930s, the state structure, represented by an imposing colonial rule, appeared to have retained only a few traces of the Joseon era.

To be sure, the Joseon dynastic state was itself a formidable institution, comprising a highly systematic collection of hierarchically arranged organs responsible for deliberative, juridical, and managerial functions. These agencies extracted resources (both material and human), exercised policing and defense functions, and governed social interaction within the state's sovereign territory. The long history of such a centralized administration, in fact, firmly cemented durable, normative patterns of state authority. Nevertheless, the Joseon system was also rationalized toward definitively ancient ideals, and in committed conformity to the neo-Confucian social ethos.

The late nineteenth century, an era characterized by persistent contact with foreign influences beyond China, brought forth a *re-rationalization* of this state structure in accordance with a new set of guiding principles rooted in imperialism: first, an overriding concern to relieve external and, to an extent, resultant internal pressures through the creation of new governing functions and institutions, often in emulation of the Meiji Japanese state; then, soon after the turn of the twentieth century, the implementation, under Japanese control, of a more coercive and penetrative state that sought to maximize the interests of foreign rule. The increasing breadth of state responsibilities, which accompanied the diversification of society and economy, also necessitated an enormous expansion of the state itself, whether measured in personnel or material inputs, or in the degree of social presence and intervention. Over the colonial period (1910–45), the state grew fourfold in personnel, over twofold in personnel relative to population, and over twentyfold in invested financial resources, establishing a regime that far exceeded the scope and mobilizational capacity of any Korean administration that had preceded it.

Much of this increase took place in the final decade or so of the colonial era, when military expansionism turned the state into a mechanism for wartime mobilization. As this chapter will show through its explorations of the wartime state as well as of systematic land surveys both before and after the annexation, the colonial state's remarkable growth was, in many ways, an extension of the trajectory, largely drawn by military imperatives, that had begun in the late nineteenth century. At another level, however, two features of the state's development belied notions of progressive rationalization and systematization: the fragmentary, often bifurcated structure of the central state from the late Joseon era through the reforms culminating in the establishment of the Government-General in 1910; and the organizational disjunctures of foreign rule itself, as the challenges of implanting and normalizing a conquest state resulted in multiple, often divergent demands tugging at the colonial regime.

The Joseon Central Administration and Tongni Amun *Agencies of the 1880s*

The reign of the monarch, Gojong (1864–1907), witnessed the emergence of a central state system in Korea that stood in stark contrast to the Joseon model that he had inherited (see appendix). Indeed, the comprehensive changes to the governing order during Gojong's forty-four years on the throne appear all the more extraordinary considering that the existing structure—notwithstanding the abuses associated with the dominance of royal in-law clans in the nineteenth century—was not a despotic tool but rather a systematic organization constructed in emulation of a definitive model found in classical sources.[1] When the final Joseon revision to the dynastic legal code, the *Daejeon hoetong*, was promulgated in the second year of King Gojong's reign (1865), the central organization that it decreed differed little from the basic form inscribed in the original dynastic code, the *Gyeongguk daejeon* of 1471. However, by the 1880s, as demonstrated in the establishment of the *Tongni amun* agencies, new government organs were created to meet functional needs that the old Joseon system clearly could not have foreseen, much less accommodate.

The character of Joseon statecraft can be labeled as "Korean-Confucian," a mixture of Confucian ideals and aristocratic interests, which in turn stemmed from ancient Korean patterns of social hierarchy as well as immediate political considerations regarding political access. It reflected a conscious, deliberate emulation of the models of ancient China, as found in the Confucian canonical texts such as the *Rites of Zhou* (*Zhouli*), as well as both Chinese and Korean interpretations of this tradition. The enduring supremacy of such principles was ensured through the recruitment and promotion system, centered on the state examinations, which tested and reviewed potential appointees on their familiarity with these ideals.[2] The abolition of the examinations by the Gabo Reforms in 1894 thus heralded a major rupture not only in personnel recruitment but in the principles of governance as well.

The Gabo Reforms departed from the Joseon model also in more tightly concentrating administrative authority. The Joseon state, while incorporating the localities under the systematic supervision of the central state, had also allowed room for three separate divisions of government—the High State Council (Uijeongbu), the Six Boards (Yukjo), and a third group comprising the censoring organs as well as the Royal Secretariat (Seungjeongwon)—to jostle for authority.[3] In the seventeenth century the High State Council, while remaining in existence, was replaced by the Border Defense Command (Bibyeonsa) as the supreme deliberative body, but most of the officials overlapped between these two agencies. Such a system of checks and balances, which extended in general to the relationship between the monarch and the officialdom, might have been critical to the stability and longevity of the Joseon ruling mechanism,[4] but the competition between the deliberative and administrative branches, in particular, helped also to fragment central authority. After King Taejong, the third Joseon monarch, instituted the basic model of the High State Council–Six Boards system, a series of struggles ensued during the fifteenth century over the precise hierarchy of these two branches,[5] fueled by competing interpretations of the Confucian canon and by the interests of individual monarchs, who preferred either a joint custody of supreme deliberative authority or domination by one of the two sides.[6] Meanwhile, the Three Censoring Organs (*Samsa*), staffed by ardent young Confucian idealists recruited through the examination system, came to grow sufficiently in stature to wield considerable clout.[7] The power of the censoring organs in turn reinforced the primacy of especially the Board of Personnel and the Board of Rites as the representative administrative organs of Korean-Confucian statecraft, and the fact that neither agency survived the reforms of the late nineteenth century reflected their incompatibility with the era of imperialism. Thus emerged the *Tongni amun* organs of the 1880s.

The new *Tongni amun* agencies, modeled after the *Zongli geguo shiwu yamen* of Qing China, undertook a comprehensive range of new responsibilities associated with foreign contact. The Tongni gimu amun, the first of these agencies, was founded in late 1880 with twelve departments, including those for diplomacy, military affairs, and border control, as well as those for machinery production (Gigyesa), foreign language instruction (Eohaksa), and trade (Tongsangsa).[8] A reduction in the number of departments to seven in late 1881 also eliminated the diplomatic distinction between China and other countries, including Japan, through the creation of a singular Diplomacy Department (Dongmunsa).[9] In late 1882 this agency was replaced by two new *Tongni amun* organs: the Home Office and the Foreign Office.[10] Officially, both fell under the jurisdiction of the High State Council, but like their predecessor, their authority superseded that of other organs, and the highest-ranking officials served in the *Tongni amun* positions while maintaining their posts in the traditional organs.[11]

By assuming a broad range of duties assigned to the Six Boards as well as new functions made urgent by persistent contact with the outside world, the Home Office and Foreign Office of the 1880s expressed the drive to strengthen the Korean state's position both domestically and externally through institutional restructuring. They also demonstrated the willingness of the Korean monarch and his reformist officials to meet the needs of "self-strengthening" in the new era.[12] In so doing, the *Tongni amun* agencies also showed the inadequacies of the Joseon institutional layout, in the age of sustained external contact and competition, for fostering advances in technology, military readiness, and education. The greater significance of the Foreign Office and Home Office, then, lay in their signaling the beginning of the end of the Joseon state order.

Gabo Reforms

Through two main stages in a short span of one-and-a-half years, the Gabo Reforms of 1894 to 1895—or early 1896 in the newly instituted Gregorian calendar—built on the innovations of the *Tongni amun* agencies and instituted a wholesale renovation of the Korean state. This system would survive in modified form for another decade, and arguably, another five decades, as the basic structure of central administration on the peninsula. The Gabo Reforms began with the enactments of the Deliberative Assembly, or *Gunguk gimucheo* ("Military state command"), which was established in the summer of 1894 following the occupation of the capital by Japanese troops in advance of their war against China.[13] A provisional organ of approximately twenty councilors, the Deliberative Assembly exercised sweeping powers and, in only a few months, enacted over two hundred directives that amounted to an all-encompassing reordering of state and society.[14]

In addition to eliminating slavery and the Joseon examination system, which were perhaps the most prominent reforms, the Deliberative Assembly erected a new system of central administration, which combined the former High State Council and Six Boards arrangement into a cabinet system, albeit one still overseen nominally by the High State Council, while eliminating the censoring agencies. In one fell swoop, all organs of the sprawling central bureaucracy from the 1880s, except for the Royal Household Ministry, coalesced into a single state administration. The cabinet was headed by the premier (Chongni daesin) and included the ministers of state (Daesin) of eight ministries (amun): Home Affairs, Finance, Foreign Affairs, Military, Legal Affairs, Trade and Industry, Public Works, and Education.[15] The second Gabo government, formed in late 1894—and now including leaders, like Seo Gwangbom, of the failed Gapsin Coup of 1884 who had returned from Japanese exile—took further steps at administrative streamlining, consolidation, and renaming the following year.[16]

Perhaps the most consequential series of organizational reforms came in the area of finances. In the late Joseon system the motley sources of tax revenue were handled by not only the Board of Taxation but also organs such as the Board of War. This fracturing of fiscal authority had been cited by Korean reformers as one of the root causes of the administrative weakness and widespread corruption of the nineteenth century. Among the first steps taken by the Deliberative Assembly in the summer of 1894 was to separate the fiscal and other affairs of the newly created Royal Household Ministry (Gungnaebu), which contained the numerous agencies catering to the monarchy, from those of the central government.[17] The consolidation of all fiscal administration in the Ministry of Finances (Takji amun, then Takjibu) was to follow in early 1895, along with the implementation of a modern "accounting law" (*hoegyebeop*) that eliminated ad hoc or miscellaneous taxes, standardized practices of written authorization for revenue collection and expenditures, required annualized budgets and updated ledgers, and funneled all financial affairs, with very few exceptions, through the ministry.[18]

Notwithstanding the overt reliance on Japanese models, it is difficult to deny the epochal significance of the Gabo Reforms, for they re-rationalized the state structure from one in accordance with the Korean-Confucian ethos and ancient models to one driven by the geopolitical pressures of imperialism. The Koreans spearheading these reforms—most prominently, Bak Yeonghyo, Yu Giljun, Yun Chiho, and Seo Jaepil—undertook a conscious, determined effort to dislodge society and polity from the Joseon system, and to erect a state designed to secure Korean autonomy and spur economic, social, and cultural developments along the lines of external models. These goals would remain central to state restructuring efforts thereafter, even as political control shifted from one group to another, and even after the resurgence of the Crown re-fragmented the central state.

Korean Empire Period (1896–1905)

The monarch's flight from the court, controlled by Japanese-backed officials, to the Russian consulate in February of 1896 triggered a widespread backlash against the Gabo Reforms and brought down the final Gabo cabinet, chasing most of its leaders to Japan. In the central government, however, the anti-Gabo atmosphere proved more powerful in sweeping away the *people* associated with the Reforms than the institutions. (Indeed, some Gabo figures were retained in influential positions.) The basic structure, authority, and thrust of the Gabo state would persist throughout the subsequent Great Korean Empire, or *Daehan jeguk*,[19] which was declared in the fall of 1897 as the new name and form of the Korean state, headed by a monarch now invested as an emperor. Concurring mostly with the 1897–1907 period of *Gwangmu* ("Glorious military"), in reference to the new reign for the old monarch, Gojong, the Korean Empire continued the Yi dynasty but changed the official name of the country as well as the character of the state itself.

Most notably, the imperial state, until the onset of the Japanese protectorate in 1905, was bifurcated and dominated by the monarchy—or more specifically, the Royal Household Ministry (Gungnaebu) and the various agencies and authorities under its command. The leaders of the Gabo Reforms likely did not imagine that their establishment of a Royal Household Ministry as a way to rationalize, through separation, the Crown's relationship to the government would lead to the incremental appropriation of much of the state's powers by the monarchy. Indeed, by the end of the *Gwangmu* period in 1907, approximately 150 organizational amendments had appropriated new powers for the Royal Household Ministry.[20] And the Gabo state's segregation of the royal household's fiscal affairs into the Office of Crown Properties (Naejangwon), within the Royal Household Ministry, had the ironic affect ultimately of strengthening not the central government's finances but rather that of the monarchy.[21] The Office of Crown Properties, under the direction of Yi Yongik, came to act as an independent bookkeeping entity, and within a few years it appropriated numerous sources of tax revenue from the central government and organized the Crown's vast landholdings and monopolies into a formidable financial basis. By the opening years of the twentieth century the royal household took control of the leasing of mining and fishing rights, railroad concessions, and even the national mint. Such proactive management of the Crown's financial resources also established the pattern of close state command over the macroeconomy that was to continue through the colonial period (see chapter 4).

The monarchy's relatively stout financial position worked hand in hand with its appropriation of military powers as well. These efforts strived toward increasing the prestige and standing of the monarchy as the undisputed source of political authority and, indeed, as the symbol of the country itself. In 1899 came the establishment of the Supreme Military Council (Wonsubu), which acted directly at the behest of the monarch and independently of the central government.[22] The council's measures to flex the Crown's muscle, however, which included staffing the highest military positions with loyal officials and the creation of capital and personal guard garrisons, ultimately did little to strengthen the country's overall military condition. This reality was on clear display beginning in 1904, when Korean high officials proved helpless in the face of intimidating demands from the Japanese, who landed thousands of troops in Korea in preparation for the war against Russia for preeminent control over northeast Asia.

This leads us, then, to question whether, indeed, we can classify the monarchy as a realm of the state itself.[23] Not only was it structurally segregated from the rest of the central government, but unlike the Gabo efforts to conceptually revamp the state several years earlier, the Royal Household Ministry for the most part simply seized or augmented its areas of authority. But the Crown was part of the Korean state by just about every other measure, whether in terms of exercising political authority or mobilizing resources and levying taxes. What the Crown's enhanced power actualized, then, was the institutionalization of the bifurcated modern Korean state, this time in correspondence to a split between the Crown and central government. This preceded the division of the state during the protectorate period according to nationality—with, oddly, the Japanese protectorate taking the position of the "state within the state" that the Royal Household Ministry had occupied in the Korean Empire period.

Protectorate (1906–1910)

In the aftermath of Japan's victory over Russia in the 1904–5 war, the Japanese Residency-General (Tōkanfu), proclaimed in 1905 and established in early 1906, appropriated the Korean government's foreign and fiscal affairs while taking an "advisory" role in other matters. The Resident-General—with elder statesman Itō Hirobumi as the first—served as the head of this organ to oversee the Japanese protectorate. Beneath him the protectorate was divided into two main parts: the (central) Residency-General; and its group of Affiliated Agencies (Sosoku kanshō), the composition of which shifted several times. The Residency-General contained three to four ministries depending on the year, including a separate Police Ministry (Keimubu—1906–7) and later, a Foreign Ministry (Gaimubu—1909). The Affiliated Agencies included Japanese consulates, the Rijichō, in the major urban centers with substantial Japanese populations, the Railroad Supervisory Bureau (Tetsudo kanrikyoku—1907), organs managing the Japanese courts, and agencies for postal and communication services, among others. Total outlays for the protectorate—the majority of which fell under the category of an "advance" to the Korean government (*Kankoku seifu ittaikin*)—saw more than a 2.5-fold increase from 1906 to 1909,[24] while the total number of personnel increased from slightly over a thousand in 1906 to 1,751 by the end of 1909.[25]

These personnel figures, however, do not include the dramatic expansion of the Japanese police and military presence, which provided the coercive elements necessary not only to gradually bring the Korean government and people under Japanese control, but to cultivate a new entrance point into the bureaucratic order for thousands of Koreans (see chapter 2). The momentous treaty of the summer of 1907 between the protectorate and the Korean government, which accompanied the forced abdication of the monarch, Gojong, in favor of his son, Sunjong,[26] gave the Residency-General power to approve personnel appointments in the Korean government and thus transmitted effective control over the state itself.[27] The police system was critical to this process. In August of 1907—three years before formal annexation—Japanese police officials were integrated into the Korean police system, authority over which went into Japanese hands. The former Japanese police advisor became the country's top police official (*Gyeongmu chonggam*, Jpn. *Keimu sōkan*), and other Japanese advisors assigned to the Korean provincial governments likewise now became formal police officials of the Korean state. In this way, the Residency-General's officials could claim to have been appointed by the Korean government, which now had "complete jurisdiction" over even the Japanese residents.[28] Of course, this represented Korean autonomy in name only; Japanese officials were firmly in control of the state's coercive apparatus, which expanded in the remaining years of the protectorate.

In the meantime, the Korean officialdom itself was racked with internal struggles between those favorably disposed to Japanese involvement—many from the same group of reformers who survived the downfall of the Gabo Reforms[29]—and a mixture of anti-Japanese and conservative officials who had regained their high positions in 1896 and resolutely refused to capitulate to the geopolitical tides. This conflict was visible in the 1904–5 period, overlapping with the Japanese entrance into Korea to persecute the war against Russia. The upper hand gained gradually by the cabinet officials who either were pro-Japanese or succumbed to Japanese gunboat pressures was reflected in the reordering of the High State Council system, which scaled back the possibilities of monarchical intervention in state affairs, particularly in finances, to an extent similar to that of the Gabo system of 1895.[30] This trend reflected increasing Japanese efforts to debilitate the Korean monarchy and culminated in the scrapping of the High State Council for good in the summer of 1907 in favor of a revamped cabinet system (*naegakje*).[31] The elimination of the Ministry of Legal Affairs would follow in October of 1909, although oddly, the Ministry of War continued in existence despite having been stripped of most of its functions following the disbandment of Korea's army in 1907.[32]

Colonial Central Administration, 1910–1945

These measures eventually dovetailed into the establishment of the colonial regime, or the Government-General of Korea (Chōsen sōtokufu), the organization of which was formally revealed at the end of September 1910, although the annexation itself had taken place a month earlier through the signing of the annexation treaty and the transfer of all governing authority to the new colonial regime.[33] On the surface, the new administrative order represented a melding of the two polities that had existed side by side in Korea over the previous five years: the Residency-General, including Resident-General Terauchi Masatake (Itō Hirobumi's successor) himself; and the Korean government that had increasingly come under Japanese control after the summer of 1907. The ministries (bu), meanwhile, were reduced from seven to four (Interior, Finance, Law, and Agriculture, Commerce & Industry) plus the Governor-General's Secretariat (Sōtoku kanpō, later Sōmubu), owing to the absence of the foreign and defense ministries and the subsuming of the Education Bureau under the Interior Ministry. And as with the protectorate government, the second main component of the colonial regime was the group of nearly two dozen Affiliated Agencies (Sosoku kanshō), big and small, that included the Advisory Council (Chūsuin), a body composed of pro-Japanese Koreans given titles of nobility, as well as the courts, the Communication Bureau (Yūshinkyoku) handling the postal services, the Police Headquarters (Keimu sōkanbu), the provincial governments, customs service, courts and jails, hospitals, and until 1918, the Provisional Land Survey Bureau, which became the largest state organ in the first decade (see below).[34] Indeed, the Affiliated Agencies, whether measured in financial or bureaucratic resources, were together far larger than the central Government-General (Sōtokufu) itself, serving as the site of most of the colonial state's expansion thereafter.

This general scheme remained in place until the March First independence uprisings of 1919 prompted the colonial authorities to revamp the system, purportedly for streamlining administration.[35] The Government-General's four ministries of the first decade were replaced by a system of six bureaus (*kyoku*), as agricultural and commercial matters now fell under the jurisdiction of the Cultivation Bureau (Shokusankyoku), and as a separate Education Bureau (Gakumukyoku) was revived and a central Police Bureau was created to oversee the suddenly inflated civilian ranks of police upon the dissolution of the *kempeitai* military police units (chapter 2). Three departments at a similar level (Railroad, Public Works [Doboku], and General Affairs) were subsumed under the Governor-General's Secretariat, although by 1925 a separate Railroad Bureau (Tetsudokyoku) was established among the Affiliated Agencies.[36] And in 1921 a new Monopolies Bureau (Senpaikyoku) was created to direct the increasingly prolific colonial state enterprises in ginseng, tobacco, salt, opium, and other products.

Except for the addition of a seventh bureau, that of Agriculture and Forestry (Nōrinkyoku) in 1932,[37] this arrangement remained largely intact until the late 1930s, when the campaigns to procure resources for the war commenced (see below). The Bureau of the Interior changed its named to the Bureau of General Affairs and created a National Total Mobilization Section (Kokumin sōryokuka*).* Two ministries were added in 1939, the Bureau of Planning and the Bureau of External Affairs, in order to coordinate, respectively, the mobilization campaign within the colony and the colonial mobilization measures with the larger imperial effort. By 1941 the Industry Bureau (Shokusankyoku) contained divisions for special minerals and electricity provision, and the central Police Bureau contained divisions for coordinating security efforts such as air raid defenses (*Bōgoka*) and the operation of the economic police (*Keizai keisatsuka*), who were responsible for channeling material resources and repressing unauthorized consumption and activities such as black marketeering. Over the final twenty months of the colonial regime, the most signal organizational change for enhancing the procurement of war materiel was the merging of scattered organs into three dedicated bureaus for mining and industry, agriculture, and transportation, respectively.[38]

Throughout this development the Government-General, like other colonial bureaucracies, functioned as the sturdy "backbone" of imperialist rule.[39] The vertical integration of authority in this bureaucratic autocracy was manifested most clearly in the person of the Governor-General, a Japanese military commander who was appointed by and, through the mediation of the Japanese premier, answered directly to the Japanese emperor.[40] His legislative autonomy conferred upon him powers to create special "system ordinances" (*seirei*) that pertained only to Korea, and in fact, over 80% of the 681 such laws promulgated by the Governors-General of Korea in thirty-five years of rule were in effect only in Korea.[41] This number constitutes over twice as many *seirei* as in Taiwan over fifty years, and in contrast to Taiwan, many of the most important statutes, including the Household Registration Act, maritime laws, and most laws concerning taxation, were *seirei*. And despite the metropolitan efforts to integrate the Korean administration into an empire-wide control system by establishing, for example, a cabinet-level Ministry of Colonial Affairs in 1929, in reality the regime in Korea—particularly the office of the Governor-General—successfully resisted such subordination for the most part, even during wartime mobilization.[42] As many studies and the rest of this book will demonstrate, however, the Government-General fell far short of exercising a dominant autonomy from social forces, and the Governor-General hardly acted unilaterally, much less as an absolute dictator. He stood at the top of a multipronged bureaucracy with internal rivalries and disagreements, divisions that left the regime prone to public pressure from extra-state actors, whether Japanese residents, Korean elites in business or the press, or even the Korean masses—as shown in the sensitivities surrounding popular reaction to colonial state policies following the March First uprising of 1919. And despite the continuing insistence on their formal independence by the Governor-General and his administration, the metropolitan government, with its own array of interest groups, also exerted strong influence over the colonial regime, which remained fiscally dependent on Tokyo and thus had to report to and gain approval for major changes.[43]

Indeed, the sources of revenue and the allocation of resources, both material and human, represent another key to understanding the colonial state, which underwent extraordinary growth in capacity, particularly from 1931 to 1945. Throughout the thirty-five years of colonial rule, in fact, remarkably the Government-General's published annual ledger sheet never showed a deficit.[44] This demonstrated not that the colonial regime established great efficiencies in revenue collection from the beginning, but rather that the metropolitan government provided a substantial portion of the necessary funds, labeled as "supplemental assistance" and including the Special Imperial Grace Endowment from the Japanese monarchy's own coffers.[45] The colonial regime itself underwent frequent structural adjustments in order to increase the revenue stream, and indeed this was one of the primary purposes behind the enormous investment in the colony-wide cadastral survey of 1910–18 (see below), for the land tax represented the foundation of government revenue inflows in the early colonial period. Over its first decade, in fact, the

Government-General relied upon the same basic sources of tax revenue as did the precolonial Korean government—primarily the land tax, plus consumption taxes on alcohol and tobacco, customs duties, various fees for licenses and other documentation services, possessions of public land and other holdings, and monopolies such as those over tobacco and ginseng production and distribution.

Over the 1920s and 1930s, however, the dependence on the land tax was reduced considerably,[46] replaced by other revenue sources such as customs duties, profits from public sector industries like the railroad and telecommunications, state monopolies, the issuance of bonds (including war bonds), as well as various surtaxes, particularly following the outbreak of war with China in 1937 (figure 1). Income from consumption taxes in general, particularly for alcohol, rose at a rate that corresponded to the reduction in land taxes, but perhaps the most notable increase came with the introduction of the personal income tax in 1934. A corporate income tax had been in effect since the 1910s, and in the 1920s a levy on interest income was introduced, but these had constituted only a fragment of the total revenue stream. But through several increases in the personal income tax and the number of people eligible for targeting, as well as the creation of manifold taxes on corporate, business, and interest income throughout the wartime mobilization period, the duties on earnings came to constitute the largest source of tax revenue by the 1940s.[47]

Expenditures also underwent major expansion, and as with revenues, the most notable increases came in the latter half of colonial rule (figure A.2). Total government outlays increased threefold from 1911 to 1920, doubled over the 1920s, and grew fourfold from 1930 to 1940, which amounted to a twentyfold increase over the first three decades of colonial rule, more than double the rate of increase in the gross domestic product.[48] Although the official narrative declared these increases as unavoidable steps, even in the face of austerity, to meet the infrastructural, educational, welfare, cultural, or other pressing needs of the colony, most striking was the dramatic rise in expenditures associated with industrialization, beginning in the 1930s, amidst the transformation of the colony into a critical contributor to Japanese military expansionism. Indeed the communications and transportation linkages with Manchuria, especially the railroads, became a major focal point of budgetary attention in the 1930s, as did in general the overarching demands for investment in the mechanisms of resource procurement, from extending roads and harbors to increasing state management over forests and water resources.[49] With the

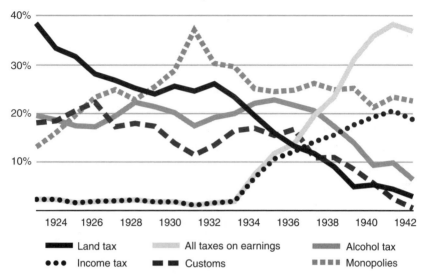

FIGURE I. Percentages of State Revenue from Major Tax Categories, 1923–1942. From Jeong Deok-ju, "Ilje gangjeomgi seje ui jeongae gwajeong e gwanhan yeongu," p. 204.

transition to total wartime mobilization, government expenditures took another major leap, doubling from 1940 to 1943 at the height of the war.[50]

LAND SURVEYS

Given the centrality of territoriality to the powers claimed and exercised by any modern state, and that the ultimate basis for the proliferation of such authority remained the increases in fiscal inputs and outlays, the land surveys undertaken by the state in Korea—the first from 1898 to 1904, and the second from 1910 to 1918—have become a focal point of research into the development of resource management and of the state as a whole. The ramifications extend to the broader issues surrounding the impact of Japanese colonialism, particularly its dependence on information for its dominion, and its relationship to efforts by the pre-annexation Korean state to rationalize fiscal administration.

As with many of the extraordinary changes promulgated by the Gabo Reforms, the stirrings of awareness of the need for a systematic overhaul of the land tax system, centered on a comprehensive land survey, had appeared several years earlier. Given that the last comprehensive survey of the country's land had taken place in the early eighteenth century,[51] government officials recognized the hodgepodge of land taxes—marred by hidden parcels, lack of clarity of ownership for a large proportion of privately owned and cultivated lands, and multiple claimants to public lands—as a main reason behind the state's shortfalls in the latter nineteenth century. This in turn prompted a debate about whether and how to undertake a wholesale reorganization of the relationship between the land tax (*jise*) and land ownership systems, particularly in light of the increasing commodification of privately owned parcels following the port opening of 1876.[52] The Gabo Reforms thus began to institutionalize key features of the rationalization of land ownership that would continue well into the colonial period, including a push to establish a single owner for each parcel of land, eliminate the tax-exempt lands (*myeonseji*) owned by certain government agencies (*yeokdunto*), consolidate all public lands under central government ownership (along with all attendant landlord rights), and in conjunction, abolish the somewhat fuzzy "cultivating semi-owner" (*jungdapju*) status of public lands having been passed down for centuries.[53] Alas, the Gabo Reform cabinets fell before these ambitions to begin the process of systematic surveying and rationalization could be realized, but as with other main features of the Gabo Reforms, the blueprint for action had been drawn, and this project would be taken up by the Korean Empire state beginning in 1898. In fact, many of the Confucian reformists behind the establishment of the empire viewed land reform as bridging the divide between core traditional values and the urgent demands for institutional change.[54]

The so-called "Gwangmu Land Survey" (*Gwangmu toji josa sa-eop*) of 1898–1904, the object of a substantial amount of scholarship,[55] actually was a two-step process: first, of undertaking a survey of all land parcels in the country; and second, beginning in 1901, of using this information as the basis for issuing titles. This began with the establishment of the Land Surveying Agency (Yangji amun), a central, independent organ charged with increasing the state's grasp of the main source of government revenue. An American, Raymond Krumm, was hired as the lead engineer (*sugisa*), responsible for training and supervising American and Korean surveyors in modern methods, with both central coffers and local treasuries providing the funds for new equipment and manpower as he traveled around the country.[56] The surveying work, beginning with the counties in Chungcheong province in 1899, was done on the spot as well as from existing documentation, and by the time the process was halted following a major crop failure in 1901, slightly

FIGURE 2. Korean survey official and American Raymond Krumm conducting the Gwangmu land survey, ca. 1901. From *Sajin euro boneun Hanguk geunhyeondaesa*, v. 1.

over a third (124) of all the counties in the country had been accounted for (figure 2).[57] The resulting land registers (*yangan*) graded each parcel of land through a traditional system of determining potential yield (*gyeolbuje*), indicated the relative location and approximate shape of each parcel, and recorded the owner (person, communal, or government body) and tenant. They also identified the "current owner" (*siju*), who would be responsible for paying the land tax for the parcel in question, and "current cultivator" (*sijak*), who was often the same person.[58]

If this first phase was designed to increase the tax yield and determine ownership of each parcel of land, the creation of the Land Certification Agency (Jigye amun) a few months after the surveying process formally ended before completion, sought to establish the principle of state-recognized private land ownership. This agency's issuance of official deeds for agricultural lands (*jeondap gwan-gye*) and homes (*gasa gwan-gye*), which were surrendered to and reissued by the government with every transaction, confirmed the state's sole authority for determining and adjudicating property ownership.[59] As with the surveying effort, the new agency directed the activities of specialist officials trained to issue titles based on the new land registers; indeed, so close were these two agencies in purpose that they were merged into a single organ (Jigye amun) a few months later in early 1902. Efforts to increase the state's authority in land transactions also were seen in the prohibition on issuing deeds to non-Koreans,[60] a move designed to halt abuses at the hands of exploitative foreigners but which actually invited further complications, especially from Japanese residents who made arrangements for Koreans to purchase plots on their behalf. Another problem, which had beset the surveying process as well, was the lack of enforcement of a single name system in the legal and household registration realms, which made it unlikely that the land registers and titles would note the "real" names of the owners.[61]

These shortcomings highlight the difficulties of assessing the historical significance of the Gwangmu land reform project, for it developed in conjunction with, and depended upon, reforms in other state realms such as household registration and local administration. The Gwangmu survey, while incomplete, was clearly systematic and authoritative in the areas for which the surveying was completed, as both the surveying of lands and issuing of deeds produced extensive new data and documentation on which subsequent efforts at reform and rationalization would be based.[62] Indeed, by early 1904, when the process was halted, two-thirds of all the country's counties had been surveyed by either the original Land Surveying Agency or the Land Certification Agency, with titles issued in five of the eight traditional provinces.[63] Another gauge of the larger impact of this project was the effect on the land taxes flowing into state coffers, which appears to have been pronounced. This revenue in absolute terms increased fourfold from 1898 to 1904, with tax yield per unit (*gyeol*) increasing threefold.[64] According to a study of this era's state budgets, the land tax increased from constituting approximately one-half to nearly three-quarters of all government tax income from 1898 to 1903, with the biggest gains coming in the last two years of this period.[65] On the other hand, these ledgers also suggested that the Gwangmu land survey did not always constitute a major state investment, and eventually the money dried up in 1902, before the project's completion.[66]

This stands in perhaps the starkest contrast with the comprehensive land survey launched upon the onset of the colonial regime in 1910, which appears to have received a great amount of state attention and resources until the end. While plans to pursue such a survey were already well developed in the late protectorate period, the process began formally the day after the signing of the annexation treaty (but before its formal proclamation), on August 23, 1910, through the promulgation of the "Land Survey Ordinance" (Tochi chōsahō) that outlined the basic procedure going forward, including the provisions for reporting ownership claims.[67] By the end of September 1910 the Provisional Land Survey Bureau (Rinji tochi chōsakyoku) came into being through one of the many imperial decrees proclaiming the commencement of the Government-General.[68] The official history of this project noted that the early and strong attention it gained in official circles reflected the imminent need for reforming both the land and taxation systems and, moreover, of clarifying once and for all the ownership of land parcels, around which there had been ongoing and innumerable disputes.[69] And in a further sign of the significance attached to this project by the colonial authorities, the bureau was headed by the Vice Governor-General, who formally sat atop an agency that underwent several changes in the first few years of existence, but which always focused on three primary tasks: the determination of ownership, the assessment of land value in order to assign tax obligations, and the study of each parcel's geological features, including its location, size, and category. Land registers and titles that recorded this information reflected a meticulous approach to surveying. Each urban or rural property, for example, was assigned one of approximately fifty grades, and its value was determined according to the property's purpose (residential, commercial, etc.) as well as its condition, while agricultural plots, for which there were 132 grades, were assessed according to their fertility and potential profitability. These assessments considered the preexisting valuations and land tax obligations, as well as the newly rationalized standard established for each province and locality. Such a process depended considerably on the bureau's new maps, which in turn accounted for regional differences and distinctive territories, such as Geumgang Mountain or the special historical cities of Gyeongju, Buyeo, and Gaeseong, in their detail.[70]

All of this indicated a degree of systematization that far exceeded the earlier attempt by the Korean Empire government, although the rationalizing goals were very similar. The deliberate pace and thorough coverage of the later project, at least, appear to have reflected the purposeful determination touted by the authorities, who envisioned from the beginning an eight-year effort.[71] The project for each district or locality proceeded through three steps: a preliminary survey that publicized and promoted the project, confirmed local administrative boundaries, and gathered existing ownership documentation and new ownership claim forms; the delineation of land categories and determination of ownership; and the resolution of ownership disputes through a process that culminated in investigations undertaken by a special committee.[72] Special committees were created, in fact, also to review maps, hiring practices, field work, and documentation.[73] The assessment of urban properties was mostly completed by 1914, after which the surveying of plots in the rural areas, the heart of the project, quickly escalated.[74] Most of this process—the on-site triangulation and standardization surveys, then the drawing up of land and tax registers, deeds, and maps—took place in the three-year span from 1914 to 1916. The project came to a close in 1918, having produced mountains of data and voluminous documentation that were still in official use in the late twentieth century as the basis of tax assessment and land transactions.[75] In expanding the colonial state's revenue stream, the survey seems to have had the intended effect: While the rise in the land tax revenue immediately following the completion of the cadastral survey was 17%—though some provinces actually showed a decrease—the cadastral survey resulted in a 53% rise in the total land area subject to taxation.[76]

Equally pertinent for evaluating the colonial land survey was the prodigious investment of financial and especially bureaucratic resources to the effort. Indeed the outlays of the Provisional Land Survey Bureau increased nearly threefold from 1911 to 1915 and came to constitute over 5% of the total expenditures of the colonial state (table 2). At the peak of the survey in 1915, this organ deployed over 10% of all government workers—more than five thousand managers, inspectors, technicians, clerks, assistants, apprentices, runners, and contract workers (*go*)—with the majority in ranked official positions (*hannin*).[77] The ordinance promulgating the bureau in 1910 in fact had left plenty of room for an expansion of both financial and bureaucratic investments as deemed necessary,[78] and as it turned out, this growth took place immediately and continued through most of the project. And from the beginning, Korean employees, who were specially prepared for this work at government training centers, became integral to the process. Starting with approximately 600 ranked officials (managers and technicians) and 81 workers (mapmakers and clerks) in 1911, these training centers eventually graduated close to 3,500 Koreans destined for the bureau.[79] Indeed, by 1912 and 1913, Koreans constituted the large majority of the bureau's technicians, clerks, and of course laborers.[80] In 1915 Koreans occupied 78% of the 3,256 official positions in the bureau—although almost exclusively in the lower-ranked posts—and made up 76% of the 1,407 contract workers.[81]

The recruitment of thousands of Koreans into the colonial bureaucracy through the cadastral survey complicates any attempt to enter the long-running historical debate surrounding the project. The clarification of ownership and the purchase of large tracts of land by major financial institutions such as the Oriental Development Company and the Korea Development

TABLE 2 Settled Expenditures (*kessan*), for the Provisional Colonial Land Survey

	Total Expenditures of Govt. -General (yen)	Provisional Land Survey Expenditures (yen)	Percentage of Land Survey to Total	Proportion of Previous Year's Expenditures
1911	46,172,310	1,349,875	2.9%	331%
1912	51,781,224	2,085,389	4.0%	154%
1913	53,454,484	2,466,074	4.6%	118%
1914	55,099,834	3,074,939	5.6%	125%
1915	56,869,947	3,735,346	6.6%	121%
1916	57,562,710	3,322,003	5.8%	89%
1917	51,171,826	1,821,993	3.6%	55%

SOURCE: Derived from *Chōsen sōtokufu tōkei nenpō* (1918), pp. 1038–39.

Bank (see chapter 4) unmistakably stripped many people of lands the ownership of which had been either contested or unsettled. This likely also contributed to the rapid increases in tenancy that characterized the colonial rural economy. Understandably a prevailing historical judgment has viewed the cadastral survey, along with the financial and other nonstate institutions that facilitated the project, as instruments of Japanese economic conquest on the heels of the political takeover from 1905–10. While the increases in tenancy undoubtedly point to the consolidation of ownership in the hands of increasingly large landlords, however, what remain debatable are whether these landlords who benefited from the survey were mostly Korean or Japanese, and to what, if any, extent the colonial regime outright seized private Korean landholdings.[82] For the purposes of considering the project's impact on the state's administrative development in the early twentieth century, a related issue comes to the fore: the connections between the colonial survey and the Gwangmu survey of the turn of the century. For there is a consensus—notwithstanding the contention over the degree of exploitation—about the sophistication and systematization, indeed *modernity*, of the colonial survey, which can be taken as a microcosm of the colonial state as a whole. The issue becomes, then, how close to this model the Gwangmu survey itself came, and how much the Gwangmu project established a basis for the colonial one.

Persuasive in this regard are scholars who argue that, despite the sheen of modern rationality, at its core the Gwangmu land survey's overriding purpose was to increase tax revenue, particularly for the Crown, and that everything else remained secondary to this basic concern. Furthermore, the

Gwangmu survey achieved little success in establishing a comprehensive ownership standard, as demonstrated by the absence of a real name system, a lack of precision in recording addresses or plot sizes, and a dependence on the traditional method of determining potential agricultural output (*gyeol-buje*).[83] In sum, the effort remained far short of a truly modern system like that implemented by the colonial state. Unlike the Gwangmu effort, the colonial survey did away with all vestiges of the long-standing "all land is the king's land" principle, nationalized large plots for which ownership was unclear or vaguely attached to government offices, privatized tracts of mountainous regions as a means of promoting reforestation, restricted private joint ownership to officially recognized corporate bodies ("legal persons"), and in general instituted, for the first time, a highly legal-rational system that would serve as the basis of land management in Korea thereafter.[84] That the "Japanese" appropriated much land through these efforts, in other words, might have been true but also unavoidable in the process of modernizing the land system.[85]

Scholars who stress the continuities between the two efforts, on the other hand, point out that the Gwangmu survey's intent and organization reflected the push to apply essentially new rationalities to a practice that had been in existence for centuries, and while this project remained incomplete, systematic on-site surveying took place for a major proportion of the plots, followed by the issuance of deeds that acted as exclusively legal documentation.[86] Hence this process reflected the state's exercise of an expanded, legal-rational, indeed modern sense of authority, while bolstering the state's position as a promoter and protector of private property. Indeed, there is little doubt also that the broader purpose of both land surveys was first and foremost the clarification of ownership in order to assess tax liabilities more precisely and efficiently, and while the technical and administrative advances deployed in the colonial survey were impressive,[87] the differences with the Gwangmu survey could be seen as one more of degree than of kind. As Edwin Gragert has demonstrated, the colonial survey mostly accelerated patterns in private landholding, tenancy, and even state registration practices that had been developing for decades, and indeed, colonial exploitation processes benefited considerably from the ingrained systematization of land ownership in Korea.[88] And as Choe Won-gyu has detailed, the entire period from the Gabo Reforms to the colonial cadastral survey witnessed increasing efforts to streamline ownership for the purpose of increasing the state's revenue collection, which had the effect of laying much of the groundwork for the colonial effort.[89] Finally, there were clear bureaucratic continuities between the two regimes. A background investigation into the Korean technicians (*gisu*) who worked in the opening year of the colonial survey, for example, shows that one-quarter of them, nearly fifty, began their surveying careers in the pre-annexation Korean government, including several who participated in the Gwangmu survey itself.[90] There is much to support, in other words, the picture of the state's reform of the landholding system as a continuum from the late nineteenth century to the early colonial period, a consistent effort at resource mobilization and the application of ever more administrative (and mobilizational) rationalities.

THE WARTIME MOBILIZATION STATE

This accumulation of rationalities came to a head in the late 1930s and early 1940s, when the colonial state, in contributing to the Japanese war effort, attempted to exercise an altogether new level of social domination. As chapters 2 and 3 will detail, the organizational basis for wartime mobilization was the construction of a close administrative connection between the central and local governments through special mobilization agencies. These units pursued campaigns in the 1930s for increasing agricultural, and then industrial, output and for engendering a "spiritual" reorientation of the populace, following similar efforts implemented in Japan. Indeed, the increasing assertiveness of the metropolitan government in Tokyo directly effected major structural changes to the colonial state, which by the 1940s could be considered a provincial component of the imperial government.[91]

The second Sino-Japanese war of the modern era, triggered by the Marco Polo Bridge incident of July 1937, led to the transformation of the Korean colony into a major military-industrial base. Tellingly, wartime mobilization began with a focus on the ideological mobilization of the population. The National Spirit Total Mobilization Movement, in tandem with the same campaign announced in Japan in 1938, reflected the belief, as Governor-General Minami Jirō put it, that the spiritual component of a country's people would have the most decisive impact on achieving victory in such a "holy war."[92] In the colony this campaign began with the establishment of the Korean League for Total Mobilization of National Spirit (Kokumin seishin sōdōin Chōsen renmei). This network of committees and agencies, connecting the center to the localities, formed the conduits for actualizing

surveillance and education directives as well as for disseminating and enforcing wartime behavioral guidelines for food, clothing, shelter, ritual activities,
and social customs. Though formally overseen by the Governor-General and
Vice Governor-General, the league functioned as an extra, almost parallel
administration within the colonial state, with advisory committees overseeing correspondent spirit mobilization leagues down to the provincial, county,
township, and village levels. This network culminated in the thousands of
neighborhood patriotic associations (*aikokuban*), each comprising about ten
households, that encompassed in principle everyone in the colony.[93]

Following the Japanese imperial government's next escalation of wartime
mobilization through the Imperial Rule Assistance Movement (*Daisei yoku-
san undō*) in 1939, the Government-General recast its own efforts by establishing the Korean League for National Total Mobilization (Kokumin
sōryoku Chōsen renmei) in 1940, which integrated the organizational framework of the National Spirit Total Mobilization Movement with the Rural
Revitalization Campaign that had begun in 1932 (chapter 2).[94] The Total
Mobilization League, headed formally by the Governor-General and Vice
Governor-General and led by high officials of the colonial state, was deemed
to consist of "everyone in Korea as well as participating organizations."[95] It
sought to "bring to complete realization the self-sacrifice of the home front"
on the way toward establishing a "high-level national defense state structure"
(*kōdo kokubō kokka taisei*) in accordance with the plans emanating from the
metropole. The Supreme Committee (Shidō iinkai) of the Total Mobilization
League gathered together the head of every ministry, as well as military and
civilian officials and notables from business, education, and other realms of
the social elite, to form planning and advisory committees at every level of
colonial government administration. This apparatus also integrated over
seventy major public associations—business, occupational, cultural, student,
regional, local, etc.—often with names that switched to or added the tag of
"Total Mobilization" (*sōryoku, sōdōin*). These agencies articulated the mobilization directives sent down to the administrative organs and officials in the
provincial and local governments, who in turn organized local branches of
the Total Mobilization League. By 1941–42, approximately 65,000 district-
or village-level leagues, 430,000 neighborhood patriotic associations, and
nearly 4.5 million households (out of approximately 4.8 million) had been
integrated into the league.[96] The mobilization campaign led by the league
developed, in sum, a mechanism that aimed to regulate the daily lives of
nearly the entire population in some form or another.[97]

The primary aim of this constant flow of regulations and restrictions, however, lay in procuring and increasing material and human resources.[98] Such measures, planned and promulgated by central organs, transmitted to local bureaucracies, and implemented mostly by neighborhood patriotic associations, ranged from encouraging savings and enforcing the recycling of waste to stamping out ostentatious rituals for weddings and funerals. Beyond these efforts to manage behavior, the Government-General of course tried to enact a dramatic shift in the colonial macroeconomy toward war-oriented industry and commerce, including a renewed focus on mining, machine tools, military vehicles, chemicals, and other predominantly heavy industry ventures.[99] The ministry-level Department of Planning (Kikakubu) established in 1939 surveyed the availability of resources in the colony and directed the procurement drive, particularly through the state's control over the production, distribution, preservation, and recirculation of natural resources.[100] In addition to the enormous increases in consumption and income taxes beginning in the mid-1930s (above), extra bonds and fees were levied, some of which fell under a "Special Tax Law [in commemoration of] the China Incident" (Chōsen Jina jihen tokubetsu zeirei) proclaimed in 1938.[101]

Although in effect all government organs participated in some capacity, separate ledgers were kept for the mobilization campaigns, which showed that the bureaucratic components created to manage the process, from the central league and committees to their equivalents in the localities, required a substantial financial commitment. The sources of funds, including donations, numbered only a few, but the largest amount of dedicated revenue, perhaps not surprisingly, came from extra money provided by the Government-General's central treasury (Kokko bojōkin). The total revenues budgeted for mobilization increased precipitously, from approximately one hundred thousand yen in 1938 to nearly eight hundred thousand in 1941 and then nearly two million by 1944: a rise of over 1,800% over a seven-year span. The targets for the budgeted outlays in that period were far more numerous—over forty categories—and demonstrated the broad scope of mobilization: along with salaries, travel fees, and other human resources expenses, mobilization funds went also to indoctrination and cultural campaigns, publishing efforts, and communication (radio, recordings, films) expenses, among others.[102]

To what extent this enormous investment made a significant difference in the colonial state's procurement of resources, or in molding the people's outlook, is not only difficult to measure but fraught with contradictory evidence and inconsistent judgments in the documentation. The official history noted, for example, that the government's goals for production increases were met successfully for 1941 and 1942.[103] But for every glowing official report on the rising industriousness and strengthening awareness of the people, there are accounts from other observers suggesting, as other parts of this book will show, distress, resistance, and the mundane, coerced, and performative nature of the mobilization activities.[104] What cannot be doubted is the determination of the colonial state to arrange and enforce dramatic changes in everyday life, particularly regarding economic activities. Gim Yeong-hui, for example, has detailed the wide range of mobilization measures followed in Hwanghae province, based on that provincial league's detailed overview from 1941: visiting Shinto shrines and war memorials; donating material goods; working on public cleanup and construction efforts; observing bans on hoarding, black marketeering, and price gouging; intensifying recycling and saving; foregoing the use of luxury items or any display of conspicuous consumption (such as in weddings); even following guidelines for what to eat.[105] Indeed restrictions on food and drink proved especially disruptive, for the wartime economy limited significantly the availability of not only staples such as rice, but also alcohol and other garnishments to the customary diet.[106] But beyond the struggles and grousing over these and other hardships—having to wear only colored clothing, for example, as traditional white garb required too much upkeep, so the reasoning went—these austerity measures did not reach the threshold of arousing widespread, organized opposition, as people mostly slogged through the war.[107] Still, it remains questionable whether the mobilization delivered enough of a gain in the war effort to counterbalance the severe deprivation, which bestowed a dark legacy in subsequent Korean history and in the collective memory of the late colonial period, indeed of the colonial experience as a whole.[108] Much could be said of the growth of the wartime state as well, for as Brandon Palmer has found, in its efforts to gain soldiers and industrial labor, the wartime colonial state fell far short of putting forth a domineering, efficient, secure, or even sincere effort at procurement and social control.[109]

CONCLUSION

Whether one views these mobilization measures as the logical outcome of the administrative growth of the Government-General or as an aberration amidst extraordinary circumstances, the wartime colonial state left a lasting, largely baneful imprint and reflected the core realities of state growth on the peninsula dating back half a century. For throughout the process, the circumstances of imperialism, particularly the demands of war and militarization,[110] consistently drove the organizational and institutional development of the early modern state. From the initial state strengthening efforts in the 1880s in response to—and emulation of—imperial powers, and the systematic, sweeping changes of the Gabo Reforms under the protection of a Japanese military preparing for war against China in 1894, to the "Glorious Military" reign (*Gwangmu*, 1897–1907) of the Great Korean Empire, war and its prospects spurred state making as a defensive measure by the Korean state at the turn of the twentieth century. Needless to say, the succeeding colonial regime, the primary institutional manifestation of Japanese imperialism on the peninsula, was strongly militaristic in character, from its top official, the Governor-General, to its heavy-handed pacification priorities in its first decade that triggered the massive resistance movement of 1919. The colonizer's response to the March First demonstrations introduced, in the form of Cultural Rule, a reprieve from this military orientation, but by the late 1930s, a war-driven regime stamped the last decade of colonial rule to cap more than a half-century of state growth inscribed by imperialism.

As tempting as it is to reduce state development in this era to the rationalities of militarized imperialism, however, until the mobilization of the late 1930s and 1940s, the state in Korea never pursued war, though often it was an expression of war's repercussions. The growth in the state's coercive power and institutional systematization, furthermore, followed its own logic and dynamics, characterized by precipitous increases in fiscal and bureaucratic resources and a rationalization of state organization toward both more efficient administration and more effective rule. The Gabo Reforms, for example, took numerous steps to increase and clarify revenue sources, including the separation of monarchical revenues from those of the state. As it turned out, the succeeding Great Korean Empire overturned the original intent of these reforms, as the Crown appropriated most fiscal powers and resources on its way toward constituting the heart of the state itself. The overarching path toward a re-rationalization of state organization continued apace, however, as seen in the revamping of the household registration system in 1896 (chapter 7) and in the cadastral survey pursued by the central government beginning in 1898.

Indeed, as seen in their respective land surveys, the continuities between the Korean- and Japanese-run states were as striking as the ruptures. And on both sides of the temporal divides between Korean and Japanese rule (1905, 1907, or 1910), the state was characterized by cleavages. The late Joseon state, in fact, had long been administratively fragmented, and the *Tongni amun* organs of the 1880s, an expression of modernizing reform, prolonged this problem by operating next to, instead of replacing, the existing agencies. The Gabo Reforms briefly attempted to reconstitute a unity to the central state, but its small provision for administrative partitioning—the segregation of the monarchical agencies—paved the way toward a firmer institutional division in the succeeding Great Korean Empire between the ascendant Crown and a supplicating central government. The imposition of the protectorate further splintered the Korean state by adding a secondary state—soon to become primary in 1907—on the peninsula.

The colonial regime aimed to put a stop to this tendency through an emphatic administrative consolidation, but it, too, was organizationally Janus-faced, on several levels. First, in reflecting the strong continuities with the precolonial state, and in response to the legitimacy gap of foreign rule, the colonial regime depended upon the appointment of a great number of Korean officials. This feature, highlighted by the thousands of Koreans deployed to implement the land survey of 1910–18, became clear immediately following annexation and continued to mark the colonial state until the end. Second, the colonial state oscillated between coercion and social immanence as its preeminent manner of rule. The first decade, characterized by pacification as the overarching priority, was followed by the period of Cultural Rule in which the state was re-rationalized toward the dispersal of power and feedback mechanisms. This approach, though, was overrun by an intensively mobilizational wartime state that nevertheless fell well short of exercising totalizing power. Finally, the colonial government, like its predecessor on the peninsula, structurally reflected the multiple, often conflicting rationalizations of the modernizing state, from the competing institutional actors within the officialdom who represented different constituencies and interests, to the constraints against the transfer of Japanese models amidst the challenges of effecting popular identification with a foreign conquest state. As chapter 2 will show, such competing rationalities characterized the relationship between the central state and its provincial and local extensions as well.

The Centrality of the Periphery

DEVELOPING THE PROVINCIAL AND LOCAL STATE

"IN RECENT TRENDS [around the world], the [central] state's sphere of direct administration has been shrinking and gradually distributed to the provinces, driven by issues closely connected to the people's welfare," wrote Mizuno Rentarō, the Vice Governor-General (Seimu sōkan) of Korea, in 1920.[1] Mizuno's invocation of global trends and his emphasis on the proper response to Korea's current historical stage recycled the time-tested rhetoric of the civilizing mission that had accompanied the Japanese takeover a decade earlier, but this narrative of internal demands and external models also reflected the dual development of local administration throughout this era. On the one hand, the increasing attention and resources devoted to administering the localities represented the ever-growing state ambition of comprehensive oversight and guidance, but on the other, this growth suggested—as Mizuno's explanation did—a rising awareness of the need to accommodate local practices and absorb local responses to state policies and actions. In sum, this increasing centrality of the periphery in the longer arch of early modern state growth signaled, depending on circumstances, both an extension of the central state and its devolution.

These phenomena could also be considered two sides of the same coin—that the institutional growth in local government represented both the carrot and the stick of the expansionist modern state: the need to address the welfare of the overwhelming majority of the population while simultaneously keeping the people in line through a disciplining central mechanism. Maintaining the balance between both demands, particularly when they represented contrasting administrative interests, remained a major challenge. This was especially the case in the colonial period, when the Government-General, while enjoying considerable autonomy, served also as a kind of provincial government in relation to the metropole. And another set of circumstances proved just as formidable: the strong centralism of Confucian statecraft as envisioned and practiced in the late Joseon dynasty. The Korean reformers at the turn of the twentieth century did not fundamentally alter this general principle, which was manifested in the relative mobilizational weakness and informality of local administration, but the Japanese, in their process of conquest, had little choice but to concentrate on the localities, if only to suppress resistance. In the 1920s, the heightened distribution of authority, resources, and attention to local government through Cultural Rule shifted the focus toward absorbing extra-state feedback and accounting for local particularities. But the increasing wartime mobilization of the 1930s returned power to the capital, which used local administration as a mechanism for achieving centralizing goals.

In analyzing the development of local administration through this thematic duality of centralization and localization, the present chapter explores organizational changes from the late Joseon to the late colonial period, with a focus on two main themes and their institutional manifestations: the enforcement of rule in the localities, as seen through the growth of the police system; and local autonomy, as shown in local councils and mobilizational organs. Running through both themes will be two outcomes integral to the larger story of the local state in this era: the extent and manner by which state revenues were dispersed to and generated by local institutions; and the personnel effect, or the recruitment and actions of local officials. The colonial period, in particular, brought forth a dramatic expansion in the size of the state, particularly as measured by the number and function of state workers, and this growth mostly came in the realm of local government.

CENTERING THE MARGINS

The development of local government in Korea from the late nineteenth to the mid-twentieth century was largely one of broadening and filling—filling the institutional gap separating the capital from the provinces and localities through an increase in powers, agencies, resources, infrastructure, and officials in the localities, and the creation or extension of sites of interaction between the state and populace. This process engendered the further penetration of centralizing forces, to be sure, but the increasing transfer of bureaucratic attention, financial resources, and civilizing impulses to the areas where most of the people lived also transformed local administration from an appendage of state power to arguably its core.

Late Joseon Era

It is generally acknowledged that one of the major advances instituted by the Joseon government was the implementation of a local administration system over the entire realm. Whereas only a fraction of the localities came under the jurisdiction of a centrally appointed official during the Goryeo period (918–1392), within a half-century after its founding the Joseon dynasty reorganized local administration and dispatched a magistrate to preside over each of the over three hundred counties, as well as a governor, vice governor, and commanding military officers for all of the eight provinces.[2] There remained, however, an invisible boundary between central and local political administration, beyond which the central government rarely ventured. From the vantage point of the capital, local administration was successful if local officials could collect their tax quotas, manage the grain distribution system in times of need, marshal corvee labor and military duties—usually substituted with a cloth payment—and were not so venal as to instigate a rebellion. In the latter Joseon dynasty, however, as seen in the frequent bouts of corruption in local administration, which the government tried to curb by circulating "secret inspectors" (*amhaeng eosa*),[3] these local officials were not integral parts of the Joseon administrative framework. This stemmed from a variety of factors, including the prevailing Confucian model of statecraft that privileged the center, the strong centralizing tendencies of Joseon politics and society, and perhaps most important of all, the geographical, political, and perceptual gulf separating the capital from the localities.

To illustrate this point, one can review the structure and personnel of the Provincial Office, or Gamyeong, headed by the provincial governor (*gwanchalsa* or *gamsa*), and of the county headquarters (*gwana*), commanded by the country magistrate (*suryeong*).[4] The complexity of the Provincial Office reflected the variegated and comprehensive duties of provincial government—managerial, juridical, fiscal, military—for which the governor was responsible and largely autonomous in fulfilling. Among the few centrally appointed officials who together constituted the official class (*gwanwon*) at the provincial government seat was the vice governor (*dosa*), whose responsibility was "generally to look after administration and people's circumstances," share inspection duties, and observe the propriety of administration, much as a censor in Seoul might.[5] Next came the various military and constabulary units, as well as the mid-level bookkeepers and managers drawn from the hereditary class of clerks, the *hyangni*, who handled the day-to-day administration. These clerks manned the Yukbang, or Six Chambers, which covered the same responsibilities (personnel, taxation, and so on) as those of the Six Boards (Yukjo) in Seoul.[6] The provincial governor and the few centrally appointed officials thus remained beholden to bureaucratic actors who were much more familiar with local conditions—as stipulated by law[7]—a situation that was even more acute for the country magistrates, who also had to contend with local elites whose social status was often higher, and who remained even more dependent upon the *hyangni* clerks.[8]

Despite their hereditary status as subservient officials, the *hyangni* were the indispensable lubricant of Joseon local administration. Their specific functions were missing from the otherwise extensive dynastic code, rendering them the foremost of the many customary actors in local government even while standing effectively as the state to the average person. They monitored the pulse of the community through their day-to-day contacts with the people in order to carry out their duties in tax assessment and collection, distribution of relief grains and other interim welfare measures, conscription for labor service, and policing. They were responsible for cataloging, recordkeeping, and accounting, and they updated the household registers and other documents that kept track of the tax burdens of local inhabitants.[9] Understandably, given that they were not provided official stipends, the potential for abusive and corrupt behavior on the part of these "functionaries," a familiar trope in traditional folklore, remained of primary concern to the county magistrate. This magistrate-clerk relationship, which represented the meeting of centrally dictated standards with local particularities, would prove equally critical to the development of local government at the turn of the twentieth century, particularly since the descendants of the *hyangni* appear to have ridden the devolution (or evolution) of their duties in the new administrative systems to take commanding roles in local society.[10]

Gabo, Korean Empire, and Protectorate Periods, 1894–1910

Problems in local government became a pressing issue in the latter part of the nineteenth century due to the increasing intensity of insurrections against corrupt officials and clerks, many of whom appeared to have manipulated resources such as local granaries and levied arbitrary taxes and fees. Between the 1862 *Imsul* rebellions and the 1894 *Donghak* uprisings, however, little was done to enact fundamental reforms of such systemic issues in local administration,[11] and even the Gabo Reforms ultimately proved of limited consequence in integrating the localities more firmly under central control. At the close of 1894, for example, the reformers established a system in which central inspectors would be sent periodically to investigate local conditions, although not in secret, unlike the *amhaeng eosa* system.[12] Such efforts extended to the codified specification of the number and function of local officials, including their salaries, in the spring of 1895, when the Gabo cabinet implemented a systematic restructuring of local administration that subordinated it definitively under the reorganized Ministry of the Interior.[13]

The Gabo rationalization efforts also sought to establish new agencies that would replenish the central coffers and undertake surveys to gauge the availability of human and material resources, including the morass of scattered quasi-public lands (*yeokdunto*) like the property attached to post stations and provincial military bases, over which various state claimants had rent collection authority. To increase tax revenues, the Gabo government in the spring of 1895 promulgated a sweeping change that attempted to separate those organs and officials who levied the tax burdens into a new network of nine Tax Agencies (Gwansesa) supervising 220 Collection Offices (Jingseseo) and employing over a thousand dedicated bureaucrats throughout the country.[14] Alas, those likely staffing the new collection agencies came predominantly from the ranks of the *hyangni*, the only local figures with the requisite skills. This probably explains why the entire effort was suspended in the fall, and local taxation management was returned to the county magistrate and his clerks the following year.[15] For their part, the *hyangni* themselves, in recognizing such measures as an existential threat, resisted, but they also adjusted to the new order by striving for newly designated official roles, such as the police, and by deploying their local knowledge and connections to refashion their social and administrative positions.[16] They largely succeeded, in short, in reiterating their indispensable place in local society and administration, even as their traditional roles came under increasing assault.

Such a dynamic was emblematic of the recurring adjustments and struggles in local administration in response to shifting demands, particularly from the central state.[17] Illustrative in this regard were the difficulties in abiding by the reporting requirements of the new household registration system promulgated in 1896 (see chapter 7). Some local officials appealed for more time or more resources, such as money to print the new registration forms, while others asked for clarification and direction when encountering locally specific problems.[18] Their superiors in Seoul appear to have been demanding. Several times the central officials ordered their local counterparts to revise the "incorrect" or low figures sent in earlier, while on other occasions reprimanding them or even ordering them punished for either deliberately or negligently submitting shoddy numbers.[19] But a larger problem lay in the simple fact that the new registration system, as did other reforms that directly affected local administration, attempted to interject central prerogatives into the spheres of direct interaction with the people, where long-standing practices suddenly required basic changes.[20] Further aggravating the situation were more aggressive revenue collection efforts on the part of the Great Korean Empire state, particularly the Office of Crown Properties (see chapter 4), and growing opposition from both elite and populist organizations, such as the Iljinhoe ("Advance in Unity Society"), over corruption, taxation, land tenure, and local power in general.[21] Local officials, caught in the middle among these competing pressures, also had to keep up with major political changes at the center, not the least of which was the incremental shift in sovereignty itself.

In the subsequent protectorate period, through two rounds of restructuring in 1906 and 1908,[22] the provincial and local governing system became fortified toward the goals of pacification and, eventually, the transfer of control to the Japanese. The governors and magistrates, for example, were entrusted with increasing authority and many more responsibilities, especially in matters of security. The treaty between the protectorate and the Korean government in the summer of 1907 that gave the Japanese effective power over personnel resulted in considerable foreign presence in each provincial governor's office. Within a year, the governors gained authority to appoint and dismiss all officials under their jurisdiction—all officials, that is, except for the Japanese.[23] Meanwhile, most of the police force, while remaining independent of the provincial governor, came under the jurisdiction of the central police ministry (Gyeongsicheong), which the Japanese also controlled (see below).

The centrality of local government, particularly policing, in the Japanese takeover process was exemplified in the Rijichō network of Japanese consulates during the protectorate. Just as the Residency-General served as a parallel state alongside the Korean central government, the Rijichō functioned as the Japanese counterpart to the Korean local state. As the official Japanese history of this period explained it, Rijichō consulates were established in early 1906 in each of the "most important localities" in Korea—i.e., those urban areas with significant populations of Japanese settlers—and were designed to oversee matters involving those residents.[24] By the end of 1907, there were thirteen such consulates in the country with more than one hundred upper-level officials and over five hundred employees associated with the police and constabulary units. This system soon expanded to include Rijichō branches (*shichō*) with Japanese officials who worked in Korean local government offices, and in the final two years prior to annexation, the Rijichō had the power to act directly on the local scene, reporting to the Resident-General after the fact.[25] This set the stage in 1908 for the wholesale appointment of new Korean governors and magistrates, the overwhelming majority of whom remained in their posts following annexation.

Colonial Period, 1910–1945

In the opening decade of colonial rule, most Japanese officials in Korea were part of the dual tandem of physical coercion, the military and civilian police, which reflected the rather straightforward local governing objective of security maintenance. Indeed, few organizational adjustments were deemed necessary when the colonial regime was promulgated in the fall of 1910. The personnel changes in the preceding three years, including the appointment of pro-Japanese Korean county magistrates and provincial governors, had ensured that local administration fit Japanese designs for rule.[26] The names of a few posts changed, but the organization of the provincial and county governments differed little from that of the Korean state of the late protectorate period.[27] Instead of attempting to alter significantly the existing local administrative units, the Government-General implemented a shift in bureaucratic responsibilities, particularly in fiscal matters. In 1914, through redistricting measures, townships (*men*, Kor. *myeon*), which were formally the constitutive divisions of a county, were rearranged and reduced in number by half. This was a prelude to the proclamation of a new township system (*mensei*) in 1917 as the "foundation of local administration,"[28] to signal the regime's renewed emphasis on fiscal administration, which sought to bypass or remove what were considered byzantine and ineffective institutions. In completing a transition begun in the protectorate period,[29] the township chief (*menchō*) and township office (*men jimusho*), though not completely independent of the county government, were assigned primary responsibility over the levying and collection of a shortened list of fees and taxes mostly linked to land ownership, and eventually for managing and distributing funds for a wide range of local administrative expenses, including infrastructure upkeep, water cooperatives, welfare, and hygiene

FIGURE 3. Seoul Municipal Government Headquarters (foreground, right) and the Government-General Headquarters (background, left), late 1920s. Courtesy of the Saitō Makoto Memorial Hall, Oshu City, Japan.

efforts.[30] Through these measures the provincial, municipal, and county governments came to collect approximately 40% of the colony's tax revenues in the 1920s and 1930s, with each local office containing a Finance Department that managed the land tax, as well as fees and consumption taxes on alcohol, tobacco, and other items within their respective jurisdictions.[31]

The colonial state's response to the March First uprisings of 1919 became an even more significant turning point in local administration. The introduction of what was touted as the less imposing and more responsive Cultural Rule, the institutional manifestation of which came predominantly in the realm of local government, ironically had the effect of expanding significantly the colonial state. As described by official histories, these reforms, on the one hand, represented an adjustment to the concentration of authority in the central administration during the first decade of colonial rule, and on the other, a recognition of the need to devote greater attention to the "people's sentiments" (*minshin*), a self-professed cornerstone of Cultural Rule. The administration of Governor-General Saitō Makoto highlighted the ramping up of inspection tours of localities undertaken by him and Vice Governor-General Mizuno Rentarō, for example (figure 4).[32] And in early 1921 the regime even appointed five People's Condition Observation Officers (Minjō shisatsu jimukan)—Jang Heonsik, Yi Beomik, Hong Seunggyun, Yi Jongguk, and Namgung Yeong—who traveled around the countryside as goodwill ambassadors to meet with local notables and other prominent figures. These Observation Officers were deemed to have relayed the "spirit" (*seishin*) of

FIGURE 4. Governor-General Saitō on a visit to the Gapsan County Headquarters, South Hamgyeong Province, late 1920s. Courtesy of the Saitō Makoto Memorial Hall, Oshu City, Japan.

the Government-General and reported to the capital their views on the effectiveness of local administration.[33] The administrative focus of these Cultural Rule adjustments, however, lay with the provincial headquarters, which gained greater authority and autonomy in the second decade of colonial rule.[34] And most instrumental in presenting a less imposing state presence in the localities was the elimination of the military police units and subordination of all noncapital police officials under provincial government control.[35]

Fiscal resources and infrastructural investments also began to flow outward as time passed. By 1930 provincial and local expenditures had increased nearly twentyfold (1,900%) over the first two decades, compared to a fourfold expansion in the central government (see figures 5–10). Prior to the colonial regime nearly all of the operating budget for the provincial and local governments had come from the central treasury, but through the creation of a separate budget ledger (*do jibangbi*) in 1909, the year prior to annexation, provincial and local government offices gained the authority to directly collect a variety of local taxes and fees to fund their operations.[36] Once in the 1920s,

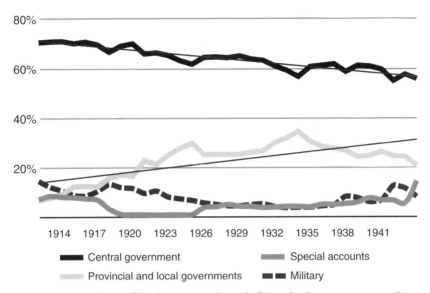

FIGURE 5. Expenditures of the Government-General of Korea by Category, 1911–1943. From Gim Nang-nyeon, ed., *Hanguk ui gyeongje seongjang, 1910–1945*, p. 468.

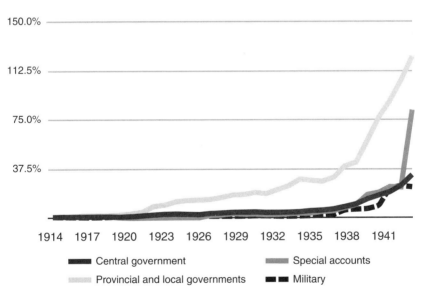

FIGURE 6. Rate of Increase of Expenditures, 1911–1943 (yen). From Gim Nang-nyeon, ed., *Hanguk ui gyeongje seongjang, 1910–1945*, p. 468.

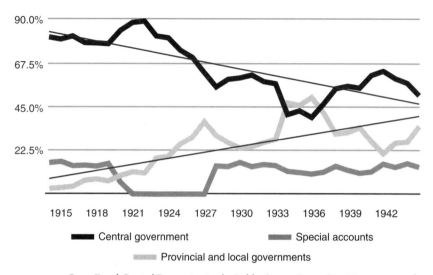

FIGURE 7. Gross Fixed Capital Formation in the Public Sector. From Gim Nang-nyeon, ed., *Hanguk ui gyeongje seongjang, 1910–1945*, p. 473.

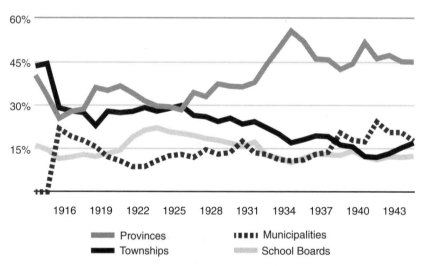

FIGURE 8. Allocation of Provincial and Local Government Expenditures. From Gim Nang-nyeon, ed., *Hanguk ui gyeongje seongjang, 1910–1945*, pp. 480–81. The figures for "School Boards" combine the separate ledgers for the associations that managed the Japanese resident schools (*gakko kumiai*) and for those running the Korean schools (*gakkohi*).

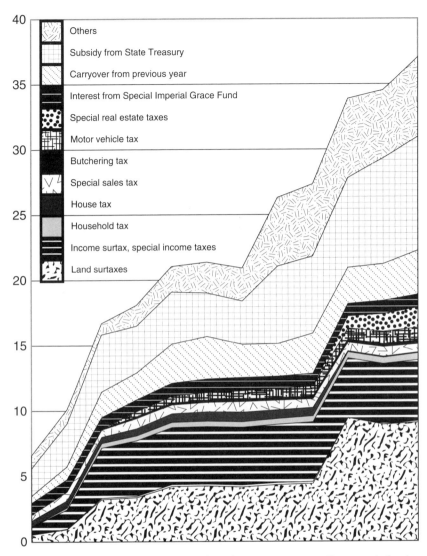

FIGURE 9. Revenue Sources for Provincial Funds, 1918–1929. From *Chōsen sōtokufu tōkei nenpō* (1930), pp. 736–37.

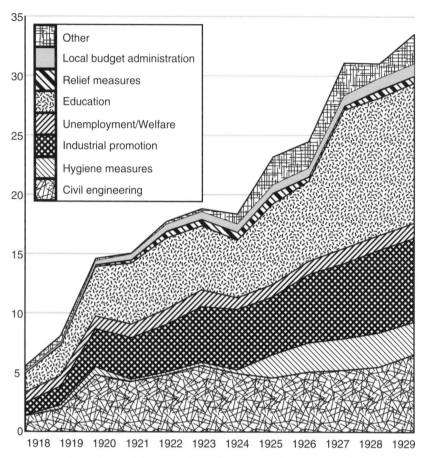

FIGURE 10. Expenditures for Provincial Funds, 1918–1929 (millions of yen). From *Chōsen sōtokufu tōkei nenpō* (1930), pp. 736–37.

province-level revenue streams expanded greatly in both scale and scope, particularly through increases in income taxes and the land surtax. These revenues came to fulfill more than half of the provincial offices' operating budgets, which continued to be supplemented by contributions from the central treasury as well as by interest earnings from the 30 million-yen Special Imperial Grace Fund (Rinji onshikin), of which the majority was designated for provincial governments to finance schools (mostly for the Japanese residents) and welfare and relief measures (figure 8).[37] In addition to education, provincial government outlays, which eventually used over half of the central treasury's allocations to local offices, were directed mostly toward construction projects and, increasingly, hygiene measures. Municipalities, for

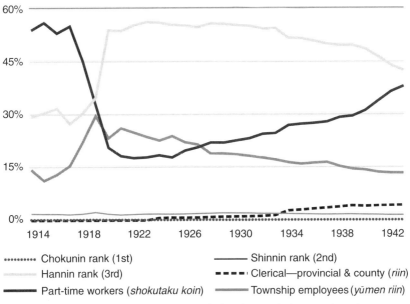

60% ───

45%

30%

15%

0%

1914   1918   1922   1926   1930   1934   1938   1942

············· Chokunin rank (1st)   ──── Shinnin rank (2nd)
──── Hannin rank (3rd)   ■ ■ ■ ■ Clerical—provincial & county (*riin*)
──── Part-time workers (*shokutaku koin*)   ──── Township employees (*yūmen riin*)

FIGURE 11. Colonial Public Employees, Ranked and Unranked. From Gim Nang-nyeon, ed., *Hanguk ui gyeongje seongjang, 1910–1945*, pp. 482–83.

their part, used most of their funds for infrastructure and schools, while the townships and villages, particularly following the 1917 fiscal reorganization that centered local revenue management in the townships, increased dramatically the range of their revenue sources, through various surtaxes and fees, as well as of their spending activities. Bureaucratic wages remained the largest expense item, but these local units also began to channel outlays toward infrastructure, hygiene measures, and policing.[38] Such trends toward greater dispersal of fiscal powers to the provinces and localities began to end in 1934, when the provincial Finance Departments were eliminated through the consolidation of revenue management into five Bureaus of Taxation (Zeimu kantokukyoku) that oversaw ninety-nine regional Tax Offices (Zeimusho),[39] a move that strikingly resembled the brief attempt (above) by the Gabo Reforms in 1895 to revamp tax administration through a similar network of Tax Agencies and Collection Offices.

The increasing attention to local government was seen also in the explosive growth of government workers over the last fifteen years of colonial rule, particularly of part-time employees and salaried officials holding the lowest (*hannin*) of the three major bureaucratic ranks (figure 11). As anticipated

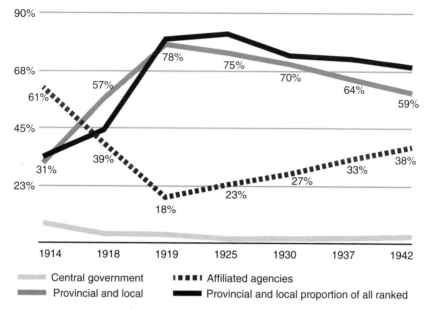

FIGURE 12. Proportion of State Employees by Large Category. From *Chōsen sōtokufu tōkei nenpō* (1914), pp. 832–51; (1918), pp. 1186–1209; (1919), pp. 598–615; (1925), pp. 722–37; (1930), pp. 677–85; (1937), pp. 456–64; and (1942), pp. 400–9.

since the 1910s, the large majority of this expansion came in local government (table 3), which increased in proportion from approximately 30% of all ranked officials in the opening years of colonial rule to nearly 80% by the early 1920s before steadily decreasing in proportion—even while expanding in absolute numbers (figure 12).[40] But these figures do not include the major portion of personnel working in the Affiliated Agencies, such as those for the railroad, postal and communication services, and the courts and prisons—among the largest such organs—who were deployed mostly in the provinces. It is safe to say that, counting them, the ratio of colonial officials and other state workers in the localities constituted well over 85% from the 1920s onward. (The Government-General, or the central state organs, accounted for less than 5% of the total state employees in the same period.)[41] As for Koreans, while those holding the highest positions—occupying the top two ranks of *chokunin* and *shinnin*—actually declined beginning in the mid-1920s, their appointments to the third-tier *hannin* posts seem to have held steady, and the proportion of Koreans in the lowest positions as clerks and part-time wage workers and runners increased substantially from the mid-1920s (figure 13). These included the Korean bureaucrats and workers who constituted what may be

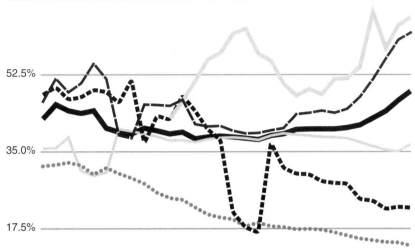

70.0%

52.5%

35.0%

17.5%

0

1915   1918   1921   1924   1927   1930   1933   1936   1939   1942

■■■■ Chokunin rank (1st)   ━ ━ Part-time workers

        Clerical—provincial & county   Hannin rank (3rd)

        ●●●●● Shinnin rank (2nd)   ━ Total

FIGURE 13. Ratio of Korean Government Employees in the Colonial State. From Gim Nang-nyeon, ed., *Hanguk ui gyeongje seongjang, 1910–1945*, pp. 482–83.

TABLE 3 Percentage of State Officials Relative to Population, 1913–1941

1913	0.31%	1923	0.38%	1933	0.43%
1914	0.30%	1924	0.37%	1934	0.44%
1915	0.30%	1925	0.37%	1935	0.45%
1916	0.32%	1926	0.38%	1936	0.48%
1917	0.25%	1927	0.38%	1937	0.51%
1918	0.23%	1928	0.39%	1938	0.54%
1919	0.30%	1929	0.40%	1939	0.58%
1920	0.34%	1930	0.39%	1940	0.62%
1921	0.36%	1931	0.40%	1941	0.68%
1922	0.37%	1932	0.41%		

SOURCE: *Chōsen sōtokufu tōkei nenpō*; Gim Nang-nyeon, ed., *Hanguk ui gyeongje seongjang, 1910–1945*, p. 483.

considered a new ruling elite (see below), cultivated by the forces of state expansion and, eventually, state-led mobilization for war.

These personnel patterns, then, form a picture of state making in Korea that increasingly targeted the localities in fortifying the regime's administrative and mobilizational capacities. Such expansion of the local administration also sustained a balance of rationalizations between extending central prerogatives and control, on the one hand, and the accommodation of local interests, on the other, which mirrored a general attempt to manage the tensions between enforcement and mediation, domination and resistance. These dualisms in turn raise basic questions about local administration's place in the exercise of state power as a whole: What constitutes state authority at the site of contact for most of the population, the localities? For an expanding, modernizing state, could effectiveness be measured primarily by increases in revenue collection, or by the degree of social stability, or by the revitalization of local society, including the inducement of social mobility, through administrative penetration? For Korea, specifically, what was the balance between direct and proxy rule implemented by an increasingly ambitious native state, and then a foreign conquest state? In highlighting these issues, this section examines two institutions: a police system that served as an enforcement and input mechanism for the localities; and local rule, the institutions and practices of which eventually were integrated into a totalizing mobilization for war. In both instances, we find further indications of the growing centrality of the periphery in the institutional rationalities of state development in Korea, and in turn, the increasing capacity—notwithstanding the excesses of wartime—of local government to effect broader changes in both state and society.

The Police and Local Administration

Michel Foucault used the term "policing" and the "police state" in reference to the Western European state's exercise of biopower through its direct, wide-ranging engagement with the population, and not to its narrower, more preventative role.[42] But in Korea from the late nineteenth century to the end of the colonial period, the police operated more closely to the expansively conceptualized expression of state authority as a whole. Its responsibilities ranged from simple enforcement of law and order—inspection, incarceration, investigation, summary dispute resolution, even summary punishment—to active participation in the realms of public health, population surveys, education, and even economy and religion, as the chapters in Part II of this book will detail. In this capacity the police officer's duties came close to the idealized notion of the "magistrate," an administrator and judge as well as a keeper of the peace. And although it was ultimately directed from the center, from the beginning the modern police system was conceived as a matter of local administration—the originating General Police Agency of the Gabo Reforms in 1895 was assigned to the capital city's municipal government, for example. Furthermore, by constituting a major portion of the local positions, where, as noted above, the bureaucratic expansion was mostly located, the police had an outsized and multilayered impact on the exercise of state authority. The versatility and range of police activity in the localities, then, allowed it to function as an experimental cauldron for state making, representing the most common site of interaction between the state and its people. To a significant degree in this era, the police in effect was the state.

Policing as a microcosm of state administration appears to have been envisioned by the Gabo Reform leaders, who clarified that the purpose of the police would be to enforce the codified law but also to undertake a vast range of responsibilities. The closest counterpart to a policing institution in the Joseon system had been a capital-based group of constabularies and a processing center for apprehending and incarcerating criminals, the Podocheong.[43] In the provinces and localities, policing was handled by the *hyangni* clerks and their underlings, but these duties had not been integrated into the systematic vision of Joseon statecraft.[44] The informal and versatile practices of local administration in a predominantly agricultural setting, in sum, required little systemic policing. This also explains perhaps why, in the re-rationalizing state at the turn of the twentieth century, policing was vested with such sweeping functions, to serve more or less as the facilitator of modern state expansion, much as it did in Meiji Japan.[45] This is at least the impression given by the establishment, in the summer of 1894, of the General Police Agency (Gyeongmucheong) of the Five Wards of Seoul, subsumed in the Interior Ministry, which also supervised local police offices in the country's original treaty ports of Incheon, Busan, and Wonsan. Staffed by a police commissioner (*gyeongmusa*), vice commissioner, and scores of police supervisors, clerks, prison guards, and patrolmen (*sungeom*), these police forces, in addition to law enforcement, assisted with a wide range of spheres in which the state exerted regulatory control—from businesses, markets, and manufacturing to roads, bridges, and other infrastructure, religious and cultural activities, disaster prevention, and matters related to public health (see chapter 8).[46] *The Independent* newspaper (*Dongnip sinmun*), which began publishing in the spring of 1896, reported frequently on the variety of activities of the new police, at times to admonish but more often to encourage better performance and hence to prove its comprehensive significance to the establishment of order, hygiene, the rule of law and due process, and a functional state.[47] The newspaper also voiced frustration at the lack of clarity regarding this organ's administrative standing, which gave rise to abuses.[48] The General Police Agency, in fact, would eventually alter its name and go back and forth between autonomy and subordination vis-a-vis the Interior Ministry in the opening years of the twentieth century.[49]

The halting extension of this system to the rest of the country reflected the challenges of conceptualizing and streamlining local administration's relationship to the center.[50] A provincial police network under the jurisdiction of the Interior Ministry was finally implemented in early 1896 by the post-Gabo government.[51] This system elaborated on the different roles of the administrative and juridical police,[52] with the former focused on preventing harm and criminality, while the latter was responsible for assessing, investigating, and assisting in the prosecution, under the guidance of prosecutors and judges, of criminal behavior. In the summer of 1898 came an expansion of patrolmen's duties to include local functions such as household registration surveys, firefighting, and even road maintenance.[53] Most notable in this revision were repeated instructions for patrolmen to obey their superiors, as well as a detailed listing of offenses committed by patrolmen and the punishments for them, ranging from reprimands and demotions to fines and dismissals. Such attention to controlling abuses suggests that central officials still faced major difficulties in integrating and systematizing local policing.

Into this environment came the forces of Japanese imperialism beginning in 1904 through the outbreak of the Russo-Japanese War. The influx of Japanese soldiers would serve as the frontline for the waves of incoming Japanese military police brigades (*kempeitai*) and civilian policemen who would provide the coercive support for the establishment of the protectorate in 1906 and generally act as the indispensable instrument of foreign domination, a process culminating in the annexation of 1910.[54] Following the war's end in 1905, many of these soldiers remained to form the core of the armed forces protecting Japanese residential quarters, commercial interests, and railroad lines, and to assist both the protectorate and Korean governments in putting down the Righteous Army guerrillas. The number of Japanese residents climbed to approximately 30,000 at the end of 1905, and accordingly the number of Japanese civilian police officials increased over twofold following the protectorate's establishment. According to the Residency-General, a year into its existence there were close to a thousand Japanese police officials, divided into "advisors" for the Korean government and others serving the Japanese community.[55]

The protectorate's organization reflected a focus on policing from the beginning. Initially the Police Ministry constituted one of three ministries, along with General Affairs and Agriculture and Industry. By 1907 police matters were handled by the Division of Provincial Affairs (Chihōbu), which coordinated the civilian police attachments to the Rijichō consulates with the military police forces dispersed in the provinces. The number of Japanese police advisors in the Korean local government offices grew in accordance with the further institutionalization of the Rijichō network, and by the summer of 1907, the takeover of the Korean police system was secured, as the protectorate, now in charge of personnel matters in the Korean government, integrated Korean police officials into a unified police apparatus.[56] This extraordinary series of developments was starkly revealed in the bureaucratic roster of the Interior Ministry for the Korean government in 1908, which shows Maruyama Jūshun, formerly the top Japanese "advisor" (*gomun*) to the Korean Central Police Agency, now serving as the police commissioner, and a Korean, Gu Yeonsu, in the number two position. In most of the major provincial and local police agencies, one finds the same layout of a Japanese police official in the commanding post and several Koreans, together with some Japanese, in subordinate positions.[57]

As for the resources devoted to policing, the figures published by the Residency-General, which managed the Korean government's finances, showed that approximately one-fifth of the 85% rise in Korean expenditures between 1906 and 1907—just shy of 6 million yen—came in the area of "pacification" and policing, and notably in the "expansion of police duties in the provinces." By 1909 local police forces took up nearly 60% of the total expenditures for provincial or local government, or over 40% of the expenditures of the Ministry of the Interior, which in turn carved out approximately 13% of the Korean government's overall expenditures.[58] (These were similar to the ratios for 1908 as well.) There was also a remarkable growth in the number of

TABLE 4 Number of Japanese and Korean Civilian Police Officials and Officers (*junsa*), 1910–1937

	Japanese	Korean		Japanese	Korean
1910	2,266	3,428	1924	11,125	7,333
1911	2,305	3,702	1925	11,125	7,333
1912	2,319	3,078	1926	11,129	7,333
1913	2,339	3,397	1927	11,129	7,333
1914	2,421	3,240	1928	11,307	7,363
1915	2,344	3,228	1929	11,398	7,413
1916	2,349	3,272	1930	11,398	7,413
1917	2,245	3,190	1931	10,601	8,168
1918	2,131	3,271	1932	11,166	8,162
1919	8,294	7,098	1933	11,166	8,162
1920	10,515	7,861	1934	11,149	8,177
1921	12,168	8,582	1935	11,232	8,177
1922	12,189	8,582	1936	11,462	8,262
1923	12,168	8,479	1937	12,161	8,481

SOURCE: *Chōsen sōtokufu tōkei nenpō* (1930), p. 334; (1937), pp. 270–71.

police officials during the protectorate: Korean policemen swelled to over 2,000 civilian and 2,300 military police by 1909, and they were joined by over 3,200 Japanese civilian and 4,400 Japanese military policemen.[59] (The Korean Empire police system had contained only a fraction of this amount.) The Korean military police officers actually were given the lower rank of "assistants" (*bojowon*), but when the Residency-General undertook a nation-wide recruiting campaign for Koreans in the fall of 1908, over 4,000 men apparently answered the call.[60] In the middle of 1909, civilian police officials, including Japanese advisors, constituted approximately half of the nearly 11,000 ranked officials in the Korean government, with the overwhelming portion of these officials assigned to the provinces and localities.[61] This would establish a seminal feature of the subsequent colonial period as well: the centrality of policing to the expansion of local administration, and the signal impact of Korean police officials in the development of the colonial state.

In the opening years of colonial rule, police administration was concentrated in the Central Police Agency (Keimu sōkanbu), which also was in charge of the *kempeitai* military police divisions dispersed throughout the country. From the capital Keijō (Seoul), this agency operated a system of thirteen provincial Police Headquarters (Keimusho) that supplied the offi-

TABLE 5 County Police Stations (Keisatsu-sho) and Township Police Substations (Keisatsukan shuzaisho), 1910–1930

	Police Stations	Substations		Police Stations	Substations
1910	107	269	1921	251	2,366
1911	106	456	1922	251	2,373
1912	106	464	1923	251	2,426
1913	106	498	1924	250	2,410
1914	105	508	1925	250	2,301
1915	100	522	1926	250	2,303
1916	99	515	1927	250	2,306
1917	99	529	1928	250	2,302
1918	99	532	1929	250	2,311
1919	251	2,354	1930	250	2,320
1920	251	2,354			

SOURCE: *Chōsen sōtokufu tōkei nenpō* (1930), p. 334.

cials for both the provincial and county governments. The rationale behind such tight integration of all policing functions stemmed from the primacy, still, of pacification of armed resistance and propagation of coercive power in the first decade. But in addition to suppressing what were deemed "rioters" (*pōto*) and "assassinations" (*ansatsu*), the police forces around the colony were charged with enforcing publication restrictions and censorship rules, protecting telegraph and telephone lines, and guarding ports and coastlines. They also oversaw a growing list of functions related to "hygiene" (*eisei*) and began supervision over livestock inspections as well.[62] In the meantime, the ranks of military policemen grew to just over 7,700 by 1912, an increase of one thousand from the end of 1909.[63] The number stabilized to approximately 8,000 very conspicuous military policemen around the colony the rest of the decade. Outnumbering the civilian police, these units belonged to the Government-General's central military apparatus and stood as an imposing representation of what was dubbed "military rule" in the 1910s.

In hindsight, the Government-General, as did many other observers both in Korea and Japan,[64] deemed this policing presence of the first decade to have been overbearing, especially that of the military police, the mobilization of which around the colony to suppress the March First demonstrations undoubtedly contributed to the violent excesses of the regime's response. "Although the temporary addition of five hundred patrolmen managed, for the time being, to successfully achieve pacification and protection [in the March First episode]," the Government-General noted delicately in its 1922 official history of the colonial police system, "the urgent social demands of the time calling for reform required that the police system also undergo a renovation."[65] The new police system thereafter was a critical component of the broader reform of local administration promulgated in the fall of 1919, which laid the administrative foundation for the Cultural Rule approach of the 1920s and early 1930s. The military police forces were abolished, though it appears many of these soldiers simply changed uniforms and were folded into the civilian police force, the numbers for which in the opening years of the 1920s corresponded to the addition of the former military policemen to the pre-1920 civilian figures.[66] But this new organization also reflected the state's decentralization of the 1920s, as the General Police Headquarters was turned into a ministry (Keimukyoku) and most police agencies and officials came under the control of provincial Police Departments (Keimubu). These provincial agencies performed a wide range of duties beyond what the colonial police under central control had done in the 1910s, particularly in supervising those people associated with public health: hospital officials, physicians, pharmacists, nurses, midwives, even dentists and barbers.[67] Most policing, however, was handled directly by county administrations, each of which contained a separate police station, with one to two dozen officials and patrolmen, which in turn also supervised the township-level policing stations, each usually with three to six patrolmen (tables 4 and 5). These local policing activities ranged from hygiene campaigns to the management of feedback channels and education centers. As Matsuda Toshihiko has shown, such heightened attention to local policing reflected the publicized goals of a "popularization of the police" (keisatsu no minshūka) during Cultural Rule, resulting in a larger but less intrusive police presence that catered to individual localities and to improving its public image. The flip side to this turn was just as pronounced, however: the "policification of the people" (minshū no keisatsuka), or the increasing integration of local society with cooperative bodies, such as neighborhood watch associations or firefighting brigades, organized by the local police.[68]

It was this latter tendency that came to prevail over the 1930s and into the wartime mobilization period, which brought forth a gradual reversion to the more overtly coercive roles that the police had played in the protectorate and early colonial periods. The organization of provincial police forces, now bolstered by the structures of heightened surveillance and regimentation cultivated more subtly during Cultural Rule, reflected this trend toward a wartime footing. The Publications Police, for example, not only grew more vigilant in censorship but also clamped down on unauthorized publishing activity following the closure of most Korean-language newspapers and magazines by 1940. A separate Air Defense Division (Bōkūkei) was established in each provincial police department to supervise the construction of air raid shelters and to coordinate drills. Most telling, perhaps, was the expansion of activities enforcing the increasingly stringent controls over economic activity: An Economic Police Section (Keizai keisatsuka) in the provincial government offices was mobilized to prevent black marketeering, to oversee the distribution of rations, and generally to enforce the channeling of material resources toward the war effort.[69] Though not deemed originally as an official activity, local police officials and patrolmen, including the economic police, also became involved in selecting and corraling thousands of people destined for hard industrial labor.[70]

Korean policemen eventually played an integral role in such wartime deprivations and excesses, a result of trends that had been developing over the course of the colonial era, including the division of colonial policing according to ethnicity, the concentration of policing in the provinces and localities, and the formidable numerical composition of police forces in the colonial state. The police consistently represented over 65% of the colonial officialdom from the 1920s to 1940s and mostly were attached to local administration, following the transfer of policing authority to provincial governments through the 1919–20 reforms. Fewer than 1% of colonial police officials belonged to the General Police Headquarters, while a substantial group of officials and patrolmen worked for the provincial and municipal governments, and the vast majority—well over 90%—were based in the county governments.[71] (Indeed, most of the ranked, salaried local officials in the colonial state were policemen of one kind or another.) The highest police positions, including those in the central Police Headquarters, the provincial Police Departments, and the county Police Offices, were almost exclusively the preserve of Japanese officials, with scattered Koreans increasing their presence lower down the ladder, particularly in county Police Offices and lower-level police stations.[72] Koreans did, however, constitute approximately half of all local patrolmen,[73] and given that Koreans comprised about 40% of all colonial local officials over this time, as noted above, it is safe to conclude that most of the local expansion in ranked positions for Korean officials came in the arena of policing. Korean policemen thus constituted a major proportion of not only the colonial police force but of the entire colonial official class. Here lay the significance of the police in ultimately sustaining the colonial system: despite misgivings about their ultimate loyalties, the regime was compelled to integrate Koreans *en masse* into the most conspicuous and requisite institution of the colonial state, the local police force, following the calamities of March First.[74] As it turned out, this phenomenon anchored the broader expansion of local government through the recruitment of Korean officials and again showed the primacy of local government in securing foreign rule.

Domination and Autonomy

Just as the police system, through its recruitment practices, could attenuate the forces of domination emanating from the center, local councils and other institutions that represented the interests of local society mediated between direct and secondary rule, a critical balance in the story of the early modern Korean state. For the practices of local administration through proxy agents underwent several transitions, as the boundary between centralization and localization shifted according to political circumstances and, in the colonial period, corresponded considerably to the ethnic divide. From the vantage point of the sovereign center, every effort to impose rationalities and standardization in the localities—whether for administrative, civilizing, pacifying, extractive, or mobilization purposes—required at least a modicum, and usually far more, of accommodation to local particularities. How and when this negotiation took place, and when it did not, determined the trajectory of local autonomy as a countervailing force against central domination, and in turn the rationalization of local rule as a whole. Here we find the critical place of buffer institutions and practices, the go-between agencies and people who served as representatives, both formal and informal, of the commanding core as well as of the particularizing and resistant locality. These mediating forces continued to play a critical role even as the impulses of total mobilization attempted to appropriate them.

To the leaders of the Gabo Reforms of 1894–96, the most immediate task was to address long-standing problems in the levying and collection of taxes, a process that had been plagued for decades by inefficiencies and graft. As noted above, although the Gabo Reforms targeted in particular the hereditary clerks, the *hyangni*, for removal from the new local administrative system, ultimately little could be done to replace these officials' expertise. But the Gabo restructuring efforts also sought to increase local self-rule as part of a larger attempt to revise not just the structure but the concept of local government. In one of the earliest actions pursued by the Deliberative Assembly in the late summer of 1894, the Gabo leaders established local councils (*hyanghoe*), constituted at the sub-county level of townships (*myeon*) and consisting of "wise elders" who gathered to deliberate and implement measures regarding the application of laws, local medical care, and other issues.[75] These local councils were nothing new—they had long been in existence in the Joseon era—but what the Gabo leadership institutionalized was a council devoid of any social status or administrative requirements, in contrast to the Joseon councils that were composed of local aristocrats or specific office holders. These councils underwent two more revisions in 1895 and 1896, with each step expanding their organization, categories, and tasks while further integrating them into the formal local administrative framework.[76] Such measures might have amounted to mostly an attempt to codify a long-standing customary practice, but they also created institutional openings for the entrance of new social elements as mediating forces between central directives and local interests.

These trends were further encouraged by the next major step in local councils, which took place in the immediate aftermath of the March First uprisings of 1919. As part of its much-touted Cultural Rule efforts to offer greater autonomy to the provinces and localities through the recruitment of more Korean local officials,[77] the colonial regime erected advisory (*shimon*) councils for the provincial, municipal, county, and selected township level governments, in addition to establishing school boards (*gakko hyōgikai*) and school cooperatives (*gakko kumiai*) for the Koreans and Japanese, respectively. Initially, these local councils had little legislative authority, and their members were drawn from local notables who were appointed by the provincial governors, mayors, and county magistrates. But by 1930 the provincial assemblies and local councils had gained deliberative power for certain local matters, such as public schooling (see chapter 6), and hence their activities were closely followed and reported by the popular press. Councilors and assemblymen, furthermore, were elected. Koreans mostly filled these positions—though proportionally less than the Japanese[78]—just as they filled the ranks of thousands of other posts that developed in the latter half of the colonial period. It was through this dynamic that Koreans came closest to exercising a measure of political autonomy, or at least self-determination, under colonial rule.

This is perhaps the most important insight from a recent debate on local administration, and by extension local politics and society, in the colonial era. Yun Hae-dong became a focal point in this exchange through his monograph, *Jibae wa jachi* (Domination and Autonomy),[79] which explored the balance between centralization and localization in the colonial administration. Yun's study is largely an investigation of limitations—the challenges of penetrating local society at the lowest level, the villages, through the rationalization of local administration centered on the township (*men*). The township, formally a component of the county, constituted the centerpiece of colonialist efforts to effect a wholesale change in local administration, particularly in the revenue system, by bypassing the county office and establishing a direct administrative connection between the provincial government and the village. As noted above, steps taken toward this end, which began in the opening years of colonial rule but extended trends in place since the protectorate period, included the assignment of most local fiscal affairs to the township office and the formal promotion of the township head (*menchō*) as the top local official. While the upgrading of the township ultimately could not overcome the ingrained practices of village autonomy and elite networking, the accompanying introduction of bureaucratic discipline and the cultivation of new local leaders introduced a regimentation that helped to better integrate local society when it came time to mobilize for war. Hence the long-term development of this township-centered local administration reform, while limited in scope, demonstrated the partial successes of what Yun labels a typically "colonial" and "modern" approach to rule—technocratic, impersonal, formal, and bureaucratic—which he asserts paved the way for the further tightening of control in the postliberation era.

According to Ji Su-geol, however, the reason Yun could find only limited effectiveness in such township-centered local administration is because, despite the ambitions of this particular rationalization, local administration continued to revolve around the county offices (*gunchō*). Furthermore, through his studies of local society in Chungcheong and Jeolla provinces during the colonial period, Ji has argued that, though formally deprived of meaningful fiscal power, the county magistrate (*gunshu*), the traditional administrative head, retained his leading position in local administration and local life; in fact, he exercised a supervisory role over the township chiefs, whose qualifications as administrators (or local notables) were much lower.[80] As commonly depicted in literary works of the 1920s and 1930s,[81] the county magistrates, the majority of whom, unlike in the late Joseon, were Koreans drawn from the area they served, also determined the makeup of the array of local associations and cooperatives, headed almost exclusively by fellow local notables—businessmen, educators, landlords—who regulated the dispensation of material as well as symbolic, cultural, and social resources. It was mostly through this kind of informal and even traditionalist arrangement that the colonial state functioned at the local level, Ji argues. This matrix of local elites also dominated the provincial and local assemblies, councils, school boards, and school funding councils that the Government-General promoted, with much fanfare, as repositories of local autonomy in the era of Cultural Rule.[82] Although the membership in these bodies was determined through elections, the franchise only went to those who met a high economic threshold, and most of the councils, despite official claims to the contrary, usually did not function as deliberative bodies or even as advisory organs, but rather as simple markers of prestige. Significantly, however, this did not mean that the county magistrates and local notables corresponded to the traditional aristocracy or their descendants, and in fact they often were composed of newly rising social elements, particularly the *hyangni* and their descendants. By exploiting advantages from their former duties and by nimbly adjusting to the demands of the new era, the *hyangni* graduated from the informal status of unsalaried local functionaries to dominant actors in both the formal administration—through their employment as county magistrates, township heads, clerks, and policemen—and the informal networks of new elites who helped to regulate local society in colonial times.[83]

To Yun Hae-dong, however, these local elites can be better analyzed through disaggregation, and he finds a clear difference between the established, mostly landed elite whose influence faded as time passed,[84] and the thousands of members of what he calls the "secondary ruling class" (*junggan jibaecheung*). It was the latter group's "double-sided" character, i.e., their mediating roles as representatives of both the villages and the local administration, for which they were specifically cultivated and trained by the colonial state. Many if not all of these officials, whom the regime labeled optimistically as "core figures" (*chūken jinbutzu*), appear to have benefited decisively from the expansion of primary schooling during this era, and thereafter were nurtured through various vocational schools and other government-sponsored training centers to provide an organic, disciplined foundation of "practical leadership" that displaced the traditional patchwork of local elites.[85] Although most of these "core figures" employed by the local government offices belonged to the nonsalaried, nonranked mass of temporary and part-time workers whose numbers swelled in the late colonial era, their administrative roles functioned as a vehicle for social mobility for thousands of up-and-comers. They were employed by or otherwise attached to the network of formal state institutions, as well as to the more informal civic associations and rural cooperatives, that together constituted the ruling network. And although they faced definite limits in freeing themselves from their attachment to state interests in order to become better accepted in village politics, members of this newly rising secondary ruling class—some of whom, as Yun acknowledges, eventually overlapped with Ji Su-geol's "local notables"—played a critical role in forming a distinctively colonial public sphere while functioning as the engine of local administration.[86]

This process was epitomized by the Rural Revitalization Campaign (*Nōson shinkō undō*) of the 1930s, a major episode in the history of this era and a bridge that connected the heights of Cultural Rule in the 1920s to the wartime mobilization measures beginning in the mid- to late 1930s. Regime officials envisioned it as a comprehensive, totalizing effort—not only to solve urgent economic problems in the rural sectors, but eventually to reorient the mind and spirit of villagers and to renovate modes of communal life, including local administration. But the germinating motives were largely preventative: The precipitous drop in grain prices stemming from the global Depression—a product, in turn, of policies of the 1920s originally to increase rice production for export to Japan, then to restrict exports in order to prop up falling prices in the metropole—triggered a severe downturn in the rural areas, characterized by mass defaults on mortgages for agricultural land and a correspondingly explosive rise in tenancy and excess labor.[87] The resulting dislocations to village life and the heightened vociferousness of peasant actions fueled by leftist revolutionary ideologies prompted Governor-General Ugaki Kazushige to initiate the campaign in the fall of 1932.[88] The objective was to stabilize the agricultural sector before the spiraling downward conditions threatened the economic and political underpinnings of colonial rule itself.

Formally the goals of the Rural Revitalization Campaign were expressed as increasing food supply, eliminating household debt, and achieving a balance in household budgets. The mechanisms, however, were firmly bureaucratic, grounded in local administration and resulting in the mass hiring of additional officials and state workers. It created and mobilized many intermediate organizations, from village, county, and provincial-level rural revitalization committees (*shinkōkai*) composed of local notables and government officials to leaders of semiofficial groups such as schools, credit and water cooperatives, and businesses.[89] Central and provincial government organs sent down instructors, paperwork, and guidelines, while local committees organized lectures, conducted surveys, and selected specific villages for targeted rehabilitation plans, which included propagating better agricultural techniques and tools as well as lessons in self-improvement, household management, and "spiritual" regeneration (chapter 3). The colonial state also instituted tax incentives and organized financial cooperatives to help peasants escape crushing debt and become owner-cultivators as a way of promoting personal investment in one's agricultural livelihood.[90]

In gauging the effectiveness of these programs in achieving the stated goals in material welfare, we can first turn to extensive reports published by the colonial regime itself, which show notable improvements in the villages and households targeted for renovation between 1933 and 1938: a rise in household incomes and numbers of owner-cultivators, and a decrease in household debt and food shortages. By the end of the campaign in 1940, the Government-General claimed that, out of the 2.3 million rural households eventually targeted, nearly 900,000 (~40%) "showed prospects of gradual improvement" in the three goals of achieving food increases, debt relief, and household budget balance.[91] Such evidence appears to have led to the decision in 1935, just a few years into the campaign, to shift the public focus from personal-, household-, and village-level improvements to the colony-wide pursuit—with the name of the campaign likewise expanding to include also "mountain and fishing" communities—of a totalizing renovation in the collective body and spirit. And recruiting, training, and mobilizing select members of the local population as the "core figures" described above remained a focal point of reorganizing designated rural communities and their means of agricultural production.[92]

This dynamic, clearly shown in the state employee statistics of the 1930s and 1940s, cultivated the emergence of a new local elite, but it also accelerated the polarization of village communities along class, educational, and political lines[93]—the opposite of the original intent, which was to mitigate the hazardous socioeconomic effects of the worldwide depression. Many of these new elites cultivated by the campaign, for example, appear to have turned against the colonial state in favor of causes for rural welfare or of leftist agitation.[94] For while the Rural Revitalization Campaign sought to further encourage a sense of self-determination and mutual investment in local life among the rural populace, the intrusive, insistent, and forceful imperatives of the center aroused strong opposition. The resistance to the campaign came eventually from within the regime as well. Korean-language newspapers reported that some officials, including provincial governors and high figures in the central government, advised a tapering of the movement rather than its escalation in 1935, in the wake of vociferous opposition from the regimented villagers as well as of evidence that local officials were falsifying results. Some observers, in fact, referred to the heavy-handedness of the campaign and the determination to force it through as a "Terauchi-style" (*Terauchi-shiki*) approach to rule, a scornful reminder of the "failures" of Terauchi Masatake, Governor-General of the 1910s.[95]

Such trouble signs did not prompt a rollback in the campaign; indeed, its organization laid the groundwork for the mobilization of the wartime period. As the colonial regime itself acknowledged, the Patriotic Village Production Movement (*Nōson seisan hōkoku undō*) and the National Spirit Total Mobilization Campaign of the wartime period were piggybacked onto the structure of the Rural Revitalization Campaign, to which were added new organs to mobilize factory labor and local financial institutions such as mutual aid production associations (*shokusankai*).[96] By the time the full National Total Mobilization Campaign was under way in 1940 (chapter 1), almost all state organs and public groups were folded into the official mobilization efforts. The patriotic neighborhood associations (*aikokuban*), the approximately ten-household units into which all households were collectivized, became the dominant channels for controlling everyday economic life, including the promotion of agricultural production and the regulation of consumption. Village and local autonomy, touted as critical to Cultural Rule and even as a driving motivation behind the Rural Revitalization Campaign, was largely dissolved, replaced by the firmer network of central control that connected these units to provincial and county-level associations.[97] The drive to tighten oversight beginning at the lowest communal level also led to the appointment of a remunerated village chief (*kuchō*) to head each of the over sixty thousand village leagues (*buraku renmei*) in the colony.[98]

An example of the impact on local administration and local life from such measures comes from Mok township in Cheongyang county, South Chungcheong province, which Yi Seong-u has detailed through an examination of local records. These sources show a pronounced degree of mobilization down to the lowest levels of society. From the heads of neighborhood patriotic associations and village leagues to the leaders of the township and county mobilization organizations, all public figures and governing units were integrated vertically, with each higher-level organization maintaining supervision and surveillance over the behavior of those immediately below. This resulted in highly regimented, ritualistic patterns of behavior, summarized in a 1940 official report from a village league chief on the observation of the monthly Patriot Day (*Aikokunichi*) by all the households, comprising four patriotic neighborhood associations, under his watch. On those days, everyone gathered to "raise the [Japanese] flag, bow to the emperor, observe a moment of silence for the troops, and then spend two hours in service activity mending the local roads and fixing the wells, etc.," he wrote. "And in our daily lives, we have been striving to preserve resources and cut down on consumption, especially in rice" by mixing it with other grains. The account ends with the village league chief thanking the head of the township mobilization league and other officials for their inspection of and earnest feedback regarding the neighborhood associations.[99]

The formulaic language in such reports, which demonstrate the pervasiveness of the mobilization, also suggests a largely performative quality to these activities that likely overstates the extent to which these residents achieved the publicly stated goals, much less understood or adopted them.[100] Additional production campaigns in the early 1940s, for example, offered many indications—poor grades in inspection reports, or small-scale resistance in the private realm that the colonial authorities often chose to ignore[101]—of difficulties in implementing the mobilization measures, and evidence of greater agricultural yield was mixed. While the Government-General's statistics show a dramatic recovery in the value of agricultural output from the depression in the early 1930s, these wartime gains paled in comparison to the growth in the colonial economy as a whole, especially for the construction, mining, and manufacturing sectors.[102] Furthermore, the austerities resulting from the channeling of peninsular resources to the battle fronts outside Korea led to severe impoverishment and an intensification of village-level conflict, as the new local officials, such as the village league chiefs and township leaders, came under the chronic strain of mediating between state demands and either local resistance or simple disregard.[103] In sum, the broader balance between centralization and localization, a main feature hitherto of modern state development in Korea, was ruptured by the intense intrusion of central power over the course of the latter 1930s and into the 1940s. The resultant conflicts and tensions set the stage for the explosion of tragic events once the forces of state mobilization descended upon villages in the postliberation (1945–50) and Korean War (1950–53) periods.[104]

CONCLUSION

The mixed record of these wartime measures' coercive and extractive capacities demonstrated the limits of centrally driven state pursuits at the local level. To be sure, in terms of institutional development, as measured in financial and human resources, a relatively straightforward development path characterized local administration in early modern Korea. From a relatively minor role in the late Joseon state, beginning with the Gabo Reforms provincial and local government developed along a trajectory of increasing systematization and integration into the central order. And through the distribution of centrally connected police forces around the country and appointment of pro-Japanese Korean provincial and county chiefs in the 1908–10 period, the localities also served as a critical site of the Japanese takeover, and then of the institutionalization of foreign domination in the early colonial period.

As shown in the dispersal of authority to the provinces, counties, townships, and villages beginning in the 1920s, however, the finer points of colonial state power also depended upon attentive consideration of local conditions. For while the advancements in bureaucratic infrastructure surely helped to bridge the gap between center and periphery—as demonstrated starkly in the penetrating ambitions of the Rural Revitalization Campaign of the 1930s—just as important was the buffering role of provincial and local administration. To use a spatial analogy, if the growth of local administration in this era was a top-down process in which state authority extended outward horizontally into the provinces and localities, and then penetrated vertically into the depths of communal interaction, the process of cultivating state authority through local mediating elements was undertaken from the bottom-up. The reconstitution of the police—which, beginning with the Gabo Reforms, developed into a comprehensive stand-in for the state—epitomized this transition and appears to have strengthened the state's capacity to achieve stability while increasing its extraction of resources. One could argue, in fact, that the localization of a comprehensive (civilian) police force and the incremental allowance for local autonomy following the March First uprisings of 1919 were critical to the maintenance of colonial rule.

This increasing turn to provincial and local government highlighted the state's dialectical development between the center and periphery, and between domination and autonomy. Major fiscal and security priorities came to be actualized substantially outside the capital, leading to greater state expansion, but this in turn compelled constant adjustments and allowance for local conditions. Such a dynamic was visible in the Gabo Reform measures to exclude the hereditary clerks, the untenable workings of which led to a tempering of state ambitions and the reintegration of traditional actors in subsequent restructuring efforts. Another telling example was Cultural Rule itself, which reflected an awareness of the limitations, indeed the counterproductiveness, of the heavily concentrated, coercive presence of policing and other state mechanisms of the 1910s. Cultural Rule's open pursuit of greater attentiveness to the localities further decentralized fiscal and administrative authority and spurred, among other outcomes, major bureaucratic growth in the localities. This phenomenon was embodied in the Korean personnel, particularly police officials, who came to constitute over half of the local officialdom by the latter colonial period. While the colonial state encountered definite limits in penetrating the long-standing networks and practices of local life, the absorption of tens of thousands of Koreans into local administration—as policemen, managers, clerks, and social notables in local councils and even in wartime mobilization organs—facilitated the critical absorption of interests and particularities on the ground. This attenuated the forces of domination and standardization emanating from the center and reinforced the social immanence of state authority as a whole.

THREE

Constructing Legitimacy

SYMBOLIC AUTHORITY AND
IDEOLOGICAL ENGINEERING

MODERN STATES, FORMED IN THE cauldron of competition and rapid expansion of both powers and obligations, have had to refine and strengthen their legitimacy in relation to not only the people but also competitors, both internal and external, for political power. States could not rely solely upon greater bureaucratic efficiencies to justify their rule; they had to establish and constantly invoke extra-institutional, nonmaterial rationalizations, ultimately with the understated goal of gaining a modicum of popular support—that the state somehow expressed the will of the people.[1] Even modern monarchical states had to account for such internal demands, often inspired by external models, for legitimation beyond the customary, if only to mobilize the populace more effectively and gain its acceptance of a new social order necessitated by economic diversification and expansion. Marxian analysis of this process, which sees it as superstructural to class domination, gained greater cogency through the work of Antonio Gramsci, who viewed commanding ideologies, following material developments, as reflecting a comprehensive hegemony that pervades the cultural and psychological orientation of the populace.[2] As the foremost institution behind the expression of this hegemony, modern states generally have depended considerably upon such discursive engagement to construct or maintain this "air of naturalness" enveloping their assumptions of legitimacy.[3]

The particularities of this common pattern lay in how the authority of an emergent modern state was wielded ideologically, as well as how ideology per se was targeted. Ideological practices could take the form of overt calls and unilateral measures to either induce or coerce particular behaviors, but also of more regularized, institutionalized, even quotidian pursuits to integrate state interests into social relations. Illustrative in this regard is the example of

Meiji- and early twentieth-century Japan, which Sheldon Garon has found to have exercised its authority less through domination than through what he deems an intensive form of "social management," which penetrated non-state actors and convinced them to help regulate society.[4] Whether for welfare or public health programs, or when dealing with religious or women's organizations, the Japanese state turned toward public campaigns, among other outlets, for exercising its powers of moral suasion—Garon's translation of *kyōka* (Kor. *gyohwa*, "edifying" or "civilizing")—in order to effect civic partnerships, and hence social consent, for its authority. This demonstrates that much of the task for modern (interventionist) states lay not in imposing control but in coaxing a recognition of the connection between state actions and people's lives.

As this chapter shows, such wielding of the state's symbolic power in order to effect certain behaviors and perceptions was on conspicuous display in the Japanese colony of Korea as well, reflecting primarily the need to rationalize foreign rule, in the sense of both justification as well as administration. This reinforced the centrality of the civilizing project to the modern state's *raison d'etat* in Korea. But there were several other legitimations that came to the forefront beginning with the Gabo Reforms of 1894–95, including the capacity to carry out internal reforms as well as to protect the country from external threats. Performance, in other words, became a hallmark of articulations of the modern state's legitimacy, including the powerful, self-referential rationale of a better-functioning state. A more competent state would ensure material improvements, the cultivation of national identity and integrity, and more popular input. In fact, even as statism, an assertion of the state's separation from and command over society, became the de facto foundation for an autocratic governing order under monarchical sovereignty, constructions of state legitimacy, including from state actors themselves, also accommodated more collaborative, even popular bases of state authority. Through an examination of the mechanisms and rationalizations of state legitimacy, this chapter, as well as the rest of this book, will analyze how both statist domination and social integration drove the early modern state's endeavors to strengthen legitimacy—by engaging in ideological engineering and coercion, to be sure, but also by cultivating and massaging popular sentiments. This chapter will furthermore demonstrate how precolonial developments foreshadowed such turns in the colonial era. Indeed, we find that some features of the state as an ideological resource, including its efforts at moral suasion, were anything but novel in Korea.

From a modernist perspective, a remarkable feature of the Joseon state, even given its high degree of systematization, was its core existence as a moralistic institution, a fount for the ethics governing social structure and interaction. Since its beginning, keepers of this state cast their policies and actions in moral terms, and the steady concerns of Joseon statecraft throughout its five-century history centered on how to refine the state's powers of moral suasion, how to streamline its exercise of authority in order to maintain the accepted, hegemonic framework of the social order. As imprinted into the *Gyeongguk daejeon* dynastic code of 1471, the Joseon state was founded on an unmistakably ideological basis, and it is difficult to label this ideology as anything but what it appeared to be on the surface: Confucian (or to be more precise, neo-Confucian). To be sure, Joseon Confucianism was versatile and selective in application, often supporting contradictory and opposing tendencies in the sociopolitical system and even condoning patently un-Confucian actions and behaviors, but as the guiding principle of statecraft, Confucianism bequeathed a definitive moral purpose, as well as structure, for Joseon administration.[5] Ritual, for example, was given an integral place within this system,[6] and bureaucratic organization, in turn, came to reflect moralistic priorities. The high status of the Board of Personnel and the Board of Rites in the Six Boards (Yukjo), the top administrative agencies of the central state, was one notable feature. Just as significant was the establishment of powerful censoring organs to oversee the Confucian propriety of governmental actions, and the erection of scholarly institutions, such as the Hall of Worthies (Jiphyeonjeon),[7] Central Confucian Academy (Seonggyun-gwan), and Royal Library (Gyujanggak), designed to further Confucian research and thereby to reinforce the role of Confucian ethics in the country's institutions. The monarch himself was obligated by this moral oversight system to adhere to Confucian (Mencian) ideals of popular support in both his public and personal behavior.

The moral order emanating from the monarch extended to the aristocratic scholars, managerial and social semi-elites, schools, shrines, and other extra-state actors responsible for maintaining proper social relations, but none was as essential as the state bureaucracy. State officials, in fact, carried both administrative and didactic functions—with the latter effectively deemed more important—and acted as both a symbol and source of state legitimacy. Indeed, nearly all state agencies down to the level of county governments practically acted as censoring organs for the propagation of Confucian morality, and hence served as the ethical anchor of Confucian statecraft. To be sure, in this capacity bureaucrats also served to absorb mass sentiment; from formal admonitions, lawsuits, and petitions to the more informal interaction between clerks and subjects in the localities, these outlets constituted the means by which officials integrated popular input into the maintenance of the moral order. But this ideal of popular support was eclipsed by the more powerful Confucian inclination toward paternalism.[8] Integral to this system, then, was a hierarchical consciousness and social structure in which state officials and social elites viewed the populace as dependent upon moral guidance from above. Such an exercise of symbolic authority fortified state centralization while contributing to another main feature of statecraft in the Joseon era, indeed in Korean history as a whole: the durability and relative stability of dynastic rule.

All of these key components of the premodern state's legitimacy—the conduits for popular input, the sovereignty of the moral monarchy, and the enduring primacy of moral suasion (*gyohwa*) in statecraft—would retain their significance through modification and extension beginning in the late nineteenth century. Despite the many shifts in projecting the state's symbolic authority in accordance with political transitions, throughout this period sovereignty always rested with the monarch, whether Korean or Japanese, with the state and its bureaucracy serving as the chief executor of this authority. This principle provided a bulwark against republicanism—and in the colonial period, Korean self-rule as well—and other serious challenges to monarchical sovereignty. Nevertheless, such alternative visions were incorporated into a growing list of sources for state legitimacy—from tradition to administrative efficiency, material improvements, and external imperatives— but all implicitly grounded in popular consent and invoking the collective good. And these rationalizations were expressed and instilled through an equally broad range of ideological mechanisms and maneuverings, from publications to campaigns and spectacles.

VISIONS AND EXPRESSIONS OF STATE LEGITIMACY

Beginning with the Gabo Reforms, caretakers of the state embraced varying justifications of state authority, and likewise a discursive multitude, from discussions of specific state roles to the meaning of the state itself, developed in both the state and extra-state realms. This was particularly true in the immediate precolonial period, which was characterized by increasingly open-ended articulations of the ideal state. Not surprisingly the bustling intellectual activity of the turn of the twentieth century reflected Korea's precarious position in the geopolitics of imperialism. Discussions of remedies revolved around the issue of how to become "wealthy and strong" (*bugang*) like the formidable countries that both enlightened and menaced Korea. Given the tradition of paternalistic domination in Confucian governance, Korean thinkers understandably turned to the state as the entity to lead their beleaguered country's path toward wealth and strength. The participants in the debate—educators, political activists, governments officials, and others—attempted to reconcile the new models and ideas from the West, as well as from contemporary Japan and China, with the equivalents from the Korean-Confucian tradition.

In culminating the enlightenment movement's influence on politics since the 1880s, the Gabo Reforms of 1894–96 institutionalized a major rupture in Korean statecraft by proposing that the state's legitimacy and organization were based on rationalities beyond Confucianism or native conventions. While not toppling the monarchy, the Gabo governments, under Japanese military protection, reformulated the central state and justified their deeds on the need, and their capacity, to bring about fundamental, sweeping change. The utterances of the Deliberative Assembly of 1894 clearly pointed toward a bureaucratically centered state authority that, while not openly challenging monarchical sovereignty—though most of the Gabo leadership likely preferred some form of constitutional monarchy—almost ignored the Crown's standing in the new order.[9] The monarchy itself had little to contribute to this shift except to express support for the general spirit of renovation, even expressing shame for the condition in which the country found itself.[10] But a confrontation between reformist officials and the Crown was brewing, and soon following the Japanese assassination of Queen Min in the fall of 1895, the Gabo government was sacked through a mass uprising mobilized by royalist political forces.

Even after the monarchical restoration of 1896–97, however, the government could not escape the Gabo influence. The central state, now led by more moderate officials but still constituting the bureaucratic counterpart to the monarchy, continued to pursue a largely reformist agenda. More important, perhaps, was the rise of a vernacular press through the launch in the spring of 1896 of *the Dongnip sinmun* newspaper, or *The Independent*, as its English edition was called, another major innovation. The organ of the Independence Club (*Dongnip hyeophoe*) under the direction of Seo Jaepil (Anglicized as Philip Jaisohn), the *Dongnip sinmun*, generally considered the first modern Korean newspaper, took the role of popular advocate for reform and of watchdog over government affairs. Not surprisingly the Crown remained wary of the potential challenges to its authority by this and other organizations and publications,[11] which represented a legacy of the enveloping "spirit of Gabo" that had continued within and beyond the state. The Crown, while institutionally appropriating a dominant position, in fact remained often at odds with not only extra-state voices but also reformers in the central state. Royal advisors and other traditionalist critics of the Independence Club accused it of harboring republican motives, which indeed its newspaper had intimated through a proposal for a national assembly or privy council to help deliberate and draft the country's laws (a proposal taken up by other publications as well).[12] The paper's push for a greater popular voice in governmental affairs as a way to increase the state's accountability, in fact, brought it to the brink of questioning the monarch's stranglehold on sovereignty itself. The increasing tension between the Crown and enlightenment activists led to a crackdown on the *Dongnip sinmun* and the forcible closure of the Independence Club in late 1898, but the monarchy also appropriated the thrust of the enlightenment movement by dedicating considerable energies to promoting monarchical legitimacy, and eventually by integrating the tenets of international law into its traditionalist claims to absolute authority.

Indeed the formal outline of the "Imperial System" (*Dae Hanguk gukje*) proclaimed in the summer of 1899, almost two years following the empire's establishment, is notable on two counts: first, the restorationist thrust of the Korean Empire shines through in the preamble's specification of the ancient Zhou dynasty as its guiding model, much as the early Joseon system did; and second, although the legitimacy of the monarchy clearly rests on the connection with the Joseon founder, the concepts and terminology for the empire's legitimacy are in the vocabulary of late nineteenth-century international law. Strikingly, the rest of the ten articles following the first one, which establishes the empire's autonomy, reinforces the absolutism of the monarchy, with each article covering a specific realm of governance over which the emperor has total command.[13] A target, then, of this proclamation clearly was the countervailing sentiment among officials and reformists for a bureaucratically led state modernization movement, which presumably would contain elements of popular sovereignty.[14] Such a motive accounts also for this declaration's appropriation of the enlightenment movement's populist discourse and eventually paved the way toward the Crown's adoption of an increasingly nationalist tone, not only in response to geopolitical threats, but also as a defensive means of shoring up the Crown's political legitimacy within the state.[15]

This was a common phenomenon, of course, in East Asia and other places. As Liah Greenfield has detailed, nationalism became almost a de facto movement ideology that drove seminal political, social, even economic developments and often engulfed aspiring modern states, which had little choice but to embrace this wave.[16] In incorporating nationalism as a core component of the state's legitimacy, governing forces in East Asia drew upon a combination of traditional Confucian rhetoric and globally circulating ideologies of state making. Prasenjit Duara, in his study of the newly constructed state of Manchukuo (1932–45), deemed this process the crafting of a "symbolic regime of authenticity" that cultivates its standing as the sole or primary arbiter of national identity.[17] Monarchies represented perhaps the most convenient vectors of the semiotic and ideological components for maintaining or, in places like Manchukuo, erecting a modern state with claims to nationalist legitimacy. But as seen in the 1911–12 revolution that overthrew the Qing dynasty in China, nationalism could drive republican visions of modern legitimacy as well. The tide, in fact, had been turning in this direction in precolonial Korea. Nationalism eventually was adopted by almost all contending parties and ideals, but its impact on the formulation of state legitimacy was diffuse and versatile, and in envisioning the future shape of a modern Korean state, other notions proved more emblematic of the evolving discourse on the modern state's legitimacy.

The Precolonial Debate: Concepts and Terms

Two key concepts lay at the center of the competing visions of the state, as expressed in the emergent realm of publishing. Both addressed the basic relationship between the governing institution and its people, and hence the place of popular political participation in determining state legitimacy: the notion of the "state" itself, or *gukga*, which normally translates into English as "state" but for important reasons retains also a second emphasis, then as now, of something akin to "nation" or "country"; and the notion of the citizenry, or *gungmin*, which also, depending on usage, could refer to "nation" or "people." In general terms, it was a debate that pitted, on the one side, a perspective that prioritized the strengthening of the Korean state's stature and extractive powers, and on the other, an increasingly assertive vision of a new relationship between the state and people that squarely emphasized the latter. And following the sudden fall of their country into protectorate status in 1905, this discourse reached another stage, as "self-strengthening," or *jagang*, became the operative slogan for enlightenment activists,[18] some of whom even resigned themselves to the loss of political autonomy and focused rather on improving Korea's internal conditions. At the other end were those who sought immediate escape from Japanese imperialism and came to see a strong state institution, the *gukga*, as the fitting tool for self-strengthening.

Tracing the evolving formulation of *gukga* in these publications yields considerable insights into this formative period, for the new meanings involved a wide array of concerns regarding the state and its people, including political legitimacy, sovereignty, and even rights. In the Joseon dynasty, *gukga*, the roots of which stretched back to the Confucian classics, had referred to the dynastic government, even to the monarchy itself. In contrast, many enlightenment intellectuals conceived *gukga* rather as a much broader collectivity whose components included, but did not equate to, the governing order. Such a broadening of scope appears also to have taken place in China and Japan (*kuo-chia, kokka*) as well. Soon, however, thanks to the attractiveness of German constitutional theory and the pull of social Darwinism, many East Asian intellectuals embraced a statist notion of *gukga*, which equated it to the ruling authority. Koreans who adopted this view stressed that "the *gukga* is the supreme organ of rule" that protects the people because it transcends the selfish interests of individual social sectors, and that only when the people "absolutely submitted to the *gukga* [the state]" would Korea survive in the world of imperialism.[19] Historians such as Bak Chan-seung and Gim Do-hyeong have argued that this statist perspective gained supremacy among the Korean enlightenment intellectuals,[20] but the original, collectivist conceptualization—that only such a model could preserve a role for the people's voice—retained its standing as a favored view and appeared in numerous other editorials and essays, and even in the school textbooks, of the 1905–10 period.[21]

This contrast between populist and state-centered views appeared in a concomitant debate on citizenship and rights (*gwolli*), initiated by Yu Giljun, a central figure in the Gabo Reforms and, through his widely read tract on enlightenment ideals, *Seoyu gyeonmun* ("Observations from Travels to the West," 1895), one of the most influential Korean thinkers of the era.[22] In this work's chapter on "The People's Rights" (*Inmin ui gwolli*), Yu declared that all people were equally endowed with fundamental, "heaven-endowed" rights, and through his chapter on "A Country's Rights" (*Bangguk ui gwolli*)—i.e., vis-a-vis other sovereign countries—he introduced the notion of citizenship. Just as each country must exist on a formal level of diplomatic equality in relation to other countries, a country's laws must "protect the people's rights," and indeed a country's ability to fend off attack depended on its government's capacity to implement just laws that protected every individual's rights equally.[23] This formulation of a citizenry (*gungmin*, or *inmin*) as defined by the possession of equal rights came to prevail at the end of the nineteenth century, as shown, for example, in an editorial of the *Hwangseong sinmun* newspaper on the "equal rights of the *gungmin*": "The state's [*gukga*] duty to properly govern the citizenry [*gungmin*] is derived from its ability to uniformly protect the citizens' rights, just as the citizens' duty to follow the authority of the state derives from their receiving equal protection from the state."[24] The second clause of this statement, stressing the citizens' obligations to the state, also began to take on greater weight in conceptualizing this relationship. In fact, as the notion of a citizenry came under further refinement, citizens increasingly came to be defined by their common duties, such as taxes or military service, as much as by their equal rights. Often the calls referred to the citizens' uniform commitment to a generic goal, such as rallying for national resolve and purpose, or simply patriotism. As one widely read pamphlet published in 1905 put it, to attempt to exempt oneself from such responsibilities constituted nothing other than the abandonment of one's duties—and, by extension, of one's qualifications—as a citizen.[25]

Despite the strong undercurrent of nationalism in these two visions—collectivist and statist—of the modern state, both perspectives, tellingly, also provided support for proponents of Korea's subservience under or absorption into the Japanese empire. The Japanese protectorate officials, of course, as well as their Korean supporters, wielded the statist argument for Japan's dominant hand, insisting that Korea's ills stemmed fundamentally from a mismanaged and weakened state administration. But there were also Korean mass movements that advocated absorption by Japan on populist grounds, the most prominent of which was the Iljinhoe, or "Advance in Unity Society," which came to push for expanded popular political participation and more representative government. The Iljinhoe leaders, with a membership that might have numbered in the tens of thousands, eventually promoted Korea's annexation into the Japanese empire as the best (and only) path toward achieving a more just political system and escaping the ravages of Western imperialism. Unfortunately for its disillusioned membership, the Iljinhoe would be closed down upon annexation in 1910.[26]

Collectivist and Statist Rationalizations of Colonial Legitimacy

Did notions of popular support as a primary component of state legitimacy, too, pass away with the loss of Korean autonomy? In starkest terms, legitimacy was never an issue. The succinct annexation treaty formalizing the Japanese conquest, as well as a public declaration at the end of August 1910 by the Korean emperor, simply stated that sovereignty passed from the Korean to the Japanese monarch through the wishes of the former, who would remain a junior partner of sorts in the imperial hierarchy. Beyond that, the treaty and royal edict that announced the annexation stated that the colonial state would be left in the hands of the imperial bureaucracy, headed by a military official, the Governor-General, appointed directly by the Japanese emperor.[27] This reflected the blunt realities behind the annexation from the Japanese perspective: the establishment of a strong colonial state and the pacification of the resistance, both violent and otherwise, to Japanese domination as the only path toward eliminating the security threat from a weak Korean state.[28] But as Peter Duus has detailed, other ideological forces behind the Japanese takeover also began to intensify in the protectorate period and contributed to the move toward annexation. Most prominent among them was an ethnically based disparagement of Korean customs, culture, and history that lent itself to ready judgment on the incorrigibility of Korean behavior, despite the efforts and good intentions of the Japanese-directed administrative reforms during the protectorate.[29] The quintessential civilizing mission, then, became self-evident as a powerful rationale behind the annexation, and it would pervade the colonial state's approach to rule as well.

Hand in hand with this rationalization was that of assimilation (Jpn. *dōka*, Kor. *donghwa*), an ideal that was frequently touted but not meaningfully pursued. Although commentators in the press found in assimilation an appealing logic of legitimation behind the annexation, colonial officials tended to tamp down expectations of realizing this goal, likely because they recognized its potential to highlight the inherent contradiction of colonialism itself: The overcoming of difference through assimilation could ultimately shatter the basis of foreign rule. Hence the regime promoted a gradualist assimilation policy while doing little to remove the barriers—whether in education or in bureaucratic or business opportunity—that preserved the ethnic gap between the colonizer and colonized. Mark Caprio has deemed this a characteristic of peripheral colonialism, a type that stood between internal colonialism, i.e., state-led nation building, and external colonialism, which focused on economic exploitation, usually of a geographically distant colony. Command over Korea, as Japan's latest and most important example of peripheral colonialism, drew upon decades of experience in implanting Japanese dominion over territories extending from Hokkaido to Okinawa and Taiwan.[30] While all these examples featured assimilationist rhetoric, in Korea Japanese rulers recognized that assimilation was a more remote possibility and likewise had little appeal to the colonized, given Korea's long history as an independent state and culture, and given the country's history of hostilities vis-a-vis Japan dating back centuries. This led, then, to a focus on touting the benefits of accepting not Japanese identity or culture as much as Japanese state administration, along with its accompanying pledge of a universalistic modernity.

In the terms of the Korean debate preceding colonization, then, the opening years of colonial rule finalized the shift toward statism in determining political legitimacy: in return for the promises and accomplishments of strong, efficient, and just administration,[31] coupled with major investments in infrastructure and other economic incentives, Koreans would submit to foreign rule and carry out their responsibilities under the new governing authority. Commitments regarding Koreans' political participation, meanwhile, including those toward their "rights," were left unspoken. Even the Koreans' citizenship status became somewhat hazy. The annexation treaty, for example, simply punted this issue through the declaration of Koreans' status as "subjects of the empire" (*teikoku no shinmin*). The new colonial administration issued broad pledges of material and other benefits, to be sure, including tax amnesties, payouts to social elites who quietly acceded to the new order, promises of bureaucratic appointment, and general improvements in public health, educational access, and religious freedom.[32] Indeed the early colonial state's message, both for internal circulation within the bureaucracy and external consumption through government publications, was that the power of good administration, overwhelming and comprehensive in its positive impact, could gain acceptance of colonial rule by highlighting the stark contrast with the precolonial Korean government. This was a dependable trope in the propaganda, such as the *Annual Reports on the*

Administration of Korea (*Chōsen shisei nenpō*), which began most major chapters on state responsibilities—land management and taxes, public health, etc.—with a brief detour to the corruption and inefficiencies of the preceding Korean government, indeed often of the Joseon era as a whole, while usually glossing over or ignoring the modernizing reforms of the precolonial period. This was followed by paeans to what were described as stunning improvements following the implantation of the new regime in 1910.[33]

Early retrospectives on the colonial administration appearing in the state-run Korean-language newspaper, *Maeil sinbo*, also provide telling examples of this narrative. In May of 1911, the newspaper editorialized on the "successes" of this administration over the first year and issued a reminder about the "transitional period" in which Korea still found itself, which required a strong, steady, and even forceful hand of the state (*gwanheon*).[34] This point sought to refute criticisms of the heavy-handed, militarized approach of colonial administration (*mudan jeongchi*, Jpn. *budan seiji*) exemplified by the strong presence of the military police and by restrictive policies such as the Company Law, which required formal licensing for all enterprises.[35] Two years later, in a serialized retrospective on the occasion of the third anniversary of colonial rule, the ordering of the areas touted was telling: reforms of government administration, then investments in infrastructure such as railways and postal services, and then details of state efforts to increase agricultural yields and improve public health, as well as other areas.[36] In 1915, in a far more extensive five-year retrospective editorial series called the "Progress Report on the Administration of Korea," the newspaper flipped this ordering of emphasis, opening with plaudits for material improvements before moving on to good policy.[37] But the credited source of these material changes remained the effectiveness of state administration, which is said to have constituted the "third most important element of success" in the colonial enterprise, following the Japanese emperor's good graces (first) and his firm commitment to Korea (second).

These bromides to the Japanese monarchy aside, the official expressions of colonial rule's accomplishments and justifications, even in their formulaic narrative, reflected the Government-General's awareness of the need to close at least some of the profound legitimacy gap resulting from the annexation. Sovereignty officially lay in the Japanese emperor, but this had little to do with the challenges on the ground, and certainly colonial officials could not expect that the traditional recognition accorded the bureaucracy would autonomously extend to the Government-General. Indeed, in nonofficial colonial-era publications, even in the first decade, one finds vigorous debates about the manner of colonial rule, topics that fell under the general rubric of the "theory of ruling Korea" (Jpn. *Chōsen tōchiron*, Kor. *Joseon tongchiron*). Whether Korea (and Taiwan), for example, should be governed as an extension of the homeland (*naichi enchō*), an argument for gradual assimilationism, or as a separate political entity with considerable autonomy (*jichi shugi*), occupied much of the attention from informed observers and commentators.[38] This discursive sphere, which often was driven by Japanese residents in the colony and sometimes involved sitting government officials, further revealed colonial rule as a legitimating strategy and ideological construct. It also stressed a less statist, more collectivist side to the colonial state, one that accounted for popular response and attempted to balance divergent ideas of how to govern Korea, such as the influence of more liberal ideologies and practices emanating from the metropole, with the irrevocable reality of foreign domination.

Legal constraints also denied the colonial state an overarching uniformity. Legality had always been central to the legitimation discourse that the Japanese deployed to take control of the peninsula, from the coerced agreements immediately preceding the Russo-Japanese War in 1904 that allowed Japanese soldiers to encamp on Korean soil, to the 1905 protectorate treaty, the 1907 agreement dethroning the longtime Korean monarch while giving the Japanese veto power over the top officials, and the 1910 annexation treaty facilitated by pro-Japanese Korean high ministers. Much of this insistence on formal legal support for imperialist actions was meant for international consumption,[39] as well as to reinforce the rhetoric of the civilizing mission. Beginning with the flurry of imperial and other ordinances issued on the day of the annexation's proclamation (August 29, 1910), almost every significant action and policy undertaken by the colonial state was backed by formal documentation published through the government gazette (*Chōsen sōtokufu kanpō*), which bureaucrats were expected to take as the effective law of the land.[40] Ordinances even addressed matters as routine as police discretion regarding flogging and other forms of summary punishment.[41] Furthermore, this legalistic regime, conscious of possible struggles over jurisdiction with the Japanese government, remained ever conscious of the response from homeland bureaucrats and even the Japanese Diet, both when devising ordinances specific to Korea and when considering the applicability of metropolitan laws.[42] The Governor-General mostly enjoyed autonomy, but he depended financially on the Japanese Diet and could not readily contradict the Japanese Home Office in matters, such as the civil code, that were on the level of fundamental law.[43] Finally, the Governor-General faced potential opposition from within the colonial administration, including judges who might be more inclined to follow metropolitan or imperial standards or allow for particularities within the colony in opposition to administrative directives.[44] All of this came on top of concerns about what kind of resistance the colonial state's laws and measures might arouse from both the Koreans and Japanese settlers. Such sensitivities grew particularly acute following the eruption of the March First Independence Movement of 1919.

Colonial administration underwent a dramatic shift in the aftermath of the jolts to the system inflicted by the March First uprisings and their violent repression. If the opening decade continued the protectorate period project of conquest built on legitimating narratives of security and the civilizing mission, the hostile Korean response to the realities behind this narrative prompted an abrupt change to both the manner of colonial rule and the language justifying its continuation. The first decade's predominantly statist discourse of colonial legitimacy, in other words, was turned into something with more collectivist features in the ensuing decade. Political reforms in contemporary Japan, in the throes of "Taisho Democracy," also contributed significantly to the change in tone, as a navy admiral, Saitō Makoto, was installed in the fall of 1919 as the new Governor-General—and destined to govern the colony for most of the ensuing decade—in conjunction with the liberalizing administration of Premier Hara Kei in the metropole. Saitō's government shepherded the much-heralded period of Cultural Rule (or "cultural politics"—*bunka seiji*), in contradistinction to the disapproving label, as noted above, of "military rule" attached to the previous decade. Cultural Rule referred to a tempered approach to colonial administration, to be sure, but it also served as an enveloping phrase for the promotion of Korean identity, cultural distinctiveness, and even limited autonomy.[45]

The motivation and goal behind this turn were well articulated by Hashimoto Tetsuma in 1921 through what appears as a semiclassified booklet meant to be circulated among high government officials and other elites, *The Future of Rule in Korea* (*Chōsen tōchi no shōrai*). In emphasizing the need to overturn long-held but misinformed conventional wisdom about Japanese dominion in Korea, Hashimoto couched the colonial enterprise in terms of morality and Japan's civilizational self-esteem. Seen in this way, he claimed, Cultural Rule constituted the only viable path in the wake of the lamentable approach of the first decade, which stripped the Koreans of any sense of pride in their native identity:

The militarism [of colonial rule's first decade] disregarded the Koreans' freedom, disrespected individuals and their dignity, and completely brushed aside
their perspectives, treating Koreans as insignificant things [*butsu*]. Above all,
[military rule] denied them any rights or standing befitting a civilized people
... Is this the best that our country [of Japan] can do? I believe that ... our
country not just should strive to be a strong country, but at the same time
must be one of righteousness and justice [*seigi no kuni*] ... Hence I believe
that we must pursue [a policy of] culturalism as soon as possible.[46]

Hashimoto also rebuked the heavy-handed ways with which Western powers,
such as the United States and Britain, dealt with their own minority or colonized populations—an approach that he claimed as having "stained their histories as civilized nations." Very much reflecting a consciousness of the West—
and particularly their representatives in Korea, the foreign missionaries—as a
rival civilizational model, Hashimoto warned that continued mistreatment of
Koreans would only lead them into the arms of Westerners.[47] Cultural Rule
would present, then, the opportunity for Japan to demonstrate a novel, more
enlightened path on the global stage.

Such an ideal of promoting Korean interests and particularities characterized not only the administrative approach but also the prevailing mood of the
1920s and continuing into the 1930s. The long list of examples demonstrating
this shift has been well chronicled:[48] The colonial state sponsored thorough
studies of Korean culture and customs, including traditional Confucian rituals and ceremonies, and even funded a major Korean history compilation
project, in the hopes ultimately of buttressing the colonialist message of a
primal civilizational intimacy, if not unity, with Japan. It even established
special administrative units beginning in 1921 to sponsor various "social
projects" (*shakai jigyō*) in the realms of religion, education, and culture.[49]
More importantly, the authorities allowed increased Korean self-expression
through native newspapers, magazines, and radio broadcasting. The explosion
of publication activities in the 1920s, in particular, had a far-reaching impact
on modern cultural and ideological development, as Korean intellectuals used
print as a platform for a wide-ranging, thoughtful discussion—and often
heated debate—on a host of topics, including nationalism and the legitimacy
of colonial rule. Associational energies were also let loose, resulting in a boom
in social organizations and activities, many of which were designed overtly to
prepare Koreans for eventual political autonomy. In sum, if the colonial state
justified its takeover and manner of rule through an emphasis on good

administration and material benefits in the first decade, following March First the focus shifted to the regime's (exclusive) capacity to facilitate the Koreans' efforts to modernize their own society and culture. Assimilation, that much-touted ideal from the first decade to which almost no one, especially the Japanese residents in Korea, had aspired, was now considerably softened in favor of a focus on stable coexistence and native development under the domain of a multiethnic, multicultural colonial rule.[50] Assimilation, in other words, would amount to political unity under a single system, not a cultural unity, much less an ethnic melding. The colonial state's legitimacy would now be based on its supervisory function of encouraging Koreans to cultivate their modern subjectivity and on absorbing inputs from the population regarding this common goal. As a Korean author promoting Cultural Rule in a news magazine put it, the sentiments and even criticisms of the "people" (*minjung*) lay at the heart of this new, "most progressive" approach of the Government-General, which now sought to "realize culturalism with the utmost dedication."[51]

There is no need to overstate this change. Japanese officials were firm in their refusal to grant Koreans their political independence,[52] and the Government-General remained an authoritarian state: no significant officials were elected, the rights of expression and assembly were limited, publications continued to be censored, and political organizations like the Korean Communist Party, founded in 1925 but immediately hounded underground, were suppressed. But the expansion of outlets for Korean expression of collective identity, combined with inputs for political autonomy (chapter 2), patchily permitted the colonial state under Cultural Rule to pursue what might be described as *managerial* legitimation: an overarching statism that nevertheless fostered semiliberal practices and perceptions as its primary rationalization for maintaining efficacy. This was the case, at least, until the Manchurian Incident of 1931, which marked the beginning of the rollback of Cultural Rule priorities through a dramatic shift in the Governor-General's office, pressures from the imperial government, and the general transformation of the colony into a base for military resources and adventures. For the colonial state's ruling narrative, the eventual transition to a full wartime mobilization in the late 1930s entailed an intensified campaign to force identification with not only the war effort but with Japanese-ness itself, which required the curious (re-)appearance of monarchical nationalism as the basis of legitimation.

IDEOLOGICAL ENGINEERING: SYMBOLS AND CAMPAIGNS

In Korea, the uncanny resemblances between the two major state efforts of monarchical nation building—the first at the turn of the twentieth century undertaken by the Great Korean Empire, and the second in the late 1930s and early 1940s carried out by the wartime colonial state—stemmed from political overlaps: the modeling of the Korean Empire's monarchy after that of the Meiji, and the wartime state's intensive efforts to tap into and reorient national identities that had thoroughly been shaped into form at the turn of the century. But these two episodes also bookended an extended period in which the state could not rely on nationalism to engineer its authority ideologically. For nearly three decades, the colonial state in fact deployed a range of symbolic mechanisms and campaigns largely divorced from the promotion of Japanese monarchical sovereignty or from the embrace of Japanese ethnic identity. These approaches, while reflecting the uneasy circumstances of a foreign conquest state attempting to maintain its hold on a colonized population, also exemplified the civilizing mission and internal colonization practices inherent to the modern state, and they drew often upon a common pool of symbolic resources deployed by the monarchy-centered campaigns as well.

Imperial Ceremonialism

As with the colonial regime, the precolonial state faced daunting obstacles in fashioning a self-enclosed rationality of legitimacy in monarchical sovereignty. This was particularly the case because the bureaucracy represented a viable alternative to the Crown's claims at a moment when Koreans were exploring various paths toward modern statehood, whereas in contrast the colonial administration served as an instrument of the monarchical state. The leaders of the Gabo Reforms, as noted above, rationalized their actions on performance—the capacity and vision to bring about a fundamental reordering of state and society—but their association with a foreign power, Japan, constrained their ambitions and vision. Particularly following the Gabo Reforms' downfall in early 1896, the Crown became the focal point of almost all such attempts, nationalist and otherwise, even when it had to contend with bureaucratic and other political forces. Indeed, the ideological maneuvering of the monarchy often worked as a means of blocking any rival notions of state legitimacy.

The king's flight to the Russian legation in early 1896, which brought about the sacking of the Gabo government through a popular uprising, led to the discomfiting sight of the Korean monarch, formally in charge, being unable to venture outside the protective shell of the Russian consulate due to fears of the Japanese and like-minded hostile forces within the Korean ruling order. This certainly did not project a sense of security and confidence in the monarchy's legitimacy, much less its capacity. So when, after more than a year, the king finally did emerge out of seclusion, it was to reinvent himself—or more specifically, the Joseon monarchy and the polity it ruled—in imperial eminence with claims to equal standing in the community of nation states. His coronation as emperor through the formal declaration of the *Daehan Jeguk*, or Great Korean Empire, took place through a ritual sacrifice, both celebratory and solemn, at a specially designed altar, the *Wongudan* ("Round Hill Altar"). The *Dongnip sinmun* newspaper, in its English edition, expressed great enthusiasm in its report on the ceremonies, which, interestingly, were held in the predawn hours of October 12, 1897. The festivities, though, had begun the previous afternoon:

His Majesty, the Emperor, left the Gyengwon [Gyeongun] Palace at half past two on Monday afternoon, and, with great splendor and pageantry of both Oriental and Occidental fashions, with several regiments of soldiers, carriers of flags, wooden hammers, gilded stirrups, silvery wooden swords, together with numerous dignified strutting officials, went to the Sacred Altar [Wongudan]. His Majesty inspected the various arrangements in connection with the ceremony in person with His Imperial Highness the Crown Prince. His Majesty wore the yellow robe upon which the sun, moon, stars and various animals were embroidered in gold. His hat was the jewelled crown after the fashion of the Ming dynasty . . .

The entire length of the route from the Palace to the Sacred Altar was lined with soldiers and police and either side of the street was temporarily fenced off by awnings. Many private and public buildings were decorated with flags and thousands of people watched the procession from high places about the city. Everything was orderly and the details of the programme were admirably carried out. His Majesty and the Crown Prince stayed in the Sacred Altar until four o'clock and returned to the Palace. About two o'clock Tuesday morning the Imperial party went again to the Altar and performed the coronation rituals.

On the upper platform several tables were placed and upon them the usual sacrificial food was arranged and the Round Hill was brilliantly lighted. His Majesty rose and reverently bowed to Heaven, and a high dignitary—Grand Master of Ceremonies—read loudly the prayer which was composed for the occasion. The gist of the prayer was that through Heaven's blessing His Majesty takes upon himself the title of Great Emperor of Great Josun [sic], which was done in accordance with the will of Heaven. Heaven may bestow upon the Emperor continual blessings and guide him in directing the affairs of the Empire. After the completion of the prayer and offering of various sacrificial animals His Majesty and the Crown Prince again bowed. Then the Emperor took a seat and received the congratulations of the Ministers of State and other civil and military officials who arranged themselves on the different terraces according to their rank and bowed to the Emperor nine times.[53]

"Pageantry of both Oriental and Occidental fashions" may very well sum up the symbolic project of legitimation undertaken by the monarchical state throughout the precolonial period, as this phrase crystallized the great challenge of following contemporary practices of ideologically projecting state power, while simultaneously relying on the customary basis of the Yi monarchy's sovereign authority. As Andre Schmid has argued, in this process of monarchical reinvention, the long-standing East Asian repertoire of symbols and rituals was creatively reinscribed with specifically Korean and nationalist significance.[54] In so doing, the monarchical state was not alone. The coronation, for example, lent itself to different interpretations even from the same observer. The *Dongnip sinmun*'s celebratory Korean-language report of this event contained much of the same flowery description of the showy proceedings as in the English version, but the Korean report framed this event less as an appeal to monarchical legitimacy and more as another call to strengthen national consciousness: The throng of onlookers in the afternoon parade "held aloft the Korean flag to express their patriotism," and their participation in the proceedings reinforced the equal standing of the Korean monarch and his subjects (*sinmin*) to their counterparts around the world, even inspiring the Korean people to strive to achieve recognition, through their continual improvement, as a "top-ranking country" (*ildeungguk*).[55]

The challenge for the Crown was to channel these burgeoning nationalist sentiments, together with their discursive and symbolic resources, toward the pursuit of a specific brand of nation building under the absolutist monarchical state. In this effort, the Crown was not alone. As the art historian Mok Su-hyeon has found, a comprehensive range of visual symbols was devised to establish the empire's autonomy and thereby to bolster, for both external and internal consumption, its exclusive claim to having enacted the modern nation-state in Korea. This began with the flag itself, featured

FIGURE 14. Emperor Gojong returning to Gyeongun Palace from Wongudan Altar during Coronation Ceremonies, October 1897. At top left and middle is the recently designated flag to represent the empire. Courtesy of Jeong Seong-gil, Hwaseong Thema Museum.

prominently in the above description of the coronation procession (see figure 14). Although conceived as a national flag in the 1880s, its widespread dissemination began in the early Korean Empire period, and thereafter the flag or its central element, the circular *taegeuk* image, appeared ubiquitously as a national symbol in newspapers and magazines, government documents and buildings, currency, stamps, streetcars, and other representations of modernity. Other images were created to enhance the monarchy's imperial aura, including traditional East Asian designs to represent the monarch himself, his family members, their palaces, and the meritorious service badges that they bestowed.[56] The efforts to promote the idea of national unity under the Crown's authority also led to the promulgation of official national holidays, such as the emperor's birthday and the empire's foundation day.[57] The emperor's *bona fides* as a modern monarch in the age of high imperialism were further supported by his appearance, as seen in some well-known images of the time, in resplendently martial Kaiser garb befitting the official term for his reign, *Gwangmu* ("Glorious Military"). The Crown also deployed a nascent yet highly suggestive techno-nationalism through its sponsorship of major infrastructural projects such as the Seoul streetcars and the first railway (see chapter 4). Such material, infrastructural, and architectural transformations of the showcase capital were designed to reinforce the Crown's centrality as the source of nationalist political authority.[58]

The effectiveness of these efforts at heightening the perceptions of the monarchical state's legitimacy is difficult to gauge. On the one hand, based on the evidence from contemporary observers and publications, the popular association of the monarchy with the emergent nation-state appears to have held firm, as even enlightenment activists hailed the emperor as a symbol around which to rally nationalist sentiment. But this connection might have pertained only to a specific monarch, Gojong, and what's more, nationalism and the quest for a modern state might have proved more durable than the attachment to the monarchy. This is what Christine Kim suggests in her analysis of the imperial progresses of the next (and final) Korean monarch, Sunjong, in 1909, the year before annexation and two years after the forced abdication of his father by the Japanese protectorate.[59] Contrary to the intent of Resident General Itō Hirobumi, who believed that parading the feeble monarch on grand tours around the country would raise popular support for the protectorate's caretaker role in the Korean government and even allay suspicions about Japanese intent, the processionals, which traveled along the newly built railways as well as in carriages and horses bedecked in royal splendor, might have had the opposite effect. The appearance of the Korean emperor aroused passionate nationalist responses that led not to support for the protectorate but rather to charges of manipulation at the hands of both the Japanese and Korean political leaders. The resulting expressions of anti-Japanese sentiment, in fact, divorced both Korean nationhood and statehood from the monarchy, which came to be seen as subservient to bureaucratic forces—precisely the reverse of what the monarchical state had tried to instill from the beginning of the Korean Empire period. The popular distaste for Japanese involvement, and specifically for Itō, that this episode triggered might have led to his assassination half a year later by An Junggeun, which in turn appears to have finalized the Japanese decision to annex the country.

Colonial Spectacles

Perhaps due to the folly of the royal progresses of 1909, the colonial state mostly steered clear of overt appeals to the sovereignty of the Japanese monarchy in its discursive efforts to strengthen its tenuous hold on authority, notwithstanding the publicity surrounding the marriage of the Korean crown prince to a Japanese princess. Interestingly, some propaganda projects, such as the *Annual Reports* in English that sometimes included resident foreigners' testimonies, were targeted at foreign audiences, as if the Japanese remained dependent on Western approval for their most recent and challenging imperialist venture. Japanese residents in Korea, too—who numbered well over one hundred thousand in the early colonial period—also needed to be reassured of their continuing privileges and opportunities.[60] But most of the public relations work to overcome the colonial state's legitimacy gap, or at least to reduce resistance, was targeted squarely at the Korean audience. To complement a steady stream of officially sanctioned press accounts touting the benefits of the colonial administration, as discussed above, the colonial state devoted considerable sums and attention to constructing symbols of the technologies and forwardness of the colonialist enterprise. These included the annual Korean Art Exhibition from 1922 to 1944, held in the Government-General Museum, that featured contemporary works as well as cultural artifacts,[61] which enabled a more direct experience of the message by bypassing the illiteracy of the mass of visitors to whom these presentations were targeted. In the era of high imperialism, as Timothy Mitchell has suggested, such staged objectifications of colonial possessions served as showcases for the civilizing mission and hence as representations of the colonizer's "order and truth."[62] They functioned, in other words, as instruments of colonial rule. Indeed, in colonial Korea, the state stood as the indisputable purveyor of these spectacles.

The most intriguing such moments were the grand colonial expositions of 1915, 1929, and 1940. The first, called officially the Korean Products Fair (*Chōsen bussan kyōshinkai*), was held on the grounds of the Gyeongbok Palace in Seoul in September and October of 1915 to commemorate the fifth anniversary of Japanese rule. This project mobilized 18,000 people in the colony, including many Government-General bureaucrats, and featured exhibits of artworks and cultural artifacts, education-related items, and over 40,000 objects produced throughout the peninsula since annexation, ranging from agricultural, marine, and manufactured products to the technologies used in "colonization" activities (in the economic sense: *takushoku*) and those resulting from the Japanese emperor's "Special Grace Fund" (*Onshikin*). The staging strategies, then, stressed the tangible, mostly material transformation of the peninsula since annexation and were meant to imbue an overwhelming sense of imperialist preeminence and progress.[63] Along these lines, particularly striking were the exhibits showcasing the benefits of colonial administration, such as those related to public health, the police, and infrastructure, which stemmed from the overt aim of contrasting the "old with the new," i.e., the pre-annexation administration with that of the colonial government.[64] A promotional write-up in one of the official Korean-language journals of the time, *Sin Mungye* (New Culture), urged Koreans to take advantage of this unique opportunity, made possible "by the kind auspices of the authorities," to view how Koreans, now armed with a "new spirit" made possible by the new administration, were making their mark on "twentieth-century civilization": While we Koreans beforehand could make such products, our leaders could not cultivate our talents to the fullest extent.[65]

If the 1915 exhibition emphasized the material benefits of Japanese rule, the 1929 Korean Exposition (*Chōsen hakurankai*), held in the same locale, focused on "cultural development" as well as on industrial promotion. Like its 1915 predecessor, this enormous project was planned and administered by the colonial regime, which established temporary bureaucratic agencies and dedicated dozens of officials and workers, who in turn mobilized four thousand people for the opening ceremonies alone.[66] Eventually drawing over a million visitors, the exposition featured a spate of dance, music, and acrobatics performances as well as demonstrations of Korean folk tales, traditional artisanal techniques, and even films.[67] Signing up for the venture were dozens of major publishers, enterprises, and social organizations, as well as civic representatives from the colonial provinces and other territories in the Japanese empire such as Taiwan and Osaka.[68] Hong Kal's analysis of the visual cues in the 1915 and 1929 exhibitions demonstrates how they reflected the evolution of colonial rule, in the first decade, from primarily that of a civilizing force to that, in the second decade, of coexistence and coprosperity within the vision of a multicultural Japanese empire. For example, whereas in 1915 the Gyeongbok Palace was blocked by a massive modern building at the forefront of the exhibition, and with Korean products displayed next to more advanced Japanese ones to signify the overtaking of Korean backwardness by Japanese advancement, the 1929 exposition was much subtler. For one, the Korean buildings were not obscured but rather highlighted, and the celebration of Korean cultural forms and products underscored the meta-banner of prosperous coexistence under Cultural Rule.[69]

Likewise, the final exposition a decade later, the Great Korean Exposition (*Chōsen daihakurankai*) of autumn 1940, demonstrated the decisive turn toward a wartime pursuit of assimilationist mobilization as the driving pur-

FIGURE 15. Weaponry on display at the Great Korean Exposition, 1940. From *Chōsen daihakurankai no kaikan*, 1940.

pose behind colonial administration. Organized by the Japanese-language organ of the Government-General, the *Keijō nippo* newspaper, the 1940 exposition's primary goals were articulated as a commemoration of the thirtieth anniversary of colonial rule, of the 2,600th anniversary of the mythical founding of the Japanese imperial house—in coordination with celebrations around the empire—and of the "holy war" for building a "new East Asian order."[70] As before, many of the galleries introduced the peninsula's industrial products and Korean historical narratives, but the former stressed their military utility and the latter now stressed the trajectory of Korean history as originating with Japanese connections and thereafter slowly returning to the imperial fold. The most conspicuous contrast with previous exhibitions, however, was the group of exhibits glorifying the war effort, already well under way, as the logical extension of the imperial reign (figure 15): an array of tanks and warplanes, displays of weapons used recently in the China war, galleries exhorting expressions of gratitude to the Imperial Army, and other tributes that underscored the call for the Koreans' accelerated embrace of the emperor-centered Japanese identity.

The deployment of such extravaganzas to buttress the colonial state's evolving legitimization narrative does not mean that they had the desired effect, of course. Todd Henry, in his detailed overview and analysis of these exhibitions, has uncovered a wide range of responses, both from the mass of visitors, who often failed to detect the intended messages while partaking in the spectacle, and from commentators, many of whom were harshly critical of the economic and cultural costs.[71] As with the imperial progresses of 1909, in other words, the colonial exhibitions took on a life of their own, acting as sites of contestation as much as of information and persuasion. This was a risk worth taking, apparently, for colonial authorities eager to effect a more immediate, direct transmission of colonialist messages to the subject people, who remained mostly illiterate (particularly in Japanese), through visually oriented experiences and thereby to overwhelm as well as overcome the legitimacy gap of foreign rule.

Spiritual Campaigns

The grand colonial exhibitions, then, signaled major transitions in the colonial state's legitimating pursuits and the regulation of popular perception, particularly as they took a turn toward intensive social mobilization over the 1930s. Chapter 2 discussed the wide-ranging significance of the Government-General's Rural Revitalization Campaign (*Nōson sinkō undō*) of 1932–40, initiated by Governor-General Ugaki (1931–36), to the development of local administration in the latter half of the colonial period. Indeed, even its name (*Nōson sinkō*) and likely much of its strategy came from the regime's effort to stunt the social-revolutionary and nationalist sentiment that had spread among the increasingly impoverished peasantry, particularly in the wake of the collapse in grain prices due to the worldwide depression.[72] But while institutional measures to improve the material conditions in the countryside were critical to achieving the goals of price stability, personal debt relief, and production increases, Ugaki's systematic state program, veering close to a physiocratic policy, stressed the spiritual and moral basis of economic decay and prioritized the injection of industriousness and frugality, a "spirit of autonomy and self-reliance," among the peasantry.[73]

The conduits for such spiritual training were the local committee members of the campaign (*Nōson sinkō iinkai*), composed of area notables such as public officials, landlords, educators, and businessmen, as well as instructional efforts, such as lecture tours, that the Government-General readily conducted for various causes. They ventured to implant an ethos, or "self-awareness" (*jikaku*),[74] of the value of diligence in order to effect a wholesale change in the peasants' lifestyle and habits. These were viewed as generally mired in "evil thoughts" (*akushiso*) and "bad customs" (*rōshū*), such as ignorance and sloth, that reflected the general decline in social mores amidst runaway materialism and capitalism.[75] In terms of political authority, the idea was that instilling such a spirit of self-discipline and self-cultivation would naturally lend itself to the peasantry's internalization of submission to the colonial state and even loyalty to the Japanese imperial cause.[76]

While stopping short of the intensive assimilationism of the wartime years—the movement mostly stuck to the call for "harmony" between the metropole and colony (*naisen yūka*) and for the customary loyalty to the state[77]—the originating motives, messages, and ideological mechanisms of the Rural Revitalization Campaign represented an unmistakable reorientation of, if not a rupture to, the accommodating approach of Cultural Rule. Through a reading of Governor-General Ugaki's diary from 1934, for example, Yi Yun-gap has found that Ugaki had already conceived of incorporating more explicitly the ideals of absolute loyalty to the emperor and to the "national essence" (*kokutai*) into the Rural Revitalization Campaign in preparation for a larger push in spiritual indoctrination.[78] Indeed, by the third-year retrospective of the campaign, in 1935, Ugaki pronounced the effort a good start but one requiring far greater dedication for the next step, the stakes for which would be at another level altogether: "Korea's rejuvenation and the empire's prosperity." Everyone in the colony shouldered the responsibility of achieving this "highest and most important project for the peninsula," for like "a single drug that cures all ills," the project of rural revitalization had comprehensive implications. Ugaki likewise couched the consequences of failure in near-apocalyptic terms for Korea's many deep-seated problems and extended these potential repercussions to the East Asian region as a whole.[79]

It comes as little surprise, then, that these discursive strains, as with the organizational infrastructure, would eventually be folded into the comprehensive mobilization campaigns following the commencement of the war against China in 1937. In fact the decisive shift is most associated with the inauguration, in 1936, of the rule of Governor-General Minami Jirō, who even before the China Incident had spoken of the "cultivation of the national spirit" (*kokumin seishin no tōya*) as his primary responsibility, along with the intensified cultivation of the colony's industrial potential.[80] Spiritual mobilization was comprehensively institutionalized in 1938 via the Total Mobilization of National Spirit campaign, first in Japan, then across the peninsula through the establishment of the Korean League for the Total

Mobilization of National Spirit (Kokumin seishin sōdōin Chōsen renmei). This network connected agencies and advisory committees in the capital to corresponding institutions scaled down to the localities and culminating in the neighborhood patriotic associations (see chapter 1). In the inaugural issue (June 1939) of the league's monthly organ, *Sōdōin* (Total mobilization), Kawashima Gishi, the league's president (*sōsai*), proclaimed its goals as promoting and actualizing the "Japanese spirit" among all 23 million inhabitants of the peninsula and thereby contributing to the "New East Asian" order.[81]

The journal, which changed its name to *Kokumin sōryoku* (National total mobilization) to become the organ for the Total National Mobilization campaign in 1940, was filled with updates on the war, reports on league and other official activities around the peninsula and empire, nationalist (Japanese) paeans and anti-Western polemics, academic essays and philosophical ramblings, inspirational poems and tales, exhortations for personal sacrifice and material donations, and generally relentless reminders of everyone's importance to the war effort, particularly in spiritual fortitude.[82] Although touted as a means of communication for the disparate league entities and of publishing readers' contributions, the narratives and advertisements show that the emphasis lay with this journal's function as the medium for transmitting central directives to the localities. Many of the articles in the early issues, particularly the exhortatory pieces, even appeared bilingually, while later issues often included the *furigana* phonetic markings for Japanese-language pieces—signs of targeting marginal and even nonelites in the countryside who likely were working in some capacity for local authorities. One such essay was penned by Yun Chiho, the prominent educator and erstwhile leader of the Independence Club in the 1890s, who urged Koreans to assist the war effort by settling—and hence reclaiming—what was once the Korean "homeland" of Manchuria.[83] The Cultural Rule encouragement of "harmony" between the metropole and colony, in sum, was replaced by calls, such as Yun's for reviving a primordial Japanese-centered northeast Asian unity, for the total sublimation of Koreanness and the strengthening of Koreans' status as "imperial subjects" (*kōkoku shinmin*).

In pushing not only an identification with the Japanese polity and war but also a dissolving of Korean ethnic identity, this total assimilationist slogan of a "United Body of Japan and Korea," or *naisen ittai*, encapsulated the wartime colonial state's pursuit of a comprehensively nationalist mobilization. *Naisen ittai* was mined for meaning at various levels, from the simple message of adopting Japanese ways and acting more Japanese to academic treatises that contextualized the slogan in the flow of grand historical forces. Prominent businessmen, educators, cultural figures, officials, and others gave talks, wrote books and newspaper columns, and were trotted out in rallies to encourage Koreans to sacrifice for the war not only by embracing Japanese identity through the symbolic unity of *naisen ittai*, but by discarding one's Koreanness altogether.[84] In a book published by the Korean League for Total National Mobilization in 1941, *Essence of the National Body and naisen ittai* (Kokutai no hongi to naisen ittai), for example, the lead author, Otaka Chōyū, a professor of law at Keijō Imperial University, appealed to Koreans' sense of regional identity by urging them to adopt the "Japanese spirit," a cultural force described as absorbing the best lessons of traditional East Asian civilization with a tempered adoption of modern (Western) enlightenment. If Koreans, he added, raised their cultural level and actualized *naisen ittai* to create on the peninsula an extension of Japan—specifically its emperor-centered "national body" (*kokutai*), billed as the perfect compromise between democracy and dictatorship—Korea could become the base for the Greater East Asian Co-Prosperity Sphere in the entire Asian mainland.[85]

The colonial state's wartime ideological campaign went far beyond sloganeering, of course; a full spate of public rituals and behaviors was implemented in order to instill the proper spirit. "Unity of thought," in fact, was articulated as the first of three main components (along with "total training" and "increase in production") of the Total Mobilization Campaign, with everyone expected to "exalt the Japanese spirit" and to "perfect *naisen ittai*" through visits to Shinto shrines, daily rituals, and by "recognizing the true history of Korea" as primordially connected to Japan's.[86] Local bureaucratic and league organs instructed households to hang the Japanese flag on the monthly "Patriot Day" and gather for holidays celebrating the military (e.g., "Navy Memorial Day" [Kaigun kinenbi], May 5),[87] or for the anniversaries of the Manchurian Incident of September 1931 and the China Incident of July 1937. There were even official celebrations of the birthday of the Meiji emperor, three decades after his death. On such occasions village leagues and other local groups assembled to bow to the Japanese emperor, sing the Japanese national anthem, pray for Japanese soldiers, and recite slogans hailing the Greater East Asian Commonwealth.[88] Following the establishment of a Central Information Committee (Chūo jōhō iinkai) as well as its provincial and local counterparts in 1937, a dedicated Propaganda Department (Jōhōka) within the Governor-General's Secretariat was formed in 1941 to coordinate ideological campaigns disseminated through radio, newspapers and other publications, films, special exhibits, lecture series, and even picture shows (*kami shibai*).[89]

CONCLUSION: CONSTRUCTING REGIMES OF LEGITIMATIONS

No revolution took place in Korea in the era examined in this study, but within the framework of monarchical sovereignty a wide range of rationalizations of state legitimacy emerged, including tradition, populism, nationalism, external demands and recognition, statism, administrative capability, material improvement, welfare and public services, and two distinctive appeals to nationalism under colonialism: the first, multiculturalist in orientation, and the second, emphatically assimilationist. Such an abundance of legitimations reflected the turbulent political history of the peninsula at this time, including the prolonged, forced displacement of a systematic monarchical state with a colonial state that itself underwent significant transitions. While retaining the core notion of the state as a source of social edification—a regulator of the social norm and a purveyor of civilization—visions of the modern state, whether from state officials or external observers, also revealed a strong mindfulness of popular support. Such an orientation, for example, was articulated in collectivist understandings of the state based on ideals such as social equality, citizenship, and the incorporation of popular voices.

Geopolitical factors also came to frame rationalizations of state legitimacy. The states of the Gabo Reforms and the subsequent Great Korean Empire, legitimated on different grounds, both reflected a keen awareness of the international ramifications of their claims of authority—the former as an agent of independence from Chinese domination, the latter as a nationalist monarchical state achieving equal standing with other nation states in the age of high imperialism. Alas, the recognition from abroad could not preserve national autonomy, and this helps to explain the appeal of statism during the subsequent Japanese protectorate period beginning in 1905: Only as an independent, commanding actor over the population could the state pursue urgent reforms needed to block external threats. Indeed, those who transformed the protectorate into a tool for the Japanese conquest implemented this legitimation narrative under the banner of security concerns, for Japan and for the northeast Asian region as a whole.

The ensuing colonial state, while retaining a sensitivity to external forces, mostly was justified on the premises and promises of superior administration, as well as on material advances originating therefrom. The debates over the colonial state's standing that arose in the 1910s shifted the discursive range away from justifying colonialism and toward achieving a balance between integration and autonomy for the colonial state, as well as for the colonized people, under the Japanese empire. But even a colonial state maintained by physical coercion heeded the necessity of cultivating legitimacy, as the eruption of the March First independence demonstrations of 1919 made clear. Following the violent suppression of the uprising, the new reign of "Cultural Rule" called for increased public input and promoted greater tolerance, indeed an embrace, of Korean culture, traditions, and identity. The civilizing mission of the colonial state, then, shifted abruptly from the disparagement of Korean customs and behaviors to a vision of coexistence, maintained by responsive administration, between the metropole and colony. The implementation of such a managerial legitimation came through a comprehensive, penetrating network of ideological conduits, from propaganda and lecture circuits to popular culture.

The most pronounced exercise of ideological engineering came via state-sponsored campaigns, rituals, and spectacles, such as the grand exhibitions of 1915, 1929, and 1940 that transitioned from the administrative-materialist basis for colonialism in the 1910s, to Cultural Rule of the 1920s and early 1930s, then finally to the intensive mobilization for war. This latter shift from Cultural Rule to wartime mobilization was also facilitated by projects such as the Rural Revitalization Campaign of the 1930s, which blended into the campaign for National Spirit Mobilization in 1938, and then into total assimilationist mobilization under the rubric of a Japanese-centered pan-Asianism. Strikingly, however, the wartime turn to a ritualistic, traditionalistic nationalism as the basis for state legitimacy showed remarkable parallels to the approaches taken by the Great Korean Empire state four decades earlier. In both settings, the upsurge of a monarchy-dominated legitimation relied on the invented emblems of both popular and heavenly endorsement for traditional authority. As bookends for the evolution of state legitimacy in this era, then, nationalism in the service of a civilizing, moralizing state also constituted an extension of the legitimating rationalities of the preceding Joseon dynasty.

PART TWO

Rationalizing Society

FOUR

State and Economy

DEVELOPMENTALISM

THE MODERN STATE'S CAPACITY TO cultivate and manage material resources constitutes perhaps the signal factor determining its relative power and social impact.[1] This now commonly accepted view of the primacy of political economy stemmed from a conceptual transformation in the modern world in which the growing mobilizational and administrative powers of the state often responded to, promoted, or controlled the material forces unleashed by geopolitical competition and international trade. This was precisely the context, in the late twentieth century, in which South Korea came to industrialize at a record-setting pace and earn its regime the designation of a classic "developmental state." But this developmentalist orientation, as many historians now acknowledge, likely had earlier origins, and in fact played a major role in shaping and defining the modern state in Korea as the notion of an economy itself came into form.

DEVELOPMENTALISM AS CONCEPT AND HISTORY

At least in the English-speaking world, the term "developmental state" seems to have entered the academic lexicon only in the 1980s through Chalmers Johnson's influential study of Japanese state-led growth, *MITI and the Japanese Miracle: The Growth of Industrial Policy, 1925–1975*. Johnson reasons that Japan emerged as a developmental state because of the country's status as a "late developer" whose overriding goal was to catch up to more advanced industrialized countries, for military, economic, and other reasons such as international prestige and diplomatic leverage. Since then other scholars have applied such a concept to places (and eras) beyond twentieth-century Japan, particularly since most modern states could be deemed to have been late developers in some form or another.[2] While remaining careful not to over-generalize the concept of a developmental state, we can fruitfully extend its analytical utility beyond these late developers of the past or the "developing" states of the more recent past to consider a range of issues surrounding the political economy of modern state making.

One could begin by suggesting that, indeed, many if not most modern states became developmental, for they had to contend with external political, commercial, and military forces that compelled a focus on internal material growth and hence pursued policies that targeted specific macroeconomic outcomes. In a wide range of historical contexts, developmentalism, if defined as the application of a state's growing powers of economic planning, market intervention, and industrial promotion,[3] has been nearly inseparable from the processes of nation building and state making. Related to, but not neces-sarily dependent on, Weberian rationalization, developmentalism then rep-resents the logical extension of the modern state itself. The centrally planned economies of the communist bloc were glaring examples of this dynamic, and despite the stifling constraints on extra-state sectors that proved fatal for this system in the long run, many of these countries, including North Korea, indeed underwent fundamental industrial transformation.

North and South Korea, in fact, present an illuminating test case for exam-ining the origins and growth of developmentalism, for while these two states in the second half of the twentieth century diverged widely, both drew upon a common historical foundation to forge a rapid industrial transformation, and in the south, a growth sustained indefinitely. For all of Alexander Woodside's recent insights about the forwardness of traditional East Asian statecraft,[4] which he located in the paternalistic Confucian bureaucratism of China, Vietnam, and Korea, undoubtedly this statecraft never pursued nor even envi-sioned the drive for continuous material expansion, on a national scale, that eventually characterized all three countries. For these East Asian states, then, the trigger that unleashed such latent state capacities to drive economic devel-opment, if they existed at all, came in the early modern era beginning in the late nineteenth century. Industrialization in South Korea (or even in North Korea), then, cannot be attributed solely to the postcolonial period, however intensified these processes became in the 1950s and '60s. The origins lay earlier.

Although conspicuous challenges to this view have arisen,[5] the prevailing thinking outside the peninsula and among a growing group of scholars in South Korea, especially economic historians,[6] is that the origins lay in the industrialization of the 1930s, and especially in the intensive mobilization for Japan's war effort from 1938 to 1945. Carter Eckert, most notably, has shown that capitalism-cum-industrialization in Korea resulted from the colonial state's overriding interests in political and military exploitation, that from its beginnings industrial growth was a handmaiden to state power.[7] The historical extension to the postcolonial Korean regimes seems almost self-evident, for the features of the colonial and postcolonial industrialization efforts were strikingly similar: the overarching notion that a national economy is a self-enclosed entity that can be controlled; state guidance in macro-industrial development, including market intervention in setting prices and determining comparative advantage; the suppression of labor resistance; the strategic allotment of resources from state-controlled financial instruments; and coordination with nonstate economic entities by a dedicated, skilled bureaucracy.

Was this set of features, then, sufficient to consider the colonial state in Korea a developmental state? As suggested above, to a certain degree all colonial states, at least those in the era of "high imperialism" from the late nineteenth to early twentieth centuries, could be considered inherently developmentalist, if one conceives of developmentalism as a rationality of material expansion through the state's regulatory control over economic engines, including market mechanisms. The idea of "colonial developmentalism" can thus approach the level of a redundancy. But it would be wise to narrow that concept to the state's pursuit of a coordinated path toward industrial growth, an effort that went beyond exploitation of natural resources and appropriation of agricultural surplus—beyond, in other words, the characteristics of a classic (overseas) colony.[8] We can also consider two features of state developmentalism that, while not given as much attention in the literature on state making, were particularly pronounced in the strengthening of a developmentalist orientation. First is the primacy of state investment in communication and transportation infrastructure, which literally paved the way for greater state penetration, extraction, and surveillance while inducing industrial growth, urbanization, and an accumulation of the technical and managerial skills necessary for further development. This did not make the state in Korea distinctive, of course, but rather part of a generalizable pattern of early industrializing states throughout the world, including those of the United States, Sweden, Japan, and even Britain, as well as of colonial states.[9] Intensive infrastructure construction was also closely connected to the second prominent feature in Korea's case: the steady effort to establish or strengthen state legitimacy, as seen in the state's strategic application of macroeconomic policies to realize, reinforce, and justify political authority. This process was actually central to the Great Korean Empire's deployment of an early form of techno-nationalism, which was revived, though in modified form, by the colonial state, especially in the wartime period.

What acts as a restraint on declaring the colonial regime a developmental state was its lack of nationalist legitimacy, which in other cases around the world appears to have been a common force for mobilizing the populace toward a dedicated, state-led industrialization.[10] But this connection between legitimacy and developmentalism was hardly straightforward—that is, it was not limited to a dynamic in which the state's legitimacy was a causal prerequisite for the developmentalist drive. One also finds that a state could pursue developmentalism in order to establish or strengthen its legitimacy.[11] Indeed, it is well accepted that among the goals of President Park Chung-Hee's state-led industrialization drive in 1960s South Korea was to bolster, if not to "manufacture," his regime's legitimacy, given that he took power through a military *coup* and constantly had to contend with boisterous opposition.[12] But as this chapter demonstrates, such a connection between state legitimation and state-led industrial growth began earlier than in the 1930s—in fact, even before the colonial period itself.

This is not to declare that a developmental state existed in Korea in the first half of the twentieth century, nor to draw a straight line between the end of the colonial period, much less the end of the nineteenth century, to the end of the twentieth. Rather, this chapter, by exploring state financial, regulatory, and ideological practices, applies developmentalism as an analytical tool to assess the patterns of state-led efforts at cultivating industrial growth in Korea, and to query how this process affected the emergence of the modern state and of notions of a national economy.

DEVELOPMENTALISM IN THE GREAT KOREAN EMPIRE, 1897–1905

The economy, and more specifically, government finances, had been the focal point of Korean government reforms for several decades, if not most of the nineteenth century, so chronically short had fallen state coffers. The corruption that surged in tandem with these revenue shortages appears to have driven the largest mass uprisings in dynastic history during the second half of the nineteenth century, as the structural and political problems in fiscal management reinforced the increasing sense of siege from imperialist forces and left the central state teetering on the brink of crisis from the 1860s onward. The several rounds of government responses, beginning with changes to the local taxation system in the 1860s and culminating in the Gabo Reforms' comprehensive administrative overhaul of 1894–96, failed to stabilize this situation and furthermore did little to effect a shift in the economy's basic character (see chapter 2). At the close of the nineteenth century's last decade, as economic historians have found, neither state finances nor the overall economic condition was fundamentally any better than what they had been a century earlier, and in fact might have been worse.[13]

The Great Korean Empire (Daehan Jeguk), the state formally proclaimed in 1897 upon the restoration of the Joseon monarch's authority, might have constituted—as it turned out—the last concerted attempt to overcome this impediment. The Korean Empire endured, formally, until the 1910 Japanese annexation of the country as a colony, but its significance for our purposes lay in the 1897 to 1905 period, when the state was dominated by the Crown. The Royal Household Ministry (Gungnaebu), which had been segregated by the Gabo Reforms of 1894–96 in order to weaken the connection between the monarchy and a restructured state aspiring to be modern, roared back into prominence and overturned the Gabo Reforms' hierarchy between the monarchy and central administration. By the end of the 1890s, the Royal Household Ministry, or at least its major organ, the Office of Crown Properties (Naejangwon), was wealthier and more powerful than the formal central administration and took the lead in forging state sponsorship of major economic projects.

The Social Darwinian Call for Industry

The motivations for undertaking such efforts by the Korean Empire state were many, ranging from the economic and political to the diplomatic and military, but the basic idea of equating material strength with a nation's well-being was pervasive in the discourse dating back to the 1880s,[14] which in turn was keenly attuned to the broader ramifications of imperialism. The notion of state leadership in strengthening the economy in an era of interstate competition, then, was clearly in the air well before the Gabo Reforms—as seen, for example, in the translations and short editorials appearing in the government news journals of the 1880s.[15] By the spring of 1896, one year before the proclamation of the Korean Empire, the *Dongnip sinmun* newspaper (*The*

Independent), the self-designated watchdog of government abuse and undue foreign influence, began to sound alarm bells about the urgency of economic strengthening for national survival. Among the recurring rhetorical strategies was to draw a connection between the decline or destruction of civilizations and their internal material weaknesses. In an 1897 editorial entitled "Business and Manufacturing Are the Paths toward National Wealth,"[16] for example, the paper noted that China and Egypt were contemporary examples of countries that failed to adapt to the emerging dominance of industry (over agriculture) and to the need for developing a national manufacturing base, and hence these old civilizations either fell into economic dependency or were on the verge of becoming conquered altogether. In the social Darwinistic environment of high imperialism, the correspondence among economic vitality, military prowess, technological advancement, and national strength (and survival) appeared increasingly certain.[17]

The wariness of imperialism and of its direct connection to Korea's economic conditions elicited more explicit calls for the Korean government itself to help save the country through economic strengthening. The early efforts led by the Great Korean Empire, or more specifically, the Crown, to incur foreign debt in order to promote industries in advanced technologies, such as the telegraph, streetcars, and the railroad (see below), appeared, on the one hand, to provide hope for achieving the necessary changes, and on the other—due to these projects' dependence on external forces and capital—to heighten the sense of urgency to maintain autonomy while doing so. This worrisome ambivalence was evinced in numerous editorials, leading up to and following the Russo-Japanese War of 1904–5, that appealed for state leadership in building a viable manufacturing and industrial base.[18] A focus on industrial growth as the basis for military strength, and hence for a strong state as well, also appeared in the writings and public activities of many of the seminal political and intellectual figures of this period—particularly An Changho, Seo Jaepil, Jang Jiyeon, and Bak Eunsik—all of whom located Korea's weaknesses in this arena to a social ideology that devalued commerce, technological innovation, and manual labor, and to a state that had too long adhered to this ethos instead of overcoming it.[19]

The Crown's Developmentalist Projects

The reformist discourse of this period, as expressed especially in newspapers, influenced government policy through, among other connections, the revolving door of state officials and enlightenment activists that at times spun quickly. Many of those officials who headed the Gabo Reforms from 1894 to 1896, in fact, had helped to institutionalize the application of modern technologies for state strengthening through the creation, beginning in the 1880s, of departments within the new *Tongni amun* agencies for mining, machinery, and the telegraph. This provided the groundwork for the establishment, during the Gabo Reforms, of a consolidated Ministry of Agriculture, Commerce, and Industry (Nongsanggongbu) in 1895, a cabinet-level agency that continued into the Korean Empire period. Published budgets of the central government from the closing years of the nineteenth century reveal that, despite its name, this ministry's primary focus lay in modern public works, with almost all of its expenditures going toward constructing the telegraph system and postal service.[20] From 1898–1902 (table 6), these two projects consistently took up 85% of the ministry's budgeted allowance and 5% of total government expenditures, minus the nebulous figures designated for "Imperial Household Expenses" (*Hwangsilbi*).[21] Given the huge allocations for military units designed to protect the monarchy and the capital city—a reflection of the dangers attributed to both imperialism and internal political rivals—and the overwhelmingly agricultural character of the Korean economy at the time, the figure of 5% for the two infrastructural projects of telegraph and the post represented an enormous sum.

By 1900, these two functions were transferred to the newly established Office of Communications (Tongsinwon) under the Royal Household Ministry. This move was part of a larger pattern in which the Crown appropriated most of the government's revenue sources and took the leading role in guiding economic and industrial activity during the Korean Empire period. Such steps were taken, on the one hand, to ensure the supremacy of the monarchy in the governing order, and on the other, to establish the Korean monarchical state on equal footing with the imperial powers that tenaciously threatened its very existence. In either case, the Royal Household Ministry acted in effect as the preeminent governing body by the turn of the twentieth century. Its primary economic agency, the Office of Crown Properties, was headed by the most influential government official of the time, Yi Yongik, who directed the Crown's sponsorship of these early commercial and industrial projects. Much of this institution's vast financial base came from late Joseon revenue sources, with others appropriated more recently. The rents from farmland attached to government organs and post-station lands (*yeokdunto*) constituted the overwhelming proportion of this

TABLE 6 Great Korean Empire Budgeted Expenditures (*won*)

	1898	1899	1900	1901	1902
Total Revenues	4,527,476	6,473,222	6,162,796	9,079,456	7,586,530
Total Expenditures	4,525,530	6,471,132	6,161,871	9,078,682	7,585,877
Normal Expenditures			5,558,972	8,020,151	
Imperial Household Expenses	500,000	500,000	655,000	737,361	900,000
Interior Ministry	1,225,655	1,262,892	1,337,801	982,599	973,410
Finance Ministry	892,197	2,037,907	879,300	764,324	578,736
Military	1,251,745	2,447,351	1,636,704	3,594,911	2,786,290
Central Police Agency				426,039	276,154
Ministry of Agriculture, Commerce, and Industry	189,230	259,004	377,136	70,117	40,892
Postal Expenses	73,000	106,041	140,350		
Communications Expenses	87,000	115,484	177,000		
Office of Communications				398,080	374,910
Postal Expenses				160,350	173,580
Telegraph Expenses				217,000	180,000

SOURCE: Takjibu, "Seip sechul chong yesan-pyo," 1898–1902.

revenue stream,[22] and these resources were supplemented by profits from monopolies and mining operations that the monarchy came to control. Additional income came from various "miscellaneous taxes" (*japse*), including those from maritime, fishing, salt, paper, cloth, water transport, and other economic activities.[23] The central government, by contrast, was left with few revenue sources aside from household taxes, a portion of the land taxes, and some revenues from mining leases, and it even had to occasionally borrow money from the Royal Household Ministry to keep itself afloat.[24]

Where did the Crown's revenues go? A central target for its developmental efforts was infrastructure, particularly the use of electricity, the expansion of the telegraph and streetcar lines, and the construction of the country's first railroads. From the beginning of electrification in Korea the monarchy had been the center of attention, as the first (incandescent) electric lights were installed in the Gyeongbokgung palace in 1886 by none other than the Edison Electric Company.[25] Soon, electrical plants were also installed in other palaces, streetlights went up in 1898, and by 1903, over three thousand lamps were illuminating the capital city. While the Royal Household Ministry left much of the electrification efforts in private hands, it took control of the telegraph (and eventually telephone) through the Office of Communications in 1900. This agency spearheaded the construction of extensions to the nascent telegraph network, which steadily constituted one of the major items for the Crown's expenditures. The ledgers for the Office of Crown Properties, for example, show frequent outlays to various provincial and local governments for what are labeled simply as "electrical expenses" but clearly were in reference to the construction and operation of telegraph lines and relay stations.[26] Recent studies have reiterated the telegraph system's growing significance in the state-led efforts for electrical development, indeed to the larger fiscal health of the state as a whole—both the central government and the Crown—and have highlighted this technology's centrality in the overarching aura of advancement and strength promoted by the Korean Empire state.[27]

Even more conspicuous along these lines were the Seoul streetcars, which came into operation in 1899 and became the most recognized symbol of the modernizing changes of the capital city and the country itself, so prominently was the streetcar featured in narrative accounts and early photographic (and even filmic) images of the time. Funded mostly by the Crown in a joint venture with an American business, which built the cars in Korea and operated the system with Korean workers, the Seoul streetcars harnessed power from an electrical plant constructed on the eastern outskirts of Seoul and ran on lines extending from the East Gate to the center of the city, close to the grounds of the main royal palace. With the Korean *taegeuk* image—by now a familiar symbol of the Korean Empire that appeared on not only the national flag (as it still does, for South Korea) but on the covers of newspapers, journals, and public buildings—clearly emblazoned on the sides of the cars (figure 16), and with the prominent display of accompanying electrical lines and poles along the rail line, the streetcars symbolized the Crown's efforts to reshape the economic and cultural landscape through the promotion of industrial infrastructure.

The same could be said of the establishment of the Railroad Service (Cheoldowon) in 1900, again within the Royal Household Ministry. The first rail line in Korea, that between Seoul and Incheon, had opened in the fall of 1899 with great fanfare and all the attendant gasps of wonder that accompanied the advent of the railroad around the world. As expressed in the

FIGURE 16. A Seoul trolley car, ca. 1902. From *Cassier's Magazine* 22.1 (May 1902).

press coverage of the first rail line, the prevailing belief was that the railroad, like the streetcars, signaled a fundamentally new era, and that it opened the door for Koreans to experience miraculous social and economic changes as well as to catch up to the rest of the world, thereby enhancing Korea's international standing.[28] The monarchy sought to capitalize on this enthusiasm for the railroad's manifold significance by promoting its further development under royal auspices—hence the creation of the Railroad Service as well as of the Western and Northern Railroad Bureau (Seobuk cheoldoguk) soon thereafter, which oversaw the construction of the trunk lines connecting the capital to the northern provinces. The initial segments of these lines were indeed laid by the Royal Household Ministry, and like the original rail line connecting Seoul to the Incheon port, they were later extended by the Japanese, whose construction of the Korean railway network went hand in hand with the takeover and exploitation of Korea as a colony.[29] Such a connection was unforeseen and certainly would have been unwelcome by the officials in the Royal Household Ministry who found the trains a valuable vehicle—both materially and symbolically—for achieving larger political and economic aims.

The Office of Crown Properties took the lead in cultivating noninfrastructural projects as well, such as in mining, that would allow the monarchy to assert its control over commercial enterprises. In early 1898 the Crown prohibited any further concessions to foreigners of mines and railroads, and later that summer all mines that had previously been under the jurisdiction of the Ministry of Agriculture, Commerce, and Industry began to be transferred to the Royal Household Ministry—a process that, within two years, placed nearly all major mining operations, and their revenues, under royal control.[30] Such efforts reveal the growth of what one might call an early form of nationalist protectionism, with a focus on self-sustaining, autonomous growth as a counterpart to external competitors (and threats). The imperial government considered or enacted proposals, for example, to restrict the activities of outside, particularly Chinese, merchants,[31] limit foreign ownership of Korean land, drive out all foreign military forces, control the currency in circulation and imprint it with national symbols, and prohibit the export of grains during years of poor harvest. An increasingly mercantilist stance emanated from outside the government as well, driven especially by newspapers such as the *Dongnip sinmun* and *Hwangseong sinmun*, which, in addition to promoting the development of native industries and commercial prowess, harped on the need to revise the unequal treaties that had given foreign merchants the upper hand in the domestic commercial sphere.[32]

In 1899, the Crown rode this sentiment to connect the country's sprawling networks of merchants and peddlers into a system of economic support for the monarchical state. Even as the establishment of private companies accelerated in the Korean Empire period,[33] the Royal Household Ministry exerted stronger control over commercial activity through its dispensation of registrations and licenses to merchants and domestic trading companies in return for protections and monopolies. On the one hand, such relationships were meant to strengthen the Crown's political position. Those merchants and peddlers who enjoyed special and monopoly privileges, for example, were deployed as shock troops to suppress the Independence Club and other political opponents, or potential opponents, to the monarchy.[34] On the finance side, these efforts were meant to unify the wholesale monopoly activities, under the Crown's command, of the porters, peddlers, and merchant guilds, for the ultimate purpose of increasing revenue streams for the Crown.[35] But they also represented a dedicated mercantilist approach of targeting certain commercial sectors for state investment and of fending off competition from foreign competitors in the name of protecting the state's power and the people's welfare.[36]

This integration of merchant activity into the systemic goals for the monarchical state was expressed clearly in the government-run Commercial Affairs Company, or Sangmusa, the successor to a series of agencies since the

1880s that had regulated merchant activity. The 1899 *Sangmusa jangjeong*,[37] or "Regulations for the Commercial Affairs Company," accompanied the formal proclamation of this new organ. These regulations represented an early effort at formulating a state-led, nationwide economic development policy within the context of a global (or at least regional) trading system, premised on a reorientation of perspectives and practices regarding commercial activity. They revealed, then, a strong interest not only in overturning the traditional disregard for commerce, but in forging a new national ethos of pursuing material growth. The opening article of these guidelines, in fact, stated that strategic investment (*gakchul jabon*) was the key to the success of the new agency and of the state itself. This idea was further elaborated in Article 7, which claimed that investment in commerce was necessary for realizing the state policy of achieving national wealth and strength (*bugang*). Other articles reiterated the need to integrate government oversight of local commercial activities with the aims of the Sangmusa at the center, to prevent abuses by both merchants and government officials, and to encourage manufacturing and trade as integral components of the nation's commercial vibrancy. Through these principles, the Korean Empire approached a holistic declaration of a national economic policy that emphasized commercial growth, protection against external economic forces, and the leadership of the monarchical state.

The increasing flow of revenue from the Commercial Affairs Company and similar efforts appears indeed to have provided the financing for further industrial efforts, including government-run projects in transportation and manufacturing.[38] In 1900 the Office of Communications set up the Seoul Telegraph Training Center (Hanseong jeonbo hakdang), which by 1905 supplied over one hundred technicians for the expanding telegraph network.[39] The Crown also erected technical training schools in commerce and industry,[40] including one specifically to teach mining techniques. Spurred by its oversight of railroad projects, the Office of Crown Properties even standardized the modified adoption of the metric system for weights and measures in 1902.[41] And around the same time, the Royal Household Ministry under Yi Yongik's direction instituted a currency reform to further monetize economic activity, in response to the growing inflation and instability caused by the circulation of different coins and currencies, an untenable situation that had newspapers crying for relief for some time.[42]

Most of the new currency issued by the government mint, Jeonhwanguk, however, came to be earmarked for use by the monarchy for its various projects.[43] And in real terms adjusting for inflation, the Crown's income was limited by a revenue collection system that employed middlemen merchants as transmitters, an arrangement vulnerable to irregularities and abuse, including by the royal household itself.[44] Efforts to standardize the financial system culminated in the establishment of a central bank in 1903, but it ultimately failed to attract enough financing from foreign interests before it was overtaken by the imposition of a Japanese overseer in 1904 through the start of the Russo-Japanese War. This stood as a prelude to the implementation, a year later, of the Japanese protectorate, which took over management of the Korean government's financial affairs. The Crown initially retained much of its fiscal independence, but in the name of institutional reform, the Residency-General reallocated most of the Royal Household Ministry's revenue sources to the Korean central government, and particularly after the forced abdication of Emperor Gojong and the transfer of control over government appointments to the protectorate in the summer of 1907, the Korean monarchy became nearly powerless, preceding in this regard the rest of the Korean government by three years.[45]

In the Developmentalist Historical Trajectory

In evaluating the economic development efforts of the Crown in the 1897–1905 period, it is difficult not to conflate them with the fate of Korean autonomy itself, so strong is the historical pull of the Japanese takeover. Scholars attempting to look beyond Japanese imperialism as the sole cause of Korea's loss of sovereignty have tended, with good reason, to highlight the Korean state's weak fiscal basis, and particularly its troubles with revenue collection.[46] Even semifavorable evaluations of the Great Korean Empire's economic development activities appear to wistfully note that the Japanese protectorate stopped such efforts before they could get under way and, in their place, implanted the juggernaut of "colonial modernization."[47] This "too little, too late" view has approached the level of a trope, while other scholars have been less forgiving. Yi Yun-sang, a specialist on the economic history of this era, finds—again, implicitly, with 1905 in mind—that in the end the Korean Empire did not have much to show for all its efforts, except to hinder the higher priority of strengthening the "real" state, i.e., the central government that seemed so weak and even impoverished compared to the Royal Household Ministry.[48] He argues that much of this failure stems from the empire's preeminent goal of enhancing the monarchy's power and stature.

Indeed, a systematic, comprehensive effort at commercial or industrial development was never fully attempted, for the Office of Crown Properties, under Yi Yongik's direction, neglected small merchants and manufacturers and instead concentrated on consolidating exclusive revenue sources and licensing monopolies.[49] Economic historian Yi Yeong-hun has put it even more bluntly, arguing more or less that the Crown's policies were simply predatory, with most of the income generated via taxation and the mint channeled toward the monarch's personal needs (protection, ceremony, lifestyle), and little toward durable investment.[50] The result, in any case, was a state fiscally incapable of fending off imperialism.

If we step back for a moment, however, from a preoccupation with the Japanese takeover and instead focus on how the Korean Empire's economic projects fit into the historical trajectory of state growth in Korea, we find core features of state developmentalism that one readily locates later in the colonial and post–Korean War periods. While the degree of coordinated planning and the monetary scale of the investment seem much smaller than in later eras, the Korean state, and the Crown in particular, cultivated specific economic sectors and likewise allocated substantial human and fiscal resources to them. Furthermore, an inordinate level of investment was directed toward promoting public works projects, particularly in new technologies, as the driver of material growth. The broader significance of these developments has been continuously examined since the 1990s. Yi Tae-jin, the most prominent participant in a rising tide of scholarly interest in the empire's industrial projects, has furthermore accentuated the role of the monarch, Gojong, from the 1880s onward. In exemplifying the now common, if not quite orthodox, perspective on the Korean Empire, Yi sees these measures as having laid an autonomous path toward modernization—that is, until the Japanese, sensing a threat to their imperialist aspirations, stopped them.[51] Rather than seeing these unmistakable advances as having been destroyed or distorted by Japanese imperialism, however, one is more inclined to view them as having been intensified by the developmentalist orientation of Japanese rule.

Indeed, both the Korean and Japanese regimes viewed state control over macroeconomic forces, including the construction of the transportation and other infrastructure, as keys to the viability of their respective states. The founding of the Great Korean Empire in 1897 attempted to reinvigorate the traditional identification of the Crown with the country itself, but there were now far greater stakes: national survival. Playing catch-up, a major factor in developmentalist efforts later in the 1960s,[52] was central to the policies and projects of the Korean Empire, as observers at the time noted.[53] The Crown's move in 1899 to prohibit any further mining or commercial concessions was indicative of this approach, as were the granting of monopoly commercial licenses to domestic merchants and the appropriation of control over all railroad development in the opening years of the twentieth century. This awareness of demonstrating internal strength in the face of external pressure was clearly on display in the regulations of the Commercial Affairs Company as well, with their explicit connection of commercial vibrancy with a readiness to resist imperialism.

Meanwhile, the Crown, still smarting from the efforts of the preceding Gabo Reforms to separate the affairs of the monarchy from that of the central administration, faced ongoing political challenges to its authority, such as from the Independence Club. As Seo Yeong-hui has demonstrated in her study of the Korean Empire's politics, a resolute, stable execution of the Crown's policies could only begin after the Independence Club and its supporters were suppressed in late 1898 and early 1899, and that even afterward the wariness of these and other looming pressure sources remained at the forefront, almost to the point of obsession, of the Crown's concerns.[54] In response, the Crown attempted to rekindle the splendor of a powerful, indeed absolutist monarchy by forging an enveloping aura of technological advances and commercial prowess while appropriating the circulating nationalist and enlightenment ideas that connected state strength to material advancement.

COLONIAL DEVELOPMENTALISM

Perhaps not surprisingly, finances constituted the first realm of state administration that fell under Japanese sway in the takeover process beginning in 1904 through the Russo-Japanese War. That year the Korean cabinet agreed to employ a Japanese advisor, Megata Tanetarō, to reform and manage the state's financial affairs, an effort that focused on shoring up the tax base and streamlining the bureaucratic order more than on promoting industrial growth.[55] Megata transformed the hitherto privately held Dai-ichi Bank into the Korean state's central bank in 1904, through which further fiscal measures, such as currency reform and the reorganization of tax levying and collection mechanisms, were pursued by the protectorate. In the fall of 1909 these efforts coalesced into the establishment of the Bank of Korea (Hanguk eunhaeng), which, despite its name and formal status as the Korean government's central bank, was run by the Japanese. As it turned out, this institution became a holding pen for the incorporation, in the spring of 1911, of the Bank of Chosen (Chōsen ginkō), which issued the Bank of Chosen *yen* note, the currency of colonial Korea (and later, Manchuria), and would remain at the center of developmental pursuits through most of the colonial era.[56]

The Colonial State's Developmental Efforts

The banking sector as a whole, under the guidance of the Bank of Chosen, became the institutional basis in the colonial period for state-directed economic growth policies, which included not only the financing of public works but also the promotion of increasingly high-value industrial sectors, the sponsorship of Japanese and Korean commercial activities and entrepreneurs, and the encouragement of the migration of Japanese capital and settlers to the peninsula. The latter activity was a particular focus of attention for the Oriental Development Company (Toyō takushoku kabushiki kaisha), which formed as a semiprivate enterprise in 1908 but soon worked closely with the colonial regime to nationalize land holdings and purchase vast tracts of real estate, and to dangle these resources to would-be settlers and businessmen from Japan.[57] The final component in this developmentalist triumvirate of financial institutions, the Chosen Industrial Bank (Chōsen sangyō ginkō), was established in 1918 and served as a source of financing to mostly settler and metropolitan businesses but also, crucially, to Korean enterprises. It eventually surpassed even the Bank of Chosen in paid-in capital and remained, particularly in the second half of the colonial period, the primary financial instrument for implementing state-directed industrial growth.[58]

In the first decade of colonial rule, however, industrial growth hardly registered in official economic policy. The promulgation of the Company Law at the end of 1910, a move publicly touted as a deterrent to "the establishment of illegal or bubble corporations,"[59] dampened native Korean industry by requiring that all new enterprises gain preapproved licensing by the central colonial government, a stipulation that proved burdensome. It appears also to have given the tens of thousands of Japanese settlers as well as favored members of the Japanese business class a leg up during the opening years of the colonial period. The government statistics for the number of workers according to industry in the 1910s, which meticulously maintained separate counts for the Japanese and Korean residents, showed an enormous gap in the manufacturing and commercial sectors.[60] There simply were few Koreans engaged in them, in relative terms. This squared with the original economic vision of Korea as a classic colony, with the focus on promoting efficiencies in the agricultural sector and on creating a consumer market for Japanese-manufactured goods. Despite the optimistic tone of some Japanese business-men regarding potential growth, the colonial regime's approach reflected more the prevailing perspective—exaggerated in its claims, as we have seen—that Korea at the moment of annexation possessed little meaningful industry to speak of.[61]

Crucially, however, infrastructure construction that had begun in the late nineteenth century continued apace, particularly through the extension of the rail lines from the capital to all four corners of the peninsula. In terms of both human and material resources, in fact, agencies devoted to the railroad, such as the Railroad Bureau (Tetsudokyoku), remained among the largest in the colonial state, and by 1938 the costs of managing, constructing, and main-taining the rail system constituted nearly one-half of state expenditures (see below). The steps initiated in the Korean Empire period toward bolstering the modern postal and communication systems also continued, and even a nascent telephone system was implemented in the first decade of colonial rule, which in turn required an increase in government employees to man the switching stations and maintain the machinery.[62] While remaining over-whelmingly agricultural, the landscape of the colonial economy in the 1910s was dotted with such indicators of modern infrastructure. Communications and transportation, in fact, would consistently attract the bulk of state investment over the course of colonial rule.

In the second decade colonial economic policy in many ways reinforced Korea's standing as an agricultural base, and in fact the sudden rise in grain prices in Japan in 1918, and the "riots" that followed, prompted a push to further stimulate the colony's agricultural production in order to raise the availability of cheaper Korean rice. The "Plan to Increase Rice Production" (*Sanmai zōsan keikaku*), based on projects to develop new parcels and convert fields into paddies, assisted by state-sponsored local water cooperatives, and funded through sources such as bonds issued by the Oriental Development Company, brought forth consistent gains in Korean rice exports and reached a level that eventually took nearly half of all the rice produced in the colony to Japan by the end of the 1920s.[63] But this decade also witnessed a shift toward cultivating a greater role for manufacturing and industry in the colonial economy, part of the unfolding of the "cooperative capitalist development" initiated under Cultural Rule.[64] The Company Law, designed to limit Japanese commercial encroachment in the colony as much as to keep the focus on agriculture in Korea, was rescinded in 1920, and incentives, such as the removal of customs duties between the metropole and colony, further encouraged Japanese investment in Korea.[65] And the colonial Industrial Commissions, the conferences of top government officials and business leaders (both Japanese and Korean) convened to study and strategize comprehensive industrial growth plans for the colony—and emblematic of state developmentalism in the late colonial period—began in 1921, and were held again in 1936 and 1938.[66] Meanwhile, native Korean manufacturing efforts also began to grow, particularly in the light industries of textiles, ceramics, and food processing. The most prominent of such companies was Seoul Spinning and Weaving Company (Gyeongseong Bangjik), the famed textile firm studied by Carter Eckert and, more recently, Ju Ik-jong, as the representative Korean enterprise of the time.[67] This company was the quintessential beneficiary of the colonialist developmentalism that patronized certain large enterprises, most of which were Japanese, for targeted growth in strategic sectors through a variety of state favors: a loosening of credit from state-owned or state-directed banks, subsidies and tax credits that encouraged expansion, and intervention in labor relations to tamp down on unrest.

This state-guided growth intensified in the 1930s, spurred by two events of global significance: the Great Depression, which caused a precipitous drop in agricultural prices and forced a renewed attention to rural society (chapters 2 and 3) as well as a reconsideration of the agriculturally centered colonial economic policy;[68] and the 1931 Manchurian Incident, the staged bombing of the Japanese-controlled South Manchurian Railway that the imperial army used to justify its invasion of Manchuria, which led to the establishment of the semicolonial state of Manchukuo the following year. Koreans followed these events closely, none more so than entrepreneurs like Bak Heungsik or the Gim brothers of Seoul Spinning and Weaving, who envisioned, and eventually realized, commercial growth in the frontiers of Manchuria. The colonial state joined the greater cause of connecting the two territories' economies, as rail and shipping lines extensively criss-crossed northeast Asia in service to Japanese expansionism. This set the stage also for heavy industrialization, as Korea quickly turned into a manufacturing base for Japanese military and commercial advance into the mainland. Helped by the Bank of Chosen's reduction of prime interest rates to record lows in the wake of the Depression, the early 1930s witnessed the first major influx of Japanese corporate investment in the colony—along with an acceleration of Japanese settler migration—which implanted factories for textiles, fertilizer, and machinery, among other products.[69] Hydroelectric plants popped up in the northern part of the peninsula, and the heavy industrial sectors of chemicals, armaments, and even shipbuilding blossomed, as major Japanese companies, including *zaibatsu* conglomerates such as Mitsubishi and Mitsui, established operations in Korea.[70]

Such changes of course carried the strong imprint of state planning. According to the analysis of hundreds of data sources undertaken by the Naksungdae Economic Research Institute, the industrialization of colonial Korea was due much more to capital accumulation than productivity growth, and the source of this capital was predominantly the state.[71] The Government-General's expenditures increased from constituting approximately 10% of Korea's gross domestic product at the start of the colonial period to approximately 20% three decades later in 1940. The state's portion of paid-in capital investments in the colony, in fact, surpassed that of the private sector in the early 1930s and eventually move beyond 60% of the total. Where those funds went, however, was just as telling: State outlays concentrated heavily in public works, particularly in the construction and maintenance of infrastructure, which accounted for over half of the Government-General's expenditures by the late 1930s.[72] When measured in terms of fixed capital formation (figure 17), communication and transportation always took in an overwhelming proportion of state investment—receiving roughly 63% in the late 1910s to over 80% by the late 1930s.[73] The public railroad system, in particular, was a recipient of state largesse, taking in 27% of the total Government-General expenditures in 1930, and nearly 45% ten years later at the height of the war (table 7).[74] As the official history of the Bank of Chosen proudly proclaimed in 1935, the expansion and development of the railways, almost all of which was state-owned, made possible the "flourishing of industrial culture" (*sangyō bunka . . . no yūshū*) in Korea.[75]

These trends also fueled urbanization. The buildup of transportation infrastructure, in particular, geographically contracted the colony and facilitated migration to urban centers. The population figures were dramatic: From 1917 to 1937, the percentage of rural households shrank from 82% to 72%, which, while not changing the overall profile of the colony as a primarily agricultural economy, signaled the beginnings of a major shift. In that same two-decade time span, the three major metropolitan areas of Seoul (Keijō-fu),

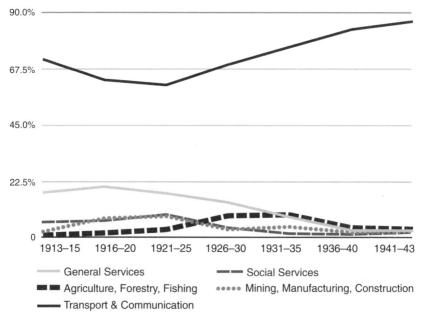

FIGURE 17. Percentage of Fixed Capital Formation, Government-General of Korea. From Gim Nang-nyeon, ed., *Hanguk ui gyeongje seongjang, 1910–1945*, pp. 488–89.

Busan (Fusan-fu), and Pyongyang (Heijō-fu) witnessed nearly threefold increases in their respective size. Seoul's population increased 184% (Busan, 187%; Pyongyang, 178%) in that period to over 700,000, compared to an increase of 32% for the colony as a whole. (The number of Japanese residents nearly doubled in that time span, but that still represented less than 3% of the total population in 1937.) Meanwhile, according to Government-General statistics the increases in the two occupational categories of "industry" and "commerce and transportation" were 88% and 59%, respectively (again, notwithstanding the large discrepancies in raw numbers between Japanese and Koreans, the effects of which were minimal for the overall figures).[76] Of course, the forces behind this urbanization came not only from the growth of industry and infrastructure, which accompanied greater factory employment in or near the cities, but also from push factors: rural immiseration, particularly through the rising commercialization of agriculture that resulted in greater tenancy, and then the shock of the Great Depression.[77] By 1940, over 38% of the gross economic output in Korea came from the manufacturing and construction sectors, which had grown an extraordinary twenty-

	Total Expenditures from Government-General Special Accounts	Railroad Construction and Maintenance Expenditures	Total Investment in State-Owned Railways
1910	17,815,654	6,144,904	
1911	46,172,310	8,418,016	9,234,242
1912	51,781,225	8,767,647	9,643,425
1913	53,454,484	8,469,387	8,661,647
1914	55,099,834	7,321,953	7,634,117
1915	56,869,947	7,618,077	8,004,432
1916	57,562,710	7,434,505	7,705,111
1917	51,171,826	5,998,408	6,152,026
1918	64,062,720	9,745,329	11,093,883
1919	93,026,893	14,980,222	15,749,711
1920	122,221,297	15,327,829	16,329,371
1921	148,414,003	18,287,158	18,855,531
1922	155,113,753	21,710,999	22,987,197
1923	144,768,149	14,999,904	16,475,266
1924	134,810,178	10,001,842	10,306,672
1925	171,763,081	9,906,505	12,017,799
1926	189,470,101	14,948,338	17,736,682
1927	210,852,949	23,367,388	25,290,524
1928	217,690,321	26,804,546	28,687,883
1929	224,740,305	22,771,905	23,378,972
1930	208,724,448	12,052,344	12,478,975
1931	207,782,798	21,829,325	21,989,919
1932	214,494,728	18,906,988	19,812,344
1933	229,224,139	19,412,042	20,955,831
1934	268,349,402	18,497,852	20,697,637
1935	283,958,943	34,891,975	37,117,886
1936	324,472,357	34,424,623	38,321,878
1937	407,027,104	63,041,650	68,940,016

SOURCE: *Chōsen sōtokufu tōkei nenpō* (various years).

seven-fold since 1911, compared to a growth of under sixfold in agriculture (figure A.1).[78] By 1941, the percentage of rural households dropped to two-thirds of the total (from 82% in 1917), even as the colony's population grew another 10% since 1917 to 24.7 million. Seoul's population swelled to nearly a million, but the growth in Pyongyang's population, which reached 330,000, accelerated at an even faster rate, a reflection of that city's increasing importance in wartime industry.[79]

All of these trends accelerated in line with war mobilization beginning in the late 1930s. Although official figures after 1941 are spotty, growth rates in urbanization, industrial production (primarily in heavy industries and especially in munitions), infrastructural investment, and total economic output appear to have jumped considerably in the first few years of wartime and continued until 1944, with the colonial state playing a leading role.[80] The relentless drive to supply the battle fronts, however, also resulted in severe deprivation in the final few years of colonial rule, as consumption and income taxes rose precipitously (chapter 1), state controls over industrial production were tightened to meet military demands, and state-owned companies, state-sanctioned cartels, producers and wholesalers associations, local rationing agencies, and other integration effects of the penetrative command economy appropriated ever more material resources for military use.[81] To what extent these stringent measures of the wartime period represented a departure from pre-mobilization practices or merely an intensification of earlier tendencies can be debated. Unquestionably, in terms of a state developmentalism that cultivated the input of major industrial firms, associations, and sectors in the growth of the Korean economy as a whole, the wartime policies extended a trajectory that had been established earlier.

Colonial Developmentalist Discourse

That the colonial state directed this material transformation is indisputable, but just as striking was its utility for bolstering the regime's legitimacy. Initially, as noted above, the developmentalist rhetoric connecting colonial rule to the promotion of commercial or industrial growth was somewhat muted. To be sure, the early colonial regime established training centers and other institutions to promote industry, and the 1910 Imperial Rescript on the Annexation declared that "All Koreans, being under Our direct sway, will enjoy growing prosperity and welfare, and with assured repose and security will come a marked expansion in industry and trade." But the annexation treaty itself, full of blustery language on the beneficial transfer of sovereignty and on the amalgamation of the two royal families, failed to mention economic development as a goal beyond the general allusion to "promot[ing] the welfare" of law-abiding Koreans (Article 6).[82] The undercurrent of the opening decade's official narrative for both domestic and foreign consumption—as evident in the 1915 Korean Products Fair (chapter 3), the *Administrative Annuals* published by the Government-General, and other channels such as public speeches and press coverage—was that the growth in material conditions under colonialism, especially in agricultural production and infrastructure construction, constituted the substance and proof of Japanese rule's salutary impact.[83]

Economic advances became more firmly tied to the legitimation rhetoric of foreign rule in the ensuing Cultural Rule period of the 1920s. But as Jun Uchida has shown, despite the lobbying of both Japanese settler and Korean business interests for major increases in state investment, the regime hesitated to formally promote industrialization, as it could complicate the original vision of Korea as an agricultural supplier for the metropole.[84] At the first colonial Industrial Commission (Sangyō chōsa iinkai) in 1921, this sense of ambivalence, as well as of transition, became apparent in the utterances of the two highest officials of the Government-General, both appointed in 1919 as purveyors of Cultural Rule. In his remarks Vice Governor-General Mizuno Rentarō, while reiterating the importance of cultivating industries in Korea, stressed the need for a gradual, "systematic" approach (keitōteki hattatsu) in line with the Japanese empire's economic growth plans, given the colony's immature stage of development. This did not deviate substantively from the general importance attached to the "welfare" of Koreans in the original annexation narrative, and more importantly, reinforced the primacy of raising Korean rice production.[85] Governor-General Saitō Makoto, however, suggested a turn toward a more nonagricultural trajectory as his main charge, even stating that "promoting the welfare of the people through the cultivation of industry constitutes the key [yōtei] to colonial rule [Chōsen tōchi]." Furthermore, in signaling a revisionist view of the original intent of colonial rule, Saitō claimed that such an ideal of prioritizing industrial growth, however challenging, had *always* been the "main objective" (honsi) and "core component" (hongi) of the annexation.[86]

A telling indicator of this shift appears in the memoir of official-turned-businessman Bak Yeongcheol, who began his bureaucratic career, aided considerably by his father's standing as one of the richest men in Korea, as a military official attached to Japanese interests before the annexation. He worked as a county magistrate in the opening decade of colonial rule before ascending to positions as a provincial vice governor, then governor of Gangwon province in the 1920s until his retirement into the realm of finance and business at the close of the decade. His *Memoir of Fifty Years* (Gojūnen no kaiko, 1929), which includes many of his observations and actions as a colonial official, conspicuously identified economic growth as not only the top priority for him personally, but that of the Government-General as well. As a good capitalist, Bak viewed such an approach as ultimately driven by the state's promotion of free-market principles, like the protection of private property, which he claimed was the "first" action undertaken by the colonial regime for the sake of the people's welfare.[87] But also notable was Bak's ready channeling of his own perspective into that of the Government-General itself, as if the increasing primacy of industrial and commercial development had always been presumed. He suggested, for example, that from the beginning the colonial state's "central policy" was to foster material improvements, and that its most "urgent" state project lay in building up the transportation infrastructure, a refrain echoed by official publications of the time that stressed the sweeping benefits of railway development, its utility as a "basic mechanism of rule" (*tōchi no konpon shisei*).[88] Even in the late 1920s, he insisted, the most important task for Koreans remained "stability of life" (*seikatsu no antei*), which he explained as an improvement in economic conditions, particularly as the basis for sparking within Koreans a fruitful diligence and even a zest for entrepreneurship. "This is why," he claimed, "since the annexation, the Government-General, in pursuing improvements in its administration of sectors such as industry [*sangyō*], education, agriculture and forestry, engineering [*doboku*], law, police, etc., exerted its greatest efforts in the development of industry."[89]

Such articulation of the industrial economy's centrality in the state became more definitive as time passed. Under the reign of Governor-General Ugaki Kazushige—the same figure who instituted the Rural Revitalization Campaign in response to the Depression's impact on the rural sector—the colonial regime in the mid-1930s began more explicitly to associate industrial growth to the larger purpose, and even fate, of the Korean colony. It declared a fundamental transition from an agricultural economy engaged in "primitive industry" (*genshi sangyo*) in order to meet demands for grain production to a "modern great industrial economy" in the service of imperial interests.[90] Ugaki and his successor, Minami Jirō, proclaimed that the promotion of industry addressed the "continental crisis" set into relief by the events in Manchuria—which, in bringing about the integration of Korea and Manchuria, would facilitate the Japanese commercial, demographic, and military expansion into the continent—and thereby opened the path for Koreans to enjoy fully the fruits of the empire.[91] In a speech given to educators in 1934 on the "Future of Korea," for example, Ugaki stressed that "the true development and improvement of Chosen will begin now" and even declared that the fate of the Japanese empire as a whole hinged on how well he and others could direct this shift in the colony's economy.[92]

As it soon became clearer, what Ugaki, Minami, and the other leaders of the colonial regime had in mind when envisioning Korea's "true development and improvement" was, above all, its economic utility for imperial expansionism. If the Cultural Rule regime under Saitō Makoto had proclaimed a gradual economic transition beyond agriculture, the Manchurian Incident of 1931 and particularly the China Incident of 1937 let loose an articulation of Korea's material standing—indeed, its standing in general—as an industrial base for achieving military aims. To be sure, at one level it was a matter of course that not only Ugaki and Minami but all colonial Governors-General, who were also army commanders (except Saitō, from the navy), would view both their roles and the peninsula itself primarily in military terms,[93] but until the 1930s such a vision had been superseded by the larger pursuit of Korea's industrial development for purposes inherent to colonial rule. With the onset of total war, however, imperialist legitimations for industrial development overwhelmed colonialist ones. Even the calls for constructing the Greater East Asian Co-Prosperity Sphere (*Dai tōa kyōeiken*), the euphemism for a Japanese-dominated economic bloc in opposition to the West, became couched in confrontational rallying cries for the martial defense of Asian civilization.[94] The justifications for militarized industrialization served, then, as a handmaiden and symbol of the colony's full integration—economically, administratively, and culturally—into the empire's pursuit of war and turned the colonial state, both discursively and institutionally, into a military organ, if not beginning the dissolution of a separate existence itself.

CONCLUSION

The emergence of militarized industrial growth as an instrument of government power capped the extended process by which the economy itself eventually became a fundamental, abiding object of state interest beginning in the late nineteenth century. This in turn followed a common pattern behind the materialist transformation of the state in the modern world, in which nurturing a macroeconomy—indeed, into existence—became a prime objective for regimes aspiring toward greater social authority domestically and heightened standing internationally. As Timothy Mitchell suggests, the full spate of bureaucratic concerns and technologies, of imperialist and self-strengthening drives, and of military and territorial rivalries, might have created the (national) economy as not just a new concept, but a definitive entity in itself.[95] While it is not possible to locate the precise moment when concerns over economic growth came to occupy such a preeminent place in Korean statecraft, from the late nineteenth century to the end of the colonial period, the state's approach to the economy passed unmistakably and irreversibly from a physiocratic to a mercantilist, then industrializing focus. And through these transitions the emergence of the macroeconomy as a distinctive sphere of state control and of industrial development as an overriding state goal came into sharper relief, particularly as material conditions within the peninsula became more clearly connected to the extended circumstances of imperialism, colonialism, and war.

Indeed the role of economic development in nation building, state making, and other political goals beginning in the late nineteenth century suggests at least a recurrence of familiar patterns, if not direct connections, over a longer period of time than is commonly perceived. State-led economic nationalism, for example, while having to wait until after liberation in 1945 to gain full force, began in the precolonial period, as seen in the growing chorus in enlightenment discourse, and particularly in the activities of the Crown during the Great Korean Empire. As shown in this chapter, the resurgently monarchical state turned toward a proto-developmentalist techno-nationalism to strengthen its internal and external standing. Through its vast land and mine holdings and tax sources, the Royal Household Ministry and the Office of Crown Properties, as arms of the absolutist monarchy, directed the mobilization of manpower and resources toward transportation and communication networks, commercial enterprises, and industry. Infrastructure projects, in particular, contributed to the development of a national market—with the first streetcars, for example, being manufactured within Korea—and hence also of a national identity tied to industrial technology, all the while advancing the state's extractive capacities. Indeed, even the concessions to foreign companies for various large-scale projects, which traditionally have been perceived as a sign of weakness, can actually be viewed as an early example of the state's paternalistic regulation over business. In the colonial period, the state's regulatory control over the internal market, including through an exponential increase in infrastructure investment and, later, the cultivation of enterprise capital, sharpened the instrumentality of economic growth for the purposes of state strengthening and development. The neo-mercantilist policies of protectionism through tariffs, monopolies, and currency controls, for example, as well as the management of financial organs in the service of the state's quest for resources and comparative advantage, characterized both the precolonial and colonial states.

These connections in turn clarify the colonial regime's place in the trajectory of modern state growth in Korea. Colonialism at one level can be taken largely as an attempt to displace the traditional bases of political legitimacy with material growth, in which case developmentalism can be considered definitional to the colonial state, just as it became a common feature of modern states in general. For Korea, one could argue convincingly that economic exploitation became the main purpose of Japanese rule, if not originally then certainly soon thereafter, in effect overriding the early justifications of security and the civilizing mission (chapter 3). What constrains this interpretation, however, is that colonial developmentalism worked within, and remained largely dependent upon, the bifurcation of society between Japanese settlers and the Koreans, and later upon the related division between a collaborationist population (both Japanese and Korean) and the rest. Not only did economic growth in the colonial period profit mostly the Japanese, as capital and control remained predominantly in the hands of Japanese settlers or bourgeoisie, but the colony's working—and mobilized—classes were almost exclusively composed of Koreans.

In other words, if the colonial regime functioned as a developmental state, it remained somewhat incomplete, limited in its capacity to deploy nationalist appeals for industrial mobilization. In contrast to the Korean Empire state, which achieved far less in state-led industrial or infrastructural growth but could tap into the strengthening discursive connections between national identity and economic welfare, the colonial state eventually faced conflicting developmentalist rationalizations of its legitimacy. The claims of material improvement as the undercurrent of the colonial state's legitimation narrative, which reached its peak during Cultural Rule as the regime loosened state controls in an effort to unleash entrepreneurial energies, was overwhelmed by the juggernaut of total war, when developmentalism as colonialist legitimation appealed less to promises of a better material future for the colony than to the baldly military pursuits of imperial Japan, the mass assimilation into which was demanded but never realized. It would take the trials of the postliberation period, on both sides of the national divide, to witness the full force of military developmentalism being mobilized for genuinely nationalist ends.

FIVE

State and Religion

SECULARIZATION AND PLURALISM

GENERALLY, IN THE REALM OF religion, modern state making in Korea aligned with global trends, as the state institutionalized its increasingly broad regulatory powers over religious institutions and practices, even the clergy. Most modern states, in fact, have had to wrestle with integrating often nebulous religious groups and traditions into the bureaucratic channels of public administration. For the process by which the state encroached upon or overtook religions touched on core issues of modernity itself: the locus of collective loyalty, the goals of social restructuring, the impact of external influence, and perhaps most of all, the standing of well-established cultural orthodoxies. In this way, the state was one of many, though perhaps the most formidable, challengers to religion's comprehensive command over truth. The long-standing rivalry around the world between Church and State, to use a shorthand, stemmed from the fact that both entities strived for final authority in communal identity, social organization, and behavior.[1] One might go so far as to suggest that religion and state, particularly as they came into the institutionalized forms that are familiar today, served as mutual metaphors: Religion emulated the state in its extensive claims over behavioral norms and truth; and for its part, the state attempted not only to regulate religions but also to act in a religious capacity, including through its attempts to control individual actions, even beliefs.

How this process unfolded in early modern Korea was complicated, as it was in other social realms, by the colonial state's function as both an extension and displacement of the preceding dynastic state, particularly since the latter had long established an intricate relationship with religious forms in general and Confucianism in particular. Such problems were addressed by major reforms in the late nineteenth century, which in many ways laid the groundwork for the colonial approaches. And cutting across this era's dynamics between state and religion was the rationalization of public secularization, as well as the state's promotion of its major component, religious pluralism.

STATE SECULARIZATION IN THEORY AND PRACTICE

It is now widely accepted that the secularization thesis, forwarded systematically beginning in the 1960s but broached by a number of prominent social theorists ranging from Max Weber to Karl Jaspers even earlier, has proven problematic if not entirely misguided. To start, asserting that modern people became less religious or that religion has played a diminished social role simply flies in the face of facts.[2] But even if the sense of secularization is limited to the declining influence of religion in the public realm, which can be considered a genuinely global phenomenon, as with so many other attempts to universalize the experience of modernity, the degree and character of secularization was too closely tied to each region's historical circumstances for generalization to be viable.[3] The same holds true for the narrower issue of state secularization, and much of the problem is semantic: Can any modern state, with all of its new functions that unavoidably fell outside the purview of religion, be free from secular considerations?[4] Obversely, did modernizing states need to undergo a process of discarding religious affiliations? If so, this principle was belied by many examples, from prewar Japan to contemporary Iran and even the United States. Indeed the demands of modern states around the world were met by various expressions of religious interests from an equally wide range of traditions; in short, a multiplicity of church / state relationships emerged in line with national particularities.[5]

Given, however, that the release from religious imperatives constituted a signal feature of states in much of the modern world, the notion of state secularization can help conceptualize the rationalities of the state's relationship to an evolving realm of modern religion. But here, too, we encounter a problem of definition: Should secularity be measured by religion's influence on the state, or vice versa? If the latter, is the state more, or less, secular the more it regulates religious life? In considering religion's impact on the modern state, as well as the state's authority over religion, it appears that in state secularization the former tendency must be weak and the latter strong, resulting in the state's separating from, regulating, and even suppressing religious organizations and activities.[6] In gaining command over the religious realm, modern states have sought to treat all (sanctioned) religions the same—or repress all religions—in order to instill equalized loyalty to the state. Secularization, in this sense, fit the larger program of homogenizing the populace in order to maximize mobilization, extraction, and subjugation, a process of displacing religion's extensive hold over the people with identification with the state—or the nation or party, as the case may be.[7]

For exploring state secularization in Korea, we can begin by considering contemporaneous Japan, for the Japanese eventually implanted core features of the Korean state through colonial rule, and because Japan, with a similar premodern statecraft ideology (neo-Confucianism) and core religious undercurrent—shamanism, later institutionalized and politicized into Shinto, plus a range of Buddhist institutions and practices—became a model of modern change even before the Japanese takeover. And while Japanese leaders in the Meiji era (1868–1912) established a rationalized, technocratic state, they also constructed Shinto as both a religiously derived civic ethos and a quasi-state religion, an ambiguity that provided room for the implementation of a semi-theocratic state in the late 1930s and early 1940s.[8] Another example comes from the *Kulturkampf*, or "civilizational struggle" launched by the Prussian state against the Catholic Church in the 1870s. By using legislative and bureaucratic measures designed to strip the clergy of its long-standing public influence and the Church of its socioeconomic foundation, the Bismarckian regime, with the backing of liberals who considered the Church a regressive impediment to the modernizing ambitions of the imperial, recently unified German nation state, severely restricted clerical activity. And upon meeting resistance, the state arrested or exiled recusant priests, appropriated Church property, and generally harassed the substantial population of Catholics in Prussia.[9] Though the repression of the clergy and of the laity's associational activities did not reach such levels in Korea, in conceptualizing religion, or at least popular religions, as a subversive element and in using this as the basis for subduing religion's social influence, the *Kulturkampf* found a parallel in early twentieth-century Korea.

These and other examples help formulate the present chapter's working definition of state secularization: first, the separation of the state's functioning and legitimacy from religious imperatives, and second, the subordination of religion to the modernizing state's expansion of authority. The former considers the state's escape from dependence on religion in conjunction with religion's retreat to the private realm, while the latter gauges the degree to which the state in Korea surveyed, regulated, and reified the realm of religion. As this chapter will show, state secularization in early modern Korea involved, first, de-Confucianization through the organizational separation of Confucianism from the state, which effectively ended any semblance of state establishment. For the purposes of legitimation, however, Confucianism might actually have been strengthened through the state's promotion, even exploitation, of Confucianism as a civic religion or a supra-religious ethos, not unlike what took place during the Joseon era.[10] Second, secularization consisted of the state's increasing regulation over both popular and congregational religions, especially in the colonial period. This process involved, first and foremost, the suppression of political activity on the part of religious figures. The flip side of this approach was the promotion of pluralism, which took the form of co-opting well-established religions and of classifying non-favored religious groups as deviant, with the aim of stamping out religiously based or religiously inspired movements in opposition to the state.[11] At one level, secularization through pluralism represented a reification of religion itself through classification and bureaucratization, but it also aimed to bolster the state's claims as an entity that served all religious interests through its commanding authority.

CONFUCIANISM AND THE STATE IN THE JOSEON DYNASTY

In measuring the degree of state secularization in early modern Korea, we must first consider whether the Joseon dynastic state of premodern Korea could have been "religious"—that is, predominantly governed, guided, or inspired by religious interests. This requires a judgment on the nature of Confucianism: Was it a religion? Setting aside, for the moment, whether the notion of "religion" itself as a distinctive, exclusive institutional-cultural entity can apply to the realities of premodern non-Western societies such as Korea,[12] the dominant religio-ethical position of Confucianism can indeed be said to have rendered Joseon a religious state. Furthermore, if "state religion" is defined by the state's promotion of ritual practices among its subjects and by its meting out penalties to those who do not follow, then indeed Confucianism constituted a state religion in the Joseon era. Monarchs, in fact, personally led state worship services that integrated liturgical elements from various institutionalized and folk religious practices, whether the impetus came from regularized ceremonies in the calendar year or from special circumstances, such as the need to gain relief from droughts or other cosmological phenomena.[13]

The monarch's participation in these rituals, however, said more about his (and his ministers') personal beliefs regarding spiritual appeasement and sanction than about the obligations of his subjects. The king did not need to perform these rituals in order to maintain *religious* authority, but rather for political reasons (and, again, sometimes as a matter of personal faith as well),[14] for his legitimacy was politically and customarily based, not religiously based. One could suggest, in fact, that the Joseon monarch in this capacity approached Weber's ideal type of a "caesaro-papist ruler who exercises supreme authority in ecclesiastic matters by virtue of his autonomous legitimacy."[15] Furthermore, there was no "Confucian church" independent of the state; indeed Confucianism required the state to operate. Even Confucian academies in the countryside ultimately depended on the same system of social, symbolic, and legal recognition doled out by the state (or the Crown). This dependence on state sanctioning came into sharp relief in the mid-nineteenth century when the Prince Regent, in the name of fiscal reform and the drive to eliminate corruption, closed dozens of major Confucian academies throughout the country.[16]

The Joseon state, furthermore, did not impose upon the general population particular private rituals to the exclusion of other kinds of rituals. Shamanistic and Buddhist ceremonies among the populace were not only tolerated but even incorporated into state functions, with monarchs as well as high officials often taking part in hybrid forms of state ceremonies, as noted above. County magistrates and provincial governors, in fact, often sponsored regular festivities celebrating local shamanistic / Buddhist guardian deities and other manifestations of folk religion.[17] Even ostensibly Confucian ritual practices that arose from local dynamics were often supported, if not co-opted, if the central state or monarch found it useful. One example comes from the state's sponsorship, in the second half of the nineteenth century, of local shrines to a legendary Chinese military hero, which underwent an explosion in popularity due to a combination of various local and national developments.[18]

Joseon Confucianism, in other words, held a central place for rituals and for the notion of state-sponsored ethical norms, but it was not preoccupied with supernatural or otherworldly concerns, especially in matters of statecraft. Its practitioners among the scholar-official elite regarded Confucianism first and foremost as a highly rational and systematic blueprint for ethics, with a strong philosophical, even metaphysical basis for prescribing social behavior, which constituted, in effect, the essence of morality.[19] In fact, Confucians saw their "faith" as a bulwark of rationality in opposition to the Buddhist establishment, which was shoved out of the state and stripped of much of its economic power and public influence at the beginning of the Joseon dynasty. Somewhat in a Hegelian sense, then, the elites of the Joseon era viewed the state, through its propagation and practice of Confucianism, as a kind of civic religion, the ultimate representation of the public good above the fray of private interests.

The Confucian state's relationship to devotional religions emanated from this superiority complex, resulting in a hierarchical form of religious pluralism: Let the common people (and elite females) believe and even worship what they wish, as long as popular religious activity did not interfere with, much less challenge, the structures of political and social domination (in a eerily similar stance practiced by some autocratic states today). In fact, the ideal was that popular religion, when controlled in this way through integration with the social hierarchy, could be employed for achieving social harmony and stability, which after all was the ultimate goal of Confucian statecraft—and indeed of most state ideologies before the modern era. This partly explains the relatively enthusiastic, albeit perilous, embrace of Catholicism in the late Joseon era among especially the sub-aristocratic hereditary local clerks, the *hyangni*,[20] a phenomenon that reflected their roles as mediators of local social order between the aristocratic and lower populations. This is also why the religiously inspired challenges to this state-led order in the nineteenth century—manifested in two of the largest rebellions in the Joseon dynasty in 1811–12 and 1894[21]—collectively applied such a shock to the system: They violated the long-standing principles of this premodern version of secularism, in which popular religions were countenanced insofar as they respected the macro structures of hierarchy and authority that emanated from the Confucian state.

RELIGION AND STATE MAKING AT THE TURN OF THE CENTURY, 1894–1910

Even if they had taken command, the leaders of the 1894 Donghak Uprising—so named because the rebellion was organized by local leaders of the Donghak religion, which arose in the 1860s as a combination of Confucian ethics, Western monotheism, and native spiritual traditions—would probably not have implemented a religiously based or even religiously inspired state system. Suffocating local corruption sparked the unrest, and despite a comprehensive set of demands for sociopolitical reform that could be considered religiously inspired, the Donghak leaders stopped far short of calling for a theocratic order.[22] Over the long term, the remnants of Donghak did in fact arouse concern among state officials over social movements associated with religion. In the near term, however, the uprising's impact was more indirect: It set in motion a chain of events that ultimately resulted, through the formal detachment of Confucianism from the state by way of the Gabo Reforms of 1894, for example, in an overturning of basic components of Joseon statecraft.

Little explicitly was said about religion in the hundreds of ordinances promulgated by the Deliberative Assembly of 1894, which is striking, given that just about every other realm of political and social life was targeted for near-revolutionary change. The one exception might have been the 1895 lifting of the centuries-long ban on Buddhist monks from entering the capital city,[23] a measure that reflected the Gabo leadership's modernizing sensitivities toward greater tolerance for "religion" (see below). Otherwise, the Gabo state's intervention in the realm of religion came about more indirectly through bureaucratic reform, such as the separation of the monarchy's affairs from the central governing order, the elimination of the Board of Rites and the scattering of its former functions, such as diplomacy, into various segments of the new system, and perhaps most consequentially, the abolition of the Confucian examination system in recruiting government officials.[24] The new state's relationship to religion in general and to Confucianism specifically received less attention, one is led to believe, either because religion had no place in the new order, or because—and more likely—Confucianism's continuing presence as an enveloping ethical system was taken for granted. In either case, the long-standing centrality of Confucian rituals and learning in the state began to weaken.

The settling of the state's relationship to religion thereafter during the Great Korean Empire came about somewhat haphazardly, and sometimes violently. As detailed in chapter 3, an elaborate series of ceremonies that can be described as sacral marked the formal designation of the Joseon state as the Great Korean Empire and the monarch as an "emperor" in October of 1897. They included the monarch's performance of an ancestor worship ceremony at the newly established *Wongudan* state altar, mixing strands of Confucian and other cosmologies in a formal plea for blessings for the new imperial venture. These developments had the potential to evolve into a quasi-religious "cult of authority,"[25] or the identification of the state with a priestly monarch that was implemented in Meiji Japan, but eventually the influence of both Korea's past and more recent history precluded this turn. For these rituals were designed not to instill legitimacy in the monarchy itself—this had long been internalized in Korean civilization—but rather to establish the Crown's absolutist power in relation to competing elements among the elite and, just as importantly, to proclaim the viability of the restorationist state in international circles.

Indeed the Korean Empire had to maintain an openness to the presence of foreigners as codified in the country's treaties with Western powers from the 1880s, which required guarantees of freedom from repression for Korean followers of foreign religions. Despite their wariness, the monarch and conservative officials faced constraints, based on these Westerners' legal status, when trying to curb foreigners' evangelizing efforts.[26] When such activities, especially those of the Catholic Church, whose mostly underground history on the peninsula amidst severe persecutions dated back more than a century, clashed with local officials and elites in ways that at times led to tremendous bloodshed at the turn of the twentieth century as well, the Korean state, under diplomatic pressure, entered into formal agreements with foreign clergy to formally establish a wall of separation, i.e., non-interference, in each other's spheres.[27]

In some quarters of officialdom, these troubles appear to have highlighted the need to establish a traditionalist firewall against foreign religious incursions, and Confucianism, naturally, presented the most logical candidate as Korea's religious bulwark. In 1899, Sin Giseon, a notoriously conservative statesman of this time who was serving as vice premier, issued a formal declaration of Confucianism's preeminence in Korea, "Revering Confucianism and Reforming the Central Confucian Academy," in the form of a "Royal Edict" that presumably was authorized by the monarch.[28] "How can we consider our country's religion to be anything but the way of Confucius [*Gongbuja ji do*]?" he asked rhetorically, and proceeded to laud the teachings of the Confucian classics, the central expressions of Confucian morality such as loyalty and ritual, as well as the fundamental Five Relationships (*oryun*) in social interaction. The newly established Great Korean Empire, in maintaining the honorable tradition of the five-centuries-old Joseon dynasty, was likewise based on Confucian teachings, he noted. Sin decried the recent rush toward adopting foreign models, which he suggested led to the abandonment of Korea's eminent values, and even blamed the rash of recent troubles, including the 1895 assassination of the Korean queen, on these impulses. Korea's survival and flourishing as a civilization could only be attributed to Korea's great "religion" of Confucianism, he stated, and henceforth in the Great Korean Empire as well, Confucianism should serve as the guiding hand.[29]

Sin's proclamation, then, reflected the increasing crystallization of the idea that particular religions stood as defining features of modern nation states (in fact, it explicitly states so), as well as the ongoing reconceptualization of Confucianism itself into a religion. Indeed in the opening years of the twentieth century, various "Confucian" societies cropped up, eager to retain social influence, if not dominance, in the face of the emergence and revival of popular religions and the loss of Confucian preeminence in statecraft.[30] The "Confucianism as [the country's] religion" debate actually had begun in contemporary China and developed within the discursive context of social Darwinism, with a clear eye toward Christianity's ostensible ties with civilizational strength and advancement—that is, Confucianism must be, or can be, China's (or Korea's) answer to Christianity.[31] In the closing years of the nineteenth century, Korean newspaper articles and editorials touted the direct connection between Western power and Christianity, amidst general observations on the significance of religion to a country's political system, and hence also to its relative standing in the community of nations.[32]

In official circles, however, this temptation to forge a tight bond between a refashioned Confucian "religion" and the state in purported imitation of imperialist powers proved insufficient in getting Confucianism established formally as the Korean Empire's state religion. In the promulgation of the "State System of the Great Korean Empire" (*Dae Hanguk gukje*) later in the summer of 1899 (chapter 3), there is no mention of Confucianism's centrality to the state despite the invocation of very traditionalist language and customs identifying the empire as an absolute monarchy. Although Confucianism's influence throughout the premodern era had been firmly wedded to that of the state, when it came time to redeploy this tradition, the new imperial state passed.[33]

Of course, it did not help the cause of Confucian advocates that, starting with the Gabo Reforms and especially in the vernacular newspapers that began publishing in the 1890s, Confucianism provided a convenient target and model *against which* to envision the intellectual and institutional basis of the modern state, a discourse that reverberated throughout East Asia at the time.[34] But a stronger force behind the disengagement of the state from Confucianism might have been the well-established secularity of the Joseon state itself, in which Confucianism served more as a governing ideology than as a state religion. When scrambling for survival in the new era of imperialist pressures and international competition, after all, Confucian statecraft proved ineffective to the task at hand. On the whole, notwithstanding traditionalist stalwarts such as Sin Giseon, there seems to have been little opposition to the shedding of the state's overt identification with Confucianism, whether as expressed in the Korean press or by the intelligentsia.

In fact, neither the Gabo Reform nor Korean Empire regime, which took preliminary steps such as reorganizing Buddhist clerics under a uniform state-regulated system,[35] exerted much effort to issue a broad ruling on its relationship to religion as a concept or social realm. One of the few exceptions was an open condemnation in 1905 of what was considered the duplicity of "shamans and fortune tellers" (*mubok*), accompanied by the formal prohibition of their activities in the capital.[36] As suggested above, this kind of official response to what were viewed as superstitious, socially disruptive sects, had a long pedigree in Joseon statecraft and, as we will see, would occupy a central role in the colonial government's approach to regulating religion as well. Otherwise, Confucianism, and religion as a whole, retained little formal significance from the standpoint of the post-Gabo, precolonial state. Confucianism certainly did not wither away after it was shed from the state—it remained central to official calls for loyalty and hence to the construction of legitimacy, to public education (see chapter 6), and to family law (chapter 7)—but whether as a state ideology or a state religion, it gave way to new notions of the state as well as of religion itself, and then eventually to the reestablishment of a state religion in the late colonial era.

THE COLONIAL STATE AND RELIGION: FROM PLURALISM TO THEOCRACY

The colonial state faced many roadblocks to the implementation of Japanese rule, but the challenges of prying the Koreans away from religious loyalties or of contending with a native religious element tied to political power were not among them. In the public realm, Confucianism as the official state ideology had been widely discredited, while in the private sphere, devotional Koreans found their access to churches, Buddhist temples, shamans, and other sources of spiritual solace and community continuing as before. The tensions with nationalists associated with the Protestant and native Cheondogyo religions were not enough to impede the progress of colonization in the initial period of Japanese rule, and following the 1911 incident involving Protestants (see below), the colonial state sought to institutionalize a normative relationship with religious organizations on the principles of a secular state.

This relationship was centered, first, on designating religion as a distinctive social realm that the state would regulate through surveillance, licensing, and both direct and indirect control of internal matters, and second, on promoting religious pluralism, though within the bounds of officially recognized religious entities. The systematic expression of this approach appeared five years into colonial rule, in 1915, when the Government-General of Korea issued its expansive "Regulations on Religious Propagation" (*Fukyō kisoku*), advertised as a guarantor of religious freedom, but which also clearly and systematically placed religious activity under state dominion.[37] Though religious histories have commonly perceived this ordinance as targeting Protestant missionary activities[38]—for good reason—it also forwarded a vision of the colonial regime's dealings with all religions in Korea, including those promoted by the Japanese. The 1915 edict expanded upon regulations that had been in place since the protectorate period, when Japanese Buddhist evangelizing activities, which catered to the Japanese settler community but had also attempted to incorporate their Korean counterparts, were reined in to prevent unnecessary conflict.[39]

The 1915 Regulations on Religious Propagation extended the network of official evangelizing offices (*fukyō kanrisho*) into a highly interventionist system overseeing proselytization activity: anyone who wanted to engage in religious promotion, or sought to erect a church, temple, or any other place or worship, had to gain formal approval from the Government-General after having supplied very detailed information about himself and his proposed activities (Articles 2, 3, and 9).[40] Although the new law's officiousness may have seemed daunting—and in its long life as the fundamental legal principle governing the colonial state's relationship to religion, the degree of its enforcement was inconsistent, which exacerbated the problem—in essence the ordinance's message and purpose were to resoundingly disestablish religion from the state. Hence it went further than the contemporary practices in Japan proper that differentiated the political from religious realms, notwithstanding the Meiji-era bifurcation of Shinto into its religious and civic manifestations. As with colonies worldwide, but to perhaps a greater degree, Korea appears to have served as a testing ground for state policies targeting social activity that would have proven difficult to implement in the metropole. Indeed, if Japan since the Meiji era had displayed the melding of religious life and political legitimacy in the form of the priestly monarch (the emperor, or *Tennō*),[41] then Korea would present the model for maintaining a clear separation between political and religious spheres as a way for the former to control the latter.

The structure of the Government-General also reflected this approach: The Bureau of Religious Affairs (Shūgyokyoku), subsumed first under the Department of Education within the Interior Ministry, then later as a "Religious Affairs Section" under the ministerial-level Education Bureau, became a notable preserve for high-ranking Korean bureaucrats and academics tasked with efforts to observe, study, and direct religious life.[42] Like so many features of Korean society, religious practices became the object of anthropological scrutiny from both private and official researchers, who produced thick ethnographic volumes. These studies represented, to be sure, the familiar colonialist fetishization of the subject population as objects of the civilizing project, but for categorizing and evaluating Korean religion, also the colonial state's efforts to clarify the boundaries of acceptance between well-institutionalized, and hence more controllable, religions, and the rest. The first article of the 1915 Regulations on Religious Propagation, in fact, specified what "religion" referred to: Shinto, Buddhism, and Christianity. Under the pursuit of pluralism, then, religions came to be disentangled from the state but also reclassified, with the strong implication that only such recognized religions could evangelize. Everything else, according to Article 15, would be viewed as something like religion, but not quite. They would be considered "pseudo-religions."

Acceptable and Unacceptable Religion

The introduction and spread of this concept of "ruiji shūkyō" ("quasi-" or "pseudo-religion") well illustrated the colonial state's efforts to delineate acceptable from less-acceptable (or unacceptable) religion. When the Regulations on Religious Propagation broached the term, it actually flipped the two words—*shūkyō ruiji*, or "religion-like"—to note that groups so categorized also would fall under state control.[43] Foremost among these quasi-religious groups were the offshoots of the Donghak religion, the movement that had begun in the 1860s as a kind of nativist response to Catholicism, was persecuted by the Joseon state, then reappeared with a fury in driving the peasants' uprising (Donghak Uprising) of 1894 before being suppressed by Korean and Japanese military forces. The Japanese wariness of Donghak's nationalistic, rebellious past appears to have remained strong even with the onset of the protectorate, as Donghak's remnants turned toward organizing a native religion under the new name of "Cheondogyo" ("Church of the heavenly way"). This religion's leaders played a central role in the March First independence demonstrations of 1919 (as did Protestant and even Buddhist leaders), and the lingering suspicions of Cheondogyo compelled the colonial authorities to heighten surveillance of all such "pseudo-religions" in the 1920s. This came even amidst a general liberalization of state control over associational and civic activities under Cultural Rule. Indeed, the nonreligious cultural endeavors of Cheondogyo flourished, and there appeared little justification for the colonial state to further suppress this organization.

But other "pseudo-religions" also gained strength, in both numbers and variety, throughout the 1920s and well into the 1930s, which raised concerns both in and outside the government. The popular press, in fact, began to sound the alarm about these groups, which actually helped to disseminate the notion of pseudo-religions itself. Numerous accounts of the misbehavior or legal troubles of these religious organizations appeared in the newspapers, usually with the scornful tone of the enlightenment thinkers of the recent past regarding what were considered backward traditional practices.[44] The colonial police, under whose jurisdiction all matters pertaining to pseudo-religions fell,[45] apparently could use all the help it could get, for several of these religious movements that grew to substantial size were denounced for engaging not only in fraud but also in nationalistic activity, even murder.[46]

One of the most systematic attempts to survey and comprehend this phenomenon appeared in a bulky Government-General study in 1935, entitled *Korea's Pseudo-Religions* (*Chōsen no ruiji shugyō*) and authored by Murayama Chijun, one of the leading folklorist-officials of the colonial era.[47] Filled with voluminous detail, including statistics on each of over eighty such pseudo-religions falling under five main groups (Donghak, Daoism, Buddhism, Confucianism, and others), this book revealed the official view of not only these popular beliefs, but of the social role of religion as a whole. Maruyama saw pseudo-religions as a reflection of social strife and instability, but also as the product of Korea's long (precolonial) history of class exploitation, Confucian domination, and political corruption—in other words, the familiar characterization of Korean society that had justified the Japanese takeover and continued to serve as legitimation for colonial policies. In fact, claimed *Korea's Pseudo-Religions*, so thorough had been the suppression of the popular voice and yearning in the Joseon era that even sects could not flourish until the Donghak religion of the 1860s, which had acted as a counterpart to the appeal of Catholicism.[48] The halting of social and material decay with the onset of colonial rule, this rationale went, eliminated the need for any such movements, which played merely a "transitional role" on the path toward an efficient colonial order that would avert social unrest.[49] In any case these movements were not even actual religions, if religions are supposed to represent the expression of a spiritual understanding of the world. Maruyama concluded, then, that beginning with Donghak, such pseudo-religions were first and foremost political-social movements in the guise of religion, and that this was where their potential for disruptive behavior lay. The evidence was damning: the multiple instances of a refusal by followers of these pseudo-religions to obey the law or even to recognize the authority of the state, and the prominent role played by the Cheondogyo leaders in the largest such demonstration of this attitude, the March First uprising of 1919. Political resistance—often code for nationalist activity—and social agitation, then, were the motivations and ultimate goals of these pseudo-religions.[50] It was precisely this offense—that they crossed the bounds of what the colonial state considered the proper realm of religion and hence violated the tenets of religious pluralism—that warranted closer surveillance and, if necessary, prohibition.[51]

To be sure, the legal tolerance of these religious movements, as well as the promotion of religious pluralism itself, reinforced the colonial state's comprehensive authority over religious life in the wake of the disestablishment of Confucianism, but they also reflected a rationalization of the colonial state that is usually dismissed but might have been decisive: the acknowledgment of, at times bordering on begrudging respect for, the significance of Korean customs and traditions, particularly during the period of Cultural Rule.[52] Such an approach was also convenient, of course, because the Japanese shared the stoutest of these traditions: Confucianism, Buddhism, and even shamanism, if one takes Shinto as institutionalized shamanism. The colonial state highlighted its efforts to cultivate friendly religious organizations, including, for a time, with even the nativist organizations of *Daejonggyo*, a following that worshipped the mythical founder of the Korean people.[53] Until the eve of wartime mobilization, which eventually enforced a dissolution of all religious organizations through integration under state control, even these "pseudo-religions," most of whom claimed descent from traditional cultural practices, were not wholly suppressed, and in fact the authorities appeared more concerned with *Japanese* religious organizations attempting to spread into the colony.[54] While closely monitored, the Korean pseudo-religions rose and fell along with the cultural and social tides, endowed with little potential to challenge fundamentally the colonial order. Those that *could* pose such a challenge were the well-established, institutionalized religions, which the regime did its best to co-opt.

Understandably, Buddhism, the most common religious tradition with Japan, became a major target of state patronage.[55] In fact, both Korean and Japanese Buddhist monks had begun mediating Japanese missionary activities in the late nineteenth century, a trend that eventually led Korean Buddhism to serve as the receptacle for an enormous—and, in retrospect, discomfiting—amount of Japanese influence.[56] Buddhism's special standing under colonial rule was inscribed early, through the Temple Ordinance (*Jisatsurei*) of June 1911, which required government permission for temples to form, reorganize, and to buy and sell property and possessions. They even had to draft formal internal rules and report any changes to them to the Government-General.[57] Eventually, as shown in the meticulously recorded approvals of requests from Buddhist temples to appoint or reappoint their abbots (*shūji*), as well as to incorporate certain buildings or to disband themselves, the Government-General commanded and intervened in the internal workings of the Buddhist establishment to an extent unimaginable in the late Joseon era.[58] The regime trumpeted this strong engagement with the Buddhist orders as an effort to help protect their properties and cultivate their religious activities—propagation, education, charities, etc.—including the erection of Evangelizing Offices in population centers beyond the mountainside temples.[59] Such state outreach was, for the most part, reciprocated by the Buddhist clergy, who deemed their efforts at modernizing Buddhism as benefiting from state sponsorship and cooperation.[60]

Confucianism, not formally recognized as a religion by the 1915 Regulations but increasingly endowed with special standing as a kind of supra-religion, also enjoyed state graces. Publicly staged, traditional Confucian ceremonies, for example, continued with the Government-General's blessings, indeed its participation.[61] As part of the larger effort to pacify the colony in the early years after annexation, funds were provided for Confucian associations, study societies, and schools as well as other forms of support. Following the commencement of Cultural Rule, in 1920 a Confucian Advancement Society (Yudo jinheunghoe) was established under state auspices by local elites, formally to assist the Government-General through the promotion of Confucian values in the countryside. This appears to have worked. Contrary to what one might expect from groups representing mostly the former Joseon aristocracy, many Confucian groups around the country acquiesced to the colonial government's efforts to co-opt them as special cultural entities. For the Confucian intellectuals, the greater motive was in maintaining Confucianism's social and ideological supremacy and in preserving their traditional, mostly local elite standing.[62] The colonial state was happy to comply and in fact found much that was useful in promoting Confucianism as a recognized interest group, which—paradoxically, perhaps—appeared to offer little ideologically to those resisting foreign conquest but much to those who were implementing it.

Christianity, though, did not enjoy such favorable treatment, despite its impressive numbers: over 450,000 adherents by the mid-1930s, according to official count.[63] For one, Christianity did not fall into this category of common cultural heritage between the metropole and colony, and that begins to explain the often tense relationship between the colonial authorities and especially Protestant organizations and clergy. Even before the annexation in 1910, Japanese observers in Korea had eyed the growth of Korean Protestantism with great suspicion, fearing its potential as a bastion of Western-inspired, anti-Japanese nationalism. American and Canadian missionaries, whose activities beginning in the late nineteenth century had spurred the growth of Korean Christianity in general, but especially of Protestantism, functioned continually as examples of a non-Japanese path toward civilizational advancement, after all.[64] In some ways these Western missionaries represented the most painful thorn in the side of the regime, which had to tread carefully before attempting any crackdown on Westerners' activities in an era when the Japanese remained sensitive to perceptions and pressures from the outside.[65] There seems no other explanation, for example, for allowing Protestant parochial schools to remain operating for three decades in open defiance of expressed colonialist goals concerning public education (see chapter 6).

Not surprisingly, following annexation the primary source of strife between the colonial state and Christianity arose from the strong association of Protestant leaders, both Korean and foreign, with nationalism. This began with the notorious "105 Incident" of 1911–15 (often called the "Conspiracy Case"), in which 105 Christians were arrested for allegedly conspiring to assassinate the Governor-General, Terauchi Masatake.[66] The lack of evidence and international pressure, given that the roundup also nabbed some foreign missionaries who spoke of harassment and torture, served to absolve most of the accused of the charges. But the conflict reemerged with the spring 1915 revision to the Regulations on Private Schools (*Siritsu gakko kisoku*),[67] which required all private schools, their educators, and their curricula and textbooks to be licensed by the Government-General along the same lines as public schools. Although some of these regulations allowed a five- or ten-year grace period for implementation for private schools already in existence, Christian educators found the prospective intervention in their curricular prerogatives, particularly the restrictions on religious instruction and the stringent requirements for teachers, alarming and difficult to accept.[68] From the perspective of the regime, this measure simply reinforced the original pursuit of separating religion and state, and hence of furthering the principles of pluralism and religious freedom. As Sekiya Teisaburō, head of the Education Department, framed it when defending this ordinance, Christian schools actually restricted religious freedom because they bound students to a certain sectarian orientation in their education.[69] Another blow came later the same year, as noted above, through the 1915 Regulations on Religious Propagation, the registration requirements of which appear to have made life for Christian pastors and leaders uncomfortable, if not necessarily restrictive.[70]

The most serious breach between the two sides took place amidst the March First independence protests of 1919, which resulted in the death, injury, or incarceration of tens of thousands of demonstrators. Protestant leaders, from those signing the Declaration of Independence down to local pastors, stood at the forefront of organizational support behind the demonstrations. And Western missionary leaders, though formally not targeted by the regime, were nevertheless rebuked by colonial officials and openly suspected of instigating and assisting the Protestants' central role in the uprisings.[71] As seen in the sometimes brutal treatment of churches during the uprising, which included burnings with parishioners trapped inside the compounds, the colonial state considered the Protestants' actions a severe infringement upon the domain of the state, and at the very least a violation of the prohibition of religious organizations from political activity.[72] Thus ended the rocky first decade of colonial rule between the state and and Christian church.

The shock of the uprisings, however, led to a public outreach effort by the Cultural Rule regime to be more responsive to Protestant leaders' concerns. This included an amendment to the Regulations on Religious Propagation, which now allowed religious leaders to report on their plans and actions instead of having to gain formal approval before commencing their activity.[73] In the 1920s and the first half of the 1930s, a working truce ensued between Protestant organizations and the colonial state. The regime, in fact, permitted Christian educators to maintain a modicum of autonomy and religious workers to engage fairly freely in their evangelizing and "social enlightenment" (*shakai kyōka*) activities, though of course within the bounds of acceptable—i.e., nonpolitical—behavior.[74] Indeed Protestant churches enjoyed a strong growth trajectory in the number of converts, or so indicated the government statistics gathered through the official registration system, as decreed in the Regulations on Evangelization.[75]

Toward a Theocratic Order

This coexistence was shattered, however, by the increasingly militarized and coercive footing of the colonial regime in the 1930s. In the sphere of religion, this decade eventually brought forth a major rupture from the mostly accommodationist stance of Cultural Rule. And as with the tensions of the 1910s arising from the original colonial regulations over parochial education, Christian schools again took center stage in this conflict. Colonial authorities viewed them as potential incubators of behaviors that could undermine state goals, chronic reminders of the struggle for loyalties, and sites of contention between the modernizing state and modernizing (in the guise of preserving traditional) religion. In the face of stern threats from the authorities, members of the more conservative Protestant orders objected fervently to the requirement, beginning piecemeal in the early 1930s and becoming finalized in 1935, that Korean schoolchildren, even those attending private schools, participate in Shinto ceremonies at school as a way of demonstrating their civic loyalty to the Japanese emperor and, later, unity for the war effort.[76] Some Protestant leaders—particularly the northern Presbyterians based in Pyongyang, who were told rather bluntly by the colonial Education Minister that they would no longer be allowed to "mix Christianity with schooling"[77]—resigned their positions as principals or closed down their schools and seminaries outright rather than abide by the order. The main Presbyterian assembly, however, from whom the northern assembly had split due to differences over the shrine visitation requirement, eventually joined the other Protestant denominations and Catholic church in acceding to the regime's demands. And by 1938 these leaders issued a formal resolution recognizing the compatibility of such rituals with their religious beliefs, pledging cooperation with the spiritual mobilization campaign, and declaring themselves loyal subjects of the Japanese emperor.[78] The Government-General eventually integrated all churches and other religious orders into state-sponsored organizations and outlawed suspicious religious activities, particularly those that had the whiff of nationalist or foreign influence.[79] The final act of repressive regimentation came in 1942, when almost all foreign missionaries were expelled from the colony as the Japanese empire's war against China transitioned into a campaign against the United States and Great Britain.[80]

This rupture appears to have been severe, both for Koreans who had to withstand an intensified state intrusion into the devotional sphere, and for the history of modern Korean state making. Hitherto the state had proceeded along a path, set in the closing years of the nineteenth century and building upon a secularist statecraft practiced in the Joseon dynasty, of noninterference in the religious realm as a way to reinforce the state's broader regulatory authority over religion. For the colonial regime prior to wartime mobilization, despite the tensions with Christian and Cheondogyo leaders over their nationalist proclivities, such an approach had helped maintain a mostly stable, gradual naturalization of foreign rule. Even with the shrine visitation requirements in the mid-1930s, the colonial authorities tried to reassure wary and embittered Christian leaders that Shinto ceremonies constituted a civic duty, not a religious one—arguing, in effect, that Shinto's place in the social order should be viewed as something akin to Confucianism's traditional standing.[81]

By the end of the 1930s, however, it became clearer that such practices, which ritually signified obedience to the existing head priest of the Shinto religion (the Japanese emperor) and the commemoration of the war dead, constituted religious exercises. The religious elements of this supposedly civic ideology became more openly promoted, including Shinto liturgy and a cosmology that established the basis of the emperor's dominion through his ancestors' divine origins.[82] Shinto altars (*kamidana*) came to be installed not only in schools, but also in government offices and even private work spaces, with the language of the government ordinances and official newspaper reports now freely incorporating explicitly religious terms in articulating the purposes behind these setups.[83] In 1938 the Government-General launched a project to build a public Shinto shrine for every township—the progress of which appears to have varied according to region—and those Koreans unable to make the visit were expected to mount Shinto altars within their own homes.[84] Eventually newspapers carried instructional articles on the method and meaning of Shinto rituals to be carried out at home. Even civil ceremonies came under state control, with certain wedding halls, under the direction of the mobilization authorities, accepting only those willing to discard the "English-American" practices and adopt the "holy style" (*shinshiki*) of (the sparser) Shinto rituals.[85] In sum, the colonial regime increasingly parroted the melding of ideological, "spiritual," and religious mobilization taking place simultaneously in the metropole, which amounted to the imposition of the emperor-centered Shinto, itself a relatively recent construct, as the indisputable state religion.[86] Notions of religious pluralism were dispensed with or overwhelmed by calls for a return to the ancient "unity of ritual and politics" (*saisei itchi*)[87]—the implementation of a theocratic order centered around the Japanese emperor—even in the Korean colony where such invented traditions, to say the least, faced greater difficulties in resonating with the populace.

CONCLUSION

The imposition of state Shinto into the colonial governing order of the late 1930s and 1940s shattered the rationalizing trajectory of state secularization through religious pluralism since the late nineteenth century and hence stood as an example of not only delusion but also gross hypocrisy on the part of the civilizing state. To be sure, this path had been trod before, though less intensively, in the efforts to sacralize the Korean monarchy as a national symbol during the Great Korean Empire four decades earlier. Unlike what resulted later in the wartime mobilization period, however, this precolonial process did not pursue a state establishment of religion through a primordial melding with monarchical authority. Only the late colonial state moved to do this, and in fact it went much further: It sought to saturate the public sphere, including nearly every government office, with Shinto rituals and altars.

These efforts also undermined efforts to constrain the public impact of religion in order to establish the state's supreme regulatory authority over it.

In its struggle against religious entities for truth claims and ultimate loyalty, in fact, the modern state in Korea helped to reify religion as a distinct social sphere through its objectification under state regulation.[88] This process was predicated on the granting of permission for religious orders to propagate, but only in conformity to state-guided norms of organization and practice. This approach, however, constituted not a displacement of religion as much as a reconfiguration of the state's relationship to the formerly semireligious role of Confucianism in Korean statecraft. The Gabo Reform governments of 1894–96 eliminated the Board of (Confucian) Rites and abandoned the most powerful, long-standing institution of Confucianism's dominion over statecraft: the state examination system for recruiting officials. In the ensuing Great Korean Empire period, the monarch, in attempting to implement absolutist control over government, incorporated Confucian religious symbolism for legitimation. But the state under his command also formalized a relationship of mutual recognition with popular religions, including native Korean movements, Christianity, and a reconstituting Buddhism. This approach continued with the subsequent colonial regime.

The first major colonial pronouncement of the state–religion relationship, the Regulations for Religious Propagation of 1915, emphasized the state's regulatory power over all evangelizing activities, and in doing so promoted religious freedom only within the bounds of properly religious, and not political or social, activity. This principle appears to have resulted in the division of religions into those that were officially recognized, i.e., those that were allowed to engage in proselytization, and those that were not officially recognized because, presumably, they were not allowed to proselytize. Christianity presented a major challenge to this arrangement from the vantage point of Japanese authorities. Such suspicions appear to have been overcome during the period of Cultural Rule, but in the third decade of the colonial period, government officials appear to have perceived even Christianity along the lines of the so-called "pseudo-religions" that they had categorically excluded from state recognition. These pseudo-religions, it was declared, were more political than religious movements, aimed at disrupting the public order in the name of spiritual activity, and hence requiring not only tight surveillance but, if necessary, suppression. Control through classification as a sect was a dependable stratagem around the world for states seeking to solidify their comprehensive social authority under the guise of the civilizing mission.[89] In fact one could argue that the Confucian state of the Joseon dynasty had taken a similar approach.

Joseon statecraft had been sufficiently effective in naturalizing the state's authority, however, that the original association with Confucianism could be abandoned fairly smoothly. Over five hundred years, the Joseon state eventually sloughed off the Confucian training wheels, and Confucianism itself, one could say, became secularized—if ever it was indeed predominantly "religious"—through its primacy in statecraft, which kept at bay any potential challenge to state power by popular religions. By the time these religions became liberated, so to speak, from Confucian domination in the early twentieth century, the Confucian state was evolving into an even more ambitious regulatory institution. Hence "de-Confucianization" stands as somewhat of a misnomer; the state remained firmly Confucian, just not formally. For the process of modern state making, Confucianism retained some of its value in statecraft but became disposable as a religion.

Indeed, concerns over the broader public impact of religions as a competitive force significantly colored the growth of the modern state's relationship to religion, particularly during colonial rule. The result in Korea, as in many other historical contexts, was a "secularization from above," in Nikki Keddie's formulation,[90] and often the motivations were not on controlling religion *per se* as much as on a generalized program of expanding state authority over society by enfeebling any object of popular loyalty and identification beyond the state. States could achieve this objective by suppressing religion, fashioning a state religion or theocratic order, or promoting religious pluralism. As we have seen, the state in early modern Korea eventually pursued all three rationalities, but the broader trajectory was to rationalize through pluralism, which, in the hands of the state, could also be a key component of secularism itself.[91]

SIX

Public Schooling

CULTIVATING CITIZENSHIP EDUCATION

THE MODERN STATE'S CONSTRUCTION and regulation of public education overlapped considerably with its dominion over other social realms. As with population tracking, schooling constituted a well-established, normally extra-state premodern institution targeted for takeover by emergent modern states. As with regulatory control over religion, it offered a medium through which the state could mold loyalties and authority structures. And as with public health, it functioned as an indispensable institution of social welfare. To be sure, public schooling, conceived through the ideals of universal education, disseminated the skills and knowledge demanded by increasing economic diversification and scientific understanding. But more importantly, as shown in the enlightenment practices and discourses of northwestern Europe in the eighteenth and early nineteenth centuries,[1] schooling could inculcate behavior and perspective. The curriculum and other aspects of public education reflected a particular territory's history and contemporary circumstances, but the drive toward mass schooling invariably normalized the relationship between the state and the people, as well as among the people themselves—that is, schooling shaped what it means to be a *citizen*.

Little wonder, then, that citizenship, in conjunction with other concepts such as the "state" as well as "society," came to be prioritized in the school curriculum, alongside basic skills such as literacy and mathematics. Citizenship education, in fact—or "civics" as it came to be known in places such as the United States[2]—proved critical for instilling the population's identification with and allegiance to the nation and / or the state amidst the circumstances of competing nation-states. Hence a public education system stood as a *strategic* institution if not entirely an idealistic or altruistic one, a necessity as much as a service. And whether the schools were privately or state run, the state's intervention through regulation, credentialing, and licensing signaled its dominion over education, and vice versa: schooling's centrality in the functions and ambitions of the modern state.

Indeed the overarching rationalization behind public education appears to have lain in the replication and reinforcement of the core drives of modern state making itself, including infrastructure construction, the promotion of hygiene and public health, urbanization, nationalist mobilization, and the administrative homogenization of the people. The state's efforts to civilize and discipline its citizens (or subjects) to be "modern"—how to behave and what to believe, how to tell time and follow a schedule, how to be industrious and orderly—reflected the vision behind public education as well. And in contrast to newspapers and other conduits for social edification, when it came to schooling, the state took emphatic and increasingly exclusive control. Compulsory or semicompulsory schooling provided a reliably steady source of pliant individuals (children as well as their teachers) in an enclosed, structured setting;[3] it was a matter of course that schools would not only propagate knowledge and skills, but also instill an embrace of the constructed narratives of social morality, including state authority. Indeed, the "morals" component of public education sought to induce loyalty, naturalize surveillance, and effect the acceptance of a reenvisioned social order and collectivity—whether termed society or the nation—under the state's guidance.

In Korea, as elsewhere,[4] such social integration through citizenship education faced a host of challenges, particularly under colonial rule. But while the historiography of colonial education in Korea is plentiful, it rarely considers the role of citizenship, focusing instead on schooling's largely unchanging instrumentality in exerting foreign control.[5] Even less do these studies contextualize such changes within the state's development throughout the early twentieth century, particularly the major shift represented by Cultural Rule in the 1920s and 1930s. This chapter aims to do both.

What follows will first examine the expansion of public schooling in early modern Korea both institutionally and, through an analysis of the critiques of state actions and policies, discursively. This will be followed by a case study of citizenship education, particularly through the examination of education policies and textbooks on "self-cultivation," or ethics. Several questions will remain central to this inquiry. First, how did public education, from the state bureaucracy to the schools themselves, reflect developments in broader state rationalities from the late nineteenth century to the end of the colonial period? Second, how did the purpose and concept of citizenship education change accordingly? And finally, what was the role of Confucianism, the dominant rationale behind learning for centuries? As we shall see, Confucian morality, as the underlying ethos of citizenship education throughout the era, often facilitated major transitions in the state's relationship to schooling, including the intensified effort to turn citizens into "imperial subjects" during the war.

STRIVING FOR PUBLIC EDUCATION

Notwithstanding its potent legacy as a guiding principle, Confucianism did not provide a blueprint for the modern school system in Korea. Indeed, the most notable aspect of the education system in the late Joseon dynasty was that there was really no integrated "system," at least one that extended beyond bureaucratic training. The Joseon state's primary interest lay in cultivating the higher philosophical command required of civil servants and the technical skills required of functionaries, such as clerks, interpreters, physicians, scientists, accountants, legal specialists, and even artists. And due to the close relationship between Confucian education and social standing—that is, because schooling reflected and certified elite status—the state had little trouble finding a ready and eager supply of civil servants through the restricted examination and recruitment systems. Other formal education in the Joseon era was run either privately or by local official actors, such as country magistrates and *hyangni* clerks, in village schools (*seodang*), local schools (*hyanggyo*), and Confucian academies (*seowon*). The curricular focus for all of these institutions was the common Confucian ethos, but there was little organizational coordination. And although in Confucian statecraft the point of government itself ultimately was edification, the lack of a dedicated central agency for education is notable. Among the Six Boards, or ministries, in the Joseon state, the Board of Rites (Yejo) came closest to this function through its administration of the state examination system and maintenance of records on local schools, even as these schools fell into decay over the last two centuries of the Joseon.[6]

As noted in chapter 5, that the Board of Rites, hitherto responsible for Confucian observances and ceremonies, was eliminated through the Gabo Reforms of 1894 is telling, given that the functions of the other Six Boards mostly found an equivalent in the restructured order. In the summer of 1894 a new Ministry of Education (Hangmu amun, then Hangmubu) was established to reconstruct and regulate a state education system through a dedicated bureaucracy. In early 1895, in a sign of the rising tide of support for a new approach to schooling, the monarch himself issued a general pronouncement (*Gyoyuk joseo*) declaring education "the basis of the nation" and specifying that it would no longer be dominated by Confucian epistemology but rather by the "new learning," i.e., practical knowledge and understanding of the larger world. In the spring of 1895 a reconstituted Ministry of Education (Hakbu) came into being, this time with concrete results. A Training Center for Legal Officials (Beopgwan yangseongso) and the Seoul Teachers College (Hanseong sabeom hakgyo), for example, were established, soon followed by an agency administering the state-run Foreign Language School (Gwallip oegugeo hakgyo).[7]

Finally, in the summer of 1895 came forth the most detailed expression heretofore of the Gabo government's new education orientation, the Ordinance on Primary Schools (*Sohakgyo-ryeong*).[8] Following an opening declaration that "primary schooling constitutes the foundation of civic education," the law specified that the Ministry of Education would not only initiate but control every facet of the new school system, including the licensing of teachers and the approval and publication of textbooks, as well as three kinds of primary schools (*sohakgyo*): public schools run by the central government (*gwallip hakgyo*), public schools run by provincial and local governments (*gongnip hakgyo*), and private schools (*sarip hakgyo*). The curriculum of the two grades of primary schools, elementary (*simsang*) and advanced (*godeung*), spanned the fields of the new learning, including math, geography, history, foreign languages, and even physical education. The fundamentals of reading and writing the vernacular as well as of Chinese characters (*seupja*) were also stressed, but significantly, before any of these subjects was listed, the ordinance designated ethics, or *susin* ("self-cultivation"), as the first topic, for both the elementary and higher grades.[9] As detailed below, this emphasis, borrowed from contemporary Japan but also incorporating a long-standing Confucian valuation of self-cultivation in social morality,[10] would form the basis of civic education—and constitute the first topic in the curriculum of all public schooling[11]—throughout the early twentieth century, and hence also underscore schooling's significance in engendering loyalty and identification with the state.

Several government-run schools were soon erected in Seoul, and by 1896 the first school in the provinces appeared in the city of Cheongju, followed by the establishment of a middle-school system in 1899.[12] But the pace of implementation of a nationwide public school system lagged, partly due to vociferous resistance from Confucian traditionalists in the countryside, but primarily because the government did not dedicate sufficient attention or resources.[13] A handful of state-run bureaucratic training schools (in law, medicine, agriculture, etc.) and foreign language schools successfully produced graduates destined for government service in areas such as the customs service and postal system.[14] By the opening years of the twentieth century, however, public elementary schools—that is, those funded (or subsidized) and licensed by the state—numbered only fifty-one, supplemented by another forty-seven recognized as public schools run by local notables and officials.[15] By 1907, these numbers had fallen to ten state-run schools, almost all of which were for foreign language training in Seoul, and fifty local primary schools, now called "normal schools" (*botong hakgyo*), which by early 1908 had 243 employees catering to a total of 6,140 students, according to government figures.[16] Contemporary observers, however, roundly criticized the conditions of these schools as unbefitting a modern education system. This was a sore point particularly for enlightenment activists who complained in exasperation, through newspaper editorials and journal articles, of the gap between this reality and their (and, presumably, the government's) vision of public education, which for some even included compulsory schooling.[17] For its part, the protectorate, which was interested primarily in keeping track of the schools popping up for Japanese settlers, did little to help expand public schooling for Koreans, even after its effective takeover of the Korean state in 1907; the number of public primary schools, for example, failed to reach even one hundred.[18]

What helped to fill in the shortfall, however, was the explosive growth in private schools beginning in the 1890s, but especially in the first decade of the twentieth century, when many of the most renowned educational institutions came into existence through extra-state initiatives.[19] These schools included the Hwimun Academy in Seoul founded by Min Yeonghwi, the Osan School in Jeongju founded by the noted entrepreneur and nationalist educator Yi Seunghun, and the Daeseong School in Pyongyang founded by the celebrated independence activist An Changho.[20] By 1908 the Korean government found itself having to issue an official reminder, through the "Private School Ordinance" (*Sarip hakgyo-ryeong*), that these schools, too, fell within the regulatory purview of the Education Ministry.[21] By the summer of 1910, just before the annexation, a state survey listed 2,082 licensed private schools, disproportionately in the northern half of Korea, and only 155 public schools—a ratio of 13:1.[22] Given the likelihood that many schools operating more informally were neither accredited nor counted by the government, the number of private schools at the time likely far exceeded the official tally.[23]

Colonial Public Schooling: Segregation and Expansion

The colonial education system would eventually seek to rein in this oversized impact of private schooling.[24] But the regime's more pressing task was to reorganize and expand the public schools and to fortify its comprehensive regulatory authority over education in the colony. This process was considerably complicated, however, by the segregation of primary schooling between Koreans and Japanese. While the Japanese residents would be served by a school system that, with the exception of the availability of Korean language instruction, mirrored that of the metropole and achieved universal access,[25] the situation for the colonized was very different.

Exactly one year following annexation, on September 1, 1911, the Government-General issued its "Korean School Ordinance" (*Chōsen kyōikurei*), which laid out the parameters of the education system for the native population.[26] It featured a three-tiered division of Korean schools into primary, secondary, and postsecondary levels. Elementary schools, which offered a four-year program for children ages eight and above, were in turn divided into those that focused on agriculture, handicrafts (*shukō*), and commerce (*shōgyō*), respectively, in the order of the number of schools.[27] The curriculum for these primary schools was be centered on the familiar topics of ethics (*shūshin*), mathematics, and reading and writing, with the language arts divided into two segments: a larger focus on Japanese and the shorter subject of Korean.[28] Secondary schools (*kōtō futō gakko*), which offered a four-year course to graduates of primary schools, were divided into regular high schools, girls' high schools, and vocational schools (*jitsugyō gakko*) specializing in agriculture, commerce, or industry.[29] Qualified graduates from the first two categories of high schools could enter the teacher training programs offered by the national high schools (*kanritsu kōtō futō gakko*), while others could enter technical training colleges (*senmon gakko*).[30] (Keijō Imperial University, the first and only university, was established in 1926.)

Other measures in the 1910s furthered the Governor-General's capacity to standardize the curriculum, assign textbooks, control the training and hiring (and presumably firing) of teachers, and open and close individual schools. This authority would extend to private schooling as well, as specified in the 1915 revision of the Regulations on Private Schools (*Shiritsu gakko kisoku*). This ordinance required certification by the Government-General of all private schools and permission by the authorities for their teachers, curricula, and textbooks, even for religious education. Some of the most stringent of these demands were postponed for five to ten years, which Sekiya Teisaburō, head of the Education Department, touted as an acknowledgment by the regime of the special circumstances of Christian schools in particular. But he could hardly veil his disapproval, denigrating the condition of such parochial schools and characterizing those who ran them as lazy, negligent, even impudent. What was most offensive, he noted, was their refusal to upgrade their teaching of the Japanese language by hiring Japanese-speaking teachers, which deprived the students of the most important skill—proficiency in the "national language"—demanded of proper citizens.[31] Perhaps not surprisingly, over the long term the number of private schools that could remain open by conforming to these requirements dropped precipitously, from over two thousand in the early colonial period to approximately six hundred by the mid-1920s.[32]

The assertiveness of the Government-General's regulatory prerogatives in all matters concerning education, even for private schools, was indeed partly a manifestation of the mistrust between the Japanese officials and Western missionaries (and Christians in general), but it also reflected the ongoing bureaucratization of education, particularly the curriculum, since the Gabo Reforms established the Ministry of Education in 1894. In addition to erecting training centers for bureaucrats and teachers, as well as constructing and operating the first public schools across the country, the precolonial education bureaucracy also began to churn out dozens of textbooks, ranging from elementary readers and geographies to books on history (Korean and otherwise), arithmetic, and foreign languages.[33] These efforts paled in comparison, however, to the extra-state publications from 1895 to 1910, the proliferation of which matched the burgeoning of private schooling in this period. As noted above, it was this unbridled privatization of schooling that was targeted by the colonial regime, which openly questioned even the need for private schools.[34] Many of the textbooks, as well as schools, that were suspected of nationalist leanings were banned just before and immediately following the annexation (see below).[35]

In spite of such actions, however, in the opening decade of its reign the colonial regime did not place a high priority on expanding availability for the colonized, and compulsory education, which was not even formally declared a goal until 1938,[36] remained a pipe dream. By 1918, the government had established only four high schools, two girls' high schools, and four technical training colleges for the entire colony. The accessibility of primary education was not much better. While the number of teachers for Korean primary schools increased more than twofold (from 995 to 2,216) from the beginning of the decade (with the rate of increase among Japanese teachers higher than that for Korean teachers), fewer than 500 public elementary schools, with an enrollment of approximately 75,000 students, were servicing a Korean population of 16.7 million people—a ratio of over 1:220 and representing an accessibility rate of less than 5% of eligible students (the figure for contemporary Japan was likely above 90%).[37]

The availability of primary education increased considerably, however, in the second decade of colonial rule amidst growing public agitation (see below), and thereafter remained on a trajectory of growth that would resemble the situation in the Japanese colony of Taiwan.[38] To what extent this criticism effectively mounted pressure is difficult to gauge, but the Cultural Rule administration, headed by Governor-General Saitō Makoto and Vice Governor-General Mizuno Rentarō, cited education reform, which was initiated through various commissions and other measures, as among their most important accomplishments.[39] The late-1919 reorganization promoted to the ministerial level the Education Bureau (Gakumukyoku), which also incorporated a Religious Affairs Section (Shūgyoka) that integrated all endeavors related to social education. In the 1920s the Education Bureau further institutionalized vocational training and established teacher training colleges (sihan gakko) in the provinces to replace the hitherto short course in the secondary curriculum, which reflected the dispersal of authority that characterized Cultural Rule.[40] School expenditures, too, were decentralized, as education took a third of the provincial government outlays (chapter 2) and as local school cooperatives and boards took over the raising and dissemination of education funds.[41] All of this fueled a major drive toward constructing, initially, a Korean public elementary school for every three townships and wards, and then one for every township and ward—a goal that appears to have been largely achieved by the end of the 1930s.[42] Clearly, however, the most dramatic increases in educational access, as measured by the number of primary schools and students, took place in the 1920s (table 8).

The influence of Cultural Rule was visible in the revised Korean School Ordinance of 1922, which emphasized the new mantras of eliminating

TABLE 8 Ratios of the Korean Population to Each Public Primary School and Each Student, 1913–1941

	School	Student		School	Student
1913	41,448	369	1928	12,760	42
1914	40,892	332	1929	12,481	42
1915	38,921	314	1930	11,974	42
1916	38,284	278	1931	11,079	41
1917	38,201	253	1932	10,568	41
1918	35,601	228	1933	10,003	38
1919	31,371	221	1934	9,617	34
1920	26,390	220	1935	9,344	31
1921	22,595	167	1936	8,843	28
1922	19,120	113	1937	8,663	25
1923	16,776	76	1938	8,446	22
1924	15,295	60	1939	8,104	19
1925	14,930	56	1940	8,051	17
1926	14,221	51	1941	8,043	16
1927	13,356	48			

SOURCE: Derived from *Chōsen sōtokufu tōkei nenpō* (1930), pp. 614, 622–30; (1937), pp. 226–27; *Chōsen tōkei yōran* (1941), p. 167.

discrimination while respecting Korean traditions and realities. In contrast to the original law of 1911, the new ordinance began by stating that all education, for both the Japanese and Korean children, would be covered by this document, in effect declaring a single public school system in the colony. The segregation between Japanese and Korean schools, however, remained intact, and indeed the ordinance promptly noted, in the second clause, that the new regulations covered almost exclusively schools for "those who speak Korean" while reiterating that the schools for "those who speak Japanese" would run in accordance with existing, separate rules.[43] And in spite of the colonial officials' strained insistence that the "content of education would be the same,"[44] the maintenance of ethnic segregation, notwithstanding the significant expansion in the number of schools, curbed efforts at improving educational access for the colonized. By 1930, for example, there were approximately 1,650 public primary schools serving 470,000 students among a Korean population of nearly 20 million (table 8), which increased fivefold the accessibility rate from the late 1910s, but left very high ratios for primary school student to population (1:42) and primary school to population (1:12,000). This was in striking contrast to the situation for Japanese residents, for whom the corresponding ratios in 1930 were 1:8 for primary school student and 1:1,060 for primary school.[45] Given the precipitous drop in private schooling in the 1920s, as noted above, as well as the continuing deterioration of demand for the hundreds of village schools (*seodang*) around the colony, the shortage of public schools, especially at the post-elementary level, also manifested itself in the sudden increase of Koreans heading to Japan for middle and high school education. This development—the *Donga ilbo* reported that close to 2,700 such students were enrolled in Japanese schools by the summer of 1925—was originally encouraged by the Government-General, but it also highlighted the stark deficiencies in schooling opportunities for Koreans in their homeland.[46]

Not surprisingly, these conditions turned into a running target of criticism, particularly in the Korean-language press. Newspapers such as the *Donga ilbo* and *Joseon ilbo*, which began publication in 1920, zeroed in on education as a priority area of coverage, and while reports of school openings and of the deliberations of school boards were plentiful, so were the fervent objections to the education plight of Koreans. Ironically the impetus for such expressions of discontent came from the Cultural Rule regime itself, which promoted the work of school councils, textbook revision committees, and other agencies that allowed public feedback, and publicized its surveys, studies, and statistics on education reform. The newspapers used this information to push for more curricular attention to the target audience and actual environment—namely, Korea, not Japan. In just its second week of publishing, for example, the *Donga ilbo* carried a stinging three-day editorial series demanding that the authorities stop forcing Korean schools to teach in Japanese.[47] For its part, the *Joseon ilbo* wondered why the Government-General continued to present a Japanese-centered historical narrative in the textbooks read by Korean children—such as using the term "subjugation of Korea" (*Joseon jeongbeol*) for the Hideyoshi invasions of the 1590s—and pointed out that, in general, using Korean, not Japanese, historical figures and examples would make more sense.[48] This point appears to have found resonance in actual changes to the primary school textbooks (see below).

The most consistent and pointed protests, however, targeted the enormous gap in public education opportunities and services between Japanese and Koreans. The ongoing "crisis of access to schools" (*iphangnan*), Korean observers claimed, came not from the lack of demand for modern public schooling, which was portrayed consistently as feverish,[49] but rather from the policies and practices of the colonial regime. The largest mass protests since March First, sparked in Gwangju in 1929 by the stark gap in educational conditions between the two ethnic communities, epitomized this simmering tension.[50] Newspaper editorials and reports abounded of the strikingly low schooling rate for Korean children, despite the substantial gains made in school construction over the 1920s. Using both official figures and the newspapers' own investigations, the publications meant to raise alarm: In Yuseong township of Daejeon county in 1922, a public elementary school for the thirty resident Japanese households, but none for the 1,099 Korean households; in Korea as a whole in 1927, a 2% primary schooling rate in relation to total population for Korean schools, versus a 15% rate for Japanese schools; in Gangwon province in 1930, merely 24,000 Korean elementary students out of a school-eligible population of 170,000; in a town in Siheung county in 1931, a public elementary school serving twenty Japanese households, with the 100 Korean households left fending for themselves in a makeshift, private learning center; in Incheon municipality in 1934, one elementary school student per twenty-one Koreans, versus one per seven for Japanese; in 1935, fifteen years after the start of the intensive drive to construct more Korean public schools, a schooling rate for eligible Korean students stuck at 10%; and so on.[51]

Although these numbers spoke for themselves, the Korean newspapers, especially the *Donga ilbo*, did not hesitate to level strident accusations of discrimination, as when the paper in 1925 related charges of bias against the educational authorities of South Pyeongan province, who overrode the objections of the Pyongyang city council and even disregarded the Korean School Ordinance in refusing, at the last minute, to let eligible Korean children enroll for the school year.[52] Indeed in the mid-1920s the *Donga ilbo* launched a series of *exposés* examining the monetary realities behind this seemingly intractable problem. With an increasing tone of scorn and mistrust directed at the colonial regime, these articles claimed not only that the spending for Japanese schools and pupils far outpaced that for their Korean counterparts, but that the authorities were effectively robbing the Koreans by directing a far greater share of the tax revenue toward Japanese schools, despite the fact that Koreans, in constituting over 95% of the population, paid greater amounts into the pool. In sum, despite the repeated "excuses" given by the authorities for this situation—that Korean households paid less in tuition than the Japanese, that not enough Koreans could pay school fees at all, or other reasons why there simply was not enough money to build more classrooms and schools—discrimination remained the primary cause of this reality.[53] Even after the *Donga ilbo* was shut down for a year in 1936 following a famous fit of nationalist defiance,[54] its publishers and editors, though chastened and no longer able to publish explicit criticisms, refused to drop the issue of Korean educational access as a major theme in its coverage.[55] The newspaper, in fact, did not always need to fashion its own critiques; often, it merely reported the embittered protests raised in school board meetings at the township, municipal, or provincial levels by local elites and educators.[56]

This constitutes one of the more striking features of the resistance to colonial state policy and administration, particularly during Cultural Rule: There were multiple outlets, despite the mechanisms of censorship and repression, for nonstate actors to voice opposition and attempt to effect change. These outlets centered on the press, to be sure, but also on the very state agencies, like local councils, that were meant to mollify the population through a modicum of local rule. Public education, in particular, appears to have aroused fervent pushback, perhaps because it, more than any other social sector, laid bare the basic contradiction of colonial rule in Korea: on the one hand, the heightening of conditions and therefore expectations for further improvement, and on the other, the limitations placed on removing the discriminatory foundations of foreign rule without jeopardizing the legitimacy of the colonial enterprise. Japanese observers, too, recognized this precarious situation,[57] and when it came time to mobilize for total war in the late 1930s, the regime formally abolished segregation, but this did little to achieve school integration, as we will see below. There is compelling support, then, for viewing colonial Korea as a "dual society," in which ethnic bias was systematic and fundamental to its functioning. While in general such a judgment tends to overstate the binary, in public education the colonial state did indeed lag behind expectations, which the regime itself raised, for a modernization of its institutions for the colonized, and the result amounted to compromising the gains made in other sectors, such as infrastructure and public health, that the colonial state could justifiably tout.

The long-term fiscal trends appear to bear this out. While the Cultural Rule reforms of the 1920s brought forth a major increase in investment in public schooling, as a proportion of the resources committed by the colonial regime—which increased even more dramatically, particularly in the 1930s—the funds for education remained below 4% of the total after the initial surge in the early 1920s (table 9).

TABLE 9 Education Expenditures, 1913–1943

	Total Government-General Expenditures for Education (Thousands of Yen)	Proportion of Government-General Total Expenditures	Proportion of Local Government Expenditures for Korean Public Schools (*gakkōhi*)
1913	1,149	2%	15%
1914	1,317	2%	12%
1915	1,415	2%	12%
1916	1,709	3%	13%
1917	1,802	4%	12%
1918	2,574	4%	13%
1919	3,312	4%	14%
1920	5,585	5%	19%
1921	7,633	5%	21%
1922	7,992	5%	22%
1923	6,838	5%	21%
1924	7,248	5%	20%
1925	5,915	3%	20%
1926	6,835	4%	19%
1927	7,361	3%	18%
1928	8,193	4%	17%
1929	8,303	4%	16%
1930	8,116	4%	17%
1931	7,227	3%	13%
1932	6,906	3%	12%
1933	7,030	3%	10%
1934	8,837	3%	12%
1935	10,812	3%	13%
1936	11,671	4%	13%
1937	12,550	3%	13%
1938	14,475	3%	
1939	16,635	2%	
1940	22,416	3%	
1941	28,182	3%	
1942	32,855	3%	
1943	37,861	2%	

SOURCE: Derived from data in Gim Nang-nyeon, ed., *Hanguk ui gyeongje seongjang, 1910–1945*, pp. 480–81, 486–87.

The colonial state, then—not unlike its native counterparts of the Gabo Reforms or the Korean Empire—could not come close to realizing the ideals of schooling as a sweeping tool for social change. Despite the pressing demands from both within and outside the regime, the possibilities and priorities of resource allocation, along with the inherent logistical difficulties of constructing enough schools, rendered this a very difficult goal to reach.

This hardly meant, of course, that public schooling itself failed to develop, or that the state's actions to increase its control over schooling bore little consequence. The sizable increase in the number of Korean schools following the inauguration of Cultural Rule, for example, enabled the colonial state to displace private schooling from its preeminent perch and to tighten curricular uniformity toward promoting state-sanctioned notions of social order, a process evinced in Government-General documents showing the meticulous management of schools through its licensing authority.[58] Such approaches intensified over the 1930s. As detailed in chapter 5, schools became an early staging ground for the implementation of coerced religious observances in veneration of the Japanese emperor, and they were later targeted for more arduous forms of wartime mobilization, including restrictions on using the Korean language in schools and the drafting of student soldiers in 1944 for the front lines. These measures, which dominate the Korean perspective on colonial education today[59]—just as the wartime hardships overwhelm the narrative of the entire colonial period—can also obscure major shifts in colonial public education and the longer arch of education's role in modern state making. This latter theme can be better illustrated by examining citizenship education, which shows how efforts to instill an allegiance to the state through public schooling facilitated the broader practices of strengthening state legitimacy.

DEVELOPING CITIZENSHIP

From the earliest attempts to implement a primary schooling system by the Gabo Reforms, citizenship education, infused with Confucian social morality, remained a consistent focus in fostering an identification with the state. This was the case, at least, until the wartime mobilization period beginning in the late 1930s, when loyalty to the state was conflated with, and even displaced by, loyalty to the imperial nation, and as both the meaning and term for citizenship changed.

Gungmin, or *kokumin* in Japanese, was the most common word for both citizen and citizenry throughout the early modern period. But often, depending on context, the term could also refer to country, the "nation" (or "national") in the American sense of a social-legal collectivity, or to the ethnic nation, or *minjok* (Jpn. *minzoku*). In fact the versatility of *gungmin*, which made it a revealing marker for the development of citizenship itself, stems from the term's etymology. Literally the "state's [or country's] people," it refers to something more expansive than *citizen*, or an identity of belonging to a smaller-scale, even voluntary community, often in opposition to the state.[60] Chapter 3 detailed how, as with *gukga*, or "state," the idea of *gungmin* initially emphasized the populace's rights and the state's responsibilities as part of a collective pact. Much of the spirit behind this discursive formation, from its initial expressions in the 1880s to the Gabo Reforms, came from a drive to effect social leveling—that through citizenship, everyone held an equal standing in relation to the state.[61] But as with the debate over *gukga*, over the course of the twentieth century's opening decade, the balance eventually shifted toward prioritizing the citizenry's (equal) *obligations* to the state, such as military service and taxes. Even the more collectivist views agreed that the failure of citizens to fulfill their responsibilities—and to exercise their rights—weakened the state both internally and externally.[62]

Naturally, state leaders sought to use schools to further engender a state-centered notion of citizenry. Citizenship education's centrality to the emerging school system was already evident in the 1895 Royal Edict on Primary Education described above, which listed *susin*, or self-cultivation, as the first required topic—a standing within the public school curriculum that would not be relinquished through the end of the colonial period. A long-standing core Confucian concept,[63] *susin*, which in essence was equivalent to ethics (or "morality"), now encompassed a wide range of lessons on individual behavior, family relations, and social interaction as well as on the state, society, and national identity. This comprehensive character of *susin* was apparent in the first textbook, in 1895, published by the Ministry of Education, *Gungmin sohak dokbon* (Elementary reader for the citizens [or nation]), which begins with a lesson on Korea's (Dae Joseon-guk) standing in the world and on the glories of its monarchy, as well as with a declaration that "the most urgent matter" for schoolchildren (or "subjects": *sinmin*) was to study and follow Confucian social tenets.[64] Like this work, the government's initial textbook-publishing efforts were limited to elementary readers, which were also used for *susin* lessons, as well as geographies and histories.[65] The earliest works specifically devoted to *susin* date from the early protectorate period and highlight a substantially Confucian curriculum centered on citizenship education.

A representative example comes from a 1906 mid-level *susin* textbook, *Jungdeung susin gyogwaseo*, written and published by the Hwimun Academy (Hwimun uisuk), a private school founded by Min Yeonghwi.[66] Like others, this text gained clearance from the Education Ministry and indeed was used in the public schools,[67] but significantly, it was originally published before the Japanese-controlled Education Ministry's efforts, beginning in 1908, to restrict textbooks deemed inappropriate, including those with anti-Japanese and overly nationalistic overtones.[68] This textbook, then, provides a helpful glimpse into officially sanctioned, Korea-centered views on state and citizenry, a topic covered in the chapter on "Lessons Regarding the Country" (*Gukga e daehan juui*), which follows other chapters on personal conduct, respect for parents, and so on. Here, while *gukga* appears as the equivalent to "country," the sovereignty of *gukga* is pointedly located in the Korean monarch himself, and in turn in the Joseon dynastic house, to whom the proper stance of the *gungmin*, or citizens, is loyalty, sacrifice, and subservience.[69] Notwithstanding the change of the country's name from "Joseon" to "Daehan Jeguk" to reflect the new polity beginning in 1897, then, this narrative conceives of state legitimacy traditionally, through the connections to the Joseon dynasty, and hence to the long-established norms of monarchical authority. Indeed, the next section, on "Loyalty to the Monarch" (*Chunggun*), explains that one's qualifications as *citizen* (*gungmin*) hinge on how well one submits to royal authority in this time of imminent danger.[70] This attempt to induce a stronger acceptance of the state's supremacy by appealing to a sense of national peril, common in this period,[71] can also be found in the chapter on "Citizenry," where the term *gungmin* is conflated with another word gradually coming into greater use—*minjok*, or "nation"—in reference to those belonging to a single "race" (*injong*). "Our nation" has always absorbed various other peoples, the narrative states, but regardless of how a *gungmin/minjok* is formed, the overriding goal is to preserve its independence (*dongnip*), which can be accomplished only through the cultivation of the nation's language and customs, and through an awareness of its history.[72]

This fuller understanding of citizenship as more or less equivalent to membership in an ethnic nation is also connected to a *gungmin*'s duties regarding education—namely, that each proper citizen must become educated. Education, in fact, constitutes a citizen's most basic responsibility, as a following section on "The Primary Duty of Education" states. In a passage that encapsulates the enlightenment discourse, which equated modern learning to national strength and renewal,[73] the textbook notes that the state must institutionalize compulsory schooling in order to cultivate the proper skills, knowledge, and character among the people. This would allow the country itself to flourish, whether through good ideas or upstanding government officials—a traditional notion—or in training the people in industry as a way of enriching the country as a whole. But interestingly, the articulation of the ultimate purpose of education refers back to the Confucian sentiment that education instills the proper "spiritual" orientation of hierarchy, duty, and loyalty (to one's country and monarch).[74] Such a connection between citizenship education, nationalism, and Confucian morality, which not coincidentally also drew from Japanese equivalents dating back to the 1890s, characterized the "Ethics" and other textbooks up to the early protectorate period.[75]

Colonialist Approaches: Confucianism Begetting Nationalism

Following the effective Japanese takeover of most higher-level government functions in the summer of 1907, such Confucian values would also become the fallback basis for the *susin* curriculum, as nationalist articulations of citizenry became prohibited in government-approved textbooks. A section containing lessons on government and society from the primary school ethics textbook (*Botong hakgyo hakdoyong susinseo*) published by the Ministry of Education (Hakbu) in 1908, for example, contains hardly any mention of citizenship. Amidst chapters on themes ranging from "Occupations" and "Public Consciousness" to "Hygiene" and "Taxes," the only allusions to the citizenry appear indirectly, in the chapters on the "Imperial Monarchy" (*Hwangsil*) and, somewhat oddly, "Good Officials" (*Yangni*). In proper Confucian fashion the monarch is presented as a paternal figure to whom his subjects (*sinmin*) are duty-bound to extend their filial affection and loyalties. The reference is to the Korean emperor, but in hindsight it appears to have been laying the discursive groundwork for annexation and the accompanying shift in loyalties to the Japanese monarch. A set of very traditional, indeed archaic, concepts and terms, then, were trotted out to function as a kind of placeholder for this transition: "In the path toward becoming a *good and faithful subject* [chungnyang-han sinmin], there is no other way than *self-cultivation and proper family bonds* [susin jega]" (emphasis added). The combination of these two terms, the former of which came, presumably, from the Meiji Imperial Rescript on Education of 1890 and the latter from the Confucian classics, would mark the colonial ethics curriculum as well. The term for citizen, *gungmin*, would not appear in this chapter, however, but rather in the following one on "Good Officials," in which it is stated simply that the state (*gukga*) seeks to advance the "peace and happiness" of the *gungmin*.[76] But *gungmin* here can just as easily be interpreted as "the nation" or "the people," even "the subjects," given the way this term is used in the preceding chapter on the monarchy.

This dilution (or expansion) of the concept of *gungmin* reflected also the diminishing and ultimate disappearance of coverage of political or government matters, including the *gukga* itself, in the official textbooks of the protectorate period's closing years. A government-approved translation of a Japanese elementary *susin* textbook published in the fall of 1908, *Chodeung yullihak gyogwaseo*, for example, reduces the coverage of *gungmin*—found in the book's concluding chapter on the *gukga*—to very generalized calls for awareness of the three responsibilities of obeying the law, paying taxes, and military service.[77] Another officially approved elementary *susin* textbook, *Chodeung susin,* published the next year, in 1909, for use in private schools, contains no separate coverage of *gungmin*.[78] By the spring of 1910, just a few months prior to annexation, the Ministry of Education's handbook for Korean educators and education bureaucrats, *A Study of Primary Education (Botong gyoyukhak)*, showed that even the mention of *gungmin* in the ethics curriculum had all but disappeared. Teachers were asked, instead, to reiterate basic lessons in (Confucian) "morality" (*dodeok*) and even to move Korean schoolchildren beyond traditional Confucian mores, to an embrace of the "advancements of modern society," in those areas for which "our country" was sorely deficient: hygiene, cleanliness, discipline, diligence, resourcefulness, sincerity, and public spirit.[79] In this closing stage of formal Korean autonomy, when the Japanese were in control but faced dicey challenges in articulating a coherent notion of citizenship, such calls for loyalty to the state and its offerings of modern advances and enlightenment, combined with appeals to Confucian values, appear to have presented the most viable option.

Needless to say, the succeeding colonial authorities also were in no position to appeal to a Korean student's sense of patriotic duty when it came to citizenship education. Given that colonial rule suffered chronically from this legitimacy deficit, further cultivating a subservience to the state had to suffice. Even the authoritative 1911 Korean School Ordinance reflected this sensitivity, in a stunning way: Although it declared from the outset that "education [for Koreans] would take as its basis the [Japanese] Imperial Rescript on Education [of 1890] in order to cultivate loyal and good citizens," it attenuated one of the core expressions of the Imperial Rescript, which had called for "loyal and good subjects" (*chūryō no shinmin*), by replacing the reference to "subjects" with "citizens" (*kokumin*).[80] For Korean schoolchildren in the early colonial period, then, citizenship education amounted to the well-trodden lessons of obedience to the *state* and the often implicit calls to embrace Japanese governance, which offered in return material improvement garnished with the enticements of modern civilization. An appeal to nationalism, the one key precolonial element of citizenship education missing here, simply was not an option, for obvious reasons, and indeed even the basic lessons of reverence for the monarchy—"Loyalty to the Emperor"—had to tread a fine line between promoting obedience to the Japanese throne, on the one hand, and arousing attachments to the now demoted Korean monarch, on the other.[81]

These realities were reflected also in the colonial government's approach to textbooks. In a study of colonial education policy for primary schools in the first decade, Jeong Hye-jeong has found that, in lieu of undertaking a wholesale publication project to replace the existing textbooks, the Government-General chose to focus on publishing a few select works, primarily for Japanese language instruction, and left individual schools and teachers to implement the required curricular changes, including in citizenship education.[82] Many measures, as expressed in policy directives, stemmed inherently from the transition to colonial rule, such as the recognition of Japanese, now the main language of education, as the "national language" and the Japanese emperor as "the emperor" (in distinction to the "Korean monarch"), and the revision of recent history to glorify Japanese deeds in, for example, the war against Russia and in the annexation itself. But what is somewhat startling, in contrast to the emphasis in Jeong's own conclusions, is how little civic education had to change, except in shifting its references to political sovereignty from the Korean to the Japanese monarch. Even the directives to strengthen Koreans' sense of "patriotism [to the empire] and loyalty to the crown" (*chūkun aikoku*) did not diverge from the focus of pre-1907, precolonial textbooks, as noted above. There is no specific language about the need to "become Japanese" aside from a sketchy promise of membership in the Japanese empire. The lessons of history and modern civilization based on the Japanese model and taught in the Japanese language would have to suffice in order to achieve, almost osmotically, the colonialist objectives in citizenship education; anything more ambitious—that is, an attempt to turn Korean schoolchildren's allegiances toward Japan—would be naive, as Japanese officials themselves recognized.[83]

Such concerns were compounded following the March First uproar, and hence the Cultural Rule approach during the 1920s and early 1930s further soft-pedaled the teaching of citizenship.[84] Colonial education policy, still having to legitimate the bifurcated public schooling system between Japanese and Koreans, turned toward a multivalent notion of citizenship that stressed Confucian ethics as much as loyalty and duty to a political authority. Through the 1922 revision of the Korean Education Ordinance, the colonial regime publicized the pursuit of two primary goals in public schooling for Korean children: the dissemination of the Japanese language and the "cultivation of a citizen-worthy character" (*kokumin taru seikyaku o kanyō*). This term had appeared also in the original Education Ordinance of 1911, but it was not featured prominently and, more importantly, had been superseded by the call for creating "good and faithful citizens" (*chūryō suru kokumin*), an emphasis highlighted in the second clause of that law. The 1922 ordinance removed this wording about good, faithful citizens and likewise weakened the association of citizenship to loyalty as a whole. Instead it more fully pursued the open-ended implications of "cultivating a citizen-worthy character [or spirit]," a phrase found in this period across the range of official publications on education as well as in the textbooks themselves.[85]

In the chapter on "Kokumin" in the Government-General teacher's guide for the primary school *shūshin* textbook of 1923, for instance, this concept is introduced as an orientation toward caring for one's society or public realm (*yo*), and for one's country (*kuni*), rather than for one's self or family. And here, the tricky issue of the Japanese monarch's place in this spectrum is almost formulaically elided through a nod toward "gratefully accepting" the emperor's grace when serving one's country, which constituted the "most important duty of the Japanese citizen [*Nihon kokumin*]." The term *shinmin*, or "subject," noticeably is nowhere to be found, even in the context of a discussion of the people's relationship to the emperor.[86] This ambiguity is seen later in a 1933 *shūshin* textbook as well, which employs different terms for different purposes: *kokumin* in speaking of a person's relationship to the state or membership in the nation; *shinmin* or *jinmin* ("people") in reference to one's standing in relation to the Japanese monarchy and the Imperial Rescript; and even *kōmin* ("public person") when referring to one's responsibilities to the state and society at large, including the duties of voting for local councils and paying taxes.[87] But there also is slippage in usage, as seen in the chapter on the "Imperial Household and Its Subjects" (*Kōshitsu to shinmin*), when even the expression "the people's [nation's] emperor" (*kokumin no tennō*) makes an appearance in deploying the term *kokumin*, normally associated with a citizen's relationship to the state.[88]

Such interchangeability of terminology highlighted the contrasting rationalities behind Cultural Rule as a whole: on the one hand, the imperative to impose a definitively Japanese-centered notion of citizenship, and on the other, the necessities (and vows) of mollifying the colonized, including their nativist impulses. In order to become good citizens, in fact, Korean schoolchildren were encouraged to cultivate their own (Confucian) cultural traditions and sensibilities, such as "customs of fraternal affection," that promoted social harmony.[89] And in keeping with the Cultural Rule slogan of "Harmony of Japan and Korea" (*Naisen yūwa*), the authorities vowed to eliminate all discriminatory barriers between Japanese and Korean primary schooling—that is, short of integrating the two systems. This extended to the Government-General's publication efforts as well, which produced or assigned textbooks that purportedly were identical to those used by Japanese schoolchildren in the metropole, and just as importantly, ramped up production of texts on Korean culture and language.[90] *Shūshin* textbooks for Korean schools, likely in response to calls from critics, as noted above, even employed examples from Korean history to illustrate morality lessons, such as in a chapter on the "Public Good" (*Kōeki*), which told of the exemplary deeds *two centuries earlier* of a civic-minded and hard-working Korean peasant from Hamgyeong province.[91] This more accommodating approach to citizenship education, the flip side of which was a more flexible conceptualization of citizenship, could also be seen in the renewed emphasis on the common Confucian ethos centered on filial piety (*kōkō*), an unmistakable refrain in the *shūshin* textbooks of the Cultural Rule period.[92]

By the late 1930s, however, the colonial authorities began to dispense with this balancing act and emphatically promoted an assimilationist, nationalist understanding of citizenship in the curriculum. In the spring of 1938, the promulgation of the revised Korean School Ordinance, issued by the Japanese prime minister through an imperial ordinance (*chokurei*), was celebrated around the colony for formally eliminating the difference between the Japanese and Korean schools.[93] This meant that Korean schools would henceforth use the same name for primary school, *shogakko*, as those catering to Japanese residents since the beginning of colonial rule, and that the post-elementary course of schooling, including the teacher training schools, would likewise be amended.[94] This did little to change things on the ground, however, as the schools continued to operate in segregation and were even classified and recognized separately, with the schools for Koreans simply referred to as the "Korean elementary schools" (*Chōsen shogakko*).[95] A more dramatic change came from the intensification of constraints on the teaching and use of the Korean language, which Governor-General Minami Jirō, in his addendum to the 1938 Ordinance, spun as the "elimination of the distinction between schoolchildren who speak Japanese and those who do not."[96]

The restrictions on Korean language education did little more than to formalize long-standing trends,[97] but behind such organizational changes lay the more consequential turn toward using public education for instilling a reconstituted notion of citizenship: citizenship as the total internalization of Japanese identity through devotion and loyalty to the Japanese emperor and to the imperial cause of war. The regulations and newspaper coverage accompanying the 1938 revision, for example, featured a conspicuous (re-)centering of the Meiji Imperial Rescript on Education as the source of "citizen morality" (*kokumin dōtoku*), the purveyor of lessons concerning the founding of Japan and its "national essence" (*kokutai*), the source of the values of "loyalty and filial piety" (*chūkō*), and the "basis" for living as a proper imperial subject.[98] As the *Joseon ilbo* reported somewhat dispassionately, the wartime demotion of the West would even extend to the Government-General's restructuring of the curriculum away from the "Western" notion of viewing geography and history as separate topics and toward the "Eastern," "totalizing" (*haphwajuui, jeonchejuui*) approach of integrating all learning into the formation of a reconstituted citizenry.[99]

As Governor-General Minami indicated, this effort to refashion citizenship would also entail a terminological change: citizenship would be absorbed into a holistic existence as "imperial subject" (*kōkoku shinmin*, or *kōmin*), and just as previous exhortations had called for shaping the student's character or behavior to that "worthy of a citizen," now the same phrasing was used to encourage the character or behavior "worthy of an imperial subject" (*kōkoku shinmin taru*). Koreans, referred to as "peninsular brethren" (*hantō dōhō*) in education-related ordinances and official publications,[100] were by fiat formally absorbed into the Japanese ethnicity. And as the term hitherto most often used for citizen, *kokumin*, came to refer increasingly to a status not in relation to the state but rather to an existential standing as part of the ethnic nation, the conventional understanding of citizenship began to fade, and the state came to be conceived more instrumentally as the extension of imperial rule, with the source of authority lying outside the state itself. A middle-level *shūshin* textbook from 1938, for example, with its detailed chapters on the distinctive culture, spirit, sacred character, and divine origins of the Japanese nation (*kokumin*), reflects clearly this shift in vocabulary. When this work touts the unique "moral values" (*dōtoku*) of the Japanese people (*kokumin*) compared to those of the United States or China, it is in reference to the distinctive ethos not of Japanese citizens, but rather of the Japanese nation, to which all Korean schoolchildren now belonged.[101]

This process culminated in the promulgation of the *kokumin gakko* primary education system in March of 1941, in modified emulation of the corresponding transition having taken place in the metropole.[102] Here, as shown in the ordinance's repeated stress on the "path toward becoming an imperial subject" (*kōmin no michi*), the term *kokumin gakko* for elementary schools referred not to "citizen schools," but rather to "national schools" in tandem with the rendering of *kokumin* to nation and of citizenship to subjecthood. *Shūshin* remained the first and foremost topic in the revised curriculum—with the others being science and math, physical education, arts, and vocational training—but its content, which constituted the substance of membership in the *kokumin* (Japanese nation), required complete mastery of Japanese history, along with command of the Japanese language. The new ordinance's second clause, covering the main points of focus for the *kokumin gakko* system as a whole, provides a blunt indication of this expansive but intensively nationalist reorientation of primary schooling and the concomitant dissipation of citizenship into subjecthood:

1. All of education must ultimately contribute to the glory of the Japanese empire and arrive at a self-awareness of what it means to be an imperial subject (*kōkoku sinmin*);

2. As loyal imperial subjects, Koreans must strive to achieve the realization of total assimilation with the Japanese nation (*naisen ittai*);

3. Students must learn clearly the distinctive features of the culture, standing, and destiny of our country [Japan];

4. All learning, training, and edification must be united into a single existence within the imperial subject;

5. And students must learn pristine Japanese, which must be the language of all instruction, and use the language precisely in order to further cultivate their standing as imperial subjects. The same applies to Japanese history, culture, and customs.

Such a turn toward the National (or Nationhood) School in 1941 amidst unabashedly assimilationist rhetoric represented, then, a logical outcome of the wartime mobilization measures begun a few years earlier, but the revised concept of citizen as subject also harkened back to the more extensive and nationalist understanding expressed in the ethics textbooks of the early protectorate period of 1906–7, just prior to the Japanese takeover. The reversion to a collectivist notion of *kokka* ("the state"), the meaning of which shifted to "country" or even "nation" (in the political sense), paralleled the transition of *kokumin* from citizenry to ethnic nation. This is shown in the middle-level *shūshin* textbook of 1943, in which the elaboration of the connection between "the path toward becoming an imperial subject" and a variety of themes, including politics, economy, religion, and world affairs, appears as an explication of the tenets of *Kokutai no hongi* ("Basic Principles of the National Body"), a Japanese government booklet promulgated in 1937 and by the 1940s in wide circulation in the colony. Indeed in this *shūshin* textbook the notion of *kokka*, as the collectivity, is used interchangeably with and ultimately absorbed into the overarching concept of *kokutai* ("national body"). *Kokutai*'s special meaning extended beyond the idea of a nation or country, however, to encompass a totalizing collectivity— "national character," "national essence," "national entity," or "national polity"—stemming from the supreme sovereignty of the Japanese imperial line.[103] Indeed, notes the textbook, among the main ideological systems around the world, it is this imperial sovereignty that distinguished Japanese *kokutai* not only from liberalism and communism, but even from fascism, with which it admittedly shares important features. The responsibility of imperial subjects is to internalize these essential truths of Japanese civilization, particularly concerning the founding of the imperial monarchy (and hence of Japan itself), in order to recognize, act upon, and sacrifice themselves—in death, if necessary—for their shared core identity.[104] Hence, as explained in the chapter on "Education and the Path toward Becoming an Imperial Subject," the primary goal of "the education of the nation's people" (*kokumin no kyōiku*), upon which hung the nation's fate, was the proper grasp of the interconnectedness between the nation, its history, and its *kokutai*.[105] Thus came full circle the journey of the notion of citizenship as taught in the public schools, back to the wide-ranging, largely Confucian concept, inextricably bound to national identity and loyalty to the monarchy, that was found in the discursive sphere, including in textbooks, of the Korean Empire period.

CONCLUSION

The implementation of the *kokumin gakko* or "national school" system epitomized the colonial shift in the concept of citizenship from identification with the state to unquestioning loyalty to the emperor and absorption into the (Japanese) nation: the monarchy replaced the state as the object of loyalty, the notion of subjecthood overwhelmed that of citizenship, and the term that had hitherto designated the citizenry, *kokumin*, came instead to reference the ethnic nation. But as the evolving meaning of "self-cultivation" in the textbooks had demonstrated, citizenship education underwent several rationalizations even before the annexation. Beginning with the enlightenment-period emphasis on both statist and collectivist notions of citizenship that informed the Gabo Reforms, this concept promoted monarchical nationalism during the Korean Empire period before 1907, and then developed into the post-1907 insistence, under Japanese domination, on statist citizenship divorced from ethnically derived considerations of loyalty and identity. The difficulties of assimilationism led the early colonial state to maintain the focus on crafting a political, cultural, and *administrative* rationalization of citizenship—that is, one premised on social behaviors and obligations, to be sure, but most of all, on a person's obligatory relationship to state authority.

Such a detachment between national identity and citizenship progressed further during Cultural Rule in the 1920s and early 1930s, when the promotion of Korean cultural identity became part of the broader goal of stabilizing colonial administration and stressing material advances, as shown in the heightened attention paid to constructing new public schools. Despite the strides made in this endeavor, however, universal or compulsory schooling for Korean children was never approached. In a reprise of the precolonial denunciation by enlightenment activists of the state's relative inattention to public education, the colonial system became the object of open wrangling between the regime's representatives, who touted the dramatic increases in educational access, and those who condemned the languid pace of progress and continuing segregation. Indeed the dual-track system separating Korean from Japanese primary schools until the late 1930s lay at the heart of the challenges to implementing a sustainable form of citizenship education in the colonial context, as the rationalities of public schooling clashed with those of colonial rule itself. This was the problem that the wartime mobilization measures to force a totalizing integration sought to overcome.

As jarring as this final shift was, however, it also reconstituted the conceptual strands of a holistically nationalist citizenship from the Gwangmu period (1897–1907) of the Great Korean Empire, indeed all the way back to the Gabo Reforms (1894–96). This was when the monarch and reformist officials proclaimed the primacy of education in the great cause of modern change and introduced the modern public school system as well as its attendant notion of "self-cultivation" (*susin*), or ethics, as the centerpiece of citizenship education. Such a vision of citizenship, as expressed most forcefully in the circulating newspapers and journals, found its way into the textbooks of the precolonial period as well, and in that discursive field citizens came to be defined by their (equal) obligations to the state and society, and eventually to the monarchy and nation as well. The cultivation of this expansive nationalism through schooling became apparent in the pre-1908 textbooks' emphasis on ethnic identity, Korean history, and loyalty to the Yi royal house, as well as on the tight bond between these entities. Indeed the internalization of this configuration by all faithful citizens was deemed the purpose of education itself in the new era, just as it became some three decades later during wartime mobilization under colonial rule.

Facilitating this increasingly firm standing of public education in the state's civilizing mission was the comprehensive extension of state authority in education. Primary schooling, in particular, served both as a replacement for private and informal schooling and as a conduit for state-sanctioned views on the normative social order. How better, after all, than through schooling to instill a naturalization of the unprecedented penetration and dominion of the comprehensive regulatory state as this kind of state was being invented? The rationalities of public schooling, then, constituted state making by another name—indeed to the extent that specific policy orientations in approaches to governing, such as Cultural Rule, might have acted not just as the instigator but also the facilitator of the state's focus on social edification.[106] Furthermore, by dedicating bureaucratic and material resources, by regulating the educational enterprise through the accreditation of schools and teachers, and by publishing and approving (and prohibiting) textbooks, the emergently modern state in Korea helped to reify education itself as a distinct social realm.

This is how Confucianism came to play a critical role in shaping education as a sphere of state control. In the Joseon era, with no state-sponsored education system to speak of beyond the confines of bureaucratic training and a loose collection of local schools, and with no counterpart to the notion of citizenship, schooling was geared toward an allegiance to Confucian ethics and hence to the normative social order. Within this framework Confucianism, while being mostly discarded as a system of statecraft, engendered the modern transition to the increasingly definitive structure of loyalties culminating in the state, either in itself or as the agent of monarchical sovereignty. As Korean reformers and monarchists, as well as Japanese colonialists, knew very well, the Confucian heritage, with its insistence on faithfulness to a social order promulgated and headed by the monarchical state and managed by its officials and rules, provided a powerfully convenient basis for instilling the lessons of modern citizenship. As the underlying repository of basic social values amidst major shifts, such as the return to a nationalist conceptualization of citizenship in the wartime mobilization period, Confucian ethics became a handmaiden to citizenship cultivation through public schooling, and hence to the solidification of the state's preeminent standing in modern education.

SEVEN

Population Management

REGISTRATION, CLASSIFICATION, AND THE REMAKING OF SOCIETY

A BASIC ACTIVITY OF THE MODERN STATE HAS been a preoccupation with locating, counting, and categorizing: money, resources, and especially people. An accurate count and feasible classification of the population provided state officials with a viable sense of the tax pool, as well as with the information required to mobilize and regulate, whether for surveillance, conscription, or other purposes. Indeed, the administrative priority of assessing and collecting taxes accounted for much of the attention to record-keeping in premodern states and likely provided the formative motivation behind state making, if not writing itself.[1] In premodern Korea, the long institutional history of household registration (*hojeok*) served primarily this purpose, but it fell far short of gaining an accurate sense of the population. As the problems in late nineteenth-century state revenues highlighted, the household registers, which epitomized both the strengths and shortcomings of the Joseon state, hardly met the needs for increasing mobilizational and surveillance capacities in an era of international competition.

And so began the revamping of this stalwart institution in line with the major extension of bureaucratic reach into people's lives. The renewed approach to population tracking highlighted critical components of modern state making: the accumulation of data and knowledge, the imposition of social categories and imaginaries through the processes of mapping and ordering the population, and hence the construction of society largely through administrative imperatives. Given the Korean state's long-standing reinforcement of the social hierarchy through the household registration system, it was this capacity to perceive, conceive, and thus help establish a new social order through identification measures that proved most illuminating in the development of the modern state's management of the population.[2] The state's capacity to remake society came about not just by serving as an institutional vehicle for social mobility (chapter 2), but also through its systematic, variegated, sometimes divergent efforts at accounting for, studying, and delineating the people.

GOVERNMENTALITY, BIOPOWER, AND POPULATION MANAGEMENT

In this respect, Michel Foucault's understandings of governmentality and biopower, which arose from his extensive efforts to conceptualize modern state development in Western Europe, will prove illuminating for this (and the next) chapter's analysis of what took place in early modern Korea. For with these concepts Foucault articulated a basic shift in the character and aims of the state—indeed, to the extent that this was definitional to the modern state— toward a systematic interest in the qualities and inclinations of the people. The traditional "subjects" became a "population," a term referring not only to people but also to a (biological) "set of processes to be managed at the level and on the basis of what is natural in these processes."[3] The state became infused with a comprehensive, systematic, recurring effort at redefining its authority in relation to this population, a method of political rationalization that Foucault characterized as *governmentality*.[4] The bureaucratic development of the governmentalized state reflected a churning experimentation with the science of statecraft ("the study of the rationalization of governmental practice in the exercise of political sovereignty"),[5] including the application of various regulatory mechanisms, accumulation and manipulation of information, and control over resources in order to realize a disciplined internalization of state authority— what he famously termed "the conduct of conduct." And governmentality's extensive concern with the biological ("natural") traits of the people—how to measure them, analyze them, cultivate and manipulate them—entailed what Foucault called the state's exercise of *biopower*.[6]

The state's main apparatus for such an approach to population management was policing, which took advantage of the "penetrable naturalness of population."[7] As discussed in chapters 1 and 2, Foucault considered many early modern European states to have been "police states" in this broader sense of the term—states that deployed policing as "the art of developing forces," that is, of measuring the resources, possibilities, and limitations inherent to the population. Policing thus became the main instrument for a key component of governmentality, that of gathering and applying information, particularly statistical information,[8] and hence for ensuring the optimization of the population's health and welfare. Foucault actually claimed that the final stage of governmentality in European state formation moved beyond that of the police state in its *raison d'etat*,[9] but the extensive impact of policing in the expression of biopower remained central to the further development of modern statecraft around the world, as the case of Korea shows. For Korea, as elsewhere, the state practices of population management in the early modern era also were closely bound to social leveling, or the homogenization of the populace, which was designed to facilitate mobilization, the collection of revenue, and the integration of everyone under state authority. Here also, the representational power of statistical data helped rationalize the state's exercise of biopower: The lumping of people into a mass, from which large-scale patterns in the natural principles regulating birth, life, death, and other phenomena could be discerned, allowed little room for traditional social distinctions. For the modern state to derive meaning from statistical information, it had to create "practical equivalences," as Bruce Curtis puts it, among the population.[10] It had to consider everybody the same.

On the other hand, what also distinguished the modern state was the expansive scope of its measures to classify people, including counting, registering, and licensing them through what Pierre Bourdieu calls the state's hold over "informational capital"—its prerogatives in labeling things and imposing standards, or its "homogenization of all forms of communication"—as a means to legitimate its authority.[11] Even the act of publicizing this information, as reports and statistics, served to reinforce state power. But such practices of objectifying society as a means of regulating it, or "seeing like a state," to borrow James Scott's term,[12] also imposed social boundaries and categories by squeezing messy realities into simplified slots in order to facilitate comprehension. These schemes invariably altered and helped reify social stratification, in terms of the distribution of privileges, by sanctioning particular forms of both collective and individual identity.[13]

This chapter analyzes the extent to which such attempts at social recategorization and homogenization unfolded in early modern Korea by investigating changes in the household registration system, and by following the trajectory of two efforts at population management: delineating occupations and assigning surnames. It argues that, while the state stopped far short of constructing a social structure according to its own terms (if this is even possible to measure), in meticulously counting, studying, labeling, and articulating the macrostructural changes taking place in Korean society—i.e., in exercising governmentalized biopower—state practices shaped the realities and perceptions of a changing society as a means of fortifying state authority. But this was far from a seamless process, and the inconsistencies and untidiness of the state's efforts revealed as much as the uniformities and efficiencies. Just as important, even in the wartime mobilization period of the late 1930s and early 1940s, the state tempered its approaches to tracking the population with loftier concerns regarding legitimacy and state efficacy.

Additional motivations came from the circumstances of imperialism and colonial rule. A stimulating, illuminating body of scholarship has analyzed the colonial construction of knowledge about the population, mostly through the state, and how such actions affected the subject populations' perceptions of themselves as much as the manner of rule. One of the most dramatic recent claims has come from Nicolas Dirks, who argues that the British colonial state not only utilized but in effect manufactured caste distinctions in its Indian subject population.[14] This was not necessarily a sinister campaign as much as a by-product of the British goal to reduce what appeared as an impossibly complex phenomenon into an administratively manageable form. As critics of this argument have shown, however, it is easy to assign too much credit (or blame) to the colonial state for this deployment, through household registers and the census, of classificatory schemes that to a considerable extent were derived from precolonial administrative forms.[15] A double dose of state surveillance power was visited upon the subcontinent's population, in other words, and the trajectory of this development across the precolonial / colonial divide remains critical to understanding colonial practices in Korea as well. While the purposes of Japanese colonialism in Korea, bolstered by increasingly intricate state mechanisms for surveying the population, injected new features of governmentalized biopower into the administration, depending on the circumstances and times, the colonial state's measures often constituted an appropriation of precolonial ways, or a concession to the inertia of customary behaviors, and often both.

POPULATION TRACKING THROUGH
HOUSEHOLD REGISTRATION

Household registration stands as one of the main institutions of the late Joseon state that remained at the center of the modern state through the colonial period, and indeed, to the present day. The arc of its historical development over this era demonstrated at once the constancy of the fundamental purpose of household registration, which was to facilitate taxation and mobilization, and the multiple motives that often set the state's pursuit of efficiency at odds with its efficacy and legitimacy. The maintenance of this balance, in turn, bespoke the challenges of developing a governmentalizing, modernizing regime of biopower that could keep abreast of the ever-changing population.

Late Joseon Household Registration

The early and impressive state centralization of the Joseon dynasty met one of its greatest challenges in the levying of tax and service obligations on the populace, the management of which fell primarily upon the central government's Board of Taxation (Hojo, literally "Board of Households"). Here, household registration, which also buttressed an extensive system of state granaries and other relief institutions that were deployed cyclically as well as in emergency situations like famine,[16] served as the primary means of state population tracking. At the lowest reaches of administration, the Joseon government depended mostly on local actors, notably the hereditary clerks (*hyangni*), to levy and collect tax revenue and determine the availability of manpower for military and corvee labor service. These clerks were also responsible for conducting the triennial household registration survey for each locality, which listed each household's head, his year of birth, clan identity,[17] "four ancestors" (*sajo*),[18] the same information for his wife (who was identified by surname or her father's name), and other family members, slaves, and their ages. A marking of each adult's official "status" (*jik* or *jigyeok*), usually denoting one's public service obligations or privileges, also appeared, the significance of which will be discussed below. This was all vital information, but in collecting such data the central administration did not intervene at the point of contact through which this knowledge was gathered and negotiated. As Yi Hun-sang has noted in his case study of Sacheon county, in the late Joseon era, and in particular the nineteenth century, the compilation of household registers reflected the autonomy of local government as much as its subservience to central demands.[19]

The substantial amount of freedom given to the local officials, however, also created a substantial potential for abuse and irregularities, and the results were household registers that, as commonly acknowledged,[20] failed to provide an accurate accounting of the population. By the 1860s and '70s, the central government began tackling revenue shortages by, among other measures, eliminating the aristocratic exemption from the household (military-) cloth tax, but stopped short of a major reform.[21] The effort of the 1880s, however, transferred much of the oversight responsibility of household registration to newly constructed organs,[22] and this set the stage for the Gabo Reforms of 1894–95, which laid the groundwork for basic changes to the household registration system in several ways. First, the Gabo government immediately had all local governments undertake a comprehensive survey of the local population and household numbers, as well as of all resources, such as land, in the possession of the local administration.[23] Direct management of the household registration system now fell into the hands of the Household Registration Bureau (Panjeokguk) in the newly established Ministry of the Interior, and the General Police Agency was given responsibility for securing the household surveys.[24] Finally, as part of the ongoing rationalization of state finances, the Gabo governments undertook the first of several attempts in this era to remove entrenched local actors and officials from the revenue levying and collection process.[25] These reforms called attention to the integral connection between local administration, fiscal management, and household registers, but as shown in chapters 2 and 4, Gabo efforts to overhaul the local taxation system faced a host of obstacles to implementation and failed to yield notable improvement. It would take a revamping of the registers themselves to initiate fundamental reform.

The 1896 and 1909 Reforms

In early September of 1896 the Korean government proclaimed a new household registration system through Royal Decree No. 61 ("Hogu josa gyuchik")—the first, momentous step toward revitalizing this enduring yet besieged state institution. As Bak Jeongyang, the Minister of the Interior, put it in proposing the new system: "The counting of the households and population represents the basis of protecting the people, yet until now the compilation of household registers has been plagued by incorrigible abuses such as avoidance of registration and nonregistration. From now on we wish to completely eliminate the messy, convoluted practices of the previous system and introduce simple regulations for implementation throughout the country."[26]

Each household was now responsible for the proper functioning of this task, and those who failed to live up to their registration responsibility would

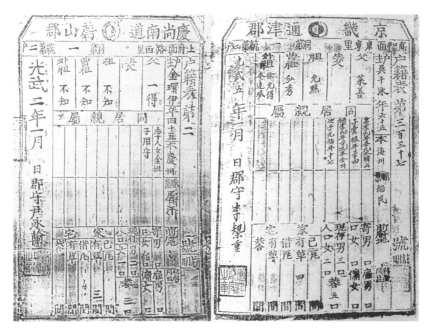

FIGURE 18. A butcher's household registration form from Ulsan County, S. Gyeongsang Province, 1898 (left), and that of a fisherman's household, from Tongjin County, Gyeonggi Province, 1901.

lose their "people's rights" (*inmin ui gwolli*) and face punishment, a warning that extended to every official in the chain of command.[27] The new system also demanded that local officials conduct a household survey every year and even issued a standard "household registration form" (*hojeok-pyo*) to be completed by local officials, which sheathed the information with a modern bureaucratic gloss (figure 18). Several spaces in the form demanded much of the same information as before: household's address, the name, number, and age of family members, clan identity (*bon*), and a listing of the household head's four ancestors. Other parts of the form listed nonrelative dependents (*gigu*) living in the household, as well as servants (*goyong*)—a reflection of the continuation of bound servitude despite the official abolition of slavery in 1894. Indeed, that the form still required information on the "four ancestors" and clan identity appeared incongruous with the broader aim, since Gabo times, of abolishing hereditary status differentiation.

In many other ways, however, the 1896 registration regime clearly pointed in a new direction. Most significantly, the state's interests now lay primarily with gauging the economic makeup and standing of each household—that is, who, regardless of familial connections, lived under the same roof, literally: The registration form sought information on whether the dwelling was owned or rented, on its size, and on whether its roof was made of straw or tile. And in line with the desire to track current residence, each household was assigned a distinct "household number" and required to list the household's previous location and date of move to the current address. The underlying goal of this new registration system, then, was to account for every household and every person at all times,[28] i.e., to increase the visibility of not only the tax pool but the conditions of the population as a whole. This also explains the demand for listing a specific occupation for the household head, whereas the late Joseon household registers had noted a public status that usually signified a household's tax and service obligations to the state.[29]

The 1896 system, though, appears not to have made major strides in rendering the population more visible, due in part to continuing dependence on traditional bureaucratic actors and to opposition from a skeptical populace fearing a greater tax burden.[30] And even a decade after its original implementation, the system suffered from a lack of administrative and material resources.[31] For such reasons, in 1909 the Korean government, under the command of the Japanese protectorate, promulgated a new "civil registration law" (*minjeok-beop*).[32] The advances of this arrangement were similar in extent to the 1896 system, but also retreated somewhat from the population tracking ambitions of the earlier reform. Most notably, the 1909 procedure, by asking for each household member's rank order (in the case of children) and relationship to the household head, indicated that the household should consist not of people living as a single economic unit, as with the 1896 system, but rather of people who belonged in the same family through marriage and patrilineal ties, as the Japanese practices did. Indeed the new registers recorded every household member's full name, birth parents, clan identity, and birth date, in addition to one's "sinbun" (Jpn. *mibun*), or life status, by indicating how each individual joined the household (birth, marriage, concubinage, adoption) or left it (death, divorce, establishment of a separate household). And as with the 1896 revision, the 1909 system, even as it eliminated the "four ancestors" requirement, deferred to customary practices by making room for each household head's clan identity (*bon*) as well as the possibility of extant servants, whose information was appended (*bujeok*) to the master's register. Significantly, however, omitted from the required items of information was the household head's occupation, a curious change that would prove significant, for the information on occupation in the household registers would not reappear. In its place was a space for the household's "permanent address" (*bonjeok*), which was understood as the household's residence address, but which soon came to designate a lifetime address—the one into which all household members were first registered, usually right after birth—and hence the same as that, usually, of one's father, regardless of where one actually lived. Even with the revamping of the colonial registration regime later in the wartime period, the basic features of this 1909 household registration system would remain in place, indeed until the end of the twentieth century.

Such changes, however, spoke to the administrative continuities of this era as much as to the conquering motives of Japanese imperialism. Just as Japanese measures in reforming land registration and surveying methods represented more often the intensification of pre-annexation efforts (chapter 1), the 1896 and 1909 revisions of the household registration system anchored an overarching process of re-rationalizing population tracking. These measures sought greater administrative efficiency, to be sure, but not necessarily a greater quantity of information—as seen, for example, in the 1909 system's scaling back of ambitions for recording everyone's current whereabouts or of the household head's occupation. Furthermore, while one of the novelties of the 1909 civil registration system was to reinforce the concept of a household centered in the nuclear family (*ie* or *ga*), much as it did in Japan, this measure's allowances for long-standing conventions, such as the Korean surname and clan traditions, bespoke also the confluences with the 1896 system. A blunt implantation of the Japanese model, in other words, did not necessarily drive the 1909 reform, as contemporary Korean observers also recognized.[33]

The Colonial Registration Regime

Korean customs, especially in matters regarding the family, would remain a special feature of the colonial registration system as well. When the Government-General issued the sweeping Korean civil code (*Chōsen minjirei*) for the colony in the summer of 1912, what stood out were Articles 10 and 11, which stated that matters concerning "relationships among Koreans," specifically family and inheritance issues, would be exempt from the provisions of Article 1 that ordered the application of the existing Japanese civil, commercial, and other statutes in the colony. Rather, for these matters, "customary practices" (*kanshū*) would be followed as long as such solutions did not infringe upon public order.[34] While subsequent amendments to Article

11 of the civil code carved out exemptions for matters regarding marriage age, divorce, custody, and a few others,[35] the basic principle of following Korean customs when it came to family law was maintained until the wartime mobilization period (see below), even as this aroused opposition from bureaucrats and legislators back in the metropole who sought greater standardization across the empire.[36]

The household registers, in fact, can be considered representative of a major facet of the civil law system introduced by the colonial state: its deference to—if not the creation of—Korean customary law. Marie Kim has recently shown that the colonial authorities' efforts to devise and emphasize customary law in the civil code protected their autonomy from interests intent on imposing Japanese legal practices.[37] Kim also argues, however, that this emphasis on Korean customs incorporated calls by Japanese jurists, since the protectorate period, to undertake a temperate approach to implementing Japanese laws in Korea in acknowledgment of significant cultural differences. Reflecting a prevailing perspective on Japanese colonial administration since being articulated by Gotō Shimpei, the first Governor-General of Taiwan, such voices recognized that a sudden, heavy-handed imposition of Japanese practices would "risk a total or partial failure of the new colonial legal order" amidst efforts to persuade Koreans of the desirability of state reforms.[38] A mindfulness of the civil code's impact on state legitimacy, in other words, resulted in a substantial accommodation of native practices, conventions, and perceptions from the beginning of the colonial period, an approach that would expand considerably under Cultural Rule in the 1920s and early 1930s. The propaganda value of this was also deemed useful, as official publications, like the Government-General's *Administrative Yearbook (Chōsen sōtokufu shisei nenpō)*, touted the colonial state's sensitivity to Korean traditions and circumstances in its handling of registration matters.[39]

Administrative decentralization also facilitated the input of customs. In line with the reorganization of local administration in 1914, the revised civil registration system promulgated in 1915 transferred responsibilities away from the central police forces and toward the municipal wards (*dong*) and townships (*men*), which henceforth maintained the records and managed the process.[40] (Such records still remain mostly in those offices today in South Korea.) This approach was maintained in the revision of the household registration system, proclaimed in November 1922 through the "Korean Household Registration Law" (*Chōsen koseki-rei*) and implemented half a year later, which specified penalties for noncompliance and for the dereliction of official duties, such as shoddy record-keeping. Tellingly, the revised system also required the provision of receipts and explanations for local officials' decisions regarding updates to household registers, such as for adoption or marriage-related issues, and granted a definitive right to appeal. Furthermore, the supervision of the registration system, including the arbitration of disputes between officials and residents, was transferred from governors and county magistrates to judges and the local courts, where the study and explication of Korean customs and the construction of Korean customary law evolved dialectically as colonial rule progressed.[41]

What resulted from this effort to accommodate traditions, customs, and local particularities was a household registration system that aspired to meet a wide range of demands, only some of which might be considered studious efforts at population tracking. The attempt to standardize the variegated real-life outcomes of customary behaviors produced, in the end, a veritable hodgepodge of court rulings and administrative practices. Countless adjudications of domestic disputes sought to provide guidance and establish precedent in finding the proper balance between legal rationalities and customary conventions, all having a direct bearing on how a municipal or township office could navigate the intricacies of Korean family practices as they affected household registration.[42] Thick manuals filled with court rulings, legal briefs, bureaucratic communications, and revisions to ordinances were compiled for the sake of puzzled officials. And later in the wartime mobilization period, upon the onset of rationing and conscription, an organization devoted to clarifying and ordering the enigmatic mix of household registration and family customs even published a monthly journal.[43]

Extant registers also evince this concession to traditional practices. For one, the continuity in the colonial registers of a designation for clan seat, or *bongwan* (Jpn. *hongan*), can be explained by a desire to better differentiate the population (see below), but also to accommodate the traditional avoidance of intra-clan marriage, an alien matter to Japanese officials and jurists that required thorough explanation.[44] Perhaps no issue proved as perplexing, however, or as wide-ranging in significance, as the ins and outs of Korean adoption practices and its related phenomenon, concubinage.[45] The prevalence of concubinage, for example, appears also to have constituted the most common reason for Koreans, including women, to file divorce petitions at the household registration windows of local government offices, which at times required comically bewildering responses from befuddled clerks.[46] As for registration practices, as expired household registers from Eonyang county in the southeast demonstrate,[47] distinctions were maintained for a concubine's children, or *seoja*, who legally belonged in the same household as the "legitimate" children but often were recorded after the wife's children regardless of age, for this had long been the established practice in Korean registers of the past as well as in the published Korean genealogies of the present.[48] Officially, as the 1909 *minjeok* regulations and 1922 revised ordinance reiterated, the two sets of children were equal,[49] and the patrimonial principle of "one family, one register" should have brooked no practical difference between a concubine's child and a wife's child.[50] But the statutes, beginning with the introduction of the 1909 civil registration system, also left some important matters unsettled.[51] This appears to have been deliberate; concubinage was so ingrained and concubines' children so numerous that powerful customary biases could not but shape bureaucratic practices. Multiple matters of family law, after all, and hence also of household registration, were directly affected, including the recording of marriage (or remarriage) and divorce, recognition of adoptions, and the ordering of a household's children. This latter issue, which determined inheritance rights and caused many disputes, was especially challenging and extraordinarily complex, as court rulings and administrative orders demonstrate. The working solution, it appears, was to have the judges, clerks, and others fudge the general equality of the wife's and concubine's children with tacit acceptance of customary practices—for example, to prioritize the wife's children in inheritance regardless of age or current circumstances.[52]

In accommodating such traditional elements in the household registration system, then, one had to accept the trade-offs in bureaucratic rationalization. This explains administrative practices that might have been directed toward one set of rationalities, like the need to account for customary behaviors, in coexistence with others, such as greater standardization and correspondence with the Japanese civil code or family system. Interestingly, this latter motive explains why the colonial household registers continued to specify everyone's "permanent address"—or *honseki*, which designated a person's (patrilineal) relationship to his or her natal household—as the basis of legal identity regardless of actual domicile.[53] As it turned out, this did not necessarily facilitate population tracking. The household registers were meant to do a lot of things, but an accounting of everyone's whereabouts appears not to have been one of them.

This theme of rationalization in the colonial household registration system has recently been highlighted by Takashi Fujitani's stimulating study of the mobilization of the colonized Korean population for the war (and of its remarkable similarities with contemporary US handling of Japanese Americans). Fujitani argues that the colonial state largely neglected the upkeep of the household registration system until the war years, and that this reflected the lack of interest in viewing the Koreans as a "population" targeted for the exercise of governmentalized biopower.[54] The welfare or health (or location) of the Korean populace, in other words, was not deemed sufficiently valuable to merit attention and care, until the shortage of manpower for the war compelled the need to know where everyone was, if only to ensure a supply of soldiers. Hence the regime declared the end of all discriminatory measures against Koreans and directed unprecedented attention toward ordering the household registers.[55] Although Fujitani does not address this issue specifically, one would deduce from his argument that the household registration system's long-standing allowance for customary practices also reflected administrative inattention to, following general disregard for, the colonized—again, until wartime mobilization made administrative standardization paramount.

To test this claim, we can consider the extent to which the colonial registration regime—fueled by the demands of conscription, rationing, and other features of intensive mobilization—did indeed change after 1938. First, we can note that Fujitani's connection between registers and wartime mobilization is borne out by the fact that, if nothing else, the ordering of social groups, neighborhood associations, rationing, conscription, and other mobilizing measures depended upon accurate registration information. But it was not simply a matter of better managing or even fixing the existing household registration system, for these registers, while able to identify who was eligible for mobilization, were never intended to keep track of everyone's whereabouts.[56] Rather, to find the people for conscription and to distribute rations, the colonial state revamped a supplemental registration system that had been in place since the beginning of colonial rule. Local offices, in fact, had all along maintained a separate "[new] residence registry" (*kyojū tōrokubo*), which required some but not all of the same information, such as one's clan identity, as the household registers.[57] Consulting these residence registers was required, for example, when in 1923 a round of smallpox inoculations demanded that local officials identify the addresses of those needing vaccination.[58] The accuracy and upkeep of these residence registers, however, were compromised by the fact that they generally depended on self-reporting by newcomers to a given locale.[59]

To close this loophole, a new system of "residence registers" (*kiryūbo*), implemented through the "Korean Residence Ordinance" (*Chōsen kiryūrei*) in the fall of 1942, specified that everyone who lived outside his permanent address (*honseki*) for more than ninety days must notify local authorities of his new or temporary address, under the threat of heavy penalties for not reporting.[60] Perhaps more consequentially, municipalities, townships, and villages—together with the police and local mobilization units such as patriotic neighborhood associations—now had to keep track of everyone in their respective jurisdictions by cross-checking the residency registers with existing household registers, which required sending notices to other local government offices if a new resident's permanent address lay in another jurisdiction. These measures appear to have worked; in short order the new residence registration system appears to have "found" an enormous number of people—41% of the total population—living away from the permanent address, as well as almost 3% of the population who had never been registered in the first place. However, as Yi Myeong-jong has shown, the authorities themselves recognized that much of this disorder had resulted from acts of evasion, as conscription had been anticipated for some time.[61] The chronic difficulties in juggling disparate records in the face of avoidance and deliberate misrepresentation in the documents, which were also reflected in newspaper reports and exhortations until the end of the war, made keeping track of everyone an elusive goal.[62]

The issue, then, of whether the wartime registration system facilitated the colonial state's breakthrough into genuine governmentality remains unclear, for this notion is premised on a judgment that the less intensive management of registers before the war reflected a lack of state interest in the population's biological conditions or life circumstances. The prewar registration system, after all, was not rationalized toward the goal of tracking the people's whereabouts for the sake of rationing and conscription. Does this mean that the pursuit or practice of governmentality and biopower was lacking? This is difficult to argue. First, in important ways the novelty of the wartime registration regime constituted one of degree as much as kind. It required a more thorough oversight of existing registration practices rather than the introduction of a wholly new one, and furthermore it did not depart fundamentally from the goals and functions of earlier registration practices dating back to 1896.[63] This would suggest, then, that the wartime measures constituted the culmination or intensification of the registration system's long-term development rather than a departure from them. If we do not insist on the exercise of governmentality or biopower as a zero-sum game ("either full governmentality or none at all"), and if changes to the registration system are taken in the context of the broader challenges of population tracking over time, then we must account for state practices that tried to achieve a balance between administrative rationalities and the efficacy of rule, which included accommodating long-standing and ingrained family conventions. The state's prewar registration system, in other words, more likely reflected not disinterest but rather the opposite. This possibility is highlighted also when examining state efforts to classify and homogenize the population.

SOCIAL LEVELING, OCCUPATIONAL LABELING, AND SURNAMES

State classification schemes to effect social leveling and homogenization, too, reflected the balance of opposing rationalities and conflicting goals. This section examines two such approaches to make the people and social structure more visible to the state: the recording of occupational diversification and the assigning of surnames. Both population tracking methods attempted to facilitate social leveling through simplification and standardization, even while pursuing administrative rationalities that would better differentiate the population as well.

Occupational Categorization

Occupational diversification, a product of urbanization and industrialization, can be said to induce greater social stratification than leveling, but for delineating the population, the state in Korea, as with states around the modern world, sought foremost to dampen the force of long-standing hereditary status categories. For this, occupation represented a secure, albeit potentially fluid category for recognizing, and hence assigning, new social identities. But the state's interest in and process of tracking occupational proliferation proceeded in fits and starts and through less-than-uniform approaches. Often, the manner by which state officials chose to classify occupations was driven more by political exigencies, such as the urge to apply the categories used in Japan, than by the goals of social leveling or even administrative efficiency. Indeed, to some extent it appears that, in this regard, the colonial period actually witnessed a regression of sorts.

To be sure, precolonial practices did not bring forth a complete shift from hereditary status to occupation (or class) as the primary means of social differentiation, but the two rounds of major reforms of the household registration system, in 1896 and 1909, clearly encouraged such a progression. In formal terms, as noted above, the information demanded in the household registers went from *jigyeok*, a reflection of one's (mostly hereditary) state service eligibility and obligations in the late Joseon era, to *jigeop*, one's occupation or means of economic livelihood, beginning with the 1896 reform. While the customary labels of *yangban* (aristocracy), commoner, low-born, etc., appear to have held sway in everyday interaction, the 1896 system, in requiring an occupational label attached to each household head, freed local officials to start disregarding the long-standing, mostly ascriptive titles. Extant registers from areas ranging geographically from the northern frontier regions to localities in the southwest (Haenam), southeast (Dongnae), and east coast (Pyeonghae) show that most household heads marked "farmer" (*nong, nongeop*) for occupation, but the registers also display considerable variety.[64] In coastal areas such as Tongjin county of Gyeonggi province, some household heads, not surprisingly, are listed as "fisherman" (*seonmin*), while in the Incheon area many merchants (*sang, sangmin, sangeop*), including rice peddler (*misang*) or wood merchant (*moksang*), are identified. Household registers from 1904 in the Mapo area south of Seoul offer up an impressive array of occupations, from oil merchant (*yusang*) and liquor distributor (*jusang*) to cavalryman (*gibyeong*) and horse breeder (*ma-eop*).[65] For the old aristocracy, the traditional listing of someone's official title continued, but interestingly, in the absence of office or official title, the designation for many *yangban* still signaled hereditary status—*sa, sain,* or *samin*, which ironically one cannot readily find in the Joseon registers—or aristocratic lifestyle (*yu, yuhak* ["Confucian"]).

This combination of old and new practices continued even after the introduction of the *minjeok* civil registration system of 1909. A collection of approximately 225 *minjeok* household registers—in this case, expired ("removed") registers (*jejeokbu*) separated out from functioning registers after new households were formed through death, marriage, and so on—in Gongju county (S. Chungcheong province), for example, displays a striking mixture of traditional status signifiers with modern occupational indicators.[66] Unlike its 1896 predecessor, the 1909 registration form did not include a separate space for occupation, but local officials were encouraged to append one of seven broad occupational labels anyway, including a curious category in reference to the former nobility.[67] Indeed, approximately half of the surveyed Gongju registers specified the household head's occupation, but each of these was also given a traditional status designation of either commoner (*pyeongmin*) or noble (*ban*). Interestingly, the former status of household servants is not marked in the Gongju forms, but they are accounted for nonetheless through supplemental registers (*bujeok*) attached to their masters' registers, just as the 1909 law directed,[68] and tagged with the occupational label of *goyong*, which the 1896 form had actually accommodated through a separate space in the form.

When the Central Police Bureau of the Korean government, under the supervision of the Residency-General, aggregated the information in all the 1909 registers, almost every household was placed in one of nine occupational categories. These included "day laborer" (*ilga*), which likely accounted for the house servants. Several others, though, seem to have come straight out of the classical East Asian social categorization scheme: farmer, merchant, artisan, even "scholar" (for *yangban*).[69] However, in places like Gongju, the household registers were just as likely not to indicate an occupation at all, and other evidence suggests (see below) that this was the case throughout the country. Wishful statistical sampling and other maneuvers to smoothen the results, then, likely served as the basis for these aggregate results, a reflection of the bureaucratic messiness behind the counting enterprise, including the intrusion of shortcutting, error, ignorance, and bad faith.[70] But the more important point is that the precolonial state, beginning with the 1896 revision, sought to account for occupational proliferation through the household registers, however imperfectly and awkwardly, even if this meant having to accommodate long-standing customs, such as the taboo associated with traditional outcaste groups, that compromised the uniformity of the project.

Perhaps for this reason, the household registers soon stopped indicating occupation, as seen in the registers for Eonyang county in S. Gyeongsang province.[71] Eonyang was a typical rural area, with most of the population composed of tenant farmers and small-scale owner-cultivators. The occupational range in the 1910 registers, however, for the township of Sangbuk, which contained the county seat for Eonyang, reveals a greater variety: most of the household heads (693) engaged in agriculture, but many were in commerce (151) and day labor (40), as well as a smattering of civil servants (10) and those in "industry" (3).[72] In the opening years of the colonial period, still under the 1909 *minjeok* system, approximately half of the households in expired registers from Eonyang township indicated an occupation for the household head (and sometimes for a nonhousehold head),[73] such as merchant, restaurant owner, physician, butcher, and government official ("clerk"). Within a few years into the 1910s, however, one finds a striking falloff of occupational tracking. Only about 5% of registers thereafter record an occupation, the overwhelming proportion (over 90%) of which are labeled as farmers.[74] It is hard to believe that this area grew more rural, and indeed the "new residence registers" in the township, averaging three or four annually throughout the colonial period, demonstrated increasing higher occupational variety as time went by.[75] Rather, tracking occupations no longer became a priority or requirement of the registration system.

Eventually, achieving a more definitive accounting for the colonial population, including its occupational diversity, became the function of the census, as neither the household nor residence registers could carry out this task.[76] Although the state had attempted a comprehensive population count independent of the household registers in 1907, and a simplified census survey was attempted in 1925,[77] it was not until 1930 that a full, systematic census took place in Korea, as part of an empire-wide survey, the first of which had begun in 1920. The colonial state proceeded to conduct a full census—literally, the "survey of national strength" (kokusei chōsa)—only once more, however, in 1935, along with a simplified survey in 1940. In contrast to the household registration system, which depended considerably on self-reporting and checks carried out by the police among their countless other tasks, these census projects mobilized dedicated bureaucratic resources and focused on the economic more than familial conditions of households.[78] But despite the exhaustive breakdown of the population according to biological measures such as age, gender, and birth and death rates, as well as to geographical distribution down to the townships and wards, only the 1930 census delineated the population with detailed occupation labels. In addition to applying ten "large categories" (daibunri)—farming, fishing, mining, industry, commerce, transportation, civil service and self-employed, house worker (kaji jiyōjin), others, and none—which slightly expanded upon those of the Statistical Annual (Tōkei nenpō), the 1930 Census Report further broke down the occupations into forty-one "mid-level categories" and nearly four hundred "small categories," which showed an occupational proliferation previously suggested by household registers from the opening years of the colonial period. However, although they allowed for several occupations unique to Korea, such as that of slash-and-burn farmer (kadenmin), the occupational divisions were mostly modeled on those used in Japan.[79] The subsequent 1935 and 1940 census surveys, moreover, reverted to using only the large categories. Total war mobilization, however, appears to have required more detailed information. In reflecting the primacy of resource procurement, for example, an ad hoc population survey ordered in 1944 introduced a new categorization scheme: Each person was tagged with, first, one of nearly ninety different "industries" (*sangyō*), then a specific occupation, then a specialty skill or job within that occupation.[80]

Surnames and Assimilation

The imperatives of wartime mobilization also shaped an aspect of population tracking that modern states have commonly used to effect societal agglomeration: the assignment of surnames.[81] Despite the commotion attached to it by contemporary propagandists and postcolonial historical conventions, this maneuver, the so-called "sōshi kaimei" (Kor. *changssi gaemyeong*) measure introduced through a revision of the civil code in 1939,[82] appears to have been more complex than making Koreans take Japanese names to identify with the war effort. The rationalities of administrative standardization were just as important, as was the broader movement toward the Japanization of the family system. These points in turn direct attention to name management in the longer-term development of state biopower.

While most Koreans by the late Joseon era had surnames and even clan identities, the diminishing, yet still substantial number of *nobi* slaves and social outcasts, for the most part, did not. As discussed above, through revisions at the turn of the twentieth century, the state required that everyone appearing in the household registers possess the same personal information. But the government took a measured approach, in full consideration of the complexities and sensitivities involved. The 1896 household registration form in fact accommodated the continuing reality of bound servitude by providing spaces for both "boarders" (*gigu*) and "manservants" (*goyong*). These two categories of people usually referred to former domestic servants still residing in the master's household even after the legal abolition of slavery in 1894;[83] but they were indicated only by number in the new registration form, and hence the touchy issue of their surnames and clan seats did not present immediate difficulties. The same did not hold true, however, for the nonresident servants and other traditionally base groups—the *baekjeong* (butchers and tanners) and Buddhist monks—who now had to declare separate households and hence to fill in the blanks for name, clan, and "four ancestors."[84] For some localities, these separate registers have been preserved, and they hint at the manner and pace by which these groups, from an administrative vantage point, were becoming integrated into the fold of regular society.[85] In the extant registers for the *baekjeong* butchers from a locale in Ulsan county, for example, while all fourteen recorded surnames and clan identities for the household heads, most simply listed "unknown" (*puji*) for the four ancestors. ("Unknown" also appeared occasionally for commoners as well.) For the Buddhist monks, the registration records show the reverse: While they continued to be registered through their ordination names, i.e., without surname, their fathers' names and clan identities did appear, as did their listings for ancestors, compared to the *baekjeong*, with greater frequency.

The succeeding 1909 *minjeok* registration system maintained this requirement for a household head's surname and clan identity, even as it eliminated the spaces for ancestors. Though firsthand accounts are few about which or how people who previously existed on the margins of society gained surnames and clan identities through the 1896 and 1909 measures, circumstantial evidence, as well as stories passed down to later eras, paints a general picture of servants and others either awkwardly negotiating a clan identity with local clerks, or simply being assigned one.[86] (And despite the incompleteness of the extant household registers from this period, durable patterns appear to have been set in motion well before this time.)[87] Beyond the force of long-established customs of patrilineal lineage identity and of the prohibition of same-clan marriage, maintaining this marker of "clan seat" likely reflected the administrative rationality of differentiating a population with low surname variability. This drive to render individuals more visible to the state was also seen in colonial regulations, making it difficult to change one's official, registered name. Such measures sought to circumvent the customary practices of giving children multiple names, for use in different contexts and stages of their lives, or of not even giving a formal name to girls.[88] These standardization steps facilitated the transition to the solution that most modern states, including that of South Korea, ultimately adopted: a system of citizen identification numbers (like the American social security number).[89] Hence, however draconian it might seem on the surface, the effort by the wartime colonial state to register Koreans with Japanese names can be considered an extension of these earlier efforts.

Administratively, the "creation of [Japanese] surnames" measure required relatively minor amendments to the Korean civil code and the Korean household registration ordinance (*Chōsen kosekirei*) in late 1939.[90] Belying the enormity of its implications, including the importation of the Japanese (nuclear) family system and thereby also the disturbance of Korean patrilineal principles, the order was simply, almost nonchalantly introduced as an addendum (*fusoku*) attached to the revised civil code: "Within six months of the beginning of implementation [February 1940], Korean household heads must select a *shi* surname and register it with the government office of their municipality, township, or village." The term *shi* (or *uji*; Kor. *ssi*) referred to Japanese surnames, in contrast to *sei* (Kor. *seong*) for denoting Korean surnames, and hence the term *sōshi* (Kor. *changssi*), or "creation of *shi*" became the common parlance for this measure.[91] Press accounts announcing this move in late 1939, in fact, tended to refer to it as the introduction of the "*shi* system," the core feature of a supposedly ancient Japanese family model.[92] And while technically Koreans were not precluded from using their Korean surnames as their *shi*, it was commonly understood that they would take— or, more often, construct—a Japanese-style surname.[93] The Government-General touted an 80% registration rate (for households) of new *shi* surnames by the time the registration period came to a close in August of 1940.[94] Soon, however, this rate was deemed 100%, for those household heads who failed to comply were simply registered by the state with their Korean surname as their household's *shi*, just as the addendum to the civil code originally noted.[95] This *shi* would henceforth be the official surname for everyone in the household, including the household head's mother and spouse, as in Japan.

Governor-General Minami Jirō, the political force behind this move, publicly denied any coercion, insisting that these registrations were voluntary, a claim reiterated by other colonial officials.[96] He had to tread carefully; given that this move constituted state intervention in core family matters and disturbed deeply embedded cultural norms regarding social identity, it could have proved counterproductive to the strengthening of the colonial state's authority amidst wartime mobilization and even to the sustainability of colonial rule itself. These were the concerns expressed by strong resistance from bureaucratic, business, and other influential circles in both Japan and Korea, and not only from those, such as colonial police officials, concerned with maintaining order once the ability to differentiate Japanese from Koreans diminished.[97] These opposing voices appear to have produced a tempering of the original thrust of this measure and a realignment with the previously gradualist approach of colonial policy. Intriguingly, for example, the imposition of Japanese surnames in 1940 did not eliminate the clan seat identifier in the household registers. In fact, neither this measure nor the 1942 residence registry system even required the deletion of the original Korean surname in the registers—it called for "creating a *shi*," not necessarily for replacing the Korean *seong*. Korean household heads could keep their Korean surnames in their registers, which remained necessary for matters such as preventing same-clan marriages.[98] And the pressure for Koreans to change their registered given names ("kaimei") did not approach that for creating *shi* surnames.[99] So while the name-change measure did indeed heighten colonial governmentality during wartime, it circumvented, more than overrode, the prevailing acknowledgment of Korean particularities regarding family law and customs.

These realities also imply a critical feature of assimilation, which from an administrative standpoint was another means of further homogenizing the population—this time between the ethnicities of the colony and the metropole. Assimilation was thus declared a primary justification for the 1939–40 *sōshi* registration measure, couched in the language of adopting the Japanese family system (*ie*) while breaking down the power of traditional patrilineal ties in Korea, particularly as manifested in the ancestral clan organizations. These ties were said to have been enabled by precolonial registration practices that allowed households to be composed of family members (wives, concubines, adopted children) even with different surnames. In response, the colonial regime had incrementally developed the household registration system in a way that, while considerate of Korean customs, institutionalized the equal standing of all families—and household heads—through increasing emulation of Japanese practices. In wartime, the authorities had to take the final step in this process: the embrace of the Japanese model of unifying households under a single (Japanese-style) surname for the sake of uniting the Korean people under a singular loyalty to the Japanese nation and emperor.[100] In fact, claimed the colonial Minister of Legal Affairs, the introduction of the *shi* system was partly in response to calls from many Koreans who desired such a step as a true sign of assimilation.[101]

Mizuno Naoki, though, has shown extensively that the *sōshi* measure, despite the heavily promoted assimilationist ideals, actually did little to eliminate markers of ethnic difference. Indeed, most of the new *shi* surnames that Koreans registered were in fact easily discernible constructions. Devising these sometimes awkward Japanese-sounding surnames appeared as confounding and variegated as the precolonial attempts at assigning surnames forty years earlier: some names were extensions, through the addition of one *kanji* character, of one's Korean surname, while others were based on one's clan identity, hometown, or ancestor.[102] And as noted above, the household registers, for their part, did little to eliminate signs of Koreanness. This maintenance of distinction amidst the public pursuit of sameness, in sum, underpinned contrasting demands for the colonial regime, which had to balance imperatives to streamline administration, promote assimilation, and deflect criticism of discriminatory colonial policies with the enduring political and cultural need to preserve social difference, the fundamental basis for Japanese rule. Earlier in the colonial period, in fact, the Government-General had moved to forbid Koreans from taking names that might lead people to "mistake them for Japanese" (*naichijin to magirawashiki*), either as newborns or thereafter, and had maintained this stance despite calls from within the bureaucracy and from public intellectuals to encourage Koreans to take Japanese names.[103]

That the colonial authorities refrained from taking this step until wartime might indeed suggest that assimilation was never taken very seriously until wartime, but it also underscores their awareness of the risks in pricking core elements of the Koreans' sense of identity. Indeed, for most of the colonial period, the generally measured administrative approach regarding the family system reflected the recognition, in the words of the colony's top legal official, Miyamoto Gen, "that to use legal authority to force through drastic changes [to overturn customs] would have been not only contrary to the integrity of the law but needlessly provocative, and hence would have invited disaster."[104] The relatively dramatic and sudden departure from these practices through the name change measure in 1940 can thus be interpreted in several ways: First, as another step, however excessive and haphazard it appeared on the surface, in standardizing surname conventions for administrative purposes, a process that had begun in the late nineteenth century; second, as a major breakthrough in the effort, since the onset of colonial rule, to weaken traditional lineage ties and in their stead to implant the Japanese family system, now including Japanese-style surnames, as a facilitator of assimilation;[105] and finally, as yet another sign, despite the publicity, of assimilationism's continuing tepid reality,[106] and hence as a heavy-handed, almost desperate move.

Indeed, the deeper impact of the name change order is doubtful, notwithstanding the ideals and motives behind this measure and its subsequent dramatization as a symbol of colonial oppression. For one, in daily interaction the use of Japanese names appears to have been uneven and bound to remain mostly confined to formalities.[107] Even beyond any sense of national grievance and cultural violence, Koreans had many reasons to reject registering new surnames. Changing one's formal name, for example, often could not be confined to the household registers; major transactions, such as for real estate, that required identifying documentation tagged to the household registers, were also affected. And many Koreans joined mass registrations, led by their clan organizations, of a uniform *shi* surname in order to maintain their traditional patrilineal bonds, which directly undermined one of the major justifications for implementing this policy in the first place, as noted above.[108] The measure was, in this way, an example of what Ann Stoler and Frederick Cooper have observed as a generalizable pattern of high imperialism, that "colonial states were often in the business of defining an order of things according to untenable principles that themselves undermined their ability to rule."[109]

CONCLUSION

The wide-ranging ramifications of population tracking, from exemplifying registration rationalities to accelerating the disruptions of wartime mobilization, reflected its incremental development over the early modern era. Whether legitimized as social leveling or cultural assimilation, the remaking of society by the modern state's practices of population tracking came first in the service of administrative rationalization. Points of data collection, ranging from revamped household registers to residence registers and census surveys, increased the complexity of classification efforts, to be sure, but at another level the aims of population tracking pointed toward simplification: The homogenization of the people through the reduction of occupational diversity into set categories, as well as the assignment of standardized surnames, family units, and other biosocial markers across the population, were designed to make everyone more visible, manageable, taxable, and available for mobilization.

This picture of an ever-rationalizing classification and registration regime, however, represented only a part of the story of state population tracking in early modern Korea. In fact the modernizing state's ambitions were constantly tempered by conflicting demands and rationalities. The most challenging and imposing was the enormous weight of customary practices, which both the precolonial and colonial states had to accommodate, to an extent beyond the state's regulation of other social realms. These considerations were manifested in the 1896 household registration system's incomplete integration of social outcast groups, for example, or the colonial regime's maintenance of traditional family markers, such as ancestral identity or concubines' children, despite their ostensible incongruence with administrative rationalities. Such constraints also magnified competing bureaucratic claims, as shown in the colonial state's turning toward a census survey or a residence registry to gain data that the household registers could not provide, or in the evolving methods to fashion a categorization scheme that would reflect more accurately the ongoing occupational diversification. Further adding to this mix was the desire to apply empire-wide standards in the colony, most notably through the gradual, careful introduction of the Japanese family system—or at least of its administrative manifestation in household registration. This process culminated in the intriguing effort to incorporate, during wartime, the recourse to which many modernizing states, including that of precolonial Korea, eventually turned: the standardization of methods to designate names and family relations, including even the assigning of surnames. This imposition of Japanese surnames for the cause of cultural integration and administrative efficiency, though, actually failed to eliminate the markers of ethnic differentiation in registration or social interaction.

Such an outcome, however, demonstrated more the shortcomings of wartime mobilization measures in general, which, in attempting to overcome the legitimacy gap of colonial rule through forced assimilation, upset the longstanding balance, however precariously maintained, between the efficiency and efficacy of colonial rule. In implementing the overarching rationalization of equalizing the populace through an accommodation of both customs and bureaucratic goals, the registration regime in early modern Korea remained mindful of both legitimacy and administrative rationality, and hence demonstrated governmentalized biopower at work. Legitimation, in reinforcing state authority, also came via the universal obligation of reporting. The mundane exercise of an officious requirement—mostly at the site of registration, the local government office—fulfilled the primary aim of governmentality: the self-reflexivity of the populace as contributors to the state's maintenance of the social order, which furthermore reinforced social homogenization by requiring that all people be so registered. This does not mean, of course, that everyone fully complied with this responsibility to actualize or update his visibility to the state.[110] But by channeling administrative mechanisms and resources to guide communal behavior and produce knowledge, the regime of classification and registration helped forge the state's preeminent standing in the making of early modern society.

EIGHT

Public Health and Biopolitics

DISCIPLINING THROUGH DISEASE CONTROL

ONE COULD READILY ARGUE that the administration of public health most distinguished the modern state from its predecessors, just as issues of health and hygiene came to frame much of the notion of modernity itself. Indeed, if the modern state's viability hinged on its capacity to secure the physical well-being of the population, then public health extensively aligned with the state's claims and ambitions: to offer protection from both human and natural threats; to edify, discipline, and civilize the population; to improve material conditions; and to induce particular behaviors and perspectives. Understandably, this transposition of the modern state's control, in the name of public health, down to the level of the personal also elicited fervent resistance. Whether in inoculating villagers, quarantining travelers and transporters, or inspecting prostitutes or butchers, such state actions were often viewed as a violation of the tacit boundary between the individual and the governing authority—between, in a sense (though not necessarily stated in these terms), the private and public realms. In these interstices of contestation between state claims in the name of the greater good and counterclaims insisting on the limits of such intervention, the workings of state power and legitimation were revealed.

In early modern Korea, these forces shaped the balance between public health as a tool and reflection of the state's regulatory authority, on the one hand, and a populace that both accepted these measures and questioned their motives and execution. The result was the reckoning of a broad range of issues concerning the state's role in medicine, sanitation, and health, indeed state authority as a whole. Public health included the construction and management of hospitals, certification and regulation of doctors and nurses, and a host of other functions, from firefighting and road maintenance to health care, and, of course, combating infectious disease. And because disease control necessitated intervention in personal behavior and individual bodies, it required an administrative mechanism that, in instituting both the macro-level exercise of biopower and the micro-level disciplining of behaviors and perceptions, perhaps came closest to exemplifying the governmentalized state envisioned by Michel Foucault.

BIOPOLITICS, DISEASE CONTROL, AND THE INSTRUMENTALITIES OF PUBLIC HEALTH

As with population tracking, an examination of disease control as a state rationalization can draw extensively from Foucault's centering of biopower and governmentality in modern Western Europe, marked by the emergence of not only the rationalities of modern public health that became familiar later—government bureaucracies dedicated to medical care, sanitation systems, even the roving activities of the hygiene police[1]—but also a statecraft that tied the health of a state, as it were, to that of the population. This resulted in state intervention in a variety of spheres: infrastructure (roads, sewage, clinics); economy (social welfare, factory conditions); schooling (hygiene education, inoculation of schoolchildren); even religion (suppression of faith healers). Foucault framed this development as part of the modern state's increasing turn to biopolitics, the "extensive complex of ideas, practices, and institutions focused on the care, regulation, disciplining, improvement, and shaping of individual bodies and the collective 'body' of national populations."[2] Biopolitics constituted the cumulative application of the state's capacity to "manage life" in order to effect governmentality's ultimate objective of inculcating a normative mode of behavior.

One can see, then, how governmentality, which encompassed the entire sweep of state measures to analyze social conditions and shape personal conduct, arose organically out of Foucault's early forays into the origins of modern medical diagnoses. In *The Birth of the Clinic*, he posited that the intensive targeting of the body as the object of medical practice at the turn of the nineteenth century entailed the formation not only of the object (the body) but also of the subject (the examiner, clinician), who held "the sovereign power of the empirical gaze."[3] The objectification of the body, in other words, could not be divorced from the subjectivity of the person(s) engaged in the "seeing and saying" concerning the body. When transposed to the level of an entire population, such corporeal mapping enabled a conceptualization of the populace as an organic entity that required medical upkeep, but also the subjectification of the state itself as it constantly expanded and redefined its scope of authority—that is, as it underwent a process of governmentalization. The clinician's diagnostic probe of the human body, then, historically spurred, accompanied, and allegorized the state's exercise of biopower over the populace. The modern state's acute interest in shaping individual behavior, meanwhile, was organically tied to its comprehensive concerns over contagion, and indeed Foucault locates the origins of modern disciplinary actions and mechanisms, including those of the state, in the systematic response to the plague in Europe.[4] This led to the moment when medicine achieved "a political status"—and hence the transition, in modern terms, to not only the birth of the clinic but also the origins of public health.[5]

The notion of state responsibility over the physical welfare of the population also had a long-standing history in Korea. The Joseon state, in fact, operated an extensive network of medical agencies staffed by officials dispatched around the country to care for public servants, dispense pharmacological advice and products for local healers, and respond to emergencies. An elite core of state physicians in the capital, furthermore, managed this nationwide system and directly cared for the royal family and high officials.[6] But although Confucian ethics, as discussed in earlier chapters, also propounded a cosmic connection between individual cultivation and the family, state, and all Under Heaven, there was little emphasis on a direct link between the state's capacity to ensure the people's health and the strength of the state itself, and by extension, of the nation and civilization over which it ruled. Such an indexing of the state through its public health system arose amidst Korea's "opening" in the late nineteenth century, particularly through the influence of contemporary Japan.

Much has been written about the formation of the Japanese public health system in the Meiji era (1868–1912), including its extensive impact on state making and imperialism. Sabine Frühstück has shown that the "modern health regime" in Japan, which also included the intensified disciplining of sexual practices, accounted for an array of officials, physicians, educators, and institutions behind the state's expansive approach to public health as a signifier of the larger society, indeed of the "national body" (*kokutai*) itself. And from the beginning, military imperatives largely directed the developments in Meiji public health, from the concerns over battlefield sanitary conditions to the construction of licensed brothels, which further ensured that such patterns would extend beyond Japan's borders through imperialism.[7]

Japanese notions of *eisei* (Kor. *wisaeng*)—the expansive term for "hygiene" originally fashioned out of classical Chinese precedents by Nagayo Sansai—made a particularly lasting impression in East Asia. Meiji officials like Nagayo had drawn considerably from the Prussian model that called for an aggressive, interventionist approach to public health within a broader range of state responsibilities, especially in social welfare and education.[8] Japan's participation in vanquishing the Boxer Uprising in 1900 and its subsequent occupation of the port city of Tianjin facilitated the transmission of this Meiji public health system to China. Ruth Rogaski has found that, by the turn of the twentieth century in much of China, this same word, *weisheng*, which the author translates as "hygienic modernity," functioned as an all-encompassing concept for health, hygiene, and even cleanliness, and as a measure of China's civilizational progress.[9] The Japanese concession in Tianjin served as a laboratory for testing Meiji advances in public health, as *eisei* officials coordinated their activities with a growing hygiene police force that enforced sometimes draconian measures on the Japanese concession's majority Chinese population. But the Japanese also established a reputation for reliability and innovation among even the European powers in Tianjin, who eventually turned to Japan for assistance.[10]

As Rogaski and others have pointed out, this dynamic constituted the application of hygiene as an instrument of colonial rule, a topic that has been endowed with considerable scholarship. While germs may have acted as an invisible weapon of conquest by killing off millions in earlier colonial encounters, in the age of high imperialism from the late nineteenth to early twentieth centuries, colonial regimes focused on blocking the ravages of contagion—if mostly for the sake of the colonists. These measures also reflected ongoing public health changes globally in response to increasing urbanization and breakthroughs in bacteriology and immunization, with colonial settings often serving as the stage for new, usually contested approaches to medicine and policy.[11] Likewise, Japanese practices of scientific imperialism—from their reliance on ethnography to the transposition of lessons in tropical medicine from warm-weather outposts such as Taiwan—were used to legitimate the civilizing mission of colonial rule.[12]

The historical meanings of the onset of biological medicine, particularly its impact on the instrumentalities of political domination in modern Korea, have gained considerably from recent scholarly attention. In their foundational, exhaustive studies on the history of Korean medicine, Sin Dong-won and Bak Yun-jae, for example, have detailed the dual significance of Western medicine's introduction into Korea—its medical impact and political utility, as well as the inseparability of the two.[13] Likewise, in examining the long history of Korean efforts to particularize medical practices in the face of universalizing forces, Soyoung Suh finds that the promotion of biomedicine, by the colonial state as well as by Japanese and Korean physicians, was part of a larger scientist shift that deployed modern science as a ruling mechanism. Similarly, in extending David Arnold's conceptualization of the "colonization of the body" as an instrumentality of colonial rule,[14] Jin-kyung Park has detected the practices of a "corporeal colonialism" in the objectification of particularly the *female* body—that of wives, concubines, "modern girls," factory workers, prostitutes, entertainers—as a target of surveillance, medical study, and discipline. The resulting "investigative regime," Park notes, played a critical role in the imperializing and colonizing process, encompassing a bureaucratic and medical establishment that forwarded biomedical, pro-natalist practices.[15]

Other studies have extended the investigation of gender in colonial biopolitics to the realm of the family as a whole. Sonja Kim, for example, excavates how the development of institutions and discourses concerning the Korean population's health, beginning in the precolonial period, illuminate the formations of gender and sexuality in early modern Korea. The state, understandably, figured prominently in this process, especially through its efforts to promote ideals of hygiene, family, and procreation. But also notable were the challenges to such measures, whether coming from Western missionaries, practitioners of native Korean medicine, or customary behaviors.[16] Gim Hae-gyeong's study on the colonialist promotion of an idealized domesticity, which compelled a reorientation of long-standing perceptions of health, happiness, and well-being, illustrates the close ties between the subjectification of motherhood and the state's advancement of the (nuclear) family, particularly the health and hygiene of children, as an object of regulatory surveillance.[17]

All of these groundbreaking works have emphasized the administrative, indeed political instrumentalities of the public health regime in early modern Korea. While relying considerably on these studies, the present chapter focuses on this regime's reflection of broader state-making forces, and especially on disease control as a leading indicator of such connections. For the battle against infectious disease constitutes the signal representation of the "police state" in Foucault's expansive conceptualization, a state that deployed officials in both the comprehensive and narrow means of "policing"—that is, from management of the populace down to a targeted disciplining of personal behavior.[18] Whether in surveillance, quarantining, or education, disease control epitomized the circular legitimation of the (police) state's authority in early modern Korea: only the state could enact such measures, and the exercise of this authority in turn justified its rule. But this general ideological impulse of the interventionist state was also part of a larger discursive field that, in turn, complicated and challenged statist aims as well.

MECHANISMS: DISCIPLINING BETWEEN COERCION AND CONSENT

The groundswell in state responses to combat highly infectious diseases in the modern world reflected the need for "a multiple gaze," in Foucault's terms for clinical observation, and often at the center of these efforts stood a police force that undertook a wide range of actions, from discovery to burial, quarantining to food control.[19] Likewise, due to their extensive disciplinary role and proximity to the populace, the police in early modern Korea were the face of the state to most people, as well as the most visible and authoritative component of an increasingly expansive and assertive public health system.

Cholera and the Construction of Public Health

The early Gabo Reform efforts to create a dedicated public health system did not necessarily envision this police centrality. The Deliberative Assembly's establishment of the new Interior Ministry in mid-1894 designated only the Hygiene Bureau (Wisaengguk) to look after the "prevention of contagious disease, as well as medicine, pharmaceuticals, inoculation, and other such matters."[20] Soon thereafter, though, with the founding of the General Police Agency within the Interior Ministry, the police took primary responsibility for an extraordinary range of sanitation matters, including "the prevention and disinfection of contagious disease, vaccination, distribution of food and water, dispensation of medicine, livestock, meat production, and burial sites," as well as the disposal of trash and human waste.[21]

Further articulation of this Gabo public health system appeared in the summer of 1895 when cholera broke out in Japanese military stations in Manchuria and then spread quickly southward into the peninsula.[22] As suggested by Sin Dongwon, the Gabo state's response made significant strides:

The central government allocated substantial resources to the effort, issued a host of new legal measures, and dispatched foreign medical experts as well as native officials. The lack of coordination between those officials sent from the capital and local counterparts, with both groups having to deal with confused and uncooperative populations, resulted in the failure to prevent thousands of deaths in the northern part of the country and to stop the contagion from eventually reaching the capital. But once there, the anti-cholera efforts proved somewhat more successful, as police officers and foreign physicians were mobilized for immediate inspection duties, including of individual homes, and patients were quarantined or confined to isolation hospitals until things quieted down.[23]

On the heels of this episode, the central state's approach to tackling cholera and infectious disease in general appears to have matured quickly. The original blueprint for preventing and treating epidemics was expanded to a systematic analysis of contagious disease, as seen later in the thorough bureaucratic instructions on the six types of contagion.[24] The revised cholera prevention guidelines issued by the Interior Ministry in the fall of 1899 were a case in point:[25] Cholera, the "most terrible" (*maengak*) scourge in the world, is caused by bacteria, and the most vital task in tackling this disease is to stop the spread of bodily fluids by disposing of tainted liquids such as sewage, and by isolating patients and those with whom they have come in contact. Preparation for epidemics included a Training Center for Vaccination Officers (Jongduui yangseongso) that produced dozens of officials destined to staff vaccination centers and other medical agencies,[26] as well as a reorganized Hygiene Bureau that aimed primarily at integrating local public health officials and clinics.[27] This might have also been a way to parcel out traditional medicine to the realm of treatment,[28] while the more intensive bureaucratic efforts could focus on prevention and emergency response. When cholera broke out again in 1902, killing thousands, the Interior Ministry dedicated enormous sums of money to eradicating the "wicked air" (*yeogi*) in the capital, with the General Police Agency quickly establishing a temporary field hospital, mobilizing scores of officials at the central to local levels, and assigning both native and foreign doctors to the cause of the "people's hygiene" (*inmin wisaeng*).[29]

Following the effective takeover by the Japanese protectorate, the Hygiene Bureau underwent further restructuring in the summer of 1907,[30] but it continued to rely on the information and material collection activities, including in-house inspections, of the police. These now joint Japanese–Korean police units included a "hygiene police" network (Kor. *wisaeng gyeongchal*, Jpn. *eisei keisatsu*) that was established in the major cities and port areas where the thirteen Japanese consulates (Rijichō) were located, and targeted, among other maladies, venereal disease from prostitution (see below).[31] These inspections were assisted by advisory doctors (*gyeongmu gomunui*) dispatched by the new, Japanese-run Daehan Hospital (Daehan uiwon) in Seoul, into which the administration of all public health functions in the country— including hospitals, doctor certification, and medical schools—had been transferred earlier that year.[32] And to the assistance of this hospital's efforts came the Seoul Sanitation Society (Keijō eiseikai), a group established under the auspices of the Japanese crown prince that oversaw waste removal and general hygiene enforcement in the capital city.[33] When cholera broke out in the fall of 1907 just ahead of his scheduled visit to Korea, the Residency-General initiated a state of emergency to contain the disease.[34] In its publicity the protectorate hailed the systematic, comprehensive, and particularly the military character of this campaign, which included not only high army officers in command, but military and police officials engaging in around-the-clock surveillance and enforcement.[35]

These actions also aroused a fierce outcry from some residents, however, as policemen forced their way into homes, even to women's quarters, if they suspected unsanitary conditions or a hidden cholera sufferer. A vicious cycle developed in which Koreans came to fear, through the rumor mill, terrible fates in isolation hospitals, which led them to evade sanitation officials and police inspectors, who in turn imposed themselves more vigorously on individuals' homes and behaviors. Understandably, the frightened residents on the ground, as well as observers later, saw these steps as inherent to the Japanese takeover,[36] but such disciplining, which to Japanese officials presented the biggest challenge to carrying out their public health duties,[37] was an approach that had already been envisioned, though not fully implemented, by the Gabo Reforms. And out of this development emerged the core features of the colonial disease control system as well: the reliance on the hygiene police to enforce inspection and inoculation measures, with all the attendant issues surrounding coercion and resistance entailed therein.

Colonial officials, in fact, chose not to establish an independent, central public health agency equivalent to the Hygiene Bureau of the precolonial era. Rather, they consolidated most of these duties into the hands of the Central Police Headquarters' Hygiene Section (Eiseika), comprising the Health Division (Hokenkei) and the Vaccination Division (Bōekikei), and infused with commanders from the military police (*kempeitai*), over whom local civilian authorities exercised little authority.[38] Aside from expanding the list of infectious diseases from seven to nine, for example, the 1915 "Decree on Preventing Communicable Disease" (*Densenbyō yobōrei*) introduced little that differed from similar edicts in Korea dating back to the late 1890s. It did, however, intensify the summary powers of the Central Police Headquarters to mobilize bureaucratic resources in case of an epidemic, and of police and other hygiene officials to enforce measures restricting people's actions and movements.[39] A final novelty was the Police Commissioner's capacity, with the consent of provincial officials, to establish "hygiene cooperatives" (*eisei kumiai*), local communal bodies responsible for refuse removal and sanitation enforcement. By the end of 1915, there were reportedly over nine hundred such cooperatives around the colony.[40] With the onset of Cultural Rule, the autonomy of the local hygiene police was formally strengthened when each provincial Police Department gained a Sanitation Section (Eiseika). This office directed the province's hygiene officials, including "public physicians" (*kōi*), or country doctors who also attended to sanitation and disease prevention matters in the more remote areas of the colony.[41] Such a police-centered public health administration, which differed notably from that in Japan, would remain largely intact the rest of the colonial period.[42]

Indeed, colonial police officials undertook an extraordinary range of public health duties. In addition to those involving quarantining and forced hospitalization, inspection, traffic restriction, drug circulation, prostitute examination, and inoculation that had been established earlier in Korea, colonial police responsibilities also included oversight of water and sewage lines, constructing waste disposal facilities, handling of dead bodies, inspecting butcher shops and livestock, conducting household surveys, and applying disinfectants. The colonial police also played a major role in public education campaigns, whether to supervise inoculations at schools, help organize rural hygiene associations, or sponsor hygiene fairs and public lectures. This in turn required coordination with both private and public medical institutions, particularly the network of government-run "Charity Hospitals" (*Jikei iin*) that had been established in the protectorate period and continued as the main source of state medical care throughout the colonial era.[43] But the police's main public health duties lay in disease control, especially in preventing epidemics by administering vaccinations and operating dispensaries, but also in regulating chronic diseases. They even diagnosed and provided initial treatment for dozens of infectious diseases, from typhus, smallpox, and cholera to more chronic, but widespread, ailments such as tuberculosis, gastrointestinal disorders, and venereal disease.[44]

Toward the end of the colonial period's first decade, in 1919, the Government-General could point to notable improvements in disease control. The number of Koreans having been vaccinated against smallpox and cholera annually was reported at 1.2 million, after having climbed to 1.5 million, or almost 10% of the population, in the middle of the decade. And the police had quarantined more than 20,000 ships and close to 700,000 seaborne travelers, both sailors and passengers, over suspicions of contagion in 1919.[45] But the mortality rate from cholera and most other contagious diseases did not improve significantly, even for the Japanese residents, whose record of survival actually was no better, and at times worse, than that for the Korean population. The death rate of patients from the 1919 cholera outbreak actually increased from the 1916 figures for both populations, from 60% to over 65%, although significantly the total number of deaths for the Japanese population decreased slightly, while that for the Korean population increased exponentially, a signal that the infection rate for Koreans increased substantially (table 10). Still, in comparing the two ethnic populations as a whole (and not just the patients), we find that, while the death rate from the 1919 cholera epidemic was about the same (just over .05%) for both groups, for the Japanese in the 1916 epidemic it had been an astoundingly high .07%, or seven out of every ten thousand Japanese residents in the peninsula, which was over ten times the ratio for Koreans (.006%).[46] Japanese patients continued to die at a surprisingly high rate in the two cholera epidemics of 1920 and 1926 as well.[47]

Nevertheless, by the middle of the second decade of the colonial era, the struggle against cholera and other contagions such as plague began to achieve a measure of success, thanks to continuing vigilance in inspections of ships, trains, restaurants, meat-packing facilities, and suspected homes. Despite the periodic outbreaks, including a smallpox scourge that spread to ten out of the thirteen provinces and killed over 300 people in early 1933,[48] renewed efforts at vaccination—nearly three million annually by the late 1930s, as well as targeted efforts such as 300,000 vaccinations in the northern provinces in 1941[49]—also brought forth notable gains, with many Koreans voluntarily seeking inoculation. And in all of these measures, the police stood at the forefront.[50] Internal police reports from the mid-1930s noted that, thanks to inspections and border control efforts, cholera, notwithstanding the occasional outbreaks from Manchuria, had all but disappeared as a major concern

TABLE 10 Cholera Patients and Deaths in Years of Outbreaks, 1907–1938

Year	Deaths*	Death Rate of Diagnosed Patients (number of deaths)	
		Koreans	*Japanese*
1907	291	81% (161)	72% (117)
1916	1,253	61% (1,022)	60% (230)
1919	11,533	68% (11,339)	66% (179)
1920	13,568	56% (13,453)	62% (110)
1922	23	55% (21)	100% (1)
1926	159	63% (156)	100% (3)
1929	15	83% (15)	(None)
1932	38	54% (36)	67% (2)
1938	32	64% (32)	(None)

SOURCE: Derived from *Meiji yonjū-nen Kankoku bōeki kiji* (1908), pp. 90–91; *Chōsen sōtokufu tōkei nenpō* (1919, 1930); *Chōsen bōeki tōkei* (1943), pp. 4–7. *Total deaths include "foreigners" (*gaikokujin*).

by the early 1930s, and that even smallpox prevention had shown substantial improvement due to public education and inoculation campaigns.[51]

VD and the Disease Control Regime

With such flash pandemics gradually coming under control by the beginning of the colonial regime's third decade, its attention turned to more chronic but communicable ailments, including leprosy, tuberculosis, and particularly venereal disease.[52] VD eventually became one of the most consistently daunting challenges for colonial disease control, and its implications extended to a range of cultural and social realms. A major body of scholarship has investigated venereal disease in the instrumentalities of colonial and imperial domination, and the particularities of colonial Korea have likewise been covered by recent research.[53] These studies have found that, as with the measures against cholera, much of what was implemented in the colony extended approaches in the metropole, but also that the colonial dynamics of differentiation and discrimination intensified and altered such efforts. Notions of racial purity intersected with assumptions about the sociocultural context of sexually transmitted disease to produce a state response that was at once cutting-edge and tempered: at the forefront of administrative and scientific approaches, but heeding customary practices regarding sexuality and gender, and steered by the demands and biases of a foreign conquest regime.

Although VD was certainly not absent in Korea beforehand,[54] as a scourge demanding state control venereal disease spread initially from the encroachment of Japanese soldiers for the imperialist wars against China in 1894–95 and particularly Russia in 1904–5, which resulted in the permanent encampment of these soldiers during the protectorate. The Residency-General drew a range of lessons from the Meiji experience of dealing with VD, such as the acknowledgment and curbing of soldiers' sexual behaviors, and perhaps most revealingly, the licensing of controlled access to prostitution. Lying behind such steps was the understanding that, in the case of overseas areas (like Taiwan), Japanese soldiers—and Japanese men in general—needed protection from tainted native women.[55] While this bias eventually gave way to the lumping of all prostitutes into a single category, official efforts to combat venereal disease continued to associate VD primarily with prostitution and likewise targeted female behavior.[56] (Even the conventional name for VD, "blossoms and willows disease" [karyūbyō], used a euphemism for courtesans.) The roundup of prostitutes by the Japanese police force initially singled out those servicing the Japanese quarters around the country, but it nabbed others as well. For example, in early 1906, within a week after the formal establishment of the protectorate government itself, 139 Korean gisaeng courtesans were brought into a police station in Seoul for health examinations. Newspaper coverage of this procedure relayed accounts of the fear and humiliation that these women experienced while undergoing sometimes harsh and invasive (speculum) examinations, which, as with the house inspections for cholera, initiated a frightful cycle of evasion and intervention.[57] But the Residency-General itself only saw results, including a crackdown on exploitative practices in the prostitution business, the examination and certification of thousands of prostitutes, and hence the securing of the safety from, or at least the control of, often deadly venereal diseases.

Under colonial rule, such roundups continued, even as the licensed prostitution system expanded.[58] In dealing with the gisaeng and others who offered sex services,[59] for example, in 1916 the colonial Police Ministry issued a comprehensive set of "Regulations for Establishments that Employ Gisaeng and Barmaids" (Geigi shakufu chokukyo eigyō torishimari kisoku) and "Regulations on Hostess Bars and Prostitutes" (Kashizashiki shōgi torishimari kisoku) as part of new laws on sanitation in restaurants and inns.[60] Such businesses and their employees were now required to register with the local police office in order to gain a license, and gisaeng—presumably those who worked in the pleasure quarters—had to pass health examinations by physicians under police supervision in order to acquire the necessary health certificate.[61]

As time passed into the 1930s, however, it became clear that VD constituted an extensive, urgent problem well beyond the circles of courtesans and prostitutes.[62] After tuberculosis, venereal disease—primarily syphilis, cancroid, and gonorrhea—turned into the most widespread ailment in colonial Korea, with the number of those afflicted reaching into the sensationalistic range.[63] Official statistics from state-run hospitals suggested that, while relatively few were dying (mostly of syphilis), tens of thousands every year were suffering from sexually transmitted diseases. In 1939 the regime counted almost 19,000 patients as having been treated in public hospitals that year for venereal disease (*karyūbyō*), with patients about evenly split between males and females.[64] In the decade from 1928 to 1937, the number of women in the three categories of prostitutes, *gisaeng*, and barmaids (*shakufu*) who were examined for venereal disease went from just under 300,000 to almost 400,000. While this could have been considered progress, the infection rate witnessed only moderate gains, declining from around 6.5% (approximately 18,500) of those examined in 1928 to 4.6% (slightly under 18,000) in 1937.[65] Despite the advances in treatment since the beginning of colonial rule,[66] the colonial state's measures to combat venereal disease, which did not coalesce into a concerted campaign until 1937, simply were not enough to control its spread, as news reports and even its own publications indicated.[67] And the real extent of sexually transmitted illnesses beyond the grasp of the police force and public health services likely was far greater. Indeed, newspaper reports, which tracked this growing problem in increasingly anxious tones, put the numbers of infected persons in Korea at more than a half-million by the close of the 1930s.[68]

This rising tide of concern over venereal disease leads uneasily, albeit unavoidably, to a consideration of its impact in wartime mobilization, particularly in contextualizing the most controversial and, for many, most horrific feature of this closing period of colonial rule: the military prostitution networks of the so-called "comfort women" (*eianfu, wianbu*) in the battle fronts of Japanese expansionism. Several studies have weighed in on the relative impact of historical-cultural and socioeconomic "push" factors, on the one hand, and the often brutalizing powers of the colonial state, on the other, in determining this system's functioning within Korea.[69] But regardless of this balance and of the deplorable calculus of exploitation that drove it, the extensive network that connected Korean villages and pleasure quarters to the frontline brothels cannot be divorced from the state's long-standing management of prostitution in Korea, and particularly from the cumulative Japanese experience in combating both VD and battlefield contagions. This close connection between prospects in war and command over infectious disease, now readily accepted as a matter of course, was recognized early in Japan. Credited with achieving hygienic victories in their war against Russia and in other imperialist ventures at the turn of the twentieth century, the Japanese undoubtedly took this success as justification for both their campaigns of conquest and their practices of colonial rule.[70]

DISEASE AND MEDICINE IN THE DISCURSIVE FORMATION OF THE STATE

Disease control, as a measure of modern civilization, hence reflected the viability of the modern state's claims to advancement and legitimacy. In the emergence of a public health discourse in early modern Korea, issues of mass hygiene and particularly of disease control came to mirror the emerging debate surrounding state authority and modern change. Cleanliness and health stood for civilization itself and thus involved issues of sovereignty and political authority, which in turn framed the state's public health measures within the pursuit of scientific modernity. Such discursive formations, often wielded to justify state actions, came from nonstate actors as well, demonstrating the potency of the ideals of hygienic modernity in also challenging the state.

Hygienic Civilization and Enlightenment

This close connection between state-directed public health and civilizational standing in Korea was a novelty of the late nineteenth century, but once this link took hold, it became a versatile discursive tool for a variety of perspectives concerning the state. Well before the Gabo Reform measures of 1894, a biomedical government hospital was established, with great fanfare,[71] in 1885, and just as significantly, public calls for state intervention in matters of health and hygiene likewise increased. Famously, Gim Okgyun and Bak Yeonghyo, two of the ringleaders of the failed coup attempt of 1884, had cited the late Joseon administration's deficiencies in this realm as justification for their actions and reform programs.[72] The official gazetteers of the 1880s, often seen as forerunners to the modern newspaper, also elaborated on this connection between national strength (or advancement) and public health, indeed down to the level of individual behavior.[73]

This enlightenment discourse was reflected clearly in Yu Giljun's *Observations from Travels to the West* (*Seoyu gyeonmun*, 1895). Yu discusses the matter in his chapter on the "Government's Responsibilities," in which he cites oversight over "health" (*yangsaeng*) as one of the most important. He also focuses specifically on the preeminent need to stop contagion, the harm from which was "more severe than a conflagration unleashed by war." The government must implement strict laws against the spread of contagious disease and be willing to punish violators severely, which would be justified on grounds that "even the person who is severely punished benefits [from this system] by avoiding the contagion." Here Yu draws a connection between the collectivity and the individual that would become more prominent in legitimating government intervention in the public health system. For the state and its police force, he notes, "failing to strictly restrict [disease-causing] pollution in a major city would be akin to unleashing a tiger in the middle of a market."[74] In becoming the director of the Hygiene Bureau following the cholera outbreak of mid-1895 discussed above, Yu helped ensure that these ideas would be implemented.

The strengthening of public health efforts in the subsequent Great Korean Empire was prodded by growing demands in the popular press for more urgent state attention to hygiene. The *Hwangseong sinmun* newspaper argued, for instance, that the country's fate directly hinged on its capacity to train people for implementing a system of (modern) medicine and hygiene, and that supplying clean water to the capital city through underground mains should come before the construction of streetcars or streetlights.[75] This paper also kept close watch on disease outbreaks both within and outside the country (particularly in Japan), reprinted official public health directives, explained government actions, and advocated state measures that would bring the country in line with advanced nations.[76] In the spring of 1899, for example, the newspaper, in announcing the recent class of graduates from the Training Center for Vaccination Officers, reported that they immediately called on the government to expand inoculation centers to the provinces, regardless of cost.[77]

The *Dongnip sinmun* newspaper, however, was the most prominent advocate of taking public health as a holistic, systematic reflection of national character. Like other papers, the *Dongnip sinmun* kept track of appointments to the Hygiene Bureau, lobbied for specific sanitation measures, and reprinted ordinances from relevant agencies. But it also published works on hygiene and medicine by pioneering figures such as Ji Seogyeong, offered lessons on how to live hygienically, and returned often in its editorials to the theme of connecting hygiene, particularly the state's public health measures, to enlightenment or advancement.[78] A typical editorial from July of 1896 praised recent attempts by the Interior Ministry to post notices around the capital banning defecation, urination, and spitting in the streets, sales of tainted food, and other unhealthy practices. "These efforts can succeed only if the Minister of the Interior, the Mayor of Seoul, and the Chief of the Hygiene Bureau exert the greatest efforts at civilizational advancement," noted the editorial, "and if the Police Chief assists this process by discovering the principles of civilizational advancement for the sake of the country."[79] The newspaper also hailed the "enlightenment motive of the government" in recent measures to clean up streets and streams, and asked rhetorically, If not for an enlightened officialdom, who would pursue such steps toward advancement?[80]

In reiterating the urgency of state leadership, then, this newspaper was also engaging in a policy debate about government priorities, and clearly, hygiene constituted one of the most urgent matters, if not the most important one. In one of its final salvos on this recurring debate, the *Dongnip sinmun* bluntly stated that the government should stop wasting money and efforts on items such as an imperial military brigade or the Privy Council (Jungchuwon). The attention should be redirected toward hygiene and health. If the government wants to send students to Japan for training, have them get educated in sanitation and vaccination, not "political science." Seemingly simple measures such as clearing the streets of refuse, building hospitals, and funding public bathhouses would be money much better spent, the newspaper argued.[81] Even the conventionally accepted national goal of building a "rich country" should take a backseat to a more urgent task: "Health of the nation is more important than wealth of the nation," is how the paper put it in its English-language page.[82]

Colonialist Expressions and Practices of a Civilizing Public Health Regime

Not surprisingly, these calls from Korean activists at the turn of the twentieth century were roundly shared by outsiders as well. Still, it is difficult to overstate the prominence of perceived deficiencies in hygiene as a sign of the country's remedial, indeed irremediable condition in the conventional Japanese (and general foreign) view of Korea. From visitors and scholars writing travelogues to officials drafting secret government reports, Japanese observers became almost obsessed with the dirtiness of the Korean people.[83] In assigning blame, these accounts naturally targeted Korean customs, but more to the point, the incompetence of the state. Filth served as a handy symbol of Korea's political and civilizational decay, as problems in public health were conflated with a general corruption of Korea's government affairs.

Such a discursive recourse to the civilizing mission, of course, accompanied imperialist takeover and colonial rule around the globe. Research into various colonial settings has excavated the ideological instrumentality of public health in colonialism—the notion, as Shula Marks put it, of "the triumph of science and sewers over savagery and superstition" that reflected, supported, and constructed the hierarchies of difference and the legitimation of foreign rule.[84] For East Asia, as Ruth Rogaski and others have asserted, the Japanese further developed this discursive tool into a systematic understanding of scientific colonialism. Such ideas were melded into colonialist practice by figures such as Gotō Shimpei, the first Governor-General of colonial Taiwan and author of a well-known paean to modern biopolitics, *Principles of National Hygiene* (*Kokka eisei genri*, 1889), and his protege Nitobe Inazō, one of the founders of Japanese "colonial studies." Such scholar-officials framed the implementation and justification of Japanese colonial rule on the provision of cleanliness and health.[85]

A representative example of this perspective in Korea comes from a Japanese-language report of 1909, "General Hygiene Conditions in Korea" (*Kankoku eisei ippan*), published apparently under the auspices of the Hygiene Bureau in the Korean Interior Ministry but clearly a Residency-General document. Many of the sections use the trope of describing public health efforts by native Korean governments, then dismissing them as all having been ineffective or incomplete. Late Joseon attempts to survey the condition of the population, for example, were woefully inadequate, and it took the onset of the protectorate, with its use of the police, to arrive at an accurate understanding. Korean Empire measures to increase the numbers of licensed physicians and apothecaries are likewise said to have not improved things at all, and consequentially there were far more prostitutes in the country than physicians or valid pharmaceutical dispensers.[86] And perhaps most damningly, according to this report, the Korean government was wholly unprepared to enact its 1899 regulations to control contagion, with the result that there remained thousands of victims—both Korean and Japanese—of epidemic diseases such as cholera, typhoid, and smallpox in the peninsula.[87] The message was clear: Public health—"the most urgent matter" at the time, in the words of the first *Annual Report* of the Residency-General—required a strong, systematic, mobilizational state, the absence of which in Korea necessitated foreign assistance. Korean officials were not unaware of this urgency, for the Korean government had invested over ten thousand *won* a year toward these public health measures, but the administration was incapable of effectively using those funds. Intent had to be followed by execution, so the narrative went, and acting alone—without Japanese help—the Korean government could not follow through.[88]

Following annexation in 1910 these vows to help were replaced by a blunt elaboration of hygienic conditions, which were roundly deemed terrible,[89] and the promises of a civilizing governmentality that justified a holistic and robust intervention in people's lives in order to achieve public health objectives. Targeting both the material and cultural shortcomings of Korean society, this irrepressible association of civilizational progress with cleanliness, which had become increasingly resonant in Korea since the late nineteenth century, now intersected with racialized social hygiene to provide ideological grounding for state action, particularly as envisioned and directed by the hygiene police.

"The health of the citizenry exerts a great influence on a country's development," wrote Itahigashi Giyū, a police supervisor (*keimukan*), in his preface to a voluminous handbook, *Korea Hygiene Digest* (*Chōsen eisei yōgi*, 1918).[90] This work, one of several encyclopedic guides to public health administration published in the colonial era, contained overviews of Korea's hygiene history and conditions, as well as the latest academic and bureaucratic perspectives on "hygiene studies" (*eiseigaku*), a discipline touted as a distinct scientific specialty that combined chemistry and ecology. Transcending health and medicine, hygiene studies focused on the balance and harmony between external, environmental elements (air, soil, water, food) and the human body. As with enlightenment-period discourse, the significance of personal hygiene for the greater good is repeatedly emphasized, but this work goes further to suggest decisively high stakes for a society's level of advancement. Indeed, through a mix of spiritualism ("hygiene thought"), communitarianism (individual responsibility for the collectivity), and social Darwinism, the *Korea Hygiene Digest* argues that other measurements of social progress—people's morality, their degree of civilization, etc.—are actually superstructural to the basis that is hygiene. Hence it remains imperative to teach individuals the critical importance of their awareness and behavior in this regard—the condition of which, even in Japan, remained sadly behind that of the West. In short, the protection of the populace as a whole depends on hygiene education. Individual and societal hygiene, in fact, are as close as "lips and teeth."[91]

This phrase, "mutual dependence like lips and teeth" (*shinshi hosha*), appears also in a work published by the Police Department of South Pyeongan province in 1913, *General Lessons on Hygiene Policing* (*Eisei keisatsu kōgi ippan*).[92] This work, like the *Hygiene Digest*, stresses the connection between individual hygiene and public health, but it goes a step further and views the hygiene police as a stand-in for the state itself: "States [*kokka*] deploy the police to intervene in protecting the health of the masses out of a desire to nurture a healthy citizenry." In fact, as expressed in the lead chapter, "The Concept of Hygiene Policing," the *General Lessons* takes the hygiene segment of the police—or simply, the hygiene police—as more of a practice than an institution, with a special standing compared to other police duties, given that its authority extends to constraining the freedoms of people who have not committed a crime.[93]

The *Korea Hygiene Digest* of 1918, by contrast, emphasizes instead the limits of hygiene police work. Suggesting strongly a collectivist—that is, nonstatist—bent ("the state [*kokka*] develops out of the people [*kokumin*]"),[94] this work's treatise on "Hygiene Administration" reiterates that the primary duty of the police, as well as of the state, is to "protect the public interest" (*kōkyo no rieki o hogo*), a phrase used repeatedly. Therefore, restraints on people's freedoms take place only in extraordinary circumstances, and only with legal sanctioning. When such circumstances do arise, such as the outbreak of an epidemic, the actions of the hygiene police—whether to quarantine carriers of infectious disease, confine patients in isolation hospitals, force immunizations, or seize goods and property—are justified in accordance with the overriding responsibility of the state, in general, to restrict an individual's rights when they infringe on those of others. Otherwise, the work of the hygiene police under normal circumstances could be considered simply as "hygiene promotion administration" (*jochō eisei gyōsei*), such as assisting public physicians and public health officials, or carrying out educational functions.[95]

These differences in perspective bespeak the challenges, most of all the cultural challenges, of conceiving and executing public health administration in the colony. The Government-General's *Annual Reports*, for example, while remaining transparently propagandistic, expressed an awareness of the limits to which the colonial state could implement its public health measures, for they depended on the collective impact of individual habits and actions. While reiterating the urgent need for a "great reform" and the "improvement of the [Korean] people's level of culture [*mindo no kōjō*]," the 1915 *Annual Report* also emphasized the "consideration of the people's sentiments [*minjō*] when guiding public perspectives [*mini*]" through new hygiene regulations.[96] Likewise, the *Korea Hygiene Digest*, amidst recounting the extensive reforms in public health following annexation, cautioned that the scale and pace of these changes had to "proceed gradually upon consideration of the people's degree of advancement, customs, and feelings."[97] Indeed, internal reports as late as 1935 also reveal colonial police officials being consistently confounded by what they encountered in hygiene conditions and practices, suggesting that the problems were deep and resistant to the standard solutions of dedicating more material and human resources.[98]

Given such challenges, public health measures, particularly in disease control, had to accompany, and often trail, major shifts in popular behavior and perception, the shaping of which required dedicated efforts at ideological engineering. The Government-General, particularly after the start of Cultural Rule, pursued a variety of public outreach measures, which ran the gamut from accommodating to mildly threatening, in order to garner acceptance of often invasive and coercive state actions, as well as to promote changes in personal hygiene practices. In demonstrating responsiveness to popular concerns, it issued press releases in Korean-language newspapers announcing upcoming hygiene "surveys" of certain districts or provinces,[99] as well as official statements by police officials or hygiene bureau chiefs in times of disease outbreaks.[100] Officials also wrote magazine pieces and even took to the radio to broadcast policy explanations and lessons about hygienic living.[101] On a more overtly propagandistic level, the regime also published works detailing its extensive efforts to combat epidemics, such as cholera in 1919, and to educate the populace through roving lectures held in marketplaces, festivals, and schoolhouses (figure 19).

The school curriculum, too, of course became a public health apparatus, particularly for conveying understandings of the relationship between personal and communal welfare. Lessons about disease prevention, and hygiene in general, began naturally with the first and foremost subject, ethics (or "self-cultivation"), the generalized thematic heading for teachings regarding one's duties as a citizen (chapter 6). The narratives included coverage of

FIGURE 19. A government hygiene lecture at a local market, 1920. From *Shashin Chōsen no gaikan*. East Asian Library, University of Southern California.

scientific facts, to be sure, but also reminders of one's moral obligations for the greater good. The seventh chapter in a 1933 ethics textbook for Korean elementary schools, for example, even features an image of common Koreans faithfully standing in line at a makeshift inoculation center to illustrate the text's message about preventing contagion (figure 20). Indeed, the caption for the graphic, featuring a blaring megaphone, signals that these people were responding to a public "hygiene campaign."

Such campaigns also sought to break down the wall of fear from adherence to customary understandings, which additionally were blamed for spreading rumors of the harm of biomedical methods. Colonial police officials catalogued these beliefs in serialized magazine studies and official publications such as *Superstitions about Hygiene* (*Eisei ni kansuru meisin*), published by the Hygiene Bureau of the South Gyeongsang Provincial Police Department in 1933, which decries "the preponderance of superstitions that might be amusing, but also absurd" and therefore posed a danger to public safety.[102] It proceeds to list thirty-five such superstitions, ranging from home remedies to widespread notions about graves, childbirth, and spirits. Many of these perceptions were seen as rooted in the shamanistic understanding of spirits as disease agents, and hence these studies, like those detailing the

染病がよくはやります。
これは人々の衛生に對す
る考が進んでいないため
です。それですから春秋
の大そうじをていねいに
し、種痘その他傳染病豫防
などを進んでしなければ
なりません。

第八　公益

全羅南道の西倉公立普通

十八

豫防は易く
治療は難し
衛生宣傳

FIGURE 20. Page from a "self-cultivation" textbook, 1933. Graphic caption: "Hygiene Campaign: Prevention is easy, treatment is hard!" From Chōsen sōtokufu, *Futō gakko shūshinsho*, v. 4 (1933).

"pseudo-religions" (chapter 5), reflected the regime's efforts to comprehend the cultural impediments to foreign rule through ethnographic reductionism, a common practice of modernizing public health regimes.[103] And as with the condemnation of pseudo-religions, often the Korean press parroted the authorities' warnings of folk remedies and other embedded behaviors. Such pronouncements were in line with the general thrust of newspaper reports and editorials that connected personal hygiene with the social good, and in turn public health with civilizational status.[104]

Perhaps no ailment garnered as much press attention in the colonial period as venereal disease, which killed more than most other maladies but did not feature prominently in government surveys and pronouncements, and in fact was rarely even mentioned in the *Annual Reports*.[105] In the public discourse beyond these official perspectives, however, venereal disease aroused persistent curiosity and concern.[106] Exhortations in magazines and newspaper articles for greater personal responsibility, condom use, and avoidance of various unclean practices—and of unclean people—began to appear in the 1920s,[107] for example. And print ads, even those in government organs, began to draw attention to sexually transmitted disease, as Japanese pharmaceutical companies, tapping into the circulating discursive association of venereal disease with the excesses of modern urban life, peddled a variety of remedies.[108] As with the coverage in the popular press, advertisements in women's magazines conceived of VD as an index of civilization—that the private sexual behaviors of individuals reflected the health and welfare of the entire society, particularly the population's capacity to realize common ideals of domesticity and procreation.[109]

Discursive Resistance to Colonial Disease Control

By the 1930s, however, it was also not uncommon to see VD appearing in the serialized novels, as the chronic suffering of characters stricken by recklessness (males) or poverty-driven prostitution (females) stood as running symbols of the underbelly of colonial society.[110] Indeed, newspapers and magazines did much more than reinforce the paternalistic, instrumental ideology pushed by the colonial authorities; they also raised doubts and leveled severe criticisms about the colony's public health conditions, deploying the language of civilization and enlightenment to question the colonial state's commitment to the very goals it espoused—namely, cleanliness, hygiene, and disease prevention. Such criticism ranged from general grievances, for example, about the lack of physicians, facilities, and information,[111] to targeted attacks at government agencies for disregarding sanitation needs, which were viewed as a basic, if not the primary, responsibility of the state.[112] Some of these critiques, furthermore, contained a nationalist edge. A lead editorial in the *Joseon ilbo* newspaper in late 1925 called out the new (Japanese) mayor of Seoul (Gyeongseong), for example, for publicly espousing a reformist-oriented "hygiene first" policy, when in reality—as demonstrated by the city's projected budget—his office devoted few resources toward constructing hygiene facilities such as waste disposal sites, public toilets, or isolation hospitals. This was yet another case, this editorial noted, of City Hall's discriminatory and shabby treatment of the capital's 300,000 residents, who were once again being duped by false promises while continuing to suffer from years of poor sanitation.[113] More than a decade later, in 1938, a stinging article in the *Donga ilbo*, titled "Pathetic Municipal Hygiene Facilities," extended its condemnation of sewage conditions in newly annexed districts of Seoul to raise questions about whether this neglect was rooted in bias. In contrast to "advanced" cities in the metropole (*naeji*) such as Tokyo, Osaka, or Nagoya, the paper noted, the capital of Korea, even while approaching status as a "global city," had only half as many public toilets per capita, which provided stark statistical evidence for complaints heard from tourists.[114]

These public criticisms exemplified the discomfiting ambivalence of the ideology of scientific rationality in hygiene matters, which could both bring extra-state actors in alignment with state interests or set them in opposition according to their perceptions, interests, and even ethnicities. Such a dynamic was apparent in the awkward relationship between Japanese and Western purveyors of health and hygiene, as both groups saw themselves as the most faithful representatives of scientific modernity. Westerners, however, had established a strong beachhead in Korea as authoritative sources of medical modernity, independent of and preceding Japanese claims—indeed, perhaps above all, as *medical* missionaries. Their lofty standing as the embodiment of Western advancement would invariably complicate and challenge the ideological grounds for Japanese actions, just as it did in education, religion, and other matters that proffered an alternative, often contrasting vision of enlightened modernity.[115] It is not clear to what extent colonial officials found threatening the medical activities of the relatively few Westerners, who were limited, by the latter half of the colonial period, to running a couple of major private hospitals and various dispensaries scattered around the peninsula. But there is plentiful evidence that the authorities were sensitive to, and aggravated by, the Western practitioners' offering a competitive contrast to colonialist visions,[116] even as the Westerners were forced to abide by stringent medical accreditation standards established by the regime.[117]

Unlike with the strife over school visits to Shinto shrines in the 1930s (chapter 5) Western residents never publicly challenged the regime in matters of medicine or public health, and as noted above, they were equally disparaging of Korean folk and oriental medicine, if not more so, than the colonial officials or Korean elites were.[118] But records of the missionaries' meetings and their formal reports reveal a legitimation of their ongoing medical activities, despite the practical absence of any reason to continue them, based on their self-perception as altruistic providers of not only Christian teachings but American / Western science and medicine, and hence of a favored alternative to the colony's public medical system.[119] As Jo Hyeong-geun has argued, however, such a position was a privilege afforded by the Westerners' lack of official responsibilities in the wider realm of public health, in contrast to the position of the colonial state, and furthermore constituted more of a correlative than oppositional stance to the Japanese promotion of hygiene and biomedicine.[120] Indeed the colonial regime found in these Westerners, despite their often grating presence, a useful ally in disseminating the doctrine of hygienic modernity and hence attempted to negate their disruptive potential through co-optation rather than coercion[121]—that is, until the totalizing imperatives of the war against the United States and Great Britain necessitated the expulsion of these Westerners from Korea in 1942.

CONCLUSION

As the epitome of modern biopolitics and the governmentalized state, public health, and particularly disease control, demonstrated not only how individuals came to be disciplined in the name of the greater good, but also how state power in Korea expanded through its efforts to control bodies and behaviors. The dedicated public health administration oversaw an expanding number of hospitals, clinics, examination centers, and other facilities, and undertook an increasing range of regulatory functions such as inspections, interventions, immunizations, and the licensing of everybody from physicians to prostitutes. The state also deployed a range of social education campaigns, which included makeshift inoculation centers, roaming lectures, and lessons conveyed through the media and schools of the connection between personal hygiene and social responsibility.

What was perhaps most notable about this administrative attention to disease and cleanliness in Korea was the dominant role played by the police. Such a role was advanced by enlightenment activists such as Yu Giljun and enacted by the Gabo Reform state, which established the Bureau of Hygiene to function alongside the General Police Agency. This organizational relationship between policing and public health was further solidified by the protectorate and colonial regimes, which endowed the police with extensive authority to devise public health measures and to comprehensively enforce them. Understandably, then, much of the understanding and reporting about public health came from the policing agencies, and likewise policing organs stood at the forefront of bureaucratic mobilization to combat contagious diseases, whether epidemic (cholera) or chronic (VD). As promoted by the colonial police, an interpretation of the emerging science of "hygiene studies" even came to theorize the preeminence of public health in assessing society as a whole—that in fact hygiene constituted the basis of civilization and thus determined the relative standing of nations.

While not necessarily going this far, an increasingly influential discursive position in the late nineteenth century came to prioritize hygiene, and more generally public health, as the foremost concern for the modern state, and hence viewed a state's strength as invariably bound to common practices of cleanliness and hygiene. State officials, too, promoted this conceptual link. Just as one had to take care to control the whereabouts of his and his household's bodily fluids in order to escape the ravages of cholera, to prevent the spread of venereal diseases one had to subject himself (or more often, herself) to checkups and inoculations or to follow state guidelines of domesticity. The reification of public health as a distinctive social realm, then, became solidified through its function as perhaps the most extensive and ambitious segment of the state's civilizing mission in the name of rationality, progress, and modernity. Such a goal was also evident in the various attempts by the authorities, joined by social elites and Western medical practitioners, to restrict "superstitious" folk remedies and even to attack the decidedly high-minded traditions of oriental medicine.

This ideological accord, however, could also be appropriated to question and even rebuke the regime's premises and performance. Indeed, the realm of health, hygiene, and disease control was particularly conducive to generating pushback against the state. The problems in this arena, after all, were more tangible than for sectors such as religion or even education, and rationalizations to control bodies and behaviors naturally engendered strong resistance. As with the enlightenment discourse in general, the budding consensus about the value of biomedicine and the scientific approach to public health constituted an intellectual repository from which both the state and its opponents could draw. The legitimizing of colonial rule, even before it formally commenced, had tapped into the discursive instrumentality of hygienic modernity: Japanese statecraft, with its know-how, resolve, and resources, would finally bring resolution to this "most urgent matter" that had fallen victim to the incompetence of the native Korean state. Even before the Japanese takeover, however, enlightenment activists were applying this understanding to question state priorities and premises, and in the colonial period, this dissent developed into a critique, whether on scientific, rationalist, or nationalist grounds, of state performance in sanitation, to say nothing of its problems in containing disease. At a larger level, as seen in the conspicuous show of state responsiveness to public health concerns through the popular press, as well as in the acknowledgment in both publications and internal documents of the need to adjust colonialist goals to suit native conditions, the absorption and interplay of such resistance was the stuff of state legitimation itself.

Conclusion

THE MODERNIZING STATE IN KOREA underwent extensive diversification and growth in its regulatory, extractive, and symbolic capacities from the late nineteenth century to the end of Japanese colonial rule in 1945. And as with other societies in the era of interstate competition, these developments accompanied an increase in state rationalization, including institutional specialization and a more systematic and commanding relationship with various social sectors. Rationalization, however, also extended to the means by which state actors came to perceive, analyze, and articulate these social sectors, which in turn induced a reflexivity in the state itself.

As this book has argued, this manifold reflexivity of modern state making in Korea, which characterized both the state and the population it governed, was one of constrained, competing, and cumulative rationalities. In a compelling example of Foucaultian governmentality, the balancing and integration of these multiple rationalizations demonstrated a dialectical, recurrent process of administrative adaptation and experimentation that sought to instill the responses of self-disciplining and self-governing within the population. Much of this behavior resulted from a "state effect" produced by the people's regularized interactions with the state. But governmentality also operated through feedback and pushback, through the absorption of conflicting demands and goals.

Each regime that ruled Korea in this era, including the Joseon dynastic state, underwent such an overarching experience of rationalization in tandem with shifts in broader goals and circumstances, such as socioeconomic diversification, industrialization, and imperialism. Taken together, these developments paint a fascinating picture of this era and of its historical connections. In revisiting the main findings of this study, this conclusion will suggest how such processes of rationalizing Korea through the state contribute to a reconsideration of broader themes in modern Korean history, particularly the impact of colonialism.

Toward a More Holistic View

This book has found that, while the governing system became the core, indispensable instrument of Japanese rule, colonialism also generated a variety of modern administrative techniques, many of which intensified the efforts that emerged in the late nineteenth century.[1] The durability of these forms, first articulated in the Gabo Reforms of 1894–95, owed much to the influence of contemporary Japan. But both the precolonial and colonial regimes also drew upon ideals and models circulating around the world.

The undeniable continuities over the ostensible rupture of the 1910 annexation reveal state making in early modern Korea as one of incremental growth, as the rationalities of diversification, specialization, standardization, and domination developed cumulatively. This book demonstrates, then, the fallacies of the picture of a rampaging colonial state replacing a hopelessly traditionalist and enfeebled one, a story adhered to both by narratives that presume colonial rule as an exploitative juggernaut and by the notion of colonial modernity, which tends to discount precolonial developments. Furthermore, as shown often in this study, the colonial state itself underwent several makeovers, with the middle period of Cultural Rule representing perhaps the peak of the systematic application of administrative rationalities inherent to a governmentalized state. And notwithstanding the droning official narrative of the takeover, the annexationist regime of the 1910s built upon the rationalizations of the Gabo Reforms and the Great Korean Empire, whose leaders had followed distinctive paths toward erecting a modern state but also drew upon the long-standing statecraft foundation laid by the Joseon dynasty.

Indeed the legacies of the Joseon state suffused the patterns of social interaction and intervention in the modern one. In the sphere of religion, the Joseon dynasty established a model of state secularism through its arm's-length control over Buddhism and folk religious practices in the name of an enveloping, civic, and semireligious Confucian ideology. And even as Confucianism as an administrative blueprint became discarded through the Gabo Reforms, it remained indispensable to refashioning the relationship between the state and people under the notion of citizenship, propagated through schools and other channels. Joseon practices in population manage-ment through the household registration system and other instruments, furthermore, showed that how the state categorizes the people and diagnoses collective features and problems could render society into more comprehen-sible form. And perhaps most consequentially, the Joseon state pursued a core purpose of social edification through moral suasion, with statecraft rational-ized toward this end not just through philosophical grounding but also through administrative systematization and social interaction.

Systematization and social interaction also characterized, of course, the early modern state in Korea from the late nineteenth century to the end of colonial rule. The difference with the Joseon state lay in the much greater capacities for extraction and mobilization, enabled by leaps in the technolo-gies of surveillance and communication, amidst dramatic expansion of the economy, diversification of society, and precipitous shifts in political rule, even in sovereignty itself. Most of these changes resulted from imperialism, which triggered and loomed over state reforms beginning in the late nine-teenth century, served as the undercurrent to state making under colonial rule, and throughout this era framed the state in the impulses of war and militarization. From the assigning of surname standards to the deployment of nationalist appeals under the banner of a sacralized monarchy, imperial-ism also provided the backdrop for the striking parallels between the Great Korean Empire state, from 1897 to 1905, and the wartime mobilization state, from the mid-1930s to the early 1940s. The latter represented, in this sense, the culmination of the logic of imperialism as it drove state making in this era. Alternatively, imperialism's facilitation of hyper-nationalist coercion and metropolitan fiats might have steered the late colonial state toward a digres-sion and even a regression from the path of increasing governmentalization.

This possibility is highlighted by the connections that have readily been drawn, though not without strong objection, between colonial developmen-talism and the postliberation states' industrialization campaigns, especially in South Korea beginning in the 1960s.[2] With the implementation of war-time mobilization beginning in 1938, including strenuous measures to raise revenues, target certain heavy industries for much higher outputs, and mobi-lize the populace for greater economic production and sacrifice, the colonial state appears to have dramatically reoriented Korea's economy. Upon check-ing the figures, however, Gim Nang-nyeon has found that in fact the South Korean developmentalist state resembled more the *pre*-wartime colonial state in its allowance for market forces and relative *lack* of intervention and controls, and that in any case, the continuities between the late colonial and postliberation periods are much clearer in the intensive industrialization pursued by North, rather than South, Korea.[3]

The complexities of this issue also suggest that the notion of a developmental state in Korean history must account for more than statistical evidence and patterns of state intervention; it should consider also the role of macroeconomic management as a broader rationalization of the state. Here again, one sees that continuities extended over a longer period and fit common patterns around the world of state-directed and state-protected early industrialization.[4] Indeed, if the postliberation examples of powerful developmentalist states in North and South Korea found their origins in the mid- or late-colonial drive, then in examining the emergence of the early modern Korean state, colonial developmentalism cannot be divorced from precolonial patterns beginning in the Great Korean Empire period.

In trying to demonstrate the coloniality of Japanese colonialism, then, we benefit from recognizing that the boundaries of political control—whether in 1905, 1907, 1910, or 1945—transmitted as much as disrupted. We should consider, in other words, the historicity of colonialism in the broader framework of the emergently modern. This book suggests, for example, that colonialism was not only a practice and ideology, but itself a rationality—a rationality of state making, as much as modern state making was a rationality of colonialism. Indeed, even militarization and war making itself, in a Clausewitzian way, could be considered extensions of the broader phenomenon of modern statecraft coming into form. This in turn appears instructive for considering the Korean colonial experience as a component, and likely an intensification, of an expansive process of modern change, not necessarily its emblem or catalyst.

The Colonizing and Civilizing Thrust of Managerial Legitimation

Having said this, however, the modern era in Korea was indeed very much framed by the colonial, and for the state this reality was most clearly on display in the range of discursive tools to establish or strengthen state legitimacy. These included an extensive slate of propaganda outlets as well as campaigns and spectacles like the coronation ceremonies in 1897 for the founding of the Great Korean Empire. Here, the traditional legitimacy of the Joseon dynasty was refreshed in the circulating discourses of international law and nationalism to express the absolutist authority of a sacralized monarchical state, an approach replicated forty years later. Beyond such appeals to customary authority, the precolonial Korean state also turned toward populism, nativism, infrastructural growth, and foreign recognition as legitimations. These, too, were reprised by the succeeding colonial state, which added security concerns and material expansion—both agricultural and industrial—as well as public services such as medical care, disease control, and sanitation. It also devised policies, such as Cultural Rule and the Rural Revitalization Campaign of the 1920s and 1930s, that provided the discursive and symbolic subtexts for measures in public education, social welfare, and economic growth.

What most fully encompassed the range of legitimizing rationalities in this era, however, was public administration itself, or the premises and promises of a better performing state. This self-referential rationalization of state legitimacy, which this study has called managerial legitimation, was broached by the Gabo Reforms of 1894–95, later became central to justifying the Japanese takeover, and thereafter served as a consistent ideological resource for the colonial regime. Under Cultural Rule, the pursuit of managerial legitimacy fostered semi-liberal practices and perceptions within statist autocracy, as competing and resistant social forces, from Christian clergy to vociferous critics in the press, were absorbed and massaged as much as suppressed. Interestingly, managerial legitimation also incorporated nationalism—first the promotion of Korean identities and customs as part of the multiculturalist approach of Cultural Rule, and then the uncompromisingly Japanese-centered imperialist nationalism of wartime. This latter turn constituted an attempt to exact sacrifices for the military industrialization drive, which served as the potent capstone to the growth of developmentalism—a state rationalization for achieving material expansion, to be sure, but political legitimacy as well.

Finally, the *raison d'etat* remained wedded to the enterprise of social edification. The civilizing thrust of the Confucian Joseon state was sustained by the reformist precolonial state and eventually melded into the premises and objectives of the colonial state, which declared that Japanese colonial rule *in itself* constituted social reform.[5] Indeed, both Confucianism and the discourse of modern civilization served as conveniently powerful repositories for basic lessons of social order and communal loyalty. The civilizing and colonizing imperatives of the state, in short, were mutually constitutive, and even before the onset of colonial rule. The rationalization of dividing religions into those officially recognized and the "pseudo-religions" was, for example, very much a colonialist endeavor, but it was also part of a longer-term pursuit of state secularization through the promotion of religious pluralism. Japanese imperialism absorbed and extended, in this way, an internal colonization effort by the native Korean state already under way since the nineteenth century.

For all the scholarly attention paid to the colonial impact on Korea's modern transformation, this study's findings remind us that such change, while heavily affected by Japan's own experience, preceded colonization and remained a product of multiple inputs and legacies. These include native traditions and internal modernizing efforts, as well as the less conspicuous but lingering Western impact, which also preceded colonization. The emergence of the modern state in Korea thus demonstrated, and to a great extent determined, the transnational, very hybridized character of Korean modernity. This takes us, in turn, toward a consideration of the longer arc of modern Korean history and of the real extent of Japanese influence in state legitimation patterns. The northern and southern regimes that emerged after liberation in 1945 conspicuously relied upon something that the colonial state, notwithstanding its wartime efforts, could not readily draw from: nationalism. The northern regime soon came to base its legitimacy on the anticolonial and anti-imperialist nationalism that clearly functioned as a reaction to colonial forms. But in instilling a nationalist dynastic state, the North also depended on the semiotics of legitimation and mass ideological mobilization from earlier periods extending back to the precolonial state.

It appears also that the North Korean revolution of the immediate post-liberation period maintained the trajectory of increasingly managerial legitimation, one that prioritized the regime's claims of implanting rational, civilizing change through administrative reform while maintaining the extensive information inputs and propaganda outputs that had accrued since the turn of the twentieth century.[6] But even more striking in this sense was what emerged in South Korea, particularly under the reign of Park Chung Hee in the 1960s. Park, without a basis of legitimacy after taking power in a military coup, stressed the merits of what he called "administrative democracy" (*haengjeongjeok minjujuui*) in erecting the twin governing pillars of anticommunism and industrialization.[7] Administrative democracy can be considered a variant of managerial legitimation, which highlighted bureaucratic performance outcomes as central to state legitimacy throughout the early modern era.

The State as a Mobilizing Agent of Modernity: Reifying, Socially Embedded, and Fragmented

Efforts at state legitimation also applied more pointedly to rationalizing the state's command over individual social sectors, for which it played a formative role. In fact the development of every major social realm covered in this book could be considered largely a product of its relationship with the state; and in turn, each of these realms further shaped and sharpened the character of the state itself. The disestablishment of religion, or the pursuit of state secularism, for example, accompanied a broader de-Confucianization of the early modern Korean state, which not only sloughed off Confucianism as the dominant source of statecraft, but also placed it into a reconstructed realm of "religion"—now including Christianity and Buddhism, and eventually Shinto as well—that became segregated from and subordinated under the state. This regulatory recognition of a few select religions while restricting unsanctioned religious groups brought forth major administrative expansion and stirred confrontations with both laymen and clerics, but this, too, further refined the distinction between the two dialectically emergent modern spheres of state and religion.

More reminiscent of their premodern foundations were education and public health, domains with which the Joseon bureaucracy had engaged more routinely. But here, too, the modernizing state, particularly the colonial state, took involvement to another level. Of course public education by definition was an invented state domain, but mass schooling came to be reified through the state's widening efforts to regulate it—including even private schooling—through curricular uniformity, textbook compilation and publication, and teacher training and appointment. Similarly, the state's more systematic interest in disease control and sanitation both fashioned and expanded the ideas and institutions of public health. The proliferation of ordinances and organs tackling the problems that resulted from urbanization, social mobility, industrialization, and war helped construct a realm of microbes, hygiene, social edification, and policing that together constituted a far more distinctive and extensive notion of state control than in the Joseon era. Furthermore, as with education, this actualized sphere of public health came to constitute a major index of civilizational status, state performance, and hence state legitimacy.

Perhaps no realm was as much a creation of the state as "society" itself, or more specifically social categories that came to be analyzed and shaped by the administrative rationalities of population tracking. Whether through household registration or the census, the population became more visible to the modernizing state, if not necessarily coming more into focus. State officials even intervened at the basic sites of private relations, including the family, in order to better know the mostly indecipherable. And they turned to standardization procedures, such as classification schemes for occupation and new conventions for surnames, on two separate occasions. In fact the striking parallels between the precolonial and colonial interventions in this regard testified to the persistence of state measures to reorganize, homogenize, and at times better delineate society.

Such self-serving state efforts to remake society, however, hardly distinguished what happened in Korea. Bureaucratic knowledge production practices in the other major Japanese colony of Taiwan, for example, were even more pronounced and appear to have come close to actually bringing that society into tangible form.[8] As James Scott has shown, the modern state in general, through its instruments of surveillance and domination, began to "read" social relationships in a way that reified its categories and prerogatives of control.[9] Such an objectification of society, which can be considered an intensification of Weberian bureaucratization, turned the population and the infinite variety of social dynamics into a comprehensible, yet sometimes grossly simplified form, the consequences of which often were tragic. Ultimately the conversion of social relations into distinct realms of surveillance and control through classification constituted a companion to territorialization, or the state's conversion of land into territory. The reification of social distinctions required, in fact, the same actions of drawing boundaries—that is, of putting things in their proper spatial and temporal order.

The rationalizing impulses of the state as a cohering and organizing force, however, did not result in a clean separation from society, and in fact this book has revealed a state far removed from pristine autonomy. This challenges the still prevailing view of the modern state, and particularly the colonial state in Korea, as exercising a kind of "demonic omnipotence" commanding absolute submission.[10] Such a notion of a uniformly domineering colonial regime, promoted by different scholarly communities for opposing purposes, has been proven simply inaccurate, and it furthermore elides consideration of Koreans' agency as well as of the makeup of the "state" itself. In demystifying the modern state in Korea, particularly that of colonial rule, one must recognize, again, that it shared common features found in other modernizing states: In their quest for greater authority and capacity, state officials had to cultivate ties to an extensive range of social actors, in a process that Ziya Onis has emphasized as a need for the state to achieve the "embedded autonomy" of infrastructural rather than despotic power.[11] Such a state penetrates, mobilizes, and organizes civil society through adaptation, negotiation, cooperation, and absorption of feedback and resistance.

To be sure, the state also takes on a life and justification of its own, driven by the ambitions of state officials, the momentum of power, and the accumulation of financial and other resources. In Korea, however, such a growth-oriented state was also fragmented along several lines. As this book has shown, the divisions within the state were as intrinsic as its ostensible uniformities. Organizationally, the late nineteenth-century reforms, particularly the *Tongni amun* organs of the 1880s, further fragmented an already divided Joseon state. The Gabo Reforms consolidated rule into a single administrative structure, only to leave room for the Crown to retake a dominant position in the subsequent Great Korean Empire beginning in 1897. This bifurcated state, co-ruled by a monarchy that commandeered most of the economic resources and a supplicating central bureaucracy that nevertheless undertook major reforms, fell to the conquering ambitions of Japanese imperialism, which maintained a weakened Crown under the guise of Korean sovereignty during the protectorate period of 1905–10. The succeeding colonial state, however—while institutionally more coherent—featured its own internal divisions over jurisdiction and resources. Shifts in the ruling figures of the regime, particularly the Governor-General, led to major changes in broader approaches and philosophies. But as with the Gabo Reforms and the Korean Empire, leaders of the colonial state also had to reconcile their ambitions with the influence of various external actors, such as journalists, public intellectuals, businessmen, religious figures, and others who provided not only ideas and support but also stern resistance.

Indeed the dispersal of state power appeared just as critical as its consolidation. Although by no means consistently or smoothly implemented or even planned, for example, the development of the local state and its mediating elements came to constitute a core state rationalization. The centrality of the periphery became more evident as time passed, as measures to transfer greater authority over finances, policing, and public health to the provinces and localities accompanied the heightened cultivation of local actors and interests, particularly during Cultural Rule. This represented, on the one hand, the attempt to negotiate central prerogatives with local needs, but at a broader level, it reflected the balancing of the state's civilizing and disciplining impulse with an absorption of customary, even primal and "irrational" elements of collective identity and culture. Such constraints on administrative rationalizations were seen also in the reformist precolonial states, but they became even more important to the colonial regime, which revealed a strong awareness—indeed, wariness—of the strength of Korean customs and other particularities.

That such expressions of nonconformity, indeed resistance, were absorbed as well as repressed bespoke the diversity of agency in the colonial state. Countless press reports detailed meetings between colonial officials, including members of local governing bodies such as provincial assemblies and school boards, and representatives of civil society, such as educators, religious leaders, and local elites, who often raised fervent objections. Even the propaganda accentuated the regime's mindfulness of opposition to certain state measures, such as those involving education or hygiene and public health. One is tempted to dismiss these acts as indicators of little more than well-oiled discursive manipulation, given the sprawling apparatus of censorship, but such measures also resulted from the insecurities of foreign rule. As this book has demonstrated with examples throughout the era, the authorities were consistently conscious of resistance, and indeed even the late colonial records reveal a strong sensitivity to the uncertainty of their dominion.[12] Nothing better illustrated, then, the metaphorical workings of Yun Hae-dong's "colonial gray zone" than the evolving relationship between the regime and the wide range of nonstate actors who operated within the gaping space between compliance and struggle.[13] The imperatives of total war ultimately dissolved the question of whether the tensions—or contradictions—that arose from these prolonged practices would either be attenuated through more effective governmentalization or develop a momentum that exploded the system altogether. But until then, the colonial state's management of this opposition, largely through co-optation, integration, and incremental change, proved vital to its workings.

None of these considerations, of course, changed the fundamentally discriminatory nature of colonial rule. The ethnic divide between Japanese officials and settlers, on the one hand, and the mass of Koreans on the other, was integral to the functioning of the Government-General, which after all was a conquest state. But within this truism lay a great differentiation across the two ethnicities—both within the state and in the vast majority lying outside it—in terms of backgrounds, interests, and expectations, and colonial officials eventually found themselves prioritizing ethnic coexistence, particularly during Cultural Rule, in order to more fully achieve a governmentalized integration of social elements under state command. Indeed the rationalities of both administration and legitimation depended upon the incorporation of large numbers of Koreans into the state order, starting with the retention of most Korean officials at the moment of annexation and the training of thousands more of the colonized for undertaking the land survey of 1910–18. As the site and agent of such attempts at co-opting and assimilating various subaltern groups—whether marked by ethnicity, class, status, or region—the expanding state solidified its supreme instrumentality in crafting modern society.

One could consider, then, the totalizing wartime measures aimed at coercive assimilation, particularly through the lower-ranking officials' interactions with the populace, as the culmination of unceasing state efforts, since the late nineteenth century, to increase capacities for mobilizing both material and bureaucratic resources. Here the comprehensive role played by the police as the effective stand-in for the state proved indispensable. In turn, this finding offers intriguing signs pointing to the interventionist regimes that emerged in postliberation Korea, for the colonial model appears to have provided a blueprint and foundation for the postcolonial growth of the state as the indisputable source of social power. But there was a difference between domination and mobilization, with the latter proving more potent because it penetrated and absorbed society sufficiently to induce social actors and institutions to work collectively in service to the state.[14] This was, in short, a governmentalized state cultivated for its mobilizational capacity, a hallmark of the Korean regimes in both the South and North, as well as a signal feature of the modern state, from the beginning, as a supreme agent of Korean modernity.

APPENDICES

TABLE A.1 Population, Colonial Period, 1910–1941

	Total Population (Naksungdae)	Total Population (Tōkei nenpō)*	Growth Rate (Tōkei nenpō)	Korean Population	Japanese Population
1910	16,338,840	13,313,017		13,128,780	171,543
1911	16,614,967	14,055,869	5.58%	13,832,376	210,689
1912	16,895,760	14,827,101	5.49%	14,566,783	243,729
1913	17,181,298	15,458,868	4.26%	15,169,923	271,591
1914	17,471,662	15,929,962	3.05%	15,620,720	291,217
1915	17,767,782	16,278,389	2.19%	15,957,630	303,659
1916	17,934,799	16,648,129	2.27%	16,309,179	320,938
1917	18,103,386	16,968,997	1.93%	16,617,431	332,456
1918	18,273,558	17,057,032	0.52%	16,697,017	336,872
1919	18,445,329	17,149,909	0.54%	16,783,510	346,619
1920	18,796,087	17,288,989	0.81%	16,916,078	347,850
1921	18,974,650	17,452,918	0.95%	17,059,358	367,618
1922	19,154,909	17,626,761	1.00%	17,208,139	386,493
1923	19,154,909	17,884,963	1.46%	17,446,913	403,011
1924	19,336,881	18,068,116	1.02%	17,619,540	411,595
1925	19,522,945	19,015,526	5.24%	18,543,326	424,740
1926	19,821,646	19,103,900	0.46%	18,615,033	442,326
1927	20,124,917	19,137,698	0.18%	18,631,494	454,881
1928	20,432,828	19,189,699	0.27%	18,667,334	469,043
1929	20,745,451	19,331,061	0.74%	18,784,437	488,478
1930	21,058,305	20,256,563	4.79%	19,685,587	501,867
1931	21,414,190	20,262,958	0.03%	19,710,168	514,666
1932	21,776,090	20,599,876	1.66%	20,037,273	523,452
1933	22,144,106	20,791,321	0.93%	20,205,591	543,104
1934	22,518,341	21,125,827	1.61%	20,513,804	561,384

(continued)

	Total Population (Naksungdae)	Total Population (Tōkei nenpō)*	Growth Rate (Tōkei nenpō)	Korean Population	Japanese Population
1935	22,899,038	21,891,180	3.62%	21,248,864	583,428
1936	23,173,826	22,047,836	0.72%	21,373,572	608,989
1937	23,451,912	22,355,485	1.40%	21,682,855	629,512
1938	23,733,335	22,633,751	1.24%	21,950,616	633,320
1939	24,018,135	22,800,647	0.74%	22,098,310	650,104
1940	24,301,959	23,709,057	3.98%	22,954,563	689,790
1941		24,703,897	4.20%	23,913,063	717,011

SOURCE: "Naksungdae" figures from Gim Nang-nyeon, ed., *Hanguk ui gyeongje seongjang, 1910–1945*, p. 521.

*The Government-General's Statistical Annual, *Chōsen sōtokufu tōkei nenpō* (*Tōkei nenpō*), appears to have considerably undercounted the Japanese settler population in the first few years of the colonial period.

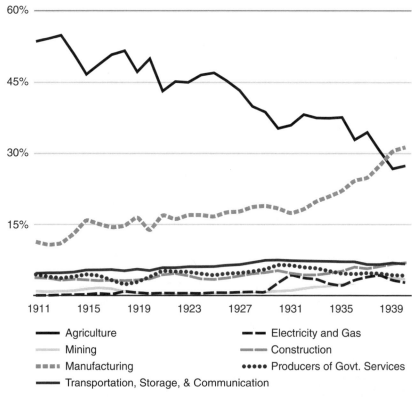

FIGURE A.I. Percentage of Gross Output by Economic Activity. From Gim Nang-nyeon, ed., *Hanguk ui gyeongje seongjang, 1910–1945*, pp. 365–66.

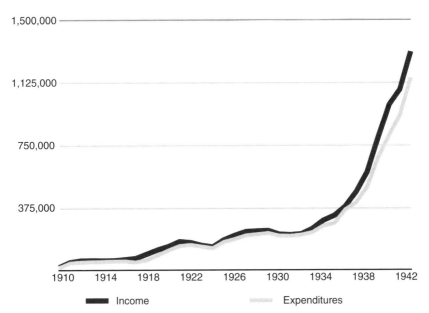

FIGURE A.2. Government-General's Income and Expenditures, 1912–1942 (thousands of yen). From Gim Nang-nyeon, ed., *Hanguk ui gyeongje seongjang, 1910–1945*, pp. 474–75.

State Organization Chart, Gabo Reforms, 1894–1895

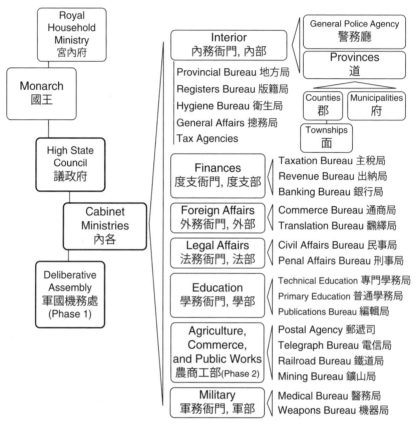

FIGURE A.3. State Organization Chart, Gabo Reforms, 1894–1895. Phase 1: 1894.6–1894.11; phase 2: 1894.11–1895.10.

State Organization Chart, Great Korean Empire, 1902

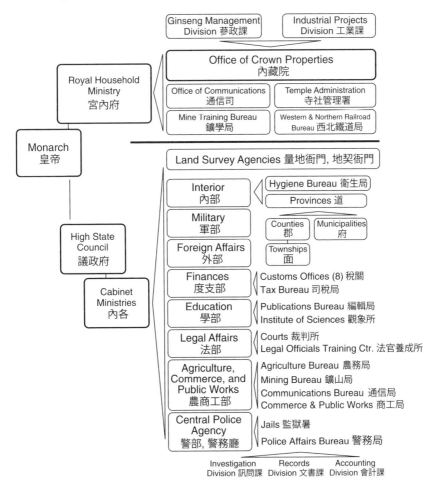

FIGURE A.4. State Organization Chart, Great Korean Empire, 1902.

State Organization Chart, Colonial Government-General, 1921

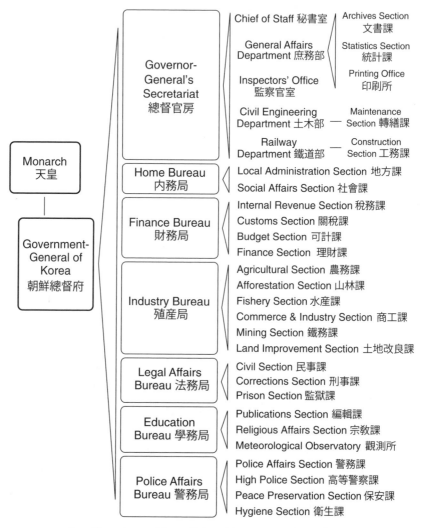

FIGURE A.5. State Organization Chart, Colonial Government-General, 1921.

Affiliated Agencies 朝鮮總督府 所屬官署

Advisory Council 中樞院
- Investigation Section 調查課
- Publication Section 編輯課

Communications Bureau 遞信局
- Electricity Section 電氣課
- Post Offices 郵便局

Courts 裁判所
- Supreme Court 高等法院 — Appeals Courts 覆審法院
- Inspectors' Office 高等法院檢事局 — Local Courts 地方法院

Prisons 監獄 — Local Prisons (15) 監獄分監

Monopoly Bureau 專賣局
- Management Section 業務課
- Manufacturing Section 製造課

Government-General Hospital 醫院
- Medical Departments (11) 各分課
- Medicine Section 醫術課
- Nurses & Midwives Training Ctr. 看護師助産婦養成所

Charity Asylum 濟生院
- Orphans Department 養育部
- Agency for the Blind and Deaf 盲啞部

Customs 稅關
- Surveillance Section 監視課
- Customs Duties Section 稅務課
- Inspection Section 檢查課
- Customs Guard Stations (15) 稅關監視署

Local Land Investigation Committee 高等土地調查委員會

Government Secondary Schools 官立學校

Provincial Governments 各道
- Finance Department 財務部
- Police Department 警務部 — High Police Section 高等警察課
- Home Affairs Department 內務部 — Peace Preservation Section 保安課 — Sanitation Section 衛生課

Charity Hospitals 慈惠醫院　Municipalities 府　Counties 郡 — Townships 面

State Organization Chart, Colonial Government-General, 1942

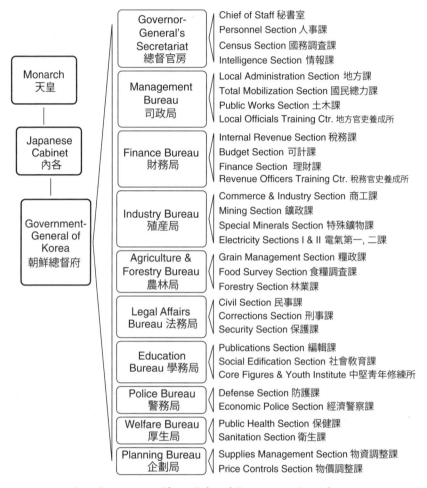

FIGURE A.6. State Organization Chart, Colonial Government-General, 1942.

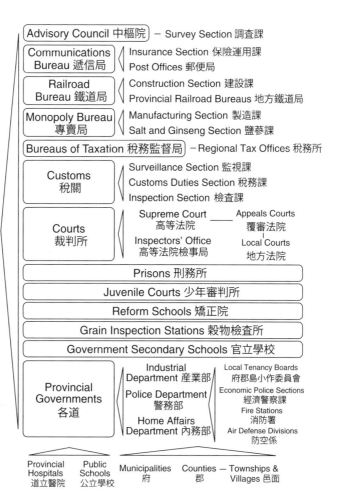

Affiliated
Agencies
朝鮮總督府
所屬官署

Advisory Council 中樞院 — Survey Section 調査課

Communications
Bureau 遞信局
Insurance Section 保險運用課
Post Offices 郵便局

Railroad
Bureau 鐵道局
Construction Section 建設課
Provincial Railroad Bureaus 地方鐵道局

Monopoly Bureau
專賣局
Manufacturing Section 製造課
Salt and Ginseng Section 鹽蔘課

Bureaus of Taxation 稅務監督局 — Regional Tax Offices 稅務所

Customs
稅關
Surveillance Section 監視課
Customs Duties Section 稅務課
Inspection Section 檢查課

Courts
裁判所
Supreme Court
高等法院 ——— Appeals Courts
覆審法院
Inspectors' Office
高等法院檢事局 — Local Courts
地方法院

Prisons 刑務所

Juvenile Courts 少年審判所

Reform Schools 矯正院

Grain Inspection Stations 穀物檢查所

Government Secondary Schools 官立學校

Provincial
Governments
各道
Industrial
Department 産業部 — Local Tenancy Boards
府郡島小作委員會
Police Department
警務部 — Economic Police Sections
經濟警察課
— Fire Stations
消防署
Home Affairs
Department 內務部 — Air Defense Divisions
防空係

Provincial
Hospitals
道立醫院
Public
Schools
公立學校
Municipalities
府
Counties — Townships &
郡   Villages 邑面

NOTES

INTRODUCTION

1. For a recent, systematic reconsideration of both the short-term and long-term colonial legacy in South Korea's political culture and institutions, including those of the state, see Jung Geun-sik and Yi Byeong-cheon, eds., *Singminji yusan, gukga hyeongseong, Hanguk minjujuui*. In English, see the recent study on colonial cultural continuities: Theodore Hughes, *Literature and Film in Cold War South Korea: Freedom's Frontier*.

2. In this study "early modern" is taken as a period within the longer "modern" era, or that from the late nineteenth century to the present day, and not as a period that preceded the modern.

3. Max Weber, *Economy and Society* v. 1, pp. 54, 56. Norbert Elias spoke of this monopolization as part of a broader process of social rationalization that culminates not necessarily in the modern state but rather in the final struggles for interstate or intercivilizational domination. See Elias, *Power & Civility: The Civilizing Process* v. 2, pp. 235–36, 319–36.

4. Weber actually articulated two ideal types of rationality as among the four primary orientations behind social action: behavior that is instrumentally rational (*zweckrational*), driven by goals and expectations of success; and value rational (*wertrational*), driven by beliefs and ethics, regardless of expectations of success. Clearly the rationality most associated with his systemic analysis of modern society, particularly through bureaucratization, was instrumental rationality. This is the formulation that will be used in this study. Weber, *Economy and Society* v. 1, pp. 24–26.

5. Weber, *Economy and Society* v. 1, pp. 223–26; v. 2, p. 954.

6. Weber's conditions for the "position of the official" in the modern (Western) bureaucracy, for example, appear to apply to Joseon: Office holding is a "vocation" for those who hold bureaucratic positions—a regular job for which the official is granted "secure existence" in return for his service; the official enjoys "distinct social esteem" as a member of an entity somewhat floating above the general populace; he

is appointed by a superior authority, not elected; he receives compensation for his services; and he moves up the administrative hierarchy as time passes. See *From Max Weber: Essays in Sociology,* pp. 198–211, 229, 240–41.

7. For an engaging examination of the development of modernization theory out of population studies and other social-scientific analyses of colonialism, see Samantha Iyer, "Colonial Population and the Idea of Development."

8. Michel Foucault, *Security, Territory, Population* (hereafter, STP), pp. 276–77.

9. Bernard Cohn, "History and Anthropology: The State of Play," p. 215. Cohn writes: "What would seem to be the defining feature of modern societies is the explicitness by which ruling groups are concerned with control of the internal and external 'others' and the proliferation of institutions—the police, prisons, social welfare agencies, hospitals, schools and codes (sanitary, criminal, building and occupational)—directed toward civilizing the colonized and controlling the masses at home."

10. Colin Koopman, "The History and Critique of Modernity: Dewey with Foucault against Weber," pp. 210–13.

11. Yun Hae-dong's book by that name, *Singminji ui hoesaek jidae,* was published in 2003, and much of his subsequent work, including on colonial local administration, has further developed this concept and taken it in directions that have compelled him to rethink a wide range of historical conventions, including national history and the "colonial modernity" paradigm. For a more recent expression of his thinking, see Yun Hae-dong, *Singminji geundae ui paereodokseu,* Chapter 2. A recent English-language distillation of some of his concepts uses the term "publicness" instead of public sphere, mostly in order to distinguish the notion, which applies to the colonial realm, from the Habermasian one. See Hae-dong Yun, "Colonial Publicness as Metaphor."

12. Timothy Mitchell, "State, Economy, and the State Effect," pp. 76–97. Similar terms have been forwarded by other scholars, including "state form," "state system," and "state idea." Peter Bratsis notes that even Max Weber, early in his career, once wrote that the state functioned largely as an idea. Bratsis, "Unthinking the State: Reification, Ideology, and the State," Chapter 10.

13. See David Scott, "Colonial Governmentality," p. 201; Bernard Cohn, "History and Anthropology," pp. 215ff; Pierre Bourdieu, "Rethinking the State: Genesis and Structure of the Bureaucratic Field," pp. 53–75.

14. Christopher Pierson, *The Modern State,* pp. 10, 23.

15. This was the case despite the implementation of elections, with restricted voting, for local advisory offices and school boards during the colonial period. See chapter 2.

16. STP, p. 287

17. Benedict Anderson, *Imagined Communities,* Chapter 6.

18. See Andre Schmid, "Colonialism and the 'Korea Problem' in the Historiography of Japan: A Review Article."

19. For a recent expression of this view, see Song Ho-geun, *Simin ui tansaeng—Joseon ui geundae wa gongnonjang ui jigak byeondong.* Song argues that a collective

social subjectivity arose in Korea largely between 1860 and 1910, when the loss of autonomy abruptly and irrevocably cut off this development.

20. For a representative work of this group, see Gim Nang-nyeon, *Ilje-ha Hanguk gyeongje.*

21. Theda Skocpol, "Bringing the State Back In: Strategies of Analysis in Current Research," pp. 9–10.

22. Kyung Moon Hwang, *Beyond Birth: Social Status in the Emergence of Modern Korea,* Chapters 1–2.

23. James Palais, *Politics and Policy in Traditional Korea.* See also chapter 4.

24. Yi Tae-jin has been probably the foremost champion of reconsidering more positively the standing of the Korean Empire, and particularly its monarch. See Yi Tae-jin, *Gojong sidae ui jaejomyeong.* For a less sympathetic portrait of the Korean monarch but a more systematic analysis of the political and geopolitical forces surrounding him and his empire, see Seo Yeong-hui, *Daehan jeguk jeongchisa yeongu.* See also the compilation of discussions and papers from some of the many scholars working on this issue, *Daehan jeguk eun geundae gukga inga?*

25. Recent works have greatly enhanced our understanding of the protectorate period's role in the Japanese takeover, a topic covered earlier in the groundbreaking work by Peter Duus, *The Abacus and the Sword: The Japanese Penetration of Korea, 1895–1910.* See Jun Uchida, *Brokers of Empire: Japanese Settler Colonialism in Korea, 1876–1945;* and Yumi Moon, *Populist Collaborators: The Ilchinhoe and the Japanese Colonization of Korea, 1896–1910.* See also Alexis Dudden, *Japan's Colonization of Korea: Discourse and Power,* for more on the construction of legal sanctioning for the takeover.

26. For an English rendering of this agreement, see Henry Chung, *Korean Treaties,* pp. 213–14. For the political and monetary dealings behind its signing, see Duus, *The Abacus and the Sword,* pp. 180–82.

27. In October of that year Japan's finance minister, Megata Tanetarō, was appointed an advisor for finance matters, and American Durham Stevens was appointed foreign affairs advisor. Stevens would be assassinated in 1909 by Koreans in the nascent immigrant community in the San Francisco area.

28. The text of the treaty can be found in Fukuda Tōsaku, *Kankoku heigō kinenshi,* pp. 551–53.

29. The Korean government agreed to the following provisions: "The Korean government . . . accepts the leadership of the Protectorate in matters of government reform" (Article 1); "In important matters concerning the laws issued by the Korean government, the approval of the Protectorate must be gained" (Article 2); and "The Korean government . . . will appoint Japanese officials recommended by the Protectorate in the Korean government" (Article 5). Yi Wanyong, newly named Premier, and Itō Hirobumi, elder statesman of Japan and for three years the Resident-General, were the two signers. Unlike previous treaties, this one was printed in the Korean government *Gazette,* though without explanation, in a brief special edition entitled "Korean-Japanese Concord" (*Hanil hyeobyak*). *Gwanbo* 1907.7.25.

30. Uchida, *Brokers of Empire,* p. 396.

31. A conspicuous and influential skeptic of recognizing the colonial regime as a viable modern state, Bak strongly implies that the ethnic bifurcation of the populace (Japanese and Korean) under colonial rule overwhelms any consideration of a uniform colonial state or society. See the English-language version of his ground-breaking study: Park Chan Seung, "Japanese Rule and Colonial Dual Society in Korea."

32. Uchida, *Brokers of Empire*, pp. 24, 121–22.

33. Gim Nang-nyeon, ed., *Hanguk ui gyeongje seongjang, 1910–1945*, pp. 468, 478. Based on an analysis of various data points, including official published statistics, this study arrives at a figure of 46.1 million yen for 1911 and 1.53 billion yen for 1943.

34. Most of this liberalization has been attributed to the onset of party-centered politics under the premiership of Hara Kei, who took great interest in the colonies. See Michael Schneider, "The Future of the Japanese Empire, 1914–1931." Schneider finds that Cultural Rule constituted both a declared reorientation of colonial policy and a wide-ranging discursive reconsideration, within the metropole, of the relationships between the components of the empire. For coverage of the impact of Hara Kei's premiership on Taiwan, see Ping-hui Liao and David Der-Wei Wang, eds., *Taiwan under Japanese Colonial Rule, 1895–1945*, Chapters 1 and 6.

35. This irony was not unique to Korea, of course. See Michael Robinson's study, *Cultural Nationalism in Colonial Korea, 1920–1925*, for more on the intense ideological confrontations between conservative nationalists and their fierce critics on the revolutionary Left. In addition to the many studies examining the maturation of Korean literature and literary culture during Cultural Rule, other recent works have examined the cultivation and construction of Korean traditions through archaeology, art history, ethnography, and mass culture. See Hyung Il Pai, *Heritage Management in Korea and Japan;* Virginia Moon, "The Grafting of a Canon: The Politics of Korea's National Treasures and the Formation of an Art History"; and E. Taylor Atkins, *Primitive Selves: Koreana in the Japanese Colonial Gaze, 1910–1945*, Chapters 2–3.

36. Takashi Fujitani, *Race for Empire: Koreans as Japanese and Japanese as Americans during World War II*, loc. 6492. This phrase, the "completion of governmentality," itself is somewhat vague, suggesting that somehow the colonial state had met an imaginary standard beyond which further development would amount only to an elaboration of a successfully achieved governmentality.

37. See Charles Tilly, *Coercion, Capital and European States: AD 990–1992*, Chapters 1 and 7.

38. Todd Henry, *Assimilating Seoul: Japanese Rule and the Politics of Public Space in Colonial Korea, 1910–1945*.

39. Fujitani, *Race for Empire*, locs. 5410–12.

40. Coincidentally, excepting population tracking, the remaining four spheres were the ones specifically cited by an early colonial propaganda work as areas for which the new administration promised improvement over the decrepit native Korean state: industry and material well-being, education and civility, freedom of

religion, health and physical well-being. See Chōsen sōtokufu, *Chōsen tōchi sannen-kan seisaku* (1914), Appendix.

41. In Korean, for example, see Jeong Il-seong, *Inmullo bon Ilche Joseon jibae 40 nyeon, 1906–1945*. In Japanese, see Okamoto Makiko, *Shokuminchi kanryō no seiji-shi*. In English, see Yumi Moon, *Populist Collaborators*; and Todd Henry, *Assimilating Seoul*.

42. Michel Foucault, *Discipline and Punish: The Birth of the Prison,* pp. 168–69.

43. Fujitani's study also provides extensive coverage of how the demands of conscription spurred changes in state policy and functions.

44. STP, p. 293.

45. Marie Seong-Hak Kim, *Law and Custom in Korea*. See also chapters 1 and 7 of the present study.

46. Jonathan Xavier Inda, "Analytics of the Modern: An Introduction," p. 9.

CHAPTER ONE

1. See *Hanguksa* v. 23, p. 13; James Palais, *Confucian Statecraft and Korean Institutions,* p. 25.

2. In fact, neither the form nor content of the state civil service exam, the *munkwa,* changed fundamentally in the 503 years it was administered. See Song Jun-ho, "Joseon hugi ui gwageo jedo," pp. 73–74. The Confucian canon—Four Books, Five Classics, and other works—plus poetry and essay composition remained the basic content.

3. This survey leaves aside the various institutions responsible for catering to the needs of the royal household. Despite their involvement in politics, these organs did not sustain a major administrative role.

4. See Edward Wagner, *The Literati Purges,* Conclusion; and James Palais, "Stability in Yi Dynasty Korea."

5. See John Duncan, *The Origins of the Chosŏn Dynasty,* pp. 230–33. For a run-down of the back-and-forth struggle between these two divisions in the fifteenth century, see *Hanguksa* v. 22, pp. 80–88.

6. The "Three Advisors," the model for the State Council (Uijeongbu) in the Joseon, was not mentioned in the *Rites of Zhou,* which placed the "Six Ministers" at the top of the administrative hierarchy. See James Palais, *Confucian Statecraft and Korean Institutions*, pp. 593–94.

7. See Edward Wagner, *The Literati Purges.*

8. The remaining five were: Gunmulsa (military supplies), Seonhamsa (management of all government ships), Giyeonsa (coast guard), Jeonseonsa (personnel), and Iyongsa (accounting and finances). See Gim Pil-dong, "Gabo gyeongjang ijeon Joseon ui geundae-jeok gwanje gaehyeok ui chui," p. 25.

9. The former Sadaesa (China relations, or "serving the great," department) and Gyorinsa (foreign relations, or "exchange with neighbors," department) were

combined. Yi Gwang-nin, *Gaehwapa wa gaehwa sasang yeongu,* p. 11. See also Choe Byeong-ok, "Gyoryeon byeongdae yeongu," pp. 101–3, for a description of the military administration following the revision.

10. Respectively, the Tongni gunguk samu amun, or Naemu amun, and the Tongni gyoseop tongsang samu amun, or Oemu amun. Gim Pil-dong, op. cit., pp. 37ff.

11. Martina Deuchler, *Confucian Gentlemen and Barbarian Envoys,* p. 94; C. Kenneth Quinones, "The Prerequisites for Power in Late Yi Korea, 1864–1894," p. 211. Gim Hong-jip is an example of such an official.

12. See Martina Deuchler, op. cit., pp. 92–93.

13. *Beomnyeong* v. 1, p. 2 (1894.6.25); "Gun-guk gimucheo," *Gwanbo* 1894.6.28. The decree establishing the Deliberative Assembly listed Gim Hong-jip as president (chongjae), Bak Jeong-yang as vice president (buchongjae), and sixteen councilors (hoeuiwon). The number of councilors would fluctuate slightly over the next few weeks. See Yu Yeong-ik, *Gabo gyeongjang yeongu,* p. 139. The English translation of Deliberative Assembly for the Gun-guk gimucheo comes from W. H. Wilkinson, *The Corean Government* (1897).

14. For a listing of the approximately two hundred resolutions passed by the Deliberative Assembly, see Wilkinson, *The Corean Government,* Appendix 1 (English), or Yu Yeong-ik, *Gabo gyeongjang yeongu,* Appendix 3 (original Chinese and Korean).

15. "Uijeongbu gwanje" and "Gak amun gwanje," *Beomnyeong* v. 1, pp. 4–13 (1894.6.28); *Gwanbo* 1894.6.28. The responsibilities of the former Board of Personnel and Board of Rites were doled out to the Ministries of Finance, Education, and Law. The Six Boards had had subordinate agencies, but they were not arranged according to set standards for name or function, did not account for all functions suggested by the Boards' names (e.g., financial for Board of Taxation, military for Board of War), and often overlapped in responsibility with independent organs. Through the first round of the Gabo Reforms, all the independent organs were incorporated into the ministries, with each specialty area accounted for by a division (*gwa*), which was part of a larger bureau (*guk*), which in turn was part of a ministry (*amun*). Significantly, each ministry contained a Bureau of Accounting (Hoegyeguk).

16. *Beomnyeong* v. 1, pp. 143–44 (1894.12.16). The following spring, the Ministry of Public Works merged with the Ministry of Agriculture and Commerce, and the traditional term of "amun," which the Gabo Reforms had employed to label the ministries, was replaced by "bu," a term that would designate cabinet ministries until the second decade of the colonial period. See *Beomnyeong* v. 1, pp. 198–200, 203–7 (1895.3.25). The Japanese state did not employ the term "bu" (Japanese: "fu")—Japanese ministries were called "shō"—but the greater difference was that in Japan, there were separate army and navy ministries, and a separate Ministry of Communications (Teishinshō).

17. "Kungnaebu kwanje," *Beomnyeong* v. 1, pp. 4–5 (1894.6.28), 68–71 (1894.7.18).

18. The exceptions were the few provisions for the autonomy of finances for the royal household (Article 37). The monarch is actually mentioned very rarely in the

nearly fifty articles of this Accounting Ordinance, as in Article 4, for example, which notes that any extraordinary expenditures required his approval. See Beom-nyul #2, "Hoegyebeop," *Gwanbo* 1895.3.30. See chapter 2 for more on the Gabo fiscal reforms.

19. See Wang Hyeon-jong, *Hanguk geundae gukga ui hyeongseong gwa Gabo gaehyeok,* pp. 424–26. The only noteworthy indication of change in the governing structure came in the fall of 1896, when the cabinet's name fell back to the Joseon designation of "Uijeongbu" and the premier now was given a title that amalgamated the old and the new: Uijeong daesin. See *Gwanbo* 1896.9.26. Beyond this cosmetic step, however, the organization remained unchanged, even when the "imperial" government was declared in 1897. Indeed, when the cabinet, Uijeongbu, changed its name back to "Naegak" ("Cabinet") in 1907, it was little more than an acknowledgment, pushed through by the Japanese protectorate, of the realities of the central system in place since the Gabo Reforms.

20. Its original dozen or so divisions, with approximately 160 officials, eventually added departments responsible for communications infrastructure in 1899, railroads in 1900 (the first railroad line having opened in 1899), police in 1901, and mining and transport in 1902. Seo Yeong-hui, *Daehan jeguk jeongchisa yeongu,* pp. 78–84. See below and chapter 2 for more on the empire's bureaucratic system.

21. See Christine Kim, "The King Is Dead: Monarchism and National Identity in Modern Korea," p. 19ff. Kim notes that the central government, so weakened by the siphoning off of revenue sources by the Crown, was forced to take out a loan from the Office of Crown Properties, which was granted (with interest!).

22. Christine Kim, op. cit.; Seo Yeong-hui, op. cit., p. 80.

23. Gim Dae-jun, who ignores the Office of Crown Properties in his major monograph on state finances of this period, does not consider the Royal Household Ministry as belonging to the Korean state.

24. *Tōkei* (1910), pp. 565–66. The total expenditures went from 2.6 million yen in 1906 to 6.5 million in 1909. In 1909 the grants to the Korean government constituted approximately 70% of the total.

25. *Tōkei* (1909), p. 1009.

26. This occurred following the discovery that Gojong had sent a secret Korean mission to a global conference on colonial issues in The Hague in 1907 to plead for international support in defending Korea against Japanese actions.

27. By 1909, Japanese officials constituted nearly 45% of the full-time officials in the Korean government, with a substantial presence in all ranks. *Tōkei* (1909), p. 614.

28. *Shisei* (1906–7), pp. 118–20, 172–73. Approximately 20% of the increase in the Korean government's expenditures from 1906 to 1907 was for the Interior Ministry, overwhelmingly for the expansion of local policing.

29. Yi Wanyong is the primary example of this kind of Gabo-era reformer who played his political cards well enough in the 1896–1904 period until the arrival of the Japanese provided an external source of assistance for his political ambitions. In this period Yi Wanyong was pro-American, pro-Russian, pro-Japanese, or a

combination of two characteristics, depending on the time and circumstances. But in fact most of the "pro-Japanese" Korean high officials of the post-1907 treaty period had spent the previous decade in exile in Japan following the fall of the final Gabo cabinet in early 1896. See Hwang, *Beyond Birth*, Chapter 2.

30. See Gim Dae-jun, *Gojong sidae ui gukga jaejeong yeongu*, p. 55. The second revision to the High State Council system, in the spring of 1905, appears in *Gwanbo*, 1905.3.1, pp. 184–85. Yi Wanyong was not in this cabinet when this proclamation appeared, but it did include four of the notorious "traitors" (*maegungno*) who were to join Yi in conceding to Japanese demands later that year.

31. The announcement came in a special edition of the government gazette that simultaneously promoted Yi Wanyong from a vice minister to premier. *Gwanbo*, 1907.6.15–18. The cabinet ministers were now called "Gungmu daesin" and the premier, "Naegak chongni daesin."

32. *Beomnyeong* v. 6, pp. 24–29 (1907.8.26), pp. 40–41 (1907.9.4).

33. "Shōsho," *Kanpō* 1910.8.29; Chokurei no. 319, *Kanpō* 1910.8.29; Chokurei no. 354, "Chōsen sōtokufu kansei," *Kanpō* 1910.9.30; and Chōsen sōtokufu kunrei no. 2, "Chōsen sōtokufu jimu bunshō kitei," *Kanpō* 1910.10.1.

34. The organizational responsibilities and structure for these Affiliated Agencies were also promulgated on September 30, 1910. See Chokurei nos. 355–68, *Kanpō* 1910.9.30.

35. *Chōsen shisei nijūgonen-shi*, pp. 317–18.

36. The rail system had been under the supervision of the South Manchurian Railway Company, but through the 1925 measure it became independent of the company and came to administer not only the public but private railroads in the colony as well. *Shisei* (1922), p. 29; (1925), p. 40.

37. *Shisei* (1935), p. 27.

38. Gim Min-cheol, "Jeonsi chejeha (1937–1945) singminji haengjeong gigu ui byeonhwa," p. 306.

39. D. K. Fieldhouse, *Colonialism, 1870–1945*, p. 26.

40. Article 3 of the imperial ordinance that promulgated the "Government-General system" on September 30, 1910 noted somewhat vaguely that the Governor-General, "through the Prime Minister of the Cabinet [of Japan]" (*naikaku sōri taishin o hete*), reported to the emperor and gained the emperor's approval. This wording appears elsewhere, including for the Governor-General's appointment powers for the highest-ranking officials under his command (Article 6). Like the Governor-General, the Vice Governor-General was appointed directly by the emperor. The official narratives into the 1930s insisted that the Cultural Rule reforms eliminated the original military commander requirement for the Governor-General, but a civilian, as it turned out, never occupied this post throughout the colonial era, although a naval commander, Saitō Makoto, held the post in the 1920s. See, for example, *Shisei* (1935), p. 27.

41. Only 16.6% of the *seirei* were implementations of Japanese or imperial laws. Han Seung-yeon, "Jeryeong ul tonghae bon chogdok jeongchi ui mokpyo," pp. 197–99. For more on the juridicial authority of the Governor-General in relation

to the metropolitan state, including its legislature, see Marie S. Kim, *Law and Custom in Korea,* pp. 152–54.

42. Edward I-te Chen, "The Attempt to Integrate the Empire: Legal Perspectives," pp. 245, 261–66.

43. Chokurei no. 407, "Chōsen sōtokufu tokubetsu kaikei kisoku," *Kanpō* 1910.9.30.

44. Gim Nang-nyeon, ed., *Hanguk ui gyeongje seongjang, 1910–1945,* pp. 474–75.

45. The originating imperial ordinances of the Government-General included a decree that specified the necessity for "supplemental funds" (hojūkin) to maintain balance under the "Special accounting regulations" (Chōsen sōtokufu tokubetsu kaikei kisoku) in Korea. Chokurei no. 406, *Kanpō* 1910.9.30.

46. As a reflection of the Government-General's early-colonial encouragement of agricultural investment, the land tax rate remained very low compared to that in Japan—1.3% of assessed value—until the last few years of colonial rule. See Gragert, *Landownership under Colonial Rule,* pp. 116–17.

47. Income taxes took in an average of 30% of all tax revenue in the 1937–43 period, during which its rate of increase was almost 700%, far higher than any other major category. See Jeong Deok-ju, "Ilje gangjeomgi seje ui jeongae gwajeong," pp. 203–4.

48. This figure includes military expenses, which never went over 15% of the total and were usually well below 10% during the 1920s and 1930s. For a sense of the inflation rate over the same period of 1911–40, the price of brown rice and barley increased a little over threefold. Gim Nang-nyeon, ed., *Hanguk ui gyeongje seongjang, 1910–1945,* pp. 353, 412, 468.

49. *Shisei* (1938), pp. 64–70.

50. Gim Nang-nyeon, ed., *Hanguk ui gyeongje seongjang, 1910–1945,* p. 468.

51. The records of this survey are held in the Gyujanggak Library and available online. For example, Namhaehyeon gyeongja gaeryang jeonan ("1720 new registers for Namhae county"), Gyu 14712.

52. *Daehan jeguk ui toji josa sa-eop,* pp. 193–94.

53. *Daehan jeguk ui toji jedo wa geundae,* pp. 60–63, 69–70.

54. See John Duncan, "The Confucian Context of Reform."

55. See Gim Hong-sik, ed., *Daehan jegukki ui toji jedo; Daehan jeguk ui toji josa sa-eop;* Jo Seok-gon, *Hanguk geundae toji jedo ui hyeongseong;* and Choi Won-kyu, "The Legalization of Land Rights under the Great Han Empire."

56. *Yangji amun an* I (1898.7–1899.12) (Gyu 17817). This collection of documents of exchanges between the Yangji amun and the Foreign Ministry (Oebu) includes the articles of agreement with the American ambassador, Horace Allen, designating the duties, pay, and other matters for the American advisor, "Keoreom" (Krumm), who was to receive the "utmost protection" as he conducted his work in the provinces (Article 5). His appointment was for five years. Allen sent a report to Washington, dated July 16, 1898, in which he noted that "An American, Mr. R. Krumm . . . has been engaged as chief engineer of the Korean Government 'for the direction of all engineering work, such as the laying out of irrigation works, roads, bridges,

fortifications, etc.' . . . Mr Krumm is now engaged with the engineering force of the Seoul-Chemulpo Railway." *Consular Reports: Commerce, Manufactures, Etc.* (1898), p. 304. For more on Krumm's work, see Gragert, op. cit., pp. 20, 28.

57. *Daehan jeguk ui toji josa sa-eop,* pp. 17–18.

58. Most of the registers, of which there were different categories depending on which officials constructed them and where they were originally housed, are currently held in the Gyujanggak Library of Seoul National Library and are available to view online. The format of the registers varies according to locality and province, but the same basic information appears for each locale and each parcel, including location, size, productivity, owner, and tenant.

59. *Daehan jeguk ui toji jedo wa geundae,* pp. 65–67. Notices to local officials were printed in the government gazette, *Gwanbo,* in order to inform landlords that they needed to take their old deeds to county and local offices to exchange them for the new deeds. See, for example, the many such notices cited in *Daehan jeguk ui toji josa sa-eop,* pp. 273–75.

60. This restriction was specified through a "correction" of a royal proclamation of late 1901 outlining the "Land Certification Agency personnel and rules pertaining to their duties" (Jigye amun jigwon geup cheomu gyujeong). "Jeongo," *Gwanbo* 1901.11.11 (Article 10). This restriction did not apply to the original open port areas. For the original decree, see *Hwangseong sinmun,* 1901.10.25.

61. *Daehan jeguk ui toji jedo wa geundae,* p. 67.

62. Gragert, op. cit., p. 29.

63. *Daehan jeguk ui toji jedo wa geundae,* pp. 30–31.

64. *Daehan jeguk ui toji jedo wa geundae,* p. 32. According to contemporary Homer Hulbert, the government investment of the equivalent of $200,000 had yielded an increase in land tax revenues to $782,709. See Gragert, op. cit., p. 28.

65. Gim Dae-jun, *Gojong sidae ui gukga jaejeong yeongu,* Chapter 3.

66. Edwin Gragert's American sources suggested that, at its peak in 1901, the survey was one of the largest government budget items. Gragert, op. cit., p. 28.

67. *Ilje ui Changweon-gun toji josa wa jangbu,* pp. 187–88, 193. The period of submitting claims in this area lasted 45 days, from December of 1912 to January of 1913, and the Provisional Land Survey Bureau commenced its surveying work in October of 1913, taking 390 days to complete.

68. Chokurei no. 361, "Chōsen sōtokufu rinji tochi chōsakyoku kansei," *Kanpō* 1910.9.30.

69. Chōsen sōtokufu rinji tochi chōsakyoku, *Chōsen tochi chōsa jigyō hōkokusho* (1918), pp. 6–7. The colonial regime proclaimed that its effort started from a clean slate due to the terribly inefficient and exploitative Joseon system. While acknowledging the Gwangmu survey, this narrative states that its many flaws and failure to finish meant that all the effort ended up "amounting to nothing." And in a familiar trope, the narrative notes that it was not until the reforms instituted under the direction of the protectorate, including proper training of specialists, that meaningful changes took place. The colonial regime undoubtedly relied on documentation from the Gwangmu effort, however, and, as Edwin Gragert has found, many of the

surveyors and administrators of the colonial project had worked on the previous survey. See Gragert, op. cit., p. 71.

70. *Chōsen tochi chōsa jigyō hōkokusho* (1918), pp. 1–4 (preface). See also Governor-General Terauchi Masatake's 1916 exhortation to bureau officials to exert a dignified, sincere effort to bring to a close this "grand project," the success of which he deemed essential to "a balanced taxation system," which in turn was the "basis for establishing [the state's] finances and the entire apparatus of administration." "Kunshi," *Kanpō* 1916.7.3.

71. *Shisei* (1911), p. 25.

72. Jo Seok-gon, *Hanguk geundae toji jedo ui hyeongseong*, Chapter 2.

73. *Chōsen tochi chōsa jigyō hōkokusho*, pp. 37–40.

74. Chōsen sōtokufu rinji tochi chōsakyoku, *Chōsen tochi chōsa jigyō gairan* (1915), p. 13.

75. Gragert, op. cit., p. 72.

76. *Chōsen tochi chōsa jigyō hōkokusho*, pp. 681–86. This increase was far more pronounced for dry fields than paddies.

77. *Chōsen tochi chōsa jigyō hōkokusho*, p. 659.

78. "Rinji tochi chōsakyoku kansei," *Kanpō* 1910.9.30.

79. *Chōsen tochi chōsa jigyō gairan* (1915), pp. 43–44. This source notes that, based on the wisdom gained from the survey done in Taiwan, the colonial authorities emphasized the need for training and deploying "native people" for the colonial cadastral survey.

80. Chōsen sōtokufu rinji tochi chōsakyoku, *Shokuinroku* (1912), p. 39; (1913), p. 54.

81. *Chōsen tochi chōsa jigyō gairan* (1915), p. 39. This data also showed the great disparity in salaries between the two groups in the early colonial period: Japanese officials received between three and four times more than their Korean counterparts, while the gap was a smaller twofold for the contract workers. The ethnic division of labor appears clearly in the most complete set of local documents from the survey to have been preserved and analyzed, those from the county of Changwon that a team of scholars has been examining since the early 2000s. Almost invariably, the documents, such as the land ownership claim forms (*tochi shinkokusho*) or the on-site inspection reports (*jitchi chōsapo*), that specify the land survey officials reveal a Japanese supervisor (*kansain*) overseeing and certifying the surveying work of Korean inspectors (*chōsain*) and surveyors (*sokuryōin*). The former two officials were listed as "technicians" (*gishu*) or "clerks" (*shoki*), while some of the surveyors appear to have been contract workers. See the statistical tables and sample documents in *Ilje ui Changwon-gun toji josa wa jangbu*, pp. 47–48, 61–67, 86, 91.

82. Edwin Gragert argues that this appropriation by the Japanese was minimal and overstated. Gragert, op. cit. pp. 73, 131. A sign of the colonial cadastral survey's social and cultural impact comes from its being viewed as an opportunity for not only Korean landlords but Korean officials attached to the project to enrich themselves or gain bureaucratic advancement. This is what is suggested in the chapter on "Upward Mobility" [*Chulse*] in Yi Giyeong's renowned socialist novel *Home Town*

(*Gohyang*), in which the path to glory of the parvenu protagonist is described as having benefited from his involvement in the survey. Yi Giyeong, pp. 112–14.

83. Yi Yeong-ho, "Daehan jeguk sigi ui toji jedo wa nongmincheung bunhwa ui yangsang," pp. 212–14.

84. Lands belonging to religious entities such as Confucian and Buddhist temples, as well as Christian churches, were required to be designated as semi-corporations when claim forms (*tochi shinkokusho*) were submitted, a step that was touted as part of a general effort to account for traditional Korean customs and practices in the surveying process. See Chōsen sōtokufu kunrei #33: "Rinji tochi chōsakyoku chōsa kitei," *Kanpō* 1913.6.7, Articles 1, 8, 9. Clarifying and selling forest and mountain tracts were actually done through a separate survey, which began in 1911 and took much longer than the cadastral survey. See Yi U-yeon, *Hanguk ui sallim soyu jedo wa jeongchaek ui yeoksa, 1600–1987*, pp. 239–42.

85. Jo Seok-gon, op. cit., 364–65.

86. Wang Hyeon-jong, "Gwangmu yangjeon jigye sa-eop ui seonggyeok," pp. 104–6. Wang was part of a research team, the "Toji daejang yeonguban" ("Land registers research group"), of more than a dozen scholars who exhaustively examined Gwangmu land registers and deeds, among other documents, from various locales and published an authoritative study, *Daehan jeguk ui toji josa sa-eop*. This work generally, though with exceptions, forwarded the idea of a systematic, advanced Gwangmu project serving as the foundation of modern notions of state regulation of private property. *Daehan jeguk ui toji jedo wa geundae* (Land surveying and the modern era) is this group's retrospective compilation of publications that appeared in the wake of that scholarly project.

87. For a lively analysis of the technical advances and methods of the colonial survey, see David Feldman, "Triangulating Chōsen: Maps, Mapmaking, and the Land Survey in Colonial Korea."

88. Gragert, op. cit., pp. 2–3, 29, 52–53, 86. Gragert notes also, however, that the major flaw of the precolonial land system—its decentralized nature, i.e., that much of the land was owned by disparate public entities such as the Crown—was not resolved by the Gwangmu cadastral survey, although the trends pointed in this direction before this survey was halted.

89. Choe Won-gyu, "Hanmal ilje chogi gongto jeongchaek gwa gugyu minyu bunjaeng," pp. 163–66.

90. These colonial survey technicians who had worked for the Gwangmu survey included Gim Yunha, who began training in 1899 and started surveying work in 1901, and Gang Daeseong and Jo Myeongho, both of whom entered the government English school and the surveying training institute of the Finance Ministry (Takjibu) in 1899, and then began their surveying work the following year. Korean technicians comprised 189 out of 255 technicians in the colonial project's Surveying Division (Sokuryōka) of the Colonial Bureau by the end of 1910, 54 of the 84 clerks in the Research Division (Chōsaka), and 3 out of 19 technicians and clerks in the highest division, the General Affairs Division (Shomuka). Out of these three, Gim Gyubyeong had worked as a technician for the Gwangmu survey, while another,

Mun Sangok, had begun his training in 1905. This analysis is based on the data from the online bureaucratic rosters (Kor. *Jigwollok,* Jpn. *Shokuinroku*) from 1908 to 1943, gleaned from published rosters of the time, found in the National Institute of Korean History's "Korean History Database" website (db.history.go.kr), and in the published collection of 3,150 Korean officials' resumes from the first decade of the twentieth century, *Daehan jeguk gwanwon iryeokseo.*

91. In late 1942, for example, wholesale personnel changes in the highest ranks of the colonial officialdom took place as part of the establishment of the Ministry of the Greater Commonwealth (Daitōashō) in Japan proper. *Kokumin sōryoku* 4.11 (Nov. 1942), p. 7.

92. Minami Jirō, "Renmei jidojin ni nozomu" (1939), p. 5.

93. *Sōdōin* 1.1 (June 1939), pp. 41–45. Chapter 3 analyzes the Spirit League in greater detail.

94. *Kokumin sōryoku* 2.11 (Nov. 1940), pp. 2–4.

95. Kokumin sōryoku Chōsen renmei, *Kokumin sōryoku Chōsen renmei yōran* (1943), p. 11.

96. *Shisei* 1941, pp. 459–61; Gim Yeong-hui, *Ilje sidae nongchon tongje jeongchaek yeongu,* pp. 319, 346–47.

97. Gim Yeong-gil, "Gungmin chongnyeok Joseon yeonmaeng ui samuguk gaepyeon," pp. 237–38, 266–67.

98. For more on the state efforts to mobilize and sometimes coerce labor—directly and indirectly, officially and unofficially—see Brandon Palmer, *Fighting for the Enemy*, Chapter 4.

99. Carter Eckert, "Total War, Industrialization, and Social Change in Late Colonial Korea," pp. 12–13.

100. The South Korean National Archives hold several internal documents of the Department of Planning, including reports sent from gunpowder manufacturing firms regarding their organization, output, material needs, and plans to contribute to the mobilization process. Kikakubu, *Shōwa 15-nen butsudō chōsho—kayaku* [1940 materials report—gunpowder], National Archives #88–1.

101. This ordinance detailed new tax rates for existing taxes—such as the corporate income tax, the rates for which more than doubled—and created new taxes on various capital gains. *Kanpō,* 1938.3.31.

102. Kokumin sōryoku Chōsen renmei, ed., *Chōsen ni okeru kokumin sōryoku undōshi* (1945), pp. 150–53.

103. *Shisei* (1941), pp. 461–64, 67.

104. The clampdown on publications after 1940 restricted expressions of resistance, but one can see this in the frequent, subtle entreaties for more positive responses to the relentlessly droning calls for sacrifice. An example comes from the April 1941 edition of *Samcheolli* magazine, wherein the Korean head of the Government-General's Social Edification Office (Shakai kyōikuka), Gye Gwangsun, gave detailed written responses to questions as part of a series of interviews with high officials to facilitate better communication between the authorities and people. At one point, Gye states, "It's really sad that, out of ignorance, [some people] hold a

skeptical attitude or express dissatisfaction and grievances in response to new [war-time] policies. The people should trust and follow the authority of the [colonial] government and dedicate themselves toward service to the greater good in their own way." In the same tone, Gye also reiterates that officials like himself must not abuse their power or act heavy-handedly, for this would impede the transmission of the proper perspectives to the people. Gye Gwangsun, "Chongdokbu godeunggwan jessi-ga jeonsi-ha Joseon minjung e jeon haneun seo" (1941). See also *Todd Henry, Assimilating Seoul,* Chapter 5; and Yun Chung-no, "20 segi Hanguk ui jeonjaeng gyeongheom gwa pongnyeok," p. 98, for further discussion of the coercive structures to induce proper execution of wartime tasks, the mostly performative orientation of the exercises, and of the preference by officials to quantify these performances over evaluating the people's level of sincerity.

105. Gim Yeong-hui, pp. 310–11.

106. See the case study of a locality in Chungcheong province by Yi Seong-u, "Jeonsi chejegi (1937–1945 nyeon) ilje ui nongchon tongje jeongchaek gwa geu silsang," pp. 148–50.

107. An internal police report from 1940, for example, stated that while there was nothing suggesting an uprising, the quantity and quality of violations against control measures were increasing. Yun Hae-dong, *Singminji ui hoesaek jidae,* p. 31. For a literary depiction of this kind of agitated stasis at the end of the colonial period, see Yi Taejun, "Before and After Liberation," in Sunyoung Park, ed. and transl., *On the Eve of the Uprising and Other Stories from Colonial Korea.*

108. Gim Yeong-hui, pp. 357–60. Gim suggests, as do others, that these mobilization structures established the foundation for dictatorial institutions in Korea following liberation.

109. Palmer, op. cit., pp. 6, 13, 111.

110. Charles Tilly has argued that, in Europe at least, state making was very much an institutional product of the imperatives of war making, from revenue collection and conscription to the extension of administration itself. See Tilly, *Coercion, Capital and European States: AD 990–1992,* or the rather provocative expression of this thesis in Tilly, "War Making and State Making as Organized Crime." Here Tilly argues that the modern state, with its claims to provide protection through its monopolization of legitimate violence, engages essentially in racketeering through its taxation practices. Of course the reverse argument is equally persuasive: that war making diverted and squandered financial resources necessary for sustained economic expansion. See Weber, *Economy and Society,* v. 2, p. 921.

CHAPTER TWO

1. Chōsen sōtokufu naimukyoku, *Kaisei chihō seido jissi gaiyo* (1922), p. 7.

2. The famous national "almanac" (*jiriji*) compiled during King Sejong's reign attests to the systematization of the basic Joseon local administration system by the mid-fifteenth century. *Sejong sillok,* vols. 145–55.

3. These inspectors held the power to relieve and arrest, on the spot, local magistrates engaged in illegal activities. Yi Hui-gwon, *Joseon hugi jibang tongchi haengjeong yeongu,* pp. 288–89.

4. For a complete description of the structure of these organs and offices, see Yi Su-geon, *Joseon sidae jibang haengjeongsa,* pp. 221, 230–31; and Yi Jon-hui, *Joseon sidae jibang haengjeong jedo yeongu,* pp. 18–20, 206–7.

5. There were also two technical officials sent from Seoul: one pharmacologist (*simyak*) and one legal official in each province. See Yi Hui-gwon, op. cit., pp. 37, 39–40. This responsibility for judging the propriety of the province's county magistrates ("popyeom") was wide-ranging and constituted one of the two primary duties—the other being administrative—of the provincial governor as well as of the vice governor.

6. Yi Su-geon, op. cit., pp. 222–23.

7. This was the law of avoidance, which kept local officials away from their home areas out of concerns for corruption through local connections. See James Palais, *Politics and Policy in Traditional Korea,* pp. 12–13.

8. These are among the well-known critiques offered by perhaps the most prominent exegesis on local administration problems in the late Joseon, *Mongmin simseo,* by Jeong Yagyong. An English translation of this work has recently been published: Yagyong Chong, *Admonitions on Governing the People.*

9. Yi Su-geon, op. cit., p. 275.

10. Kyung Moon Hwang, *Beyond Birth,* pp. 181–89.

11. Sun Joo Kim, "Taxes, the Local Elite, and the Rural Populace in the Chinju Uprising of 1862," pp. 1017–20.

12. *Beomnyeong* v. 1, p. 148 (1894.12.16).

13. The county magistrate remained the only official specified, however, while "other employees," presumably the clerks, constabulary personnel, and runners were "determined ad hoc [*byeoljeong*]." This was the case for clerks and administrative specialists, or *jusa,* as well, as the ordinance simply stated that the total number of *jusa* for all provincial government offices would be 330, with their distribution to be determined by the Minister of Home Affairs, not the provincial governor. See *Beomnyeong* v. 1, pp. 239–41 (1895.3.26). Two months later, the Gabo government even overhauled the provincial layout, from the eight provinces (*do*) system that dated back to the early Joseon dynasty, to that of twenty-three smaller provincial regions (*bu*). This measure also consolidated all the different categories of Joseon counties and county magistrates into the singular designations of "gun" and "gunsu," respectively. A further departure from Joseon practice was the assignment of police officials to each provincial office: one police supervisor, one police assistant, and one or two patrolmen. See *Beomnyeong* v. 1, pp. 398–405 (1895.5.26); *Gwanbo* 1895.5.29–30. Soon after the final Gabo cabinet fell in early 1896, however, the provincial divisions reverted to a modified version of the Joseon eight-province arrangement, with several large provinces divided into the northern and southern halves, that exists to this day, at least in South Korea. And following Joseon practices, Seoul was designated a special administrative zone, with its mayor equal in rank to that of

a provincial governor, while several locales gained the status of municipality (*bu*): Gwangju, Gaeseong, Ganghwa, Incheon, Dongnae (Busan), Deogwon (Wonsan), and Gyeongheung. *Gwanbo* 1896.8.4.

14. The Tax Agencies—presumably one for Seoul and each of the eight provinces—and Collection Offices together employed almost 900 government collectors (*jingse jusa*). These collectors were to collect only the specified amount and only from those designated by the orders, established in writing, of the tax levying officials. See Chingnyeong no. 56, "Gwansesa geup Jingseseo gwanje," *Beomnyeong* v. 1, pp. 248–50 (1895.3.26); Chingnyeong no. 71, "Suip gyuchik," *Beomnyeong* v. 1, pp. 321–26 (1895.4.5).

15. *Gwanbo* 1895.9.7; *Gwanbo* 1896.8.4. See also Yi Yeong-ho, *Hanguk geundae jise jedo wa nongmin undong*, pp. 103–5; and Hwang, *Beyond Birth*, p. 397.

16. Yi Hun-sang, "Gabo gyeongjanggi jibang jedo wa gunsa jedo ui gaehyeok geurigo jiyeok sahoe ui dae-eung." This study of the local responses to these reforms in the county of Dongnae (now part of Busan) has found that, among other consequences, the order to eliminate the local military stations in the summer of 1895 caused significant economic disruptions.

17. In one example of a compromise solution to the conflict of central control and local resistance, Yi Hun-sang shows that the Dongnae magistrate of the second half of 1895, Ji Seogyeong—a prominent figure of this era—selected the individual township heads (*myeonjang*), but only from people who were nominated by local actors. Yi Hun-sang, "Gabo gyeongjanggi," pp. 328–38.

18. *Gaksa deungnok*, Gyu 18154, 1894.11.19; Gyu 18022, 1904.6.20, 1904.6.27, 1900.5.22, 1906.8.7.

19. *Gaksa deungnok*, Gyu 18154, 1897.2.18; Gyu 18022, 1898.5.17, 1898.9.3, 1900.9.25.

20. Jo Seok-gon, "Gwangmu yeon-gan ui hojeong unyeong chegye e gwanhan sogo," pp. 155–56.

21. See Yumi Moon, *Populist Collaborators*, Chapters 5–6, for a detailed accounting of the destabilizing activities of the Iljinhoe at this time. See also Yi Yeong-ho, *Hanguk geundae jise jedo wa nongmin undong*, Chapters 2 and 4. Corruption, by all accounts, remained a major problem in the countryside at the turn of the twentieth century. Hwang Hyeon, in *Maecheon yarok*, detailed many such incidents of corruption, as did foreign observers such as Horace Allen and Homer Hulbert. On New Year's Day of 1906, the Korean government itself, while not abolishing the provincial and local system instituted in 1896, issued a stern warning that the continuing maladministration, waste, and fraud of the provincial and county governments would henceforth be sternly punished. *Beomnyeong* v. 4, pp. 474–75 (1906.1.1).

22. The first round came in the fall of 1906, which implemented a simpler layout of personnel: A governor, a reestablished vice governor, and police commissioner (*gyeongmugwan*) were now the only high-ranking officials in the provincial governor's office, joined by a small group of eight or fewer specialists (*jusa*) and four or fewer police supervisors (*chongsun*). The county magistrate's office was even sparser, with only two required positions—the magistrate (*gunsu*) and a clerk (*seogi*) in each office. *Gwanbo* 12:819–21, *Beomnyeong* v. 5, pp. 184–87 (1906.9.).

23. *Gwanbo* 13:639–40 (1908.6). The revisions of the following month, in July of 1908, established divisions of the interior and police (Gyeongmubu and Naemubu) within each provincial government, and "tax offices" (*semuseo*), then "finance offices" (*jemuseo*) in the local administrative districts. *Gwanbo* 1908.7.23.

24. The provision for the Rijichō appears in Article 3 of the 1905 protectorate treaty. In 1906, the Residency-General determined that there would be a Rijichō consulate in ten localities, but this later changed to thirteen: Seoul, Incheon, Busan, Masan, Mokpo, Gunsan, Jinnampo, Pyongyang, Wonsan, Seongjin, Cheongjin, Daegu, and Sinuiju. Each Rijichō office was headed by a director (*rijikan*), and included one or two vice directors, secretaries, a police division, and interpreters.

25. For more on the function and history of the Rijichō in Korea, see Fukuda Tōsaku, *Kankoku heigō kinenshi,* pp. 556–57; *Shisei* (1910), pp. 15–20.

26. See the proclamation of the provincial and local government system in Royal Ordinance (*chokurei*) #357, *Kanpō* 1910.9.30.

27. As was the case during the previous fifteen years, a province was broken down into counties (*gun*) and municipalities (*fu*), which were the same twelve districts that previously had been home to the Rijichō, i.e., urban areas with substantial Japanese communities. The provincial administration under the governor was divided into two divisions, or *bu*: Division of the Interior (Naimubu), which had been in place earlier, and the Division of Finance (Zaimubu), which replaced the Division of Police (Keisatsubu) as the second division. The *fu* municipalities at the beginning of the colonial period were the same localities for Rijichō offices from the late protectorate period.

28. See the official history of the development of the township system in *Chōsen shisei nijūgonen-shi* (1935), pp. 239–41. The officials were the township chief and the clerks (*shoki*), among whom were also the planning committee members, all salaried, and unsalaried district heads in each of the smaller administrative districts within each *men*.

29. *Shisei* (1906–7), p. 191.

30. Through a survey of local landlords' records in the county of Gurye, Yi Jong-beom has found in the ledgers that, over the 1910s, the surcharges paid by landlords were restructured to two main fees, which were paid not to the village head but directly to the township head. And these fees were designated for the upkeep of the new *men*-centered administration, particularly for the salaries of the township officials. See Yi Jong-beom, "Hanmal ilje-cho toji josa wa jise munje," pp. 602–4.

31. Jang Deok-ju, "Ilje gangjeomgi seje ui jeongae gwajeong e gwanhan yeongu," pp. 198–99. Through an analysis of published figures, Chang finds that the ratio between central tax revenues (*kokuzei*), including customs duties, and provincial and local taxes (*chihōzei*) was approximately 6:4 in the 1920s and 1930s. Beginning in 1938 under wartime mobilization, however, the proportion of revenues taken in by the central state began to climb, and by 1943 it took in nearly 80%. See also Son Nak-gu, "1923–24 nyeon Joseon chongdokbu ui semu gigu dongnip jeongchaek," pp. 82–84. Son argues that opposition from various quarters within and outside the

Government-General, including the Korean propertied class, helped scuttle an attempt by the colonial regime in the mid-1920s to revamp the revenue system through, among other means, establishing a general income tax, which would not be implemented until 1934.

32. Dozens of high-resolution images of Saitō's inspection tours around the colony can be found on the website, "Uri yeoksa net," from the National Institute of Korean History (http://contents.history.go.kr/photo/1920.do). Accessed February 2015.

33. *Chōsen shisei nijūgonen-shi*, pp. 63–64, 319. All five Observation Officers eventually took higher office as governors or vice governors in the 1920s and 1930s. See also *Chōsen tōchi hiwa*, pp. 260–68; and Gang Dong-jin, *Ilbon ui Hanguk chimnyak jeongchaeksa*, p. 183. Furthermore, in the fall of 1919, fifty-one Korean local elites recommended by provincial offices as dependably "pro-Japanese" were sent through a five-day crash course, including an audience with the new Governor-General Saitō Makoto himself, on the basics of the upcoming "new administration" in order to relay reassurances to the Korean masses. These local elites even received a commemorative gift. *Joseon tongchi bihwa*, p. 142.

34. *Chōsen shisei nijūgonen-shi*, p. 318. The functional distribution within each provincial office, furthermore, was substantially diversified and expanded. A Police Department (Keimubu) joined the Home Affairs and Finance Departments of the previous decade, then later in the 1920s, a Department of Industry (Sangyōbu) was installed in the Gyeonggi, North Gyeongsang, and South Gyeongsang provincial offices. Each of the departments was in turn further subdivided into specific divisions (*ka*) headed by a director (*rijikan*), one of whom usually was a Korean.

35. *Chōsen sōtokufu kansei to sono gyōsei kiku*, pp. 67–70.

36. Gim Ok-geun, *Ilje-ha Joseon jaejeongsa nongo*, pp. 223–24.

37. *Shisei* (1935), p. 543.

38. *Tōkei* (1930), pp. 746–53.

39. *Shisei* (1935), pp. 31, 528. Part of this revision was the establishment of the general income tax, inheritance tax, and beverage tax (*seiryō inryōzei*).

40. Richard Devine, "Japanese Rule in Korea after the March First Uprising: Governor-General Hasegawa's Recommendations," pp. 532–34.

41. See figure 12. The precipitous changes between 1918 and 1919 were the result of the post–March First reforms, including the recategorization of military police as salaried, ranked civilian police. But this shift in the police constituted only about one-third of the personnel changes.

42. STP, pp. 315, 322–27, 339–41.

43. See Code of Punishments (*Hyeongjo*), "Capturing Thieves" (*Podo*), *Daejeon hoetong* v. 4, pp. 76–82.

44. According to Zhu Xi himself, the Confucian ideal taught that a good government maintained proper social order primarily through the proper display of virtue and ritual, and only secondarily through (the threat of) punishment. See William Shaw, *Legal Norms in a Confucian State*, p. 14.

45. As Robert Spaulding has found, in contemporary Japan "political power was not personified by the remote and seldom-seen elite of the Diet, Cabinet, and higher civil service, but by the ubiquitous civil police" and other lower-end officials such as tax clerks and school teachers. See Spaulding, "The Bureaucracy as a Political Force," pp. 36–37.

46. "Gyeongmucheong gwanje jikjang," *Beomnyeong* v. 1, pp. 38–41 (1894.7.14), p. 17 (1894.7.1), p. 85 (1894.8.6).

47. In just the first four months of publication, *The Independent's* reports included notices of the following police activities: apprehending petty thieves (1896.4.23), major thieves (1896.6.16, 1896.8.13), remnant Donghak rebels (1896.8.1), gamblers (1896.5.23), counterfeiters (1896.5.7), and corrupt officials (1896.6.20); recording household registration information (1896.5.7); preventing unauthorized construction (1896.5.23); enforcing weapons restrictions (1896.6.2); taking in abandoned infants (1896.6.18); and issuing sanitation notices (1896.7.16). Interestingly, the newspaper's editors, led by the Christian doctor Seo Jaepil, also seemed particularly keen on the police's duties to suppress shaman activities ("sorcerers," "devil worship") (1896.5.23, 1896.5.28, 1896.6.2, 1896.6.13). See chapters 6 and 8 for more on this connection. Criticisms were also directed at the Police Agency's disregard for the medical condition of prisoners (1896.8.22, 1897.3.6).

48. *The Independent*, 1897.3.6, 1897.4.7.

49. From 1900 to 1902, for a period of twenty months, the Central Policy Agency (Gyeongbu) functioned as an independent ministry. Im Jun-tae, "Hanguk geundae gyeongchalsa sogo," pp. 399–403. Another revision in early 1902 specified a maximum of 142 total officials and police officers nationwide. *Beomnyeong* v. 3, pp. 352–57 (1902.2.16).

50. A revision of the local policing system in early 1905 specified that each of the twelve ports and municipalities with centrally appointed police officials would employ two supervisors (*chongsun*) and at least one patrolman (*sungeom*). See *Beomnyeong* v. 4, p. 31 (1905.2.26).

51. Chingnyeong #113, *Beomnyeong* v. 1, p. 437 (1895.5.10); Naeburyeong #3, *Beomnyeong* v. 1, p. 482 (1895.6.5); *Beomnyeong* v. 2, pp. 2–3 (1896.1.8).

52. This duality was modeled after that of contemporary Japan. *Beomnyeong* v. 1, pp. 41–47 (1894.7.14).

53. Naeburyeong #15, *Gwanbo* 1898.8.1.

54. Military police units had been in Korea since the early months of 1896, when they came to protect Japanese telegraph lines immediately following the fall of the Gabo Reforms. *The Independent* newspaper ran many reports (for example, 1896.4.7, 1897.1.23, and 1897.8.24) of both cooperation and clashes between Korean and Japanese police over jurisdiction. Japanese policemen also ventured into the interior. A news item in the *Hwangseong sinmun* of 1899.5.29, for example, reported that Japanese police officials in Incheon embarked on a survey trip of fishing grounds in Chungcheong province along with a representative from the Incheon Japanese Chamber of Commerce (Sangeop hoeuiso).

55. *Shisei* (1906–7), pp. 108–13.

56. *Shisei* (1906–7), pp. 10–11, 118–20.

57. *Daehan jeguk jigwollok* (1908), Naebu, Gyeongsicheong & Do gwanchaldo (Guksa pyeongchan wiwonhoe website, accessed February 2012). With the exception of the South Hamgyeong Province interior division, the director of each provincial interior ministry (*naemubu*) as well as provincial police ministry (*gyeongmubu*) was already Japanese. See *Daehan maeil sinbo* 1906.9.8 for more on Maruyama.

58. *Shisei* (1906–7), pp. 172–74; *Daehan jeguk jigwollok*; *Tōkei* (1908–9), pp. 583–87. The proportion appears to have remained the same the following year, according to the published budget, when local policing funds would constitute 42% of the Interior Ministry's budget. See *Hwangseong sinmun*, 1910.1.6 and 1910.1.7.

59. In 1908, there were, respectively, 1,862 Korean civilian police officials and 3,128 Japanese, with the corresponding totals for 1909 being 2,077 and 3,259. As for military police, in 1908 there were 2,374 Koreans in 1908 and 4,234 Japanese. The corresponding figures for 1909 were, respectively, 2,369 and 4,392. *Shisei* (1908–9), pp. 58–60.

60. *Shisei* (1906–7), p. 127. One suspects that some of these Korean recruits to the *kempeitai* came from the former Korean army, which was disbanded beginning in 1907.

61. *Tōkei* (1908–9), pp. 613–18.

62. *Shisei* (1911), pp. 61–69; (1915), pp. 29–33.

63. *Tōkei* (1917–18).

64. See Matsuda Toshihiko, *Nihon no Chōsen shokuminchi shihai to keisatsu*, pp. 267–68. Matsuda notes that, while there was widespread agreement about the need to reform the colonial police system, particularly through the abolition of the military police and their close ties to the army units on the peninsula, the long-term vision for the post–March First reforms differed significantly between the Japanese government led by Hara Kei, who wanted the new police to facilitate the extension of home rule to the peninsula, and the colonial bureaucracy, which prioritized above all the strengthening of pacification powers through an increase in civilian police forces in the countryside. The intensive, rapid implementation of the latter priority would establish the enforcement basis for implementing Cultural Rule. See also Joseon chongdokbu, *Joseon tongchi bihwa*, pp. 43–44, 115.

65. *Chōsen sōtokufu keisatsu no gaiyō* (1922), p. 3.

66. *Chōsen sōtokufu keisatsu no gaiyō*, pp. 4–5. Maruyama Tsurukichi, the Government-General's Police Commissioner at the time, claimed that over 10,000 new patrolmen had to be recruited, and the goal was to take 3,000 new recruits from Japan, as well as an additional 5,000 who had been patrolmen in Japan, with the remaining to consist of former Japanese and Koreans attached to the military police in Korea. *Joseon tongchi bihwa*, pp. 119–23.

67. *Chōsen sōtokufu keisatsu no gaiyō*, p. 17.

68. Matsuda, pp. 459–87. Matsuda notes that the "popularization of the police" ideal was a direct extension of similar developments in the metropole, which in turn was a result of the political liberalization in Japan that came to exert significant influence over the administration in Korea following March First.

69. *Chōsen jijō* (1943), pp. 262–63.

70. Matsuda, pp. 684–87.

71. The following is a breakdown of the 20,769 police officials in the colonial state in 1938: 71 commandants (*keishi*), who mostly staffed the central Police Headquarters and provincial Police Departments; 477 commanders (*keibu*) and 895 lieutenants (*keibubo*), who mostly headed the county Police Offices; and 20,326 patrolmen (*junsa*), who comprised 98% of the total. This was representative of the proportions throughout the colonial period after 1919. *Shisei* (1938), p. 538.

72. See *Chōsen keisatsukan shokuinroku* (1932). As of 1932, out of the top five positions in each of the thirteen provincial offices—sixty-five total posts around the colony—only four were held by Koreans, with one occupying the post of higher affairs division chief (*kōdō kachō*), and the remaining three taking the fourth-highest post of provincial security division chief (*hoan kachō*) in South Pyeongan, Hwanghae, and South Gyeongsang province, respectively.

73. This was the natural result of the Cultural Rule goal of having each of the more than two thousand township-level police substations (*shuzaisho*) around the colony staffed by at least one Japanese and one Korean patrolman. *Joseon tongchi bihwa*, p. 118.

74. This dilemma, of having to staff half of the 15,000 new civilian police positions with Koreans of questionable loyalty and motivations, apparently remained a source of great concern in the early years of Cultural Rule. *Joseon tongchi bihwa*, pp. 79–84. But according to the Government-General's own figures, the demand for such positions among Koreans was extraordinarily high: ten to twenty applicants for every post. Chung-chih Chen, "Police and Community Control Systems in the Empire," p. 236.

75. *Daehan jegukgi jeongchaeksa jaryojip* v. 7, p. 1 (1894.7.12).

76. The major revisions of the fall of 1895 included the delineation of local councils into three types (village, township, and county levels) and an expanded list of areas of responsibility: education, household registers, granaries, road upkeep, industry promotion, and revenue collection, among others. *Daehan jegukgi jeongchaeksa jaryojip* v. 7, pp. 32–33 (1895.10.26).

77. In perhaps an indication of ideals outpacing realities, Japanese premier Hara Kei declared that even Koreans resistant to colonial rule would be hired if they were influential and respected in their respective localities, so determined was the new Cultural Rule regime to locate talented Koreans who could contribute to the new administration. Joseon chongdokbu, *Joseon tongchi bihwa*, p. 165.

78. *Shisei* (1935), pp. 532, 535, 537.

79. Yun Hae-dong, *Jibae wa jachi—Singminji chollak ui samgungmyeon gujo*.

80. Ji Su-geol, "Iljeha ui jibang tongchi siseutem gwa gun danwi." Ji finds also that these local "agents" (*kkeunapul*) cultivated by the regime exerted a baneful influence through their continuity—both in the patterns of local society and in the actual people themselves—into the postliberation era. Ji, "Ilje gun-gukjuui pasijeum gwa 'Joseon nongchon jinheung undong.'"

81. The matrix of local officials, particularly surrounding the township chief, local clerks, and local constables, appears as a common trope in the literary depictions of

local life. Regarding the hierarchy between the county magistrate and the township chief, one of the more interesting scenes appears in episode 45 of Gang Gyeong-ae's famed proletarian novel of the mid-1930s, *Ingan munje* ("The Human Predicament"). In his capacity as the local township chief, a main character, depicted as a representative of the exploitative and largely inscrutable state, arranges for a visit of the newly appointed county magistrate, who proceeds to give a lecture to assembled farmers (who appear out of fear of possible fines if absent). In his exhortations for very specific agricultural and behavioral changes in line with the Rural Revitalization Campaign, the magistrate appears as the main political figure in the locality, with one of the farmers even remarking how impressive it is that someone of such stature would know and seem to care so much about the farmers' lives. On the other hand, in a sign of the administrative reforms, the magistrate, in his remarks urging the farmers to pay their taxes properly, also reminds them of the vital fiscal responsibilities of the township office for ensuring local welfare. See Gang Gyeong-ae, *Ingan munje (oe)*, pp. 131–33. For the English translation, see Kang Kyŏng-ae, *From Wonso Pond*, pp. 102–4.

82. See Chōsen sōtokufu naimukyoku, *Kaisei chihō seido jissi gaiyo* (1922). This work by the regime touts and details the heavy representation of local Korean voices in these provincial and local councils, including school boards, as a sign of the new age of cooperation between the two ethnic communities.

83. See Hwang, *Beyond Birth*, Chapter 5.

84. A report in the magazine *Samcheolli* in 1937 appears to share the view that the traditional administrative powers wielded by the county magistrate, and even the provincial governor, had been on the decline for some time, with the magistrate consigned mostly to ceremonial duties, and the governor replaced by specialist bureaucrats heading the three main departments (interior, finance, and police) in the provincial office. See "Sipsam dojisa inmulpyeong—Chungbuk jisa Kim Dong-hun gun" (1937).

85. Chōsen sōtokufu, *Chōsen ni okeru nōsanyoson sinkō undō* (1935), pp. 67–77.

86. Yun Hae-dong, *Jibae wa jachi*, pp. 226–27, 263–65.

87. Gragert, *Landownership under Colonial Rule*, pp. 137–49. Gragert notes that the dramatic drop in rice prices, which hit some areas of Korea "like a tsunami," amounted to 50% between 1929 and 1931, with pre-1929 prices not being regained until 1934. Not unexpectedly this resulted also in the further concentration of landholdings in large Japanese corporations tied to the lending banks, and over the longer term, in the hands of Japanese investors and local Korean landlords as well.

88. Gi-Wook Shin, *Peasant Protest and Social Change in Colonial Korea*, pp. 122–25.

89. A planning committee, headed by the Vice Governor-General, was established in late September of 1932, soon followed by committees at the provincial and local levels the following month. At the county and township level, the committees were headed by the county magistrate and township chief, respectively, and included the local police chief and heads of credit cooperatives and schools. Kunrei #62, *Kanpō* 1932.9.30; Keikido kunrei #15, *Kanpō* 1932.10.15; Zenra nando kunrei #28, *Kanpō* 1932.11.28.

90. Newspaper coverage of the anticipation, promulgation, and particularly the establishment of local committees, cooperatives, surveys, and lecture sessions around the colony was extensive. The *Donga ilbo* newspaper contained hundreds of reports of such activities, for example, although its coverage was generally one of restating the goals and claims of the campaign instead of reporting whether such goals were being realized. See, for example, from the campaign's first year, *Donga ilbo* 1932.4.4, 1932.10.5, 1932.10.14, and 1933.1.12. Sample forms for officials conducting surveys of targeted households can be in found in Chōsen sōtokufu, *Nōson sinkō undō no zenbō* (1935), pp. 135–45.

91. *Shisei* (1941), pp. 453–56. Interestingly the government's statistical breakdown divided the results according to region: north, central, and south. See also Gi-Wook Shin and Do-Hyun Han, "Colonial Corporatism: The Rural Revitalization Campaign, 1932–1940," pp. 83–92. The authors argue that the vertically integrated organization of the campaign constituted a corporatist system due to the emphasis on cooperative, mobilizational, and ideological elements in a process driven by the state.

92. Chōsen sōtokufu, *Chōsen ni okeru nōsanyoson sinkō undō* (1935), pp. 18–19, 67–77.

93. Yun Hae-dong, *Jibae wa jachi*, pp. 357–58.

94. See, for example, newspaper reports from 1936 that youth members of the local revitalization committee in Jangseong county in Jeolla province were arrested on suspicion of forming a secret communist network and purchasing leftist books, while another man working in a revitalization committee in Bucheon county in Gyeonggi province was sentenced to a year in prison for engaging in a similarly suspect "ideological movement." *Joseon ilbo* 1936.10.14 and 1936.11.2, in *Ilje chimnyak-ha Hanguk 36-nyeonsa* v. 11.

95. "Chōsenbun sinbun kiji sakujō chūi kiji yōshi—*Chōsen nippo*," *Chōsen shuppan keisatsu geppo* (Korean publications police monthly report) no. 77 (1935.1.15); "Chōsenbun sinbunshi sashiosa kiji yōshi—*Chōsen chuō nippo*," *Chōsen shuppan keisatsu geppo* no. 96 (1936.8.30).

96. *Shisei* (1941), p. 456; "Nam chongdok ui yeonseol, dojisa hoeui eseo," *Samcheolli* (1940.6).

97. Yun Hae-dong, *Jibae wa jachi*, pp. 362–64, 373.

98. Gim Yeong-hui, *Ilje sidae nongchon jeongchaek yeongu*, pp. 340–41.

99. Yi Seong-u, "Jeonsi chejegi (1937–1945 nyeon) ilje ui nongchon tongje jeongchaek gwa geu silsang," pp. 137–43. Quotation from p. 140.

100. See Gim Yeong-hui, op. cit., pp. 354–55, for more examples of this kind of disinterest and ignorance.

101. Yi Seong-u, p. 151; Todd Henry, *Assimilating Seoul,* Chapter 5. See also Lee Songsoon, "The Rural Control Policy and Peasant Ruling Strategy of the Government-General of Chosŏn in the 1930s–1940s," pp. 15–22.

102. After a steady climb beginning in the late 1910s, the agricultural sector's production hit its nadir in the Depression, in 1930, and the recovery to 1929 levels did not occur until 1934. Thereafter until 1940, agricultural output approximately

doubled. In the same time span, from 1934 to 1940, the construction sector increased fourfold, mining fivefold, and manufacturing fourfold. Gim Nang-nyeon, ed., *Hanguk ui gyeongje seongjang, 1910–1945,* pp. 35–36, 365–66.

103. Yun Hae-dong, *Jibae wa jachi,* pp. 243, 264; Yi Seong-u, op. cit., pp. 154–64.

104. See Bak Chan-seung, *Ma-eullo gan Hanguk jeonjaeng,* pp. 44–48.

CHAPTER THREE

1. Christopher Pierson, *The Modern State,* pp. 22–25.

2. Antonio Gramsci, *Selections from the Prison Notebooks,* pp. 145, 373, 405–6, 530–32, 546. Gramsci perceived the state not only as a governing institution, and hence a coercive force, but also as the instrument of a particular group's more comprehensive, ideologically grounded civil hegemony.

3. Graeme Gill, *The Nature and Development of the Modern State,* p. 136.

4. A larger purpose of Garon's book, *Molding Japanese Minds,* which extends its coverage from the Meiji era to the late twentieth century, appears to be to explain the Japanese high savings rate in lieu of welfare—and hence to account for Japan's high economic growth—and to reexamine Japanese explanations (emperor system, repressive state) of their failures to resist authoritarianism and militarism before 1945.

5. See James Palais, "Confucianism and the Aristocratic / Bureaucratic Balance in Korea," *Harvard Journal of Asiatic Studies* 44.2 (Dec. 1984): 427–68.

6. This can be explained, as Martina Deuchler put it, by "the Confucian conviction that human nature can be perfected from without, regardless of whether this nature is originally good or bad." Deuchler, *The Confucian Transformation of Korea,* p. 24.

7. The *Jiphyeonjeon* is renowned for its central role in the formulation of the native Korean alphabet, but its primary function was to undertake intensive research into the clarification of ancient Confucian ideals and models, in essence refining and augmenting the canonical foundation for the newly incorporated state ideology. The *Jiphyeonjeon* did so by publishing a vast quantity of Confucian texts in the mid-fifteenth century.

8. Bak Chan-seung, "20 segi Hanguk gukgajuui ui giwon," p. 200. Bak also suggests (p. 207) that the strong paternalism of Confucian family ideology steered Koreans toward statism in the early modern era.

9. Wang Hyeon-jong, "Daehan jegukgi ipheon nonui wa geundae gukgaron," pp. 307–9.

10. One telling example of this was a royal proclamation to all his subjects a few days following the commencement of the Gabo Reforms, in which the monarch declares his culpability in the current dire circumstances and hence the need for "fundamental change" (byeonhyeok), "reform" (gaehyeok), and "renovation" (yusin) in the state. *Beomnyeong* v. 1, pp. 20–21, *Gwanbo* 1894.7.4. The document reads as if it was drafted by the Gabo officials themselves and issued in the king's name.

11. Yi Tae-jin, ed., *Gojong sidae ui jaejomyeong*, pp. 77, 273–75.

12. See Wang Hyeon-jong, op. cit., pp. 326–36.

13. *Beomnyeong* v. 2, pp. 541–43 (1899.8.17).

14. See Harada Kan, "Kenkoku kara heigō ni itaru Taikan teikoku," pp. 50–51. Harada calls the proclamation of the "Imperial System" an attempt to "privatize the state" (*kokka o kasanka*) by the monarchy, which exacerbated the confrontation between the Crown and top officials.

15. Andre Schmid, *Korea between Empires*, p. 72.

16. Liah Greenfield, *Nationalism: Five Roads to Modernity*.

17. Prasenjit Duara, *Sovereignty and Authenticity: Manchukuo and the East Asian Modern*.

18. The use of "self-help," or *jajo*, overlapped with that of "self-strengthening" in this period, with the former developing into a term in reference to reforming individual behavior and Korean society as a whole in the early colonial period. See Choe Hui-jeong, "1910 nyeondae Choe Namseon ui 'jajoron' beonyeok."

19. "Gukga ui gaenyeom (sok)" [Concept of the *gukga* (continued)], *Seobuk hakhoe wolbo* #17 (1908.5), in *Hanguk gaehwagi haksulji* v. 6, p. 452. See also Han Gwangho, "Tongchi ui mokjeongmul" [Object of rule], *Seou* #5 (1907.1), *Hanguk gaehwagi haksulji* v. 5, pp. 275–77.

20. Bak Chan-seung, "20 segi Hanguk gukgajuui ui giwon," pp. 205–7; Gim Do-hyeong, *Daehan jegukgi ui jeongchi sasang yeongu*, p. 101.

21. Kyung Moon Hwang, "Country or State? Reconceptualizing Kukka in the Korean Enlightenment Period, 1896–1910." See, for example, Seol Taehui, "Gukga ui uiui" [Meaning of the *gukka*], *Daehan hyeophoe hoebo* 3 (1908.6), *Hanguk gaehwagi haksulji* v. 3, pp. 180–81.

22. Yu had spent much of the 1880s, following his return from a trip around the world, under house arrest for his associations with the 1884 Gapsin Coup. During that time in partial incarceration, Yu drafted *Seoyu gyeonmun*, arguably the most influential work of the Korean enlightenment period, and certainly the work that had the greatest impact on the program of the Gabo Reforms, even before it was formally published. This book was modeled on a similar work, *Seiyo sijo*, by his mentor Fukuzawa Yukichi, and copied much of it, though not its chapter on the "country's rights." See Yi Gwang-nin, "Yu Giljun ui gaehwa sasang," pp. 45–92, for a comparison of the two works.

23. Yu Giljun, "Bangguk ui gweolli," in *Yu Gil-chun jeonseo*, v. 1, p. 85.

24. "Gungmin ui pyeongdeung gweolli" [The equal rights of citizens], *Hwangseong sinmun* 1899.3.13.

25. *Gungmin suji* (1905), pp. 19–21. Written anonymously and published by a local official, *Gungmin suji* appears to have enjoyed wide circulation among officials and intellectuals. In several parts of the work, such as in the final chapter on "the rights of the gungmin," *Gungmin suji* clarifies and repeats the assertions in *Seoyu gyeonmun* about the inviolability of rights and the connection between the government's protection of these rights and its external fate. Choe Gi-yeong suggests, in fact, that the anonymous author was none other than Yu Giljun, writing incognito

from his exile in Japan. Choe Gi-yeong, *Hanguk geundae gyemong undong yeongu,* pp. 22–43.

26. The Iljinhoe originated in the Donghak movement—the same one that in 1894 had led the largest uprising against the Joseon state. See Yumi Moon, *Populist Collaborators.*

27. See "Shōsho" (p. 1), "Jōyaku" (p. 3), and "Yukoku," in *Kanpō,* 1910.8.29. The expression of a desire for the annexation by the reigning Korean monarch, Sunjong, appeared in a declaration attributed to him that was published on the front page in the August 30, 1910 edition of the Korean-language colonial government organ, *Maeil sinbo,* when the paper also carried other royal decrees concerning the annexation. It stated that the conjoining of the two royal households constituted the transfer of sovereignty over Korea, which the Korean monarch deemed the best course to secure "peace in East Asia" and "the welfare of the people in the eight provinces [of Korea]."

28. The imperial edict (*shōsho*) on the annexation and establishment of the Government-General of Korea of late August of 1910 opened with a lamentation on the incapacity of Korea to be sufficiently reformed to remove itself as "the source of calamity" in Japan's security. Hence the decision, "in response to the demands of the times," to "forever annex Korea into the Japanese empire." See *Kanpō* 1910.8.29. See also a similar emphasis on mutual security as the basis for joining the two countries, with Korea taking Japan's lead, in the editorial on the "Principles of Amalgamation" in the *Maeil sinbo* newspaper of August 30, 1910 (p. 2). Often appearing in these narratives, including the imperial edict of August 29, is a portrayal of a country, prior to annexation, overrun by instability and even banditry, and hence requiring a resolute, dramatic solution. See, for example, Chōsen sōtokufu, *Chōsen tōchi sannen-kan seiseki* (1914), p. 2.

29. Peter Duus, *The Abacus and the Sword.*

30. Mark Caprio, *Japanese Assimilation Policies in Colonial Korea, 1910–1945,* pp. 8–12.

31. The transition from the Korean government to the Government-General is said to have resulted in the reduction of over 1,400 government officials and a savings of 700,000 won through gains in efficiency. Chōsen sōtokufu, *Chōsen tōchi sannen-kan seiseki,* p. 3.

32. Terauchi Masatake, "Kankoku heigō ni kan suru yukoku" (1910.8.29), in Chōsen sōtokufu, *Chōsen tōchi sannen-kan seiseki,* Appendix, pp. 1–5. Governor-General Terauchi opened the proclamation with reminders of the "generous grace" of the Japanese emperor in reference to the major financial investment to improve Korea. This document also declared a general tax amnesty in response to the "urgent need to raise the people's strength." The annexation treaty itself, in the sixth (out of eight) articles, mentions briefly a commitment to protect Koreans' "bodies and property" and to the "promotion of their material welfare" [*furiku no zōshin*]. "Jōyaku," *Kanpō* 1910.8.29.

33. This was the narrative pattern also in the extensive rundown of improvements in the first three years of colonial rule found in Chōsen sōtokufu, *Chōsen tōchi sannen-kan seiseki,* pp. 1–72.

34. "Joseon tongchi ui seonggong," *Maeil sinbo* 1911.5.5.

35. As Jun Uchida shows, this moniker was forwarded not only by Korean critics of the Government-General, but perhaps even more vociferously by Japanese settlers who criticized the regime's stripping of their special privileges in the colony. Uchida, *Brokers of Empire,* p. 134.

36. "Joseon tongchi samnyeon," *Maeil sinbo* 1913.12.21–24.

37. So Bong-saeng, "Joseon tongchi ui seongjeok," *Maeil sinbo* 1915.10.19–1915.11.02.

38. Mark Caprio, op. cit., pp. 112–29; Jun Uchida, op. cit., p. 222.

39. See Alexis Dudden, *Japan's Colonization of Korea: Discourse and Power,* Chapter 1.

40. Tōkan furei no. 50, *Kanpō* 1910.9.29. Most of the ordinances issued on the day of annexation dealt with the transfer of authority from the Korean and protectorate governments, financial affairs, and legal and commercial relationships within the Japanese empire. The first "system law" (*seirei*) formally declared that existing imperial laws and the laws of the former Korean government would still apply "for the time being."

41. Chul-woo Lee, "Modernity, Legality, and Power in Korea under Japanese Rule."

42. Ryu Seung-nyeol, "Ilje-ha Joseon tongchi seryeok ui jibae ideollogi jojak gwa gangje," pp. 122, 143.

43. Among the first imperial ordinances (*chokurei*) on the day of annexation was one that bestowed upon the Governor-General the power to issue the "system laws" (*seirei*) that pertained only to the colony. The issue of the relationship between this legislative power and those agencies in Japan proper was left vague; the imperial ordinance stated simply that the Governor-General's laws should gain approval from the Japanese prime minister's office unless it was an urgent matter. Chokurei no. 324, *Kanpō,* 1910.8.29, p. 5. See also Tōkanfu kunrei #16, *Kanpō* 1910.8.29.

44. Yi Seung-il, *Joseon chongdokbu beopje jeongchaek,* p. 372. Yi argues that all of this was settled to a considerable extent in the 1940s, when wartime mobilization's imperatives forced the streamlining of the legal system empire-wide, weakening any special provisions for the colony.

45. These goals were expressed officially by the new Governor-General of September 1919, Saitō Makoto. See Joseon chongdokbu, *Joseon tongchi bihwa,* p. 19.

46. Hashimoto Tetsuma, *Chōsen tōchi no shōrai* (1921), pp. 5–6.

47. Hashimoto, pp. 9–10.

48. See Michael Robinson, *Cultural Nationalism in Colonial Korea;* Michael Robinson, "Broadcasting, Cultural Hegemony, and Colonial Modernity in Korea, 1924–1945"; Gi-Wook Shin, *Ethnic Nationalism in Korea,* Chapters 2–3. See also Todd Henry, *Assimilating Seoul: Japanese Rule and the Politics of Public Space in Colonial Korea, 1910–1945,* which reveals the discursive variety, including among nationalist critiques, that proliferated in response to the state-led campaigns and infrastructural development in the showcase capital during Cultural Rule; and Jennifer Jung-Kim, "Gender and Modernity in Colonial Korea," which analyzes the

women's journals of the time as signifiers of major cultural and socioeconomic transitions.

49. A dedicated "Social Affairs Section" (Shakaika) was established within the ministerial-level Home Bureau (Naimukyoku), as well as in separate provincial governments, in July of 1921. In 1936 these expanding responsibilities were divided into two ministries, with an extra "Social Edification Section" (Shakai kyōikuka) created in the Education Bureau (Gakumukyoku). See Chōsen sōtokufu gakumu-kyoku shakai kyōikuka, *Chōsen shakai kyōka yōran* (1938), pp. 19–20.

50. Komagome Takeshi, *Shokuminchi teikoku Nihon no bunka tōgō,* pp. 192–93; Caprio, op. cit., Chapter 4. See also C. Miura, "The Problem of Korean Assimilation" (1921), pp. 130–34. Miura suggests that assimilation remained the ultimate goal and that the problem may have lain with terminology. He notes that, over the first decade of rule, "it was seen that the word 'assimilation' was not agreeable to the Korean people, as it savored of ultimate Japanese dominance. Hence this word should be changed to 'harmonization' or 'amalgamation,' or some word embodying a more conciliatory idea. The idea of cultural development succeeded the attempt at assimilation . . . [and] the feelings and sentiments of the Korean people considered more carefully than before." This is what he deemed "a real amalgamation of the two peoples." Miura also insists that there is no possibility for granting Korea independence, "much as we may sympathize with her national pride," for too much was sacrificed by the Japanese to gain Korea, and "in all her history we have no record of the Koreans having attained independence nor do they seem fitted for it"—a common Japanese refrain at the time regarding Korea's past.

51. Gim Sanghoe, "Munhwa jeongchi ui geunbon jeongsin" (1922), pp. 2–3.

52. *Joseon tongchi bihwa,* pp. 160–61.

53. "Coronation Ceremony," *The Independent* 1897.10.14.

54. Andre Schmid, op. cit., pp. 74–76.

55. *Dongnip sinmun* 1897.10.12, 1897.10.14.

56. In addition to the *taegeuk* symbol, three other recurring images were used for such purposes: the plum flower, the rose of sharon, and the falcon. See Mok Su-hyeon, "Daehan jegukgi gukga sigak sangjing ui yeonwon gwa byeoncheon," and Mok, "Daehan jegukgi ui gukga sangjing jejeong gwa Gyeongungung."

57. The Monarch's Birthday, according to the government-published *New Elementary Reader* (*Sinjeong simsang sohak*) from 1896, was September 8, and on that day the people (*gungmin*) were to take a break from their work, express congratulations, and hang the Korean flag in front of their homes. Hangukhak munheon Yeonguso, ed., *Hanguk gaehwagi gyogwaseo chongseo,* v. 1, pp. 373–74. According to the government ordinance of July 1909 detailing how to implement the Primary School Ordinance, schools would close for the following holidays: the emperor's (Sunjong) birthday (Geonwonjeol), foundation day of the Joseon dynasty, foundation day of the Daehan jeguk, the anniversary of the emperor's ascent to the throne, and the ancestral shrine day of the Yi monarchical house. See "Botong hakgyo-ryeong silhaeng gyuchik," in *Botong gyoyukhak* (1910), Appendix, pp. 13–14.

58. Todd Henry, *Assimilating Seoul,* pp. 24–26.

59. Christine Kim, "Politics and Pageantry in Protectorate Korea (1905–10): The Imperial Progresses of Sunjong."

60. Jun Uchida, *Brokers of Empire,* Chapter 6.

61. Mok Su-hyeon, "Joseon misul jeollamhoe wa munmyeonghwa ui seonjeon." Mok argues that the Korean Art Exhibition, which was highly publicized by the Government-General and drew tens of thousands of visitors every year, became a visual conduit for the altered recreation of contemporary Korea in accompaniment to the civilizing discourse that emphasized the colony's cultural development. See also Virginia Moon, "The Grafting of a Canon," Chapter 3, for more on the museum's exhibits.

62. Timothy Mitchell, "The World as Exhibition," pp. 218–19; and Gyan Prakash, *Another Reason,* p. 19. These two studies, coming in the wake of Benedict Anderson's pioneering work on the origins of modern nationhood, are part of a large body of stimulating scholarship on colonial museums, expositions, and other spectacles.

63. For a thorough analysis of the semiotic, classificatory, consumerist, and discursive representations of the 1915 Fair, see Se-mi Oh, "Consuming the Modern: The Everyday in Colonial Seoul, 1915–1937," Chapter 1.

64. *Shisei gonen kinen Chōsen bussan kyōshinkai hōkokusho,* v. 1 (1916), pp. 79, 123. This voluminous, comprehensive program book for the event shows that one of the exhibition spaces designed to stage the contrast between the "old and new" administration featured police-related items, including precolonial Korean contraptions and methods used for meting out punishment or capturing criminals, in addition to a special exhibit on Korean "superstitions."

65. "Sijeong onyeon ginyeom Joseon mulsan gongjinhoe e daehan gamsang" *Sin mungye* (1915.1), p. 3.

66. The official sponsor was the *Keijō nippo* newspaper, the organ of the Government-General. The basic plans for the Exposition, including details of exhibitions and targeting of bureaucratic resources, were promulgated half a year before its opening in September of 1929. Pointedly the official purpose of the Exposition was articulated as promoting industry as well as "cultural development." Kunrei no. 4, "Chōsen hakurankai jimu shōtei," and Kokuji no. 111, "Chōsen hakurankai kisoku," *Kanpō* 1929.3.29.

67. *Maeil sinbo* 1929.9.2; *Jungoe ilbo* 1929.9.12. The *Maeil sinbo* newspaper, the Korean-language mouthpiece of the regime, provided extensive coverage before the opening in order to build anticipation. The latter report, from a nationalistic Korean paper, claimed that the Exposition's opening went ahead as planned despite not being completely ready, with the colonial government having already invested 2–4 million yen in the venture.

68. "Joseon bangnamhoe gaegwan," *Joseon* (1929). Among other exhibition halls the following themes were featured: Industry, Society and Economy, Education and Art, Transportation and Construction, Electricity and Machinery, Japanese Prefectures, Taiwan, Army and Navy, Railways, and Motion Pictures. Films were shown in the Motion Picture Exhibition Hall (Katsudō shashinkan). A separate exhibition

hall was also dedicated to the Japanese firm Mitsubishi, which operated several major plants in Korea.

69. Hong Kal, "Modeling the West, Returning to Asia: Shifting Politics of Representation in Japanese Colonial Expositions in Korea." Kal suggests that this multicultural vision of the Japanese empire was a prelude to the full-throttled pursuit of the "Greater East Asian Co-Prosperity Sphere [Commonwealth]" during the Pacific War beginning in the late 1930s.

70. *Chōsen daihakurankai no gaikan* (1940), p. 3.

71. Todd Henry, *Assimilating Seoul,* Chapters 3 and 5.

72. Yun Hae-dong, *Singminji ui hoesaek jidae,* pp. 239–49. Yun suggests that the Rural Revialization Movement not only appropriated the native nationalist and socialist efforts centered in the rural areas, but effectively neutralized them. See also Albert Park, "Visions of the Nation: Religion and Ideology in 1920s and 1930s Rural Korea," Chapter 5.

73. Ugaki's analysis of the rural problem was expressed in many outlets, including a proclamation issued at a meeting of provincial governors in June of 1932. See Yi Yun-gap, "Ugaki Gajeusige chongdok ui siguk insik gwa nongchon jinheung undong ui byeonhwa," pp. 48, 53–54. See also Gi-Wook Shin and Do-Hyun Han, "Colonial Corporatism: The Rural Revitalization Campaign, 1932–1940," pp. 79–83.

74. This term for "self-awareness" or "self-consciousness," coupled with the term for hard work, appeared frequently in publications to promote or explain the campaign. See, for example, the use of "jagak bullyeo" (self-awareness and strenuous effort), "jabun gongnyeo" (individual diligence and collective effort), and "jagak balbun" (self-awareness for stimulating hard work) to describe the necessary ingredients for success in the campaign, by the Gyeonggi provincial governor in his introduction to a Korean-language pamphlet that touts the movement's accomplishments but reiterates the need to further work at realizing "good customs and beautiful habits" (*yangpung misok*). Gyeonggi provincial government office, *Nongchon jinheunghoe yaksok* (1936), pp. 3–4.

75. Chōsen sōtokufu, *Chōsen ni okeru nōsanyoson sinkō undō no dai ichiji nōka kōsei keikaku jisseki* (1935), pp. 21–23; Chōsen sōtokufu, *Nōson sinkō undō no zenbō* (1935), p. 40.

76. Mun Young-joo, "Rural Rehabilitation and Colonial Subjects during the 1930s," pp. 167, 170.

77. *Nongchon jinheunghoe yaksok,* p. 5. Gim Yong-cheol, "Ugaki Gajeusige ui Joseon tongchigwan," p. 157.

78. Yi Yun-gap, pp. 73–75.

79. *Chōsen ni okeru nōsangyoson sinkō undō no dai ichiji nōka kōsei keikaku jisseki,* pp. 31–32.

80. Minami Jirō, "Nentō shokan" [New year's thoughts], *Chōsen gyōsei* 1.1 (1937), pp. 4–5.

81. *Sōdōin* v. 1.1 (1939.6), p. 3.

82. See, for example, Gim Yeonsu, "Shinteki o semuru kakugo" [Determination to smite the main enemy], *Kokumin sōryoku* 4.12 (December 1942), pp. 47–48, in

which Gim, the head of the Social Services Department (Kōseibu) of the League, urges the readership to dig in psychologically for a long confrontation against the British-American forces in this, the one-year anniversary of the commencement of the "Greater East Asia War." This was one of several contributions to this journal made by perhaps the most prominent collaborationist businessman, Gim Yeonsu, head of the Gyeongbang textiles company.

83. Yun Chiho, "Tōa no shinkensetsu to naisen ittai" [*Naisen ittai* and the new construction of East Asia], *Sōdōin* 1.1 (June 1939), pp. 21–23.

84. Probably the most notorious public figure was the novelist Yi Gwangsu, who promoted even the eradication of the Korean language. For more on Yi's collaborationism, see John Whittier Treat, "Choosing to Collaborate: Yi Kwangsu and the Moral Subject in Colonial Korea," pp. 88–90. Treat argues that Yi, fueled by a social Darwinistic fatalism, viewed the absolute embrace of Japanese identity as the only solution to the existential problem of being both modern and Korean.

85. Otaka Chōyū, *Kokutai no hongi to naisen ittai* (1941), pp. 77–79, 84–85.

86. Morita Yoshio, ed., *Chōsen ni okeru kokumin sōryoku undōshi* (1945), pp. 106–7. Morita served as a leader of the *Ryokki renmei* ("Green flag league"), a group formed to assist in the mobilization campaigns in Korea. For more on Morita, see Jun Uchida, *Brokers of Empire*, pp. 342–43, 368–69.

87. *Sōdōin* 1.1 (1939), pp. 46–48, contains detailed instructions on properly observing Navy Memorial Day.

88. See Yi Seong-u, "Jeonsi chejegi (1937–1945 nyeon) ilje ui nongchon tongje jeongchaek gwa geu silsang," pp. 143–47.

89. *Shisei* (1941), pp. 469–71. The propaganda films in particular have gained considerable scholarly interest with their recent rediscovery and release.

CHAPTER FOUR

1. This principle is well articulated by Theda Skocpol: "A state's means of raising and deploying financial resources tell us more than could any other single factor about its existing (and immediately potential) capacities to create or strengthen state organizations, to employ personnel, to coopt political support, to subsidize economic enterprises, and to fund social programs." Skocpol, "Bringing the State Back In," p. 17. For more on the emergence of this equation between a state's strength and security, on the one hand, and notions of "wealth" and management of resources, on the other, see Foucault, *Security, Territory, Population*, p. 294.

2. Bruce Cumings, for example, has forwarded the notion of a northeast Asian developmentalism beginning in the first half of the twentieth century, when Japan, through its colonization of Taiwan and Korea, eventually exported its model throughout the region. He labels these states as "BAIRs," for "bureaucratic-authoritarian industrializing regimes," a more specific reference to the indispensable requirement of a powerful, indeed nonliberal, state in the process. See Cumings, "Webs with No Spiders, Spiders with No Webs: The Genealogy of the Developmental

State," p. 70. And Atul Kohli has applied this model of an interventionist, developmental state beyond East Asia in his comparison of postcolonial states in South Korea, Nigeria, Brazil, and India—all having in common the experience of colonial rule but forging diverse postcolonial paths toward industrial growth. The countries that experienced the most success, he notes, were those in which the state played a dominant, indeed intrusive role in negotiating colonial legacies with postcolonial demands. Kohli is particularly struck by Korea's colonial heritage, which, to be sure, "left behind a considerable density of entrepreneurship in South Korea," but, more significantly, established the behavioral patterns of a "bureaucratized, penetrating, and architechtonic state." See Kohli, *State-Directed Development*, pp. 55, 61.

3. Hugo Radice has defined the developmental state's workings as being driven by "the principle that existing price relativities and other market signals should be deliberately distorted, through selective tariffs, subsidies and access to finance, in order to induce a step-change in the pace and direction of capital accumulation." Radice, "The Developmental State under Global Neoliberalism," p. 1154.

4. Alexander Woodside, *Lost Modernities*.

5. There is a body of literature that denies the colonial ties to the South Korean (or North Korean) developmental state, on the grounds that the most consequential features of development and / or the developmental state emerged after liberation. See, for example, Wonik Kim, "Rethinking Colonialism and the Origins of the Developmental State in East Asia."

6. A representative work from this group of economic historians is Myun Soo Cha and Nak Nyeon Kim, "Korea's First Industrial Revolution," p. 28. The authors conclude that the basis for the take-off of industrialization was set in the colonial period, when the colony achieved higher rates of economic growth than the average around the world, though not nearly the level achieved in post–Korean War South Korea. The primary difference was the much higher rate of educational opportunity in South Korea, which stood in contrast to the much lower levels of both education and income distribution in the colonial period. More recently, however, Kim (Gim Nang-nyeon) has also concluded that the continuities between the late colonial and postliberation periods in terms of industrialization were far stronger for North Korea than South Korea, particularly in the degree of state intervention in market mechanisms. The North Korean state, in short, followed the pattern established by the colonial regime of the 1930s and especially the wartime period much more closely than its southern counterpart. See Gim Nang-nyeon, "Singminji Joseon gyeongje ui jedojeok yusan."

7. Carter Eckert, *Offspring of Empire*. See also Bruce Cumings, "Colonial Formations and Deformations: Korea, Taiwan and Vietnam."

8. For well over a century, this has been a prevailing view of the origins of the Meiji imperialism that eventually engulfed Korea, and for almost as long, the distinctiveness of the Japanese version of this common pattern of imperialism has been considered the result of Japan's defensive, backward, insecure position in the era of high imperialism. See Duus, *The Abacus and the Sword*, Chapter 1, Conclusion.

9. Ha-Joon Chang, *Kicking Away the Ladder*, pp. 31, 40, 47. Chang shows that almost all states adhered to nonliberal, nonclassical policies in their earlier stages of

economic development as a means of nurturing native markets and industries, including especially intensive infrastructural investment. See also Ziya Onis, "The Logic of the Developmental State," p. 124; and Graeme Gill, *The Nature and Development of the Modern State,* pp. 30, 127–28, for more on the purposes of the modern state's investment in infrastructure.

10. Meredith Woo Cumings, ed., *The Developmental State,* "Introduction," pp. 4–10, 21–24.

11. See Chalmers Johnson, "The Developmental State: The Odyssey of a Concept." Ziya Onis's review of the developmentalist state literature concerning East Asia in the 1980s suggests that the mostly authoritarian East Asian regimes overcame legitimacy shortages precisely because they led states in a threatening geopolitical context (the Cold War), and hence could mobilize nationalist sentiment. Onis, op. cit., pp. 116–17. Michel Foucault has written that, in Europe, the right of states to exercise regulatory control over the economic activity within its territorial jurisdiction flowed directly (and logically) from its preestablished right to rule—that is, legitimacy begat developmentalism. This dirigiste authority of the "police state," so central especially to continental (German) statism, was challenged by liberalism's insistence on limiting the state's powers through the rationality of free economic activity, which denied the state's authority over all economic activity within its borders on grounds that the sovereign (or the state) simply was incapable of having this kind of knowledge or capacity to control. See Foucault, *The Birth of Biopolitics,* pp. 16, 106.

12. See, for example, Byung-Kook Kim and Ezra Vogel, eds., *The Park Chung Hee Era,* locs. 4530, 4549.

13. On state finances and economic conditions of the late nineteenth century, see Gim Jae-ho, "Joseon hugi jungang jaejeong ui unyeong," pp. 41–74; Yi Yun-sang, "Gabo gaehyeok-gi geundaejeok jose jedo surip sido wa jibang sahoe ui dae-eung."

14. Yu Seung-nyeol, "Hanmal ui sangeop ipguk noryeok gwa sanggwon suho undong," pp. 65–66.

15. An editorial in 1883, for example, in the *Hanseong sunbo* ("Seoul News"), the first quasi-newspaper published in Korea, claimed that in Western countries the state not only assisted in providing capital to would-be entrepreneurs but in fact ensured that companies would gain a profit from their venture. "Hoesa-ron" [On companies], *Hanseong sunbo* (1883.11.20), in HSSS 1, pp. 38–41. Seo Yeong-hui finds that the Crown, too, began envisioning this connection between industrial growth, on the one hand, and royal authority and national strengthening ("buguk"), on the other, back in the 1880s, with Meiji Japan, not surprisingly, serving as the model. Seo, op. cit., pp. 106–8.

16. "Jangsa wa jejo ga buguk ui gil," *Dongnip sinmun* (1897.8.7).

17. See "Ijen cheonha geunbon-i nongsa-ga anira sangeop ida" [Now the basis of the world lies in industry, not agriculture], *Jeguk sinmun* (1901.4.19), and "Gongsang ija ji geummu" [Urgent tasks of (revering) artisans and merchants], *Hwangseong sinmun* (1898.11.19), HSSS 1, pp. 822–23.

18. See, for example, the editorial of the *Hwangseong sinmun* in the 1899.3.6 issue, which contrasted the feeble efforts of the Korean state (or Crown) with the

extraordinary growth of commerce and industry in contemporary Japan. See also "Nara gyeolttan naeneun geunini mulgeon jejo haneun ja-ege ittseum" [Blame for the country's destruction lies with (our) artisans], *Jeguk sinmun* (1906.12.8, 1906.12.10), HSSS 1, pp. 752–55, which called for immediate reform in the ethos and quality of native manufacturers in order to turn around the country's precarious standing following the establishment of the protectorate; and "Gongeop-eul bulga geubgeup jangnyeo" [The need for focused encouragement of industry], *Hwangseong sinmun* (1906.7.25), HSSS 2, pp. 33–35, which called on government leaders to waken the people's potential by establishing a foundation for industrial growth, including schools, training centers, and overseas study opportunities.

19. See, for example, Jang Jiyeon, "Daehan jaganghoe yeonseol: Siksan munje" [Speech for the Korean self-strengthening society: Industry], *Hwangseong sinmun* (1906.4.30). This speech was notable for, among other things, its focus on the significance of exports in order to maintain a balance of trade and hence to avoid becoming "slaves" to outside powers.

20. Takjibu, "Seip sechul chong yesanpyo" (1898–1902).

21. Ibid. With the exception of 1901, the budget allocations for the Imperial Household Fee were given in suspiciously rounded numbers (e.g., "500,000 won," "655,000 won," "900,000 won"), though they were fairly consistent in constituting 8–12% of the total government expenditures. See also the account of the state budget in *The Korea Review* (1902), pp. 120–22. Here it shows that the budget allocation for "Post and Telegraph" (353,580 *won*) was by far the largest allocation to any agency and nearly equaled the total for the entire Royal Household Ministry. This magazine contained dozens of news items every year related to the building or use of telegraph lines.

22. Yi Yun-sang, "Daehan jeguk ui jaejeong unyeong gwa geundae gukga ui gyeongje-jeok gicho," p. 221. Yi suggests that the Crown's land tax revenue likely exceeded that of the central government.

23. Seo Yeong-hui, "Gukga-ron cheongmyeon eseo bon Daehan jeguk ui seong-gyeok," p. 81. The vastness of economic resources controlled by the Crown is suggested by the voluminous records of the communication between the Office of Royal Properties and its many minions, including provincial and local officials, around the country. These documents, held in the Gyujanggak Library at Seoul National University, are published as *Hullyeong johoe jonan* (8 vols.) and *Naejang-weon gakdo gakgun sojang yoyak* (3 vols.).

24. Yi Yun-sang, op. cit., p. 103.

25. Min Suh Sohn, "Enlightenment and Electrification." This installation came through a special arrangement following the first Korean diplomatic embassy to the United States in 1883.

26. *Naejangwon hoegyechaek* (1890s). See also *The Korea Review* (1901), p. 176, for figures on the government's telegraph receipts.

27. Gim Yeon-hui, "Daehan jegukgi, saeroun gisul gwanwon jipdan ui hyeong-seong gwa haeche"; O Jin-seok, "Hanguk geundae jeollyeok saneop ui baljeon gwa Gyeongseong jeongi (ju)."

28. *Dongnip sinmun*, 1899.9.19.

29. Jeong Jae-jeong, *Ilje chimnyak gwa Hanguk cheolto*. See also Peter Duus, *The Abacus and the Sword*, Chapter 4, for more on the processes through which the Japanese gained and developed the railroad concessions.

30. *Beomnyeong* v. 2, p. 375 (1898.6.23); Jo Jae-gon, "Daehan jeguk ui siksan heungeop jeongchaek gwa sanggongeop gigu." This did not mean necessarily that foreigners were excluded from the process. Indeed foreign technicians, engineers, educators, and their know-how were encouraged to be deployed at the mines, and holdovers from previous concessions, including a lucrative gold mine at Unsan in the north, continued to depend on foreigners—in this case, American prospectors. Seo Yeong-hui, *Daehan jeguk jeongchisa yeongu*, p. 118; Donald Clark, *Living Dangerously in Korea*, Chapter 11. It was also announced that ownership of the Seoul Electric Company, which operated the streetcar system, would be transferred to the Royal Household Ministry. *The Korea Review* (1901), p. 219.

31. Kirk Larsen, *Tradition, Treaties, and Trade: Qing Imperialism and Chosŏn Korea, 1850–1910*, p. 242.

32. See Yu Seung-nyeol, "Hanmal ui sangeop ipguk noryeok gwa sanggwon suho undong," pp. 72–84, which details growing tensions between foreign and native merchants in this period, with foreign governments, especially that of Japan, applying pressure and objecting to the Korean government's protectionism. Yu also suggests that overturning the results of these Korean policies was one of the motivations behind the Japanese prosecution of the Russo-Japanese War in 1904–5.

33. The first Korean companies appeared in the mid-1880s, but there were few until the Gabo Reforms period, after which, for several years, more than ten new operations were established annually. However, the major explosion of new companies came in 1899, immediately following the establishment of the Korean Empire's developmental drive. In 1899 the number of new companies went from thirteen to forty, with most of the gains coming in companies engaged in manufacturing, mining, trading, and commerce. The number of companies newly erected remained high for several more years. In this era emerged also the first modern Korean tycoons. Jeon U-yong, "Hanin jabonga ui hyeongseong gwa seonggyeok."

34. Seo Yeong-hui, *Daehan jeguk jeongchisa yeongu*, p. 116.

35. Seo Jin-gyo, "Daehan Jeguk-gi Sangmusa ui jojik gwa hwaldong."

36. So said also one of the early newspaper advertisements heralding the new mission of the Commercial Affairs Company in late 1899. See Jo Jae-gon, op. cit.

37. *Sangmusa jangjeong*, 1899. Digital access provided by *Dongnip ginyeomgwan*.

38. Yi Yeong-hak, "Daehan jeguk ui gyeongje jeongchaek," pp. 82–83.

39. Gim Yeon-hui, op. cit., pp. 197–208.

40. "Sangmu hakgyo gwanje." *Beomnyeong* v. 2 (1899.6), p. 509.

41. Seo Ho-chul, "The Process of the Metric System's Acceptance in Korea and Its International Context."

42. See, for example, "Hwapye kkadalge da jungneunda" [Everybody's suffering because of the currency problems], *Dongnip sinmun* (1899.9.22); and "Geugui

jeongni hwapye" [Urgent need for fixing the currency issue], *Hwangseong sinmun* 1903.10.30, HSSS 1, pp. 415–17, 935–36.

43. Yi Yun-sang, "Daehan jeguk ui jaejeong unyeong," p. 222.

44. Yi Yeong-ho, "Daehan jeguk sigi Naejangwon ui oehoek unyeong gwa sangeop hwaldong."

45. Peter Duus, op. cit., p. 211.

46. Gim Dong-no has suggested, for example, that the state's chronic financial shortages, particularly from the inability to collect the tax revenue that was due, caused the failure of reform efforts, not only by the Korean Empire but also by the Gabo Reforms that preceded it, to kick-start an industrialization drive, despite the fact that state officials possessed sufficient "separation" from economic elites and interests to undertake such a movement. Gim, "Hanmal ui gukga gaehyeok undong gwa jawon dongwon." See also Young-Iob Chung, *Korea under Siege,* pp. 63–64.

47. Seo Yeong-hui, *Daehan jeguk jeongchisa yeongu,* p. 123; Gim Yeon-hui, op. cit., p. 208, 217.

48. Yi Yun-sang, "Daehan jeguk ui gyeongje jeongchaek," pp. 126–27.

49. Yi Yun-sang, "Daehan jeguk ui jaejeong unyeong," p. 230.

50. Yi Yeong-hun, "Daehan jeguk-gi hwangsil jejeong ui gicho wa seonggyeok," Naksungdae Institute of Economic Research Working Paper Series, August 2011, pp. 14–16.

51. Yi even dismisses the many criticisms of Gojong's self-centered and puzzling actions as reflecting a victor-centered, pro-Japanese narrative. In fact, he finds the leadership of the Independence Club, the longtime antagonist to the Crown, as having been so beholden to foreign ideals that they failed to see the larger Japanese designs behind them. Yi Tae-jin, *Gojong sidae ui jaejomyeong,* pp. 74–88, 275.

52. For more on the quest for legitimacy as a central feature of Park Chung Hee's industrialization policy, including his own acknowledgment of this connection, see Kim and Vogel, *The Park Chung Hee Era,* locs. 4530, 4549, 4886.

53. Gim Yeon-hui, op. cit.

54. Seo Yeong-hui, *Daehan jeguk jeongchisa yeongu,* pp. 42–63. The monarch's struggles against the enlightenment figures dated back to the 1880s, when the most radical among them attempted a coup against the government in 1884. The 1894 Gabo Reforms under Japanese military protection, which stripped the Crown of much of its authority, only deepened Gojong's contempt, and even after the suppression of the Independence Club in 1899, the Crown had to fend off plots to implement a republican governing order amid mounting suspicion that the enlightenment figures who had fled to Japan in 1896 were devising further attempts to overthrow him. But as the author notes, while the monarch mistrusted the people behind the enlightenment movement, he largely adopted the movement's ideas, except outright republicanism. See Seo, pp. 110–11.

55. Infrastructural growth, particularly the railroad, continued apace, along with changes that sought to increase the yields from state-owned mining and marine products operations, but there were no major new industrial projects introduced during the protectorate period.

56. *Economic History of Chosen* (1921), pp. 66–71.

57. See Karl Moskowitz, "The Creation of the Oriental Development Company: Japanese Illusions Meet Korean Reality," pp. 74–75; and Peter Duus, op. cit., pp. 381–83. See also *Prospectus of the Oriental Development Company* (1921), Chapters 1–2. The headquarters of the ODC moved from Seoul to Tokyo in 1917, in line with the expansion of the ODC's activities to other areas of East Asia.

58. Eckert, *Offspring of Empire,* pp. 87–91.

59. Government-General of Tyosen, *Annual Report on Administration of Tyosen* (1937–38), p. 140.

60. *Tōkei* (1919), pp. 72–77. In 1919 the colonial government counted approximately 40,000 Japanese residents belonging to households primarily engaged in agriculture, 40,000 in industry (*kōgyō*), and 100,000 in commerce and transportation. The corresponding figures for Koreans were, respectively, 14.25 million, 350,000, and 100,000. The ratios, then, were 4:4:10 for Japanese, and 1,425:35:10 for Koreans.

61. See Yamaguchi Sei, *Chōsen sangyō-shi* (1911), v. 2, pp. 384, 570.

62. *Tōkei* (1918), pp. 458–61.

63. By the end of the 1920s the project was relying on bond funding through both the Oriental Development Company and the Korea Development Bank (Chōsen shokusan ginkō). See the report sent by the Government-General to the metropolitan Treasury Department (Ōkurashō) in "Sohwa sanyeondo sanmi jeung-sik gyehoek toji gaeryang sa-eop jageum gwangyeseo" [Documents related to funding for the rice production increase plans and land development projects, 1929], pp. 131–33. See also Gragert, *Landownership under Colonial Rule,* pp. 112–16.

64. Eckert, op. cit., pp. 232–33.

65. Chung, *Korea under Siege, 1876–1945,* p. 93.

66. Eckert, op. cit., pp. 103–6.

67. Ju translated Eckert's book into Korean and published an expansive study of this company in a recent work that also critiques Eckert's classic study. Whereas Eckert stops short of drawing direct connections to the postliberation period and considers the complex interworkings of interests and loyalties in the company leadership's relationship to the colonial state from which it derived its existence and welfare, particularly in the wartime period, Ju is unabashedly approving of their proactive, innovative character and more certain that the company's leaders pioneered the model for the South Korean economic miracle. The titles of the two works also reflect this difference: Eckert's is "Offspring of Empire," while Ju's is "Scouts of a Great Army." See Ju Ik-jong, *Daegun ui cheokhu—Ilje-ha ui Gyeongseong bangjik gwa Gim Seongsu, Gim Yeonsu.*

68. Gim Nang-nyeon, *Ilje-ha Hanguk gyeongje,* pp. 170–71.

69. *Chōsen Ginkō nijū gonen-shi* (1935), pp. 154–55; Eckert, op. cit., p. 72.

70. Dennis McNamara, *The Colonial Origins of Korean Enterprise: 1910–1945,* pp. 51–54.

71. Myung Soo Cha and Nak Nyeon Kim, "Korea's First Industrial Revolution, 1911–40," pp. 16–17.

72. Gim Nang-nyeon, ed. *Hanguk ui gyeongje seongjang, 1910–1945*, pp. 190–91.

73. Ibid., pp. 488–89.

74. National Office of Statistics (Tonggyecheong), Republic of Korea, *Tonggye-ro dasi boneun Gwangbok ijeon ui gyeongje sahoe-sang*, p. 85. According to Young-Iob Chung, public investment in railroads exceeded "the total paid-in capital and reserves of all industrial companies in Korea, nearly one-fifth of all capital stock accumulated under Japanese rule." Chung, *Korea under Siege*, p. 121.

75. *Chōsen Ginkō nijū gonen-shi*, p. 18.

76. *Tōkei* (1917, 1925, 1930, 1937), *Kokō* ("Population") sections.

77. Recent analysis suggests, in fact, that a major downturn in the agricultural labor market, as measured especially in wages and employment, began long before the Great Depression. In the 1920s the ratio of tenant households—not even including those self-cultivators who also did tenant farming—increased from 40% to over half of the total within a decade, where it would remain for the remainder of the colonial period. Gim Nang-nyeon, *Ilje-ha Hanguk gyeongje*, pp. 125–26; Myeong Su Cha and Wu Yeon Lee, "Living Standards and Income Distribution in Korea's First Industrial Revolution, 1910–42," p. 21. For more on the impact of rural immiseration and commercialization, urbanization, and industrialization on factory labor, see Janice Kim, *To Live to Work*, Chapters 1–2.

78. *Tōkei* (1940), p. 5.

79. Chōsen sōtokufu, *Chōsen tōkei yōran* (1941), pp. 4–7, 16–17.

80. Based on various sources of statistical evidence, Huh Soo-youl (Heo Su-yeol) has found that, after nearly a decade of precipitous growth, especially in the 1940–41 period, factory and factory labor levels dropped in the last year or so of the war. He also finds that, not surprisingly, most of the heavy industrial growth was concentrated in the north, that it was oriented overwhelmingly toward munitions production, and that most of this heavy industrial investment during the war was by "large-scale Japanese capital groups," even more than by the colonial state. But it is important to note that Heo, following the statistics compiled by the US military government soon after liberation, segregated "financial institutions" from government investment, when in fact most of the financial institutions' investment was controlled by the state, as noted above. Huh Soo-youl, "Changes in the Manufacturing Industry of Korea," pp. 68–80.

81. Eckert, op. cit., pp. 107–10; Lim Chaisung, "The Development of a Control Policy over the Coal Industry and the Management of the Coal Mining Industry in Wartime Colonial Korea."

82. See the official English versions of the annexation treaty and imperial rescript in *The Annual Report on the Reforms and Progress in Chosen (1921–1922)*, compiled by the Government-General of Chosen, 1923, Appendixes A and B, pp. 241–43.

83. In a fascinating example of the more subtle measures undertaken by the early colonial state to tout the connection between its economic development policies and the rapid growth of the transportation infrastructure, the Korean-language state

organ, the *Maeil sinbo*, hired budding author Yi Gwang-su to take an extended trip around the southern provinces in the summer of 1917 and report on his travels, which were done mostly by railroad and on ferries. For details, see Gim Jae-gwan, "'Odo dap-pa yeoheng' e natanan ilje singminji gyotong chegye yeongu."

84. See Uchida, *Brokers of Empire*, pp. 229–52.

85. Gomikawa Nori, "Tenkanki no Chōsen keizai," (1937), p. 38.

86. *Saitō Makoto bunsho* v. 1, pp. 584–88. Mizunō's remarks are also recorded therein.

87. Bak Yeongcheol, *Gojūnen no kaiko* (1929), p. 261.

88. Ibid, pp. 262, 268; *Chōsen no tetsudō* (1928), p. 343. The vision for the future of the railway included establishing deeper connections with China and the Eurasian continent, and therefore the widening of Koreans' spiritual and cultural horizons.

89. Bak Yeongcheol, op. cit., pp. 604–5.

90. *Chōsen sangyō keizai chōsakai kaigiroku* (1936), pp. 7–8; Gomikawa Nori, "Tenkanki no Chōsen keizai," (1937), pp. 37–38. Ugaki's views were prominently on display as early as 1927, as he was serving briefly as the interim Governor-General, when he convened a gathering of major financial figures to rally support for the industrial turn in Korea. The government organ, *Maeil sinbo,* in offering editorial support for this policy, stressed the untapped industrial potential of Korea and dismissed criticisms that such an orientation would benefit only the Japanese. *Maeil sinbo* 1927.7.8, 1927.7.9.

91. Minami Jirō, "Nentō shokan" [New year's thoughts], *Chōsen gyōsei* 1 (1937.1), pp. 4–5. The reorientation of Korea's economic standing in the empire toward Manchuria was expressed as the ideal of considering "Korea and Manchuria as the same" (*Senman ichinyo*) in the service of the grander vision of realizing "Japan and Manchuria as one bloc" (*Nichiman ittai*). See also Mark Caprio, *Japanese Assimilation Policies in Colonial Korea, 1910–1945*, pp. 142–43.

92. Government-General of Chosen, *Thriving Chosen* (1935), pp. 79, 92. Ugaki stated that this seminal moment was upon them, "for the time of industrial development is ripe, and the future promising."

93. Eckert, op. cit., pp. 114–16, 126.

94. See, for example, the official proclamation, through an early 1941 Korean-language magazine article, of the Imperial Rule Assistance Association (Taisei yokusankai) of Japan, which declared that the "collective war of the East Asian people" must be led by the country, Japan, that, "as the pioneering civilization in East Asia, [readily] takes on this core responsibility of East Asia's defense." Korea is never mentioned as one of the Sphere's constitutive countries, in contradistinction to China and Manchuria, for the tenor of this proclamation simply takes for granted that Korea was a well-established part of Japan. "Dae donga gongyeonggwon hwangnip ui gibon gwannyeom" [Basic concepts behind the establishment of the Greater East Asian Co-Prosperity Sphere], *Chunchu* (1941), p. 97.

95. Mitchell also reiterates the central role played by colonialism in this process. See Timothy Mitchell, *Rule of Experts*, pp. 4–7; Graeme Gill, *The Nature and*

Development of the Modern State, pp. 118–19; and Michel Foucault, *Security, Territory, Population,* pp. 33–34, for his similar suggestion that the birth of the "economy" as we know it was tied to the shift from a physiocratic to mercantilist state.

CHAPTER FIVE

1. Antonio Gramsci, *Selections from the Prison Notebooks,* p. 506.

2. The most fervent advocate of burying this notion, at least as it applies to the religiousness of individuals and societies, has been Rodney Stark. See Stark's polemical but engaging essay, "Secularization: RIP."

3. While not denying the validity of this concept, David Martin has been among the most prominent advocates of historicizing secularization around the globe. See Martin, "The Secularization Issue: Prospect and Retrospect."

4. As Nikki Keddie notes, "No state today is entirely secular or entirely nonsecular. The very strengthening of a state demanded by modern economies requires considerable state control of public education, civil law, welfare and other spheres that is more secular than anything that existed in the past." Keddie, "Secularization and the State: Towards Clarity and Global Comparison," p. 24.

5. Philip S. Gorski and Ateş Altınordu, "After Secularization?", pp. 74–75; Peter Berger, "Religion and the West"; and Terrance Carroll, "Secularization and States of Modernity," pp. 362–82. Not unrelated to this problem is that the secularization thesis in general can be considered an auxiliary to the discredited modernization theories of the 1950s and '60s. See Rodney Stark, "Secularization: RIP." Stark goes so far as to insist that the concept has lost all meaning.

6. Keddie, op. cit., p. 24, contends that the separation from religion enhanced the state's control over it.

7. Indeed in some settings, such as Turkey and France and the former Eastern Bloc communist states, state secularization powerfully drove social secularization. See David Martin, op. cit., pp. 468–69.

8. See Helen Hardacre, *Shinto and the State,* and Alan G. Grapard, "Japan's Ignored Cultural Revolution," for more on the political motivations and actions surrounding the implementation of a theocratic state in late nineteenth- and early twentieth-century Japan. J. A. Josephson has recently intervened to insist on a complicated concept of a "Shinto secular" in the Meiji era, a nationalist political ethos culminating in the monarch's authority that was separated from Shinto as a religion (which also was being invented). This allowed Shinto, as a civic religion above sectarian loyalties, to command a state that officially promulgated religious freedom; in effect, there was no such thing as "State Shinto." See Jason Josephson, *The Invention of Religion in Japan.*

9. For a skillful contextualization of the *Kulturkampf,* see David Blackbourn, *Marpingen: Apparitions of the Virgin Mary in Nineteenth-Century Germany,* Chapters 3 and 7. Blackbourn calls the *Kulturkampf* a "secular crusade" by liberals and the Bismarckian state against the Church (p. 256).

10. In his rundown of various secularization theories, Olivier Tschannen has found many of them citing this phenomenon as a common feature, which he labels "generalization." See Tschannen, "The Secularization Paradigm: A Systematization," pp. 408–9.

11. For an assessment of how modern religious pluralism expressed competition and conflict between religions and the panoply of modernizing demands, including those promoted by an ascendant state, see William Swatos, Jr. and Kevin J. Christiano, "Secularization Theory: The Course of a Concept," p. 225.

12. As Robert Campany shows convincingly, the modern notion of "religion" itself, so endowed with metaphors suggesting a holistic, systematic entity ("organisms," "agents," or "fully integrated systems and as containers into which persons, ideas, practices, and texts may be fit without remainder"—p. 317), usually did not apply to "religious" practices and institutions in many historical contexts, such as medieval China, where the metaphors for religion were quite different from those in the Abrahamic sphere. He stops short of denying the institutionalized character of what we conventionally term "religions" in East Asia—Buddhism, Confucianism, Daoism, Shamanism—but the thrust of his study certainly implies the weakness of the value of institutional elements, whether temples or clerical hierarchies. See Campany, "On the Very Idea of Religions (In the Modern West and in Early Medieval China)," pp. 287–319. In pre-twentieth-century Korea, however, Buddhism, Confucianism, and the state did indeed function and were perceived as institutional entities, with internal hierarchies, rules, and material possessions. Buddhism and Confucianism, then, were not any less real than the state itself.

13. See Jahyun Kim Haboush, *The Confucian Kingship in Korea,* pp. 36–40.

14. Haboush, *The Confucian Kingship in Korea.*

15. Max Weber, *Economy and Society* v. 2, pp. 1160–61. This comes from Weber's extensive discussion of "hierocratic domination." Weber's other two ideal types of rulers in their relationship to ecclesiastical power were those whose legitimacy depended on priests, and those who also functioned as priests. The logical outcome of caesaro-papism in the modern era, one would assume, would be the kind of totalitarian state that was emerging at the end of Weber's life. Interestingly, Weber also gives a nod to traditional East Asian (i.e., Chinese and Japanese) statecraft's capacity to place the monarchy in a position of domination over "magical-ritual forces" embodied in the clergy.

16. See James Palais, *Politics and Policy in Traditional Korea,* for a rundown of these efforts by the Daewongun, the Prince Regent who undertook extensive reforms in his decade of rule following the ascendance of his young son (Gojong) to the throne in 1863.

17. For a discussion of the ceremonies to these guardians, the *Seonghwangje,* see Boudewijn Walraven, "Popular Religion in a Confucianized Society."

18. See Son Suk-gyeong, "19-segi huban Gwanwang sungbae ui hwaksan." These shrines (*Gwanwang-myo*) were named after a Chinese general from the period of Japanese invasions of the late sixteenth century. In focusing on the locality of

Dongnae (in present-day Busan), Son finds that their strong popular growth and eventual state sponsorship in the second half of the nineteenth century, through financial support and classification as a state-sanctioned ceremony, were fed by the struggle between local elites for cultural domination. The nationwide popularity of such altars, with even the central state financially supporting the worship services in the capital, suggests that the state's precarious standing in the midst of imperialist pressures led it to embrace such ceremonies, even for a non-Korean historical figure, because of the symbolic emphasis on (anti-Japanese) military glory and unbounded loyalty to the Crown. In the mid- and late 1890s, several requests came into the government for funding renovation and enhancement of existing shrines, and by March and May of 1899, the High State Council (Uijeongbu) approved an enormous sum of money for reconstruction of a shrine in the capital following fire damage. See *Gaksa deungnok*, Jiryeong #15 (1899.3.15), #35 (1899.5.15).

19. See Don Baker, "A Different Thread: Orthodoxy, Heterodoxy, and Catholicism in a Confucian World."

20. Son Suk-gyeong, op. cit., p. 233; Bak Chan-sik, "Hanmal gyoan gwa gyomin joyak," p. 63.

21. A variety of factors, including religious inspiration and legitimation, played a role in these uprisings, though all three were sparked by local corruption. For more on the role of geomantic prophecy in driving the 1811–12 revolt in northern Korea, see Sun Joo Kim, *Marginality and Subversion in Korea: The Hong Kyongnae Rebellion of 1812*, Chapter 4.

22. As George Kallender shows in his recent study of Donghak, while the uprising's leaders rode a messianic doctrine of social reform that, given its impulses in response to imperialism, can be called "ideological religious nationalism," they did not preach religious exclusivity, much less a religious infusion of the state with Donghak theology. George L. Kallender, *Salvation through Dissent: Tonghak Heterodoxy and Early Modern Korea,* pp. xx–xxi, 114–17.

23. Mark Andrew Nathan, "Buddhist Propagation and Modernization: The Significance of P'ogyo in Twentieth-Century Korean Buddhism," p. 12.

24. See *Gwanbo* 1894.6.28 and 1894.7.14 for a rundown of the administrative reorganization.

25. Richard K. Fenn, *The Spirit of Revolt: Anarchism and the Cult of Authority.*

26. For more on the back-and-forth through recourse to diplomatic and legal maneuvering between Korean officials and Protestant missionaries in the closing decades of the nineteenth century, see Sung Kwang Cha, "Contesting Obligations: American Missionaries, Korean Christians, and the State(s), 1884–1910," Chapter 1; and Donald Clark, *Living Dangerously in Korea,* pp. 14–15.

27. See Bak Chan-sik, op. cit. Korean Catholics had suffered through relentless oppression and three major persecutions from 1801 to 1866, which likely killed thousands of native converts and dozens of foreign missionaries in hiding. For more on the imagery and ideological strategies of state edicts that ordered these mass killings, see Franklin Rausch, "Like Birds and Beasts: Justifying Violence against Catholics in Late Chosŏn Korea."

28. *Gwanbo* 1899.4.29. The form of such a royal edict, "jochik," was one in which the monarch himself is credited with issuing the words, but a minister's name appears at the end of the text to denote the author. In this case, the author, Vice Premier Sin Giseon, is one of the more interesting political figures of this era, a symbol of staunch Confucian conservatism as well as political opportunism. According to Hwang Hyeon's memoir, *Maecheon yarok*, Sin, though a representative of the anti-enlightenment, traditional Confucian elite, was forced by the monarch to abide by the nationwide "Hair-cutting Ordinance" and cut off his traditional "top-knot" in favor of a Western hairstyle. Interestingly, later in 1908 he headed one of what were considered pro-Japanese groups, for which he was excoriated, even being named one of "Three Pro-Japanese Slaves" by the *Maeil sinbo* newspaper. See Seo Yeong-hui, *Daehan Jeguk jeongchisa yeongu*, pp. 56, 111; Hwang Hyeon, *Maecheon yarok*, v. 3 (1902) no. 56, v. 6 (1908) no. 7, and v. 6 (1909) no. 25.

29. *Beomnyeong* v. 2, pp. 467–69 (1899.4.27).

30. Taehoon Kim, "The Place of 'Religion' in Colonial Korea around 1910," p. 38.

31. Go Geun-ho, "Yugyo neun jonggyo inga?" In China, this issue was tied to calls for using Confucianism as the rational basis for radically secularizing the state and public life, a movement that eventually ventured into a repression of religion in general in the name of an anti-superstition campaign. See Vincent Goussaert, "1898: The Beginning of the End of Chinese Religion?"; and Peter Zarrow, *After Empire: The Conceptual Transformation of the Chinese State, 1885–1924*, pp. 252–54.

32. See O Gyeong-hwan et al., *Gyohoe wa gukga*, pp. 427–53, for more on the newspaper discourse of the 1890s that reiterated the centrality of religion to civilization and governance.

33. *Beomnyeong* v. 2, pp. 541–43 (1899.8.17). Not only did the imperial state decline to appropriate Confucianism as the state religion, in retreating from Gabo measures, it appears to have implemented a split use for the "Western calendar" (for official documents, diplomatic relations, etc.), which was officially implemented on January 1, 1896 (along with the switch away from the lunar calendar), and the "Eastern calendar" (for imperial state ceremonies and national holidays, most of which were recent creations). According to Im Hyeon-su, this testified to the officials' consciousness of the modern concept of state–church separation, for the state ceremonies and national holidays were devoid of any religious or supernatural element. Im Hyeon-su, "Daehan jeguk sigi yeokbeop jeongchaek gwa jonggyo munhwa," pp. 183–211.

34. See Gwon Hui-yeong, "Ilje sigi Joseon ui yuhak damnon," pp. 124–26; and John Duncan, "Uses of Confucianism in Modern Korea," pp. 435–41, for examples of late nineteenth- and early twentieth-century Korean enlightenment intellectuals' excoriation of the Confucian impact on Korean culture and civilization.

35. The Korean Empire state first attempted to reorganize the Buddhist clergy under a nationwide state-sanctioned system in 1899. Later, the 1902 Temple Ordinance established an Office of Temple Administration (Sasa gwalliseo), under the administrative umbrella of the Royal Household Ministry, in a newly constructed

monastery in Seoul. For extensive analysis of this ordinance, see Hwansoo Ilmee Kim, *Empire of the Dharma: Korean and Japanese Buddhism, 1877–1912*, pp. 152–58. And for more on these transitions in the state's approach to Buddhism at the turn of the century, including the seminal role likely played by Japanese Buddhist clergy in Korea, see Mark Andrew Nathan, op. cit., pp. 10–18.

36. This statement was issued by the Korean vice premier at the time, Min Yeonghwan. GSS 1905.4.17; *Gwanbo* 1905.4.20.

37. "Fukyō kisoku," *Kanpō* 1915.8.16.

38. An Yu-rim, "Ilje gidokgyo tongje jeongchaek gwa pogyo gyuchik," p. 40.

39. In late 1906 (11.17), the Residency-General under Ito Hirobumi issued the "Regulations Concerning the Evangelization of Religion" (*Shūkyō no senpu ni kansuru kisoku*), which established the rules and bounds of Japanese evangelizing activities in Korea. See Hwansoo Ilmee Kim, op. cit., pp. 164–67.

40. *Kanpō* 1915.8.16.

41. For more on the Meiji-era symbolic and ideological construct of the Tenno, see Takashi Fujitani, *Splendid Monarchy: Power and Pageantry in Modern Japan*. Kyu-Hyun Kim has recently suggested that, in the Meiji era at least, the political, monarchical authority of the emperor actually was segregated from and superseded (the attempts to unify it with) his liturgical or ritual role. Kyu-Hyun Kim, "The Mikado's August Body: 'Divinity' and 'Corporeality' of the Meiji Emperor and the Ideological Construction of Imperial Rule."

42. See Kyung Moon Hwang, *Beyond Birth*, p. 125.

43. It is difficult to determine how or when this term arose. Sheldon Garon suggests it was coined by the Bureau of Religions in the Japanese Ministry of Education for inclusion in a new directive to crack down on these groups in 1919. But given that essentially the same term appeared through this ordinance in Korea in 1915, likely the origins lay earlier, perhaps with the colonial authorities themselves. Sheldon Garon, "State and Religion in Imperial Japan, 1912–1945," pp. 288–89.

44. See, for example, "Yusa jonggyo-dan ui cheoltoe" [The iron truncheon of the pseudo-religions], *Joseon ilbo* 1939.8.31; "Yusa jonggyo ui bimil" [Secrets of the pseudo-religions], *Donga ilbo* 1935.1.19; "Jonggyo yusa danche-reul eomjung chwije hal bangchim—yusa danche-ga jonggyo danche ui guhal, gyodo-ga samsimmanin-eul chogwa" [How to respond firmly to pseudo-religious groups—pseudo-religious groups constitute 90% of all religious groups, with more than three hundred thousand followers], *Donga ilbo* 1935.6.7. The latter report details plans in the Government-General to convene a meeting of high officials to begin devising a response to this development. The *Donga ilbo* in particular carried extensive coverage of the pseudo-religions, reporting, for example, on the arrest and trial of the leaders of one of the most powerful such groups, the Cheongnim-gyo—one of the descendants of the Donghak religion—in the early and mid-1930s on charges of fraud and extortion.

45. *Ilje gangjeomgi jonggyo jeongchaeksa jaryojip*, p. 131.

46. The latter 1930s witnessed a sensational series of incidents centered on the Donghak-derived Baegbaekgyo movement, which was implicated in multiple mur-

ders. The *Donga ilbo* covered this extensively. See, for example, "Baegbaekgyo sageon-eun uri ege mueotser gareucheonna?" [What did the Baekbaekgyo incident teach us?], *Donga ilbo* 1940.3.20.

47. Murayama Chijun, *Chōsen no ruiji shūkyō* (1935). Murayama also authored thorough studies on Korean shamanism, geomancy, clothing, and other customs. For more on Murayama, see E. Taylor Atkins, *Primitive Selves,* locs. 1658–1795.

48. Maruyama Chijun, op. cit., pp. 1–3.

49. Ibid., pp. 10–17.

50. Ibid., pp. 845–52.

51. See Richard Devine, "Japanese Rule in Korea after the March First Uprising: Governor-General Hasegawa's Recommendations," p. 538. In his outgoing notes to his successor in 1919, Hasegawa actually recommends recognizing Cheondogyo in order to "strictly regulate it, and lead it in a more positive direction."

52. This is one of the main findings of the recent study by E. Taylor Atkins, who quotes a contemporary article in the *New York Times* (September 5, 1919) in which the new Governor-General Saitō Makoto states, "It would be absurd to think of destroying the ancient Korean language and customs. We shall continue to offer Japanese education, but there will be no coercive attempts to crush out the Korean spirit and traditions or legitimate aspirations." Atkins, *Primitive Selves,* loc. 947.

53. Seong Ju-hyeon, "1910 nyeondae Joseon eseo ui Ilbon Bulgyo pogyo hwal-dong gwa seonggyeok."

54. Several Japanese religious organizations, including Shinto derivations, came under the watchful eye of the Government-General. According to a collection of bureaucratic records from 1936, some, like the Tenri-kyo, were carefully permitted to establish evangelizing offices, while others, like the Ōmotokyo, an ultra emperor-cult movement, were banned. See *Jonggyo sawon changnip pogyo gwallija e gwanhan geon* (1936), pp. 265–68, 343–45.

55. The colonial Statistical Annual (*Tōkei nenpō*) did not contain figures for Buddhist adherents, but it kept track of the number of Buddhist temples, as well as the number of registered monks and nuns. These figures remained remarkably stable until the late 1930s, with approximately 1,300–1,400 temples, 6,000–7,000 monks, and 1,000–1,300 nuns. *Tōkei* 1918, 1930, 1937.

56. The influence, indeed domination, of Japanese customs and practices in the Korean Buddhist establishment under colonial rule has remained a sensitive issue in postliberation South Korea, though one that easily lends itself to dichotomies of resistance and collaboration. See Eunsu Cho, "Re-thinking Late 19th Century Joseon Buddhist Society," pp. 88–89. For more on the precolonial impact of Korean transmitters, particularly the monk Yi Dongin, of Japanese Buddhist influence, see Vladimir Tikhonov, "The Japanese Missionaries and Their Impact on Korean Buddhist Developments," pp. 246–59.

57. Over the long term, the 1911 Temple Ordinance bureaucratized the Korean Buddhist order and effectively segregated it from further major influence of Japanese sects, according to Hwansoo Ilmee Kim, *Empire of the Dharma*, pp. 318–35.

58. "Jinja jiin kisoku," *Kanpō* 1915.8.16; Chōsen sōtokufu, "Sawon pyeji e ttareun sayu jaesan mit juji chwijik inga sincheong gwangye seoryu" (1924), "Jonggyo sawon changnip pogyo gwallija e gwanhan geon" (1936).

59. See, for example, *Shisei* (1922), p. 191. See also Pori Park, *Trial and Error in Modernist Reforms: Korean Buddhism under Colonial Rule*, pp. 42–43. A 1929 overview of state–religion relations by a Korean-language organ of the Government-General states that, without such official measures to cultivate and protect Korean Buddhism, it would have been difficult for the faith to survive into the present day (1930s). Yi Chang-geun, "Joseon jonggyo ui jinjeon," *Joseon* 144 (1929.10), pp. 1435–38.

60. Mark Nathan, op. cit., pp. 170–81.

61. Michael Robinson, "Perceptions of Confucianism in Twentieth-Century Korea," p. 215. There exists remarkable film footage of one such ceremony, the funeral of the former Korean monarch, Sunjong, with high colonial officials in attendance.

62. Such is the finding by Gwon Hui-yeong, who takes a highly critical view of this behavior, which he claims contributed to the loss of national sovereignty. He also suggests that this somewhat reactionary impulse represented the dominant response among Confucian scholar-elites in the countryside. Indeed many if not most Confucian scholars, excepting well-known examples such as Jeong Inbo, chose not to wage an overt struggle against the Japanese takeover or colonial rule. See Gwon, op. cit., pp. 121–54.

63. *Shisei* (1935), p. 191.

64. The first Governor-General of Korea, Terauchi Masatake, was said to have found particularly distasteful what he considered the Koreans' latching on to Christianity as a foil to Japanese political power. See An Yu-rim, "Ilje gidokgyo tongje jeongchaek gwa pogyo gyuchik," p. 39.

65. The colonial officials often acknowledged this sensitivity while expressing strong hostility and suspicion toward some Westerners for undermining colonial rule through their dissemination of misinformation, a reflection of their deep sympathies for Korean nationalist sentiments. See *Chōsen tōchi hiwa* (1937), pp. 146–47. See also Don Baker, "World Religions and National States: Competing Claims in East Asia."

66. For more on this incident, particularly the thorny problems of extraterritoriality faced by the regime in trying the foreign missionaries among those arrested, see Alexis Dudden, *Japan's Colonization of Korea: Discourse and Power,* pp. 120–29.

67. *Kanpō* 1915.3.24.

68. Gam Jong-gyu, *Hanguk gyoyuk gwajeong byeoncheonsa yeongu*, pp. 86–87.

69. Seikya Teisaburō, "Sarip hakgyo gyuchik gaejeong ui yoji," *Chōsen ihō* (April 1915), in Gim Seung-taek, ed. and transl., *Ilje gangjeomgi jonggyo jeongchaeksa jaryojip—Gidokgyo pyeon, 1910–1945*, p. 95.

70. Minutes of the meetings of the Methodist Episcopal Church in 1916, for example, record ministers' aggravation at the enormous time spent to meet the

demands of the 1915 ordinance for records and information. The Presbyterians encountered similar difficulties. See An Yu-rim, op. cit., pp. 56, 58.

71. Clark, *Living Dangerously in Korea,* pp. 45–50.

72. Yi Chang-geun, "Joseon jonggyo-gye ui jinjeon" *Joseon* 144 (1929), pp. 171–72. This analysis in the Government-General's periodical refrained from explicitly invoking this official condemnation, merely noting that the extensive participation of Christian churches, "most" of whom served as staging grounds for the uprising, resulted in great misfortune for everyone involved, in Christians' misunderstanding of the colonial government, and in stagnation and loss in church membership.

73. *Kanpō* 1920.4.9.

74. *Ilje gangjeomgi jonggyo jeongchaeksa jaryojip,* pp. 131–32.

75. *Tōkei* (1937), p. 257. Though the precise number of adherents is notoriously difficult to compile, and there remains contradictory evidence, the official numbers show an increase of approximately 100,000 Christian believers to nearly a half-million (499,323) from 1928 to 1937, with Presbyterians constituting nearly three-quarters of the total. The number of officially recognized "evangelists" numbered nearly 4,000 by 1937.

76. Although there seems to have been an agreement reached in 1935 with the authorities that Christian schoolchildren and officials could delay participation in the ceremonies for a year, there were also reports of continuing coercion, misunderstandings, and ongoing resistance. See, for example, "Sinsa bulchambae munje-ro yasogyo dangguk gwa hyeobui" [Agreement with Christian educators stemming from refusal to participate in Shinto shrine ceremonies], *Joseon jungang ilbo* 1935.10.8; "Sinsa chambae geojeol si en jungdeung gyojang bulyongin" [Principals of (Christian) middle schools will be decertified if they do not participate in Shinto shrine ceremonies], *Joseon jungang ilbo* 1935.11.29; and "Sinsa chambae bulgapi-rago—jonggyo seonpo wa gyoyuk jeongchaek-eun byeolgae munje-rago" [(Authorities say that) shrine visitations are unavoidable—that evangelization and education policy are separate items], *Joseon ilbo* 1935.12.5. This latter article was pessimistic about the chances for a peaceful settlement between the regime and Christian leaders, especially missionaries.

77. "Seon-gyo daepyo hangmuguk bangmun—gijeong bangchim irago ilchuk" [Missionary representatives visit the Education Bureau—and are told in a denial of their appeal that this policy has already been settled], *Donga ilbo* 1935.12.10. These mostly foreign representatives, it was reported, were received politely, but their pleas proved fruitless in the face of resolute colonial officials.

78. See, for example, "Jinju Gidokgyo gakpa yeonhap sinsa chambae-reul sil-haeng" [Association of all Protestant orders in Chinju to participate in Shinto shrine rituals], *Donga ilbo* 1938.9.27; and Donald Clark, op. cit., pp. 209–21. For the text of the notorious 1938 declaration by the 27th General Assembly of the Presbyterian Church in Korea, see Chung-shin Park, *Protestantism and Politics in Korea,* p. 155. For the text of the Methodist Church's official position, following a meeting with the Government-General's Education Minister in mid-1936, see Choi Jae-Keun, *The Korean Church under Japanese Colonialism,* pp. 121–23. Choi notes that

this concession allowed the Methodists to keep their schools open until the end of the colonial period, though likely the schools were diluted of "their distinctive Christian character." The agonies over how to respond to this coercion—as the colonial regime probably had anticipated—engendered significant cleavages within the Protestant establishment, with the most publicized riff forming between the capital- and Pyongyang-based Presbyterian groups. As for the Catholic Church, in 1936 the clergy was reported to have received word from the Vatican's representative in Japan that participation in these rituals was not in a "religious spirit" and therefore would be allowed. See "Cheonjugyo cheuk eseon jajin chambae-reul seongmyeong" [The Catholic Church, for its part, announces (allowance for) voluntary participation], *Donga ilbo* 1936.8.2.

79. One of the more interesting such events was the repression of the colony-wide "Universal women's prayer service" (*Manguk buin gidohoe*), an annual event initiated by a foreign missionary in 1925, but whose organizers in 1940 and 1941 were arrested for anti-state conspiracy. The regime also brought in for questioning 672 participants and potential participants. These interrogation records, *Manguk buin gidohoe sageon jaryojip,* have been published in thirty-seven volumes, and are available also online through the National Institute of Korean History website. See also Jo Seon-hye, "1941 'Manguk buin gidohoe sageon' yeongu." Jo states that this represented the "decisive" event in the regime's co-optation of the Korean Christian church during wartime.

80. See Donald Clark, *Living Dangerously in Korea,* Chapters 9, 10, and 12, for more on the chronic tension between conservative Protestants and the colonial state in the late colonial period, which ultimately resulted in the shutdown of missionary activities, then finally the expulsion of all Western missionaries. The German Catholic clergy were exempt due to Japan's alliance with Nazi Germany.

81. In a letter dated December 31, 1935 and sent to George McCune, president of the Union Christian College in Pyongyang, Watanabe Toyohiko, head of the colonial regime's Education Bureau, insisted that the government did not hold "the slightest intention of interfering with the propagation of Christianity or with the confusion of education and religion," and that the shrine visitations, in essence, constituted (Confucian) ancestral ceremonies that cultivated the "national moral virtue." See Choi Jae-Keun, op. cit., Appendix 1, pp. 227–28. In one of the early clashes between Pyongyang Protestant leaders—mostly foreign missionaries like McCune—and the colonial regime, it was reported that among the objections to the state's insistence on the Shinto ceremonies as "civic rituals" and not religious ones was that Buddhist monks were participating by reading aloud from sacred scripts (*dokgyeong*). In response, the governor of South Pyeongan province apparently forbade the monks' participation thereafter. "Yasogyo hakgyo sinsa chambae munje haegyeolchaek jakjeong" [Finding a solution to problems surrounding participation in Shinto shrine ceremonies by Christian schools], *Donga ilbo* 1933.2.8.

82. This cosmology was reiterated increasingly in mobilization-period sources, including the opening sections of *Kokutai no hongi* (Essence of National Entity), a booklet widely circulated in Korea. For an analysis of this work as the culmination

of a long-standing ideological process since the Meiji period to implant a Shinto theocratic state in Japan, see Walter A. Skya, *Japan's Holy War: The Ideology of Radical Shinto Ultranationalism,* Chapter 8. Skya translates the title of this booklet as "Fundamentals of Our National Polity."

83. See, for example, *Maeil sinbo* 1937.7.16, 1942.8.16, and 1943.2.16.

84. In the Korean language press, these (mostly Shinto) terms included "gyeongsin" (worship), "bongje" (worship), "bongan" (enshrine), and "sinang" (faith), and they were couched in the grandly assimilationist goals of "gukche myeongjing" (clarification of the national essence [*kokutai*]) and propagation of "hwangdo jeongsin" [spirit of the imperial way]). See *Maeil sinbo* 1938.6.5, 1938.8.5, 1938.9.24, 1939.2.23, 1941.3.9, 1942.8.16, 1943.2.9, 1943.2.16, 1944.8.5. The Government-General announced in 1940 that various private Shinto altars and their construction materials would be included in the items falling under price controls. See *Kanpō* 1940.11.19. The *Maeil sinbo* newspaper ran dozens of reports from the late 1930s onward on successful efforts to get households to establish these in-home altars. But actual compliance probably was not as high as what these reports suggested. A case study of a locality in South Chungcheong province shows, for example, that, based on reports from patriotic neighborhood associations and other local-level mobilization organizations on how many of the households had purchased mini shrine kits, there was widespread disparity in compliance, and generally the overall adoption rate was below 30% of all households. See Yi Seong-u, "Jeonsi chejegi (1937–1945 nyeon) ilje ui nongchon tongje jeongchaek gwa geu silsang," pp. 152–53.

85. *Maeil sinbo* 1943.2.9, 1943.6.1. Undoubtedly the simplified, "holy style" of Japanese Shinto ceremonies was in accord with the broader campaign to eliminate all extraneous, apparently wasteful economic activity, which included the "Western" custom of exchanging engagement rings.

86. See Walter Skya, op. cit., for more on the triumph of this "Shinto ultranationalism" in the internal ideological developments of the early twentieth century in Japan; and Sheldon Garon, op. cit., pp. 300–1.

87. "Misogi harai no shōrei," *Kokumin sōryoku* 3.4 (1941.4), p. 121. This article was promoting the practices of *misogi harai,* a Shinto purification ritual, among the political leaders and laypeople.

88. Gim Jong-seo argues that at the turn of the twentieth century, the modern notion of what constitutes religion itself began to emerge, following the differentiation of religion from other social sectors and the stimulus provided by Christianity. Gim, "Gaehwagi sahoe munhwa byeondong gwa jonggyo insik." Don Baker, meanwhile, has argued that while this transformation was mostly a late twentieth-century phenomenon, the groundwork was laid as early as the eighteenth century with the introduction of Catholicism. See Baker, "The Religious Revolution in Modern Korean History." See also Mark Nathan, op. cit., pp. 157–81 for an insightful discussion of how Korean Buddhism in the colonial era became framed by legal measures that both endowed recognition and imposed behavioral expectations about what religions were supposed to look like and do. In Japan itself, much of this standardized perspective on religion, according to Helen Hardacre, appears to have come

from the example of Protestantism, and the ensuing struggles to adhere to this model presented Japanese Buddhism with many difficulties. Hardacre, op. cit., p. 65.

89. This is what Mart Bax suggests occurred in places such as the Netherlands, as state sponsorship of certain religious institutions served to differentiate a religious establishment from "sects." See Bax, "Religious Regimes and State Formation: Towards a Research Perspective."

90. Keddie, "Secularization and the State," p. 30.

91. Peter Berger, one of the foremost champions of the secularization thesis of the 1960s, has more recently amended his argument to claim that it was not secularism but rather pluralism, with its intrinsic promotion of voluntary association, that has characterized religion's standing in the polities of the modern world, but the case of Korea suggests that the two approaches can be mutually constitutive. See Peter L. Berger, "Pluralism, Protestantization and the Voluntary Principle."

CHAPTER SIX

1. See David Lloyd and Paul Thomas, *Culture and the State,* Chapters 1 and 4. On the influence of Schiller on the promotion of a *Bildung*-centered notion of citizenship education led by Wilhelm von Humboldt in the early nineteenth century, see Lesley Sharpe, *Friedrich Schiller: Drama, Thought and Politics,* pp. 166–67.

2. "Citizenship education" and "civics" are more or less interchangeable, though there have been attempts to be more precise in distinguishing the two terms. See David Kerr, "Citizenship Education in the Curriculum."

3. For Foucault's discussion on the role of "serial space"—the dynamic of individual pupils being attended to collectively in an enclosed classroom—in modern disciplining, see Michel Foucault, *Discipline and Punish,* p. 147.

4. Andy Green, "Education and State Formation in Europe and Asia."

5. See, for example, Leighanne Yuh, "Contradictions in Korean Colonial Education." Another example comes from a recent study that claims, through its analysis of ethics textbooks in the colonial period, that this curriculum constituted nothing less than the "birth of the modern child" in Korea. However, despite its meticulousness—even keeping statistics on keywords in the ethics textbooks over the colonial era, which the author breaks down into five periods—this work detects no significant change over the course of colonial rule: The content of ethics education was consistently "fascistic," emperor-centered, and exploitative, attempting—and succeeding, apparently—in instilling in Korean schoolchildren a colonial mentality of "slavery," thereby "distorting" the path toward the emergence of an individualistic, modern sensibility among the Korean people. See Yi Byeong-dam, *Hanguk geundae adong ui tansaeng.*

6. Even for the seventeenth and eighteenth centuries, when local schools were still in viable operation, by far the most substantial coverage in the extant reports that local schools submitted to the Board of Rites in the late Joseon, *Hakgyo deungnok,* were upkeep records—construction and change of locale, maintenance and

repair, availability of material and human resources (including slaves)—of individual schools and their Confucian altars. See *Gugyeok hakgyo deungnok* v. 1, pp. 5–7.

7. For the text of these ordinances, see *Gaehwagi ui gyoyuk,* pp. 47–52.

8. *Gwanbo* 1895.7.22.

9. A revised school system promulgated in 1906, which included "the physical development of students" in addition to the "common knowledge and skills necessary in their daily lives," still emphasized "imparting moral as well as citizenship education [*gungmin gyoyuk*]" as its main task. See *Botong gyoyukhak* (1910), Appendix, p. 1.

10. The earliest such textbooks, mostly translations, appeared in Japan in the 1870s, with the Meiji state beginning to publish its own by the 1880s and, by the opening years of the twentieth century, designating standard texts for the public elementary schools. See Mun Cheol-su and Yi Byeong-dam, "Geundae Ilbon ui chodeung 'Susin' gyogwaseo yeongu."

11. "Self-cultivation" would even be the first course throughout all four years of the earliest medical training college, attached to the central public hospital, in the colonial period. See Yi Chung-ho, *Ilje amheukgi uisa gyoyuksa,* pp. 145–46.

12. *Gwanbo* 1899.4.4. *The Korea Review* in 1901 (p. 27) contained a report on the invitation of a special instructor from Tokyo to teach in the newly opened public middle school, upon which much Education Department funds and attention were paid.

13. Gim Dae-jun's analysis of the central government's budgets during the Korean Empire period shows that the allocation for the Education Ministry (Hakbu) never exceeded 2.6% in any year between 1896 and 1905, and usually ranged from 1.5–2.2%. Funds for public schools hovered around 60–70% of those amounts. Gim Dae-jun, *Gojong sidae ui gukga jaejeong yeongu. The Korea Review* observed in 1904 (p. 126) that, "If half the money devoted to the army were spent on education we believe the net results would be far greater. It is not an encouraging sign that education is held in a sort of contempt at the present time."

14. For a foreign visitor's perspective on these schools, see J. Paske, "The Corean School System," *East of Asia Magazine* (1903).

15. Gu Hui-jin, "Daehan jegukgi gungmin gyoyuk ui chujin gwa guljeol."

16. *Tōkei* (1906–7), pp. 54–55; *Gaehwagi ui gyoyuk,* pp. 229–33.

17. Ham Jong-gyu, *Hanguk gyoyuk gwajeong byeoncheonsa yeongu,* pp. 37–38; Yoonmi Lee, *Modern Education, Textbooks and the Image of the Nation,* pp. 78–81; Leighanne Yuh, "Education, the Struggle for Power, and Identity Formation in Korea, 1876–1910," pp. 152–53, 168–71.

18. Ham Jong-gyu, *Hanguk gyoyuk gwajeong,* p. 73.

19. The first "Western-style" or "modern" schools were founded in the 1880s, including the most well-known school of the era, Baejae Hakdang, established in 1885 by an American missionary.

20. For fuller coverage of these pioneering private schools, see Namgung Yong-gwon and Gim No-yeon, *Gyoyuk ui yeoksa wa sasang,* pp. 206–11. The first private schools were established by Western missionaries in the 1880s, and the successors to

some of these institutions continue to operate today as prominent schools and universities.

21. "Sohakgyo-ryeong," Chingnyeong no. 62, *Gwanbo* 1908.9.1.

22. *Gwanbo* 1910.8.13. See also Kyung Moon Hwang, "From the Dirt to Heaven: Northern Koreans in the Chosŏn and Early Modern Eras," pp. 172–73.

23. Namgung and Gim, *Gyoyuk ui yeoksa wa sasang*, p. 264.

24. By the spring of 1911, half a year after annexation, the number of public elementary schools and public trade schools increased to 146—though most of these, presumably, were for Japanese residents—while the number of private schools was 2,131, a ratio of 1:15. See *Gaehwagi ui gyoyuk*, p. 241.

25. *Shisei* (1915), p. 338; Chōsen sōtokufu, *Chōsen kyōiku yōran* (1926), p. 32.

26. "Chōsen kyōikurei," *Kanpō* 1911.9.1.

27. *Shisei* (1915), pp. 342–43.

28. *Kanpō* 1911.9.01; *Tōkei* (1918), pp. 974–75.

29. There was also a kind of special fast-track vocational school (*kani jitsugyō gakkō*) option for primary school graduates.

30. *Shisei* (1915), p. 356. After liberation in 1945, some of these colleges turned into well-known universities in South Korea, including Korea University and Yonsei University.

31. Sekiya appeared further peeved that the students in these parochial schools were encouraged to perfect their skills in "foreign languages" (such as Korean) but not Japanese. See Sekiya Teisaburō, "Sarip hakgyo gyuchik gaejeong ui yoji" (1915), pp. 94–97. There was, of course, much more going on here below the surface. The Japanese and Western missionaries had been on a collision course over their respective cultural influence in Korea. The perspective of many of the Westerners was revealed most pointedly by Homer Hulbert, who had lived in Korea for nearly two decades and penned a classic defense of Korean sovereignty, *The Passing of Korea* (1906), just as the Japanese protectorate was being implemented. In the closing pages of this work Hulbert stressed that Western missionaries had a duty, and were in the best position, to help Koreans fend off Japanese predations, for what the Koreans most needed was the new education that Western missionaries could deliver. See Hulbert, *The Passing of Korea*, pp. 463–66. For more treatment of this theme, see chapter 8.

32. Religious schools also suffered a precipitous drop, from over 500 at the start of the colonial period to under 250 by 1925, according to the regime. *Tōkei* (1925), pp. 654–55. One newspaper reported the results of a survey of Korean private schools in the summer of 1922, which found 655 schools still in operation, of which 275 were parochial schools. *Donga ilbo* 1922.7.26.

33. Yi Jong-guk, *Hanguk ui gyogwaseo byeoncheonsa*, p. 50. The first official textbook appears to have been the *Sohak dokbon* (Primary school reader) of 1895.

34. *Shisei* (1915), p. 354.

35. The long list of banned books that "disturb the peace and order" appeared a few months after annexation. See *Kanpō* 1910.11.19.

36. As Mark Caprio points out, the 1911 Korean School Ordinance never mentions schooling as a requirement. See Caprio, "Neo-Nationalist Interpretations of Japan's Annexation of Korea."

37. Ninety-eight percent in 1910, according to Ōkubo Toshiaki, *Meiji jidai no kyōiku* (1933), pp. 52–53; *Tōkei* (1918), pp. 36, 974–77. By 1918 there were approximately 700 Japanese school teachers and administrators and 1,500 Koreans in Korean primary schools. These were approximately 2.5-fold and 2-fold increases, respectively, since 1911. One scholar puts the rate of Korean elementary schooling at 3.7% in 1920. See Gang Yeong-sim, "Ilje sigi 'chungnyang-han sinmin mandeulgi' gyoyuk gwa hakgyo munhwa," p. 234.

38. By 1933, almost forty years into colonial rule, elementary schools took in 37% of the Taiwanese. Fujii Shōzō, "The Formation of Taiwanese Identity and the Cultural Policy of Various Outside Regimes," loc. 1963.

39. Jeong Il-seong, *Inmullo bon Ilje Joseon jibae 40 nyeon, 1906–1945*, pp. 209, 213.

40. Hong Mun-jong, *Joseon eseo ui Ilbon singminji gyoyuk jeongchaek, 1910–1945*, p. 198.

41. *Chōsen kyōiku yōran* (1926), pp. 35–36.

42. The *Joseon ilbo* reported that this goal was met in 1936 for Yangju county, for example, and that the primary schooling rate there was close to 70%. *Joseon ilbo* 1937.5.6. The colony-wide goal had originally been 1937.

43. "Chōsen kyōikurei," Shokurei #19, *Kanpō* 1922.2.6. This euphemism, so redolent of Cultural Rule sensitivities, appears to have been constructed late in the process, as the original "classified" drafts of this revision simply put the equivalents as "Japanese" (*Naichijin*) and "Koreans" (*Chōsenjin*). See *Saitō Makoto bunsho* v. 5, pp. 149–50, 170.

44. This was apparently Vice Governor-General Mizuno Rentarō's view, as expressed in the *Maeil sinbo* newspaper, the Korean-language organ of the colonial regime, in its February 7, 1922 issue. Heo Jae-yeong, ed., *Joseon gyoyungnyeong gwa gyoyuk jeongchaek byeonhwa jaryo*, pp. 328–29.

45. There were approximately 500,000 Japanese residents in Korea in 1930, according to Government-General statistics. As a point of comparison, the ratio for students in grades K–8 to population in the United States in the early 2010s was approximately 1:10, according to the US census.

46. Even extra-state actors from the Japanese resident community stepped in to promote and arrange such excursions, with the overt motivation to fill the gaps in educational access for Koreans in the colony itself. See Jeong Mi-ryang, "1920 nyeondae ilje ui jeil Joseon yuhaksaeng huwon," pp. 70, 84–85. Jeong emphasizes the hidden agenda behind this initial government sponsorship—namely, the authorities' desire to increase surveillance on these students while cultivating a more accommodating stance toward Japanese rule over the colony. See also *Chōsen kyōiku yōran* (1926), pp. 219–20. The *Donga ilbo* (1926.7.15) reported that the education authorities changed their mind about the wisdom of seeking schooling in Japan and by 1926 were insisting that Korean students not resort to this step. For coverage of the activities of a semiprivate Japanese settler organization, the Dōminka (Association of One

People), that arranged "mail-order lectures" for advanced primary and secondary curricula in the 1920s, see Jun Uchida, *Brokers of Empire,* p. 173.

47. *Donga ilbo* 1920.4.11–13. The editorial is extraordinary for the severity of its open condemnation of colonial rule, referring to it as a "regime of soldiers" that stripped Koreans of all liberties since annexation. The coerced use of Japanese in Korean schools is considered, then, as nothing less than an effort to enfeeble Koreans and rob them of their cultural identity.

48. *Joseon ilbo* 1928.10.27. Twelve years later, as news came that by 1941 the Japanese Ministry of Education (Monbushō) would provide the textbooks to be used in Korea, the same newspaper editorialized for the need to include lessons and examples drawn from Korean experiences for the new textbooks to have any meaningful effect in the colony. The colonial regime's special committee on textbooks appears to have concurred, the paper reported. *Joseon ilbo* 1940.5.28.

49. *Donga ilbo* 1922.8.7.

50. What began as a scuffle between Korean and Japanese secondary students in the closing months of 1929 quickly escalated into demonstrations against colonial education policies, which spread to other parts of the colony. By the end of the movement nearly two hundred schools and fifty thousand students had participated, resulting in the arrest or expulsion of thousands of students.

51. *Donga ilbo* 1922.8.14, 1927.1.27; *Joseon ilbo* 1930.3.16; *Donga ilbo* 1931.3.3, 1934.2.7, 1935.3.19.

52. *Donga ilbo* 1925.3.29, 1925.4.1.

53. *Donga ilbo* 1924.3.17, 1925.12.24, 1926.8.14, 1926.10.13. As the last article showed, what proved even more exasperating was that, at the time, a Korean (Yi Jinho) was serving as the Minister of Education for the Government-General. Some other statistics publicly made available by the colonial state reinforce this sense of imbalance. In the mid-1920s, for example, employees at Korean schools, including Japanese administrators and teachers, received approximately 80% of the salary of workers in Japanese schools. And family school fees (*jugyōryō*) for Japanese students constituted a smaller percentage (10–15%) of the overall fiscal input than for Koreans (15–20%), meaning that the state devoted more resources per capita to the Japanese schools to cover the rest of the expenses. *Tōkei* (1925), pp. 660–73.

54. This was when editors defaced the Japanese flag in a picture of the Korean winner of the 1936 Olympic marathon.

55. From 1937 onward the newspaper focused more of its energy on reporting and encouraging the hiring and better treatment of Korean school principals, officials, and teachers. See, for example, *Donga ilbo* 1937.11.23, 1938.3.4, 1939.2.28, 1939.3.7, 1939.3.30, 1939.11.29.

56. The paper, for example, reported that a Korean member of the school committee, at a meeting of the North Jeolla Provincial Council (Do hyōgikai) in 1933, complained that only three of the more than five hundred Korean elementary schools in the province had a Korean school principal. The council responded that this was a matter for the central government to address. *Donga ilbo* 1933.3.10.

57. Takashi Fujitani, *Race for Empire,* locs. 6156, 6194.

58. The volumes of such collected Government-General documents are held today by the South Korean National Archives (*Gukga girogwon*), including *Gakusoku henkō* (1926), which contain the colonial state's recognition of, or directions for implementing, internal rules for individual public schools. The approval for Gyeongseong (not to be confused with the capital, which in Korean bore the same pronunciation) Teacher Training High School, for example, specified that one of its school holidays would be the "Anniversary of the Beginning of the Government-General's Rule," presumably in late August. Chōsen sōtokufu, *Gakusoku henkō* (1926), p. 25.

59. See, for example, the representative coverage of the colonial period educational experience in the massive survey, *Hanguk gyoyuk 100-nyeonsa, 1880–1999,* which features a constant refrain of brave Korean resistance to continuously repressive and exploitative colonial measures. The most dramatic and overstated chapter (pp. 246–49), entitled "Educational Policies to Eradicate the Korean Nation," concludes that all the education policies during wartime uniformly aimed at extinguishing Korean culture and identity.

60. It is striking that the Korean and Japanese term most closely corresponding to "citizen" refers to membership in the country or state, not the city. This reflects in part the much longer tradition and strength of Confucian statecraft and state centralization in East Asia. Notably, the term literally for citizen—i.e., in reference to the city—in South Korea today is usually attached to groups and movements *in opposition* to the state, such as "civic groups" (*simin danche*) or "citizen movements" (*simin undong*). This interestingly resembles more the European historical path that resulted in "citizenship," dating back to the times of ancient Greece and more recently in the early modern era when the "Bürger" or "bourgeoisie" often stood in opposition to monarchical or feudal rule. To add further complexity, this term for a "city's people" (*simin*), quirkily, is also used to specify one's country of citizenship—e.g., the identification reflected in one's passport.

61. See Gim So-yeong, "Gabo gaehyeok (1894–1895) gyogwaseo sok e 'gungmin.'" Gim also argues that, up to the Gabo period, the term *gungmin* overlapped with "subject" (*sinmin*) more than with "citizen." This is debatable, but it reflects the fluidity of these terms.

62. Kyung Moon Hwang, "Country or State?" For a representative example of the collectivist, nonstatist textbook, see Hyeon Chae's work for private schools, *Yunyeon pildok* (Compulsory Reader for Children). In its chapter on "The Citizens' Rights" (*Gungmin ui gwolli*), this text insists that everyone enjoys heaven-endowed, inalienable rights that are protected even from the monarch (*ingun*) or officials (*sinha*). Hangukhak munheon yeonguso, ed. *Hanguk gaehwagi gyogwaseo chongseo* (hereafter, HGGC) v. 2, pp. 34–35.

63. Its most conspicuous appearance comes in the *Great Learning* by Confucius, as part of a larger chain of metaphysical existence connected to the family, country, and heaven.

64. HGGC v. 1, pp. 2–3.

65. These early works apparently were not in wide circulation, however, as an editorial suggested in decrying the lack of published textbooks for Korean elementary schooling. *The Independent,* 1897.06.12.

66. HGGC v. 9, pp. 159–369.

67. At the top of the cover page of this textbook, it is noted that the book had been "approved by the Education Ministry" (*Hakbu geomjeong*). Article 15 of the 1895 Royal Edict on Primary Schooling noted that textbooks not published directly by the Education Ministry could also be used with such an approval.

68. See Son In-su, *Hanguk gyoyuksa yeongu* v. 1, pp. 25–26, for a listing of the official reasons, including excessive nationalism and even the promotion of socialism, for denying the approval of textbooks. See also Ham Jong-gyu, op. cit., pp. 65–70, for the long list of prohibited books, including *Jungdeung susin gyogwaseo.*

69. HGGC v. 9, pp. 235–38, 340.

70. HGGC v. 9, pp. 340–42.

71. According to Gim So-yeong's comparison of one particular Japanese ethics textbook of the time and its modified Korean translation of 1908—just before the prohibition of such works—the Korean version in fact one-upped the Japanese original by elevating the Korean monarchy to a status as an absolute monarchy *in practice,* not just in theory as was the case, so the book says, in Japan and China. Gim suggests that this reflected the difficulties of implementing a strong state and its correspondent need for cultivating a sense of national identity in relation to the monarchy, given the urgent circumstances of the time. See Gim So-yeong, "Hanmal susin gyogwaseo beonyeok gwa 'gungmin' hyeongseong," pp. 16–17, 32.

72. HGGC v. 9, pp. 335–41.

73. Namgung and Gim, *Gyoyuk ui yeoksa wa sasang,* pp. 218–19; Michael Seth, *Education Fever,* pp. 17–18.

74. HGGC v. 9, pp. 345–48.

75. Gim So-yeong, op. cit., pp. 12–13, 20–21.

76. HGGC v. 9, pp. 665–66.

77. HGGC v. 10, pp. 520–31.

78. HGGC v. 9, pp. 83–155.

79. *Botong gyoyukhak* (1910), pp. 39–44.

80. "Chōsen kyōikurei," *Kanpō* 1911.9.1. For the official text of the original Meiji Rescript, see *Kyōiku chokugo kampatsu kankei shiryōshū,* v. 1 (1935), which also includes the Chinese, English, French, and German translations of the Rescript. The English version renders the phrase as "good and faithful subjects."

81. Gim Sun-jeon and Bak Je-hong, "Hwangguk sinmin ui yukseong: 'Botong hakgyo susinseo' e natanan chung ui byeonyong," pp. 82–95; Gim Gyeong-mi, "Botong hakgyo jedo ui hwangnip gwa hakgyo hunnyuk ui hyeongseong," p. 499; *Shisei* (1915), pp. 330ff.

82. Jeong Hye-jeong, "Ilje gangjeomgi botong hakgyo gyoyuk jeongchaek yeongu," pp. 123–53.

83. Gim Gyeong-mi, op. cit., p. 506.

84. For more on the often subtle changes in education policy that took place in politics and among politicians (and bureaucrats) in the aftermath of March First, see Chiho Sawada, "Cultural Politics in Imperial Japan and Colonial Korea: Reinventing Assimilation and Education Policy, 1919–1922," pp. 245–45, 254–56.

85. Chōsen sōtokufu, *Futō gakko shūshinsho hensan shuisho* (1924), pp. 2–5; Chōsen sōtokufu gakumukyoku, *Chōsen kyōiku yōran* (1926), p. 33; *Futō gakko shūshinsho—kyōshiyō* (1923), v. 6, pp. 1–7.

86. *Futō gakko shūshinsho—kyōshiyō* (1923), v. 5, pp. 99–100. One sees such incorporation of the term *kōmin* also in the proposed curricula for the "young men's training centers" (*seinen kunrenjo*), which were established in the late 1920s to mimic those in Japan. The first and presumably most important subject in these training centers, meant originally for mostly Japanese resident teens but later including also Koreans, was "how to elevate one's qualities as a citizen" (*kokumin taru no shishitsu o kōjō*), taught through the "ethics and public citizen department curriculum" (*Shūshin oyobi kōminka*). See Chōsen sōtokufu, *Seinen kunrenjo ninteishorui* (1928–29), pp. 701, 724, 746, for examples from the applications for certification presented by such prospective training centers in Incheon, Masan, and Sinuiju.

87. Chōsen sōtokufu, *Futō gakko shūshinsho—Yonnensei* (1933), v. 4, pp. 21–23.

88. Ibid., p. 33; see also *Futō gakko shūshinsho—kyōshiyō* (1923) v. 6, p. 1.

89. Chōsen sōtokufu, *Futō gakko shūshinsho hensan shuisho* (1924), p. 2; Chōsen sōtokufu gakumukyoku, *Chōsen kyōiku yōran* (1926), p. 33.

90. *Chōsen kyōiku yōran* (1926), pp. 149–50, 157.

91. *Futō gakko shūshinsho—kyōshiyō* (1923), v. 5, pp. 95–97.

92. The preponderance of "filiality" in the *Shūshinsho* headings can be seen in the rundown of chapters in Chōsen sōtokufu, *Futō gakko shūshinsho hensan shuisho* (1924), pp. 20–31; see also *Futō gakko shūshinsho—kyōshiyō* (1923), v. 5, pp. 179–80.

93. *Donga ilbo* 1938.4.6.

94. "Chōsen kyōikurei," Chokurei No. 103, *Kanpō* 1938.3.4.

95. *Donga ilbo* 1940.2.28.

96. "Yukoku" [Instructions], *Kanpō* 1938.3.4, p. 2.

97. See, for example, the findings from interviews detailed in Russell Vacante, "Japanese Colonial Education in Korea: An Oral History." There are many methodological problems with this study, as the author found precisely the kinds of answers about which he queried—namely, the degree of suppression and nationalistic response that the elderly interviewees could recall from their childhoods. But the one consistent, plausible response that diverged from the line of questioning, which did not probe the issue of citizenship education at all, was that the restrictions on the teaching and use of the Korean language in the public schools began early in the colonial period and accelerated through the wartime measures.

98. Such language is seen in almost all of the proclamations and commentaries of the time, including the March 1938 Middle School Ordinance, reproduced in the *Kanpō* official gazette and, for the Korean-language version, the *Maeil sinbo* newspaper. Heo Jae-yeong, *Joseon gyoyungnyeong gwa gyoyuk jeongchaek byeonhwa jaryo*, pp. 176, 223. From its inception, the Meiji Imperial Rescript had served strategically

as an ideological weapon for conservative official forces against pluralistic, individualistic, and nonstatist voices, which appear to have gained considerably in the 1910s and 1920s. See Yukihiko Motoyama, "Thought and Education in the Meiji Era."

99. *Joseon ilbo* 1939.4.19. A year later, in a similar report concerning curricular changes in South Hamgyeong province, the *Joseon ilbo* appeared much more enthusiastic about the transformation of schools into "educational organs for imperial subjects." *Joseon ilbo* 1940.5.10. In any case, the newspaper was shut down a few months later for the duration of the war.

100. See, for example, *Nihon shokuminchi kyōiku seisaku shiryō shūsei—Chōsenhen,* v. 4, pp. 5, 8.

101. Chōsen sōtokufu, *Chūtō kyōiku shūshinsho* v. 4 (1938), pp. 38–80.

102. This step had been anticipated for a while. See, for example, *Joseon ilbo* 1940.5.26. But as with the abolition of the separate term for Korean primary schools through the 1938 reforms, the 1941 introduction of the *Kokumin gakko* system did not necessarily mean that, in reality, the two sets of schools for Japanese and Korean schoolchildren were integrated, nor was such integration seriously pursued. Even amidst the total war mobilization, these deficiencies continued to draw public criticism. See Mark Caprio, *Japanese Assimilation Policies in Colonial Korea, 1910–1945,* pp. 154–55.

103. The American occupation authorities' official English translation of this notoriously difficult term rendered *kokutai* as "national entity" in order to "reduce it to its unemotional original meaning." See Robert King Hall, ed., *Kokutai No Hongi: Cardinal Principles of the National Entity of Japan,* p. 15.

104. A pronounced glorification of dying, as a form of "sacrificing for the emperor," appears in the 1940s *shūshin* textbooks. See Gim Sun-jeon and Bak Je-hong, "Hwangguk sinmin ui yukseong: 'Botong hakgyo susinseo' e natanan chung ui byeonyong," p. 102.

105. Chōsen sōtokufu, *Chūtō kyōiku shūshinsho* v. 5 (1943), pp. 25–53.

106. In his study of the political forces behind the education reform initiative immediately following the March First uprisings, Chiho Sawada suggests that instead of considering education as an extension of Cultural Rule, one should rather take Cultural Rule, as a whole, as an expression of an education-centered policy, an approach that had been implemented in ameliorating social tension in Japan proper. See Chiho Sawada, op. cit., p. 322.

CHAPTER SEVEN

1. This is what Jared Diamond, in his prominent account of the ecological origins of cultural diversity, suggests. See Diamond, *Guns, Germs, and Steel,* Chapter 12.

2. See Jane Caplan and John Torpey, eds., *Documenting Individual Identity,* Introduction.

3. Michel Foucault, *Security Territory, Population* (hereafter, STP), p. 70. This text is the transcribed lectures he delivered at the *College de France* in 1977–78 on the origins of the modern state.

4. Foucault also incorporated the epistemology of political economy and the goal of security into his expansive definition: "By 'governmentality' I understand the ensemble formed by institutions, procedures, analyses and reflections, calculations, and tactics that allow the exercise of this very specific, albeit very complex, power that has the population as its target, political economy as its major form of knowledge, and apparatuses of security as its essential technical instrument." Foucault considered governmentality as the analytically external mechanism of power that was incorporated into the state at a specific moment in time, and hence is central to a proper analysis of the modern state's emergence historically. STP, pp. 108, 118–20.

5. Foucault, *The Birth of Biopolitics,* p. 2

6. See STP, pp. 1, 10. Foucault also believed that the state transition to a governmentalized focus on population, or biopolitics, heralded the onset of liberalism as a viable alternative to absolutism, a thesis he covers in his next course, the lectures for which are transcribed in *The Birth of Biopolitics*. Foucault implied strongly that the population-centered governmentality heralded the onset of, and naturally led to, liberalism, which "let" things happen through guidance, instead of coercion. One could also suggest, however, that totalitarianism was just as much a logical end, and that a preoccupation with biopower was sufficiently versatile to lend itself to a range of modern state forms.

7. STP, p. 72.

8. STP, pp. 274–78, 326–28.

9. STP, pp. 345–48, 352–54.

10. Bruce Curtis, "Foucault on Governmentality and Population: The Impossible Discovery," pp. 508–9, 529–30. As Curtis points out, Foucault saw this transition in which the state "discovers" the population as having been informed by the premodern Christian pastoral tradition. For Foucault's discussion of Christian pastoralism and its appropriation by the modern state, see STP, pp. 125–29.

11. Pierre Bourdieu, "Rethinking the State: Genesis and Structure of the Bureaucratic Field," pp. 1, 7.

12. James Scott's book examined the monstrous outcomes of grand twentieth-century state planning projects. Scott, *Seeing Like a State.*

13. Roland Axtmann, "The State of the State," p. 267. See also Jacqueline Urla, "Cultural Politics in an Age of Statistics: Numbers, Nations, and the Making of Basque Identity." Urla's study examines the use of statistics as "instruments of social description" by both the state and those who opposed state policies.

14. Nicolas Dirks, *Castes of Mind.*

15. Norbert Peabody, "Cents, Sense, and Census: Human Inventories in Late Precolonial and Early Colonial India." Peabody finds striking correspondences between the precolonial Mughal household survey categories of caste and the early British colonial census efforts, arguing that the economic interests of the primary

bureaucratic informants to the British—merchants and other "scribal groups" who had carried out the Mughal surveys—were key to the way the colonial state came to perceive caste delineation. See also the book review of the Dirks book by Diane Mines, in *American Ethnologist* 30.2 (2003.5): 312–13.

16. See Anders Karlsson, "Famine Relief, Social Order, and State Performance in Late Chosŏn Korea." Karlsson notes that in the eighteenth century the Joseon state developed measures to provide relief in the wake of natural disasters, and to care for orphans in times of famine. In this sense, Mencian welfare concerns bequeathed to the civilizations that embraced Confucian statecraft, including Joseon Korea, a pervasive heritage of "state salvationism," in Alexander Woodside's terms: the capacity and responsibility of state policies to control conditions such as food supply and poverty. See Woodside, *Lost Modernities*, p. 68.

17. The clan identity (*seong-ssi*) actually consisted of two parts, the clan seat (*bon*) and the surname (*seong*).

18. The four ancestors, commonly listed not only for household registers but also in other contexts requiring ancestral clarification (such as an examination roster), consisted of the father, paternal and maternal grandfathers, and paternal great-grandfather.

19. Yi Hun-sang, "19 segi hojeok daejang ui jiyeok-hwa."

20. The dynastic code, the last version of which, the *Daejeon hoetong*, was promulgated in 1865, hinted strongly at a rampant problem of nonregistration; most of the lengthy section on household registration specified in exacting detail the punishments for people and officials who failed to properly carry out their duties. These penal provisions, in fact, had been appended to the original dynastic code a century earlier in the revision of King Yeongjo's era (*Sok daejeon*), further indicating that the these abuses had reached severe proportions for some time. *Daejeon hoetong:* Hojeon (Code of taxation): Hojeok (Household registration): Nuhoja (Those not registered). Furthermore, the problem did not lie exclusively with the conniving of the local clerks and county magistrates. The people themselves strenuously did what they could to avoid the levies. See Choe Hong-gi, *Hanguk hojeok jedosa yeongu*, pp. 153–58; James Palais, *Confucian Statecraft and Korean Institutions*, p. 737.

21. James Palais, *Politics and Policy in Traditional Korea*, Chapter 5; Gim Ok-geun, *Joseon wangjo jaejeongsa yeongu*, pp. 377–80.

22. See Gojong Sunjong sillok (hereafter, GSS) 1890.3.19; GSS 1890.11.22. Ideas for improvement could be seen in memorials and gazetteer articles in circulation in the 1880s and 1890s. Typical was an editorial in the *Hanseong jubo* ("Seoul weekly") in 1886, which put forth as a model for government reform Western practices, which were said to include information on the people's "status, gender, age, wealth, life or death, and marriage" situation. "Seol tonggye" [On statistics], *Hanseong jubo* 1886.9.6, in *Hanguk sinmun saseol seonjip* (hereafter, HSSS), v. 1, p. 131.

23. Yi Hun-sang, "Gabo gyeongjanggi," pp. 355–58.

24. GSS 1894.12.07; GSS 1895.4.29, *Chingnyeong* 85. The records, for example, of the Mapo area households, *Mapo bunseo hogu seongchaek*, currently held by the

Republic of Korea's Government Archives, date from 1904 and were compiled by the Western division of the Seoul Police.

25. See, for example, GSS 1895.4.5, *Chingnyeong* 71. A strong indicator of the Gabo government's seriousness of purpose regarding government financial reform appears in the published "Explanation of the 1895 Budget." This work's lament about the continuing difficulties of balancing the budget, of gathering local tax revenue into central government coffers, of reforming local government toward this end, and of controlling "sundry expenditures" (*yesan oe jichul*—a subtle dig, it appears, at the unpredictable expenses associated with the royal household, such as the private guards), is supported with precise calculations of expenditures and revenues. See "Gaeguk 504-nyeon yesan seolmyeongseo." See also chapters 2 and 4.

26. *Gaksa deungnok,* Gyu 17721, 1896.9.1.

27. *Gwanbo* 1896.9.4, 1896.9.8.

28. Son Byeong-gyu, "Myeongchi hojeok gwa Gwangmu hojeok bigyo yeongu," pp. 292–95.

29. A tremendous variety of such official statuses appeared in these Joseon registers, and a major portion of these markers indicated one's actual working activity. See Song Yang-seop, "Joseon hugi sinbun jigyeok yeongu wa jigyeok cheje ui insik." See also Yi Jun-gu, *Joseon hugi sinbun jigyeok byeondong yeongu,* Appendix 1.

30. The *Dongnip sinmun* newspaper, in an 1898 article on "Hojeok abuses," claimed that the new registration system actually created more problems than it solved, with the primary fault lying in the lack of proper information relayed to the local clerks and communities. With the new registration forms in their hands, the newspaper noted, the *hyangni* clerks came knocking at the door claiming only to carry out orders to conduct a new household survey, but the people suspected that the survey's sole purpose was to levy more taxes; hence many of them bribed the clerks to keep them off the new registers. *Dongnip sinmun* 1898.9.9.

31. The *Mansebo* newspaper's editorial of May of 1907, for example, decried the shabby condition of the paper, the ink, and other aspects of the registration form itself. See *Mansebo* 1907.5.7.

32. *Gwanbo* 1909.3.6, 1909.3.23.

33. See, for example, *Hwangseong sinmun* 1909.2.16.

34. *Kanpō* 1912.3.18.

35. Nakata Tenbyō, *Chōsen kosekirei yōgi* (1923), p. 14; and Nakahara Shigeru, *Chōsen koseki hikkeishū* (hereafter, CKH) (1930), Appendix, pp. 2–3.

36. Yi Seung-il, *Joseon chongdokbu beopje jeongchaek,* pp. 369–70.

37. Marie Seong-Hak Kim, *Law and Custom in Korea,* pp. 151, 158. Kim's larger argument in this work is that customary law was invented by the colonial state and simply was nonexistent in Korea during the Joseon era, when laws were almost exclusively geared toward penal and administrative matters. Kim, pp. 3–6.

38. Marie Kim, pp. 173–74; Yao Jen-To, "The Japanese Colonial State and Its Form of Knowledge in Taiwan," locs. 1300–15.

39. "Shin koseki seido," *Shisei* (1923), p. 368.

40. One of the official reasons was to benefit the local government offices financially. See *Shisei* (1923), p. 368.

41. Nakata Tenbyō, *Chōsen kosekirei yōgi,* pp. 4–6, 19–20, 33–36; Marie Kim, p. 175.

42. For a thorough analysis of court cases involving customary law in the colonial period, see Sungyun Lim, "Enemies of the Lineage: Widows and Customary Rights in Colonial Korea, 1910–1945." As the title of her work suggests, Lim finds that the colonial state's primary motive was not to overturn long-standing patriarchal practices and principles, but rather to weaken, against often fierce resistance, the hold on inheritance and family customs of the patrilineal descent groups. Lim asserts that, in so doing, the colonial state and Korean litigants both played a major role in standardizing and, frankly, inventing Korean customary family law.

43. The journal, *Chōsen koseki* [Korean household registration], was published by the Chōsen koseki kyōkai [Korean household registration association] and carried bureaucratic guidelines as well as statistics and reports on the progress of various measures. The manuals included two compilations by Nakahara Shigeru, a court clerk in Busan: *Koseki jimu hikkei* [Handbook of household registration work] (1927), which interestingly included glosses of Korean grammatical particles to the Japanese text in another sign of the abundance of Korean local officials; and the *Chōsen koseki hikkeishū*, which included a forward by the sitting Minister of Legal Affairs (*Hōmukyokuchō*) in the Government-General.

44. CKH, Appendix, pp. 208–9.

45. Sungyun Lim suggests, rather, that widows might have served as the most representative of these legal complexities. Widows were featured most prominently in adoption disputes, which took up 70% of all family court cases. Lim, "Enemies of the Lineage," Introduction.

46. Most divorce petitions from women arose from distress over the practice of concubinage by their husbands. See K. Gija, "Hojeok-changgu e natanan insaeng ui huibigeuk" (1939).

47. The analysis of this section is based on the computerized data pulled from expired registers from 1911 onward in Eonyang county (in today's Ulsan) by the Naksungdae Economic Research Institute.

48. Strikingly, the published genealogies, many of which were fabricated, were seen as authoritative by some officials. The 1930 bureaucratic manual, in fact, designated Korean genealogies as the definitive source for determining kinship in case of dispute. CKH, Appendix, p. 211.

49. See Articles 57, 61, and 70 of the 1922 ordinance. CKH, Appendix, pp. 20–23. The formal instructions accompanying the introduction of the civil registration system of 1909 had suggested also an equality between wife and concubine, stating that recording the concubine in the register "be in accordance with that of the wife." "Minjeokbeop jiphaeng simdeok," Articles 3 and 10, *Gwanbo* 1909.3.23.

50. This was the goal and ideal expressed both by colonial state officials and outside commentators. See Nomura Chōtarō, *Chōsen kosekirei gikai* (1923), p. 8; Hong Yang-hui, "Singminji sigi hojeok jedo wa gajok jedo ui byeonyong" (2006), pp. 190–94.

51. The 1909 civil registration system, while suggesting that all children of the household be recorded in order of birth, also reiterated that a concubine's children be specified, and that instead of the wife's name, a concubine's child *can* (not *must*) record the biological mother—that is, the concubine herself. A revision in 1915 suggested that the concubine's children be listed behind the wife's children. The 1922 major revision, while more direct, still appeared to leave the matter somewhat undecided. See "Minjeokbeop jiphaeng simdeok," *Gwanbo* 1909.3.23; Kunrei no. 47, *Kanpō,* 1915.8.7; CKH, Appendix, p. 20.

52. Administrative rulings in responses to judges' inquiries demonstrated the complexity and sensitivity of recording concubines' children in the registers. For example, in 1924 a judge in Pyongyang wondered how to handle the case of a man who married his concubine following the death of his wife. Was it simply a matter of elevating the registered designation of the concubine's sons and thereby integrating them into the same status as that of the first wife's sons? In response, the Government-General's Ministry of Legal Affairs stated that the integration of the two sets of children should take place in the registers, but in terms of inheritance, at least, the original order (wife's children, then original concubine's children) should be followed, even if the father later married the concubine. A year later, in response to an inquiry from a judge in Seoul, the Ministry stated that, "in accordance with customs," even if the wife's son was in utero at the time of the household head's (father's) death, that son would, upon his birth, gain inheritance priority over the concubine's children, although the latter would briefly enjoy that designation before the wife's child was born. CKH, pp. 212–13, 358–59.

53. Yi Jeong-seon, "Hanguk geundae hojeok jedo ui byeoncheon," pp. 303–6.

54. Fujitani, *Race for Empire,* locs. 1026, 1776. Fujitani cites memos declaring a new concern for the health and welfare of the Korean population, due to the acute problems of population shortage for the war.

55. Fujitani, locs. 1605, 1771, 5994.

56. Yi Myeong-jong, "Ilje malgi Joseonin jingbyeong eul wihan giryu jedo," p. 84.

57. As part of a larger local history project, the Naksungdae Economic Research Institute input the data from expired residence registers of Eonyang county from the 1910s to the 1970s.

58. "Chōsen shutōrei shikō kisoku," Furoku, Article 1, *Kanpō* 1923.5.23.

59. See Yi Seung-il, "Joseon chongdokbu ui Joseonin deungnok jedo yeongu," pp. 27–29; and Bak Hui-jin, "Ilje Eonyang jiyeok giryu gagu ui bungeo," pp. 63–65.

60. "Chōsen kiryūrei" and "Chōsen kiryū tetsuzu kisoku," *Kanpō* 1942.9.26. Such newcomers were considered "residents" (*kiryūja*) and thus had to report. The penalty for not reporting (such as "sloth") was up to 10 yen. Fujitani also mentions the new residence registers but appears to conflate them with the household registers. Fujitani, *Race for Empire,* locs. 1789–1813.

61. A dedicated survey of registers of eligible males for conscription (age 20 and below) was begun in early 1943, and it also found roughly 40%, or about 2.5 million, in need of some kind of correction in the registers. Not coincidentally, this was the

approximate percentage of prospective conscripts whose addresses were unclear, according to a provincial survey in the fall of 1943. *Maeil sinbo* 1943.1.26. Yi Myeong-jong, "Ilje malgi Joseonin jingbyeong," pp. 93–94, 97–99. Brandon Palmer shows that the colonial authorities dedicated great efforts and resources simply to uncover the extent, for a variety of reasons, to which the registers were inaccurate and the Koreans were avoiding their registration obligations. See Palmer, *Fighting for the Enemy*, pp. 108–10.

62. Formal requests to correct one's age also appear to have clogged the bureaucratic machinery. Yi Myeong-jong, op. cit., pp. 99–100. For reports and editorials in the official organ calling for sustained vigilance and cooperation in straightening the registers (now referred to as "hojeok giryu"), see *Maeil sinbo* 1943.7.11, 1944.5.10, 1944.6.30, 1945.1.28.

63. As with the 1896 household registration system and 1911 residency registers, for example, the new residence registers of 1942 conceived of households as *setai* (not *ko*, as in the household registers) in order to track not necessarily families but rather people who lived together and engaged in common economic activity. The new residence registers required that a new resident specify his relationship to both the "head of [*ko*] household" and "head of the [*setai*] household" to which he belonged. "Chōsen kiryū tetsuzu kisoku," *Kanpō* 1942.9.26. See also Yi Seung-il, op. cit., pp. 32–35.

64. Household registers from the following counties were examined: From the old documents collection of the National Central Library of Korea, Goksan (Hwanghae province, 1900) and Tongjin (Gyeonggi, 1901). From the Museum of Jeonbuk National University (for various years), Pyeonghae (Gangwon), Damyang (S. Jeolla), Jinju (S. Gyeongsang), Haman (S. Gyeongsang), Bonghwa (N. Gyeongsang), Sunchang (S. Jeolla). From the Gyujanggak Library, Goksan (Hwanghae, 1896), Byeon-gye (N. Hamgyeong, 1903), Chosan (N. Pyeongan, 1902), Haenam (S. Jeolla, 1899, 1908), Incheon (Gyeonggi, 1898).

65. *Mapo bunseo hogu seongchaek* (1904). This proliferation of registered occupations squares with Jo Seongyun and Jo Eun's analysis of the Seoul area registers and O Seong's survey of registers from five counties in Gyeonggi province, which for their part reveal many other listings for "jigeop," such as cloth dealer (*posang*) and even maker of musical instruments (*akgong*). See Jo Seongyun and Jo Eun, "Hanmal ui gajok gwa sinbun"; O Seong, "Hanmal Gyeonggido jibang ui hoju guseong ui yangsang."

66. This random, albeit representative, sampling of the expired *minjeok* registers (*jejeokbu*) from the 1909–12 period was held in the Gongju municipal government office, *hojeok* division, when the author examined them in 2002.

67. See Yi Heonchang, op. cit., p. 35.

68. See "Minsekihō no setsumei" (1909), pp. 8–10, for comments on the need for "supplemental registers" to accommodate the "so-called nobi [slaves]."

69. These figures were published as the *Minjeok tonggyepyo* [Statistical charts of the civil registers, 1910], which provide occupational breakdowns for all the townships throughout the country.

70. Son Byeong-gyu, op. cit., pp. 306–9. On the problems surrounding sample case studies of even the ostensibly straightforward category of age in the Indian colonial census projects, see Timothy L. Alborn, "Age of Empire in the Indian Census, 1871–1931."

71. This locale is now part of the city of Ulsan on the southeast coast.

72. See *Minjeok tonggyepyo* (1910), p. 261.

73. This analysis comes from the data of expired registers from 1911 to 1977, which total over 45,000 individuals, input by the Naksungdae Economic Research Institute. For the colonial era, 18,000 individuals were recorded.

74. The percentage of "farmers" in the registers goes from approximately 75% of all households in the first full year of colonial rule (1911) to 90–95% thereafter, through the wartime mobilization period of 1938–45. This may not be significant, given that usually occupations were not listed at all.

75. See Bak Hui-jin, "Ilje Eonyang jiyeok giryu gagu ui bungeo," p. 72. Based on data from residency registers (*geoju deungnokbu*) gathered for Eonyang township by the Naksungdae Economic Research Institute. This was likely related to greater attention to another regular duty of local officials, which was to report figures for the Statistical Annual of the Government-General (*Chōsen sōtokufu tōkei nenpō*), the occupational categories of which were slightly different from that of the 1909 system. It appears that village elders maintained a list of their respective populations and simply supplied the occupational breakdown according to these categories when the local clerks came around for the annual survey.

76. In fact the household registers in some localities produced an over-count of the population, as people who listed their permanent address in a certain locale remained on the registers even after they had moved away. See Bak Hui-jin et al., "20 segi hojeokbu ui ingu gijae beomwi wa girok ui jeonghwakseong."

77. An abbreviated census was undertaken in 1925, the results from which were published as a "Simplified Census Report" (Kani kokusei chōsa hōkokusho), which did not track occupations. *Kanpō* 1925.5.28.

78. An article in a government monthly stated that the 1930 census planned to mobilize 72,000 surveyors who were to visit households beginning on October 1 to either gather the completed census forms or do a direct survey. Kawano Setsufu, "Sohwa onyeon gukse josa sihaeng e chwihayeo" (1930), pp. 4–8. For the 1935 survey, over 52,000 census takers drawn from local officials, residents, and others (for an average of 93 households surveyed for each surveyor) began their work at noon on October 1 and finished in two months. A special Interim Census Division was established in the Governor-General's office to oversee the entire effort, and corresponding special agencies were established at the provincial and local levels. See *Showa jūnen Chōsen kokusei chōsa hōkoku, kekka-hyo, zensen-hen* (1935), pp. 1–7. Furthermore, like the residence registers, the census surveys labeled their basis unit for household *setai,* not the *ko* of the household registers, and generally included everyone who lived together *and* depended on a common livelihood, regardless of familial relations—just as the 1896 household registration system (but not the 1909 system) had done. A person or group of persons who lived separately, or who engaged

in another occupation, was said to constitute a separate *setai*. See Chokurei #396, *Kanpō* 1930.1.10; Furei #8, Kanpō 1925.2.25; and Furei #75, *Kanpō* 1935.5.27. In early 1944, in fact, the base unit for household, again, was *setai* instead of *ko*, just as it was for the census reports of the 1930s and the 1911 and 1942 residence registration systems. See Yi Seung-il, op. cit., pp. 32–36.

79. See *Showa gonen Chōsen kokusei chōsa hōkoku, zensen-hen, kekka-hyo* (1930), Appendix, pp. 7–8; Naikaku tōkeikyoku, *Kokusei chōsa tōkeito* (1930).

80. *Kanpō* 1944.2.19. This division into, first, "industries" was apparently a corrective to the incompleteness of the 1935 census, which stopped at labeling people's occupations. This general shift toward wartime categorization imperatives was reflected in the figures of an earlier state publication as well: Chōsen sōtokufu, ed., *Chōsen jijō* (1943), pp. 7–8. What stands out in this work is that, by 1942, almost 120,000 households were listed as engaged in mining.

81. For a helpful overview of how assigning surnames have gone hand in hand with the development of state interests to increase surveillance and extraction, from ancient China to recent colonial states, see Scott, *Seeing Like a State,* pp. 64–73.

82. Technically, "creation of surnames and revision of given names."

83. The 1896 ordinance (Article 4 of "Hogu josa sechik") defined "gigu" as people who, because they are not self-reliant and do not have families, cannot form separate households themselves. A corresponding explanation of who should constitute the "goyong" is not included, presumably because it was well understood at the time. Indeed the *Daejeon hoetong* dynastic code of 1865 used the same term in reference to the recording of *nobi* slaves on the household registers.

84. See *Gaksa deungnok* (Gyu 18022), 1899.5.15; Oe Gakbugun gongcheop jeo-gyo 1898.7.30 (Gyu 18022), Naebu panjeokguk 1 chaek, Hamgyeong namdo, bogo 37-ho; Oe Gakbugun gongcheop jeogyo 1899.7.10 (Gyu 18022), Naebu panjeokguk 1 chaek, Hamgyeong bukto, bogo 37-ho.

85. The *baekjeong* registers surveyed here are "Ulsan-gun dohan hojeok-pyo," which cover the period from 1898 to 1904, while those for the Buddhist monks, "Ulsan gaksa chalseung hojeok-pyo," cover the period from 1900 to 1904.

86. Considerable variations likely arose depending on region. A local historian of Jeonju, Yang Man-jeong, insisted that, in the case of a *nobi* slave, the new surname-clan seat combination could not have been the same as that of either the master or local notables, for this would have greatly offended the sensibilities of the latter in an era when status consciousness remained strong (personal communication, January 2002). But historian Yi Su-geon has written that all kinds of solutions were devised; some former slaves, for example, appropriated their masters' clan identities, while others simply took the most common clan identities of the local area. Yi Su-geon, "Seongssi."

87. In South Korea today, the five clan identities with the most numerous populations are, in order, Gimhae Gim, Miryang Bak, Jeonju Yi, Gyeongju Gim, and Gyeongju Yi, and with the exception of the Jeonju Yi, these clans also appear more frequently than others in the registers from the early twentieth century. *Hanguk munhwa dae baekgwa sajeon,* p. 474. The widespread appearance of the Gimhae Gim

is particularly striking. It was by far the most represented clan identity in registers from five different counties in Gyeonggi province at the time, for example. O Seong, op. cit. The *baekjeong* registers of fourteen households in Ulsan count three Gimhae Gim households, which also outnumbered all other clans among the *goyong* servant households in Gongju in the 1909 registers. The instructions for filling out the 1909 registers, in fact, suggests offhand that the Gimhae Gim had already been well established as a fallback clan identity: "In the space for 'bon' [clan seat], it is suggested that the birthplace of the progenitor ancestor [*sijo*] be listed. For example, if the progenitor was born in Gimhae, 'Gimhae' should be written." *Gwanbo* 1909.3.23. The Gimhae Gim would continue to serve as the de facto example for bureaucratic instructions regarding Korean surnames well into the colonial period. See, for example, *Kanpō* 1915.8.7. Regarding the Miryang Bak, see Eugene Park, *A Family of No Prominence,* pp. 19, 76.

88. According to a 1911 ordinance, changing a registered name required going through the local police offices, submitting an application that included the reason for change as well as other information, and paying a 50-sen fee. Wives, concubines, and children under 20 years of age also needed to submit documentation of consent from either the husband (wives and concubines) or the head of the household. In 1915 a stern reminder was issued to provincial officials, who were now entrusted with handling these matters, that petitions for name changes should only be considered in special circumstances. *Kanpō* 1911.10.26, 1915.4.5.

89. The current South Korean system of a resident identification number (*jumin deungnok beonho*) was established in the 1960s.

90. *Kanpō* 1939.11.10, 1939.12.26 (special issue); *Manseon ilbo* 1940.1.5.

91. See also Choe Jae-seong, "Changssi gaemyeong gwa chinil Joseonin ui hyeomnyeok," pp. 349–51.

92. See *Donga ilbo* 1939.11.10, 1940.2.8, 1940.3.5; *Maeil sinbo* 1939.11.09; Mizuno Naoki, *Changssi gaemyeong,* pp. 60–62.

93. Fujitani, *Race for Empire,* loc. 7396. The first of only two articles in System Ordinance no. 20, promulgated on the same date as the amendment to the civil code, began interestingly with a prohibition on Koreans picking certain names associated with the Japanese royal family as their *shi,* and then noted that Koreans could not select another *seong,* or Korean surname, as their officially registered *shi* surname. *Kanpō* 1939.11.10.

94. This would be 3.2 million out of approximately 4 million households. Most of these registrations appear to have come at the tail end of the registration drive, and the final tally seems somewhat exaggerated, at least according to newspaper accounts. The *Donga ilbo* was reporting interim figures of 130,000 households at the three-month mark (1940.6.7), 1 million at the five-month point (1940.7.17), and approximately 1.5 million (37%) just a few weeks before the end of the registration period (1940.8.4).

95. *Donga ilbo* 1939.11.10; Sakamoto Shinichi, "Myeongchi minbeop ui seongssi jedo," pp. 173–75.

96. "Changssi gaemyeong gihoe jul ppun; gangje silsi haji malla" [Registering a new name is only meant to be an opportunity; do not implement by force], *Donga*

ilbo 1940.3.6. This report notes that the Governor-General asked the press to help "prevent misunderstandings" about aspects of the new name registration system. The colonial Minister of Legal Affairs, Miyamoto Gen, claimed that there was no obligation for a Koreans to adopt a Japanese-style surname for his registered *shi;* rather, this was an opportunity made available to those who wished to do so. Miyamoto Gen, "Seoyangja, iseong yangja geup ssi jedo" (1940), p. 289. See also *Manseon ilbo* 1940.3.9.

97. Mizuno Naoki, *Changssi gaemyeong,* 65–67, 139–41, 187–88. Jun Uchida shows that strong opposition arose also from Japanese settlers for various reasons. Uchida, *Brokers of Empire,* pp. 380–82. And Ken Kawashima has detailed how Korean day laborers in Japan turned to the tactic of adopting Japanese surnames for rental contracts in order to counteract the legalized discrimination in housing. See Kawashima, *The Proletarian Gamble,* Chapter 4.

98. Miyamoto Gen, op. cit., p. 290. This practice of keeping a household head's Korean surname while registering a *shi* surname is borne out in the Eonyang county registers.

99. Some, however, welcomed this opportunity to change their registered given names. Most of these people had been stuck with undesirable given names, such as those that indicated slave ancestry. See Yi Dae-hwa, "Changssi gaemyeong jeongchaek gwa Joseonin ui dae-eung," pp. 213–15.

100. Hong Yang-hui, "Singminji sigi hojeok jedo wa gajok jedo ui byeonyong," p. 194; Choe Jae-seong, op. cit., pp. 352–53; and Park Hwan-mu (Bak Hwan-mu), "Effects of the Name Change Policy in Onyang during the Pacific War Period."

101. Miyamoto Gen, op. cit., p. 289.

102. Mizuno, op. cit., pp. 200–10.

103. For administrative clarification on this matter from 1925, see CKH, p. 368. See also Mizuno, pp. 31, 45–54.

104. Miyamoto Gen, op. cit. (1940), p. 235. Miyamoto was referring to the regime's prewar approach.

105. Sungyun Lim asserts that the name change order, particularly through its accompanying directive allowing sons-in-law to gain inheritance rights while reinforcing patriarchal principles, reflected the final step in this long-term maneuver to facilitate assimilation through the Japanese household and family systems, and hence assimilation constituted the most significant feature of the 1939 revision itself. Lim, "Enemies of the Lineage," Chapter 4.

106. See Palmer, *Fighting for the Enemy,* p. 22.

107. A classified report from the Gyeonggi Province Police Department in the spring of 1941, for example, noted the following: "In general the new names [*shin-shimei*] are in use in places such as government offices and schools. But outside of working periods in companies, banks, and other such places, or when speaking with Japanese people, among regular Koreans there are still not a few [*sukunatosesu*] who continue to use their old names [*kyūshimei*]. This is especially the case in rural areas [*gunbu*]." Keikido keisatsu buchō, "Sōshi no riyō jōkyō ni kan suru ken" (1941), p. 3.

108. Yi Dae-hwa, op. cit., pp. 197–212. Yi finds that, although the authorities recognized the subversiveness of this behavior, they did not initially repress it because it increased the registration rate and potentially could encourage other villagers of traditionally lower status in the rural areas to register.

109. Frederick Cooper and Ann Laura Stoler, eds., *Tensions of Empire: Colonial Cultures in a Bourgeois World,* locs. 329–330.

110. The precise rate of compliance, of course, is very difficult to come by, but anecdotal evidence suggests a wide range of reasons for people to forego this obligation. In reporting marriages, for example, some either forgot or deliberately avoided reporting them in order to pursue second marriages or relationships, which often led to comical if discomfiting outcomes, such as lawsuits charging polygamy when the offended party discovered what happened. See K. Gija, op. cit., pp. 279–80. Fujitani, *Race for Empire,* loc. 5994, has found that, before the wartime period, most commoner Koreans seem not to have recognized the significance of how they were recorded in the registers. This is likely because the household head, under the oversight of local clerks, usually was responsible for reporting any changes in the household's makeup.

CHAPTER EIGHT

1. Dorothy Porter, *Health, Civilization and the State,* pp. 97, 104.

2. Edward Ross Dickinson, "Biopolitics, Fascism, Democracy," p. 3.

3. Michel Foucault, *The Birth of the Clinic,* pp. xiii–xiv.

4. Foucault situates this transition in the late eighteenth century, when the accumulation of knowledge from local state organs about the populace's health conditions systematized state interest in the population. See STP, pp. 57–63, for his views on how the targeting of individuals for disciplining was reflected in smallpox inoculation measures. See also Foucault, *Discipline and Punish,* pp. 144, 197–200, for the framing of these developments, including the shaping of modern hospitals, in panoptic disciplining. As the translator notes, Foucault's term of *surveiller* has no precise equivalent in English, but the author himself suggested using "discipline" to connote the combination of observation and coercion implied in the French word.

5. For more on the centrality of social medicine as a core state concern in the emergence of governmentality in Europe, see Foucault, *The Birth of the Clinic,* p. 34; and Bruce Curtis, "Foucault on Governmentality and Population," pp. 511–15.

6. Kyung Moon Hwang, *Beyond Birth,* Chapter 3.

7. Sabine Frühstück, *Colonizing Sex: Sexology and Social Control in Modern Japan.*

8. Yi Jong-chan, *Dongasia uihak ui jeontong gwa geundae,* pp. 202–6; Porter, op. cit., p. 106.

9. Ruth Rogaski, *Hygienic Modernity: Meanings of Health and Disease in Treaty-Port China;* Sin Gyu-hwan, *Gukga, dosi, wisaeng,* pp. 36, 42–52.

10. Rogaski, op. cit., Chapter 9.

11. The process, for example, by which a discursive site of contestation in British-controlled India emerged over the suitability and meaning of Western medicine, is a primary insight offered by David Arnold's *Colonizing the Body: State Medicine and Epidemic Disease in Nineteenth-Century India*. On the systematic impact of the "bacteriological revolution" on the notions and interventionist methods of public health in Europe, see Porter, op. cit., pp. 139–43.

12. Yi Jong-chan, op. cit., pp. 237–38. See also Liu Shiyung, "The Theory and Practice of Malariology in Colonial Taiwan"; and Michael Shiyung Liu, *Prescribing Colonization: The Role of Medical Practices and Policies in Japan-Ruled Taiwan, 1895–1945*, Chapter 4.

13. Sin Dong-won, *Hanguk geundae bogeon uiryosa*; and Bak Yun-jae, *Hanguk geundae uihak ui giwon*.

14. Arnold argues that the contested objectification of the human body in the mechanisms of colonial rule and the discourse that arose therefrom together constituted the "corporality" of British colonialism. David Arnold, *Colonizing the Body*, pp. 7–8.

15. Jin-kyung Park, "Corporeal Colonialism: Medicine, Reproduction, and Race in Colonial Korea."

16. Sonja Kim, "Contesting Bodies: Managing Population, Birthing, and Medicine in Korea, 1876–1945."

17. Gim Hye-gyeong, *Singminji-ha geundae gajok ui hyeongseong gwa jendeo*.

18. Foucault, *The Birth of Biopolitics*, pp. 5–7, 284.

19. Foucault, *The Birth of the Clinic*, pp. 25–26. Foucault considered the police's centrality to disease control as an extension of its centrality in the wide-ranging exercise of governmentalized biopower: "Health becomes an object of police inasmuch as health is also a necessary condition for the many who subsist thanks to the provision of foodstuffs and bare necessities, so that they can work, be busy and occupied. So health is not just a problem for police in cases of epidemics, when plague is declared, or when it is simply a matter of avoiding the contagious . . . ; henceforth the everyday health of everyone becomes a permanent object of police concern and intervention." STP, pp. 324–25.

20. *Gwanbo* 1894.6.28.

21. *Beomnyeong* v. 1, pp. 39 (1894.7.14), 428 (1895.5.5).

22. Much of the knowledge about cholera appears to have drawn from recent experiences in Japan, which had suffered an outbreak following the Satsuma Rebellion in 1877. See Frühstück, *Colonizing Sex*, p. 25.

23. Sin Dong-won, op. cit., pp. 148–67; "Cholera in Korea," *The Korean Repository* v. 2 (1895), pp. 339–43.

24. "Jeonyeombyeong yebang gyuchik," Naeburyeong #19, *Gwanbo* 1899.8.26.

25. "Hoyeolja yebang gyuchik," Naeburyeong #20, *Gwanbo* 1899.9.1.

26. *Beomnyeong* v. 1, pp. 608–11 (1895.11.7). Although the course of study was only one month, students had to pass a graduation exam in order to gain certification as vaccination officers. The *Dongnip sinmun* listed the names of those who

passed the graduation exam from the Training Center in the summer of 1897 (1897.7.13). In the fall of 1898, the *Hwangseong sinmun* newspaper ran a government announcement ("advertisement") on the creation of three vaccination centers in the capital while specifying the time and place for the government certification examination for prospective graduates of the Training Center. *Hwangseong sinmun* 1898.10.24. A short report in the same newspaper the next year noted that the Training Center held a graduation ceremony for fifty graduates, at which many dignitaries, including the Royal Household Minister, Education Bureau Chief, Finance Minister, Hygiene Bureau Chief, and Japanese ambassador Katō, were present. *Hwangseong sinmun* 1899.4.11.

27. *Beomnyeong* v. 2, pp. 486–87 (1900.5.29). The functions of the Hygiene Bureau were formally divided into two separate departments, that of Medical Care (Uimugwa) and Hygiene (Wisaenggwa).

28. Sin Dong-won and Hwang Sang-ik suggest that this equalized status was a way to recognize the widespread reliance on traditional medicine, and hence constituted an assertion of national identity. Sin and Hwang, "Joseon malgi (1876–1910) geundae bogeon uiryo cheje ui hyeongseong gwajeong gwa geu uimi," p. 8.

29. "Gian, Uijeongbu uijeong Yun Yongseon," 1902.7.28 (Gyujanggak #17746); *Beomnyeong* v. 3, p. 427 (1902.7.26). Internal documents of the Interior Ministry state that 50,000 won were spent on that summer's cholera epidemic, which had begun in the northern frontier areas. *Naebu georaemun*, v. 14, 1902.9.21; *Gyeongmucheong georaemun*, v. 4, 1902.9.22. *The Korea Review* (1902, pp. 363, 506) reported that the government distributed circulars around the capital with instructions on how avoid the disease.

30. The bureau now was composed of two divisions, one for health and hygiene (Bogeon-gwa) and another for medical care (Uimu-gwa), with a third added in 1908 for laboratory and vaccination work (Siheom-gwa).

31. Sin Gyu-hwan, "Gaehang, jeonjaeng, seongbyeong: Hanmal iljecho ui seongbyeong yuhaeng gwa tongje," pp. 244–45.

32. *Shisei* (1906–7), p. 381. The Daehan ("Great Korea") Hospital consolidated the main government hospital run by the Korean Interior Ministry, the medical school run by the Education Ministry, and the Red Cross Hospital into a single agency under the flag of the Royal Household Ministry.

33. *Shisei* (1906–7), p. 387; Todd Henry, "Sanitizing Empire: Japanese Articulations of Korean Otherness and the Construction of Early Colonial Seoul, 1905–1919," pp. 655–56. Henry details some of the heavy-handed and disruptive measures that this agency implemented, often in the face of resistance. Subsequent official histories of the colonial administration noted that the crown prince's donation of funds were to be directly applied to hygiene measures in Seoul. A Seoul guide book published approximately a decade after the event put this figure at 30,000 yen. See *Keijō annai* (1915), pp. 66–67.

34. For an exhaustive rundown of the protectorate's campaign against this 1907 cholera outbreak, including an overview of the organization, activities, and reports of the four main command centers (Seoul, Busan, Pyongyang, Incheon), see *Meiji*

yonjū-nen Kankoku bōeki kiji (1908). The total allocated budget provided by the metropolitan government was 105,000 yen (pp. 110–12).

35. *Shisei* (1906–7), pp. 385–6.

36. Todd Henry, "Sanitizing Empire," pp. 653–60.

37. *Kankoku eisei ippan* (1909), pp. i–ii, 11, 31.

38. The Government-General eliminated the Hygiene Bureau in 1911, and thereafter almost all public health enforcement functions fell squarely in the hands of the Police Headquarters' Hygiene Section. For more on this reorganization and on the significance of the military police element in the 1910s hygiene police work, see Jeong Geun-sik, "Singminji wisaeng gyeongchal ui hyeongseong gwa byeonhwa, geurigo yusan," pp. 232–35.

39. "Densenbyō yobōrei," *Kanpō* 1915.6.5. In a sign likely of the extra significance of this measure, a Korean-language version also appeared in the same issue of the *Kanpō* government gazette. The nine infectious diseases were cholera, dysentery, typhoid fever, two types of typhus, smallpox, scarlet fever, diphtheria, and bubonic plague ("pest"). For newspaper coverage, see *Maeil sinbo* 1915.6.9.

40. *Shisei* (1915), pp. 317–18.

41. These doctors, who numbered 157 when the system was founded in 1914 but exceeded 300 in the next decade, were originally intended to service Japanese settlers and were composed almost wholly of Japanese nationals, but eventually, by the 1920s, they included many Koreans and catered to the native population. See Bak Yun-jae, *Hanguk geundae uihak ui giwon*, pp. 267–77; and Jeong Geun-sik, op. cit., p. 249. A similar system was later revived by the South Korean government.

42. Bak Yun-jae, op. cit., pp. 330–44. Pak notes that, in contrast to the system in Korea, in contemporary Japan the civilian public health system oversaw the police in hygiene work.

43. At the beginning of colonial rule several central hospitals (including the Jaesaengwon) in the capital headed this network. In 1924, in accordance with the general dispersal of fiscal responsibility to the provinces, provincial governments began to run these regional hospitals. See Asaki Sanrō, "Joseon ui gyeongchal gwa wisaeng" (1929), p. 52; *Shisei* (1922), pp. 363–64.

44. A comprehensive survey of all these public health duties can be found in *Eisei keisatsu kōgi ippan* (1913), published by the South Pyeongan Province Police Division; and Asaki Sanrō, "Joseon ui gyeongchal gwa wisaeng," (1929), pp. 46, 50–52.

45. *Tōkei* (1919), pp. 389, 402.

46. *Tōkei* (1919), pp. 374–78.

47. *Tōkei* (1930), pp. 366–70.

48. *Donga ilbo* 1933.3.15.

49. *Tōkei* 1937, pp. 306–9; *Chōsen bōeki tōkei*, p. 248.

50. The 1926 cholera outbreak, for example, mobilized approximately 2,500 officials, of which 90% belonged to the police. Park Yunjae, "Sanitizing Korea," pp. 161–67. Park finds contemporary reports indicating people enthusiastically sought vaccination shots against cholera.

51. *Je-69 hoe jeguk uihoe seolmyeong jaryo—Gyeongmuguk* (1935), pp. 34–36.

52. Sonja Kim, "Contesting Bodies," p. 188; Park Yunjae, op. cit., p. 169.

53. A classic study remains Philippa Levine, *Prostitution, Race and Politics: Policing Venereal Disease in the British Empire*. See also Ann Laura Stoler, *Carnal Knowledge and Imperial Power: Race and the Intimate in Colonial Rule*, pp. 48–49, for a discussion of how the fear of VD through prostitution drove the institutionalization of concubinage in the European colonies of southeast Asia. For Korea, see Jin-kyung Park, "Picturing Empire and Illness: Biomedicine, Venereal Disease and the Modern Girl in Korea under Japanese Colonial Rule"; and Theodore Jun Yoo, *The Politics of Gender in Colonial Korea*, Chapter 5.

54. A foreign doctor, however, claimed that in his experience "venereal diseases are about as common as they used to be in England." O. R. Avison, "Disease in Korea," *The Korean Repository* (1897), p. 90.

55. Jin-kyung Park, "Corporeal Colonialism," pp. 107–9; Frühstück, op. cit., loc. 503.

56. Gang Hye-gyeong, "Ilje sigi seongbyeong ui sahoe munje wa seongbyeong gwalli," pp. 89–90. See Frühstück, op. cit., Chapter 1, for an analysis of this discourse in Japan and the empire in the early twentieth century. Inspection and isolation of prostitutes to control VD served as part of larger interventionist inoculation efforts in nineteenth-century Britain and the United States. See Porter, *Health, Civilization and the State*, pp. 128–32, 153.

57. Gang Jeong-suk, "Daehan jeguk ilje chogi Seoul ui maechuneop gwa gongchang jedo ui doip," pp. 206–9; Jin-kyung Park, "Corporeal Colonialism," pp. 109–10.

58. Song Youn-ok, "Japanese Colonial Rule and State-Managed Prostitution: Korea's Licensed Prostitutes."

59. In her study of colonial-era female laborers, particularly as they appear in print media, Jennifer Jung-Kim labels these somewhat indeterminately designated women as "pseudo-sex industry workers." Jung-Kim, "Gender and Modernity in Colonial Korea," p. 229.

60. *Kanpō* 1916.3.31. These regulations divided *gisaeng* into two broad categories, "shōgi" ("prostituting *kisaeng*") and "geigi" ("artistic *gisaeng*"), and designated different places where they could work. There was indeed a great deal of internal differentiation among the *gisaeng* in the colonial period. For a more thorough examination, particularly of *gisaeng* organization activities, see Jennifer Jung-Kim, pp. 210–24.

61. *Kanpō* 1916.3.31. Other requirements were that *gisaeng* prostitutes who worked in hostess bars meet age requirements (17 years old) and even show evidence of familial consent. For more on these regulations, see Gang Jeong-suk, op. cit., pp. 215–17; and Jin-kyung Park, "Corporeal Colonialism," pp. 112–13.

62. By 1937 the Government-General's newspaper appears to have acknowledged that prostitutes were not always the primary vector of VD. "Hwaryubyeong eun yeoja boda namja" [Venereal disease lies more with men than women], *Maeil sinbo* 1937.3.13.

63. One magazine article from 1922, for example, put the VD infection rate at a stunningly high 12.5%, but it does not indicate whether this percentage referred to the entire population, the adult population, the young adult population (most likely, given the article's admonitions to young adults), or the women in the sex industry. Gim Chan-du, "Joseon sahoe wa hwaryubyeong," *Gaebyeok* (1922.5), p. 96.

64. *Tōkei* (1939), pp. 312–13. Interestingly, there was one Japanese patient for every two Koreans. Given that the Japanese population represented less than 5% of the total, this suggests that Japanese residents still had far greater access to biological medicine in the colony.

65. The bulk of the infections were from gonorrhea, with the far more dangerous ailment of syphilis accounting for less than 20%.

66. Jin-kyung Park has found that the first effective treatment for syphilis, Salvasan (or "606"), which was discovered in 1909 by Nobel laureate Paul Ehrlich with help from a Japanese assistant, was used in a Government-General hospital in the city of Daegu in 1911. See Jin-kyung Park, "Corporeal Colonialism," pp. 92–93, 118–19.

67. "Jeon Joseon ye-changgi, jakbu hwaryubyeong jeomcha jeungga" [Gradual increase in VD infections among courtesans and barmaids in all of Korea], *Maeil sinbo* 1936.9.27; "Jeon illyu-reul jom meogeoganeun hwaryubyeong ui bangmyeol-chaek" [Eradicating the disease that is gradually ravaging all of humanity, VD], *Donga ilbo* 1939.4.10; *Tōkei* (1939), pp. 304–5; Jin-kyung Park, "Picturing Empire and Illness," p. 11. Gang Hye-gyeong's study of the accounts of prostitutes' VD rates in the *Donga ilbo* newspaper shows that, according to this paper's unofficial studies, the infection rates increased markedly in the capital area from the early 1920s to the late 1930s, from 10% to over 50%, and even more dramatically in the provinces. See Gang, op. cit., pp. 95–99.

68. Some fragmentary evidence comes from a 1938.3.5 *Joseon ilbo* newspaper article, which noted that a survey by the colonial postal and communication services counted over two thousand sufferers of VD among health insurance claimants in the eleven largest cities. A *Donga ilbo* report of 1939.3.6 counted slightly over 13,000 sufferers in South Pyeongan Province alone. Later that year, according to the *Donga ilbo,* which published comprehensive statistics and best official estimates, there were presently between 510,000 and 600,000 sufferers of VD in Korea at the time.

69. See C. Sarah Soh, *The Comfort Women: Sexual Violence and Postcolonial Memory in Korea and Japan,* for a comprehensive consideration of the complexities involved in delineating this balance. For connections to earlier state practices in the colonial period (and before) that led directly to the absorption of countless girls and even married women into these networks, see Song Youn-ok, "Japanese Colonial Rule and State-Managed Prostitution: Korea's Licensed Prostitutes."

70. For more on the integral place of Japanese disease control developments in the Japanese military, and vice versa, see Louis Livingston Seaman, *The Real Triumph of Japan: The Conquest of the Silent Foe* (1906), which chronicles how Japanese success in combating battlefield contagion proved decisive in the war against Russia;

Sabine Frühstück, op. cit., Chapter 1; Michael Bourdaghs, "The Disease of Nationalism, the Empire of Hygiene," p. 646; and Charlotte Furth, "Introduction," p. 12.

71. L. George Paik, *The History of Protestant Missions in Korea, 1832–1910*, p. 121. It was a well-known story in Korea: The monarch, Gojong, was so impressed by the medical care given to one of his top advisors injured in the 1884 Gapsin Coup, that he named Allen a court physician and asked him to serve as founding director of a new biomedical hospital, soon called Jejungwon. After a few permutations this institution became the Severance Hospital, still one of the most prominent medical facilities in South Korea today.

72. Sonja Kim, "The Search for Health: Translating Wisaeng and Medicine during the Taehan Empire," pp. 305–6.

73. See, for example, "Manguk wisaenghoe" [World conference on hygiene], *Hanseong sunbo* 1884.5.5, in HSSS v. 1, pp. 84–85.

74. Yu also noted that someone who spreads disease through his unhygienic behavior is no different from someone who attacks others with arrows or guns. Yu Giljun, *Seoyu gyeonmun*, pp. 172–73.

75. Editorial, *Hwangseong sinmun* 1899.10.9, 1901.10.10.

76. Editorial, *Hwangseong sinmun* 1899.5.16, 1899.9.8, 1899.10.2, 1900.10.20, 1900.11.15, 1900.12.3.

77. "Cheong seol hyangdu" [A call for establishing local vaccination centers], *Hwangseong sinmun* 1899.4.29.

78. *Dongnip sinmun* 1896.6.27, 1896.7.2, 1897.7.13, 1899.6.21. Of particular note was the newpaper's article on "Ji Seogyeong ssi ui uduron" [Inoculation theory of Mr. Ji Seogyeong], 1897.5.8.

79. *Dongnip sinmun* 1896.7.18. See also *The Independent* 1896.7.16 for one such notice.

80. *Dongnip sinmun* 1896.7.2.

81. *Dongnip sinmun* 1896.6.21. See also the editorial of 1897.4.15 in *The Independent*.

82. *The Independent* 1896.7.4.

83. See Peter Duus, *The Abacus and the Sword*, pp. 400–4; Todd Henry, "Sanitizing Empire," pp. 643–53.

84. Shula Marks, "Presidential Address: What Is Colonial about Colonial Medicine?" pp. 205, 209–10.

85. Rogaski, op. cit., pp. 153–54. For more on Nitobe's influence in Japan and Korea, see Michael Schneider, "The Future of the Japanese Empire, 1914–1931," Chapter 2; and Yi Jong-chan, op. cit., pp. 237–38. Yi relates that Nitobe (1862–1933), one of the most influential theorists of Japanese imperialism, emphasized in his treatise on the "Advancement of Medicine and the Development of Colonies" (1918) the primacy of hygiene, medicine, and science in colonial administration, so much so that they formed the basis of successful colonial rule, and without which "the colonies that we have gained through the power of the army or navy or economic development will simply burst like a bubble."

86. *Kankoku eisei ippan* (1909). This critique was used against the Government-General two decades later, when a Korean newspaper decried the continuing shortage of physicians in the colony.

87. *Kankoku eisei ippan,* pp. 1, 5–11. Interestingly, this report's sections on state oversight of butcher shops and refuse removal ignore the earlier Korean government efforts altogether.

88. *Shisei* (1906–7), pp. 380, 387. The narrative actually praised the cooperative effort of the Korean government and the protectorate to stamp out the cholera threat before the Crown Prince's visit in 1907.

89. In the English-language publication, *Annual Report on Administration of Chosen,* meant for foreigners in Korea and overseas, the chapter on "Sanitation" (later changed to "Public Hygiene") typically put the differences between the pre-colonial and colonial regimes in very stark and grossly inaccurate terms: "Under the old Korean Government nothing was done to further the public health, but since the establishment of the present regime [the colonial Government-General] various sanitary regulations have been drawn up and made effective as popular conditions called for them." *Annual Report* (1922), p. 177.

90. Shiroishi Hōsei, *Chōsen eisei yōgi* (1918).

91. Shiroishi, pp. 1–4.

92. *Eisei keisatsu kōgi ippan* (1913), p. 88.

93. Ibid., pp. 85–87.

94. Shiroishi, *Chōsen eisei yōgi,* p. 25.

95. Shiroishi, pp. 23–33.

96. *Shisei* (1915), pp. 306–7.

97. Shiroishi, p. 38.

98. This comes from the regime's Central Police Bureau report prepared for the 1935 session of the Japanese Diet. In exasperated tones, the narrative noted that, while improvements had been made over the quarter-century since annexation in terms of raising the perceptions and awareness of hygienic matters, compared to Japan and Western countries, Korea in 1935 "still could not escape its primitive [*yōchi*] condition" in public health and hygiene. Later, in a discussion of the roving "public doctors" [*kōi*] system that the colonial state first implemented in 1914, the disappointment seeps through in the report's back-and-forth between the proud efforts to increase the funds and physicians dedicated to the effort, on the one hand, and the continuing administrative and cultural difficulties, on the other. *Je-69 hoe jeguk uihoe seolmyeong jaryo—Gyeongmuguk* (1935), pp. 13–14, 24.

99. *Joseon jungang ilbo* 1934.7.6; and *Maeil sinbo* 1929.1.30, 1929.11.23, 1933.2.25, 1936.11.13.

100. See, for example, "Jeonyeondu huisaeng 300 myeong dolpa" [Smallpox victims now over 300], *Donga ilbo* 1933.3.15. The coverage included comments by Hygiene Bureau Chief Nishikame, who called for extra efforts at immunization, given the high death rate for those afflicted. Half a year later, when a pestilence outbreak in Manchuria threatened to descend southward, the newspaper's coverage, while verging on sensationalism, also included comments from the Government-

General's head epidemiologist. "Heuksabyeong jeomcha namha!" [Plague gradually moving south!], *Donga ilbo* 1933.9.22.

101. For a collection of such magazine articles and transcripts of radio broadcasts in the late 1930s by the chiefs of the Seoul municipal government's hygiene division, see Keijōfu sōmubu eiseika, *Eisei shisō fukyū no tame ni* (1939).

102. *Eisei ni kansuru meisin* (1933), Introduction. See also a similar work from 1930 by the N. Gyeongsang Police Department. The serialized magazine articles, found in the Government-General's journal *Chōsen (Joseon)* in 1928–29, focused on folk remedies for VD. Jin-kyung Park, "Picturing Empire and Illness," pp. 23–24.

103. In parts of Europe, this simplification process targeted internal groups, such as the proletariat, in assigning blame for health-related ignorance and bad hygienic practices. See Porter, *Health, Civilization and the State,* pp. 69, 98.

104. Among the many such examples from colonial newspapers are the *Donga ilbo* editorial of 1921.7.7; and "Gaein wisaeng gwa sahoe wisaeng" [Individual hygiene and societal hygiene], *Joseon ilbo* 1926.5.6.

105. Although the *Statistical Annual (Tōkei nenpō)* reported figures for courtesans and barmaids who were examined and diagnosed with different classes of VD, the *Annual Reports* never mentioned VD in their otherwise extensive section on "Infectious Diseases" or elsewhere. The chapter on police activities occasionally and briefly alluded to enforcing hygiene measures on courtesans and hostesses, but otherwise VD, even efforts to combat it, remained invisible in the propaganda.

106. For a discussion of some of the perspectives appearing in colonial-era publications on the need to raise better awareness of VD, see Theodore Jun Yoo, *The Politics of Gender in Colonial Korea,* p. 188.

107. See, for example, Gim Chandu, "Joseon sahoe wa hwaryubyeong," *Gaebyeok* (1922.5), p. 96.

108. Jin-kyung Park, "Picturing Empire and Illness." Park argues that there was collusion between these drug companies and the colonial state in pushing an idealized domesticity and a salvational ideology of Japanese medical science conquering Korean backwardness. But one could also argue that the companies and state authorities both drew from common cultural tropes in circulation—tropes that, admittedly, the Japanese colonial and imperial states had an interest in forwarding, as Park shows.

109. Gim Mi-yeong, "Ilje-ha 'Joseon ilbo' ui seongbyeong gwallyeon tamnon yeongu," p. 392; Jin-kyung Park, "Corporeal Colonialism," pp. 121–32. The same connections between VD, private (especially female) behavior and morality, and civilizational standing were in play in contemporary China as well. See Sin Gyu-hwan, *Gukga, dosi, wisaeng,* pp. 214–20; Frank Dikötter, *Sex, Culture, and Modernity in China,* pp. 129–30.

110. Gim Mi-yeong, "Ilje-ha geundae soseol-sok ui jilbyeong gwa byeongwon," pp. 11–14.

111. An early expression of criticism came from a Korean physician who editorialized in the journal *Gaebyeok* that, given the great correspondence between a country's strength and its people's consciousness of good health and hygiene

(*wisaeng*), the colonial authorities needed to divulge more statistical information about Koreans' health conditions, particularly their birth and mortality rates, so that the people could properly evaluate the government's overall performance. See Ryu Hongjong, "Minseihaksang euro boneun Joseon minjok," *Gaebyeok* 4 (1920.9), pp. 64–65. Later, the *Joseon jungang ilbo* newspaper, which was more combative than others, seized upon statistics that demonstrated a woeful lack of doctors and medical facilities in certain areas, as well as in the colony as a whole. See, for example, "Bin-yak han Joseon ui uiryo gigwan—chong ingu icheon man e uisa neun icheon-yeo" [Medical facilities of miserable Korea—for a population of twenty million, around two thousand doctors], 1934.12.25; and "Hansimhan uiryo gigwan—uisa irindang ingu gucheon, uisaeng irindang ingu sacheon" [Pathetic state of medical facilities—one doctor for every nine thousand people, one medical practitioner for every four thousand], 1935.3.19.

112. In one of its criticisms of public sanitation, for example, the *Joseon ilbo* newspaper reiterated that, "For the sake of effective public hygiene, regardless of East or West, in all countries the government must first complete everything that has to do with urban infrastructure and other matters." *Joseon ilbo* 1926.5.6.

113. "Wisaeng jeiljuui-reul seongmyeong han Umano Gyeongseong buyun ui taedo" [Attitude of Seoul Mayor Umano, who declares a hygiene-first policy], *Joseon ilbo* 1925.11.7. For more detailed analysis of the back-and-forth between the Seoul municipal government and its critics during the colonial period, see Todd Henry, *Assimilating Seoul,* Chapter 4.

114. *Donga ilbo* 1938.11.06. The lack of public toilets, noted this editorial, resulted in the "odd sight" of people going into cafes and department stores to find places to relieve themselves. Fifteen years earlier, in 1923, the *Donga ilbo* had compared Seoul unfavorably in matters of sanitation even to Japanese-controlled Dalian on the Lia-otung peninsula: "Bulgyeol jeil ui Gyeongseong" [Seoul, number one in uncleanli-ness], *Donga ilbo* 1923.3.11. See also similar criticism in *Joseon jungang ilbo* 1936.6.30.

115. Yun Hae-dong, *Singminji geundae ui paereodokseu,* p. 61; and Bak Myeong-gyu and Gim Baeg-yeong, "Singmin jibae wa hegemoni gyeongjaeng," pp. 20–21. Bak and Gim suggest that the running contrast, and sometimes tension, between Western missionaries and the Japanese, which came to a head in the 1930s, produced a complicated, ever-changing relationship that reflected a larger "hegemony strug-gle" over the minds and hearts of the Korean population. See also Sonja Kim, "Contesting Bodies," pp. 209–10.

116. For insight on Japanese suspicions of particularly the influence of American missionaries, see Richard Devine, "Japanese Rule in Korea after the March First Uprising: Governor-General Hasegawa's Recommendations," p. 539. Based partly on the precipitous decline in the number of medical missionaries in the 1930s, Yi Chung-ho suggests a deliberate colonial policy of reducing the influence of Ameri-can missionary medicine, which signaled the completion of the process in which the influence of American medicine was replaced with that of "German" medicine in the colony, indeed in the empire as a whole. Yi Chung-ho, *Ilje amheukgi uisa gyo-yuksa,* pp. 292–93.

117. For more on the credentialing requirements of Western doctors who were licensed in their home countries, which resulted in increasing failure rates in passing the tests, see Yi Man-yeol, *Hanguk gidokgyo uiryosa*, pp. 531–33. Yi concludes that this was a deliberate ploy to limit Western doctors.

118. Sonja Kim, "Contesting Bodies," pp. 69, 211; Jo Hyeong-geun, "Ilje ui gongsik uiryo wa gaesingyo seongyo uiryo gan hegemoni gyeongjaeng," pp. 140–41.

119. Jo Hyeong-geun, op. cit., pp. 147–49, 153. Hyaeweol Choi shows that these missionaries saw themselves, in contrast to Japanese, as promoting a "Christian modernity" that offered Western (scientific) advances in addition to the proper spiritual foundation. See Hyaeweol Choi, *Gender and Mission Encounters in Korea: New Women, Old Ways,* p. 11. See also Yi Man-yeol, op. cit., p. 538.

120. Jo Hyeong-geun, op. cit., pp. 125, 151.

121. An example comes from Government-General of Chosen, *Thriving Chosen: A Survey of Twenty-Five Years' Administration* (1935), pp. 74–75. Two physicians, including the head of the Pyongyang Union Hospital, are quoted as praising the medical advances by the colonial administration, which is credited for eliminating "the horror and suffering from ignorant and superstitious treatment back in the old days." See also *Ilje gangjeomgi jonggyo jeongchaeksa jaryojip,* p. 132; and Sonja Kim, "Contesting Bodies," p. 211.

CONCLUSION

1. As Peter Pels points out, some seminal techniques, not to say perspectives, of modern states, such as the census, statistical analysis, and other systematizations, were developed out of the political rationalities of colonial settings. Pels, "The Anthropology of Colonialism: Culture, History, and the Emergence of Western Governmentality," p. 176. Of course we should remain mindful of David Scott's concerns about collapsing the range of colonial experiences to variations on a single standard of modern state making. Scott, "Colonial Governmentality," pp. 194–95.

2. Similarities between Korea in the wartime period of 1938–45 and South Korea in the 1960s appear quite strong, including a government-directed focus on heavy industry, state intervention in the market, and strategic allocation of resources. See, for example, Bruce Cumings, "Colonial Formations and Deformations." For an opposing perspective, which begins with a rejection of any premise of "colonial modernity" but also includes a thorough consideration of the material, political, and personnel connections between the two periods, see Lee Byeong Cheon, "Political Economy of Korean Development after Liberation."

3. While one could point toward aggregate outputs and other macroeconomic production indicators to argue for the link with South Korea, in terms of government intervention in market mechanisms, such as prices, interest rates, and revenue sources, the North Korean regime realized better the wartime state developmentalism of the late 1930s and 1940s, claims Gim. Indeed, in South Korea following the Korean War, the extent of government controls over the market and the efforts to extract material

and human resources never approached the levels seen at the end of the colonial period. Gim Nang-nyeon, "Singminji Joseon gyeongje ui jedojeok yusan." Though coming from the opposite historiographical position, Lee Byeong Cheon has also argued that, if any period of the colonial economy resembled the South Korean development trajectory, it was the immediate *pre*-mobilization period of the 1930s. Lee, "Political Economy of Korean Development after Liberation," p. 54.

4. See Gerald Epstein, "Central Banks as Agents of Economic Development," for more on nonliberal actions of central banks in developing economies during their early stages, including the United States and United Kingdom.

5. Takashi Fujitani, *Race for Empire*, loc. 6120.

6. See Charles Armstrong, *The North Korean Revolution, 1945–1950.*

7. Byung-Kook Kim and Ezra Vogel, eds., *The Park Chung Hee Era,* locs. 1768–76.

8. Yao Jen-To hence argues that Japanese colonial rule represented not just a political rupture, but an epistemological one as well. Yao, "The Japanese Colonial State and Its Form of Knowledge in Taiwan," locs. 1226–28.

9. James C. Scott, *Seeing Like a State.* In extending the metaphor of a panoptic state's "sight," Scott deems these administrative maneuvers as amounting to a "mapping" of society in order to increase its *legibility.*

10. For a representative perspective from the Korean-language historiography, see Gim Dong-no, "Ilbon jegukjuui wa Joseon chibae ui dokteukseong," pp. 215–22.

11. Ziya Onis, "The Logic of the Developmental State." This reality tempers the view of a rationality that presupposes an autonomous state pursuing its own interests. As Graeme Gill notes, organic interdependence in relation to society is a common feature of modern states, regardless of how dominant in form or even external in origin the state was. See Gill, *The Nature and Development of the Modern State,* pp. 19, 32. See also Karen Barkey and Sunita Parikh, "Comparative Perspectives on the State," pp. 526–29.

12. Brandon Palmer, for example, finds even the wartime state's efforts at instituting conscription and other mobilization measures as "plagued by anxiety and much hand-wringing" due to the potential backlash and the lack of institutional preparation. See Palmer, *Fighting for the Enemy,* pp. 4. Takashi Fujitani, too, finds this late colonial state as "a regime not fully sure of itself, always mindful of the precariousness of its control over the people and indeed fearful that the macropolitical system of domination might unravel from the bottom up." Fujitani, *Race for Empire,* loc. 6406.

13. This space was the colonial public sphere, or "publicness," reconceived. For some examples, including the operations of local assemblies, of how this space was constructed out of collective activity in response to various state measures, see Yun, *Singminji ui hoesaek jidae,* pp. 34–39.

14. As Gim Yeong-mi has argued, the mobilizational capacity of the state is what proved most durable from the colonial period to the Korean War, then to the military dictatorship periods of South Korea. Gim, "Singminji dongwon cheje ui yeonsok gwa danjeol."

BIBLIOGRAPHY

ABBREVIATIONS

CKH   Nakahara Shigeru, *Chōsen koseki hikkeishū.*

GSS   *Gojong Sunjong sillok*, 1863–1910.

Gwanbo   *Gu Hanguk gwanbo*, 1894–1910.

HGGC   *Hanguk gaehwagi gyogwaseo chongseo.*

HSSS   *Hanguk sinmun saseol seonjip.*

Kanpō   *Chōsen sōtokufu kanpō*, 1910–1945.

Shisei   *Kankoku shisei nenpō*, 1906–1910; *Chōsen sōtokufu shisei nenpō*, 1910–1943.

STP   Michel Foucault, *Security, Territory, Population.*

Tōkei   *Tōkanfu tōkei nenpō*, 1906–1910; *Chōsen sōtokufu tōkei nenpō*, 1911–1944.

NEWSPAPERS AND JOURNALS

Cassier's Magazine
Chōsen gyōsei
Chōsen shuppan keisatsu geppo
Chunchu
Daehan maeil sinbo
Donga ilbo
Dongnip sinmun
Gaebyeok
Hwangseong sinmun
The Independent
Jeguk sinmun

Jogwang
Joseon
Joseon ilbo
Joseon jungang ilbo
Jungoe ilbo
Kokumin sōryoku
The Korea Review
The Korean Repository
Maeil sinbo
Mansebo
Manseon ilbo
Samcheolli
Seobuk hakhoe wolbo
Sin mungye
Sōdōin

REFERENCES

Alborn, Timothy L. "Age of Empire in the Indian Census, 1871–1931." *Journal of Interdisciplinary History* 30.1 (1999.7): 61–89.

An Yu-rim. "Ilje gidokgyo tongje jeongchaek gwa pogyo gyuchik" [The Regulations on Religions Propagation and the Japanese colonial regime's policies on controlling Christianity]. *Hanguk gidokgyo wa yeoksa* 29 (2008): 35–68.

Anderson, Benedict. *Imagined Communities: Reflections on the Origin and Spread of Nationalism.* London: Verso, 1983.

Armstrong, Charles. *The North Korean Revolution, 1945–1950.* Cornell University Press, 2003.

Arnold, David. *Colonizing the Body: State Medicine and Epidemic Disease in Nineteenth-Century India.* University of California Press, 1993.

Asaki Sanrō. "Joseon ui gyeongchal gwa wisaeng" [Police and hygiene in Korea]. *Joseon* 144 (1929).

Atkins, E. Taylor. *Primitive Selves: Koreana in the Japanese Colonial Gaze, 1910–1945.* University of California Press, 2010. Kindle edition.

Avison, O. R. "Disease in Korea." *The Korean Repository,* 1897.

Axtmann, Roland. "The State of the State." *International Political Science Review* 25.3 (2004.7): 259–79.

Bak Chan-seung. "20 segi Hanguk gukgajuui ui giwon" [Origins of statism in twentieth-century Korea]. *Hanguksa yeongu* 117 (2002): 199–246.

———. *Ma-eullo gan Hanguk jeonjaeng* [The Korean War in the villages]. Dolbaegae, 2010.

Bak Chan-sik. "Hanmal gyoan gwa gyomin joyak" [Church policies and religious treaties in the late nineteenth century]. *Gyohoesa yeongu* 27 (2006): 59–77.

Bak Hui-jin. "Ilje Eonyang jiyeok giryu gagu ui bungeo" [Distribution of residence registers in Eonyang in the Japanese colonial period]. *Gomunseo yeongu* 34 (2009): 61–82.

———— et al. "20 segi hojeokbu ui ingu gijae beomwi wa girok ui jeonghwakseong" [Scope of recording of household registers and the accuracy of documentation in the twentieth century]. *Daedong munhwa yeongu* 63 (2008): 301–30.

Bak Myeong-gyu and Gim Baeg-yeong. "Singmin jibae wa hegemoni gyeongjaeng: Joseon chongdokbu wa Miguk gaesingyo seongyo seryeok ganui gwangye-rcul jungsimeuro" [Colonial rule and hegemony competition: With a focus on the relationship between the Government-General of Korea and American Protestant missionaries]. *Sahoe wa yeoksa* 82 (2009): 5–39.

Bak Yeongcheol. *Gojūnen no kaiko* [Memoir of fifty years]. Keijō: Ōsaka okugo shoten, 1929.

Bak Yun-jae. *Hanguk geundae uihak ui giwon* [Origins of modern medicine in Korea]. Hyean, 2005.

Baker, Don. "World Religions and National States: Competing Claims in East Asia." In *Transnational Religion and Fading States*, edited by Susanne Hoeber Rudolph and James Piscatori. Westview Press, 1997.

———. "A Different Thread: Orthodoxy, Heterodoxy, and Catholicism in a Confucian World." In *Culture and the State in Late Chosŏn Korea*, edited by Jahyun Kim Haboush and Martina Deuchler. Harvard Asia Center, 1999.

———. "The Religious Revolution in Modern Korean History: From Ethics to Theology and from Ritual Hegemony to Religious Freedom." *Review of Korean Studies* 9.3 (2006): 249–75.

Ban Yun-hong. "Bibyeonsa ui jeongchijeok wisang" [The Border Defense Command's political standing]. *Hanguksa yeongu* 91 (1995): 99–127.

Barkey, Karen, and Sunita Parikh. "Comparative Perspectives on the State." *Annual Review of Sociology* 17 (1991): 523–49.

Bax, Mart. "Religious Regimes and State Formation: Towards a Research Perspective." *Anthropological Quarterly* 60.1 (1987): 1–11.

Berger, Peter L. "Religion and the West." *National Interest* 80 (Summer 2005): 112–19.

———. "Pluralism, Protestantization and the Voluntary Principle." In *Democracy and the New Religious Pluralism*, edited by Thomas Banchoff. Oxford University Press, 2007.

Blackbourn, David. *Marpingen: Apparitions of the Virgin Mary in Nineteenth-Century Germany*. Knopf, 1993.

Botong gyoyukhak [Studies in elementary education]. Hakbu, 1910.

Bourdaghs, Michael. "The Disease of Nationalism, the Empire of Hygiene." *Positions—East Asia Critique* 6.3 (1998): 637–73.

Bourdieu, Pierre. "Rethinking the State: Genesis and Structure of the Bureaucratic Field." In *State/Culture: State-Formation after the Cultural Turn*, edited by George Steinmetz. Cornell University Press, 1999.

Bratsis, Peter. "Unthinking the State: Reification, Ideology, and the State." In *Paradigm Lost: State Theory Reconsidered*, edited by Stanley Aronowitz and Peter Bratsis. University of Minnesota Press, 2002.

Campany, Robert. "On the Very Idea of Religions (In the Modern West and in Early Medieval China)." *History of Religions* 42.4 (May 2003): 287–319.

Caplan, Jane, and John C. Torpey, eds. *Documenting Individual Identity: The Development of State Practices in the Modern World*. Princeton University Press, 2001.

Caprio, Mark. *Japanese Assimilation Policies in Colonial Korea, 1910–1945*. University of Washington Press, 2009.

———. "Neo-Nationalist Interpretations of Japan's Annexation of Korea: The Colonization Debate in Japan and South Korea." *Asia-Pacific Journal* 44.4 (2010), http://japanfocus.org/-Mark-Caprio/3438.

Carroll, Terrance. "Secularization and States of Modernity." *World Politics* 36.3 (1984): 362–82.

Cha, Myung Soo and Nak Nyeon Kim. "Korea's First Industrial Revolution, 1911–40." Working Paper 2006–3, *Naksungdae Institute of Economic Research Working Papers* (2006): 1–51.

Cha, Myeong Su and Wu Yeon Lee. "Living Standards and Income Distribution in Korea's First Industrial Revolution, 1910–42." Working Paper 2008–2, *Naksungdae Institute of Economic Research Working Papers* (2008): 1–51.

Cha, Sung Kwang. "Contesting Obligations: American Missionaries, Korean Christians, and the State(s), 1884–1910." PhD diss., UCLA, 2011.

Chang, Ha-Joon. *Kicking Away the Ladder: Development Strategy in Historical Perspective*. Anthem Press, 2002.

Chen, Chung-chih. "Police and Community Control Systems in the Empire." In *The Japanese Colonial Empire, 1895–1945*, edited by Ramon Myers and Mark Peattie. Princeton University Press, 1987.

Chen, Edward I-te. "The Attempt to Integrate the Empire: Legal Perspectives." In *The Japanese Colonial Empire, 1895–1945*, edited by Ramon Myers and Mark Peattie. Princeton University Press, 1987.

Cho, Eunsu. "Re-thinking Late 19th Century Joseon Buddhist Society." *Acta Koreana* 6.2 (2003): 87–109.

Choe Byeong-ok. "Gyoryeon byeongdae yeongu" [Gyoryeon Byeongdae corps]. *Kunsa* 18 (1989): 73–125.

Choe Gi-yeong. *Hanguk geundae gyemong undong yeongu* [Enlightenment movement in modern Korea]. Iljogak, 1997.

Choe Hong-gi. *Hanguk hojeok jedosa yeongu* [History of the Korean household registration system]. Seoul National University Press, 1997.

Choe Hui-jeong. "1910 nyeondae Choe Namseon ui 'jajoron' beonyeok gwa 'cheongnyeon' ui 'jajo'" [Choe Namseon's rendering of "self-help theory" and the notion of "self-help" in "youth" in the 1910s]. *Hanguk sasang sahak* 39 (2011): 213–50.

Choe Jae-seong. "Changssi gaemyeong gwa chinil Joseonin ui hyeomnyeok" [The name change ordinance and the collusion of pro-Japanese Koreans]. *Han'guk dongnip undongsa yeongu* 37 (2010): 345–92.

Choe Won-gyu. "Hanmal ilje chogi gongto jeongchaek gwa gugyu minyu bunjaeng" [Land policies and ownership disputes between state and private parties in the late nineteenth century and early Japanese occupation period]. *Hanguk minjok munhwa* 45 (2012): 119–70.

Choi, Hyaeweol. *Gender and Mission Encounters in Korea: New Women, Old Ways.* University of California Press, 2009.

Choi, Jae-Keun. *The Korean Church under Japanese Colonialism.* Jimoondang, 2007.

Choi Won-kyu. "The Legalization of Land Rights under the Great Han Empire." In *Landlords, Peasants and Intellectuals in Modern Korea*, edited by Pang Kie-Chung and Michael D. Shin. Cornell East Asia Series, 2005.

Chong, Yagyong. *Admonitions on Governing the People: Manual for All Administrators.* Translated by Choi Byonghyon. University of California Press, 2010.

Chōsen daihakurankai no kaikan [Overview of the Great Korean Exposition]. Keijō nipposha, 1940.

Chōsen Ginkō. *Chōsen Ginkō nijū gonen-shi* [Twenty-five-year history of the Bank of Chosen]. Keijo, 1935.

Chōsen sōtokufu. *Chōsen jijō* [Conditions in Korea]. Keijo, 1943.

———. *Chōsen bōeki tōkei* [Disease control statistics in Korea]. 1943.

———. *Chōsen keisatsukan shokuinroku* [Roster of police officials in Korea]. Keijo: Chōsen keisatsu sinbunsha, 1932.

———. *Chōsen kyōiku no kaikan* [Overview of Korean education] (1939), in *Nihon shokuminchi kyōiku seisaku shiryō shūsei—Chōsenhen* [Collection of historical documents on Japanese colonial education policy—Korea], v. 4. Ryūkei shosha, 1987.

———. *Chōsen kyōiku yōran* [Korean education survey] (1926).

———. *Chōsen ni okeru nōsanyoson sinkō undō no dai ichiji nōka kōsei keikaku jisseki* [The revitalization movement for rural, mountain, and fishing communities in Korea—results of the first round of the rejuvenation of agricultural households] (1935).

———. *Chōsen sangyō keizai chōsakai kaigiroku* [Korean industrial commission transcript] (1936).

———. *Chōsen shakai kyōka yōran* [Overview of social edification in Korea] (1938).

———. *Chōsen shisei nijūgonen-shi* [Twenty-five years of administration in Korea] (1935).

———. *Chōsen sōtokufu kanpō* [Government gazette of the Government-General of Korea], 1910–1945.

———. *Chōsen sōtokufu keisatsu no gaiyō* [Overview of the Government-General police] (1922).

———. *Chōsen sōtokufu rinji tochi chōsakyoku shokuinroku* [Roster of officials of the Interim Land Survey Bureau] (1912).

———. *Chōsen sōtokufu shisei nenpō* [Administrative annual of the Government-General of Korea], 1910–1943.

———. *Chōsen sōtokufu tōkei nenpō* [Statistical annual of the Government-General of Korea], 1911–1944.

———. *Chōsen tochi chōsa jigyō gairan* [Overview of the Korean land survey project] (1915).

———. *Chōsen tōchi sannen-kan seiseki* [Three-year progress report on the administration of Korea] (1914).

———. *Chōsen tōkei yōran* [Statistical survey of Korea] (1941).

———. *Chūtō kyōiku shūshinsho* [Middle-level ethics textbook], v. 4 (1938).

———. *Futō gakko shūshinsho* [Normal school ethics] (1933).

———. *Futō gakko shūshinsho hensan shuisho* [Prospectus for normal school ethics textbook publication] (1924).

———. *Futō gakko shūshinsho—kyōshiyō* [Normal school ethics—teacher's guide] (1923).

———. *Futō gakko shūshinsho—Yonnensei* [Normal school ethics textbook—fourth-year curriculum] (1933).

———. *Gakusoku henkō* [Changes in school regulations] (1926).

———. "Jonggyo sawon changnip pogyo gwallija e gwanhan geon" [Documents related to the establishment of religious institutions and evangelists] (1936). National Archives, Republic of Korea (CJA 0004831).

———. *Nōson sinkō undō no zenbō* [Complete overview of the Rural Revitalization Campaign] (1935).

———. "Sawon pyeji e ttareun sayu jaesan mit juji chwijik inga sincheong gwangye seoryu" [Records of applications concerning temple possessions following the closing of Buddhist temples and certification of appointments of temple abbots] (1924). National Archives, Republic of Korea (CJA 0004762).

———. *Seinen kunrenjo ninteishorui* [Licensing documents for young men's training centers] (1928–29). National Archives, Republic of Korea.

Chōsen sōtokufu naimukyoku. *Kaisei chihō seido jissi gaiyo* [Overview of the implementation of the reformed local government system] (1922).

Chōsen sōtokufu rinji tochi chōsakyoku. *Chōsen tochi chōsa jigyō hōkokusho* [Report on the Korean land survey project] (1918).

Chōsen sōtokufu kansei to sono gyōsei kiku [Bureaucratic system of the Government-General of Korea and its administrative organization]. Yūhō kyōkai, 1969.

Chōsen taihakurankai no gaikan [Overview of the Great Korean Exposition]. Keijō nippo-sha, 1940.

Chōsen tōchi hiwa [Secret story of rule in Korea]. Chōsen Gyōsei Henshūkyoku, 1937.

"Chōsenbun sinbun kiji sakujō chūi kiji yōshi—*Chōsen nippo*" [Summary of Korean-language newspaper articles to consider censoring—*Joseon ilbo*]. *Chōsen shuppan keisatsu geppo* [Korean publications police monthly report], no. 77 (1935.1.15). National Institute of Korean History website.

"Chōsenbun sinbunshi sashiosa kiji yōshi—*Chōsen chuō nippo*" [Summary of censored Korean-language newspaper articles—*Joseon jungang ilbo*]. *Chōsen shuppan keisatsu geppo* no. 96 (1936.8.30). National Institute of Korean History website.

Chung, Henry. *Korean Treaties*. H. S. Nichols, 1919.

Chung, Young-Iob. *Korea under Siege, 1876–1945: Capital Formation and Economic Transformation*. Oxford University Press, 2006.

Clark, Donald. *Living Dangerously in Korea*. EastBridge, 2003.

Cohn, Bernard. "History and Anthropology: The State of Play." *Comparative Studies in Society and History* 22.2 (1980): 198–221.

Consular Reports: Commerce, Manufactures, Etc., v. 58. U.S. Bureau of Foreign Commerce, 1898.

Cooper, Frederick, and Ann Laura Stoler, eds. *Tensions of Empire: Colonial Cultures in a Bourgeois World*. University of California Press, 1997.

Cumings, Bruce. "Webs with No Spiders, Spiders with No Webs: The Genealogy of the Developmental State." In *The Developmental State*, edited by Meredith Woo-Cumings. Cornell University Press, 1999.

———. "Colonial Formations and Deformations: Korea, Taiwan and Vietnam." In *Decolonization: Perspectives from Now and Then*, edited by Prasenjit Duara. Routledge, 2004.

Curtis, Bruce. "Foucault on Governmentality and Population: The Impossible Discovery." *Canadian Journal of Sociology* 27.4 (2002): 505–33.

Daehan jeguk eun geundae gukga in-ga? [Was the Great Korean Empire a modern state?]. Pureun yeoksa, 2006.

Daehan jeguk gwanwon iryeokseo [Resumes of the officials of the Great Korean Empire] (1908). Compiled by Guksa pyeonchan wiwonhoe. Tamgudang, 1971.

Daehan jeguk ui toji jedo wa geundae [The Korean Empire land system and modernity]. Compiled by Hanguk yeoksa yeonguhoe toji daejang yeonguban. Hyean, 2010.

Daehan jeguk ui toji josa sa-eop [The cadastral survey of the Great Korean Empire]. Mineumsa, 1995.

Daehan jegukgi jeongchaeksa jaryojip [Sources of the policy history of the Great Korean Empire], v. 7. Seonin munhwasa, 1999.

Daejeon hoetong. Seoul Daehakgyo Gyujanggak, 1999 (1865).

Deuchler, Martina. *Confucian Gentlemen and Barbarian Envoys*. University of Washington Press, 1977.

———. *The Confucian Transformation of Korea: A Study of Society and Ideology*. Harvard East Asian Monographs, 1992.

Devine, Richard. "Japanese Rule in Korea after the March First Uprising: Governor-General Hasegawa's Recommendations." *Monumenta Nipponica* 52.4 (1997): 523–40.

Diamond, Jared. *Guns, Germs, and Steel*. W. W. Norton, 1999.

Dickinson, Edward Ross. "Biopolitics, Fascism, Democracy: Some Reflections on Our Discourse about 'Modernity.'" *Central European History* 37.1 (2004): 1–48.

Dikötter, Frank. *Sex, Culture, and Modernity in China*. University of Hawaii Press, 1995.

Dirks, Nicholas B. *Castes of Mind*. Princeton University Press, 2001.

Duara, Prasenjit. *Sovereignty and Authenticity: Manchukuo and the East Asian Modern*. Rowman & Littlefield, 2004.

Dudden, Alexis. *Japan's Colonization of Korea: Discourse and Power.* University of Hawaii Press, 2006.

Duncan, John. *The Origins of the Chosŏn Dynasty.* Seattle: University of Washington Press, 2000.

———. "Uses of Confucianism in Modern Korea." In *Rethinking Confucianism: Past and Present in China, Japan, Korea, and Vietnam*, edited by Benjamin A. Elman et al. UCLA Asian Pacific Monograph Series, 2002.

———. "The Confucian Context of Reform." In *Reform and Modernity in the Taehan Empire*, edited by Kim Dong-no et al. Jimoondang, 2008.

Duus, Peter. *The Abacus and the Sword.* University of California Press, 1995.

Eckert, Carter. *Offspring of Empire: The Koch'ang Kims and the Colonial Origins of Korean Capitalism, 1876–1945.* University of Washington Press, 1991.

———. "Total War, Industrialization, and Social Change in Late Colonial Korea." In *The Japanese Wartime Empire, 1931–1945*, edited by Peter Duus et al. Princeton University Press, 1998.

Economic History of Chosen. Chōsen ginko, 1921.

Eisei keisatsu kōgi ippan [General lessons on hygiene policing]. Heian nandō keimubu, 1913.

Eisei ni kansuru meisin [Superstitions regarding hygiene]. Keishō nando keisatsubu eiseika, 1933.

Elias, Norbert. *Power and Civility: The Civilizing Process, v. 2.* Translated by Edmund Jephcott. Pantheon Books, 1982.

Engerman, S., and K. Sokoloff. "Colonialism, Inequality, and Long-run Paths of Development." NBER Working Paper No. 1157: 1–34.

Epstein, Gerald. "Central Banks as Agents of Economic Development." In *Institutional Change and Economic Development*, edited by Ha-Joon Chang. Anthem Press, 2007.

Feldman, David. "Triangulating Chōsen: Maps, Mapmaking, and the Land Survey in Colonial Korea." *Cross-Currents—East Asian History and Culture Review* 2 (2012): 1–28.

Fenn, Richard K. *The Spirit of Revolt: Anarchism and the Cult of Authority.* Rowman and Littlefield, 1986.

Fieldhouse, D. K. *Colonialism, 1870–1945: An Introduction.* Palgrave Macmillan, 1981.

Foucault, Michel. *Discipline and Punish: The Birth of the Prison.* Vintage Books, 1977.

———. *The Birth of Biopolitics: Lectures at the Collège de France, 1978–1979.* Translated by Graham Burchell. Picador, 1981.

———. *The Birth of the Clinic—An Archaeology of Medical Perception.* Translated by A. M. Sheridan Smith. Vintage Books, 1994.

———. *Security, Territory, Population: Lectures at the Collège de France, 1977–1978.* Translated by Graham Burchell. Picador, 2009.

Frühstück, Sabine. *Colonizing Sex: Sexology and Social Control in Modern Japan.* University of California Press, 2003.

Fujii Shōzō. "The Formation of Taiwanese Identity and the Cultural Policy of Various Outside Regimes." In *Taiwan under Japanese Colonial Rule, 1895–1945: History, Culture, Memory*, edited by Liao Ping-Hui and David Der-Wei Wang. Columbia University Press, 2006, Chapter 3.

Fujitani, Takashi. *Splendid Monarchy: Power and Pageantry in Modern Japan*. University of California Press, 1996.

———. *Race for Empire: Koreans as Japanese and Japanese as Americans during World War II*. University of California Press, 2011.

Fukuda Tōsaku. *Kankoku heigō kinenshi* [Commemorative history of the Korean annexation]. Dai Nihon sitsugyo kyokai, 1914.

Furth, Charlotte. "Introduction." In *Health and Hygiene in Chinese East Asia: Policies and Publics in the Long Twentieth Century*, edited by Angela Ki Che Leung and Charlotte Furth. Duke University Press, 2010.

"Gaeguk 504-nyeon yesan seolmyeongseo" [Explanation of the 1895 budget]. Gyujanggak Library (Gyu 17893).

Gaehwagi ui gyoyuk [Enlightenment period education]. Guksa pyeonchan wiwonhoe, 2011.

Gaksa deungnok [Records of individual agencies], 1894.11.19 and 1897.2.18 (Gyu 18154), 1896.9.1 (Gyu 17721), 1899.5.15 (Gyu 18022), 1898.7.30 (Gyu 18022), 1899.7.10 (Gyu 18022).

Gam Jong-gyu. *Hanguk gyoyuk gwajeong byeoncheonsa yeongu* [History of the development of the education process in Korea]. Gyoyuk gwahaksa, 2003.

Gang Dong-jin. *Ilbon ui Hanguk chimnyak jeongchaeksa* [History of the Japanese invasion policy in Korea]. Hangilsa, 1987.

Gang Gyeongae. *Ingan munje (oe)* ["The human predicament" and other works]. Beomu, 2005.

Gang Hye-gyeong. "Ilje sigi seongbyeong ui sahoe munje wa seongbyeong gwalli" [Perception of and measures to combat venereal disease in the Japanese colonial period]. *Hanguk minjok undongsa yeongu* 59 (2009): 87–125.

Gang Jeong-suk. "Daehan jeguk ilje chogi Seoul ui maechuneop gwa gongchang jedo ui toip" [Prostitution and the introduction of the licensed prostitution system in Seoul in the Korean Empire and early colonial periods]. *Seoulhak yeongu* 11.1 (1998): 197–237.

Gang Yeong-sim. "Ilje sigi 'chungnyang-han sinmin mandeulgi' gyoyuk gwa hakgyo munhwa" [Education and school culture for "creating loyal and good subjects" in the colonial period]. *Ihwa sahak yeongu* 33 (2006): 231–59.

Garon, Sheldon. "State and Religion in Imperial Japan, 1912–1945." *Journal of Japanese Studies* 12.2 (1986): 273–302.

"Gian, Uijeongbu uijeong Yun Yongseon" [Directive from High State Councillor Yun Yongseon], 1902.7.28. Gyujanggak Library (Gyu 17746).

Gill, Graeme. *The Nature and Development of the Modern State*. Palgrave Macmillan, 2003.

Gim Chandu. "Joseon sahoe wa hwaryubyeong" [Korean society and venereal disease]. *Gaebyeok* (1922).

Gim Dae-jun. *Gojong sidae ui gukga jaejeong yeongu—geundaejeok yesan jedo surip gwa byeoncheon* [State finances in the Gojong period—establishment and development of the modern budgeting system]. Taehaksa, 2004.

Gim Do-hyeong. *Daehan jegukgi ui jeongchi sasang yeongu* [Political thought of the Korean Empire period]. Jisik saneopsa, 1994.

Gim, Dong-no. "Hanmal ui gukga gaehyeok undong gwa jawon dongwon" [State reform movements and resource mobilization in the Korean Empire period]. In *Jeontong ui byeonnyong gwa geundae gaehyeok* [Transformation of tradition and modern reform], edited by Yonse daehakkyo gukga yeonguwon. Taehaksa, 2004.

———. "Ilbon jegukjuui wa Joseon chibae ui dokteukseong" [Japanese imperialism and the special character of its rule over Korea]. *Dongbang hakji* 133 (2006): 199–242.

Gim Gyeong-mi. "Botong hakgyo jedo ui hwangnip gwa hakgyo hunnyuk ui hyeongseong" [Establishment of the normal school system and the formation of school discipline]. In *Ilje ui singminji bae wa ilsang saenghwal* [Everyday life under Japanese colonial rule]. Hyean, 2004.

Gim Hong-sik, ed. *Daehan jegukgi ui toji jedo* [Land system of the Korean Empire]. Mineumsa, 1990.

Gim Hye-gyeong. *Singminji-ha geundae gajok ui hyeongseong gwa jendeo* [Gender and the formation of the modern family under colonialism]. Changbi, 2006.

Gim Jae-gwan. "'Odo dap-pa yeohaeng' e natanan ilje singminji gyotong chegye yeongu" [A study of the colonial transportation network as revealed in the "Excursion through the southern five provinces"]. In *Gaehwagi eseo ilje gangjeomgi kkaji geundae jedo ui doip gwa ilsang saenghwal ui jepyeon* [Introduction of modern systems and the reordering of daily life from the enlightenment period to the Japanese occupation period]. Danguk daehakgyo chulpanbu, 2012.

Gim Jae-ho. "Joseon hugi jungang jaejeong ui unyeong" [Management of central finances in the late Joseon era]. In *Joseon hugi jaejeong gwa sijang* [Finances and the market in the late Joseon], edited by Yi Heon-chang. Seoul National University Press, 2010.

Gim Jong-seo. "Gaehwagi sahoe munhwa byeondong gwa jonggyo insik" [Perceptions of religion and developments in society and culture during the enlightenment period]. In *Hanguk geundae sahoe wa munhwa* [Modern Korean society and culture], v. 1. Seoul National University Press (2003): 397–420.

Gim Mi-yeong. "Ilje-ha 'Joseon ilbo' ui seongbyeong gwallyeon tamnon yeongu" [Discourse on VD in the *Joseon ilbo* newspaper during the colonial period]. *Jeongsin munhwa yeongu* 29.2 (2006): 389–417.

———. "Ilje-ha geundae soseol-sok ui jilbyeong gwa byeongwon" [Diseases and hospitals as they appeared in the modern novels of the colonial period]. *Uri malgeul* 37 (2006): 309–36.

Gim Min-cheol. "Jeonsi chejeha (1937–1945) singminji haengjeong gigu ui byeonhwa" [Development of the colonial administrative organs under the wartime system, 1937–1945]. *Hanguksa hakbo* 14 (2003): 281–315.

Gim Nang-nyeon. *Ilje-ha Hanguk gyeongje* [The Korean economy under Japanese colonial rule]. Haenam, 2003.

———, ed. *Hanguk ui gyeongje seongjang, 1910–1945* [Growth of the Korean economy, 1910–1945]. Seoul National University Press, 2005.

———. "Singminji Joseon gyeongje ui jedojeok yusan" [Systemic legacy of the colonial Korean economy]. Working Paper 2010–2, Naksungdae Institute of Economic Research Working Paper Series (2010).

Gim Ok-geun. *Joseon wangjo jaejeongsa yeongu* [History of finances of the Joseon dynasty]. Iljogak, 1990.

———. *Ilje-ha Joseon jaejeongsa nongo* [A study of government finances in the colonial regime]. Iljogak, 1994.

Gim Pil-dong. "Gabo gyeongjang ijeon Joseon ui geundae-jeok gwanje gaehyeok ui chui wa saeroun gwallyo gigu ui seonggyeok" [Efforts at modern reform of the Korean bureaucratic system and the character of the new bureaucratic organs before the Gabo Reforms]. *Hanguk sahoesa yeonguhoe nonmunjip* 33 (1992.12): 11–88.

Gim Sanghoe. "Munhwa jeongchi ui geunbon jeongsin" [Fundamental spirit of Cultural Rule]. *Sisa pyeongnon* 5 (1922): 2–10.

Gim So-yeong. "Gabo gaehyeok (1894–1895) gyogwaseo sok e 'gungmin'" [*Gungmin* as found in the textbooks of the Gabo Reforms period, 1894–1895]. *Hanguksa hakbo* 29 (2007.11): 171–208.

———. "Hanmal susin gyogwaseo beonyeok gwa 'gungmin' hyeongseong" [Ethics textbook translations and the formation of the notion of "citizens" (*gungmin*) in the immediate precolonial period]. *Hanguk geunhyeondaesa yeongu* 59 (2011): 7–45.

Gim Sun-jeon and Bak Je-hong. "Hwangguk sinmin ui yukseong: 'Botong hakgyo susinseo' e natanan chung ui byeonyong" [Cultivating subjects of the empire: Development of the concept of loyalty, as seen in the "Normal School Ethics" textbooks]. In *Jeguk ui singminji susin: Joseon chongdokbu pyeonchan "Susinseo" yeongu* [Colonial self-cultivation in the empire: A study of the "Ethics" textbooks published by the Government-General of Korea], edited by Gim Sun-jeon et al., 82–95. J&C Publishing, 2008.

Gim Yeon-hui. "Daehan jegukgi, saeroun gisul gwanwon jipdan ui hyeongseong gwa haeche—jeonsin gisulja reul jungsim euro" [Formation and dissolution of the first groups of techno-bureaucrats during the Korean Empire period—Focusing on the telegraph technicians]. *Hanguk sahak* 140 (2008): 183–220.

Gim Yeong-gil. "Gungmin chongnyeok Joseon yeonmaeng ui samuguk gaepyeon gwa gwanbyeon danche e daehan tongje" [Administrative restructuring of the National Total Mobilization League of Korea and control over official organs]. *Hanguk geunhyeondaesa yeongu* 37 (2006): 333–74.

Gim Yeong-hui. *Ilje sidae nongchon jeongchaek yeongu* [Rural policy in the Japanese colonial period]. Gyeongin munwasa, 2003.

Gim Yeong-mi. "Singminji dongwon cheje ui yeonsok gwa danjeol" [Continuities and ruptures of the colonial mobilization system]. In *Singminji yusan, gukga hyeongseong, Hanguk minjujuui* [Colonial legacies, state formation, and South Korean democracy], v. 2, edited by Jeong Geun-sik and Yi Byeong-cheon. Chaek sesang, 2012: 219–53.

Gim Yeonsu. "Shinteki o semuru kakugo" [Determination to smite the main enemy]. *Kokumin sōryoku* 4.12 (1942): 47–48.

Gim Yong-cheol. "Ugaki Gajeusige ui Joseon tongchigwan gwa nongchon jinheung undong" [Ugaki Kazushige's perspectives on rule over Korea and the Rural Revitalization Campaign]. *Joseondae jeontong munhwa yeongu* (1999): 147–75.

Go Geun-ho. "Yugyo neun jonggyo inga?" [Is Confucianism a religion?]. In *Jonggyo dasi ilkgi* [Re-reading religion], edited by Hanguk Jonggyo Yeonguhoe. Cheongnyeonsa, 1999.

Gojong Sunjong sillok [Veritable records of the Gojong and Sunjong reigns]. Tamgudang, 1986.

Gomikawa Nori, "Tenkanki no Chōsen keizai" [The Korean economy at a turning point]. *Chōsen gyōsei* 2 (1937.2).

Gorski, Philip S., and Ates Altınordu. "After Secularization?" *Annual Review of Sociology* 34 (2008): 55–85.

Goussaert, Vincent. "1898: The Beginning of the End of Chinese Religion?" *Journal of Asian Studies* 65.2 (2006): 307–36.

Government-General of Chosen. *Annual Report on the Reforms and Progress in Chosen*, 1911–23.

———. *Thriving Chosen: A Survey of Twenty-Five Years' Administration* (1935).

———. *Annual Report on Administration of Chosen*, 1923–38.

Gragert, Edwin. *Landownership under Colonial Rule*. University of Hawaii Press, 1994.

Gramsci, Antonio. *Selections from the Prison Notebooks*. Edited and translated by Quentin Hoare and Geoffrey Nowell Smith. ElecBook, 1999.

Grapard, Alan G. "Japan's Ignored Cultural Revolution: The Separation of Shinto and Buddhist Divinities in Meiji ('Shimbutsu Bunri') and a Case Study: Tōnomine." *History of Religions* 23.3 (1984): 240–65.

Green, Andy. "Education and State Formation in Europe and Asia." In *Citizenship Education and the Modern State*, edited by K. J. Kennedy. Falmer Press, 1997.

Greenfield, Liah. *Nationalism: Five Roads to Modernity*. Harvard University Press, 1993.

Gugyeok hakgyo deungnok [Hakgyo deungnok—Korean translation]. Sejong daewang ginyeom sa-eophoe, 2010.

Gu Hanguk gwanbo [Government gazette], 1894–1910. Asea munhwasa, 1973.

Gu Hui-jin. "Daehan jegukgi gungmin gyoyuk ui chujin gwa guljeol" [Promotion of and shifts in the pursuit of national education in the Great Korean Empire period]. *Yeoksa gyoyuk* 109 (2006): 185–227.

Gungmin suji [What all citizens should know]. Unpublished booklet, 1905.

Gwon Hui-yeong. "Ilje sigi Joseon ui yuhak damnon" [Korean discourse on Confucianism in the Japanese colonial period]. *Hanguk minjok undongsa yeongu* 63 (2010): 124–26.

Gye Gwangsun. "Chongdokbu godeunggwan jessi-ga jeonsi-ha Joseon minjung e jeonhaneun seo—Daedonga gongyeonggwon geonseol gwa Joseon minjung" [Written thoughts transmitted to the Korean people by high officials in the Government-General during wartime—The Korean people and the construction of the Greater East Asian Co-Prosperity Sphere]. *Samcheolli* 13.4 (1941.4).

Gyeonggi docheong. *Nongchon jinheunghoe yaksok* [Promises of the Rural Revitalization Committee] (1936).

Gyeongmucheong georaemun [Internal documents of the Central Police Agency], v. 4, 1902.9.22 (Gyu 17804).

Gyeongsangdo seonsaengan [Roster of notables of Gyeongsang Province]. Hanguk gukhak jinheungwon, 2005.

Haboush, Jahyun Kim. *The Confucian Kingship in Korea: Yŏngjo and the Politics of Sagacity.* Columbia University Press, 2001.

Hall, Robert King, ed. *Kokutai No Hongi: Cardinal Principles of the National Entity of Japan.* Translated by John Owen Gauntlett. Harvard University Press, 1949.

Ham Jong-gyu. *Hanguk gyoyuk gwajeong byeoncheonsa yeongu* [History of the development of the education process in Korea]. Gyoyuk gwahaksa, 2003.

Han Seung-yeon. "Jeryeong eul tonghae bon chogdok jeongchi ui mokpyo wa Joseon chongdok ui haengjeongjeok gwonhan yeongu" [An investigation into colonial political goals and the Governor-General's administrative powers through an analysis of the *seirei* ordinances]. *Jeongbuhak yeongu* 15.2 (2009): 165–215.

Hanguk gaehwagi haksulji [Journals of the Korean enlightenment period], 19 vols. Asea munhwasa, 1976.

Hanguk gyoyuk 100-nyeonsa, 1880–1999 [100-year history of Korean education, 1880–1999]. Daehan teuksu gyoyuk hakhoe, 1995.

Hangukhak munheon Yeonguso, ed. *Hanguk gaehwagi gyogwaseo chongseo* [Complete textbooks of the Korean enlightenment period]. 20 vols. Asea munhwasa, 1977.

Hanguksa [Korean history]. 55 vols. Guksa pyeonchan wiwonhoe, 1993–2002.

"Hanguksa deitabeiseu" [Korean history database]. National Institute of Korean History website (db.history.go.kr). Accessed on multiple occasions.

Hanguk sinmun saseol seonjip [Selected editorials of Korean newspapers]. Bang I-ryeong munhwa jaedan, 1995.

Harada Kan. "Kenkoku kara heigō ni itaru Taikan teikoku" [The Great Korean Empire, from state foundation to the annexation]. *Tōajia kindaishi* 14 (2011): 39–51.

Hardacre, Helen. *Shinto and the State.* Princeton University Press, 1991.

Hashimoto Testuma. *Chōsen tōchi no shōrai* [The future of rule in Korea]. Seieisha, 1921.

Henry, Todd A. "Sanitizing Empire: Japanese Articulations of Korean Otherness and the Construction of Early Colonial Seoul, 1905–1919." *Journal of Asian Studies* 64.3 (2005): 639–75.

———. *Assimilating Seoul: Japanese Rule and the Politics of Public Space in Colonial Korea, 1910–1945.* University of California Press, 2014.

Heo Jae-yeong, ed. *Joseon gyoyungnyeong gwa gyoyuk jeongchaek byeonhwa jaryo* [Sources on the Korean school ordinances and the development of the colonial education policy]. Gyeongjin, 2011.

Hong Mun-jong. *Joseon eseo ui Ilbon singminji gyoyuk jeongchaek, 1910–1945* [Japanese colonial education policy in Korea, 1910–1945]. Hakjisa, 2003.

Hong Yang-hui. "Singminji sigi hojeok jedo wa gajok jedo ui byeonyong" [Development of the household registration and family systems in the colonial period]. *Sahak yeongu* 79 (2010): 167–205.

Hughes, Theodore Q. *Literature and Film in Cold War South Korea: Freedom's Frontier.* Columbia University Press, 2012.

Huh Soo-youl. "Changes in the Manufacturing Industry of Korea." *Review of Korean Studies* 14.4 (2011): 51–84.

Hulbert, Homer. *The Passing of Korea.* Doubleday, Page, & Company, 1906.

Hullyeong johoe jonan, 8 vols. Gyujanggak, 1992.

Hwang Hyeon. *Maecheon yarok* [Unofficial observations of Hwang Hyeon]. Translated by Yi Jang-hui. Daeyang seojeok, 1980.

Hwang, Kyung Moon. "Country or State? Reconceptualizing *Kukka* in the Korean Enlightenment Period, 1896–1910." *Korean Studies* 24 (1999): 1–24.

———. "From the Dirt to Heaven: Northern Koreans in the Chosŏn and Early Modern Eras." *Harvard Journal of Asiatic Studies* 62.1 (June 2002): 135–78.

———. *Beyond Birth: Social Status in the Emergence of Modern Korea.* Harvard University Asia Center, 2004.

Hyeon Chae. *Yunyeon pildok* [Compulsory reader for children]. 1907.

Ilje chimnyak-ha Hanguk 36-nyeonsa [36-year history of Korea under Japanese occupation], v. 11, accessed through Hanguksa detaebeiseu, National History Compilation Committee website (http:// db.history.go.kr / item / level.do?itemId = su&setId = 1202179&position = 102; http:// db.history.go.kr / item / level.do?itemId = su&setId = 1202179&position = 103).

Ilje gangjeomgi jonggyo jeongchaeksa jaryojip [Documents of religious policy during the Japanese occupation period]. Hanguk gidokyo yeoksa yeonguso, 1996.

Ilje ui Changwon-gun toji josa wa jangbu [Changwon county's land survey and ledgers under Japanese colonial rule]. Seonin, 2011.

Im Hyeon-su. "Daehan jeguk sigi yeokbeop jeongchaek gwa jonggyo munhwa" [Calendar policies and religious culture in the Great Korean Empire period]. In *Daehan jeguk eun geundae gukga in-ga?* Pureun yeoksa, 2006.

Im Jun-tae. "Hanguk geundae gyeongchalsa sogo" [Brief treatise on modern Korean police history]. *Hanguk gongan haengjeong hakhoebo* 41 (2010): 375–414.

Inda, Jonathan Xavier. "Analytics of the Modern: An Introduction." In *Anthropologies of Modernity: Foucault, Governmentality, and Life Politics,* edited by Jonathan Inda. Blackwell, 2005.

Iyer, Samantha. "Colonial Population and the Idea of Development." *Comparative Studies in Society and History* 55.1 (2013): 65–91.

Jang Deok-ju. "Ilje gangjeomgi seje ui jeongae gwajeong e gwanhan yeongu" [Development of the tax system during the Japanese colonial period]. *Semuhak yeongu* 23.4 (2006.12): 189–221.

Jang Jiyeon. "Daehan jaganghoe yeonseol: Siksan munje" [Speech to the Korean Self-Strengthening Society: The issue of industry]. *Hwangseong sinmun* (1906.4.30).

Je-69 hoe jeguk uihoe seolmyeong jaryo—Gyeongmuguk (Explanatory documents for the 69th Imperial Diet [hearings]—Central Police Bureau [of Korea]), 1935. National Archives (CJA 0002448), pp. 13–14, 24.

Jeon U-yong. "Hanin jabonga ui hyeongseong gwa seonggyeok" [Formation and character of Korean capitalists]. *Guksagwan nonchong* 41 (1993): 1–52.

Jeong Geun-sik. "Singminji wisaeng gyeongchal ui hyeongseong gwa byeonhwa, geurigo yusan" [Formation, development, and legacy of the colonial hygiene police]. *Sahoe wa yeoksa* 90 (2011): 221–70.

Jung Geun-sik and Yi Byeong-cheon, eds. *Singminji yusan, gukga hyeongseong, Hanguk minjujuui* [Colonial legacies, state formation, and South Korean democracy]. 2 vols. Chaek sesang, 2012.

Jeong Hye-jeong. "Ilje gangjeomgi botong hakgyo gyoyuk jeongchaek yeongu" [Education policies for normal schools in the Japanese occupation period]. In *Ilje singminji jibae jeongchaek gwa Maeil sinbo—1910 nyeondae* [Policies of rule in the Japanese colonial period and the *Maeil sinbo* newspaper—1910s], edited by Suyo yeoksa yeonguhoe. Duri midieo, 2005.

Jeong Il-seong. *Inmullo bon Ilje Joseon jibae 40 nyeon, 1906–1945* [A view of the 40 years of Japanese rule in Korea through historical personalities]. Jisik saneopsa, 2010.

Jeong Jae-jeong. *Ilje chimnyak gwa Hanguk cheoldo* [The Japanese invasion and Korean railroads]. Seoul National University Press, 1999.

Jeong Mi-ryang. "1920 nyeondae ilje ui jeil Joseon yuhaksaeng huwon saeop gwa geu seonggyeok" [Official sponsorship of Korean students to Japan in the 1920s]. *Hanguk gyoyuk sahak* 30.1 (2008): 61–89.

Ji Su-geol. "Ilje gun-gukjuui pasijeum gwa 'Joseon nongchon jinheung undong'" [Militaristic fascism of the colonial regime and the "Korean Rural Revitalization Movement"]. *Yeoksa wa bipyeong* 47 (1999):16–36.

———. "Iljeha ui jibang tongchi siseutem gwa gun danwi: 'gwallyo-yuji jibae cheje'" [Local governing system and the county unit in the colonial period: "The bureaucrat-local elite ruling order"]. *Yeoksa wa hyeonsil* 63 (2006): 346–79.

Jo Hyeong-geun. "Ilje ui gongsik uiryo wa gaesingyo seongyo uiryo gan hegemoni gyeongjaeng gwa geu sahoejeok hyogwa" [Social impact of the hegemony struggle between the colonial state's public medicine and Protestant missionary medicine]. *Sahoe wa yeoksa* 82 (2009): 123–65.

Jo Jae-gon. "Daehan jeguk ui siksan heungeop jeongchaek gwa sanggongeop gigu" [Industrial promotion policy and the commercial structure of the Great Korean Empire]. *Hangukhak nonchong* 34 (2010): 941–68.

Jo Seok-gon. "Gwangmu yeon-gan ui hojeong unyeong chegye e gwanhan sogo" [Brief observations on the system of tax administration during the Gwangmu (1897–1907) years]. In *Daehan jegukgi ui toji jedo* [Land system of the Korean Empire period], edited by Kim Hong-sik. Mineumsa, 1990.

———. *Hanguk geundae toji jedo ui hyeongseong* [Establishment of the modern Korean land system]. Haenam, 2003.

Jo Seon-hye. "1941 'Manguk buin gidohoe sageon' yeongu" [A study of the "universal women's prayer service incident" of 1941]. *Hanguk Gidokgyo wa yeoksa* 5 (1996): 117–54.

Jo Seongyun and Jo Eun. "Hanmal ui gajok gwa sinbun—Hanseongbu hojeok bunseok" [Family and status in the Korean Empire period—An analysis of the household registers of Seoul]. *Sahoe wa yeoksa* 50 (1996): 96–133.

Johnson, Chalmers. "The Developmental State: The Odyssey of a Concept." In *The Developmental State,* edited by Meredith Woo-Cumings. Cornell University Press, 1999.

Jonggyo sawon changnip pogyo gwallija e gwanhan geon (1936) [Religion: Documents related to the establishment of Buddhist temples and prospective evangelizers]. National Archives, Republic of Korea (CJA 0004831).

Joseon tongchi bihwa [Secrets of rule over Korea] (1937). Translated by Yi Chung-ho and Hong Geumja. Yeongun chulpansa, 1993.

Josephson, Jason A. *The Invention of Religion in Japan.* University of Chicago Press, 2012.

Ju Ik-jong. *Daegun ui cheokhu—Ilje-ha ui Gyeongseong bangjik gwa Gim Seongsu, Gim Yeonsu* [Scouts of a great army—Seoul Spinning and Weaving Company's Gim Seongsu and Gim Yeonsu under Japanese colonial rule]. Pureun yeoksa, 2008.

Jung-Kim, Jennifer. "Gender and Modernity in Colonial Korea." PhD diss., UCLA, 2005.

K. Gija. "Hojeok-changgu e natanan insaeng ui huibigeuk" [Life's comedies and tragedies, straight from the household registration window]. *Chogwang* (1939.02): 274–80.

Kal, Hong. "Modeling the West, Returning to Asia: Shifting Politics of Representation in Japanese Colonial Expositions in Korea." *Comparative Studies in Society and History* 47.3 (2005): 507–31.

Kallender, George L. *Salvation through Dissent: Tonghak Heterodoxy and Early Modern Korea.* University of Hawaii Press, 2013.

Kang, Hildi. *Under the Black Umbrella: Voices from Colonial Korea, 1910–1945.* Cornell University Press, 2005.

Kang Kyŏng-ae. *From Wonso Pond.* Translated by Samuel Perry. The Feminist Press, 2009.

Kankoku eisei ippan [General hygiene conditions in Korea]. Naibu eiseikyoku, 1909.

Kankoku shisei nenpō [Administrative yearbook of the Residency-General of Korea]. 1906–1910.

Kankoku tōkanfu. *Daisanji tōkanfu tōkei nenpō* [Third statistical annual of the Residency-General]. 1910.

Karlsson, Anders. "Famine Relief, Social Order, and State Performance in Late Chosŏn Korea." *Journal of Korean Studies* 12 (2007): 113–41.

Kawano Setsufu. "Sohwa onyeon gukse josa sihaeng e chwihayeo" [On implementing the 1930 census]. *Joseon* (1930.3): 2–8.

Kawashima, Ken C. *The Proletarian Gamble: Korean Workers in Interwar Japan.* Duke University Press, 2009. Kindle edition.

Keddie, Nikki. "Secularization and the State: Towards Clarity and Global Comparison." *New Left Review* 226 (1997): 21–40.

Keijō annai [Information about Seoul]. Chōsen kenkyukai, 1915.

Keijōfu sōmubu eiseika. *Eisei shisō fukyū no tame ni* [For the sake of propagating hygiene teachings]. 1939.

Keikido keisatsu buchō. "Sōshi no riyō jōkyō ni kan suru ken" [Matters regarding the conditions of the usage of new surnames] (1941.3.25). National Institute of Korean History website, accessed 2012.1.11.

Kerr, David. "Citizenship Education in the Curriculum: An International Review." *School Field* 10.3–4 (1999): 5–32.

Kikakubu. *Shōwa 15-nen butsudō chōsho—kayaku* [1940 materials report—Gunpowder]. National Archives of the Republic of Korea (#88–1).

Kim, Byung-Kook, and Ezra Vogel, eds. *The Park Chung Hee Era: The Transformation of South Korea.* Harvard University Press, 2011.

Kim, Christine. "The King Is Dead: Monarchism and National Identity in Modern Korea." PhD diss., Harvard University, 2004.

———. "Politics and Pageantry in Protectorate Korea (1905–10): The Imperial Progresses of Sunjong." *Journal of Asian Studies* 68.3 (2009): 835–59.

Kim, Hwansoo Ilmee. *Empire of the Dharma: Korean and Japanese Buddhism, 1877–1912.* Harvard Asia Center, 2012.

Kim, Janice. *To Live to Work: Factory Women in Colonial Korea, 1910–1945.* Stanford University Press, 2009.

Kim, Kyu-hyun. "The Mikado's August Body: 'Divinity' and 'Corporeality' of the Meiji Emperor and the Ideological Construction of Imperial Rule." In *Politics and Religion in Modern Japan: Red Sun, White Lotus,* edited by Roy Starrs. Palgrave Macmillan, 2011.

Kim, Marie Seong-Hak. *Law and Custom in Korea.* Cambridge University Press, 2012.

Kim, Sonja. "The Search for Health: Translating Wisaeng and Medicine during the Taehan Empire." In *Reform and Modernity in the Taehan Empire,* edited by Dong-no Kim et al. Jimoondang, 2006.

———. "Contesting Bodies: Managing Population, Birthing, and Medicine in Korea, 1876–1945." PhD diss., UCLA, 2008.

Kim, Sun Joo. "Taxes, the Local Elite, and the Rural Populace in the Chinju Uprising of 1862." *Journal of Asian Studies* 66.4 (2007): 993–1027.

———. *Marginality and Subversion in Korea: The Hong Kyŏngnae Rebellion of 1812.* University of Washington Press, 2009.

Kim, Taehoon. "The Place of 'Religion' in Colonial Korea around 1910: The Imperial History of 'Religion.'" *Journal of Korean Religions* 2.2 (2011): 25–46.

Kim, Wonik. "Rethinking Colonialism and the Origins of the Developmental State in East Asia." *Journal of Contemporary Asia* 39.3 (2009): 382–99.

Kohli, Atul. *State-Directed Development: Political Power and Industrialization in the Global Periphery.* Cambridge University Press, 2004.

Kokumin sōryoku Chōsen renmei. *Kokumin sōryoku Chōsen renmei yōran* [Overview of the Korean League for National Total Mobilization]. 1943.

———. *Chōsen ni okeru Kokumin sōryoku undōshi* [History of the national total mobilization movement in Korea]. 1945.

Komagome Takeshi. *Shokuminchi teikoku Nihon no bunka tōgō* [Cultural integration in the colonies of the Japanese empire]. Iwanomi shoten, 1996.

Koopman, Colin. "The History and Critique of Modernity: Dewey with Foucault against Weber." In *John Dewey and Continental Philosophy*, edited by Paul Fairfield. Southern Illinois University Press, 2010.

Kyōiku chokugo kampatsu kankei shiryōshū [Documents related to the proclamation of the Imperial Rescript on Education], v. 1. Tokyo: Kokumin seishin bunka kenkyūsho, 1935.

Larsen, Kirk. *Tradition, Treaties, and Trade: Qing Imperialism and Chosŏn Korea, 1850–1910*. Harvard University Asia Center, 2008.

Lee Byeong Cheon. "Political Economy of Korean Development after Liberation: A Critical Reflection." *Korea Journal* (Autumn 2006): 49–79.

Lee, Chul-woo. "Modernity, Legality, and Power in Korea under Japanese Rule." In *Colonial Modernity in Korea,* edited by Gi-wook Shin and Michael Robinson. Harvard University Asia Center, 1999.

Lee, Songsoon. "The Rural Control Policy and Peasant Ruling Strategy of the Government-General of Chosŏn in the 1930s-1940s." *International Journal of Korean History* 15.2 (2010): 1–33.

Lee, Yoonmi. *Modern Education, Textbooks and the Image of the Nation: Politics of Modernization and Nationalism in Korean Education, 1880–1910.* Garland, 2000.

Levine, Philippa. *Prostitution, Race and Politics: Policing Venereal Disease in the British Empire.* Routledge, 2003.

Liao, Ping-hui, and David Der-Wei Wang, eds. *Taiwan under Japanese Colonial Rule, 1895–1945.* Columbia University Press, 2006.

Lim Chaisung. "The Development of a Control Policy over the Coal Industry and the Management of the Coal Mining Industry in Wartime Colonial Korea." *Review of Korean Studies* 14.4 (2011): 85–133.

Lim, Sungyun. "Enemies of the Lineage: Widows and Customary Rights in Colonial Korea, 1910–1945." PhD diss., University of California at Berkeley, 2011.

Liu Shiyung. "The Theory and Practice of Malariology in Colonial Taiwan." In *Disease, Colonialism, and the State: Malaria in Modern East Asian History*, edited by Ka-che Yip. Hong Kong University Press, 2009.

Liu, Michael Shiyung. *Prescribing Colonization: The Role of Medical Practices and Policies in Japan-Ruled Taiwan, 1895–1945.* Association for Asian Studies, 2009.

Lloyd, David and Paul Thomas. *Culture and the State.* Routledge, 1997.

Lo, Ming-Cheng Miriam. *Doctors within Borders: Profession, Ethnicity, and Modernity in Colonial Taiwan.* University of California Press, 2002.

Makiko, Okamoto. *Shokuminchi kanryō no seijishi* [Political history of the colonial bureaucracy]. Sangensha, 2008.

Mapo bunseo hogu seongchaek [Collection of household registers from Mapo district]. 1904. National Archives of the Republic of Korea.

Marks, Shula. "Presidential Address: What Is Colonial about Colonial Medicine? And What Has Happened to Imperialism and Health?" *Social History of Medicine* 10.2 (1997): 205–19.

Martin, David. "The Secularization Issue: Prospect and Retrospect." *British Journal of Sociology* 42.3 (1991): 465–74.

Matsuda Toshihiko, *Nihon no Chōsen shokuminchi shihai to keisatsu* [Japan's colonial rule over Korea and the police]. Azekura Shobō, 2009.

McNamara, Dennis. *The Colonial Origins of Korean Enterprise: 1910–1945.* Cambridge University Press, 1990.

Meiji yonjū-nen Kankoku bōeki kiji [Reports on the disease control efforts of 1907 in Korea]. Kankoku tōkanfu, 1908.

Minami Jirō. "Kakudo naimubuchō kaigi ni okeru Sōtoku kunji yōshi" [Overview of the Governor-General's directives to the conference of provincial interior department chiefs] (1938), in *Chōsen ni okeru kyōiku kakushin no zenbō* [Complete picture of the renovations in Korean education], in *Nihon shokuminchi kyōiku seisaku shiryō shūsei—Chōsenhen* [Collection of historical documents on Japanese colonial education policy—Korea]. Ryūkei Shosha, 1987.

———. "Nentō shokan" [New year's thoughts]. *Chōsen gyōsei* 1.1 (1937): 4–5.

———. "Renmei jidojin ni nozomu" [Expectations for the leaders of the League]. *Sōdōin* 1.1 (1939).

Minjeok tonggyepyo [Statistics of the *minjeok* household registers]. Naemubu gyeongmuguk, 1910.

"Minsekihō no setsumei" [Explanation of the civil registration law]. Kankoku tōkanfu naibu keimukyoku, 1910. National Central Library of Korea (Han 20–68).

Mitchell, Timothy. "The World as Exhibition." *Comparative Studies in Society and History* 31.2 (1989): 217–36.

———. "State, Economy, and the State Effect." In *State / Culture: State-Formation after the Cultural Turn*, edited by George Steinmetz. Cornell University Press, 1999.

———. *Rule of Experts: Egypt, Techno-Politics, Modernity.* University of California Press, 2002.

Miura, C. "The Problem of Korean Assimilation." *Japan Magazine* 12.2–3 (1921): 130–34.

Miyamoto Gen. "Seoyangja, iseong yangja geup ssi jedo e kwanhan Joseon minsaryeong ui gaejeong e daehayeo" [On the revision to the Korean civil code in regard to adoptions and the introduction of the *shi* system]. *Jogwang* (1940.7).

Mizuno Naoki. *Changssi gaemyeong* [Name-change ordinance]. Translated by Jeong Seon-tae. Sancheoreom, 2008.

Mok Su-hyeon. "Daehan jegukgi gukga sigak sangjing ui yeonwon gwa byeoncheon" [Sources and development of state visual symbols in the Great Korean Empire]. *Misulsa nondan* 27 (2008): 289–321.

———. "Daehan jegukgi ui gukga sangjing jejeong gwa Gyeongungung" [Gyeongun palace and the formulation of state symbols in the Great Korean Empire]. *Seoulhak yeongu* 15 (2010): 159–83.

———. "Joseon misul jeollamhoe wa munmyeonghwa ui seonjeon" [The Korean Art Exhibition and civilizing propaganda]. *Sahoe wa yeoksa* 89 (2011): 85–115.

Moon, Virginia. "The Grafting of a Canon: The Politics of Korea's National Treasures and the Formation of an Art History." PhD diss., University of Southern California, 2010.

Moon, Yumi. *Populist Collaborators: The Ilchinhoe and the Japanese Colonization of Korea, 1896–1910*. Cornell University Press, 2013.

Morita Yoshio, ed. *Chōsen ni okeru kokumin sōryoku undōshi* [History of the national total mobilization movement in Korea]. Kokumin sōryoku Chōsen renmei, 1945.

Moskowitz, Karl. "The Creation of the Oriental Development Company: Japanese Illusions Meet Korean Reality." *Occasional Papers on Korea* 2 (1974): 73–121.

Motoyama, Yukihiko. "Thought and Education in the Meiji Era." In *Proliferating Talent: Essays on Politics, Thought, and Education in the Meiji Era*, edited by Richard Rubinger et al. University of Hawaii Press, 1997.

Mun Cheol-su and Yi Byeong-dam. "Geundae Ilbon ui chodeung 'Susin' gyogwaseo yeongu" [Elementary "Ethics" textbooks in early modern Japan]. *Ilboneo munhak* 23 (2004): 283–304.

Mun Young-joo. "Rural Rehabilitation and Colonial Subjects during the 1930s." *International Journal of Korean History* 14 (2009): 163–86.

Murayama Chijun. *Chōsen no ruiji shūkyō* [Korea's pseudo-religions]. Chōsen sōtokufu, 1935.

Naebu georaemun [Internal documents of the Interior Ministry], v. 14, 1902.9.21 (Gyu 17794).

"Naejangwon gakdo gakgun sojang yoyak" [Summary of Office of Crown Properties documents from provinces and counties]. 3 vols. Gyujanggak, 1998.

Naejangwon hoegyechaek [Ledgers of the Office of Crown Properties], 1890s (Gyu 19116).

Naikaku tōkeikyoku. *Kokusei chōsa tōkeito* [Census survey statistical charts]. 1930.

Nakahara Shigeru. *Chōsen koseki hikkeishū* [Handbook of household registration in Korea]. Keijō: 1930.

Nakata Tenbyō. *Chōsen kosekirei yōgi* [Korean household registration ordinance digest]. Taikyū: Kyūseitō, 1923.

Namgung Yong-gwon. *Gyoyuk ui yeoksa wa sasang* [Education history and thought]. Hyeongseol chulpansa, 2007.

Namhaehyeon gyeongja gaeryang jeonan [New registers for Namhae county, 1720]. Gyujanggak Library (Gyu 14712).

Nathan, Mark Andrew. "Buddhist Propagation and Modernization: The Significance of P'ogyo in Twentieth-Century Korean Buddhism." PhD diss., UCLA, 2010.

Nomura Chōtarō. *Chōsen kosekirei gikai* [Explanation of the Korean household registration ordinance]. Ganshōtō, 1923.

Nongchon jinheunghoe yaksok [Promises of the Rural Revitalization Committee]. Gyeongidocheong, 1936.

O Gyeong-hwan et al. *Gyohoe wa gukga* [Church and state]. Incheon katollik daehakkyo, 1997.

O Jin-seok. "Hanguk geundae jeollyeok saneop ui baljeon gwa Gyeongseong jeongi (ju)" [The Seoul Electric Company, Inc., and the development of the electricity industry in early modern Korea]. PhD diss., Yonsei University, 2006.

O Seong. "Hanmal Gyeonggido jibang ui hoju guseong ui yangsang" [The makeup of the heads of households in the Gyeonggi province region during the Korean Empire period]. *Yeoksa hakbo* 152 (1996): 1–34.

Oh, Se-mi. "Consuming the Modern: The Everyday in Colonial Seoul, 1915–1937." PhD diss., Columbia University, 2008.

Ōkubo Toshiaki, *Meiji jidai no kyōiku* [Education in the Meiji period]. Iwanami Shoten, 1933.

Onis, Ziya. "The Logic of the Developmental State." *Comparative Politics* 24.1 (1991): 109–26.

Otaka Chōyū. *Kokutai no hongi to naisen ittai* [Essence of the national body and *naisen ittai*]. Kokumin sōryoku Chōsen renmei bōei jidōbu, 1941.

Pai, Hyung Il. *Heritage Management in Korea and Japan: The Politics of Antiquity and Identity*. University of Washington Press, 2013.

Paik, L. George. *The History of Protestant Missions in Korea, 1832–1910*. 1929. Yonsei University Press, 1970.

Palais, James. *Politics and Policy in Traditional Korea*. Harvard East Asian Monographs, 1975.

———. "Stability in Yi Dynasty Korea: Equilibrium Systems and Marginal Adjustment." *Occasional Papers on Korea* 3 (1975): 1–18.

———. "Confucianism and the Aristocratic / Bureaucratic Balance in Korea." *Harvard Journal of Asiatic Studies* 44.2 (1984): 427–68.

———. *Confucian Statecraft and Korean Institutions*. University of Washington Press, 1996.

Palmer, Brandon. *Fighting for the Enemy: Koreans in Japan's War, 1937–1945*. University of Washington Press, 2013.

Park, Albert. "Visions of the Nation: Religion and Ideology in 1920s and 1930s Rural Korea." PhD diss., University of Chicago, 2007.

Park, Chan Seung. "Japanese Rule and Colonial Dual Society in Korea." *Korea Journal* 50.4 (2010): 69–98.

Park, Chung-shin. *Protestantism and Politics in Korea*. University of Washington Press, 2003.

Park, Eugene. *A Family of No Prominence*. Stanford University Press, 2014.

Park, Hwan-mu. "Effects of the Name Change Policy in Onyang during the Pacific War Period." Paper presented at the workshop on "The Modern Transformation of a Korean Locality," University of Southern California, April 2010.

Park, Jin-kyung. "Corporeal Colonialism: Medicine, Reproduction, and Race in Colonial Korea." PhD diss., University of Illinois at Urbana-Champaign, 2008.

———. "Picturing Empire and Illness: Biomedicine, Venereal Disease and the Modern Girl in Korea under Japanese Colonial Rule." *Cultural Studies* (2013): 1–34.

Park, Pori. *Trial and Error in Modernist Reforms: Korean Buddhism under Colonial Rule*. Institute of East Asian Studies, UC Berkeley, 2009.

Park, Yunjae. "Sanitizing Korea: Anti-Cholera Activities of the Police in Early Colonial Korea." *Seoul Journal of Korean Studies* 23.2 (2010): 151–71.

Paske, J. "The Corean School System." *East of Asia Magazine* (1903): 24–30.

Peabody, Norbert. "Cents, Sense, and Census: Human Inventories in Late Precolonial and Early Colonial India." *Comparative Studies of Society and History* 43 (2001): 819–50.

Pels, Peter. "The Anthropology of Colonialism: Culture, History, and the Emergence of Western Governmentality." *Annual Review of Anthropology* 26 (1997): 163–83.

Pierson, Christopher. *The Modern State*. Routledge, 1996.

Porter, Dorothy. *Health, Civilization and the State: A History of Public Health from Ancient to Modern Times*. Routledge, 1999.

Prakash, Gyan. *Another Reason*. Princeton University Press, 1999.

Prospectus of the Oriental Development Company. Oriental Development Company, 1921.

Quinones, Carlos Kenneth. "The Prerequisites for Power in Late Yi Korea, 1864–1894." PhD diss., Harvard University, 1975.

Radice, Hugo. "The Developmental State under Global Neoliberalism." *Third World Quarterly* 29.6 (2008): 1153–74.

Rausch, Franklin. "Like Birds and Beasts: Justifying Violence against Catholics in Late Chosŏn Korea." *Acta Koreana* 15.1 (June 2012): 43–71.

Robinson, Michael. *Cultural Nationalism in Colonial Korea, 1920–1925*. University of Washington Press, 1989.

———. "Perceptions of Confucianism in Twentieth-Century Korea." In *The East Asian Region: Confucian Heritage and Its Modern Adaptation*, edited by Gilbert Rozman, 215. Princeton University Press, 1991.

———. "Broadcasting, Cultural Hegemony, and Colonial Modernity in Korea, 1924–1945." In *Colonial Modernity in Korea*, edited by Gi-Wook Shin and Michael Robinson. Harvard University Asia Center, 1999.

Rogaski, Ruth. *Hygienic Modernity: Meanings of Health and Disease in Treaty-Port China*. University of California Press, 2004.

Ryu Hongjong. "Minseihaksang euro boneun Joseon minjok" [Examining the Korean people through the lens of public health studies]. *Gaebyeok* 4 (1920).

Ryu Seung-nyeol. "Ilje-ha Joseon tongchi seryeok ui jibae ideollogi jojak gwa gangje" [Construction and enforcement of the ideology of those ruling Korea during the colonial period]. *Je-2 gi Hanil yeoksa gongdong yeongu bogoseo, je-4 kwon* (2011): 119–49.

Saitō Makoto bunsho [Papers of Saitō Makoto]. Goryeo seorim, 1999.

Sajin euro boneun Hanguk geunhyeondaesa [Modern Korean history viewed through photographs], v. 1. 20-segi Gonghunsa pyeonchanhoe, 2000.

Sakamoto Shinichi. "Myeongchi minbeop ui seongssi jedo" [Surname system of the Meiji civil code]. *Beopsahak yeongu* 22 (2000): 155–90.

Sangmusa changjeong [Regulations of the Commercial Affairs Company]. 1899. Digital access provided by Dongnip ginyeomgwan.

Sawada, Chiho. "Cultural Politics in Imperial Japan and Colonial Korea: Reinventing Assimilation and Education Policy, 1919–1922." PhD diss., Harvard University, 2003.

Schmid, Andre. "Colonialism and the 'Korea Problem' in the Historiography of Japan: A Review Article." *Journal of Asian Studies* 59 (2000): 951–76.

———. *Korea between Empires*. Columbia University Press, 2002.

Schneider, Michael. "The Future of the Japanese Empire, 1914–1931." PhD diss., University of Chicago, 1996.

Skocpol, Theda. "Bringing the State Back In: Strategies of Analysis in Current Research." In *Bringing the State Back In*, edited by Peter Evans et al. Cambridge University Press, 1985.

Scott, David. "Colonial Governmentality." *Social Text* 43 (1995): 191–220.

Scott, James C. *Seeing Like a State: How Certain Schemes to Improve the Human Condition Have Failed*. Yale University Press, 1998.

Seaman, Louis Livingston. *The Real Triumph of Japan: The Conquest of the Silent Foe*. D. Appleton, 1906.

Sekiya Teisaburō. "Sarip hakgyo gyuchik gaejeong ui yoji" [Overview of the revision of the Private School Ordinance], *Chōsen ihō* (April 1915). In *Ilje gangjeomgi jonggyo jeongchaeksa jaryojip—Gidokgyo pyeon, 1910–1945* [Sources on religious policy during the Japanese occupation period—Protestantism, 1910–1945], edited and translated by Gim Seung-taek. Hanguk gidokgyo yeoksa yeonguso, 1996.

Sejong jangheon daewang sillok [Veritable records of King Sejong the Great].

Seo Ho-chul. "The Process of the Metric System's Acceptance in Korea and Its International Context." *Review of Korean Studies* 11.3 (2008): 37–59.

Seo Jin-gyo. "Daehan Jeguk-gi Sangmusa ui jojik gwa hwaldong" [Organization and activities of the Commercial Affairs Company during the Great Korean Empire period]. *Hanguk geunhyeondaesa yeongu* 9 (1998): 61–92.

Seo Yeong-hui. "Gukga-ron cheongmyeon eseo bon Daehan jeguk ui seonggyeok" [The Great Korean Empire's character from the vantage point of state theory]. In *Daehan jegugeun geundae gukga in-ga?* Pureun yeoksa, 2006.

———. *Daehan jeguk jeongchisa yeongu* [Political history of the Great Korean Empire]. Seoul National University Press, 2005.

Seol Taehui. "Gukga ui uiui" [Meaning of the *gukga*]. *Daehan hyeophoe hoebo* 3 (1908): 30–31.

Seong Ju-hyeon. "1910 nyeondae Joseon eseo ui Ilbon Bulgyo pogyo hwaldong gwa seonggyeok" [Character and activities of Japanese Buddhist evangelization in 1910s Korea]. In *Ilje singminji jibae jeongchaek gwa Maeil sinbo* [Japanese colonial policies and the *Maeil sinbo* newspaper], edited by Suyo yeoksa yeonguhoe, 157–58. Duri midieo, 2005.

Seth, Michael. *Education Fever: Society, Politics, and the Pursuit of Schooling in South Korea*. University of Hawaii Press, 2002.

Sharpe, Lesley. *Friedrich Schiller: Drama, Thought and Politics*. Cambridge University Press, 1991.

Shashin Chōsen no gaikan [Pictorial overview of Korea]. 1920. East Asian Library, University of Southern California.

Shaw, William. *Legal Norms in a Confucian State*. Institute of East Asian Studies, University of California, Berkeley, 1981.

Shin, Gi-Wook. *Peasant Protest and Social Change in Colonial Korea*. University of Washington Press, 1996.

———. *Ethnic Nationalism in Korea*. Stanford University Press, 2006.

Shin, Gi-Wook, and Do-Hyun Han. "Colonial Corporatism: The Rural Revitalization Campaign, 1932–1940." In *Colonial Modernity in Korea*, edited by Gi-Woo Shin and Michael Robinson. Harvard University Asia Center, 1999.

Shiroishi Hōsei, *Chōsen eisei yōgi* [Korea hygiene digest]. 1918.

Shisei gonen kinen Chōsen bussan kyōshinkai hōkokusho [Report on the Korean Products Fair in commemoration of the fifth year of the new administration]. Chōsen sōtokufu, 1916.

Showa gonen Chōsen kokusei chōsa hōkoku, zensen-hen, kekka-hyo [Report of the 1930 Korea census survey—complete Korea volume—results tables]. Chōsen sōtokufu, 1930.

Showa jūnen Chōsen kokusei chōsa hōkoku, kekka-hyo, zensen-hen [Report of the 1935 Korea census survey—results tables—complete Korea volume]. Chōsen sōtokufu, 1935.

Sin Dong-won. *Hanguk geundae bogeon uiryosa* [History of the modern public health and medical system in Korea]. Hanul, 1997.

Sin Dong-won and Hwang Sang-ik. "Joseon malgi (1876–1910) geundae bogeon uiryo cheje ui hyeongseong gwajeong gwa geu uimi" [Formation of the early modern public health and medical system, and its meaning in the 1876–1910 period]. *Uisahak* 5.2 (1996): 155–67.

Sin Gyu-hwan. "Gaehang, jeonjaeng, seongbyeong: Hanmal iljecho ui seongbyeong yuhaeng gwa tongje" [Port opening, war, and venereal disease: The spread and control of VD in the late nineteenth and early twentieth centuries]. *Uihaksa* 17.2 (2008): 239–55.

———. *Gukga, dosi, wisaeng* [State, cities, and hygiene]. Acanet, 2008.

Skya, Walter A. *Japan's Holy War: The Ideology of Radical Shinto Ultranationalism*. Duke University Press, 2009.

So Bongsaeng. "Joseon tongchi ui seongjeok" [Accomplishments of the governance of Korea]. *Maeil sinbo* 1915.10.19–1915.11.02.

Soh, C. Sarah. *The Comfort Women: Sexual Violence and Postcolonial Memory in Korea and Japan*. University of Chicago Press, 2009.

Sohn, Min Suh. "Enlightenment and Electrification: The Introduction of Electric Light, Telegraph and Streetcars in Late Nineteenth Century Korea." In *Reform and Modernity in the Taehan Empire*, edited by Kim Dong-no et al. Jimoondang, 2006.

"Sohwa sanyeondo sanmi jeungsik gyehoek toji gaeryang sa-eop jageum gwangyeseo" [Documents related to funding for the rice production increase plans and land development projects, 1929]. National Archives, Republic of Korea (CJA0003889).

Son Byeong-gyu. "Myeongchi hojeok gwa Gwangmu hojeok bigyo yeongu" [Comparative study of the Meiji and Gwangmu household registration systems]. *Taedong gojeon yeongu* 24 (2008): 279–318.

Son In-su. *Hanguk gyoyuksa yeongu* [History of Korean education], v. 1. Muneumsa, 1998.

Son Nak-gu. "1923–24 nyeon Joseon chongdokbu ui semu gigu dongnip jeongchaek" [The Government-General's policy of establishing independent revenue agencies, 1923–24]. *Hanguk geunhyeondaesa yeongu* 59 (2011): 79–118.

Son Suk-gyeong. "19-segi huban Gwanwang sungbae ui hwaksan gwa gwanwang-myo jerye ui judogwon eul dulleossan Dongnae jiyeok sahoe ui donghyang" [Developments in the local society of Dongnae, as reflected in the expanding worship of King Gwan and competition for hegemony in the ancestral ceremonies of the King Gwan shrines in the late nineteenth century]. *Gomunseo yeongu* 23 (2003): 211–41.

Song Ho-geun. *Simin ui tansaeng—Joseon ui geundae wa gongnonjang ui jigak byeondong* [The birth of citizens—Early modernity and intellectual changes in the public sphere of Joseon]. Mineumsa, 2013.

Song Jun-ho. "Joseon hugi ui gwageo jedo" [Late Joseon examination system]. *Guksagwan nonchong* 63 (1995): 37–191.

Song Yang-seop. "Joseon hugi sinbun jigyeok yeongu wa 'jigyeok cheje' ui insik" [Research into status in the late Joseon era and the perception of a "status system"]. *Joseon sidae sahakpo* 34 (2006): 127–57.

Song Youn-ok. "Japanese Colonial Rule and State-Managed Prostitution: Korea's Licensed Prostitutes." *positions* 5.1 (1997): 171–219.

Spaulding, Robert. "The Bureaucracy as a Political Force." In *The Dilemmas of Growth in Prewar Japan,* edited by James William Morley. Princeton University Press, 2015.

Stark, Rodney. "Secularization: RIP." *Sociology of Religion* 60.3 (1999): 249–73.

Stoler, Ann Laura. *Carnal Knowledge and Imperial Power: Race and the Intimate in Colonial Rule.* University of California Press, 2002.

Swatos, Jr., William and Kevin J. Christiano. "Secularization Theory: The Course of a Concept." *Sociology of Religion* 60.3 (1999): 209–28.

Takjibu. "Seip sechul chong yesanpyo" [Total budget table of tax revenue and expenditures] (1898–1902). Gyujanggak Library (Gyu 15295).

Terauchi Masatake. "Kankoku heigō ni kan suru yukoku" [Proclamation on the annexation of Korea]. In *Chōsen tōchi sannen-kan seiseki* [Three years of policy of governing Korea]. 1910.8.29. Appendix.

Thriving Chosen: A Survey of Twenty-Five Years' Administration. Government-General of Chosen, 1935.

Tikhonov, Vladimir. "The Japanese Missionaries and Their Impact on Korean Buddhist Developments (1876–1910)." In *Makers of Modern Korean Buddhism*, edited by Jin Y. Park. SUNY Press, 2010.

Tilly, Charles. "War Making and State Making as Organized Crime." In *Bringing the State Back In*, edited by Peter Evans et al. Cambridge University Press, 1985.

———. *Coercion, Capital and European States: AD 990–1992*. Wiley-Blackwell, 1992.

Tōkanfu tōkei nenpō [Statistical annual of the Residency-General of Korea]. 1906–10.

Tonggye-ro dasi boneun Gwangbok ijeon ui gyeongje sahoe-sang [Revisiting conditions in the economy and society before the 1945 Liberation]. National Office of Statistics, Republic of Korea, 1995.

Treat, John Whittier. "Choosing to Collaborate: Yi Kwangsu and the Moral Subject in Colonial Korea." *Journal of Asian Studies* 71.1 (2012): 81–102.

Tschannen, Olivier. "The Secularization Paradigm: A Systematization." *Journal for the Scientific Study of Religion* 30.4 (1991): 395–415.

Tsurumi, E. Patricia. "Colonial Education in Korea and Taiwan." In *The Japanese Colonial Empire, 1895–1945*, edited by Ramon Myers and Mark Peattie. Princeton University Press, 1984.

Uchida, Jun. *Brokers of Empire: Japanese Settler Colonialism in Korea: 1876–1945*. Harvard University Asia Center, 2011.

Urla, Jacqueline. "Cultural Politics in an Age of Statistics: Numbers, Nations, and the Making of Basque Identity." *American Ethnologist* 20.4 (1993): 818–43.

Vacante, Russell. "Japanese Colonial Education in Korea: An Oral History." PhD diss., SUNY Buffalo, 1987.

Wagner, Edward W. *The Literati Purges: Political Conflict in Early Yi Korea*. Harvard East Asia Monographs, 1974.

Walraven, Boudewijn. "Popular Religion in a Confucianized Society." In *Culture and the State in Late Chosŏn Korea*, edited by Jahyun Kim Haboush and Martina Deuchler. Harvard University Asia Center, 1999.

Wang Hyeon-jong. "Daehan jegukgi ipheon nonui wa geundae gukgaron" [Debates on constitutional monarchy and the modern state in the Korean Empire period]. *Hanguk geundae sahoe wa munhwa* [Korean society and culture of the early modern era], v. 1, edited by Gwon Tae-oek et al. Seoul National University Press, 2003.

———. *Hanguk geundae gukga ui hyeongseong gwa Gabo gaehyeok* [Formation of the early modern state in Korea and the Gabo Reforms]. Yeoksa bipyeongsa, 2003.

———. "Gwangmu yangjeon jigye sa-eop ui seonggyeok" [Character of the Kwangmu land survey and certification projects]. In *Daehan jeguk ui toji jedo wa geundae*. Hyean, 2010.

Weber, Max. *From Max Weber: Essays in Sociology*. Edited and translated by H. H. Gerth and C. Wright Mills. Oxford University Press, 1946.

———. *Economy and Society.* 2 vols. Edited by Guenther Roth and Claus Wittich. University of California Press, 1978.

Wilkinson, W. H. *The Corean Government: Constitutional Changes, July 1894 to October 1895.* P. S. King & Son, 1897.

Woodside, Alexander. *Lost Modernities.* Harvard University Press, 2005.

Yamaguchi Sei. *Chōsen sangyō-shi* [History of Korean industry], v. 2. Hōbunkan, 1911.

Yangji amun an 1 [Regulations of the Land Survey Agency]. 1898.7–1899.12 Gyujanggak Library (Gyu 17817).

Yao Jen-To. "The Japanese Colonial State and Its Form of Knowledge in Taiwan." In *Taiwan under Japanese Colonial Rule, 1895–1945: History, Culture, Memory,* edited by Liao Ping-Hui and David Der-Wei Wang. Columbia University Press, 2006.

Yi Byeong-dam. *Hanguk geundae adong ui tansaeng* [Birth of the modern child in Korea]. J&C Publishing, 2007.

Yi Changgeun. "Joseon jonggyo-gye ui jinjeon" [The development of the Korean religious sphere]. *Joseon* 144 (1929): 1435–38.

Yi Chung-ho. *Ilje amheukgi uisa gyoyuksa* [Education of physicians in the Japanese dark period]. Gukhak jaryowon, 2011.

Yi Dae-hwa. "Changssi gaemyeong jeongchaek gwa Joseonin ui dae-eung" [Name change policy and the response of Koreans]. *Sungsil sahak* 26 (2011): 179–223.

Yi Giyeong. *Gohyang* [Hometown]. Donga chulpansa, 1995.

Yi Gwang-nin. "Yu Giljun ui gaehwa sasang—*Seoyu gyeonmun* eul jungsim euro" [Yu Giljun's enlightenment thought—Focusing on *Seoyu gyeonmun*]. *Hanguk gaehwa sasang yeongu* [Korean enlightenment thought]. Iljogak, 1979.

———. *Gaehwapa wa gaehwa sasang yeongu* [The Enlightenment Party and enlightenment thought]. Iljogak, 1989.

Yi Heon-chang. "Joseon singminjihwa ui naejeok wonin" [Internal causes behind Korea's colonization]. *Joseon sidae sahakbo* 55 (2010): 261–307.

Yi Hui-gwon. *Joseon hugi jibang tongchi haengjeong yeongu* [Administration of local rule in the late Joseon era]. Jimmundang, 1999.

Yi Hun-sang. "19 segi hojeok daejang ui jiyeok-hwa wa hyangni sahoe e isseoseo jeolhap gujo ui hyeongseong" [Localization of the household register compilations in the nineteenth century, and adjustment methods among the local clerks]. Paper presented at the Association for Social History Meeting, Seoul National University, March 23, 2002.

———. "Gabo gyeongjanggi jibang jedo wa gunsa jedo ui gaehyeok geurigo jiyeok sahoe ui dae-eung" [Reforms of the local government and military systems, and local responses to them, in the Gabo Reforms period]. *Yeongnamhak* 20 (2011): 315–404.

Yi Jeong-seon, "Hanguk geundae hojeok jedo ui byeoncheon" [Changes in the early modern Korean household registration system]. *Hanguksaron* 55 (2009): 275–328.

Yi Jon-hui. *Joseon sidae jibang haengjeong jedo yeongu* [The Joseon local government administration system]. Iljisa, 1990.

Yi Jong-beom. "Hanmal ilje-cho toji josa wa jise munje" [The problem of land surveying and land taxes from the late nineteenth century to the early colonial
period]. In Hanguk yeoksa yeonguhoe geundae sabun gwa toji daejang yeonguban, *Daehan jeguk ui toji josa saeop* [The cadastral survey of the Great Korean
Empire]. Mineumsa, 1995.

Yi Jong-chan. *Dongasia uihak ui jeontong gwa geundae* [Tradition and modernity in
East Asian medicine]. Munhak gwa jiseongsa, 2004.

Yi Jong-guk. *Hanguk ui gyogwaseo byeoncheonsa* [History of the development of
textbooks in Korea]. Daehan gyogwaseo jusik hoesa, 2008.

Yi Jun-gu. *Joseon hugi sinbun jigyeok byeondong yeongu* [Development of status titles
in the late Joseon era]. Iljogak, 1993.

Yi Man-yeol. *Hanguk gidokgyo uiryosa* [History of Protestant medicine in Korea].
Akanet, 2003.

Yi Myeong-jong. "Ilje malgi Joseonin jingbyeong eul wihan giryu jedo" [Household
registration and the implementation of the residence registry system for con-
scripting Koreans in the late colonial period]. *Sahoe wa yeoksa* 74 (2007): 75–106.

Yi Seong-u. "Jeonsi chejegi (1937–1945 nyeon) ilje ui nongchon tongje jeongchaek
gwa geu silsang" [Colonial rural policies and practices during wartime mobilization (1937–1945)]. *Hanguk geunhyeondaesa yeongu* 60 (2012): 123–59.

Yi Seung-il. "Joseon chongdokbu ui Joseonin deungnok jedo yeongu" [The Government-General's system for registering Koreans]. *Sahoe wa yeoksa* 67 (2005): 6–40.

———. *Joseon chongdokbu beopje jeongchaek* [Legal policies of the Government-
General of Korea]. Yeoksa bipyeongsa, 2008.

Yi Su-geon. "Seongssi" [Clan identities]. In *Hanguk minjok munhwa dae baekgwa
sajeon* [Great encyclopedia of Korean culture]. http://encykorea.aks.ac.kr.

———. *Joseon sidae jibang haengjeongsa* [History of Joseon local administration].
Mineumsa, 1989.

Yi Tae-jin. *Gojong sidae ui jaejomyeong* [Re-illuminating the Gojong era]. Taehaksa,
2000.

Yi T'aejun. "Before and After Liberation." *On the Eve of the Uprising and Other
Stories from Colonial Korea*, edited and translated by Sunyoung Park. Cornell
East Asia Series, 2010.

Yi U-yeon. *Hanguk ui sallim soyu jedo wa jeongchaek ui yeoksa, 1600–1987* [History
of the ownership system and policy regarding forests and mountains in Korea,
1600–1987]. Iljogak, 2010.

Yi Yeong-hak. "Daehan jeguk ui gyeongje jeongchaek" [Economic policies of the
Great Korean Empire]. *Yeoksa wa hyeonsil* 26 (1997): 56–92.

Yi Yeong-ho. "Daehan jeguk sigi Naejangwon ui oehoek unyeong gwa sangeop
hwaldong" [Commercial activities and the operation of the *oehoek* transaction
system by the Office of Crown Properties in the Korean Empire period]. *Yeoksa
wa hyeonsil* 15 (1995): 209–42.

———. "Tonggambu sigi jose jeungga jeongchaek ui silhyeon gwajeong gwa geu
seonggyeok" [Progress and character of policies for increasing land tax revenue
during the protectorate period]. *Hanguk munhwa* 18 (1996.12): 343–78.

———. *Hanguk geundae jise jedo wa nongmin undong* [Land tax system and peasant movements in early modern Korea]. Seoul National University Press, 2001.

———. "Daehan jeguk sigi ui toji jedo wa nongminchcung bunhwa ui yangsang" [The land system of the Great Korean Empire and the differentiation of the peasant class]. In *Daehan jeguk ui toji jedo wa geundae*. Hyean, 2010.

Yi Yeong-hun. "Daehan jeguk-gi hwangsil jejeong ui gicho wa seonggyeok" [Basis and character of royal finances during the Korean Empire period]. *Naksungdae Institute of Economic Research Working Paper Series* (2011): 1–18.

Yi Yun-gap. "Ugaki Gajeusige chongdok ui siguk insik gwa nongchon jinheung undong ui byeonhwa" [Governor-General Ugaki Kazushige's perspectives on rule and the transformation of the Rural Revitalization Campaign]. *Daegu sahak* 87 (2007): 33–80.

Yi Yun-sang. "Daehan jeguk ui gyeongje jeongchaek gwa jejeong sanghwang" [Economic policies and the financial situation of the Great Korean Empire]. In *Daehan jeguk eun geundae gukga in-ga?* Pureun yeoksa, 2006.

———. "Gabo gaehyeok-gi geundaejeok jose jedo surip sido wa jibang sahoe ui daeeung" [Establishment of a modern taxation system and the response of local society during the Gabo Reform period]. In *Hanguk geundae sahoe wa munhwa*, v. 1. Seoul National University Press, 2003.

———. "Daehan jeguk ui jaejeong unyeong gwa geundae gukga ui gyeongje-jeok gicho" [The Great Korean Empire's financial administration and the economic foundations of a modern state]. *Sasil ireoke bonda 4* (2004): 218–32.

Yoo, Theodore Jun. *The Politics of Gender in Colonial Korea: Education, Labor, and Health, 1910–1945*. University of California Press, 2008.

Yu Giljun. *Seoyu gyeonmun* [Observations from travels to the West]. In *Yu Giljun jeonseo* [Complete works of Yu Giljun], v. 1. Iljogak, 1971.

Yu Seung-nyeol. "Hanmal ui sangeop ipguk noryeok gwa sanggwon suho undong" [Efforts to enter the commercial sector and the movement to protect commercial rights in the Korean Empire period]. In *Hanguk geunhyeondae ui minjok munje wa sin gukga geonseol* [The national problem and efforts to establish a new state in modern Korea]. Jisik saneopsa, 1997.

Yu Yeong-ik. *Gabo gyeongjang yeongu* [The Gabo Reforms]. Iljogak, 1990.

Yuh, Leighanne. "Education, the Struggle for Power, and Identity Formation in Korea, 1876–1910." PhD diss., UCLA, 2008.

———. "Contradictions in Korean Colonial Education." *International Journal of Korean History* 15.1 (2010): 121–49.

Yun Chiho. "Tōa no shinkensetsu to naisen ittai" [New construction of East Asia and the united body of Japan and Korea]. *Sōdōin* 1.1 (1939): 21–23.

Yun Chung-no. "20 segi Hanguk ui jeonjaeng gyeongheom gwa pongnyeok—ilje gangjeomgi singminjuui jeonjaeng eseo beteunam jeonjaeng kkaji" [War experiences and violence in twentieth-century Korea—From the colonialist wars of the Japanese occupation period to the Vietnam War]. In *Singminji yusan, gukga hyeongseong, Hanguk minjujuui* [Colonial legacies, state formation, and South Korean democracy], v. 1, edited by Jeong Geun-sik and Yi Byeong-cheon. Chaek sesang, 2012.

Yun Hae-dong. *Singminji ui hoesaek jidae* [The colonial gray zone]. Yeoksa bipyeongsa, 2003.

———. *Jibae wa jachi—Singminji chollak ui samgungmyeon gujo* [Domination and autonomy—The triangular structure of the rural areas under colonialism]. Yeoksa bipyeongsa, 2006.

———. *Singminji geundae ui paereodokseu* [The paradox of colonial modernity]. Hyumeoniseuteu, 2007.

———. "Colonial Publicness as Metaphor." In *Mass Dictatorship and Modernity*, edited by Michael Kim et al. Palgrave Macmillan, 2013.

Zarrow, Peter. *After Empire: The Conceptual Transformation of the Chinese State, 1885–1924*. Stanford University Press, 2012.

INDEX

Page references in italics refer to illustrative materials: figures, photographs, and tables.

authority *(continued)*
  knowledge in, 3; in legitimation, 8–10,
    18–19, 86–87, 111, 114; in moderniza-
    tion, 254–55; police system in, 68–76;
    in public health discourse, 233; and
    religion, 148–49, 153, 165–66, 167; states
    defined by, 4
autonomy: and dependence, 20; and devel-
    opmentalism, 131; and domination,
    76–85; and imperialism, 30, 33, 91;
    industrialization in, 124; international
    status in, 114; local, 53, 84, 85; in state
    rationalization, 254–55

Bak Chan-seung, 15, 93
Bak Jeongyang, 200
Bak Yeongcheol: *Memoir of Fifty Years*,
    141–42
Bak Yeonghyo, 30, 233–34
Bak Yun-jae, 223–24
banking, 131, 133–34, 136–37
banks, 43–44
Basic Principles of the National Body
    (Kokutai no hongi), 191
behavior: biopolitics in, 220, 222; education
    in, 168; in legitimation, 86–87, 95; in
    public health, 221, 224–25; and religion,
    146, 151; in wartime, 48
bifurcation: of Shinto, 157; social, 145,
    272n31; state, 3, 26, 30, 32
biopolitics/biopower: in behavior, 220,
    222; in governmentalization, 6, 19;
    household registration in, 207, 208–9;
    in liberalism, 327n6; policing in, 68,
    196–97; in population management,
    196–98; in public health, 221–25; statis-
    tical information in, 197; surname
    standardization in, 213
Birth of the Clinic, The (Foucault), 221–22
black marketeering, 35, 75
Bourdieu, Pierre, 8, 197
brothels, 222, 232–34
Buddhism: in colonialism, 159, 160; in
    the Joseon State, 150, 151; in the
    Korean Empire, 311–12n35; regulation
    of, 152, 156, 157; in secularization,
    148
Buddhist monks, 152, 160, 213–14

budgets: in accounting practices, 30; in
    developmental projects, 125; for educa-
    tion, 319n13; in the Gabo Reforms, 30;
    household, 80–81; local, 60–61, 64, *64;*
    for mobilization, 48; in public health,
    125
bureaucracy: colonial, 15, 36; Confucian
    ethos in, 12, 88–89, 120, 311n30; and
    education, 170, 174; elites in, 68; in the
    Joseon state, 2, 5, 12; and knowledge,
    254; in land surveys, 43–44, 46; local,
    48, 53, 84, 85; in public health, 220,
    244–45; and religion, 146, 148, 152;
    social impact of, 7
bureaucratic rationalization, 4, 269n4
bureaucratic resources, 193, 228
bureaucratization, 4, 196
Busan, 137–38

cabinet system, 29, 33–34
cadastral survey, 15, 38–46, 51
capital formation, *62, 138*
capital investments, 137, 144
capitalism, 4, 111, 121, 142
Caprio, Mark, 96
Catholicism, 148, 151, 153, 158, 310n27
Catholic schools, 315–16n78
censorship, 73, 88–89, 101, 256
census, 198, 212–13, 219, 327–28n15,
    333–34n78
central government: of the colonial regime,
    34–38; consolidation of public lands by,
    39; in developmentalism, 125–27, 130–
    32; in the Gabo Reforms, 30; in house-
    hold registration, 199–200; in the
    Korean Empire, 30–32; and local gov-
    ernment, 53–68; in public health, 226;
    in public schools, 171
centralization of administration: coercion
    and absorption in, 68–85; in the colo-
    nial period, 52–53, 58–68; limits to, 84;
    local administrations in, 53–68
ceremony: Confucian, 150; in ideological
    engineering, 102–6; in the Korean
    Empire, 152–53; Shinto, 163–64, 316n81,
    317n84; state sanctioned, 150,
    309–10n19
Cheondogyo religion, 158, 159

China, 13, 93, 120, 124, 223, 311n30
Choe Won-gyu, 45–46
cholera epidemic, 225–30, *230*
Christianity, 17, 154, 157, 161–63, 166, 251
Christian schools, 162–64, 174, 315–16n78, 320n31
Church and State, 146, 147–48, 162, 166, 253, 311n33
citizen identification numbers, 214
citizenry *(gungmin, kokumin)*, 92–94, 182, 183–85, 237–38
citizenship: conceptualizations of, 187–88, 192; duties of, 94, 183–84; and legitimation, 96, 114; public education in, 168–70; in public health, 239–40; and rights, 93–94; social leveling through, 182; terminology of, 182–84, 189–92, 323n60; in textbooks, 183–85
citizenship education, 19, 168–71, 181–94, 248–49
civil code, 98–99, 203–4, 206, 213–15
civilizing: colonial, 52; courts in, 21; dispersal of power in, 255–56; education in, 7, 193; in governmentalization, 6–7; in legitimation, 95, 114, 115, 251–52; local agencies in, 53; and public health, 7, 223, 233–42, 245, 253; religion in, 157, 165; in state development, 2–3
civil service examination, 12–13, 170
clan identity, 199, 201–3, 205, 213–14, 216, 334n87
classification, 149, 166, 195, 197, 209–18, 254
cleanliness. *See* hygiene
clergy, 148, 153, 160–61, 251
clerks. *See hyangni* clerks
coercion: in assimilation, 257; in centralization, 68–85; in colonialism, 58; continuities in, 249; in legitimation, 87; in naming conventions, 215; police in, 70, 73, 74–75; in the protectorate, 33; in public health, 225–33, 239; in religion, 163–65, 181; states defined by, 4; in wartime mobilization, 50
coexistence, 101, 108, 115, 206, 256–57
Cohn, Bernard, 6–7
collaboration, 145, 313n56
collective identity, 197–98, 234, 256

collectivism: and citizenship, 191, 192; in legitimation, 93–95, 98–99, 114; public education in, 169; in public health discourse, 238
colonial developmentalism, 121, 133–43, 144–45, 250
colonial gray zone, 7, 256
colonial period/state: autonomy in, 254–55; benefits of, exhibited, 107–8; biopolitics in, 224; decentralization in, 52; disciplinary power in, 52–53; economy in, 44, 83, 134–36, 138–39; education in, 173–81, 184–92; in governmentalization, 6–7, 16–18; history and historiography of, 11, 13–18, 248, 254; household registration in, 203–9; hygiene in, 223; ideology of, 5; industrialization under, 37–38, 121, 134–36, 140; land survey, 15, 41–46, 51; legitimation of, 9–10, 95–101, 106–10, 115, 219, 245; localities in, 30, 52–53, 58–68; modernity, 11, 131, 248; organizational chart, *264–67;* police in, 35, 58, 72–73, 76; population in, *259–60;* population management in, 198; prostitution in, 232; public health in, 227–29, 235–42; as a rationality, 250; religion in, 146, 155–65, 167; and social edification, 251; spectacle in, 106–10; in state development, 2–3, 145; state functions in, 26; state making in, 34–38, 50–51; statist discourse of, 98–99; venereal disease in, 232
comfort women, 232
commerce/commercialization: Crown projects in, 125–26; in developmentalism, 128–31, 133–34, 142, 144; education in, 173; external pressures in, 6; in social ideology, 124; in war mobilization, 48
Commercial Affairs Company, 129–30, 133
communications: continuities in, 249; in developmentalism, 121, 135, 137, 144; in governmentalization, 6; homogenization of, 197; in the Joseon state, 12; Office of, 125, 127. *See also* telecommunications; telegraph system
communism, 120, 291n94
concubinage, 205–6, 331n51
Confucian civil service examination, 12–13, 27, 29, 152, 166

Confucianism: in bureaucracy, 12, 88–89,
120, 311n30; in colonialism, 159–61; in
education, 170, 184–92, 194; ethics of,
12, 151–52, 170, 184, 194, 222; in the
Joseon state, 5, 88–89, 149–51, 155,
166–67, 248; in the Korean Empire,
153–54, 166; in legitimation, 92, 100,
149, 155, 166; loyalty in, 155, 252; morality in, 88–89, 153, 185; in public health,
222; in statecraft, 10, 27, 30, 53, 54, 148;
state-sanctioned, 153–54
Confucian reformists, 39
conscription, 207, 208
construction, 64, 138–39
consumption, 35, 37, 48, 140
contagious disease. *See* disease control
continuities, 11–12, 45–46, 50–51, 203, 205,
248–50, 300n6
Cooper, Frederick, 218
co-optation, 3, 16, 244, 256
corruption, 54, 55, 122–23, 152, 236, 284n21
county administration, 54, 58, 72–75,
78–79, 283–84n13
courts, 21, 32, 34, 204, 205, 331n52
Crown Properties, Office of, 31, 57, 125–29,
132, 144
Cultural Rule: citizenship education in,
187–88; coexistence in, 256–57; education in, 175–77, 181; and governmentality, 16; harmony in, 112; in imperialism,
50, 51; in legitimation, 10, 99–100,
108–9, 115, 141, 251; liberalization in, 16,
99–100, 158; in localities, 59–60, 77–80,
82, 85; nationalism and citizenship in,
192–93; police in, 73–74; public health
discourse in, 239; rationalities behind,
188; religion in, 158, 161, 163, 166; Rural
Revitalization Campaign in, 80–83
culture: in Cultural Rule, 115; in decentralization, 256; development of, 30, 100–101,
108, 296n50; in public health discourse,
240–41; venereal disease in, 230–31
currency, 129, 130–31, 132, 133
curriculum: citizenship in, 168–69; in the
colonial period, 173–74, 176–77, 181,
184–92; in the Gabo Reforms, 171; in
public health discourse, 239–40; regulation of, 253

Curtis, Bruce, 197
customs: and Confucianism, 159; in decentralization, 256; in household registration, 201–7, 209, 218–19; in hygiene,
236; in the Joseon state, 2; in legitimation, 95, 100–101, 251; naming, 214; in
social differentiation, 210; and venereal
disease, 230. *See also* culture
customs duties, 37, 136, 145

Daehan Hospital, 227
Daejeon hoetong, 27
Daejonggyo, 159–60
daily lives, 47–48, 49, 83
decentralization, 52, 74, 84, 204–5, 256
de-Confucianization, 149, 167, 253
Decree on Preventing Communicable
Disease, 228
Deliberative Assembly, 29–30, 77, 90,
152
developmentalism: colonial, 121, 133–45,
250; concept and history of, 119–22;
continuities in, 249–50; discourse on,
141–42; education in, 142, 168; Gabo
Reforms in, 30, 125; in the Korean
Empire, 122–33; in legitimation, 13, 19,
121–22, 140, 145, 251; in the monarchy,
128, 130, 144; organizational, 50; in state
development, 144–45
differentiation, 3, 4, 201, 210, 219, 230,
256–57, 317–18n88
Dirks, Nicolas, 198
discipline/disciplinary power: centralized,
52–53; in Confucian morality, 185;
dispersal of, 255–56; in governmentalization, 6, 8, 19; public education in,
169; in public health, 224–25, 244
disease control and prevention: bureaucracy
in, 244–45; criticism of, 345–46n111;
discourse on, 233–44; in governmentalization, 19; instrumentalities of, 224–25;
in the Japanese military, 342–43n70; in
legitimation, 233, 251; police in, 224–25,
228–29, 338n19; in public health, 221–
26; regulation of, 253; in school curriculum, 239–40; venereal disease in, 230–
33; in wartime mobilization, 17. *See also*
public health

diversification, 26, 86, 168, 209, 219, 247–49
domination, 68, 76–83, 84–85, 248, 254, 257
Donga ilbo newspaper, 177–78, 243, 291n90
Donghak religion, 158, 312–13n46
Donghak Uprising, 151–52, 158, 159
Dongnip sinmun (The Independent), 90–91, 103–4, 123–24, 129, 234–35
Duara, Prasenjit, 92
Duus, Peter, 95

Eckert, Carter, 121, 136
economic activity, 49, 75, 132, *260,* 301n11, 332n63
economic development. *See* developmentalism
economic historians, 11, 120–21, 300n6
economic policy, 129–30, 134–36
economy: colonial, 44, 134–36, 138–39; developmentalism in, 143–44; growth in, 140; in household registration, 201–2; and imperialism, 124; of the Joseon state, 5; reforms in, 122–23; in state health, 220; strength of, 123–24, 133; in wartime, 49
education: accessibility of, 175–79; biopolitics in, 168; budgets for, 319n13; and bureaucracy, 170, 174; as a citizen's duty, 183–84; civilizing in, 7, 193; compulsory, 169, 172, 175, 184; in developmental discourse, 142, 168; discrimination in, 177–79, 188; expenditures on, 178–79; hygiene in, 238, 244; in legitimation, 19, 100, 183; police in, 74; reified, 193, 252; religion in, 161–62; in wartime mobilization, 17, 46–47. *See also* citizenship education; public education; schools
Education, ministry of, 29
Education Bureau, 34–35, 157, 175
efficacy. *See* legitimation/legitimacy
electricity, 35, 126–27
elites, 68, 79–80, 81, 170, 256
enforcement, 4, 15, 53, 68, 156, 227
enlightenment: in developmentalism, 133; education in, 168, 184; in governmentalization, 6; hygiene in, 235; in public health discourse, 233–35, 242–43, 245

enlightenment activism: in developmental projects, 125; and Gojong, 304n54; and legitimation, 90–92, 93, 106; in public health discourse, 235–36, 244–45; on public schools, 172, 192–93
entrepreneurship, 134, 136–37, 142, 145, 172
epidemics, 236–38, 245
equality, 114, 182, 206
Essence of the National Body and naisen ittai, 113
ethics *(susin):* citizenship education in, 192; Confucian, 12, 151–52, 170, 184, 193, 194, 222; in curriculum, 173, 182, 184–85; education in, 169–70, 171; in public health discourse, 239–40; textbooks on, 318n5
ethnic discrimination: in assimilation, 95; in coexistence, 256–57; in colonialism, 15, 76, 256–57; in education, 177–79, 188; in public health, 229–30, 242–43; in registration, 219; in salaries, 279n81; surnames in, 216–17; in wartime mobilization, 17
ethnicity, 75, 189–90, 193
ethnic nation *(minjok),* 182–83
evangelizing, 156–57, 166
expenditures: in developmentalism, 125–28, 137; on education, 175, *180;* of the Government-General, 37–38, *61, 139, 261;* of the Korean Empire, *126;* of local administrations, 58–60, *62,* 64–65; on police, 71–72; of Provisional Land Survey Bureau, *44;* in wartime mobilization, 48–49
External Affairs, Bureau of, 35
extractive powers: continuities in, 249; in developmentalism, 121, 144; in legitimation, 92–93; police in, 76; secularization in, 148; in state-making, 2, 247, 249; in wartime, 84
extra-state actors, 8, 12, 36, 88, 91, 243, 255

family customs/law, 182, 202–6, 209, 213, 215–19, 254
finance: decentralization of, 255–56; departments, provincial, 59, 64–65; in developmentalism, 129, 133–34; ministries of, 29–30, 34; reform of, 29–31, 122–23, 200; resources in, 31, 53, 60, 64–65, 132, 255

financial management, 14, 33–34, 133–34, 145, 200

fiscal authority, 29–30, 32, 50, 58–59, 65, 84–85

folk remedies. *See* traditional medicine

foreign affairs, 29, 32

foreigners, 40–41, 107, 128–29, 133, 153, 303n30

foreign language schools, 171–72

foreign missionaries: in the 105 Incident, 314n66; in colonialism, 17; in education, 174, 319–20n20, 320n31; and the Japanese, 313n56, 346nn115,16, 347n119; and legitimation, 100; medical activities of, 243; restrictions on, 161–63; shut down of, 316n80

Foreign Office, 28–29

foreign recognition in legitimation, 107, 251

foreign rule: administration rationalizing, 2–3; in developmentalism, 141; discriminatory foundations of, 179; in fragmentation, 256; legitimacy gap in, 9–10, 51, 95–101, 106–10, 219; legitimation of, 87, 95–96, 236; police in, 75–76; in public health discourse, 240–41; religion in, 164; resistance to, 15–16, 150; in state development, 26

Foucault, Michel: *The Birth of the Clinic,* 221–22; on governmentality, 5–8, 196–97, 247, 327nn4,6; on policing and biopower, 68, 196–97; on public health, 221–22, 338n19

fragmentation of the state, 3, 26, 28, 30, 50–51, 255–56

Frühstück, Sabine, 222

Fujitani, Takashi, 17–18, 206–7, 348n12

Future of Rule in Korea, The (Hashimoto), 99–100

Gabo Reforms (1894–1895): citizenship in, 192; civil service examination in, 27; Confucianism in, 152, 154–55, 166; consolidation by, 27, 51, 255; in developmentalism, 30, 125; education in, 170–71; household registration in, 200; in imperial state-making, 29–30, 50; in the Korean Empire, 30–32; land surveys in, 38–39; leaders of, 30, 31, 76, 102; legiti-

mation in, 9, 87, 89–90, 102, 251; local administration in, 55–57, 283–84n13; organizational chart, *262;* police in, 69–70; public health in, 225–26, 244; in state development, 2; state restructuring by, 12–13; tax reforms in, 29–30, 76–77

Gamyeong. *See* Provincial Office

Gapsan County Headquarters, *60*

Garon, Sheldon, 87

General Affairs, 35

geopolitics: in developmentalism, 119; in the Gabo Reforms, 18, 30, 33; of imperialism, 30, 90; in the Korean Empire, 13; in legitimacy, 92, 114, 301n11

Gim Do-hyeong, 93

Gim Hae-gyeong, 224

Gim Nang-nyon, 249–50, 300n6

Gim Okgyun, 233–34

Gim Yeong-hui, 49

goals: of classification, 209; conflicting, 247–48; of developmentalism, 122, 129–30, 144–45; in education, 161, 163, 187; ideological engineering, 109, 110, 112; of land surveys, 42; local administration in, 53, 57; police in, 74; in public health, 242; rationalizations in, 3; of registration, 208–9, 219; in religious regulation, 146, 159; of rural revitalization, 80–83; in state restructuring, 30; in wartime mobilization, 48–49

Gojong, monarch of Korea: abdication of, 14, 33, 131, 275n26; administrative reforms under, 26–29; coronation ceremony of, 103–6, *105,* 250; in developmentalism, 132; and enlightenment activists, 304n54; flight and return of, 13, 30–31; and the Jejungwon hospital, 343n71

Goryeo period, 54

Gotō Shimpei, 204, 236

governing institutions, states defined by, 4

governmentality/governmentalization: biopower in, 19; in colonial rule, 6–7, 16–18; disciplinary power in, 6, 8, 19; household registration in, 207–9; in population management, 196–98; in public health, 221–22, 237; reflexivity in, 247; in state making, 5–7, 327n4

Government-General of Korea: as the colonial regime, 34–38; developmental discourse of, 140–43; in developmentalism, 137; discrimination by, 256–57; in education, 173–74, 186–87; expenditures of, *61,* 137, *139, 261;* income and expenses of, *261;* lack of foreign policy by, 20; in legitimation, 97–99; in local administration, 58–60; military apparatus of, 73; powers of, 295n43; as provincial government, 52–53; in public health discourse, 239; reforms in establishing, 26; in religious affairs, 157, 158–61, 164–65, 313n54; in the Rural Revitalization Campaign, 81; in surname registration, 215–17; in wartime mobilization, 46–50

government workers, 43, *65,* 65–66, *67*

Gragert, Edwin, 45

Gramsci, Antonio, 86

Great Depression, 136–37, 138

Greater East Asian Co-Prosperity Sphere, 113, 143

Great Korean Exposition, 108–9, *109*

Greenfield, Liah, 92

gross economic output, 138–39, 140

gukga (the state), 92–93, 182–83, 185

gungmin (citizenry), 92–93, 94, 182, 184–85, 237–38

Gungmin sohak dokbon (Elementary reader for the citizens), 182–83

Gungmin suji, 293–94n25

Gu Yeonsu, 71

Gwangmu land survey, 39–41, *40,* 44–46, 277–78n56, 278–79n68, 280–81n90

Gwangmu period (1897–1907), 31, 50

Gye Gwangsun, 281–82n104

Gyeongguk daejeon dynastic code, 27, 88

Hashimoto Tetsuma: *The Future of Rule in Korea,* 99–100

heavy industry, 48, 136–37, 249–50, 306n80, 347n2

Henry, Todd, 18, 110

hereditary status, 55, 199, 201, 209–10

hierarchy: in education, 184; in the Joseon state, 25, 27–28, 89; in local administration, 289–90n81; in public health

discourse, 236; in religious pluralism, 151; social, 7, 27, 105–6, 151, 195–96

High State Council, 27–29, 33–34

historiography, 1, 10–18, 169

Home Affairs, Ministry of, 29

Home Office, 28–29

homogenization, 169, 197–98, 209, 213–18, 254

hospitals, 226–28, 233, 235, 238, 242–43

household registration: addresses in, 202–3, 208; children in, 205–6, 219, 331n52; in collective identity, 198; in colonialism, 203–9; customs in, 201–7, 209, 218–19; economic activity in, 332n63; evasion of, 204, 208; forms for, *201,* 201–3, 211; in Japan, 202; in the Joseon state, 198–200, 249; local administration of, 56–57, 200, 207–8; in modernization, 254; occupations in, 209–13; police in, 70; in population management, 195, 198–209; reforms of, 200–203, 328n20; in wartime mobilization, 17

Household Registration Act, 36

human resources, 36, 48–49, 56, 132, 134–35

Hwangseong sinmun, 94, 129, 234

hyangni clerks, 55–56, 69, 76–77, 79, 151, 170, 199

hygiene: cooperatives for, 228; education in, 169, 228, 239, *240;* expenses in, 58–59; financing of, 64; Japanese, 223, 244; in modernity, 220; personal, 7, 241, 244, 327–28, 329; police in, 73, 227–28, 237; in public health, 224, 233–36, 238, 244, 344nn89,98; regulation of, 253

Hygiene Bureau, 226–27, 234–36

idealized domesticity, 224

ideal state, 90

identification, 195–96, 214

identity: and citizenship, 182–83, 192; collective, 101, 146; individual, 197–98, 234, 256; Korean, 99–101, 112–13, 115, 192–93, 251; legal, 206; national, 87, 92, 102, 144, 145, 182–83; social, 209, 215; surnames in, 217, 219

ideology: Confucianism as, 155; engineering of, 18–19, 102–14, 115, 239; in the Joseon state, 2; in legitimation, 87, 92, 95,

ideology *(continued)*
102–15; motivation by, 46–47; and
national weakness, 124; and the populace, 86; in public health discourse, 236,
242–45; of statecraft, 148; in state
making, 5, 8–10, 250–52
immunization, 223, 238, 344–45n100
imperial ceremonialism, 102–6
imperialism: absolutism in, 91; colonial
administration in, 34–38; developmentalism in, 132, 143; diversification in, 26,
247; and economic strengths, 124;
external pressures in, 6; Gabo Reforms
in, 29–30, 50; ideology of, 5; Japanese
protectorate in, 32–34; Korean
responses to, 30–31; militarized, 50;
policing in, 70–76; population management under, 198; in reforms, 248; scientific, 223; in state development, 2, 25–28,
30, 35, 50; and wartime mobilization,
46–51
Imperial Rescript on the Annexation, 140
Imperial Rule Assistance Movement, 47
imperial subjects, 17, 112, 170, 190–91, 194
"Imperial System" (1899), 91–92
Independence Club, 91, 129, 133
Independent, The (Dongnip sinmun), 70,
90–91, 287nn47,54
Industrial Commissions, 136, 141
industrialization and industry: bureaus of,
35; civilizing, 7; colonial, 37–38, 121,
134–36; continuities in, 249–50; Crown
projects in, 125–26; in developmentalism, 119–20, 123–24, 130–31, 140, 144;
in diversification, 247; education in,
173, 184; heavy, 48, 136–37, 249–50,
306n80, 347n2; in legitimation, 108,
122, 141, 142; regulation of, 253; in
urbanization, 138; in wartime mobilization, 17, 46, 121, 138, 143
infrastructure: in developmentalism,
121–22, 126–28, 132, 135, 137, 138, 140,
144; discourse on, 141; discursive, 21; in
legitimation, 97, 251; local, 53, 58–59, 60,
64–65; in macroeconomics, 132–33; and
public education, 169; in state health,
220; symbolism of, 105–6
instrumental rationalization, 4, 7, 269n4

insurrections, 55–56
interest groups, 3, 36
Interior Ministry, 34, 69–71, 226, 235
international law in legitimation, 91,
250–51
international status, 114, 128, 143–44, 153
international trade, 119
interstate competition, 5–6, 123, 247, 269n3
investment: in development, 121–22, 129–
30, 132, 135–37, 140, 144–45; in land
surveys, 36–37, 41, 43; and legitimation,
96–97; in localities, 60–61, 81–82; in
public schools, 179; in wartime mobilization, 48–49
Itō Hirobumi, 32, 106

jagang (self-strengthening), 93
Japan: benefits to from development, 145;
civil code of, 206; commercial activities
of, 134; consulates of, 32, 57–58; corporate investment by, 137; courts of, 32; as
developmental state, 119; Diet of,
98–99; economic conquest by, 44;
Korean students in, 321–22n46; public
health in, 222–23; religion in, 148
Japanese colonialism. *See* colonial period/
state
Japanese emperor: birthdays of, celebrated,
105, 113; in the citizen-state relationship,
187–88; loyalty to, 111, 184–86, 189, 216;
worship of, 163–65, 181
Japanese identity, 10, 16, 96, 109, 189–90
Japanese protectorate (1905–1910): financial
management in, 133–34; historical
context of, 10–11; historiography of,
13–14; in imperial state making, 32–34;
local administration in, 57–58; policing
in, 70–72; public health in, 226–27;
statism in, 94–95; venereal disease in, 231
Japanese residents: in colonialism, 14–15; in
developmentalism, 135, 137; in Korean
localities, 57–58; in legitimation, 98,
107; in the protectorate, 33, 71; schools
for, 176–79
Japanese troops, 14, 32, 70–71
Jeong Hye-jeong, 186
Jiphyeonjeon, 88, 292n7
Ji Seogyeong, 235

Ji Su-geol, 78–79
Johnson, Chalmers: *MITI and the Japanese Miracle,* 119
Jo Hyeong-geun, 244
Joseon dynastic state (1392–1894): bureaucracy in, 2, 5, 12; centralism in, 53; Confucianism in, 5, 88–89, 149–51, 155, 166–67, 248; education in, 170; fragmentation of, 51; *gukga* in, 93; historical context of, 11–13; household registration in, 198–200, 249; imperialism's impact on, 25–26; legacies of, 248–49; legitimation of, 250–51; local administration in, 54–55; modern features of, 2; moral suasion in, 88–89; policing in, 69; public health in, 222, 233–34, 236–37; social edification in, 6, 251; *Tongni Amun* in, 26–29
Joseon ilbo newspaper, 177, 189, 242
Ju Ik-jong, 136
Jungdeung susin gyogwaseo, 183

Kal, Hong, 108
Kawashima Gishi, 112
Keddie, Nikki, 167
Keijō nippo newspaper, 109
Kim, Christine, 106
Kim, Marie, 204
Kim, Sonja, 224
Kohli, Atul, 299–300n2
kokumin (relationship to state), 187–88, 190
kokumin gakko education system, 190–91, 192
kokutai (national body), 191–92
Kokutai no hongi (Basic Principles of the National Body), 191
kōmin (public person), 188
Koopman, Colin, 7
Korea Hygiene Digest, 237–39
Korean Art Exhibition, 107, 297n61
Korean Communist Party, 101
Korean companies, 303n33
Korean Education Ordinance, 187
Korean Empire (1897–1910): Confucianism in, 153–54, 166; developmentalism in, 122–33; expenditures of the, *126;* fiscal weakness of, 133–34; in fragmentation, 255; historical overview of, 13; legitimation of, 91–92, 102–6; and local administration, 57; nationalism in, 10, 193; organizational chart, *263;* police in, 70; pubic health discourse in, 234–35; religion in, 152–53, 165; state development in, 249; state making in, 30–32, 50
Korean Exposition, 108, 297n66
Korean flag, *104,* 104–5
Korean historians, 11–12
Korean identity, 99–101, 112–13, 115, 192–93, 251
Korean industry, 134–36
Korean language education, 189
Korean League for National Total Mobilization, 47, 113
Korean medicine, 223–24
Korean officials, 51, 66, 68, 84, 85, 257
Korean police, 72, *72,* 75–76
Korean Products Fair, 107, 140
Korean Residence Ordinance, 208
Koreans: in developmentalism, 135; employed by the colonial state, 43–44, 66, *67,* 85; as imperial subjects, 112
Korean School Ordinance, 173, 175–76, 186, 188–89
Korea's Pseudo-Religions (Murayama), 158–59
Krumm, Raymond, 39–40
Kulturkampf (civilizational struggle), 148

labor resistance, 121, 136
land: agencies, 39–42; nationalized, 134; ownership of, 38–46, 58, 128–29; surveys, 15, 38–46, 51; taxes on, 36–46
Land Certification Agency, 40–41
Land Surveying Agency, 39–40
Land Survey Ordinance, 41–42
language: in education, 171, 172, 173, 189; Japanese, 174, 186–87, 190–91, 320n31
Law Ministry, 34
laws, 4, 21, 35–36, 94, 98–99, 142, 204, 239n37, 295n43
lecture circuits, 110–11, 115
Legal Affairs, Ministry of, 29, 34
legitimacy/legitimation: biopower in, 219; civil code in, 204; colonial, 9–10, 95–101, 106–10, 115, 151, 245; Confucianism in, 92, 100, 149–50, 155, 166;

legitimacy/legitimation *(continued)*
developmentalism in, 13, 19, 121–22, 140, 145, 251; discourse in, 8, 250; education in, 19, 100, 183; gap in, 9–10, 107, 110, 186, 219, 300n11; ideology in, 87, 92, 95, 102–14, 115; international law in, 19, 250–51; managerial, 9–10, 101, 115, 250–52; of the monarchy, 13, 91–92; moral suasion in, 88–89; population management in, 198; populism in, 92–95, 114, 251; and public health, 220, 223, 225, 233, 236, 245, 251; as rationalization, 8–10, 86, 251; regimes of, 114–15; religion in, 19, 100, 148, 157–59, 251–52; semiotics of, 252; spiritual campaigns in, 110–14; in state development, 3; and symbolic authority, 18–19; visions and expressions in, 89–101

liberalism, 191, 301n11, 327n6

local administrations/governments: autonomy of, 53, 84, 85; centering of, 53–68; in the colonial period, 30, 52–53, 58–68; corruption in, 54, 55, 284n21; domination through, 76–83; expenditures of, *62,* 65, 158–59; in the Gabo Reforms, 55–57, 283–84n13; in household registration, 56–57, 199–200, 205, 207–8; institutional development of, 84; police in, 68–76; in resistance, 256; in the Rural Revitalization Campaign, 80–83; in state power, 68, 255–56; township-centered, 78–79

local elites, 79–81, 256

local officials: in the Gabo Reforms, 56–57; in household registration, 199–200, 201, 210–11, 333n75; in the Korean Empire, 57; in literature, 289–90n81; pro-Japanese, 84; in the protectorate, 57–58; in public health, 226; and revenue, 53; in the Rural Revitalization Campaign, 80

loyalty: citizenship education in, 168; in Confucianism, 155, 252; and education, 169, 183, 184, 186–87, 193; to the imperial monarchy, 184–85; and religion, 146, 163

macroeconomics, 31, 121–22, 132–33, 143–44, 250, 347–48n3

macro-industrial development, 121

Maeil sinbo, 97

Manchukuo, 92

Manchuria, 112, 136–37, 142

Manchurian Incident (1931), 16, 101, 113, 136–37, 143

manufacturing, 124, 130, 135–37, 138–39

March First uprisings (1919): colonial central administration in, 34–35; and Cultural Rule, 2, 15–16, 50; in legitimation, 99–100, 115; and local administration, 59–60; military police in, 73–74; religion in, 158, 159, 162–63

Marco Polo Bridge incident (1937), 46

market economy, 249–50

Marks, Shula, 236

Maruyama Jūshun, 71

material growth, 120, 130, 132–33, 141

material improvements, 87, 100–101, 142, 145

material resources: in colonialism, 35, 135; and county administration, 79; in education, 193; of Gabo Reforms, 56; in household registration, 202; in national well-being, 123–24; in wartime mobilization, 48–49, 75, 140. *See also* resources

mediation: authority through, 84; between center and periphery, 76; and enforcement apparatus, 68

medicine, 220, 223–24, 233–44, 245, 251, 345n108. *See also* public health

Megata Tanetarō, 133, 271n27

Meiji Imperial Rescript on Education, 185–89, 325–26n98

Meiji Japan, 69, 86–87, 148, 153, 157, 222–23, 231

Memoir of Fifty Years (Bak Yeongcheol), 141–42

mercantilism, 129, 145

metric system, 130

metropolitan government, 36

migration, urban, 137–38

militarization, 6, 20, 124, 143, 249

military: development, 145; expansionism, 26, 37–38; in the Gabo Reforms, 29; and industrialization, 124; in the Joseon

state, 55; police, 35, 58, 60, 70, 73–74,
227–28, 287n54; powers of, 31–32;
prostitution in, 232–33; in public health,
223, 227
military rule, 73, 99
Minami Jirō, 46, 111, 142, 189–90, 215–16
mines/mining, 31, 35, 128–29, 133
minjeok-beop civil registration law, 202,
206, 210–12, 214
minjok (ethnic nation), 182, 183
missionaries, 160, 161, 164, 174, 243, 320n31,
346nn115,16
Mitchell, Timothy, 8, 107, 143–44
Miyamoto Gen, 217
Mizuno Naoki, 216–17
Mizuno Rentarō, 52, 59, 141, 175
mobilization: campaigns of, 110–14; household registration in, 198, 207; industrial,
145; in modernity, 253–57; public education in, 169; by the Rural Revitalization
Campaign, 80–83. *See also* wartime
mobilization
modernity/modernization: of Buddhism,
160; colonial, 11, 131, 248; household
registration in, 254; hygiene in, 244,
245; and imperialism, 132; institutional
development in, 270n9; of land surveys,
44–45; in legitimation, 101, 252; mobilization in, 253–57; movement for, 91–92;
in public health discourse, 233, 243;
public schools in, 193; rationalization in,
51; and religion, 146, 147–48; scientific,
243; and state making, 4–7; streetcars
in, 127; visions of, 114
Mok Su-hyeon, 104
Mok township, 82–83
monarchy: authority of, 183; Confucian
morality in, 88–89; developmentalism
in, 128–30, 144; Gabo influence on,
90–91; in the Korean Empire,
30–32; legitimation of, 13, 91–92,
102–6, 114, 250–51; religion in,
146–47
monopolies, 35, 37, 129, 132–33
morality, 88–89, 153, 169, 171, 185, 190,
240
moral suasion, 87–89, 99–100, 249
municipalities, 64–65, 204, 208

Murayama Chijun: *Korea's Pseudo-
Religions,* 158–59

Nagayo Sansai, 223
naisen ittai (United Body of Japan and
Korea), 112–13
Naksungdae Economic Research Institute,
137
national character, hygiene in, 234–35
national high schools, 173
national holidays, 105
nationalism: assimilationist, 114; and
Christianity, 161–62; and citizenship
education, 168–69, 184, 186, 188–92,
194; in defining the state, 94; and
developmentalism, 133, 144; and economic welfare, 145; in historiography,
11; in the Korean Empire, 10, 193; in
legitimation, 10, 87, 92, 100, 101, 104–6,
114, 250–52; mobilization of, 112–13;
monarchical, 101, 192, 324n71; multicultural, 114; protectionist, 129; in public
health discourse, 242; regulation of, 110;
religion in, 158
nationalization, 45, 134
national spirit, 46–47, 82, 111–12, 115, 185
Navy Memorial Day, 113
neighborhood associations, 47, 83, 112, 207
neo-Confucianism, 25–26, 148
newspapers. *See* popular press
Nitobe Inazō, 236
nobility, 11, 12, 210
North Korea, 120, 252, 300n6

obedience, 164, 186
objectification: of the body, 221–22, 224; of
colonial possessions, 107; of education,
193, 252; of populations, 6; of public
health, 245; of religion, 149, 166; of
society, 8, 197, 254; in state development, 3, 4
Observations from Travels to the West
(Yu Giljun), 93–94, 234
occupations, 197, 202–3, 209–13, 219, 254,
333n75
officials: centrally appointed, 54–55; in
developmental projects, 125; Japanese to
Korean ratio, 66; in the Joseon state, 5,

officials (continued)

12; in legitimacy, 88–89; percentage of in population, 67; in the protectorate, 33; in state development, 3; states defined by, 4. See also Korean officials; local officials

Onis, Ziya, 255

Ordinance on Primary Schools, 171

Oriental Development Company, 43–44, 134–35

Otaka Chōyū, 113

outreach, 160, 163, 239

pacification, 15, 50–51, 57, 71, 73–74, 95, 288n64

Palmer, Brandon, 49

pan-Asianism, 113, 115

Park Chung-Hee, 122, 252

Park Jin-kyung, 224

paternalism, 89, 90, 144, 188, 194, 242

Patriot Day, 113

patriotic neighborhood associations, 82

peasantry, 80–81, 110–11, 158

People's Condition Observation Officers, 59–60

perceptions: in legitimation, 9, 87, 101, 106, 110, 251; in public health, 221, 224, 239, 240–41, 243; in public health discourse, 236; of state enforcement, 4; of subject populations, 198, 204

performance, 9, 49, 83, 87

peripheral colonialism, 96

periphery: centering the, 52–68, 255; coercion and absorption of, 68–85

personal hygiene, 7, 237–39, 241, 244. See also hygiene

personal income tax, 37

personnel, 26–27, 32–33, 66, 81. See also human resources; local officials; officials

Personnel, Board of, 28

Pierson, Christopher, 9

Planning, Bureau of, 35, 48

police: in biopower, 196–97; central agencies, 72–73, 211; decentralization of, 255; in developmental discourse, 142; enforcement by, 15; Japanese, 33, 71, 72, 75; in legitimation, 8, 98; in localities, 53, 57–58, 60, 65, 68–76, 73, 84; pacifica-

tion by, 288n64; in public health, 73, 223–30, 237, 244–45, 338n19; regulation of, 70, 253; and religion, 158; in state expansion, 69

Police Ministry, 32, 34, 71

political economy, 119, 327n4

political-social movements, 159

populace: biopower over, 222; homogenizing of, 148; ideology and the, 86; in legitimation, 9, 87, 92–93; in religious anthropology, 157; rights and obligations of, 182–83; spiritual reorientation of, 46; and state authority, 68; state interaction with, 53

popular culture, 115

popular press: on discrimination, 177–79; on localization, 291n90; police activity in, 287n47; in public health discourse, 233–35, 239, 244, 289; and religion, 158; on venereal disease, 232, 342n68; vernacular, 90–91

population: collaborationist, 145; in the colonial period, 259–60; in governmentality, 327n6; in household registration, 205; in legitimation, 19; objectification of, 6; and primary schools, 176; statistics, 138–39

population management: biopower in, 196–98; classification in, 195, 197, 209–18; governmentality in, 196–98; household registration in, 195, 198–209; in the Joseon state, 249; in modernization, 253–54; public health in, 224–25; as rationalization, 218; in state making, 195–96; surnames in, 213–18

postal agencies, 32, 125–28, 135

post-colonial industrialization, 121, 249–50

power: dispersal of, 10, 255–56; exercise of, 68; in the Korean Empire, 31–32; in local government, 53; over bodies and behaviors, 244; political, 2–3, 8–9; political economy in, 119; and public health, 220; rationalized, 8–9

Principles of National Hygiene (Gotō Shimpei), 236

privacy and public health, 220

privatization, 45, 174

processes of rationalization, 3

production campaigns, 83

"Progress Report on the Administration of Korea," 07

propaganda: Cultural Rule in, 204; Department, 113; as a discursive tool, 250; in ideological engineering, 18–19; in legitimation, 96–97, 115; in managerial legitimation, 9–10; in public health, 239; and resistance, 256

property ownership, 40, 142

prostitution, 17, 231–33, 236, 341n60

protectionism, 128–29, 130, 133, 145, 303n32

protectorate treaty, 98–99

Protestants, 156, 161–64, 315–16n78

provincial administration/government: in centralization, 53–68; expenditures of, 60, 62, 64, 64–65; in the Gabo Reforms, 283–84n13; integration and systematization of, 84; in the Japanese protectorate, 33; police in, 70, 72–75; revenue sources for, 63; in the Rural Revitalization Campaign, 81; townships in, 78. See also local administrations/governments

Provincial Affairs, Division of, 71

Provincial Office, 54

Provisional Land Survey Bureau, 15, 34, 42–43, 44

pseudo-religions, 157–59, 160, 166, 252

publications, 73, 75, 92–93, 96–99, 100, 281–82n104

public education, 155, 168–81, 228. See also education; schools

public health: biopolitics in, 221–25, 244; civilizing, 7, 223, 233–42, 245, 253; coercion and consent in, 225–33, 239, 244; decentralization of, 255; discourse on, 233–45, 346nn115,16; disease control and prevention in, 221–26; in governmentalization, 6, 244; hygiene in, 238, 245; in legitimation, 19, 97; in modernity, 220, 223, 225, 236, 245; police in, 74, 223–30, 237, 244–45, 338n19; in population management, 224–25; public education in, 169; regulation of, 220–21, 244, 253; in wartime mobilization, 17. See also disease control and prevention

public lands, 38

public sector, 7, 37, 62

public services, 251

public works, 29, 35, 125, 132, 134, 137

Pyongyang, 137–39, 163–64, 172, 178

quarantine, 226, 229, 238

quasi-public lands, 56

railroads: in the colonial period, 35, 37–38, 128; in developmentalism, 126–29, 135–36, 142; expenditures on, 139; in the Korean Empire, 31; in the protectorate, 32

rationing, 75, 140, 207, 208

reflexivity, 5–6, 18, 219, 247

reforms: administrative, 16, 25–26; in Cultural Rule, 59–60; in developmentalism, 122–25, 130–31, 133; of education, 175–76; of household registration, 200–203, 210; of land and taxation systems, 42–43, 46; in legitimation, 97, 252; and police, 74, 288n64; of religion, 146–47, 152; sociopolitical, 152; in state power, 6–7

regimentation, 16, 74, 78, 164

registration, 19, 331–32n61. See also household registration

regulation: in authority, 196; in developmentalism, 129, 133, 301n11; as discursive infrastructure, 21; of education, 176, 253; of nationalism, 110; police in, 70, 253; in public health, 220–21, 244, 253; of religion, 146, 156–59, 162–63, 166–67

Regulations for the Commercial Affairs Company (Sangmusa jangjeong), 130

Regulations on Private Schools, 162

reification: of education, 193, 253; of public health, 245; of religion, 149, 166; of society, 3, 197, 254. See also objectification

relief institutions, 199

religion: and authority, 148–49, 153, 165–66, 167; coercion of, 163–65, 181; in colonialism, 146, 155–65, 167; Confucianism, 149–51; in education, 161–62; freedom of, 96, 153, 156, 162, 166, 308n8; hierocratic domination of, 309n15; institutionalized character of, 309n12; in the Joseon state, 248; in the Korean

religion *(continued)*
    Empire, 152–53; in legitimation, 19,
        100, 148, 157, 158–59, 251–52; modern
        conceptions of, 317–18n88; objectifica-
        tion of, 166; regulation of, 146–47,
        156–59, 162–63, 166–67; and seculariza-
        tion, 147–49; and Shinto theocratic
        order, 163–65; in state health, 220; and
        state making, 151–55, 253; in wartime
        mobilization, 17
Religious Affairs Section, 157, 175
religious pluralism, 149, 151, 156–57, 159–63,
    165
repression, 16, 148, 153, 165
residence registry system, 215–16, 219,
    332n63
Residency General (Japanese), 14–15,
    32–34, 57, 72, 231
resistance: civil society in, 254, 256; and
    domination, 68; extra-state actors in, 91,
    253, 255; to foreign rule, 15–16, 50; and
    legitimation, 99; and local administra-
    tion, 53; in modernity, 256; to public
    health measures, 219, 227, 242–44, 245;
    responsiveness to, 3; to the Rural Revi-
    talization Campaign, 81; to state mobi-
    lization, 83; and venereal disease, 231; to
    wartime mobilization, 17, 49
resources: allocation of, 36–37; bureau-
    cratic, 193, 228; financial, 31, 53, 60,
    64–65, 132, 255; human, 48–49, 56, 132,
    134–35; for local government, 53; man-
    agement of, 38–46, 121, 196; natural, 48,
    121; in public health, 226, 242–43; for
    public schools, 172; socio-cultural, 79;
    states defined by, 4. *See also* material
    resources
responsibilities: in citizenship, 183–84, 191;
    in household registration, 200–201, 219;
    in public health, 222, 225, 237, 238, 242,
    244; of states, 182
revenue: collection system for, 130–31; in
    developmentalism, 125–26; Gabo
    Reforms in sourcing, 50; from house-
    hold registration, 200; sources of, 36–37,
    38, 61, *63,* 64–65, 132; in wartime mobi-
    lization, 48–49
rice, 135, 141

Righteous Army guerillas, 71
Rijichō network of consulates, 57–58, 71
Rites, Board of, 28, 170–71
ritual, 88, 103, 113–14, 115, 150–51, 152
Rogaski, Ruth, 223, 236
Royal Edict on Primary Education, 182
Royal Household Ministry, 30–32, 125–32,
    144
rules, states defined by, 4
rural cooperatives, 80
Rural Revitalization Campaign, 80–83,
    110–11, 115, 251
Russo-Japanese War of 1904–1905, 10, 18,
    70, 98

Saitō Makoto, 16, 59, *60,* 99, 141, 175
salaries, ethnic differences in, 279n81
Sangmusa, 129–30
sanitation, 225, 228, 242–44, 246, 251, 253,
    346n112
Schmid, Andre, 104
schools: financing of, 64; for Japanese
    residents, 176–79; Korean, 171–81, 189;
    primary, 79–80, 173, 175–77, *176,* 192–
    93; private, 162, 171–74, 181, 253, 319–
    20n20; public, 176–79, 192–93; reli-
    gious, 174, 315–16n78; secondary, 173,
    175; in state health, 220; technical, 130
science, 168, 224, 233, 236, 240, 243, 245
Scott, James, 197, 254
secondary ruling class, 79–80
secret inspectors, 54
secularism, 156, 164, 248, 252
secularization, 19, 147–49, 167
security, 58, 84–85, 114, 299n1, 327n4
segregation of primary schools, 173, 175–79,
    192–93
Sekiya Teisaburō, 162, 174
self-awareness, 110–11, 190, 298n74
self-cultivation. *See* ethics
self-expression, 100
self-reflexivity, 219
semiotics, 92, 252
semi-theocratic state, 148
Seo Jaepil, 30, 91
Seoul, migration to, 137–38
Seoul municipal government, *59*
Seoul Sanitation Society, 227

Seoul Spinning and Weaving Company, 136
Seoul Teachers College, 171
Seo Yeong-hui, 133
Seoyu gyeonmun (Yu Giljun), 93–94
servants, 201–2, 211, 213, 214, 334n86
sexuality, 223–24, 230
sexually transmitted disease. *See* venereal
    disease
shamanism, 148, 150, 159, 240–41
shinmin (subject), 187–88
Shinto, 148, 157, 159, 163–65, 316n81, 317n84
shūshin textbook, 187, 188, 190
sincerity in Confucian morality, 185
Sin Dong-won, 223–26
Sin Giseon, 153–55
Sin Mungye (New Culture), 108
Sino-Japanese Wars, 18, 46
Six Boards, 27–29, 274n15
Skocpol, Theda, 299n1
slavery, 29, 201, 213, 318
smallpox, 229–30
social Darwinism, 123–24, 154, 237
social edification: in education, 175, 193; in
    the Joseon state, 6; in managerial legiti-
    mation, 251–52; moral suasion in, 249;
    public education in, 169; regulation of,
    253; state in, 114
social immanence, 3, 51, 85
social integration: citizenship education in,
    169; coercion of, 74, 78; colonial, 15, 16;
    governmentalized, 256–57; in legitima-
    tion, 87; in population management,
    218–19; in state-making, 3
social interaction, 8, 182, 219, 249
social leveling. *See* homogenization
social management, 87
social mobility, 80, 253
social norms, 114, 230–31
social order: Church and State rivalry in,
    146; Confucian ideology in, 88, 89, 194;
    education in, 181; identification mea-
    sures in, 195–96; legitimation in, 86, 251;
    primary schools in, 193; public educa-
    tion in, 169; self-reflexivity in, 219;
    social edification in, 6
social-revolutionary sentiment, 110
society: behavior in, 4, 192; bifurcation of,
    145, 272n31; categories in, 4, 6, 197–98,

253–54, 327–28n15; differentiation in,
    210; domination over, 46–49; objectified,
    3, 254; and public health, 237–38, 245;
    and religion, 156–59; standing in, 170,
    209; and state rationalization, *20,* 253
socioeconomic diversification, 86, 168,
    247–49
Sōdōin (total mobilization), 112
South Korea, 119–22, 249–50, 252
sovereignty: in citizenship education, 186;
    in the Joseon state, 89; in legitimation,
    97–98; monarchical, 104, 194; and
    political power, 2–3; in public health
    discourse, 233
Special Imperial Grace Fund, 36, 64, 107
specialization, 3–4, 247, 248
Special Tax Law, 48
spectacles, 106–10
spiritual campaigns, 110–14
spiritual reorientation of the populace, 46
stability, 6, 25, 84, 158–59
standardization: in authority, 85; continu-
    ities in, 249; in household registration,
    205–7; of information, 197; institu-
    tional reforms in, 6; in modernization,
    254; of names, 213–15, 217, 219; of occu-
    pations, 219; in state growth, 248
state: defining, 4, 92–93; strength of, 220,
    245; subjectification of, 221–22
statism, 87, 93–97, 192, 225
Statistical Annual, 212, 280
statistics, 11, 18, 21, 197, 211
Stoler, Ann, 218
streetcar lines, 126–27, *128*
Study of Primary Education, A, 185
subjugation, 148, 177, 197
Suh, Soyoung, 224
Sunjong, Emperor of Korea, 33, 106,
    294n27
superstition, 7, 155, 236, 240–41, 245,
    297n64
Supreme Military Council, 31–32
surnames, 197, 203, 213–19, 254, 334n86,
    335n88, 336n105
surveillance: continuities in, 249; in devel-
    opmentalism, 121; in governmentaliza-
    tion, 6; in modernization, 254; police
    in, 74–75; and population management,

surveillance *(continued)*
195, 198; public education in, 169; in
public health, 224, 227; of religion,
156–57, 166; in wartime mobilization,
46–47, 74–75
symbolism, 8, 18–19, 87–89, 102–14
systematization: continuities in, 249; in
land surveys, 42–46; of local policing,
70; of provincial government, 84; in
wartime mobilization, 50
system ordinances *(seirei)*, 35–36

Tax Agencies, 56
Taxation, Board of, 30, 199
Taxation Bureaus, 65
taxation system: in the Gabo Reforms,
29–30, 76–77; household registration
in, 198, 200; of the Joseon state, 5; in the
Korean Empire, 31, 132; land surveys in,
38–46; officers in, 65; population management in, 95; reform of, 42–43, 133
tax revenue: collection of, 45–46; in the
colonial period, 59; and consumption,
37, 48, 140; in developmentalism, 125–
26; in the Gabo Reforms, 56; income, 37,
48, 140; in land surveys, 44–45; land
tax, 40; local clerks in, 55; sources of, *38*;
in wartime mobilization, 48
teacher training programs, 173, 189
technical training colleges, 173
technology, 107–8, 124–25, 133
techno-nationalism, 104–5, 121–22
telecommunications, 37, 135
telegraph system, 125–28
Telegraph Training Center, 130
Temple Ordinance, 160, 311–12n35
Terauchi Masatake, 34, 82
terminology: in assimilation, 296n50; of
citizenship, 189–90, 323n60; in legitimation, 91
territoriality, 5–6, 38
textbooks: citizenship in, 193; colonial, 174,
177, 182–88; on ethics, 184–85, 318n5;
nationalism in, 174, 183–84, 324n71;
public health in, 240; regulation of, 253
Three Censoring Organs, 27–28
Tongni Amun agencies, 26–29, 51, 125, 255
Total Mobilization League, 47

Total National Mobilization campaign,
112–13
total war, 17, 143, 179, 256
townships: in the colonial period, 58;
dominion and autonomy in, 77; expenditures of, 65; in household registration,
204, 208; mobilization leagues in, 83;
police in, *73, 74*
Trade and Industry, Ministry of, 29
traditional medicine, 226, 240–41
traditions, 7, 12, 114–15, 159–60, 188, 252
Training Center for Legal Officials, 171
Training Center for Vaccination Officers,
226
transportation: in the colonial central
administration, 35; in developmentalism, 121, 135, 137, 142, 144; in the Joseon
era, 12; in macroeconomics, 132–33
treaties: of annexation, 34, 96–99, 140; in
colonialism, 14; protectorate, 33, 57,
98–99; unequal, 129
truth, in Church and State rivalry, 146, 166

Uchida, Jun, 14–15, 141
Ugaki Kazushige, 80, 110, 111, 142–43
United Body of Japan and Korea *(naisen
ittai)*, 112–13
urbanization, 121, 137–38, 140, 169, 223,
253
urban properties, 42–43

vaccination, 225–30, 338–39n26
venereal disease, 230–33, 241–42, 245,
342n63, 342nn67,68, 345n105
vice-governors, 54–55
Vietnam, 120
villages, 65, 81, 83, 208
vocational training, 175

War, Ministry of, 34
wartime mobilization: agencies in, 46–47;
censorship in, 281–82n104; census in,
213; citizenship education in, 188–92;
colonial, 16–17, 37–38; continuities in,
249; developmentalism in, 139–40;
disease control in, 17, 230–33; education
in, 181, 193; household registration in, 17,
198, 205, 206–9; in imperialism, 46–51;

industrialization in, 17, 46, 121, 139, 143; legitimation in, 10, 101, 108–9, 111–14, 115, 198; material resources in, 48–49, 75, 140; and military expansionism, 26; police in, 74–76; religion in, 160, 163–65; resistance to, 17, 49; revenues in, 285–86n31; state development in, 249; surname standardization in, 214–15

waste disposal facilities, 228

water, 58–59, 135, 228, 234

Weber, Max, 4–6, 147, 150, 309n15

Weberian rationalization, 4–5, 120, 254, 269n4

welfare, 58–59, 123–24, 141, 145, 328n16

Western medicine, 224–25, 243, 245

Western powers, 100

Western residents, 243–44

Woodside, Alexander, 120

working classes, 145

Yi Dynasty, 31

Yi Hun-sang, 199

Yi Myeong-jong, 208

Yi Seong-u, 82–83

Yi Tae-jin, 132

Yi Wanyong, 275–76n29

Yi Yeong-hun, 132

Yi Yongik, 125–26, 130

Yi Yun-gap, 111

Yi Yun-sang, 131–32

Yu Giljun, 30, 244, 293n22

Yu Giljun: *Observations from Travels to the West,* 93–94, 234

Yun Chiho, 30, 112

Yun Hae-dong, 7, 78–80, 256

THE FIRST 24

One Man. One Mission. One Day.

DAVID H. ROSEBERRY

Scripture quotations marked (ESV) are from the English Standard Version. Copyright © 2001 by Crossway, a publishing ministry of Good News Publishers. All rights reserved

ISBN Paperback 978-1-7358461-7-0

ISBN eBook 978-1-7358461-8-7

Book cover design and photograph by David Roseberry

Published by RML Books, 4545 Charlemagne Drive, Plano, Texas 75093

Printed in the United States of America

❀ Created with Vellum

DEDICATION

For Daniel.
You bring beauty to the world God so loved.

CONTENTS

THE FIRST 24

One Man. One Mission. One Day

INTRODUCTION

The First 24

ONE MAN. ONE MISSION. ONE DAY.

In 2001, the thrilling series *24*, starring Kiefer Sutherland, hit the television airwaves. It was fast-paced, gripping, and graphic. Jack Bauer, the lead character played by Sutherland, worked for "CTU," a fictional counter-terrorist unit of the US Government. The popular show was a combination of crime drama, a political thriller, and action-hero series known for its relentless use of cliffhangers at the end of each episode.

What made the series so electrifying was the framework of the show. The entire 24-episode season told a continuous story that occurred in "real-time" over 24 hours.

I intend to do the same thing in this book. *The First 24* will cover the first 24-hour day of Jesus' public ministry in Capernaum as recorded in the Gospel of Mark. The events of the opening chapter (vs. 21-45) are written to be read as one busy, important, and inaugural day in the life of Jesus. The day begins with Jesus' entrance into Capernaum. Twenty-four hours later, he leaves the vicinity to move on "to other towns and villages." Everything that happened in those 24 hours is captured in verses 21 through 45 of Chapter One. If you do the math, you'll find that the events of the 24 hours are told in exactly 24 verses. This is serendipitous—a happy accident.[1]

What follows in this book are 24 chapters investigating the events in the 24 verses covering the first 24 hours of Jesus' ministry.

No other place in the gospel account gives us this tight of view of Jesus' work and mission. There isn't another 'day-in-the-life' account of Jesus' ministry. As we will discover, the first 24 hours of Jesus' ministry set the tone and tenor for what Jesus did over the rest of his earthly ministry. As we make our way through each moment on that first day, we will investigate and elucidate the events as fully as we can. And most remarkably, in the end, we will find that every one of the events creates a series of themes or storylines that run through the rest of the Gospel. Put another way, the events and encounters, teaching, preaching, healings, and confrontations with the unclean spirits over that single day in Capernaum are like a sneak peek at what would happen over the next three years and what would finally be resolved at the Cross.

THE WHIRLWIND GOSPEL OF MARK

Each of the gospel writers, Matthew, Mark, Luke, and John, have different and distinct views of the life of Jesus. They record many of the same events in the gospels differently, as four individual writers or storytellers would do today. They chose to emphasize or explicate specific details they believed were essential to engage their audience with the Gospel's central message. Every one of the four different accounts tells the same story over the same timeframe concerning the same person, but they are all told differently. The finished products—the gospels themselves—are wonderfully unique expressions of the author's faith and belief in Jesus the Son of God.

When it comes to the Gospel of Mark, it has its own style and substance. It is a whirlwind to read. It is the shortest of the gospels. And the swiftest. The incidents described in its16 chapters occur at a breakneck speed and with breathtaking immediacy. (Mark uses the word "immediately" or a derivative of it 11 times in the first chapter alone; 41 times over the entire gospel. It's the gospel of what's happening now!)

For example, as we will see in our 24-verse investigation, in one 24-hour day, Jesus will enter the village of Capernaum, attend the town Synagogue, teach from the Scriptures, preach an astonishing sermon, cast out a fearful demon, free a possessed man, visit a friend's home down the street, heal his mother-in-law of a fever, heal dozens of others and cast out demons from others, pause for a few hours of sleep, and then leave early in the morning for prayers before sunrise. Then, the disciples come to search for him the next day. When they find him, they urge him to return to Capernaum because the crowds are waiting. Jesus tells them to keep going, to move on to the next town. And finally, before he gets far down the road, he encounters one last needy man—a man plagued with leprosy. He cleanses the man and then moves on to other towns and villages. Jesus accomplished all of this in 24 hours.

Whew! Only Mark's gospel tells the story of this day in this way. Only Mark lets us see the most amazing "first day on the job" ever!

These events, told in rapid-fire succession, don't just tell us about the exhausting work of ministry. They reveal the Lord's inexhaustible love and compassion for the people. They also show us his impressive power and energy for God's mission—what God had called him to accomplish. He does more in 24 hours than any of us would in many more days—and he does it all with seeming indefatigable endurance and energy. The first full day of Jesus public ministry shows us that, hour by hour, step by step, one episode after the other, Jesus has the power and ability to speak, preach, teach, heal, and perform miracles that confirm his identity as the unique Son of God.

All this is revealed to us in Mark's Gospel as we make our way into the first 24 hours of Jesus' public ministry.

I'm framing this journey with Jesus over 24 hours like the television series 24. Obviously, there are no pulsating digital clocks or by-the-second timers or displays. Time stamps in the New Testament are helpful, but there are only a few of them, and they are vague. Gospel writers include transitional comments: "in the morning," "later that same day," or "early the next morning." These markers help us follow the story, but they will never show us the exact time of day or how many minutes to the top of the hour. Chronological time was not an essential detail for the Gospel writers. Therefore, in this book, we will not be a slave to the "tick-tock" of a 24-hour clock. Don't expect each episode to occur in a single sixty-minute period. However, we will treat all the episodes from verse 21 to verse 45 in the order in which they occur.

A DEEP DIVE

Our deep dive will look at what happened in Capernaum during that first full day, and we will discover hidden details and clues in each event. We will also assess what the event means and what it tells us about Jesus, his purpose, and his plan. Behind every episode, event, or vignette, we will discover a deep reality in the life of Jesus—that he not only did the things we will look at; he did them with a deeper and wider purpose in mind. He was on a mission. And as we look intently into everything that he did and said during those 24 hours in Capernaum, we will find treasures and insights that paint a vivid portrait of the Lord and the reason he came.

As we take this step-by-step journey with Jesus, we will also go deeply into our faith. In the next 24 chapters of this book, we will follow Jesus and enter his ancient world. We will listen intently to the Scriptures and we feel the intensity of the interactions and the engagements that he had with others. We will realize more personally what his message was—and still is. We will be challenged in our beliefs as well. How much of what Jesus did and said do we understand? Do we truly believe? I hope that I can show you firsthand, like an eyewitness with a front-row seat to an incredible show, what these 24 verses mean for our faith and our life today.

One more thing before we start our clocks. We should note that Mark mentions five events that precede Jesus' entrance into Capernaum. Let's take a brief look at each of these previous episodes. Then, we will say a quick word about the story's setting in Capernaum. Finally, we will be ready to begin our investigation into the details of the first 24 hours of Jesus' ministry in Capernaum as told to us in the Gospel of Mark.

1. Mark and the other writers of the New Testament did not write or think of their work in individual verses. It was not until the 13th Century AD that the modern system of chapters and series came into use.

PREVIOUSLY IN THE GOSPEL OF MARK

EVENTS BEFORE JESUS'S ARRIVAL IN CAPERNAUM

Mark tells the story of Jesus so rapidly (about 11,000 Greek words over 16 chapters; roughly 1/3 of the length of this book) and so powerfully that we can be overwhelmed by its velocity. Mark is an immediate gospel. There isn't a grandiose introduction to the story; it simply starts. The first words of the Gospel of Mark get right to the point. They reveal the entire gospel message; what the story of the Gospel is about: Jesus Christ, the Son of God. Mark begins his Gospel with this end in mind: tell the readers who Jesus is.

This is very different than the other accounts of the life of Jesus. Mark does not include an extensive genealogy (as in Matthew); there is no background story of the Lord's birth and childhood (as in Luke); there is no magisterial prologue before the action begins (as in John). Mark's Gospel simply begins, "The beginning of the gospel of Jesus Christ, the Son of God." (Mark 1:1). Thus, Jesus is introduced, and his appearance is imminent.

Let's look at the five events mentioned in Mark 1:1-20. They occurred before Jesus arrived in Capernaum and set the stage for what would happen there.

EPISODE ONE: THE BAPTIST

The opening scene in Mark's Gospel is of John the Baptist appearing in the public arena. It took a rabble-rouser like John, a loud prophet, to kickstart the events of the Messiah's coming. He was a natural troublemaker and a courageous eccentric who was the answer to the 700-year-old prayer of the Jews. *When, O Lord, will the Messiah come?*

Pulling quotes from Malachi 3:1, 4:3, and Isaiah 40:3, Mark tells us that the entire prophetic body of Scripture finally imagined someone like John to come on the scene. When John the Baptist began his ministry, he came 400 years *after* Malachi had written his prophetic book and 700 years *after* Isaiah had written his. These two prophets are "bookends" to the entire body of prophetic Scripture. They are the first (Isaiah) and the last (Malachi) to speak, expressing the hope of Israel for a Messiah. The point is that the faith (and frustration) of the Jews, active and alive for over 700 years, was finally fulfilled in the life of John the Baptist.

EPISODE TWO: JESUS

In Mark's Gospel, the story of Jesus' ministry starts on the banks of the Jordan River, where John the Baptist was baptizing people for the forgiveness of sins. John was not claiming to forgive sins—only God can do that—but he sounded an alarm. The Messiah is coming. Get ready for change. John was like a weatherman blaring the forecast: "Change is coming. The Kingdom of Heaven is about to break open, and everyone whose heart is unprepared will be swept away!"

We will look closely at the baptism of Jesus later in the book, but the high point of the ministry of John the Baptist was at the Jordan when he baptized Jesus of Nazareth. The baptism of Jesus was, in effect, the Lord's inauguration. The ministry of Jesus started with his baptism in the Jordan, but it went public (in Mark's Gospel) when he entered Capernaum.

EPISODE THREE: THE DESERT

After Jesus' baptism, the Holy Spirit drove Jesus into the desert to be tempted by the Devil. We will look at this event later in the book, but for now, we should note that it happened. Many people wonder why the Spirit drove Jesus into the desert. Why the sudden push to contend with the Devil? But Jesus did not question his ordeal. It seems like he wanted to go there. It might be that Jesus knew the Devil would be roaming the wilderness and that the Lord wanted to meet the evil creature at a place of the Lord's choosing.

EPISODE FOUR: PRISON

Sometime after Jesus' baptism, John the Baptist was arrested and placed in a prison fortress in the mountains east of the Dead Sea. There had been tensions between the despot Herod and the Baptist for several years; John was very vocal about Herod's current illicit marriage. And he had every right to be.

The Herod family is the most dysfunctional family dynasty in the Bible and one of the most confusing to keep track of all the players. The backstory of the king's family tree is tangential to the ministry of Jesus. However, the Gospel writers tell sordid details about this family to show the level of sin, corruption, and immorality in the ranks of the Roman rulers.

In the footnote below, please read a quick summary of this family and what led to the imprisonment and eventual death of John the Baptist. Pay attention. It's complicated.[1]

EPISODE FIVE: CHOSEN

In the final scene before the first recorded full day of work and ministry of our Lord, Jesus chose four disciples: Peter, John, James, and Andrew. He wanted to build a team for the work ahead. These men would join others and become the Lord's agents to begin the work of the Great Commission.

The men were ordinary fishermen on the Sea of Galilee. They were likely well-known and well-established in their local businesses. They followed Jesus and experienced his teaching, ministry, and friendship for three years, and after they had received the Holy Spirit at Pentecost, they became the world-changers that we know them to be.

THE SETTING: CAPERNAUM

For all it meant to Jesus, Nazareth faded from view in the story of his adult life. Jesus is referred to as "Jesus of Nazareth" more than 20 times in the gospels, but when he left the small town and moved his base of operations to Capernaum, he never returned. Ever. He might as well have been called Jesus *from* Nazareth.

When we investigate the reason for this self-imposed, permanent exile, we find an unfortunate event when a sermon he preached early in his ministry nearly got him killed by the synagogue members.

This is what happened. The community of Nazareth came to demand what Capernaum already had seen for themselves: miracles. After all, they claimed Jesus as their hometown hero. He hailed from their town, and they wanted a share of his growing fame. In a sermon in Nazareth, Jesus told them that pride was nothing to be proud of. He said, referring to two well-known stories in their Scriptures, that God overlooks proud people like them, who see themselves as deserving insiders and expect perquisites and prestige. The sermon triggered their rage and transformed the people into a mob intent on killing their hometown boy.

With their anger roiled, the congregation pushed Jesus to the edge of a nearby precipice and prepared to throw him off to his death. But in the pushing and shoving chaos, Jesus slipped away quickly and quietly. Jesus didn't merely leave Nazareth that day. He escaped. And he never returned. The violent incident in Nazareth was an ominous sign of things to come.

Jesus moved to Capernaum, which became the scene and setting for the significant events of the first day of Jesus' ministry.

We have touched on the previous episodes mentioned by Mark in his opening verses. These events occurred before Jesus walked into the lakeside town of Capernaum and made his way to the synagogue on the Sabbath.

With these earlier episodes noted, we are ready to begin.

1. Herod the Great (the Herod at Jesus' birth) was a mad genius and brilliant architect and builder. But he was also a paranoid megalomaniac who tried to kill the infant Jesus. He failed at that murder attempt but successfully killed two of his sons.

Herod the Great also arranged the marriage of his daughter Herodias to his uncle, named Herod Philip. But then she divorced Herod Philip to marry his half-brother, Herod Antipas. (She kept it all in the family!) Herodias had a daughter, a seductress, and dancer, who performed for her stepfather Herod one evening at his request. In payment for her sultry dance and at the request of her mother, Herodias, who was sick of John the Baptist's public criticisms and condemnations, the young teenager demanded the head of John the Baptist on a silver platter.

1

OPENING SALVO

When Jesus Enters Capernaum on the Sabbath

And they went into Capernaum.

— MARK 1:21

The events listed in the first 24-hour day of Jesus' public ministry begins with his entrance into the fishing village on the shore of one of the northernmost lakes in Israel. Jesus walks into Capernaum and there is no one there.

Has a more significant historical figure ever made a less auspicious entrance? Three years later, Jesus will enter Jerusalem to great fanfare, loud cheers, and waving of bright green palm branches. The long-awaited King would finally arrive, riding on a colt. But now, in the quiet village of Capernaum, there are no cheering crowds to welcome him. There is no commotion or celebration. Today, he is entering the town alone except for the newly selected disciples. They are the freshmen followers of their rabbi

and friend, Jesus. It's a parade of five; hardly an impressive procession on this early Sabbath morning. No one is around to care.

Yet, in only a few hours, crowds will swarm around him. There
will be scores of sick people, demon-possessed sufferers, curious
onlookers, and relentless critics who come to see him. Some will
be there to watch him. Some will experience a healing touch or
witness one of his powerful voice commands over the demons. In
a sinister move, some will listen to him and begin to gather
evidence against him. And soon enough, Jesus will be overwhelmed by the press of people trying to see, hear, or touch him.
This happens within the first few hours of his public ministry, as
recorded in the Gospel of Mark.

This wasn't the first time Jesus had been to Capernaum—it seems
that people were acquainted with him. Perhaps they had seen him
before. As we said earlier, he was known as Jesus of Nazareth—a
town only two dozen miles away. Maybe they knew him, but they
didn't know *who* he was. But in any event, they never expected
what would happen today. The day begins when Jesus enters
Capernaum. It will end when he leaves the vicinity of the fishing
town 24 hours later. Today is the beginning of a new chapter in
history. It is his opening salvo.

HIS TURNING POINT

Something had changed in Jesus' manner and momentum on this
first day. A turning point seems to have occurred in his life,
perhaps only months earlier. He was always bold in his beliefs and
focused on God's purpose. But recently, something happened to
him that changed him, or we could say, charged him. He was
baptized in the Jordan. And whatever else can be said of that
experience at the Jordan, eighty miles south of Capernaum, it
initiated and propelled him into his mission.

In other words, baptism was a defining moment for Jesus. In that single event, Jesus saw the Holy Spirit descend on him in the form of a dove. And then he heard the voice of his Father in heaven speak to the masses and affirm him, the Son. They were all there in one place—the three members of the Holy Trinity: The Father, the Son, and the Holy Spirit.

Other than a vision of the Trinity seen by John and told in the Book of Revelation, this moment in the Bible is the only place where all three persons of the Trinity appear in their personage and can be seen or heard. We can do our best to understand this eternally historic moment if we believe what the gospel writers tell us about it: that Jesus emerged from the waters of the Jordan (John had just baptized him); that the Spirit, as a dove (Luke says that the Spirit came in bodily form), came over the waters of the Jordan and descended upon him, the Son; and that, from the opened heavens, the Father's voice, clear and confident, spoke over him, "This is my Son, in whom I am well pleased." (Mark 1:11)

It is a stunning occurrence because, while we know that the Trinity is an essential doctrine of the Christian faith, no one can define it fully or adequately. It is a mystery. The word Trinity is never mentioned in the Bible. The three members of the Trinity are either referenced individually or inferred from other biblical events. But no one in history had ever seen the Trinity.

Until now.

Here, at the baptism of Jesus, the Son of God, the Holy Spirit of God, and God the Father, to the extent we can fathom this moment, are all gathered in one place.

This must have changed Jesus, or, as I said, charged him. The sense of divine community and power he received and shared with the Father and the Holy Spirit surely empowered him with everything he would need for his ministry. He did not receive anything at his baptism that he did not already have. He wasn't completed by it. He wasn't 'topped off' with power and vision with it. But something happened at the Jordan that needed to happen for him to begin. He was released, fully empowered for the work ahead.

The desert came next and the one-on-one meeting with the Devil. If the Devil thought that Jesus would be weakened by hunger or tempted by insecurity, it was never going to happen. He emerged from the prolonged period of temptation and privation full of purpose and confidence. Jesus not only survived that ordeal; he thrived through it. The taunts and trials of the Devil did not defeat him. They steeled him. They sharpened him.

At his baptism, Jesus was forever attuned to the presence of God. And though no one was there to greet him, when he came to the small town of Capernaum on the northern shore of the Sea of Galilee, he was ready, willing, and able to fulfill his calling.

Next: Jesus comes to Capernaum, but he doesn't have a home there.

2

WELCOME HOME

Jesus Loves the World But He Has No Home

And they went into Capernaum.

— MARK 1:21

The town of Capernaum is situated on the northern shore of the Sea of Galilee, the largest freshwater lake in Israel. It was the perfect place for Jesus to launch a movement that would reach the masses. Many well-traveled roads nearby guaranteed that news about Jesus and his message would spread quickly through local gossip, word-of-mouth chatter, and roadside conversations. The lakeside town was near two major crossroads in the ancient world, the Via Maris and the King's Highway; tens of thousands of traders, merchants, soldiers, and travelers crossed and commuted over these ancient highways.

Capernaum was a significant enough outpost for commerce and traffic to have all the features of a growing town: a full-fledged synagogue, a detachment of Roman soldiers, and an assembly of Jewish scribes and Pharisees. For Jesus, it was the perfect place to begin.

The Sea of Galilee is a gem of a lake, sunken below sea level and surrounded by green hills. It is only sixteen miles from north to south and seven miles wide. The famous Jewish historian of the era, Josephus Flavius, called the Sea of Galilee the "Pride of Nature."[1] It is beautiful.

Jesus arrived in the lakeside community to start his ministry. We should not forget that he didn't have a natural home. He didn't have a place to call home. He would spend a few nights with friends or stay overnight here and there throughout his ministry. Later, it is revealed that he may have stayed with Peter and his family for a brief time. Undoubtedly, he often slept in caves or under the stars. Jesus never had a home.

This is a sad paradox. The New Testament states that Jesus, the Son of God, is the master architect and creator of the universe. In St. Paul's magisterial tribute to the Son of God written in a letter to the believers in Colossae, the Apostle proclaims that Jesus was the chief designer and builder of all that is seen and unseen.

> "For by him, all things were created, in heaven and on earth, visible and invisible, whether thrones or dominions or rulers or authorities—all things were created through him and for him." (Col. 3:16ff).

Yet, for all he made, he didn't have a home in the world he created.

Why? The simplest way to explain it is that people did not know what to do with him. Many people loved him. Dozens, if not hundreds, of friends, admirers, and believers followed him wherever he went. But some of what he taught made people uncomfortable; they pulled away from him.[2] They squirmed when they considered the radical nature of his teaching. Jesus even called himself a "prophet without honor" in each four gospel accounts. (Matt. 13:54-57, Mark 6:1-6, Luke 4:16-30, John 4:44)

The Fourth Gospel though, says it best. It reads,

> *"(Jesus) was in the world, and the world was made through him, yet the world did not know him. He came to his own, and his people did not receive him." (John 1:10-11)*

They did not *receive* him. Think about this for a moment. It is a stinging indictment against our human race. We rejected him. For example, consider children enjoying all the benefits and warmth of their parents' home while ignoring them as they stand on the porch of the family house—knocking on the front door in vain. It is like a son disowning his mother or a daughter rejecting her father. Is there anything sadder?

THE MAN WITH NOTHING

When we read through the gospel accounts of our Lord, we see him publicly leading, teaching, preaching, traveling, conversing, defending, and ministering to the masses. But in all of that, Jesus had a sequestered sense about him—he was alone. He stood by himself. He was not a loner—he loved people, but he was often alone.

This is the painful irony of his story. The Creator of the world, who owns everything and whose power and presence created all that is, and will be, is without a place to lay his head in the world he made. He seems strange in a land of strangers. Even though he owns the "cattle on a thousand hills" (Ps. 50:10), and they are his hills, he doesn't have an address. As Jesus entered Capernaum on the first day, he came as a permanent visitor, a resident alien. We should not forget this.

Not only is he homeless, but he is possession-less too. He owns nothing of his own. In his adult life and ministry, everything he had, every place he could lay his head, and nearly everything he used was something he had to borrow. Everything.

- Mary's womb held him—a womb *loaned* to the Holy Spirit of God.
- His stepfather raised the boy—a *borrowed* man for the role.
- The keeper of the inn provided a *borrowed* manger at his birth.
- He *borrowed* the homes of his friends: Peter, Mary, Martha, and Lazarus.
- On the most public day of his life—a day intended for fanfare and praise—he had to *borrow* a ride into Jerusalem.
- He *borrowed* the upper room for the last Passover he would ever observe.
- His wealthy friend, Joseph of Arimathea, *loaned* Jesus his tomb at his death.

Jesus had nothing of his own while he was in the world.

The only possession that could have been called his own was taken from him just before he died. A final insult. His robe was absconded by uncaring soldiers who, like every soldier, Pharisee, political appointee, and member of the fickle crowd, did not know what they were doing.

Now, as we follow him into Capernaum, we should remember that though he was never at home in the world, he still loved the world. He loved the people in the world. He lived among them. He prayed with them. He ate with them. He walked with them. He entered their homes. He fished from their fleets. He spoke to their friends. He welcomed sinners and strangers.

As he comes into the fishing town, those are the people on his mind and in his heart. He is looking for them, and he knows where to find them. He heads across town, through empty streets on this Sabbath morning, to be where the people are. He is going to the synagogue. He is going to be with the people.

Next: Jesus enters the local synagogue to start his day of ministry.

---

1. The famous Jewish historian was born 37 AD; died 100 AD. His comment deserves to be fully quoted. "One might say that nature had taken pride in thus assembling, by a tour de force, the most discordant species in a single spot, and that, by a happy rivalry, each of the seasons wished to claim this region for her own," Josephus, *The Jewish War,* 3.516 (Thackeray, Loeb Classical Library).
2. John 6:66

FIRST STEP

When Jesus Enters the Local Synagogue

And immediately on the Sabbath, he entered the syna-
gogue and was teaching.

— MARK 1:21

J esus knows where he's going and what he is doing, particularly on this first day of ministry in Capernaum. On other days over the next three years of ministry, it will appear that Jesus is very flexible about his schedule. He does not ever seem to be in a hurry as he moves from town to village preaching and teaching. But today, on his first day, there is intentionality as he enters Capernaum.

We are in the morning of a new day, and Jesus walks to the synagogue and enters the place of worship without hesitation. He is Jewish, and, like all Jewish men of his time, it is customary to attend services on the Sabbath.

There's a good reason Jesus goes to the synagogue. He comes to town on the Sabbath because he knows the people will be at the synagogue. Jesus is seeking the people. Their worship assembly is his first stop. As he begins his ministry to the people, he will not remove himself from them to a centralized headquarters in Jerusalem. He will not take the place of honor on an elevated throne in a distant palace. He does not expect people to come to look for him. He goes to the people. The Son of God makes first contact; *Jesus makes the first move.*

Other religions demand something from their believers before any spiritual engagement. But God knows that we cannot bring anything to the relationship, so he begins by bringing himself to us.

This may seem too obvious to point out, but it highlights a much greater idea that governs the ministry of Jesus. Christians believe that the Son of God *initiated* the story of our salvation. He started it. Jesus came to us. He came from heaven, entered our world, ate our food, and walked our streets. He related to us, and thus, we can relate to him. The old King James Bible put it this way: "For he knoweth our frame" (Ps. 103:14).

God knows us, and we want to be known. This is what the prophet Isaiah had longed for when he cried out, "Oh that you would rend the heavens and come down" (64:1). Jesus came from heaven; he entered our world. The Judeo-Christian faith is unique in this way.

This truth is made more explicit by our Lord himself. He comes to where the people are and finds them when they are lost. For example, in Luke's gospel, after Jesus' encounter with Zacchaeus, the short man of Jericho, the Lord declares his purpose in coming into the world: "For the Son of Man came to seek and save the lost" (Luke 19:10). He is on a search and rescue mission. He was searching to rescue us. We are the ones who are lost.

In other religions, the founding leader or central teacher usually becomes a celebrity or a noted, influential leader set apart from the rest. People seek *them* out. People stand on the outside looking in; they knock on *their* door, as it were. In Islam, for example, Muhammed became a military general and the head of state with all the rights and privileges there unto. He was high and mighty over the people. In Judaism, Moses is held in highest esteem as the people's representative, by the people, and for the people, but not of the people. He sat in judicial sessions to rule over them as a judge. People came to the Old Testament lawgiver to decide their cases and settle disputes.

In some religious faiths, there are not only high-placed people but also high places where people can go. There are high-level pilgrimage sites. In China, for example, there are sacred mountains, five for Taoists and four for Buddhists. These high places are like "Mecca," where the faithful are urged to ascend to attain further enlightenment.

CELEBRITY-FREE

In Christianity, there are no special holy men, revered women, or higher places over all others. There are no sacred mountains to ascend. There are no pilgrimages required. Of course, there are saints to be admired and emulated, but biblically speaking, they do not have a special status here or in the world to come. They do not live their human lives closer to God because of their accomplishments or personal fame. Some Christians might be famous in a worldly sense, but there are no Christian celebrities.

At its core, the Christian faith does not call believers to be more prominent and powerful or aspire to greater success or significance. Christianity is not about human efforts to be ascendant, admired, or adored. The Christian faith highlights the story of the Lord's *descent* into our world and humanity—not his ascent above it. The Christian faith is centered on God's Incarnation in the flesh when he became one with us. We speak about the Incarnation in spatial or relational terms that connect to our life: Jesus came *down* to know our life; he *entered* our sufferings, and he *took on* our sorrows; he *walked* our paths; he *knew* our problems, and he *understood* our needs.

Other religions promote high-ranking leaders and upward journeys to higher knowledge and wisdom; they call followers to spiritual advancements. However, Christianity isn't centered on human accomplishments at all. It's centered on the achievements of Jesus Christ. It is true: there is a journey at the heart of the Christian faith, but it is not *our* journey. It is *Jesus'* journey to become one of us. The Christian faith is about his descent; he came down to the rough and tumble of our lowly, daily, dusty life.

Christianity is about Jesus coming to our material world and living his life in the world like us. This makes Christianity, as Archbishop William Temple said, "the most avowedly materialistic of all the great religions."[1] He rubs elbows with us.

So, on this Sabbath morning, Jesus enters Capernaum because that is where the people are. And he enters the synagogue because that is where the people go. And he comes to the synagogue because, like all Jews, Jesus observes the Sabbath. And once he is inside the small synagogue, he has a captive audience.

Next: *What he says in his teaching astonishes everyone.*

---

1. William Temple, *Nature, Man and God* (London: Macmillan, 1949), 478.

4

ASTONISHING MESSAGE

Why the Good News is Good to Hear

And they were astonished at his teaching.

— MARK 1:22

We are following the footsteps of Jesus on his first full day of ministry, as recorded in the Gospel of Mark. It is a massive day for the Lord—a turning point in his life. He will never be able to come back to where he is now. Whatever anonymity he had going into this first day will vanish within the next hour when Jesus speaks in the synagogue. But we must not get ahead of the action. Let's go back.

It was the Sabbath that day. Jesus entered Capernaum with the intent of stopping at the local synagogue where the people had gathered for worship. The synagogue was small, holding no more than 150 people. (The ruins of a centuries-old replica of the structure are still visible today.) On the first day of Jesus' public ministry, he had a plan to deliver a message to the congregation.

Once inside the synagogue, Jesus took over. We don't know how he took the teaching position that morning. Jesus was a preacher and itinerant rabbi. He was not unknown. Was he invited to speak impromptu? Was he scheduled to speak at the local congregation? We can only imagine. Regardless, we know that Jesus took center stage and began to expound the Scriptures.

But what did he say?

Only a few times in the New Testament do we know the specific contents of Jesus' sermons. For his most famous sermon in Matthew 5, "The Sermon on the Mount," we have the entire text. Later, Jesus delivered a condensed version of the same message in a field to another group. We have the text of that sermon as well.[1] The only other sermon for which we have the detailed outline or text is the verbal indictment of the Pharisees in Matthew's gospel.[2] We have most of that sermon, maybe even all of it, and it is a scorcher. We don't have to read it all to know where Jesus is going with the eight warnings (or "woes" as they are called) for the religionists of Jerusalem. It was a stinging condemnation of the hypocrisy of the most religiously obsessed people on earth. That sermon—and a few others like it—probably got him killed.

However, at Capernaum, Jesus' full sermon text is not known to us. But we do see the theme. We see the keynote theme for all his preaching and teaching: The Gospel of God. And we also can see the subtitle for most messages ever preached by the Lord. It is given to us in Jesus' very first announcement in Mark's gospel, "The time is fulfilled, and the Kingdom of God is at hand; repent and believe in the gospel." (Mark 1:15)

This keynote was the great theme of the sermons he would preach during the three years of public ministry. It was like an overture for his entire life, teaching, travel, compassion, works, and miracles. This was the simple message of Jesus.

THE KEYNOTE

It is memorable and memorizable. Please reread it: "The time is fulfilled, the Kingdom of God is at hand. Repent and believe the Gospel" (Mark 1:15). Could anything be more powerful or provocative? Looking at it closely, this simple message of the Kingdom is what we call today a three-point sermon. Jesus preaches about (1) *relief*—the time is fulfilled. The long, long period of waiting is over. Then he speaks about (2) *hope*—the Kingdom is here. It had arrived. Today! And he ended with a clear call to action: (3) *repent*. Change the way you think.

This keynote statement about relief, hope, and repentance might have been Jesus' opening line in his sermon at the synagogue that morning. In any case, it was the phrase that launched his ministry, and it is (or should be) the central message of the church.

Over the long history of the church to come, teachers, clergy, theologians, Bible scholars, philosophers, followers of Christ, and preachers of his Word have plumbed and expounded the depth and meaning of this inaugural declaration. This message has been complicated and confused by 2,000 years of repetition, innovation, familiarity, misunderstanding, misapplication, and corruption. But the original message of Jesus was simple and profound. He had one central point to make. *The Kingdom of God had come.* It was just that simple. And there was only one adequate, appropriate, personal response to its advent: *repentance*.

We should remember that when Jesus came to preach this message of the arrival of the Kingdom, it rang true in the minds and hearts of those who heard it. It sounded like *good* news to them. His message did not begin with harsh denunciations of sin, although Jesus hated iniquity and its collateral damage in our lives. His central message though, was not to condemn people for their sins, even though we all stand condemned before a holy God.[3]

In other words, the Good News wasn't bad news. It was good to hear. The Gospel of the Kingdom seemed like fresh air to those who heard it. It came to them (well, most of them) as *great* news. It was not the bad news of threats, punishment, warnings, and fear. It was a grand announcement of a change that had arrived. There were no sweeping accusations of blame. The Gospel of God was a positive declaration calling people to do something even more optimistic: *change.*

When was the last time you left your church and used the word "astonished" to describe what you felt or heard? Jesus, in effect, blew their minds. The power with which he spoke and the content of what he said was earth-shattering. Words create worlds, and the words that Jesus preached created a world of hope that hit people right between the eyes—where the mind is. And the people thought the good news of the Kingdom was the most incredible thing they had ever heard.

Next: *The Good News didn't shock or scold the people; it soothed them. It was like a breath of fresh air.*

---

1. Luke 6:20-49. The text that we have for the Sermon on the Mount and the so-called Sermon on the Plain are probably only outlines or high-points of the message Jesus preached.
2. Matthew 23:1-36
3. John 3:18

5

FRESH AIR

Learn and Turn Instead of Turn or Burn

And they were astonished at his teaching.

— MARK 1:22

Jesus spent time in the synagogue defining, describing, and illustrating the Good News of the Gospel. Again, as Mark tells us, they were astonished; they did not want him to stop speaking. One of the most surprising aspects of Jesus' message to that congregation was that people "got it." They understood it. He was not speaking over their heads or hearts—he was speaking right to them. He was speaking their language!

What message could be simpler or more significant? As we saw in the last chapter, Jesus' sermon was a three-point message that people could remember and personalize: Relief had come to me. Hope was here for me. It was time to change my thinking.

We know that the message of Jesus was mind-blowing, but yet the people loved to hear it. But how do we know this? The answer is that they followed him; they wanted more. Jesus' proclamation of the Good News made people want to hear more about it. If we understand the central message of Jesus in this way, many other questions throughout the rest of the gospel accounts find answers.

For example, why do the people of Capernaum follow the Lord and not run from him? Their interest in Jesus is not just about getting some miraculous food or health care from time to time. The curiosity about Jesus was not only to see something extraordinary now and then. They *heard* something wonderful that greatly encouraged them. It was good news. Why did the tired and poor, the lonely and sick, the needy and the hungry, the sinners and the outcasts—why did these souls seek him instead of hiding from him? Why did the masses follow the Lord to distant and remote places? Why did the short man, a tax collector named Zacchaeus in Jericho, climb the fabled sycamore tree to perch in its branches?[1] To see for himself the one who was bringing the Good News. If he had expected judgment or condemnation, he would have been wiser to hide in the bushes, not sit in the branches.

The message of Jesus was refreshing to those who heard it. That's what fresh air is: *refreshing*. Jesus' message was often accompanied by signs, wonders, and miracles of provision. Those were always wonderful. But the people heard the Good News and it seemed good for them, with or without an accompanying miracle. They liked it because it *was* good.

In spiritual terms, these people already knew their status before God. They did not need reminding that they were sinners. The broken and impoverished lives they lived were all the evidence they needed to prove that they had sinned and fallen short of the glory of God. But they loved Jesus and the message he proclaimed because it felt like a relief to them, not judgment. It was a blessing, not a burden. They didn't feel condemned. They were comforted. Maybe for the first time, they experienced an attribute of God they had only heard about: mercy.

It is important to paint the complete picture here. Clearly, Jesus condemned the sin that embeds itself in our lives. However, he had a unique way of helping people see their sinfulness and understand their need to repent. He did not denounce sinners directly. Jesus was not usually straightforward in confronting specific people about their sins. At times, he accused people of sinful actions and behaviors; he didn't shrink from that diagnosis. But typically, the people receiving those direct accusations were Pharisees, other religious officials, and demons.

Jesus was clear: people needed to understand that they were outside the will of God and that their lives needed to change. But, the way Jesus told it, the message came to them like a thief in the night. Suddenly. Stealthily. Surprisingly. Let's look at how he spoke the truth so gracefully.

LEARN AND TURN

Jesus often delivered his message to ordinary sinners (like us) by first telling a story or parable or using a metaphor. Often, he entered a dialogue with someone, engaged in a friendship, or built a relationship bridge from his life to the life of another. Once the sinner (we are all sinners) understood the meaning of the parable the story, or the point behind a conversation, they began to see themselves. They knew they were implicated. It was as if the listeners were captured in the encounter or story, got caught up in its telling, and suddenly realized that Jesus was talking about them! In Jesus' unique and wonderful way of teaching and preaching, the people saw their sins not because Jesus pointed them out directly but because they discovered them personally. They looked through a window pane as the story unfolded, but then they suddenly realized they were looking at themselves in a mirror!

Some preachers wonder how to help modern listeners understand the depth of sin and our need to repent. What does it take to awaken the human consciousness to see personal sin for what it is? How can we help people become aware of God's holiness and the reality of our brokenness and sinfulness and repent?

Consider that Jesus did not use a direct route except a few times. As I said, explicit condemnations were reserved for religious professionals and demons. People like you and I were not promised hell and eternal isolation from God. In the context of a relationship or a parable, Jesus helped the sinners see the seriousness of an unrepentant life. The faith was not forced on them; they came to a new personal understanding about it.

Some readers might object to this observation. They cite examples of Jesus threatening listeners with hell, suffering, damnation, and eternal pain. I have read the same passages; Jesus called people to repent. However, most of the warning statements from Jesus were delivered to people as a story, a parable, or in the context of a personal encounter with the Lord.

Put another way, in all the Lord's teaching and preaching, there is no example of "fire and brimstone" preaching or "turn or burn" teaching directed at ordinary people. His teaching was, we might say, not "turn or burn" but "learn and turn." This is how people change.

We hear today that people don't like change. This is not so. The truth is that everyone loves change. We love to talk about change all the time. We tell others how much we have changed our life. We say, "I got a new my job," "I bought a new car," or "I am going to move into a new apartment." And we celebrate the news because we all love change. Almost every product advertised on TV promises to "change your life" if you use it. We love change. *But we do not want to be changed.* We don't like other people or forces pushing or pulling us into uninvited or unexpected new ways to live and think.

We love change, but we don't want to be changed by anyone, anything, or God Himself. Why? Because our will is stubborn, and sin is so entrenched in us that we can't overpower our own will. We cannot overpower ourselves. We cannot change what we do without first adjusting our minds about what we do. This is called "repentance," or changing the mind. Meaningful and lasting change must first begin as an internal desire of the heart to willingly and freely change the mind.

Next: *Some in the synagogue are dead set against this message. They are starting to take notice—and they are not happy.*

---

1. Luke 19:3

6

HIS AUTHORITY

When Jesus Makes His Dangerous Claim

He taught them as one who had authority and not as the scribes.

— MARK 1:22

We should wonder who else was there to hear the teaching of Jesus. The people of the town were there, as we have said. But there were others too. Since the synagogue Jesus entered an hour ago is an outpost of the massive Temple in Jerusalem—a satellite congregation, if you will—we can assume that the religious elite leaders were there also. Even though the scribes and Pharisees are never explicitly mentioned in this 24 hour period, we can be sure they were in attendance.

If they heard Jesus for the first time that morning, they would have noticed the same thing the people did: Jesus preached and taught with an unusual voice of authority. He references the authority of this "Good News" teaching based on himself as the giver of a new Law, not the Jewish Law as commonly understood. In other words, the letter of the Law was fulfilled by Jesus himself. Jesus is the new authority for the Law because he fulfilled the Law.

Not everyone will be blessed by this new idea. Enter the scribes.

Scribes were proud religious scholars with a pedigree that went back to the time of Ezra in the 4th century BC. These formidable students of the Law would later be called "Rabbi," and they became the religious elite of their era. Many were Pharisees, some were Sadducees, but the scribes made up most of the Jewish Supreme Court. One commentator wrote this of the scribes: "If some persons fear that they are too bad to be saved, this group ran the risk of believing that they were so good they did not *need* to be saved!"[1] They were meticulous religious authorities who made a very good living doing things they thought pleased God.

However, as proud and elitist as they were, they knew there was a limit to their authority. Even though they were a class of teachers unto themselves, the scribes could not teach the Law except by referring to the Law as their higher authority. In other words, the scribes would make their case by appealing to the traditional Law. They would teach and say, "As it is written...," pointing to the Jewish Law as their authority. They appealed to legal points that were settled law.

However, in Jesus' teaching and sermons—particularly in his most famous Sermon on the Mount—he first describes the Law as important but then refers to himself as a new authority. He begins his teaching with the incendiary statement: "You have heard it said...but I say to you." In saying this, Jesus pointed to *himself* as the new source of authority. He wasn't dispensing with the Law, he was fulfilling it. Out with the old (unfulfilled Law) and in with the new! And thus, he placed himself as the new authority, the one who had fulfilled what Law was intended to do: to be the gateway and the pathway to a life with God. Jesus was the door to that new life. He was the gate, as he mentions elsewhere. Jesus assured his disciples, "I am the Way, the Truth, and the Life." (John 14:6) He did not say the Way, the Truth, and the Law! In saying this, Jesus claimed he was God; he was the fulfillment of God's Law.

CHUTZPAH

What the religious leaders heard from Jesus that day set their teeth on edge. If only from this single experience at the synagogue, they had enough evidence against Jesus to bring him to trial, which they will eventually do. In fact, one of the running subplots in the gospels is the Pharisees' unbridled antipathy toward Jesus. Over 77 verses in the gospels highlight the hatred and contempt of these religious professionals toward Jesus.

For the religious elite, statements such as these—equating oneself with God—could not stand. And Jesus never ceased making them!

For example, a few weeks after this first day in the synagogue, a well-known incident occurred inside a home just down the street. A quadriplegic man had been placed before Jesus, hoping for a miracle healing. In an act of mercy, Jesus took pity on the man and declared that the paralyzed man was forgiven of his sins. Jesus said confidently, "Son, your sins are forgiven" (Mark 2:5). The Pharisees witnessed the entire event in horror. In their minds, this display was a heretical spectacle, and they were outraged by its presuppositions and presumptions. It was sacrilege! "Only God can forgive sins," they fumed.

But Jesus knew what was in their hearts. He wanted to prove himself; he wanted to prove that he had the authority of God.

And so, to show that he had the right to forgive sins, Jesus instantly cured the man of his paralysis with a single action. The man stood for the first time in years and walked! The man's physical cure proved that Jesus had the authority to claim the spiritual truth—that he *could* forgive sins as only God could.

Jesus was God, and he could exercise the authority of God and the power of God as well.

Today, a common term for Jesus' boldness is *chutzpah*, a Yiddish word for audacious self-confidence. Jesus' authority is not a derivative authority requiring another power, ruler, or body of writing to validate or authenticate it. Jesus is not God's deputy, standing in for a mightier and more powerful God. Jesus is God.

Such a claim is entirely and insanely false or wonderfully and gloriously true. This is still true.

Today, many people might consider themselves to be modestly religious; have a mild belief in God, and go about their daily lives. Their faith might represent an occasional source of wisdom, guidance, comfort, or peace for them. This is very common. Many people who believe at this level draw strength and comfort from a religious and spiritual connection with a higher power.

Christianity can also give us peace, wisdom, guidance, and comfort. But there is more to the Christian faith than these feelings. Much more. If Jesus, the man of the Gospel, is also the God and Lord of history, he is in an entirely different category or being. If this man is God and God is this man—and he is surely alive—then I can have a living personal relationship with him. And you can too. We can have a friendship with him, a tangible, real, personal, and present relationship for today and every day hereafter. If Jesus the man is also the God of history, then he puts a face on the faith, as it were.

In short, it means that I can know God, as I am even known by him! This is what the Apostle Paul meant when he wrote the Christians in Corinth, "...then I shall be know fully, even as I have been fully know" (I Corinthians 13:12).

Next: Jesus' teaching draws the ire and fire of the religious elite.

---

1. Daniel Akin, Christ-Centered Exposition Commentary, 2004. Pg. 26

7

SCANDALOUS TRUTH

How Jesus Taught the Deepest Mystery

He taught them as one who had authority and not as the scribes.

— MARK 1:22

We can use our imagination to visualize the moment in the synagogue when it dawns on the scribes that Jesus is undercutting their authority and the authority of the Law.

The murmuring begins. The tension in the room escalates. The people are shocked at Jesus' boldness, but, as we saw, they love the new teaching. However, it is too much for the scribes to take. Their murmuring gets louder. They start to squawk. They attempt to shout him down. After all, a teacher who claims to be God *must* be silenced. Such teaching could lead people astray. But more to the point, such teaching is an offense against God. His is a wild claim. Jesus teaches as one who has the authority of God in and of himself.

There is no mistaking the fact that Jesus makes a claim to be God. In his day-to-day ministry with people or his teaching near the Temple, he does not deny the claim when asked about it. He does not shrink from it when Pilate threatens to kill him. He does not hesitate to assert it when he encounters demons. His divinity becomes a continuous theme in his teaching, preaching, and lively debates with religious leaders. Jesus, the man, claimed to be the Son of God.

This claim is unique among all other religions. Neither Judaism nor Islam nor their central leaders/founders, Moses or Muhammed, make a similar claim.

Today, the belief that Jesus is both God and human is why many people, who may know about Jesus and appreciate the example of his life, do not identify themselves as Christian. They are not followers of Christ. They are his admirers only. They do not believe that Jesus is who he says he is, the Holy Son of God. He couldn't be. Such a dual nature is impossible. Jesus' claims are a bridge too far.

The objections by the scribes and religious elites of the day are understandable. Jesus' assertion that he was God and was the fulfillment of the Law and could rewrite them was a clear and present danger to those in power. These leaders enjoyed broad control over huge populations. They had the quasi-support of the Roman government. They had a monopoly on the large and profitable religious festival industry and the money that could be made at the regular observances of the Jews. They were fearful that Jesus' claims would threaten their comfort, control, or status. (History will prove their fears correct. Their religious hegemony collapsed as Jesus' followers increased and spread throughout the Roman Empire.)

THE INCARNATION

Without having the words or the theological categories to describe it yet, the scribes and Pharisees were instinctively worried about what is called today the Doctrine of the Incarnation. This pillar of Christianity holds that the Son of God took on flesh and became fully human while remaining fully God. This doctrine is so central to the Christian faith that you cannot be a Christian without subscribing to it. C. S. Lewis said that the Incarnation was the central miracle for all Christianity. "Every other miracle prepares for this, or exhibits this, or results from this (doctrine)."[1]

The implications of the Incarnation are enormous. It means that whatever Jesus said should be taken as literally God's Word. It means that what he did with his life should be imitated. And, as Jesus informed Nicodemus, the Incarnation means that "God so loved the world that he gave his only Son to the end that everyone who believes in him will not perish but have everlasting life." (John 3:16)

Behind the Doctrine of the Incarnation is one of the deepest mysteries that can be considered: that the sinful nature of our race separates us from God. Because of our sinful nature, we are all destined for an eternity without him. The reality of the Incarnation means that God chose to enter our world, identify with our sin, and, having fully identified with it, yet not succumbing to it, forgave us for it; forgave it in us.

But there is more and it is even more beautiful. The Incarnation means that there was a task to accomplish on behalf of humanity that required an extraordinary intervention on God's part: *to become a human being.* The Incarnation means that the solution to this problem required God to do something as radical and wonderful as becoming human to solve it.

The Apostle Paul later wrote that Jesus, who knew no sin, became sin for us, that we might become the righteousness of God.[2] This is astonishing!

The coming of the Son of God as a man was not intended to teach us good things and better ways to live. Those are good reasons, but they are not glorious enough to warrant the Incarnation. There was a tremendous task that God wanted to accomplish that only a divine being could, but a task that only a human being should. God had to come as God to do what only God could, and God had to come as a man to do only what man should. This is the mystery and miracle of the Incarnation.

Jesus fulfilled both roles—God and man—and therefore deserves our worship and praise.

These higher thoughts do not occur to the objectors listening to Jesus' teaching this morning in Capernaum. They are offended by his claim to have the authority of God. They cannot imagine that Jesus, who preaches this morning in the small Capernaum synagogue in front of only a few dozen people, is the divine ruler and judge and will save millions and millions of people as their Savior and Lord. All this is in play the day Jesus comes to the synagogue and teaches the people of Capernaum.

Next: *Another objection comes quickly. This one is from the Devil itself.*

---

1. Miracles, Chapter 14
2. 2 Corinthians 5:21

8

UNCLEAN SPIRITS

When the Evil Opposition Arrives

*And immediately, there was in their synagogue a man
with an unclean spirit.*

— MARK 1:23

Before we address the arrival of the unclean spirit, allow me a few words about terminology and Satan. For the remainder of this book, I will use a literary device—a useful word tool—to refer to unclean spirits and forces of evil. I will assign the pronoun "it" to the Devil and all other evil forces. I am doing this for the sake of clarity and precision. The Devil, by nature, is sexless and without gender. It does not need to be dignified with such a beautiful gender specific pronoun as "he" or "she".

The Devil is not made in the image of God. Nor is it a competing deity to our Lord. This is not treating Satan like a myth. For Jesus, it was very real: there is a dark, quasi-personal, spiritual force waging a fruitless war it has already lost against our God. Calling it "it" is the very least we can do for it.

Now, let us pick up the story at the synagogue. Step by step, we are tracing Jesus' activity on his first day in Capernaum. As he enters the synagogue to teach the people, we can imagine that silence falls upon everyone. The words of the Lord carry a weight and a command that quiets every person in attendance. We have assumed (reasonably) that the scribes and the Pharisees are in the meeting room too. They are silenced. But it is the silence of the dumbfounded. They vehemently object to Jesus' teaching but can't stop it. They have never heard such blasphemy. What will happen? They are not sure what can be done. The pressure to do something increases as Jesus continues his teaching. Something must give.

But then, suddenly, the situation becomes more complicated. Not only does Jesus astonish the crowd with his authority, but just when tensions and tempers are high, another man enters the synagogue.

It seems that he enters quickly. Or was the man already there? We are not told. But we are told that he has an unclean spirit. Unexpectedly, the tension between Jesus and the Pharisees slackens for a few moments, but it is replaced by the apprehensive presence of an aggressive man. We know that a public confrontation is about to take place between the unclean spirit and the Lord.

The phrase "unclean spirit" and other terms that refer to the supernatural, active presence of the Devil is used nearly 70 times in the New Testament. This makes the Devil, demons, and unclean spirits one of the leading opponents of the ministry of Jesus and of the church in the Book of Acts. It doesn't have a small part in the biblical drama. It is a major player.

Jesus is not intimidated by the appearance of this possessed man. Remember, he recently spent 40 days in the wilderness, tempted by Satan. The threat from the possessed man in the synagogue is, for Jesus, mild.

In Jesus' mind, the Devil is not a metaphor. The Devil is a real, singular force. It is the leading cause of disease, disability, physical and spiritual suffering, blindness, deafness, epilepsy, fever, and death. In the gospels, the main category of negative impact from the Devil is mental illness, but the Devil is responsible for much more. Jesus believes that all suffering—all disease and death—is the Devil's work.

This does not mean that all those who suffer in any way or have ailments or diseases or those with a disability or handicap are possessed by an evil spirit. Not at all. It is much simpler than that. Jesus believes that all suffering and brokenness in the world is the result of the devastating work of the Devil ever since the early beginnings of our race. He believed it was responsible for all human suffering, every catastrophe, and each death.

In other words, since the Fall, we have lived in a fallen world where things fall apart.

In our day, we have come to believe that illness, suffering, disease, defects, and death are permanent features of human life. They will be with us forever. We think this is nature's way—all things age, wither, rust, rot, and die. We are so used to this; that we believe it is the universal reality of the cosmos. And Jesus agrees. It is objectively true. It is universal. All things die and turn to dust. For now.

However, Jesus would not fix the blame for this on the laws of nature or the inexorable ways of an indifferent universe. He believes there is a fundamental flaw in all creation and it needs to be healed. Things need to be set right. Jesus knows it can only be set right if the Devil is ultimately put down—vanquished—finally and fully defeated by and through the Cross.

THE BATTLE BEGINS NOW

Today, in Capernaum, an important battle begins. It is only a small confrontation between the Lord Jesus and the unclean spirit. But, like many first battles and skirmishes, it will lead to all-out war.

As we read the stories of Jesus and his encounters with the Devil, we find that Jesus meets the Devil without hesitation. In the desert, perhaps only weeks before, Jesus was assailed by it. He engaged Satan personally and dismissed the temptations. They were shortcuts to what Jesus would receive anyway. However, in the account of this ordeal in the desert, Luke's Gospel says something ominous. He writes that the Devil withdrew from tempting Jesus for a more suitable time.[1]

This is a very revealing comment. It means that the Devil has a plan to take out Jesus—it wants to kill him—and it is hell-bent to make it happen. In the desert, Jesus was on the defensive; the Devil tempted him. But that would never happen again; Jesus gained the offensive there and he keeps gaining ground.

With this last point in mind, there is another way to read the encounter in the synagogue that sheds a better light on what happened there. It might be that Jesus *knew* the unclean spirit would be there. He knew that unclean spirits need a host or a home base, as it were. Perhaps Jesus went to the synagogue to confront the Devil, overcome it, and initiate the battle. Jesus is not on defense; maybe he is playing pure offense.

Given the numerous encounters Jesus had with Satan and demons, it makes sense that the synagogue encounter was not a coincidence. Jesus goes to the synagogue, knowing it will be there.

―――――

Next: Jesus plans to bring the fight to the enemy, and he knows where to find it.

―――――

1. Luke 4:13

9

THE STRONGMAN

What Jesus Believes about the Devil

And he cried out, "What have you to do with us, Jesus of
Nazareth? Have you come to destroy us? I know who
you are—the Holy One of God".

— MARK 1:24

Most of us would be terrified of the dramatic events at the synagogue at Capernaum. Our church services are usually very uneventful; our church is safe. But not on this first day of Jesus' ministry. On this inaugural day, he takes on the evil power of what he would later call "the prince of this world." (John 12:31; 14:30; 16:11). Let's set aside the question about what we believe concerning the Devil for a moment. It is far more important for us to know what Jesus thought about the Devil, and there is plenty of information about this in the gospels.

As I said earlier, it is impossible to understand the entire ministry of Jesus without admitting and accepting that Jesus is an exorcist. He cast out demons 12 times in the Gospels of Matthew, Mark, and Luke. In addition, in sending out the disciples to exercise their ministry, Jesus gave them power over unclean spirits. And they would need that power.

It is interesting to note that there are very few instances of evil spirits and demonic harassment in the Old Testament. But now, with the announcement of the Kingdom by the new King Jesus, evil spirits and malevolent forces suddenly appear. If the disciples were to advance the Kingdom, they would need spiritual protection and power. There is no mistaking it: a spiritual battle is being waged in the age of the New Testament.

So, what does Jesus believe about the Devil, and should his followers believe that? Let's see.

As we know, Jesus used parables and stories to teach profound truths. The metaphors and images within parables are not always benign, sweet stories. They can describe an exact, important point Jesus wants to make. In understanding what Jesus believed about the Devil, consider the following story or parable as told by the Lord.

Jesus routinely cast out demons from possessed people. Once a Pharisee accused Jesus of casting out demons by using the power of Beelzebub (another name for Satan). The man accused Jesus of fighting evil with evil—thus saying that Jesus was evil. Jesus dismissed the charge. He said, "If a kingdom is divided against itself, it could not stand" (Mark 3:24). He meant that all kingdoms, including evil dominions, need unified leadership. If households or empires are at odds internally, they will collapse externally. We know this is true. The aphorism "united we stand, divided we fall" is as old as Aesop.

A STRONGER STRONGMAN

But then Jesus extended the analogy. He imagined a strongman's house full of possessions. The property and possessions are held and controlled with an iron fist. They are his. The property belongs to the strongman, or so he thinks. But Jesus says there is only one way to free the goods held hostage. The only way to break a strongman's iron grip on the possessions is for a stronger man to enter the house, overpower the occupant, and bind him securely. Only then can the second and stronger man take control, break the occupant's iron grip, take the goods, and free them.

In this extended metaphor, Jesus reveals the broad strokes of his strategic plan against the Devil. We are in Satan's grip. Jesus knows that the Son of God has come and is the stronger man. Jesus plans to seize the weaker man, tie it up firmly, and take things away from its control. It is a simple plan. In the rest of the gospel stories, when Jesus meets an unclean spirit or a demon, he will bind the demon and free those held captive by it.

This is the Lord's mindset when he walks into the synagogue at Capernaum. This firm and confident attitude has the desired effect on the unclean spirit in the man. It starts to panic. It is afraid of Jesus. It is worried about what Jesus will do. "Have you come to destroy us?" (Mark 1:24). These screams of desperation come from a being who knows that its time is up; its days are numbered.

The question—have you come to destroy us? —is a dumb question. Of course, Jesus came to destroy it! Jesus comes to find the Devil and demonstrate his superior strength over it. He intends to conquer the enemy. As the parable reveals, the Lord binds the evil one, strips it of its strength, renders it helpless, and frees its possessions.

On the first day of the ministry of Jesus, the Lord engaged the Devil with this strategy in mind. Time and time again, wherever Jesus sees the effects of the Devil in play, he acts this way. He frees a demon-possessed man. He casts demons out of suffering people. He heals illnesses attributable to Satan's work. In truth, all the healings, exorcisms, miracles, teachings, and spiritual confrontations that Jesus has over his three years, beginning on this day in Capernaum—all these actions are oddly random, scattered, and incoherent until we see them all as strategic acts of war.

Christians today should bear this in mind. Jesus came and fought the battle against the evil one. And he won. Today, the strongman is still alive. It is noticeably active. But it is inert. It is tied up securely, as Jesus' metaphor explains. It will intimidate believers, but we should remember that the Devil is utterly exposed without protection. It has no superior strength. Jesus defeated it. And the property it once owned (you and me) has been set free.

In my view, we should strive to believe what Jesus believed about the Devil. No more, and certainly no less.

We will see later that the Devil is homeless. But as we see now, it is also defenseless. And by the strategic assaults of Jesus—and by his dying and rising again—it will be defeated.

Next: *The unclean spirit doesn't take defeat lying down.*

10

THE CONFRONTATION

What the Devil Believes about Jesus

*And the demon cried out, "What have you to do with us,
Jesus of Nazareth? Have you come to destroy us? I
know who you are—the Holy One of God".*

— MARK 1:24

J esus has been slow to move on from the encounter with the
unclean spirit. They are demanding a lot of attention. In the
middle of the public service, they scream out to Jesus. This
is such a dramatic moment—and the first of its kind—that we
should look at it closely. After all, the Devil is in the details here.

Remember that the sermon Jesus preached in the synagogue had
a simple, clear message of hope: *the long wait is over; the Kingdom is
here, so repent and believe!* Perhaps it was the clarity of Jesus's explanation, the conviction of his proclamation, or the intensity of his

passion that bothers the demons. Clearly, something has pushed them over the edge. There will be a consequence.

The demon-possessed man interrupts the service in the middle of Sabbath worship with a loud, violent scream. Using the human voice of its host, it demands to know if Jesus came to destroy it. They know the Son of God is an existential threat to their kind. And they are right.

With their statements, the screaming demons are telling us more than we first think. Read what the Devils say carefully: "What have you to do with us, Jesus of Nazareth? Have you come to destroy us? I know who you are—the Holy One of God."

This statement reveals several things about the demons to us.

First, we can see that the demon admits that it is not alone. They are plural. They are acting in league with other evil forces in the spiritual realm. There are others.

Secondly, they know Jesus. The carpenter might have been somewhat known in this newly adopted hometown Capernaum, but he was very well known to the evil spirits. They knew Jesus was raised in Nazareth; it calls him "Jesus of Nazareth.". Many people in the Galilean area knew the popular, local, disparaging saying about the Lord's hometown: "Can anything good come from Nazareth?" (John 1:46). Was the demon trying to disparage the Lord by reminding people of his humble beginnings? Are they inferring that Jesus came from the wrong side of the tracks?

Thirdly, and quite amazingly, the demon admits that it knows about the divinity of Christ! It understands the plan set in motion three decades earlier when Gabriel first visited Mary. On that occasion, the angel of the Lord told Mary about her Son. He said,

"The Holy Spirit will come upon you, and the power of the Most High will overshadow you; therefore, the child to be born will be called holy— the Son of God." (Luke 1:35)

Here, in the synagogue at Capernaum, three decades later, the demon was screaming out the complete identity of Jesus using Gabriel's _exact_ words! The demons knew about Jesus. It knew who he was!

Strange as it is, the demon is the first to believe the essential doctrines of the faith. Namely, that Jesus is fully man and fully God. When the Devil has its outburst in the synagogue, it reveals both natures of Jesus. Jesus is called Jesus of Nazareth, and also the Holy One of God. The demon fully admits that Jesus is the Son of God, the holy child that they all feared was coming into the world. This panicked awareness terrifies the unclean spirits.

TRUE BELIEVER?

It is interesting to note that the most informed, knowledgeable, religiously schooled entity in the synagogue, aside from Jesus, is the Devil himself. And he is also the evilest one in the room. And it shows us that what the scribes do not yet understand in full, the demons believe wholeheartedly. That Jesus is the Divine Son of God.

This situation with the demons show us something quite disturbing. It shows us that it's possible to know that Jesus is the man from Nazareth and the Holy Son of God, yet still not budge or be impacted. We should understand this as an apt warning for us: just because we know that something is true in an objective sense, as the demon did about the identity of Jesus, we can still ignore, discount, postpone, or even forget about it.

On this first day of Jesus' ministry, the Lord confronts the unclean spirit in the man. He will expel it. It is the shape of things to come for the evil forces. The Devil will continue to be overpowered, overwhelmed, and outmaneuvered until the end when our Savior is on the Cross. Then, it will be overcome.

The encounter that Jesus had with this unclean spirit gives us reason to think about how comfortable we are today with what Jesus did then. It is a personal question that this story poses to each of us. How much of his ministry can we embrace, believe in, and apply in our lives?

We know he was called to preach and teach, to announce the coming of the Kingdom. We love his sermons and lessons. We know he is a preacher. And we also know he is a healer. As he moves on, there will be a wake of happy, healthy people behind him. Praise God for this!

But only a few today are comfortable with the Lord exercising his third role: he casts out demons.

This last role of Jesus is difficult to embrace in today's world of science and materialism. Many of us are accustomed to blaming the reality of evil on human choices, systemic injustice, blind fate, or bad luck. But Jesus' engagement with the forces of darkness and unclean spirits forces us to ask a few other questions. Namely, how many of the bad things that happen to people directly result from the impact or the influences of a real, spiritual demonic presence? Or, is there a spiritual force of wickedness that rebels against God, his creation and the creatures he has made? And if there is such a force, how comfortable are we in knowing that Jesus spent an outsized portion of his time in confrontation and engagement with this evil power?

As we think about Jesus' first day of ministry in Capernaum, we must consider that it is nearly impossible to understand the mission of Jesus without coming to terms with the fact of the Devil, Satan, and the nature of evil. If we are to understand what Jesus did and why he did it—and how he did it—we cannot avoid looking at the Devil. As we discover on this first day, Jesus had a plan to confront the demons of this world and overturn their rule.

Next: *There is more coming from Jesus. He needs only to speak, and the battle is won.*

11

THE REBUKE

How Jesus Evicts the Unclean Spirit

But Jesus rebuked him, saying, "Be silent, and come out of him!" And the unclean spirit, convulsing him and crying out with a loud voice, came out of him.

— MARK 1:25

As we just saw, the unclean spirit is the first to express the great mystery of the Christian faith that Jesus is both human and divine. This scene at the synagogue is a remarkable moment for that reason alone. But another important reason to pay attention to this close encounter is what happens next. Jesus confronts the unclean spirit and casts it out.

The confrontation between them is a fantastic spectacle. We do not know precisely how it happened moment by moment, but we can imagine the scenario.

The exorcism of the unclean spirit is sudden and violent. It is loud. With only a few words spoken clearly and authoritatively over it— "Be silent and come out of him"—the unclean spirit convulses the man's body, screams through his throat, and, in an instant, is gone. It is cast out.

Having been host to this evil spirit for some time, the man lays flat on the synagogue floor, exhausted, panting heavily, weeping with relief. He might be curled up in a fetal position, but he is free. The poor man is likely stunned, in traumatic shock. Perhaps Jesus comes to the man's side and touches him; maybe he places his hand on his forehead to soothe his mind, providing comfort and peace. Does he grasp the man's hand to help him to his feet? Is the man able to stand on his own? Does the Lord embrace him and let his power enter the newly freed man?

The clash is seen and heard by everyone in attendance. Jesus' bold and explicit command, and the sudden release of the man by the unclean spirit, push the congregation into a frenzy. As Jesus attends to the man, the people break out with a cacophony of loud whoops, shouts, cheers, and exclamations of praise and wonder. They see the power of God emanate from Jesus of Nazareth, who, only minutes earlier, had been preaching and teaching in their synagogue. First, they could not believe their ears—the teaching of the Lord was astonishing. But now, are their eyes betraying them? They can't believe that they see! They look around the room where the incident happened and speak excitedly. "What is this?" some ask. Others say, "A new teaching with authority!" Still, others shout over the entire congregation for everyone to hear, "He commands even the unclean spirits, and they obey him!" (Mark 1: 27)

TWO TAKEAWAYS

We can take away two important truths from this encounter in this vignette. First, Jesus has absolute and total power over every force of darkness. For example, after its initial screaming about Jesus, the unclean spirit never speaks again. Jesus "muzzles" it (the Greek word) and does not allow the demon to say anything further. In a short, two-word phrase, Jesus orders the Devil to "be gone." And it is gone. Done!

In other words, Jesus doesn't need to pray extensive prayers and petitions. He doesn't offer any lengthy incantations. He does not speak on behalf of a power greater than himself. He is able to forcefully exorcized the demon from the poor, oppressed soul.

The second thing we take from this story is the nature and capacity of the Devil. Namely, the man's possession in the synagogue reveals the Devil's ability and creativity. They are nil. It has nothing of its own. It needs a host body. The Devil needs to piggyback on someone or something else to do anything.

The story of the Garden of Eden first introduces Satan as a crafty serpent. But note how little the snake can do. It was a parasite in paradise. It has no creative power. It can't make anything of its own. It can only distort or corrupt the things God has already made. The Devil is a cruel reality responsible for misery and mayhem today. But it has nothing of its own to use. All it can do is corrupt God's creation, capitalize on the world's fallen state, and use it to amplify terror and pain and cause rebellion against God.

For example, in the Book of Job, the terrible forces that Satan hurled upon Job's family were not its creations. The destroying winds, the consuming fires, and the murderous marauders did not originate with Satan; they were corruptions of the forces and people God had already made.

Even though the Devil is subject to Jesus in every way, and though it has nothing of its own, much of our culture today is under its dominating spell. There is no question that what is going on in the world today has all the hallmarks and fingerprints of an evil force. And Christians should be very clear on their response to its work in the world. Christians should know about what the King James Bible called the "wiles of the Devil." (Eph. 6:11) In other words, believers should know what they believe about the Devil.

This event in the synagogue should show us that Jesus has the power and the authority to speak to the Devil directly. We do not need to engage in lengthy arguments or verbal jousts with an unclean spirit or demonic force. Instead, when we are tempted or sorely tried, we can ask the Lord to come to our side and speak boldly on our behalf. He will say, in effect, "Be gone!" And with that, it will be gone.

Next: *The crowd heard him, but would they listen to him?*

12

HIS REPUTATION

Why Jesus's Message Goes Viral

*And at once, his fame spread everywhere throughout all
the surrounding region of Galilee.*

— MARK 1:28

As Jesus leaves the synagogue, having taught the Good News
and defeated the demons, Jesus hopes that people will
primarily remember the lessons of the sermon, not the spectacle
of the exorcism. It is not to be. The excitement in the building is
palpable. People witnessed something they never expected, especially at their small, out-of-the-way synagogue, a seven-day walk
north from the Jerusalem Temple. Regarding religious teaching
and public displays, the Holy City was usually the center of the
world—but not today. Today, Capernaum was in the spotlight.
What an amazing thing happened there.

News travels fast, but earth-shattering news travels even faster. The report that Jesus defeated the demons would have been passed from traveler to traveler along the roads. Capernaum then became home to a swelling crowd of people. The masses were full of peasants, farmers, fishermen, and families. In other words, people from the lower class of the locals. There were also hated tax collectors in the crowd, scorned prostitutes, and those unfortunate souls whom the religious leaders collectively called "sinners." The growing group was a mixed bag of religions and races, including Israelites, Judeans, Galileans, and even some Roman citizens.

Before the experience in the synagogue, Jesus and his disciples were alone for the first few days after he called them from their fishing fleets. Afterward, he joined the people gathered at the synagogue in relative obscurity. But then he became famous, and large crowds followed him daily. From this point in the story, and for the rest of Jesus' ministry, there were crowds of people everywhere hoping to hear what he has to say and to see what he does. He is extraordinarily successful in drawing a crowd. But that is not what he wants.

Jesus was ambivalent about crowds. While the most famous incident involving the public was on Palm Sunday when they betrayed him, earlier in his ministry, the crowds protected him. The Pharisees were always on the watch, waiting for Jesus to slip up and say something or do something that broke Jewish Law. But the crowd had his back. They protected him from malicious attacks by the authorities.

When Jesus ate with the crowds, the Pharisees accused him of being drunk and gluttonous, and again he was shielded from attack by those around him. When Jesus extended mercy to someone in the crowd, the Pharisees labeled him a blasphemer.

They wanted to take him in, but the multitudes' support of Jesus kept him safe for a time. In a way, Jesus was saved from his adversaries because of the masses of people; they were like a force field around the Savior—that is, until the last week of his life. Then they became a mob.

As the message of Jesus' healing powers and persuasive preaching went viral, the crowds that followed him grew bigger than they could easily be handled. This was when things started to get complicated.

A CROWD ALLERGY

A few Gospels say that he loved crowds of people. He looked over one large group of people gathered to hear him, and he felt deep compassion. The gospel writers describe it literally: his *guts moved* with pity. He saw the great groups of people as "sheep without a shepherd." (Mark 6:34)

On another occasion, he addressed a smaller group with a message meant for anyone in any crowd. His message is unmistakably loving:

> *"Come to me, all you who are weary and burdened, and I will give you rest. Take my yoke upon you and learn from me, for I am gentle and humble in heart, and you will find rest for your souls. For my yoke is easy, and my burden is light." (Matt. 11:28-30)*

His relationship with crowds of people grew complicated as they increased in size. The crowd in the well-known story of the loaves and fish was the same crowd that pursued him earlier and from which he was trying to escape.[1] Indeed, at some level, we can understand why he didn't always like crowds. He couldn't trust them. He loved the people in the masses, but he knew what could be in people's hearts when they met in masses.[2] And, as we see in the Palm Sunday betrayal, the crowd became dangerous for Jesus.

Fame was never the intent of our Lord. Frequently, after Jesus performed a miracle for someone in a crowd, he would tell them to keep quiet about it and tell no one what happened. Unlike most modern leaders, he did *not* want his reputation to precede him. Scholars often refer to this hesitation to go viral as the "Messianic Secret," and Jesus wanted to keep it. He tried to keep his miracle cures and feats a private matter.

Why does Jesus have an apparent ambivalence toward large crowds? The reason appears evident to us when we think about it. Crowds can be selfish. Base instincts emerge from large groups and anonymous gatherings. With minimal prompting, crowds can become hysterical. Crowds provide concealment and protect people from being held accountable for their actions. In the world of social media today, many people have been canceled by anonymous crowds and Twitter mobs. In only a few hours in Jerusalem on Sunday before the Passover, the crowds moved from crying out, "Hosanna!" to demanding his execution.

For this reason, Jesus never followed a crowd. He didn't trust them; crowds often had a mind of their own. This is in part what makes Christianity a difficult and often lonely way to live. When a believer longs for connection and comfort in a group of people —to be known and accepted—they must be aware that sometimes (often) group-think can often smudge clear lines between right, wrong, good, bad, or wise.

Finally, Jesus did not want anyone attracted to him because of his work but because of who he was. He did not want people so eager to see, receive, or "get" a miracle that they missed the Gospel's message. It was never about fame. It was always about faith.

Next: *Leaving the crowds behind for a moment, the ministry of Jesus gets very personal.*

---

1. Mark 6:30–40
2. John 2:23–25

13

THE VISITATION

When Jesus Enters the Home of a Friend

*And immediately, he left the synagogue and entered the
house of Simon and Andrew with James and John.*

— MARK 1:29

We have come through the very tense moments in the synagogue between the Pharisees and the scribes, the unclean spirit and the suffering man, and the presence of the Lord. When it was all over, Jesus left the building.

As the crowd dispersed after worship, they went to their homes. They must. It is the Sabbath. Jesus leaves the house of worship, too. He is moving on to the next opportunity to show the power of the Kingdom, and we are going with him, step by step. Shortly after he leaves the synagogue, he enters the house of Simon and Andrew. The other two recruits, John and James, are with him.

Remember, these men were new to the mission of Christ. They have been summoned to follow him only recently. They heard Jesus' sermon in the synagogue. Was it the first time they heard Jesus teach? They witnessed the extraordinary events of the exorcism. Had they ever seen anything like that? Without question, they would have been amazed at the spiritual power of their new leader. And, if we consider they are freshmen-level leaders at this point, what did they make of Jesus' promise that they would be fishers of men in a much larger way? We can imagine that all these ideas and questions swirled around the minds of these four disciples right after the synagogue moment.

And who is this unnamed woman? We know she is Peter's mother-in-law. A further answer requires some imagination. It is not far-fetched to say that she was both wife to Zebedee and, thus, mother to James and John (who were with them) and also mother to Peter's wife! She may well have been a sister to Jesus' mother, Mary.

We should also ask why Jesus went to Peter's house. Archeologists tell us that the synagogue was close to Peter's home, and Sabbath laws strongly suggested that everyone stay in their homes on the Sabbath, except for attendance at the synagogue. (Ex. 16:29) Peter's house was convenient.

But there is a more fundamental reason why Jesus went to Peter's house. He was invited.

When we surveyed the gospel accounts of Jesus, we read that Jesus always went where he was invited. One family asked him to a wedding in Cana of Galilee.[1] He went happily and took others, including his mother. When he was invited to come to Jairus's house in the foothills of Capernaum and heal his young daughter, he went immediately.[2] In Luke's Gospel, a wealthy and generous resident of Capernaum, a Centurion, asked Jesus to come to his home to heal a servant. Jesus left right away.[3] He went where he was invited.

INVITATION

Sometimes, miraculous moments occur when Jesus came upon a human need by chance or circumstance. We know that he did not address every spiritual and physical need he saw; there wasn't enough time. However, in every case, when Jesus was invited to attend, come over, dine, or be in someone's home, he went. Every time. In the story in Capernaum just cited, he even responded to someone he didn't know—but who knew him and desperately called him for help.

There is a very touching scene in Jericho that is recorded in the Gospel of Mark.[4] It involves a blind man well-known to Sunday school children: Blind Bartimaeus. His story highlights Jesus' willingness to come to the aid or help of an individual when asked.

The blind beggar in the story was living out his dark days on the Jericho roadside outside the city. Jesus, traveling south from the Galilee region, made one last journey through Jericho to Jerusalem. Near this location where the unsighted man was seated, Jesus was baptized in the Jordan three years earlier.

The beggar Bartimaeus sat on the side of the road, pleading for food and sustenance from passers-by. Somehow, he heard that Jesus was nearby, and the blind man, oblivious to the crowd of people and the scorn of the disciples, cried out in a loud voice, "Jesus, Son of David, have mercy on me!" The disciples would have none of that! His loud outbursts annoyed them, and they tried to quiet the hungry, blind man. But the man persisted and shouted his request again. When Jesus heard the man's cry, he stopped. The rest of the event is best described by Mark himself:

"And Jesus stopped and said, 'Call him.' And they called the blind man, saying, 'Take heart. Get up; he is calling you.' And throwing off his cloak, he sprang up and came to Jesus. And Jesus said to him, 'What do you want me to do for you?' And the blind man said, 'Rabbi, let me recover my sight.' And Jesus said to him, 'Go your way; your faith has made you well.' And he immediately recovered his sight and followed him on the way." (Mark 10:46ff)

Do you see the honest and sincere compassion of the Lord for this man? They had not met before. The man's request was passionate and determined. And when he asked, the Lord responded. It is one more example of the Lord's openness to the cries of those who love, need, or believe in him. In short, as we have said, Jesus will go wherever he is invited.

Given what we learned about Jesus and the vagaries of crowds in the previous chapter, we should add one more point. Jesus always responded to the personal requests of individual people. He responded to their personal, human needs. But he never followed the crowd or submitted to their demands.

Next: *The Lord goes to Peter's home, but Peter never asks him to do what he does next.*

1.
2. Mark 5:22-24
3. Luke 7:1-10
4. Mark 10:46

14

REAL MIRACLES

When Jesus Meets Peter's Mother-in-Law

*Now Simon's mother-in-law lay ill with a fever, and
immediately they told him about her.*

— MARK 1:30

As we trace the steps of Jesus on the first day of his public ministry, we see him show dominance over the spiritual forces. He has taken control of the demonic spirits in the synagogue with confidence and authority. The unclean spirit renders a plea, *nolo contendere*, no contest. It doesn't admit guilt; it simply takes the punishment. As we have seen earlier, it has not finished with Jesus. It withdrew and waited for a more suitable time.

As Jesus enters Simon Peter's home, he meets Simon's mother-in-law, who is sick with a fever. This is no small thing in the ancient world. In the time of Jesus, there was little medical care. Cuts, scrapes, and common problems that are addressed quickly in today's world might be severe enough in the ancient world to kill through infection or opportunistic diseases. People died from less than this woman had.

In this home, in one of the most tender scenes in the gospels, Jesus takes control of the physical forces askew in her body and restores her to health. The first miracle of the day was the public freeing of the man from the unclean spirit. This personal healing is the second miracle, and both divine interventions will unleash a flood of needs and requests right after sunset. But for now, we can think about all the public, private, spiritual, and physical miracles Jesus performed in all of his ministry.

In the gospel stories, there are four kinds of miracles that Jesus did in his ministry.

- *There are miracles over nature.* These would include the weather-related work of Jesus: walking on water, speaking to, and calming the storm.
- *There are miracles of provision and supply.* Jesus' multiplication of loaves and fish is his most public and famous miracle. Changing water to wine is another well-known example.
- *There are miracles of physical healing.* Most of Jesus' miracles are in this category. Matthew's Gospel records that Jesus went around preaching and teaching in all the synagogues around Galilee and "healing every disease and every affliction among the people." Jesus even raises the dead on three different occasions.
- *There are miracles over demonic forces at work in the world.* We have seen this previously in the synagogue.

These four different categories are not firmly defined. For example, we can imagine that those with physical needs are also under the spell of unclean spirits.

FOUR ARENAS OF HUMAN NEED

If we stand back and consider these four arenas of miraculous work, we see that these areas closely touch our individual lives. The miracles of Jesus were solutions to genuine problems we have. First, we need safety and shelter from outside physical forces of weather. We must have a safe place to live, protected from forces of nature. Secondly, we require sufficient food and water; we need to have sustenance. Thirdly, as we age, we need a way of getting through various illnesses and infirmities. We need adequate health care. And finally, we need to live free from fear, oppression, and spiritual danger. None of us want to take on the Devil and fight against the powers of the unseen spiritual world. We want protection from evil.

These four arenas: safe harbor, regular nutrition, health care, and spiritual security—are the four things that make life livable. Indeed, we should pity anyone who does not have all of these. Further, we do not need only one or two of them—we need them all.

These are the four essential areas of human life where Jesus focused his miraculous power. People would have ignored Jesus if he had come preaching the Good News of God but could not address these human needs. The public would have regarded him as just another sophist, preacher, or grifter with some vague pronouncement of a different religious system or a new way of thinking.

Even still, for all the miracles he did (all four Gospels record only 38 different miracles), the signs and wonders of Jesus were not the purposes of his ministry. They were not the focus of his time on earth; they are not today. The Christian faith is not characterized by miracle provisions, physical healings, or revelatory signs and wonders. Sure, many people want to see demonstrations of the power of the Christian faith. We want to see miraculous events occur in these four categories—or perhaps only one, just once! But miracles, as we will hear Jesus say later, are not the reason he came; it is certainly not what we should demand of him today.

Some people believe that power demonstrations and miraculous moments would increase the number of Christian believers. But we have evidence that miracles, signs, and wonders do not produce faith in Christ. They do not foster obedience to him. Not at all. There are exceptions in the Bible; there are accounts of people healed by our Lord, and then becoming a disciple.

But generally speaking, feasting on miracles is too rich a diet to bring lasting faith to us. If they happen, miracles can foster faith; but they will seldom build it.

This is the lesson from Capernaum itself. They were front-row witnesses to the power and glory of the Lord's public ministry. After months and months of the ministry of healing the sick and suffering, teaching in the streets, preaching from the mountain-top, and watching their town grow with an ever-widening sphere of influence, they yawned. They believed in Jesus. That is certain. But they were unwilling to repent as Jesus had told them. They believed in him, but they didn't believe him. Jesus said that though they had seen signs and wonders that would have brought repentance to Sodom, they were still in their sin. "For if the mighty works done in you had been done in Sodom, it would have remained until this day." (Matt. 11:23)

The town where Jesus anchored his ministry, the ground-zero community that witnessed major miracles more than any other town, did not believe. They did not repent. In the end, Jesus cursed the town for its hard-heartedness, faithlessness, and pride.

Next: The sick woman is healed by his touch and his word. Maybe both!

15

THE HEALING

How Three Different Stories Tell the Same Story

And he came and took her by the hand and lifted her up...

— MARK 1:31

S tep by step, we continue with Jesus through the first full day of his earthly ministry, as recorded in the Gospel of Mark. He has already astonished the people of the synagogue with his authority in teaching and his power over demons. They must have known that the sleepy fishing town would soon be center stage for much more.

Then, after the service, when Jesus enters Simon Peter's home, he notices that the mother-in-law of his newest recruit is sick with fever. The story reads as if there is some familiarity between Jesus and the woman. He knows her. They likely met on one of Jesus' early trips to Capernaum. In any event, Jesus does not hesitate—he immediately cures her illness. She is instantly freed from her suffering. We see, without a doubt, that the potent power of the Lord that can cast out a demon is safe enough to tenderly heal an older woman's body and restore her to health.

It is a very human and gentle story. And it is made warmer and more touching when we read some of the corroborating details as told in the other gospels.

One account says that Peter's family "requested him" to come and perform healing. Would Jesus come? (Of course, we now know he does.) Two stories confirm that Jesus touched the sick woman. Mark says he "took her by the hand and raised her." Luke, the physician, gives more detail about her illness. He called it a "violent fever."

Matthew, Mark, and Luke describe the same healing moment differently. Matthew reveals that Jesus touched her to heal her. Mark focuses on the touch and progressive movement: as she sits up with the Lord's help, she is healed. In other words, the fever lefts her when she makes the effort to sit up. Luke says that Jesus audibly spoke to the fever and rebuked it, as he rebuked the demons in the synagogue in his version and as he will rebuke the wind and waves later on the Sea of Galilee. Three different accounts of the story. Three methods of healing in the story. But one result: she is healed.

Jesus used a variety of methods to heal people. Sometimes he spoke. Sometimes he touched. Once, he told a blind man in Jerusalem to bathe in the pool of Siloam. Another time, he told a leper to show himself to the priests, and as the leper went, he was cleansed. In Bethsaida, he made a mud paste with dirt and spit, smeared it in the eyes of a blind man, and asked him if he could see. The man could see, but just barely. Jesus touched him again, and it worked the second time! The point is this: the methods Jesus used were unique and appropriate to the situation. The varied techniques spotlighted the power and faith of the Healer, not the mechanics of how it was done.

HOW IT HAPPENS

When we zoom out from these story and focus on other miracles of Jesus, we can be challenged, even surprised to learn that there are different accounts of the same story. The story of an event is told differently in different gospel accounts. What can modern readers make of this discrepancy and disparity between the Gospels? Shouldn't there be uniformity? Can't the gospel writers get the facts straight? Can Good News be "fake news"?

Some people might prefer a clear, news-reel type of unified replay where everything is harmonized, and there are no discrepancies or different perspectives. This is what we have come to expect (or hope) from news reporters. But a blended account like that would not give us the stereoscopic vision of who Jesus is and what he did. Our understanding of Jesus' life and ministry is richer and more remarkable because of these different accounts, timelines, emphases, and versions of his ministry.

Yet, this can be a challenge for us, to be sure. With our scientific worldview today, we are taught to look for corroborating facts, exact details, and clear and clean answers to the questions: how did this event occur? Where did it happen? Who was there?

The Gospel writers were men from the ancient world with a very different world-view. They knew that a critical event had happened—a miracle had occurred—and word of mouth repeatedly conveyed the story's details. They knew that Jesus had healed (in this case) Peter's mother-in-law. But each of them wrote the story as they had heard it—as it had been told to them —and as they wanted to have their audience understand it. They could never have imagined that someday, someone, somewhere, would like to know precisely how a miracle took place. To Mark, Matthew, and Luke, those details were not critical to the truth of a story or what that story meant in the life of the Early Church.

That the event happened was indisputable according to eyewitness testimony. But exactly *how* it happened is somewhat veiled in the mists of time

Those of us today who demand scientific accuracy for every event in the Bible might one day, after careful study and examination, discover exact methods and specific means to explain a miracle— but then miss its meaning. The stories of the miracles we read about in any of the Gospels are not meant to answer our modern questions but to prove points to ancient readers. In this case, each of the Gospel accounts of this specific miracle proves the point that Jesus had the power to heal in a very personal and private way.

Next: *Healing happened every time when Jesus was present. But for us today, it raises a question of why not now?*

16

HARD QUESTIONS

How to Understand the Mystery of Unanswered Prayer

...and the fever left her.

— MARK 1:31

As Jesus heals the woman, her health seems to change effortlessly. We are told that the fever left her. As we make our way through the first full day, we will encounter other miracles like this. One word from Jesus or, as other writers have told us, one touch from him, and she is freed from suffering.

What are we to make of this? In a way, this healing seems an easy miracle for Jesus to perform. The venue is domestic—it is a private residence. There are no crowds or detractors; no Pharisees clutching their robes or scarves, feigning their outrage and offense. And healing a simple woman's fever seems like an entry-level miracle for the Son of God.

While all this is true, it raises a complex issue for many of us today. Many of us have asked the Lord for intervention in our life, our needs, or the needs of a loved one, only to be disappointed. Sometimes, all the elements seem to be present for Jesus to perform a miracle, but he doesn't. We have faith. We have prayed for the Lord's presence. We are certain he hears our prayer. And yet, nothing seems to happen when we pray and ask for what is needed.

Who is not familiar with this? We ask the Lord for his power to work, but he doesn't seem to respond. Where is he when we need him? In other words, how do we understand unanswered prayer? Too many of us have too many of them.

As a pastor of over 40 years, I have been in these situations many times. I have been at hospital bedsides, hovering over someone's family member, praying for miraculous healing, believing by faith it would come, and inviting the presence of the Lord and the power of the Holy Spirit. And nothing happens. Again, we ask, "Why?".

This can be a crisis of faith for some of us. We know that at some point, we will be at the bedside with a loved one, or they will be at ours. The worn-out answers—"God's will must always be done," "God must have a plan," etc.—will not do. They do not address the realities we face in our hours of desperate prayer. So, what is the answer? Where is he when we pray for healing, but the illness or disease remains?

HEALING AND CURING

I can propose an answer, but it is an answer that requires us to think critically about who Jesus is and what he offers us.

Recall the story of the paralyzed man we mentioned earlier. In an incredible scene in Simon Peter's house, Jesus was teaching a large and growing crowd of listeners and critics.[1] As he speaks, there are four friends of a paralyzed man who climb up on Peter's thatched roof, tear an opening to create daylight with their bare hands, and then slowly and audaciously lower their bedridden friend right into the center of the living area, where Jesus is. Talk about chutzpah! They place their needy friend right in the center of the group; right in front of Jesus. He will have to deal with it.

What will Jesus do? The Pharisees are curious too. They will weigh and measure the words of Jesus—they are collecting evidence for his heresy trial. The people strain to hear and see how Jesus will respond to this man. Then, in a bold and confident declaration of fact, Jesus said, "Son, your sins are forgiven."

That was not the preferred outcome for the man or for the friends. They expected a curative, physical miracle where the man would be made well. The four friends were also disappointed. They had worked hard to manage this meeting; they took big risks interrupting the Master during his lecture. The people around the house waiting for Jesus' response were let down as well.

But here is the story's point and how it addresses the challenge of unanswered prayer. Jesus gave the man what he needed most: God's forgiveness. The man was spiritually and eternally healed— he was freed and forgiven of his sin. The man's relationship with God was set right for all eternity. Is there a more significant gift that Jesus can give to someone?

Then notice what happens next. The man was not only *healed* by the word of the Lord, but he was also *cured* of his paralysis. Jesus said, "So that you may know that the Son of Man has authority on earth to forgive sins..." and Jesus turned to the paralyzed man and said, "Get up! Take your bed and walk!" The man walked out freed from sin for the rest of eternity and free from suffering for the rest of his life.

Do you see it? Healing first, then curing. This is the way of the Lord. He came first to heal our relationship with our Father in heaven. That is the most significant thing. And then, as proof that he could do that, he did the cure. The man picked up his bed and walked out of the house.

There is a difference between healing and curing; Jesus came to accomplish the former and proved it by doing the latter. We can confidently say that they have been healed if a loved one has faith in the Lord Jesus. To believe is to receive healing. A cure might come, or it might not. But spiritual healing—healing for all of eternity—will always come to those who invite Jesus to enter their life.

One last point to make about healing and curing. Miracle cures are only temporary. Consider that Lazarus[2], though made alive again, would have to die again. Only healing is eternal; it lasts forever.

Sometimes Jesus performs real restorative miracles. I have seen them. Perhaps you have as well. Too many people believe that these miraculous events are just coincidences. The truth is, I have witnessed enough miraculous healings to make me keep praying for them. But not enough to believe that they will happen every time. However, healing *will* happen every time.

Next: *The story of her cure is wonderful. But we discover that there is an even bigger meaning to this extraordinary event.*

---

1. Mark 2:1ff
2. John 11:1ff

17

BIGGER PICTURE

When the First Deacon Serves Her Lord

And she began to serve them.

— MARK 1:31

Before we leave this story of healing and the home where it happened, we can step back from this close-up view of Jesus' ministry and look at the story through a wider lens. Something is going on during the first day in Capernaum that should remind us of the much bigger story of the Gospel. Let's look.

Jesus comes to Capernaum after one of the most intense moments of his life: *his baptism.* As we saw earlier, the baptism of Jesus is the only time in the Bible where we can see all three persons of the Holy Trinity in one place. The Lord, the Son of God, is in the river. God the Father is heard from the heavens above. And as Jesus emerges from the water, God the Holy Spirit descends like a dove. It was a mighty moment.

If you had been there with a movie camera, you could not have captured the event on video. But you would have picked up the audio. The Father's voice boomed from the heavens and blessed the Son. He said, "You are my beloved Son; with you, I am well pleased." (Mark 1:11)

After that high point, Jesus entered the wilderness and wasteland of the world. The sequence of the glorious baptism followed by the inglorious encounter with Satan, then the hard work of ministry in Capernaum, shows us the Gospel in miniature. Jesus came from the high and holy fellowship with the Trinity and entered our world, where he found the good, bad, and ugly. This sequence should remind us of the bedrock doctrine of the Incarnation.

As we have said earlier, you cannot be a Christian without believing that the God of all things became a man and lived among us. The high and mighty second member of the Holy Trinity came to our world, ate our food, lived in our homes, bathed as we do, and drank our water and wine. The Incarnation posits that Jesus slept, walked, eliminated waste, got wet when it rained, and skinned his knee as a child, as all of us do. As we saw earlier in this story, this is a scandal and a stumbling block for many people.

Here, in Simon Peter's house, the sequence of the Incarnation is acted out again. Jesus enters her home, finds the room where she lays, bends to her, takes her hand, and then lifts her. Do you see how the sequence of events echoes his entrance into our human story? He came to us; he finds us sin-sick and suffering. Then he reached out to us and touched our race. And he lifted us.

THE SABBATH RESTRICTIONS

To appreciate the miracle even more, we must remember that there are also known boundaries between men and women, not to mention the demands and restrictions of Sabbath keeping. These religious and legal issues drop by the wayside. Jesus hears about her illness, responds to the invitation, comes to her home, sees her personal need, and does what is needed to bring healing. He touched her. This is the Incarnation.

And, of course, she served him and everyone else in the entourage. This is remarkable. We should remember that she is bound by the customs of the Sabbath not to serve him or anyone. Food must be prepared in advance of the Sabbath so that no work or preparation is done on the day of rest. But it is not a day of rest for her. At least, not anymore! It is a day of celebration and thanksgiving. Once again, as in the teaching of Jesus concerning the Law, the old has gone, and the new has come. She gives up the observance of the Law to follow the joy in her heart.

We should do likewise.

Mark uses only about 40 Greek words to describe the healing of Simon's mother-in-law. It is a small event in the scheme of the Gospel story. Indeed, the event is often overlooked, but it is a watershed moment in Jesus' ministry. She is the first woman that Jesus healed. Her healing was the first healing of his first day. And her response to serve them set the tone for how people should respond to the ministry of Jesus.

Some feminist Bible scholars look at this healing scene with disdain. One commentator wrote that the timing of the healing is suspect—"healed just in time for supper, indeed!" [1] But this is predictable in today's culture of political correctness. This scorn takes away from the beauty of what is happening here. Some also take umbrage that she is not named. But in a way, she shouldn't be. It is in keeping with her quiet character of love and service.

We don't know what this re-energized woman did after this for her family, others in Capernaum, and possibly beyond. Many women were early adopters of Jesus' message and became church leaders as congregations sprung up in the wake of the apostles' missions and journeys. Was she one of them? Jesus' message to women was energizing and liberating. Many of them, once they heard the Lord's message, voted with their feet and followed him.

One more feature of this story should be mentioned and appreciated. When the Devil was in the desert tempting Jesus, angels "ministered to him." When Jesus heals the unnamed mother-in-law, she also "ministered to him." It's the same word. It is the word used many times in the New Testament, *diakonia*, from which we get the word "deacon."

This short, tender account is the story of the church's first deacon.

Next: *The news about both miracles today is about to go viral.*

---

1. A Feminist Interpretation of Mark, Deborah Krause, 'Mother-in-Law,' 39.

18

AT SUNDOWN

When Many Came to Receive Healing and Freedom

*That evening at sundown, they brought to him all who
were sick or oppressed by demons. And the whole city
was gathered together at the door. And he healed
many who were sick with various diseases and cast
out many demons.*

— MARK 1:32–34

As we continue with Jesus through this 24-hour day, we
know that chronological time is never mentioned. The
events in the synagogue, followed by the time and healing in
Peter's house, might have taken four to six hours. It doesn't
matter. Jesus has all the time in the world.

And now, after all that has been said and done since Jesus came to
town, and as the sun drops beneath the western mountains of
Capernaum, signaling the end of the day, the Sabbath is over. By

the calendar of the ancient Jews, days are completed at sunset and the new day begins. This is true even today.

As the Sabbath ends at sundown, the community comes back to life. Suddenly, crowds begin to mill around Simon Peter's house, where Jesus is staying. News travels fast, and the entire town has heard about the synagogue's sermon and scene. News about the woman's healing in Peter's home has also spread.

There are many in need, so they came. The sick and suffering people wanted his touch; some wanted to be free from demonic oppression. The well-worn pathways and dusty side streets near Simon Peter's small, modest home were abuzz with talk as the townsfolk bring their family members and friends.

In our own time, we have seen and heard stories of COVID-19 patients who have struggled to overcome the effects of the virus. COVID-19 has humbled every nation, every leader, and every elected official with persistence. It goes where it wants. It was (we can hope it has subsided) the worst and most lethal pandemic in 100 years. Many today remember the horrific scenes from the early days of the outbreak; emergency rooms, hospitals, and morgues filled. Around the world, at the time of this writing, the virus has killed one out of every 500 people. One of every 100 older people has perished in the United States alone.

Those numbers make the pandemic very personal; we all probably know someone who has died. For the first time in modern times, our culture has dealt with death on a large scale. Of course, the ultimate death rate is always 1 to 1. We die at the rate of one death per person, but the recent prevalence and the pace of death around us should be a wake-up call. Our lives are fragile, uncertain, and transitory.

NEEDING HIS TOUCH

Those living in the New Testament had their types of disease and death to deal with and were as helpless in preventing it as we appear to have been with COVID-19. Hundreds of people with illnesses are huddling outside Peter's house. Where is Jesus when you need him? They are hoping and praying for his healing touch.

Many of us also know about demonic power over people, albeit in different forms: hopelessness, depression, alienation from family, disabling addictions, uncontrolled anger, and lashing out. One or more may have affected someone we love or even ourselves. We can relate to the desperation of the citizens of Capernaum as they reach out to Jesus to mend their bodies, minds, spirits, and relationships. The possibility of returning to a right relationship with God's creation is overwhelmingly urgent. And when the day ended, Jesus showed he could do that. As the new day started, he was their hope.

The point is this: if we had been in Capernaum as the sun set and the Sabbath ended, we would have known someone who needed to go find Jesus. We would have known people in the line outside Peter's home. You might even have been there yourself.

The makeshift clinic outside the door is crowded, but as time draws on, it becomes clear that Jesus cannot heal or free everyone. Sadly, night is coming. The evening will end before everyone receives what they came for. If we read the account closely and think of the logistics involved, we can imagine the terrible disappointment of those who do not find what they are looking for; what they need. They will be left on the fringes of hope.

Several times in these pages, I have mentioned that the performance of miracles was not why Jesus came into the world. Later, in one of the next episodes, when the disciples find him in the morning, he will say it himself. "Let us move on to other towns

and villages, that I may preach there. For that is why I came out."
(Mark 1:38)

We should remember this today. When a loved one is sick; or we
are sick, we should pray to God for miraculous healing. We have
seen Jesus do these things in the New Testament, so we add a
phrase to our prayer. We say, "in Jesus' Name," trusting that Jesus
knows how to do it. He has healed people and can choose to do it
today. But that is not his purpose, as we have seen.

Next: *When Jesus healed people, he gave them hope for an eternity they
could now attain through Christ.*

19

OUR HOPE

The World We Want is Coming

That evening at sundown, they brought all who were sick
or oppressed by demons to him. And the whole city
was gathered together at the door. And he healed
many who were sick with various diseases and cast
out many demons. And he would not permit the
demons to speak because they knew him.

— MARK 1:32–34

We have imagined Jesus walking through his first day: teaching, preaching, healing, touching, and casting out demons. To complement our understanding of this first day, we should take the time to imagine the setting and the scenes of Capernaum as it existed 2,000 years ago. Its small homes are primitive, made with mud bricks, hand-hewn timbers, thatched roofs, and dirt floors. The houses have small rooms adjacent to one another under a single roof. Narrow cobblestone walkways divide homes from the other and meander between one dwelling and the next. The population of Capernaum is only a few thousand, and all these people live in crowded and cramped accommodations.

We can also imagine that when the sun sets and the Sabbath ends, the homes, the rooms, the streets, and the walkways jam up with all manner of people. Many of them are sick and highly contagious. Demons oppress some; those poor souls are loud and often violent. Some people are paralyzed; begging for food and water is their daily struggle. The blind, the deaf, the mute, and the lame stumble around the town, each foraging for food or shelter.

We have medical care, affordable housing, ample food supplies, government subsidies, extended families, and safe spaces to live and work. The realities faced by lower classes of the ancient world are well beyond our imagination. Life was dirty, dusty, and disease-prone. Death came early for most people.

I am trying to paint a vivid picture of the harshness and struggle of life in the ancient world because Jesus, and his ability to cure people, are fresh hope in an ugly world. Life is hard and short, and Jesus brings relief to the daily difficulties of life; he brings a vision of a life to come where the sorrows and pains of this world are no more.

This is another reason why the miracles of Jesus are so powerful. They show people the beauty and perfection of a world to come. They show what the Kingdom of God will be like. Remember his opening proclamation: "The time is fulfilled, the Kingdom of God is at hand, repent and believe in the gospel." (Mark 1:15) If anyone wonders what the Kingdom of God will be like, the signs and wonders show them a renewed life where sorrow and pain are no more.

WHAT IS NEXT

The first verses of the last chapter of the New Testament show what the new heaven and the new earth will be like. John recorded it all as a dream in the Book of Revelation.

> *"Then I saw a new heaven and a new earth, for the first heaven and the first earth had passed away, and the sea was no more. And I saw the holy city, New Jerusalem, coming down from heaven from God, prepared as a bride adorned for her husband. And I heard a loud voice from the throne saying, 'Behold, the dwelling place of God is with man. He will dwell with them, and they will be His people, and God Himself will be with them as their God. He will wipe away every tear from their eyes, and death shall be no more, neither shall there be mourning, nor crying, nor pain anymore, for the former things have passed away.'" (Rev. 21:1–4)*

This is the vision of the coming and present Kingdom of God. And coming to earth and living among us as he did, Jesus is the King coming to stake out his territory and claim it back. With Jesus as King, sickness, suffering, and spiritual oppression are on their way out. The miracles show this truth. They give people a short but wonderful glimpse of what awaits them in the new Kingdom.

Once again, Jesus believes miracles and wonders are not the Good News for people as wonderful as they are. People need to believe and trust in the Kingdom to come. After all, if the sick suddenly become well but do not grasp the glory and hope of the Kingdom, they will miss out on the best news of all—that they can become citizens of the new realm of God. Miracle cures are temporary at best. The permanent, eternal solution to a difficult life lies on the *other* side of the gates of heaven. Once Jesus has vanquished death and hell on the cross, those gates will be opened wide.

Pastor and well-known author Tim Keller invites us to think along these same lines. Miracles point us to the way things should be and, given the Cross, one day will be. He writes,

> *We modern people think of miracles as the suspension of the natural order, but Jesus meant them to be the restoration of the natural order. The Bible tells us that God did not originally make the world to have disease, hunger, and death in it. Jesus has come to redeem where it is wrong and heal the world where it is broken. His miracles are not just proofs that he has power but also wonderful foretastes of what he is going to do with that power. Jesus' miracles are not just a challenge to our minds, but a promise to our hearts, that the world we all want is coming.* [1]

If you or I had been living in the ancient world of Jesus' day, the Good News of Jesus and the miracles he performed would have sounded like the greatest news imaginable.

We learn one more detail about Jesus' ministry after sundown. Jesus mutes the demons; he does not allow them to speak! It knows who he is—and what he came to do. It knows him, and he knows it. Anything that would have come out of its mouth would have been lies, threats, and distractions to the main message of Jesus.

But this minor detail tells us something extraordinary. Demons can be silenced. Remember, it has nothing in and of itself. It must use things that do not belong to it to accomplish or promote its evil work. As we saw earlier, Jesus does not match his words with its words, word for word. He does not offer long, drawn-out incantations to rid the synagogue of the unclean spirit. He doesn't suffer this fool. He simply tells it to shut up and get out.

This small detail about Jesus' treatment of the Devil gives us a final clue about handling temptations with a Devilish source. We can call on Jesus to join us in response to any temptation that comes to us and say: "Be quiet!"

———————

Next: *The residents of Capernaum didn't realize it, but the miracles were about to end.*

———————————————

1. –Timothy Keller, *The Reason for God* (New York: Dutton, 2008), 95-6.

20

HIS RISING

When Jesus Finds a Time and Place for Prayer

*And rising very early in the morning, while it was still
dark, he departed and went out to a desolate place.*

— MARK 1:35

We can imagine the scene outside Simon Peter's house on
the first evening of Jesus' ministry in Capernaum. Many
people needing to be touched and healed of their infirmities were
present. The poor, oppressed souls and those in bondage with evil
and unclean spirits waited in the hope that they would be freed.
It seemed that everyone in Capernaum was there. Mark writes
descriptively: "And the whole city was gathered together at the
door." (Mark 1:32)

There weren't orderly lines of people waiting to take a turn.
There were no queues of sufferers politely and patiently hoping
that Jesus would address their needs. We should imagine dozens,

if not hundreds, of people clamoring for medical relief and spiritual release. There was a heightened excitement in the scores of people who had lived with debilitating problems. They could be free from pain; they could be free from fear.

Jesus moved effortlessly in and among all these sorts and conditions of people all evening long. One by one and touch by touch, Jesus strengthened and healed the sick and weakened. When those suffering under the burden of demon oppression stood before the Lord, he only had to speak a few short, commanding words, and the demons would flee. These dramatic moments continued most of the night.

As we can imagine, it was spiritually exhausting work, and sometime that evening—perhaps in the earliest morning hours of the new day—the Healer needed time to rest. Jesus was tireless in his compassion and love for people. But he was not immune from fatigue in a physical and emotional sense. When he took on our flesh, he also took on our limitations. As he grew tired and weary, like any of us, he needed sleep. There was more to do—more people to heal—but he must first lay down and sleep.

We don't know precisely when he went to lie down, but we know when he awakened. He was up before first light, preparing himself for the new day, and then left the house quietly to find an away place for a few hours alone. His purpose was prayer. Jesus always sought personal times to be in close communion with his Father in heaven. So today, in the early morning hours, Jesus found a place for prayer. Back at Peter's house, the disciples were unaware that Jesus had left the building. They were fast asleep. It would not be the last time they slept while he prayed to his Father.

EARLY TIMES AND PLACES

As we will see in the next chapter, Jesus prayed in many places and at many times throughout the day. But regularly, he sought prayer times in places of his own choosing, usually in the morning.[1] He met God in private places. He heard from God there. He cleared his mind of the trials and tempests of the previous day and waited for God to speak; he stayed with God to hear and listen.

When we read the story of Jesus' temptations in the wilderness, we often feel sympathy and sorrow for the Lord. We want his time of fasting and extreme isolation to end quickly; we want him to be with others. But being alone in the desert was not the hardship for Jesus that we imagine it would be for us. The wilderness was a place of clarity, communion, and personal contact with the Father. That's why he went to find a desolate and lonely places for prayer that morning; when he was there, he wasn't lonely at all.

We should linger at this point and note how uniquely biblical this idea is. The desert or the wilderness in the Bible is often a place of private renewal, personal awakening, and rediscovering a sense of mission and faith. We know that Moses received a life-changing commission in the desert—at the age of eighty. God spoke to him from a burning bush. David hid in the arid, quiet and lonely places of the Judean wilderness. It was undoubtedly difficult—it wasn't the luxury he loved. But he forged his faith there. He learned leadership while being alone in the desert. He wrote beautiful poetry and songs to God there. The wasteland could also be a place of rebirth for him. He found his personal courage in the desert.

The great preacher Charles Spurgeon, reflecting on the same verse in the Gospel of Mark, gives us this encouragement.

The Son of Righteousness was up before the sun. How much must our Lord have loved prayer to renounce his needed rest in sleep, in order to hold converse with his heavenly Father? He was sinless, and yet needed prayer: far be it from us to dream that we can do without it. In private, we must, like our Lord, equip ourselves for the public battle of life.[2]

Finding the time and a place for early morning prayer may be the most obvious personal application of what we learn from Jesus' daily habit. The quiet times for prayer was time which he actively sought. It was not the leftover time at the end of the day. It was the first fruit of every day harvested in the first hours of the morning. Jesus went to the desert or the wilderness or the caves or the desolate shoreline of the Sea of Galilee. That is where he listened to God, renewed his trust, and committed to the will of his Father in heaven.

Next: *There was a secret weapon that Jesus had, that we can have as well. It is the easiest and yet most difficult thing to do.*

---

1. Matthew 4:13, Mark 6:31-32, Luke 5:15-16, 9:10, and many other passages
2. C. H. Spurgeon, The Interpreter: Spurgeon's Devotional Bible (Grand Rapids, MI: Baker Book House, 1964), 509.

(21)

HE PRAYS

The Prayer Life of the Master

And there he prayed.

— MARK 1:35

W hat kind of prayer life do you have? When was the last time you sought the Lord for a clear answer or direction to a consuming question?

If we are honest, we'll admit to having mighty struggles with personal prayer. It's far easier to do something or to jump into something rather than pray. Often, we approach the significant decisions of our life more scientifically than spiritually. We make a list of pros and cons or build a spreadsheet of choices, implications, and impacts, or, when faced with a new direction to take, we "go with our gut." We "feel" our way into a choice before us. In other words, we make a semi-informed guess based on a semi-vague hunch.

If anyone in history is entitled and equipped to rely on his gut, it is Jesus. After all, he is the Son of God! But he doesn't ever guess or go with his gut. He is known in the Gospels for having a serious life of prayer. And now, after a busy day and evening in Capernaum, he rises early and heads to the hills to find a place to pray.

Jesus' prayer life is so profound and meaningful that it deserves a separate book. And indeed, many volumes have been written about it. But in effect, the prayer life of Jesus is very straightforward. He prays. And he prays often.

As we think about this idea, we discover that his prayer life is not conditioned on being in a suitable place or even at a scheduled time—even though he has relocated to a different venue in the early hours of the day. Luke records that he prayed in the desert and other lonely places. [1]Sometimes he prayed all night.[2] In the last week of his life, he went to a place by himself in the Kidron Valley and prayed so passionately that his sweat became like drops of blood. And, like the moment in the early morning near Capernaum, while Jesus prays, the disciples sleep. They did not have the experience or the maturity to wait the night in prayer. Most of us would have done the same.[3]

It doesn't matter. Jesus doesn't need friends to pray. His link is direct—a connection with his Father in heaven.

As we read through the New Testament Gospels, we find that preceding any major decision, Jesus went to pray. He prayed before a hostile encounter with the Pharisees and before he sent the disciples on a mission. He prayed when he was on the top of the mountain where the transfiguration took place.

Jesus prayed for others. Jesus prayed with others. He prayed alone. Jesus prayed all night while in nature. Jesus taught his disciples to pray in short phrases. We even read that Jesus is praying for us! Right now! [4]

The writer of Hebrews summed up the prayer life of Jesus with these words:

> *"During the days of Jesus' life on earth, he offered up prayers and petitions with fervent cries and tears to the one who could save him from death, and he was heard because of his reverent submission." (Hebrews 5:7 NIV)*

HARD TO PRAY

Many religions teach their followers to pray. They provide training classes to understand techniques for prayer. Some words are printed or memorized. There are movements and motions to make. There are body positions to hold. There are liturgical frameworks to follow. And Christianity has many of these options for prayer as well. But the Lord did not endorse any particular words, movements, repetitions, incantations, practices, postures, or processes. He prayed.

Most of us are ambivalent about prayer. We know it's crucial. We feel that it should be a principal activity. And we know that it would be more important in our life if we did it more. Most of us would admit that prayer is the easiest thing to do and is one of the most challenging.

Luke's gospel focuses on prayer more than any other record of Jesus' life and ministry. In Luke's account, we read about the episode when the disciples asked the Lord to teach them about prayer. They didn't ask the Lord about techniques and models. They didn't ask the Lord to teach them *how* to pray. They simply asked him, "Lord, teach us to pray." (Luke 11:1)

It seems to me Jesus' answer is symbolic of his life of prayer, the means, and the motive for prayer. Jesus said, "When you pray, say, 'Our Father in heaven...'" (Matt. 6:9). We know the rest of the Lord's Prayer by heart. But I think in these first words of the Lord's Prayer, we see the "secret," if you will, of Jesus' life of passionate prayer. Our prayer life will be filled with passion, purpose, power, praise, and delight when we truly understand we are praying to God, our Father in heaven.

Next: *Peter would eventually understand the need for prayer, especially for him, But he doesn't get it now.*

---

1. Luke 5:16
2. Luke 6:12
3. Luke 22:44-45
4. In order, these the passages referenced in this paragraph. Luke 19:13, Luke 9:28, Luke 5:16, Luke 6:12, Luke 11:1ff, Hebrews 7:25

22

PETER FINDS

Why Everyone is Looking for Jesus

And Simon and those who were with him searched for
him, and they found him and said to him, "Everyone
is looking for you".

— MARK 1:36–37

W e are nearing the end of the record of the first 24 hours of Jesus' public ministry. Mark has front-loaded his Gospel of the Good News of Jesus Christ with an account of a very full and busy day.

In each of the episodes we have seen, our Lord is decisive and directed. When the day began less than 24 hours ago, Jesus entered the synagogue with the disciples. There he spoke. Then he commanded the demons and freed an oppressed man. Soon after, he healed a fever-stricken woman and met with many suffering and oppressed people. Then he slept (briefly) and arose early to find his way to a place where he prayed to his Father in heaven. That was one day!

During the early morning hours, when Jesus is praying in the "lonely place," the disciples sleep in the home of Simon Peter. As the sun rises, they awaken and realize that Jesus has already left the house. They form a search party to look for Jesus, and when they find him, they tell him everyone is looking for him. There are crowds of people waiting. From the disciples' perspective, it's time to return to Capernaum and complete the healing ministry for the public. The disciples were searching for Jesus to tell him that others were searching for him.

There is a pattern in the gospels of people looking for Jesus. We might even call it a motif or a narrative feature in gospel stories. If we thought that the Christian faith was removed, remote, or academic—that is, unattached to the daily life of its followers–the stories of people looking for Jesus show us otherwise. From this first day of ministry to the final Passover meal with Jesus' disciples, the gospel story is a continuous series of appointments and meetups between Jesus and others. There are nearly 50 recorded one-on-one encounters in the four gospel narratives.

CLOSE ENCOUNTERS

One of those meetings took place at night. It was a secret session between the earnest and erudite Nicodemus and Jesus. It is one of the gospel's most famous and consequential meetings–at least for Nicodemus.[1] Nicodemus was a well-qualified Pharisee. He was educated, experienced, well-known, and well-respected among his peers. He came to Jesus under cover of darkness to have an intellectual, theological discussion. He was good at that, but before he could ask any of his prepared questions, Jesus commandeered the conversation. He turned the conversation on its head and spoke to him about faith. "Truly, truly I say to you unless one is born again, he cannot see the kingdom of God." (John 3:3)

This raised even more questions for the confused Pharisee. Nicodemus asked, how can these things be? And Jesus answered with the most famous Bible verse ever. "For God so loved the world, he gave his only Son, that whoever believes in him should not perish but have eternal life." (John 3:16). Jesus moved the conversation from Nicodemus' head to his heart—about 12 inches —in a few seconds.

The Lord's encounter with Nicodemus deeply moved the old Pharisee; he was never the same. Later in the Gospel of John, we learn that Nicodemus is the only one who broke rank with his peers and asked to tend to the limp, lifeless body of the crucified Jesus. Something happened in that nighttime conversation to change his mind and his heart. He never had all his questions answered—he didn't need to ask them all. But still, all of his questions were satisfied. They went away.

Another encounter in the gospels concerned a group of Greeks who requested a meeting with Jesus. The story is told in John's gospel and occurred late in his ministry. In Jerusalem, during a festival for the Jews, Jesus was teaching near the Temple. A small group of Greek men came to Philip, a disciple of Jesus from a town near Bethsaida in Galilee. They were searching for Jesus. They famously said, "Sir, we wish to see Jesus" (John 12:21).

Hearing their request, Philip told Andrew, and the two of them went to tell Jesus.

Oddly, the story is never concluded. We do not know if Jesus made himself available to these Greeks. We know what they said:

Sir, we wish to see Jesus. But we are not told if they ever found him. But we can be sure they did. Why? Because in every case, when someone seeks the Lord, they find him. As I said, there are nearly 50 encounters like this, and everyone who asked for a meetup with the master met him. No one was left hanging.

This was true even in the first days of Jesus' life. The Wise Men from the East were looking for Jesus. They were so intent on finding him that they asked Herod the Great for directions! He didn't know, so they continued their quest to see him, which they did. They found him on their own—a star led them to the place where they had their face-to-face with the infant Jesus. Everyone who searches for him finds him. Another way to say this is that Jesus will find a way of making himself found.

In yet another story, a large crowd was looking for Jesus.[2] Jesus had sailed across the Sea of Galilee, trying to hide from the crowd. But still, they tracked him down at the site across the lake. They sought him, and they found him. Or, as we might say, Jesus found them searching for him.

This is a remarkable point, and it offers a very personal application. Just as Jesus will come to anyone who invites him, anyone who seeks the Lord will find him. As he said in his famous sermon, "Seek, and you will find....for everyone who seeks, finds." (Luke 7:7-8)

This is the nature of our loving God. Those who seek the Lord will find him. Sometimes it might seem that God is hiding, that he is playing a "cat and mouse" game with us. We seek, but we do not find. This is what the psalmist meant when he asked the Lord not to be coy or quiet. "You have said, 'Seek My face.' My heart says to you, 'Your face, Lord, do I seek.' Hide not your face from me". (Ps. 27:8–9) But the point is still valid: those who seek will find.

Next: *The people of Capernaum would soon learn that Jesus didn't come for only themselves. He had the whole world on his mind.*

1. John 3
2. Mark 6:30

23

SHOW AND TELL

How Miracles Prove the Message

And he said to them, "Let us go on to the next towns, that
I may preach there also, for that is why I came out."
And he went throughout all Galilee, preaching in
their synagogues and casting out demons.

— MARK 1:38–39

O ur 24-hour day is nearly over, and now a slight
misunderstanding arises between Jesus and the disciples.
The newly chosen men have been watching Jesus over his first full
day. It has been an extraordinary eye-opening experience for
them. Let's go back to the moment Jesus called them into service.

We remember what he said to them: "Follow me, and I will make
you become fishers of men" (Mark 1:17). In fishing terms, the kind
of response Jesus was having in Capernaum, with crowds of

people suddenly aware of his ministry and his message and waiting around for more of it, has been overwhelming.

When the disciples find Jesus in the morning, they attempt to convince him to head back to town and pick up where he left off. The people are all there. The crowds are waiting for him. Let's get back to town and keep it going, they say. But Jesus has a different vision of what success is. He is ready to move on to other cities and villages where he can preach.

As Jesus tells his disciples, he must move on to preach in other places. And thus, he went out preaching and casting out demons.

Jesus had a simple message. No other message from anyone, anywhere, or any other time in history has ever been more profound. And it was a simple message: *The time has come. The Kingdom is here. Repent and believe.*

Jesus broadcasted the message through simple and repeatable methods: preaching and demonstrating. Indeed, the ministry of Jesus can be understood, in effect, as a three year, show-and-tell" program that could change an open-hearted person or any open-minded individual.

Perhaps I am reading my feelings into the story, but it seems to me the disciples are disappointed. How could they *not* prefer go back and finish the job? They live in Capernaum. The people waiting for their turn with Jesus are their friends. Peter's mother-in-law has recovered from her debilitating fever—she has an incredible testimony—and so do dozens of others. But there is more to be done; there is more need because there are more people.

The disciples might have seen the first day's success as a sign they should *stay* in Capernaum. They think they can live out their days in a familiar place and still fulfill their commission to be fishers of men and women. They could let the world come to *them*. They still could be "fishers of men" only now, from the banks of the Sea of Galilee! They might rather stay in Capernaum, at home, and live out their faith in their old haunts.

But in a statement that has the ring of a decree, Jesus clarifies his purpose: "Let us go, that I may preach there also, for that is why I came out" (Mark 1:38). And they go. Other places and people need to hear the gospel message as well. They will return to Capernaum. But for now, they go.

WORDS MATTER

As we think about the preaching and teaching of the Lord, we should stop and consider *how* people come to believe the Good News. He speaks the message out loud so that people can listen to it. It is just that simple. His miracles are only real-life demonstrations of his message. They are wonderful, but they are like sermon illustrations. The spoken word—or shall we be clear, the *preached* word—is the primary means of bringing people to faith and faith to people. The most important of the five human senses, the most important for receiving faith, is the sense of hearing. This truth makes the spoken word the most effective communication tool ever. Our ears connect directly to our minds and heart.[1]

Verbal preaching and teaching—speaking words—have fallen out of favor in many places. It seems old-school. Today, preachers who want to move people to faith often rely on video clips, publicly shared testimonies, or emotional music to touch people's hearts. And it does. The production value of some of the music and videos, and the authenticity of those who share their faith in God, can be moving. It is tempting to go to a church that offers only the best of these.

However, for over 2000 years, the church has used the spoken, preached Word to move hearts and change minds. Sights and sounds can amplify a sermon or teaching, but people need to *hear* words. As was mentioned earlier, words create worlds. In other words, *words matter*. And the Word of God matters most, especially when it is preached.

We need only look at the biblical story to see the power of words in action.

- In the earliest texts of the Bible, God spoke, "Let there be light!" Boom! There was light.
- He spoke to Abram and told him to leave his home and go to a new place. He went.
- God spoke words to Moses so crucial that he inscribed them on a tablet. They were short, commanding words, but they had a massive impact.
- The prophets spoke God's words, even if they spelled doom for their hearers.
- The early church discovered at Pentecost that the Holy Spirit would use spoken words of Spirit-infused believers to reach multitudes of people, even without their knowledge or knowing how.

Indeed, throughout the Bible, we see words' impact and power. The Bible is even called the Word! Jesus is called the Word! Christianity exclusively depends on words to the point that if they are not spoken—if we remain silent—people will not hear the Good News and will not come to faith. This is remarkable.[2]

Jesus' commitment to preaching and teaching using words was his primary activity. In modern times, some have used a quote attributed to St. Francis as a handy way to discount the importance of traditional preaching and teaching. "Preach the Gospel at all times. If necessary, use words." While we understand the sentiment behind this quote, it is not something Jesus would ever say. He never intended the Gospel message to be pantomimed—acted without words—to an unbelieving world. The Gospel must be proclaimed widely, announced publicly, trumpeted clearly, declared boldly, and spoken plainly. (By the way, most scholars agree that St. Francis never made this remark.)

The biography and ministry of Martin Luther comes to mind here. He dutifully read the Word of God every day. He listened to it in his monastery. He heard the Word preached there. Hearing God's Word as he read, taught, or listened in his monastery, was instrumental in converting the reformer's heart. In his day, Luther stood against the corrupt and dangerous Roman Catholic church and declared his convictions from which he would not budge. He had heard the Word of God, it had changed his heart, and he would stay faithful to the Word of God. He would stand; he could not do otherwise.

Later in his life, reflecting on the role of hearing God's Word, he gave this critical insight:

> *"If you were to ask a Christian what his task is and by what he is worthy of the name of Christian, there could be no other response than hearing the Word of God, that is, faith. Ears are the only organs of the Christian."* [3]

We should learn to listen to God's Word spoken, preached, taught, or delivered. Hearing the Word of God and preached is the lifelong duty and privilege of a person of faith. It is the way that God nurtures and nourishes us.

Next: Jesus' last encounter shows us something that has been on Jesus' mind from the beginning. This thought never escaped him.

1. I am sensitive to some readers who might question this comment regarding the deaf community. The connection between hearing functions and the human heart seems to be true even in people who are deaf. The evidence suggests that the brain responds to the perception and production of sign language in deaf people in the same way that it responds to the perception and production of speech in people who can hear. There are wonderfully informative articles on the Internet about this subject. For example https://www.healthline.com/health/what-language-do-deaf-people-think-in

2. Romans 10:14

3. Martin Luther: A Spiritual Biography by Herman Selderhuis, pg. 56

24

SHED BLOOD

When a Leper is both Cleansed and Restored

And a leper came to him, imploring him, and kneeling said to him, "If you will, you can make me clean." Moved with pity, he stretched out his hand and touched him and said to him, "I will; be clean." And immediately, the leprosy left him, and he was made clean. And Jesus sternly charged him and sent him away at once and said to him, "See that you say nothing to anyone, but go, show yourself to the priest and offer for your cleansing what Moses commanded, for a proof to them. But he went out and began to talk freely about it, and to spread the news..."

— MARK 1:40–45

We have not been a slave to clocks and modern chronology in this study. However, we have seen the passing of one full day. Jesus entered Capernaum in the morning hours of the Sabbath. Now, it is early morning the next day; 24 hours have passed since Jesus and his disciples entered the synagogue at Capernaum.

The disciples found Jesus in his place of prayer. Jesus told them he must move to other towns and villages to preach there. And so, they leave the area.

However, one man had been unable, for ritual purity reasons, to come to Peter's house. As Jesus goes out of town and into the countryside, a man with leprosy falls at the Lord's feet asking him to cleanse him. And, as we now know, Jesus will certainly do this for him. He touches the man and makes him clean. Then, he tells the man to be quiet, goes on his way, and shows himself to the priest, as Moses commanded.

Leprosy is one of the oldest known diseases. It is a wasting of the skin and tissue. It is dreadful. But there is one thing about leprosy that makes it quite different from other diseases: a severe social stigma accompanies it. Leprosy is a brand. It signifies infamy and disgrace, and those with the disease are shunned. Lepers were isolated in the ancient world because it was thought that the disease was contagious and a curse from God.

One writer said this about how the victims are tragically isolated:

> *"I have found this universally true as I have traveled around the world ferreting out these unfortunates from their hiding places. I have discovered them living among the tombs of the dead. I have visited them behind stone walls with guards at the gates to recapture them if they escaped."* [1]

There is something that happens in this story that defies all convention and tradition. Jesus *touches* the man. We can be sure that no other human has touched this man in decades. Jesus doesn't care about that. He touches the man, and instantly leprosy leaves him. The word that is used for this kind of cure is the word "cleansed." The man is cleansed of leprosy.

We understand why Jesus sternly charges the man to stay quiet about the incident. Jesus does not want fame, as we have seen. But we also understand why this man never complies with our Lord's direction. He is a changed man. He is cleansed. His life of suffering and isolation is over. The man eagerly begins talking freely about his changed life. The man keeps spreading the news.

THE WAY BACK

The Levitical Law carefully prescribes the next steps for him. Surprisingly, Jesus tells the man to comply with it. This adherence to the legal code is shocking, given Jesus's earlier teaching in the synagogue. But before we understand why Jesus is sending him to the priest to fulfill an Old Testament protocol, lets see what the Levitical process involves.[2]

In the Scripture, it is straightforward. The cleansed leper brings two birds to the priest. One bird represents the leper with the dreaded disease and the priest kills the bird letting its blood fill a small vessel. The other bird represents the new, free-from-leprosy life. The priest dips the second bird in the blood of the sacrificial bird. Then the priest sprinkles the cleansed leper seven times with the dead bird's blood. The living bird is set free in the field. Then the priest instructs the man to wash his clothes, shave every hair on his body, and bathe in water. The new man will wait seven more days, and then, after all of this, the man is declared clean and welcomed back into the community.

So why would Jesus ask this newly cleansed man to submit himself to a complicated ritual like this? There are two reasons.

First, we have seen the difference between healing and curing. Jesus has cured the man of leprosy. He is cured (cleansed), but he needs to be *healed*. Undoubtedly, emotional scars, long-term losses, and deep sorrows have plagued the man for years. He has been estranged from all people. Remember, Jesus' touch was the first time anyone had been near enough to speak to him, let alone touch him.

This man faces the reverse situation of the paralyzed man whom Jesus healed first and then cured. The paralyzed man was healed (of sin) and needed to be cured. Conversely, now that the leprous man is cured, he needs to be healed. The man has a long life ahead of him. He has been isolated for decades. Jesus wants him to be ritually restored and truly welcomed back into the fellowship of God's people. The ritual is a beautiful way of involving everyone in the community to welcome the man and have him publicly restored.

But there is another reason Jesus wants man to submit himself to the Levitical restoration process.

Remember how the ancient Jews carried out the ancient ritual? There are unmistakable references to the sacrificial death of Jesus. The dead bird's blood is sprinkled on the cleansed man, and then he is told to go and wash. He is told to shave and bathe and wait seven days—one day for every day of Creation. The cleansed man is now a new man. He is reborn. Whatever vestige of his old life that he still has will be shaved off, washed off, rubbed off, or worn off over the following seven days. Effectively, he is a new man. After waiting seven days, the man is a new creation. It is as if the man is baptized (washed) and born again. This should remind us of the Apostle Paul's famous statement: "If any man is in Christ, he is a new creation. The old has gone; behold, the new has come." (2 Corinthians 5:17)

Jesus reveals a spiritual reality taught throughout the Old Testament: true cleansing is achieved through a sacrificial offering, through the shed blood of a living creature. One bird is killed, and one bird is freed.

The day's long saga ends when Jesus tells the leper to find a priest and reenact an ancient standard. This ritual points directly to the shed blood of a living creature, bringing restoration to a sinner.

Mark started his Gospel with these words: "The beginning of the Gospel of Jesus Christ, the Son of God." (Mark 1:1) Then Jesus started his ministry in Capernaum. Some 11,000 Greek words later (Mark's Gospel uses only 11,000 Greek words), Mark comes to the story's climax with the Centurion's words at the foot of the cross. "When the soldier who had crucified Jesus saw the way he died, he said, 'Truly, this man was the Son of God.'" (Mark 15:39)

Now, at the end of the 24 hours, and as we look back to the start of the Gospel and look forward to the end of the story, it is amazing to see something we might never have noticed. The further we dive into all the details, the scenes and dialogues, events, teaching, sermons, intentions, and miracles of the Lord, the more we find references, glimpses, suggestions, evidence, allusions, and types and shadows which lead to the Cross.

Now: *Everything changed after his first 24 hours. He would never be the same after this first day. Jesus had started his ministry and articulated his message. Once people knew it and heard it themselves, they would either follow or fall back.*

1. The Social Stigma of Leprosy, Eugene Kellersberger in The Annals of the New York Academy of Science
2. Leviticus 14:1–9

EPILOGUE

Why the Cross is Always on His Mind

None of us knows when or how we will die. We cannot know those details and circumstances. But this was **not** true of Jesus. In the back of his mind, and underneath every event in his life, is the reality of the Cross he will endure and on which he will die. He knew how he would die. He knew where he would die—the great city of Jerusalem. He knew who would be responsible for ending his life. He knew what would happen; the means of his death. And, it can be argued that he knew the day and the hour of his last moments.

In other words, he knew that his life would end on a Cross.

Therefore, the entire life of Jesus, beginning in Capernaum and spreading through the countryside, villages, the hills of Galilee and Samaria, the streets of Jerusalem, and the hill of Calvary—in front of the entire story of Jesus of Nazareth is an event that he knew was coming: the Cross on the hill of Calvary.

The Cross is always on Jesus' mind because it is why he came. He came to announce the Kingdom of God, as we have seen. His appearance on the stage of history meant more than healing and casting out demons. His coming called people to a life of repentance. But it was more than that too. It was about the Cross.

As I mentioned in the Introduction, a trademark feature in each weekly episode of 24 was using a cliffhanger at the end of the hour. The audience was forced to wait until the next week or the next installment to find out what happened next. As an avid fan of the 8-season drama, it was exciting to see how all the plot lines resolved by the end of each season. Week by week (or hour by hour if binge-watching), cliffhanger after cliffhanger, the story raced toward its conclusion. Every plot line was resolved; every character was redeemed.

Our study of Mark's 24 verses depicting the 24 hours of Jesus' ministry in Capernaum has done much the same—with one important clarification: Mark's Gospel describes the facts, not fiction. The events of the Gospel story are true, but they are also like cliffhangers. How will the first day's events be resolved at the end of the story at the Cross?

As Mark would tell us, when Jesus walked into Capernaum, he set events, conflicts, teachings, healings, and situations in motion that would propel the story forward for the next three years. The dramatic events of his first full day are just the beginning of the plot line or stories that would continue daily until they meet and end at the Cross.

REDEEMED AND RESOLVED

Mark's Gospel is a remarkable feat of storytelling. In the first 24 hours of public ministry, Jesus did so much. And what is more, each event was a precursor of what he would face for the next three years. This is what is so remarkable about the first full day. Everything that started on that first day was completed on his last day at the Cross. In other words, his crucifixion, death, resurrection, ascension, and the coming of the Holy Spirit at Pentecost resolve and redeem everything that Jesus initiated in his first 24 hours.

- The Pharisees' obsession with Jesus's teaching ends when he is crucified. It seems like they have won. However, Jesus was completely vindicated by the Resurrection. He claimed to be God, one with the Father, and he was raised from the dead, as only God could do.
- The Devil's hatred toward Jesus and desire to put Jesus to death was realized when Jesus was arrested and crucified. It seemed that it had the victory. But Jesus rose from the dead. As Paul will say in future years, death lost its victory; it has no sting. Jesus was raised from the dead. The Devil was overcome.
- The crowd's support of Jesus ran off the rails as Jesus entered Jerusalem. They called for his execution, and it seemed they had their way. Their shouts to crucify him led to his death. Yet, God got his way. The death of Jesus was the means for salvation to be offered to everyone in the crowd.
- The mother-in-law, who served the Lord after her healing, could likely be one of the few women who did not deny Jesus but stood by him weeping at the sight of him on the Cross. Their witness and courage are redeemed. These women are among the first witnesses of the Resurrection. The Apostle Paul will later speak about those in Christ and included in the ancient promise to the Jews. This promise will no longer be reserved for only

male, circumcised Jews. He wrote: "There is neither Jew nor Greek, there is neither slave nor free, there is no male and female, for you are all one in Christ Jesus." (Galatians 3:28)

- The Lord's homeless and poverty, a long-standing theme in each Gospel, is fully resolved at the Cross. He was laid to rest in a borrowed tomb, but he ascended to heaven 40 days after his crucifixion. He was seated at the right hand of God. He is at home in heaven as its King.

- His deep prayer relationship and connection with the Father appeared to have been interrupted; Jesus cried that God had forsaken him. Yet, God heard him and raised him from the dead!

- Finally, the religious community of Pharisees, priests, and scribes to which Jesus insisted the cleansed leper show himself regarded the Lord as a cursed criminal who hung on a tree. (Deut. 21:22-23) Yet this cursed man appeared to a young Pharisee named Saul, who became the great apostle Paul and launched a worldwide outreach and evangelism mission in the name of Risen Lord Jesus that continues today.

Do you see it? Each episode that starts on the first day of Capernaum creates a storyline that weaves its way through the Gospel story until it reaches the Cross. All of the plot-lines that began in Capernaum end at the Cross; they end *on* the Cross. From the beginning of the first day, Jesus had a plan. As we say today, he began his ministry with the end in mind. And in Jesus' mind, the end was always the Cross. The Cross is like a watermark imprinted on every page of the written story of Jesus.

Now, at the end of the 24 hours, and as we look back to the start of the Gospel and look toward the end of the story, it is amazing to see something we might never have noticed. The further we dive into all the details, the scenes and dialogues, events, teaching, sermons, intentions, and miracles of the Lord, the more we find references, glimpses, suggestions, evidence, allusions, and types and shadows which lead to the Cross by which we are saved.

AFTERWARD

How Life's Most Important Question Finds its Answer

Looking back over the past 24 episodes, we cannot help but be impressed. Our Lord spent the entire time, one full day, giving himself to others as well as directly addressing the demons and the diseases. But of all the things he did and said in that single day, it seems that the day's most important task was preaching the Good News about the Gospel of God and demonstrating what the Kingdom will look like by releasing people from spiritual oppression and providing healing and curing for their physical bodies.

The subject of each of the gospels is, of course, Jesus. The gospels give us a clear and compelling picture of the life, ministry, death, resurrection, and ascension of our Lord. The four gospel stories from different perspectives present a unified narrative of Jesus' life. It's helpful to know how each of the gospels portrays Jesus. This quick summary might help us to understand each gospel's uniqueness:

- The Gospel of Matthew focuses on what Jesus said.
- The Gospel of Mark focuses on what Jesus did.
- The Gospel of Luke shows us what Jesus felt.
- The Gospel of John emphasizes who Jesus was.

Yet, the Gospel of Mark is not a historical text, per se. The events described are historical, to be sure. We should not doubt that. But the Gospel of Mark is a dramatic script that pulls us into the action. We are there. It is a fast-paced, action-packed drama featuring the Son of God as the lead character. And like any good dramatic script, it is best not to be skimmed and shelved. The story invites you into the first day's events and asks you to consider them deeply. As we go into the story, we take the story into ourselves!

As we saw, Jesus began slowly. First, one encounter and then another. Initially, the people of Capernaum were suspicious or uninterested. But in only a matter of hours, hundreds of men, women, and children clamored to see Jesus and to have him touch them. He was inundated with meetings, requests, encounters, confrontations, and many drop-in appointments from those in need.

Why? Because Jesus met people where they were and touched their lives at their point of need. Jesus proved himself able to solve the most persistent and widespread physical and spiritual problems they faced in their lives. He could not have fully protected them from all things that assault or afflict people. He does not put a force field around anyone. But Jesus healed the infirmities and defeated the demonic forces around them, showing everyone that the Kingdom of God had begun and started with him. In his message that day, Jesus convincingly argued that the Kingdom of God was available for all who wanted to be its citizens.

But why should we want to be citizens of the Kingdom of God? And more to the point, if we want to be its citizens, why can't we just become citizens? These two questions beg another question, a critically important question found in the earliest pages of the Bible in the Book of Job.

THE MOST IMPORTANT QUESTION

An unanswered question looms large throughout the history of the Jews and the record of the Old and New Testaments. In the earliest written book of the Bible, Job, the main character, asks this central question. It's one of the most profound theological questions ever phrased. Job asks,

> *"...how can a man be in the right before God? If one wished to contend with Him, one could not answer Him once in a thousand times."*
>
> *Job 9:2*

Throughout the Bible, Job's question is in search of an answer. How can a person be just or righteous before God? This is the looming question. This is what John the Baptist said that the Messiah was coming to proclaim. This is what Jesus preached on his opening day of ministry. And he would proclaim the message to all the towns and villages around the Sea of Galilee. This is the Good News.

It's a question that few people ask today. Why? Because the question assumes a belief in a holy and transcendent God. The question assumes that there is something incredibly holy, right, and wonderful about God, who made the universe and had the creativity to bring the spark to it.

But the question also implies something is wrong with the world we know today. And if we are honest, we see that what is wrong with the world is me. And you. Something about you and me is not right. We are not holy or righteous in any way. And we are certainly not transcendent. We all die and become dust.

So how can we be united with our Holy God? After all, we were made for God. As St. Augustine said, "Our hearts are restless until they find rest in Thee, O God." Yet, if we are honest with ourselves and clear about our sin, we know that, on our own, we could never find "rest in Thee, O God." We should all agree with the realization that King David writes in Psalm 130: "If You, O Lord, should mark iniquities, O Lord, who could stand?"

If you believe in God, this is the most important question in the world. We need somehow to achieve a state of righteousness before him that we can never reach. We must be something we can never become. What will remedy this situation? Something must give.

And the Good News of the gospel is that someone did give. Our Lord Jesus gave his life for us. His sinlessness and love are imputed to us—his life, not ours—is all that is required for eternal life. This is the Gospel of God. This is behind Jesus' hallmark statement, as recorded in the opening lines of the Gospel of Mark: *The time is fulfilled; the kingdom of God is at hand. Repent and believe the gospel.*

CONCLUSION

We are now at the end of our study. What a journey it has been! Thank you for coming along and being part of the story of the First 24 hours of Jesus minister in Capernaum.

I hope you have been both informed and inspired through the pages of this book. I have been informed and inspired in writing them! I trust that you now see the incredible purpose of our Lord. Furthermore, I trust that you understand more clearly what his message was—and still is.

And most personally, I hope you came to see first-hand what those incredible 24 hours mean for us today.

Faithfully yours in Christ,

The Rev. David H. Roseberry

24 QUESTIONS AND POINTS OF DISCUSSION

For Personal Reflections and Small Group Discussion

24 DISCUSSION POINTS AND QUESTIONS

It is always good to stop and reflect on what we read. We can do this individually as we read chapter by chapter or all at once at the end. Additionally, I wrote this book to be used in small groups and study gatherings. However, you choose to use this section, I hope it will be helpful as you read and reflect upon Mark's Gospel and my commentary.

1. **Opening Salvo:** How was Jesus' baptism a significant turning point in his life?
2. **Welcome Home:** What is your reaction to the idea of Jesus borrowing everything he needed? Is there a personal stewardship application for your life?
3. **First Stop:** Christianity is "Celebrity-Free." Please comment on how or whether this applies to the modern church and modern Christianity.

4. **Astonishing Message:** List the three points of Jesus' keynote statement. How do these three points help you clarify his purpose? Or do they muddy the water?

5. **Fresh Air:** Jesus' teaching was not "turn or burn," but we might say, "learn and turn." What is your reaction to this point?

6. **His Authority:** Why did the scribes object so vehemently about Jesus teaching with authority?

7. **Scandalous Truth:** In detail, in our own words, describe the Doctrine of the Incarnation. Why is this doctrine such an essential element of Christian belief?

8. **Unclean Spirits:** Chapter 8 includes this comment: *"Jesus believes that all suffering and brokenness in the world is the result of the devastating work of the Devil ever since the early beginnings of our race. He thought it was responsible for all human suffering, every catastrophe, and each death."* What is your reaction to this statement? Do you agree or disagree?

9. **The Strongman:** In your own words, summarize the parable of the strongman mentioned in this chapter. How does the parable shed light on what Jesus believed about the Devil?

10. **The Confrontation:** How could something as evil as an unclean spirit know the complete Identity of Jesus? What does that say to modern believers?

11. **The Rebuke:** Comment on this quote from Chapter 11: *"The Devil is a cruel reality responsible for misery and mayhem today. But it has nothing of its own to use. All Satan can do is corrupt God's creation, capitalize on the world's fallen state, and use it to amplify terror and pain and cause rebellion against God."* What do you think about it? What do YOU believe about the devil and evil forces?

12. **His Reputation:** What did Jesus think about the crowds that followed him? Why was he ambivalent?

13. **The Visitation:** This chapter starts to cover a very 'homey' story in the Gospel. What would it be like to have Jesus over to your home? Is there something you would ask him to do or help you with?

14. **Real Miracles:** What are the four arenas where we need help or support? Have you seen God provide miracles in any of them? How and when?

15. **The Healing:** Does it bother you that there are three versions of this story, and each is slightly different?

16. **Hard Questions:** How do you feel about unanswered prayer? Is there a difference in your mind between healing and curing?

17. **Bigger Picture:** Do you see an example of the Doctrine of the Incarnation in this story? The mother-in-law served him after the healing. Comment on this.

18. **At Sundown:** The crowds were filled with people like us. Reflect on the hope and the need that would bring you out to meet Jesus that night.

19. **Our Hope:** What do miracles teach us about the life to come? Comment on the last line of Tim Keller's quote in this chapter: *"Jesus' miracles are not just a challenge to our minds, but a promise to our hearts, that the world we all want is coming."*

20. **His Rising:** Comment on Jesus' need for prayer with the Father. Do you have a particular time and place? Is it a habit or an occasional occurrence in your life?

21. **He Prays:** Review this chapter in detail, perhaps looking up the many Scripture references. What is your reaction to knowing these things about Jesus' prayer life? How can we begin to pray more fervently?

22. **Peter Finds:** Who do you know who is searching for Jesus? Where would you go if someone came to you asking to meet Jesus? What would you do? Retell the story of Nicodemus in our own words (John 3).

23. **Show and Tell:** Why was Jesus intent on preaching the
    Word to many more people? How did you come to faith?

24. **Shed Blood:** How does the story of the restitution of
    the leper bring the element of the Cross into the first 24
    hours?

A FINAL WORD

Looking back over the 24 episodes, we cannot help but be
impressed. Our Lord spent the entire time, one full day, giving
himself to others as well as directly addressing the demons and
the diseases. The day's most important task seemed to be
preaching the Good News about the Gospel of God and demonstrating what the Kingdom would look like.

Thank you for reading this book and discussing it with others. I
am thankful and humbled that you would take the time to "read,
mark, learn, and inwardly digest" the truth of God's unchanging
Word. I pray that this offering of mine will assist you in your
understanding and devotion to the Lord and his work.

Faithfully yours in Christ,

David H. Roseberry

THE TEXT OF THE GOSPEL OF MARK

Mark 21-45 - ESV

MARK 1:21-45

And they went into Capernaum, and immediately on the Sabbath, he entered the synagogue and was teaching. [22] And they were astonished at his teaching, for he taught them as one who had authority and not as the scribes. [23] And immediately, there was in their synagogue a man with an unclean spirit. And he cried out, [24] "What have you to do with us, Jesus of Nazareth? Have you come to destroy us? I know who you are— the Holy One of God." [25] But Jesus rebuked him, saying, "Be silent, and come out of him!" [26] And the unclean spirit, convulsing him and crying out with a loud voice, came out of him. [27] And they were all amazed, so that they questioned among themselves, saying, "What is this? A new teaching with authority! He commands even the unclean spirits, and they obey him." [28] And at once, his fame spread everywhere throughout all the surrounding region of Galilee.

And immediately, he left the synagogue and entered the house of Simon and Andrew with James and John. [30] Now Simon's mother-in-law lay ill with a fever, and immediately they told him about her. [31] And he came and took her by the hand and lifted her up, and the fever left her, and she began to serve them.

That evening at sundown, they brought to him all who were sick or oppressed by demons. [33] And the whole city was gathered together at the door. [34] And he healed many who were sick with various diseases and cast out many demons. And he would not permit the demons to speak because they knew him.

And rising very early in the morning, while it was still dark, he departed and went out to a desolate place, and there he prayed. [36] And Simon and those who were with him searched for him, [37] and they found him and said to him, "Everyone is looking for You." [38] And he said to them, "Let us go on to the next towns, that I may preach there also, for that is why I came out." [39] And he went throughout all Galilee, preaching in their synagogues and casting out demons.

And a leper came to him, imploring him, and kneeling said to him, "If you will, you can make me clean." [41] Moved with pity, he stretched out his hand and touched him and said to him, "I will; be clean." [42] And immediately, the leprosy left him, and he was made clean. [43] And Jesus sternly charged him and sent him away at once, [44] and said to him, "See that you say nothing to anyone, but go, show yourself to the priest and offer for your cleansing what Moses commanded, for a proof to them." [45] But he went out and began to talk freely about it and to spread the news so that Jesus could no longer openly enter a town but was out in desolate places, and people were coming to him from every quarter.

(Mark 1:21-45, English Standard Version)

ALSO BY THE AUTHOR

A Field Guide to Giving

Come Before Winter (early 2023)

The First 24

The Giving Life

Giving Up

The Ordinary Ways of God

The Psalm on the Cross

The Rector and the Vestry

When the Lord is My Shepherd

ALL TITLES ARE AVAILABLE ON AMAZON

ONE REQUEST: PLEASE GO TO AMAZON AND LEAVE AN HONEST REVIEW OF THE BOOKS YOU HAVE READ, INCLUDING THIS ONE.

ABOUT DAVID ROSEBERRY

DAVID ROSEBERRY leads a non-profit ministry called Leader-Works. In this ministry, he consults and teaches church leaders across the US and Canada. He has written many books that are available on Amazon. In addition, every year, he and Fran lead life-changing trips to Israel and other important places for the Christian faith. In earlier years, David and Fran founded Christ Church in Plano in 1985, where he was Rector for 31 years. They are forever thankful to God for the incredible blessing of those years. David has served local churches and the national denomination for over 40 years of ordained ministry. He and Fran live in North Dallas. They have four children and five grandchildren. Stay in touch with the ministry of LeaderWorks at www.LeaderWorks.org.

PRAISE FOR THE FIRST 24

Innovative and yet biblically faithful, this book held me captive to the very last word. The practical examination and profound application of Mark's recording of a day in the life of our Lord Jesus is as informative as it is edifying. David Roseberry has gifted us with a deeply moving reminder that the one we claim to follow came to serve and not to be served. Every page is insightful and inspiring and challenging.

The Rev Dr Johannes W H van der Bijl, author of Breakfast on the Beach: The Development of Simon Peter *and* For the Life of the World: The Multiplication of Simon Peter.

IF you enjoy thriller action...**IF** you'd like a front row seat on "Day 1" of Jesus's ministry...**IF** studying the whole Bible feels overwhelming and you long to digest a small part...**IF** you want to experience Mark's gospel exploding from black and white into technicolor...**IF** you are weary of studying the word the "same old way" and need a creative, fresh approach...

THEN you will love this book.

Whether you are an older believer or newly discovering the Bible, this easy, yet profound read will whet your appetite and make you long to read what's next! You'll feel exhausted and exhilarated as you walk with the disciples for the first crucial 24 hours of Jesus' ministry.

Susan Alexander Yates, speaker and best-selling author of several books including, Risky Faith, Becoming Brave Enough to Trust the God Who Is Bigger Than Your World and The One Devotional. She blogs at susanalexanderyates.com

---

In framing the story of Jesus amidst the urgency of a 24-hour story, David Roseberry brilliantly evokes the chaotic excitement of the Gospel of Mark. His explanation will help a Christian believer grasp who the Trinity is and how the three persons of the Godhead function. *The First 24* will change how one reads the Gospel of Mark, but even more importantly, it will change how the reader understands his life as participating in the in-breaking of the Kingdom of God.

The Rev. Dr. Laurie Thompson, Dean and President (ret.) Trinity School for Ministry

---

Are 24 verses about 24 hours in Jesus's life enough to tell us much? With experienced preacher and writer David Roseberry as our guide, the answer is: Absolutely! Roseberry has not only captured the essence of the Gospel of Mark but the essence of Christ's life and mission. Jesus came down to earth, and Mark captures his earthly life with "down to earth" Greek. And Roseberry retells it all in a readable, "down to earth" way. With a crisp and "immediate" style (just like Mark!), Roseberry draws on his gifted experience in storytelling preaching, and guiding groups through Israel to convey the action with texture and lively theological reflection.

The Rev. Dr. Jon Parker, Associate Professor of Biblical Studies at Berry College

Using the 24-hour format to follow this first day of Jesus' life takes us into the story and teaches biblical truth. The book moves fast and Roseberry also includes many fascinating details that open up the Gospel to us. The book was just really good.

Penna Dexter, Co-host Point of View Radio Show

So good! A winner in every way. Thank you for allowing me to read the manuscript for your new book *The First 24*. I love it! It is interesting and informative. I'm buying a supply to share with others. Well done.

Mark Schupbach, LifeMark Ministries, Dallas

David Roseberry's *The First 24* will fix the immediacy of the Gospel of Mark in your mind for the rest of your life. The play-by-play of those first hours in Capernaum beautifully captures the intensity and power of Jesus' first encounters. It's a great resource for formation; the study questions at the end of 24 will provide good discussion in a small group setting or rich fodder for individual reflection.

The Rev. Cindy Telisak Ministry, Author of The Eloquent Lay Reader: A Guide to Skillfully Preparing and Delivering the Biblical Text for Your Congregation.

The First 24 is a crisp, authentic and clear. It presents the first day of Christ's public ministry for the modern reader. You'll read with fresh eyes as you hear the story again for the first time.

Sharon Fox, author, teacher, Founder Brave Penny, Shadowlands Grief Recovery Program

ACKNOWLEDGMENTS

I have had this book in my mind since I noticed that Mark told the story in Chapter One as one very busy day in Capernaum. As a fan of the television series *24*, it was only a matter of time before I made the connection between the story from Mark's gospel and the eight-season, 198 episode odyssey of Jack Bauer.

Having the idea of a book and having a book are two different realities. As concept of an actual book began to take shape, and when I had enough words written to test the approach, I sent it to a few people whose encouragement, help, and imagination gave me the courage to press on to the end. Thank you, Bruce Barbour, Chick Schoen, Cindy Telisak, and Amber Galloway. I pressed on and kept writing and filling out the chapters one at a time. To test the water again, I sent the book to a few more people to get their assessment. I felt that the manuscript I had written was trying to be something, and I had to ask a few trusted colleagues. Thanks to Eric Taylor, my son Jed Roseberry, Penna Dexter, Sharon Fox, and John Tuthill. The final step in writing this book meant I had to trust the entire manuscript to real authors who have written real books! I loved reading their encouragement so much, I put most of their comments in the section just before this one. Two other contributors to this process deserve mention. While I have never met them face to face, I am thankful for Victoria

I have enlisted the help of a certified coach whose ability to help me bring focus to my work have been very helpful. Thank you, Victoria. And also, this book is available on Audible because of the voice-over talents of Dominionfire, a top rated seller on Fiver r.com.

I am also extremely thankful for the generous donor base at LeaderWorks. The "job" I have right now is a dream position. I work with great pastors in challenging situations, provide Leader-Works Trust grants to help their congregations, and coach clergy. And I write. Were it not for the donors, I would not be able to offer these books. Thank you! You know who you are!

My most honest and loving critic is the woman whose life I have shared for nearly 40 years of marriage. Thank you, Fran, my love. I always want and value your opinion. I will never forget the too-late nights we spent for years binge-watching *24!*

David Roseberry

Fall, 2022

Made in the USA
Columbia, SC
03 November 2022

70401682R00093